American Educational Thought

Essays from 1640–1940

A volume in
Readings in Educational Thought
Chara Haeussler Bohan, Perry L. Glanzer, Andrew J. Milson, and J. Wesley Null,
Series Editors

American Educational Thought

Essays from 1640–1940

edited by

Andrew J. Milson
University of North Texas

Chara Haeussler Bohan
Georgia State University

Perry L. Glanzer
Baylor University

J. Wesley Null
Baylor University

Editorial Assistant, 2nd edition: Caroline Jernigan, *Georgia State University*
Editorial Assistant, 1st edition: Genny Davis, *Baylor University*

INFORMATION AGE PUBLISHING, INC.
Charlotte, NC • www.infoagepub.com

Library of Congress Cataloging-in-Publication Data

American educational thought : essays from 1640-1940 / edited by Andrew J.
Milson ... [et al.]. – 2nd ed.
  p. cm.
 Rev. ed. of: Readings in American educational thought, c2004.
 Includes bibliographical references.
 ISBN 978-1-60752-364-2 (pbk.) – ISBN 978-1-60752-365-9 (hardcover) –
ISBN 978-1-60752-366-6 (e-book)
1. Education–United States–History. 2. Education–United
States–Philosophy. I. Milson, Andrew J. II. Readings in American
educational thought.
 LA205.R39 2010
 370.1'0973–dc22

                                                        2009047642

Copyright © 2010 Information Age Publishing Inc.

Printed in the United States of America

Contents

Introduction to the Second Edition, 2010

Conversation and American Educational Thought

This book contains primary source readings on American educational thought from the mid 1600s to 1940. As editors, our goal is to provide teachers, contemporary scholars of education, and policymakers with the most significant arguments made on the subject of American educational thought.

Numerous questions are at the heart of the essays in this book. What is the purpose of education? What is democratic education? What does it mean to provide a high-quality education to all children? How should this goal be achieved? What curriculum should be offered to children in America, and on what basis do we justify the subjects we choose? Once the question of curriculum has been addressed, what teaching methods should be used to teach it? Should these methods be different for males compared to females? If so, why and how should this different curriculum be offered? How should educators address subjects of morality and religion? To what extent should American education prepare students for a life of work, as opposed to a life of leisure? Or, should American education provide students with both? If both, how can this goal be accomplished? Is teaching an art, a science, or a combination of both? How does our answer to this question change the teaching practices we promote? These are indeed difficult questions, but they must be addressed if we are to proceed with a sound approach to American education. In *American Educational Thought*, you will

American Educational Thought: Essays from 1640–1940, pages ix–xiii
Copyright © 2010 by Information Age Publishing
All rights of reproduction in any form reserved.

read the words of authors who provide answers to these and many other essential questions.

From William Penn to Mary Lyon to William James, these writers make arguments from all points along the ideological spectrum, an indication that no one school of thought has ever dominated conversation about American education. Essays in *American Educational Thought* range from the conservative theology of John Cotton to the romanticism of Ralph Waldo Emerson, from the Hegelian idealism of W. T. Harris to the Progressivism of John Dewey, from the democratic traditionalism of William Bagley to the child-centered developmentalism of G. Stanley Hall. Throughout this broad scope of American educational philosophy, however, one theme that holds these essays together is the ideal of democratic education. The authors no doubt disagree about what democratic education means or what its content ought to be, but they all agree that the ideal of universal education is worthy of pursuit. Every author—each in his or her own way—wrestles with what universal education entails and how the goal can be accomplished, but nobody questions the argument that every young person deserves high-quality curriculum and teaching.

In this respect, these authors merely extend the views of the first educational philosopher to make the case for liberal education for all: John Amos Comenius. Considered the father of universal education, Comenius' monumental work *The Great Didactic,* published in 1638, laid down the gauntlet for educating all young people regardless of class, gender, nationality, or ethnic identity. In one way or another, every author included here is indebted to Comenius. He laid the groundwork individually for universal education, whereas the authors in this text tackled the question collectively. In this respect, America became the first nation to take Comenius' ideal of universal education seriously. Few people could argue that America has achieved this goal in the early twenty-first century, but nobody can disagree with the point that the conversation contained in this book has been intense, passionate, and lively.

The premise behind *American Educational Thought* is simple. We believe studying this subject from a broad, interdisciplinary perspective provides the best way to ensure that educational policymakers, teachers, and the general public will make wise decisions about the future of American education. Without familiarity with the historical and philosophical context this book provides, those who make decisions on behalf of American education will inevitably operate within a vacuum and without any historical memory. No decision ever takes place outside of the stream of history, yet policymakers often proceed as if each morning is a brand new day. If nothing else, careful attention to the essays in *American Educational Thought* proves the point that "nothing is new under the sun." Contemporary educational policymaking remains a tangled web of many—if not all—of the arguments found in this text. Tracing contemporary ideas to their roots enables us to recognize which arguments hold the most truth, which have been tested, which make the most sense given our contemporary context, and which perhaps should be discarded as failed fads from an earlier age.

Improvements to the Second Edition

We made a number of improvements in this second edition. First of all, we reviewed all of our short introductions to make sure they provide the necessary context to make sense of what the author is doing. We eliminated several readings that we found not to be particularly helpful in classroom and other conversations. In addition, we added numerous works that open up new possibilities for discussion, represent more wide-ranging viewpoints, and provide even richer context for making sense of American educational thought. Examples of new readings in this edition include the National Education Association's monumental "Committee of Ten" report on curriculum from 1894, John Dewey's "My Pedagogic Creed" from 1897, Ellwood P. Cubberley's "The Certification of Teachers" from 1906, the National Education Association's 1918 "Cardinal Principles Report" on curriculum, two selections from Mary McLeod Bethune, and powerful essays from Boyd H. Bode and Isaac Kandel. All of these essays match our goal of capturing a broad range of arguments that represent the main currents of American educational thought. The result of these revisions is a more readable text that captures the central arguments from each author, places them within the context of those who came before them, and then invites comparison on the central questions stated above.

Teaching *American Educational Thought*

The idea for this book began when the four editors were assistant professors together at Baylor University. We originally designed the book for a course on American Educational Thought that was taught for the first time at Baylor in the spring of 2003. American Educational Thought has remained a required course for all students in Baylor's teacher education program. This book has served as a foundational text for the course ever since the first edition was published in 2004 under the title *Readings in American Educational Thought: From Puritanism to Progressivism.* Before the first edition of this book was published, we made these readings available to students piecemeal instead of as a single publication.

Since the publication of the first edition, we have heard from faculty at other institutions who have found the book to be useful in a variety of contexts—including courses on the history of American education, foundations of education, curriculum theory, multicultural foundations, and many others. For courses on the history of American education, *American Educational Thought* provides a good supplement to standard textbooks that offer a historical analysis, but that fail to include the primary source arguments published here. Arguments like those found here inject emotion, passion, and argumentation into courses on the history of American education, elements that have always been present in debates about the future of American education. These elements also should be present in any course on the history and/or philosophy of American education.

In the undergraduate and graduate courses where we have used this text, we have discovered that students appreciate hearing the actual arguments made by people like Thomas Jefferson, Noah Webster, Catharine Beecher, W. E. B. DuBois, and Isaac Kandel, as opposed to someone else's explanation of what these authors believed. As well, we have discovered that primary sources like these are much more discussable than textbooks. Textbooks come to us in a somewhat "anti-septic" fashion in the sense that they are presumed to be value-free and neutral. Everyone in the twenty-first century, however, recognizes that textbooks are always written from a particular perspective. *American Educational Thought* embraces this perspective-driven approach and hence presents readers with arguments from authors in their own words. The essays in this text make arguments driven by passion and reason (and sometimes both), views that students can embrace, reject, or simply appreciate. They cannot, however, ignore them. Classroom conversations are always much more enjoyable and lively when students have something substantive, meaningful, and thought-provoking to discuss.

To cultivate classroom conversation, we have found a three-part approach to conversations to be quite helpful. Each author in *American Educational Thought* tackles the subjects of curriculum, teaching methods, and the purpose of schooling in one way or another. The authors, of course, offer competing views on these three subjects, but any substantive discussion of American education inevitably must come around to addressing these crucial matters. The competing views offered here are what make the subject of American educational thought such a fascinating endeavor. Arguments like Benjamin Rush's "Thoughts upon Female Education" or Horace Mann's "Means and Objects of Common School Education" or Isaac Kandel's "Prejudice the Garden Toward Roses?" provide readers with an absorbing, unending source of conversation, reflection, and debate. These authors don't just state their views. They argue and seek to persuade their audience. Every teacher, policymaker, or student of education will find something in *American Educational Thought* to love, hate, or perhaps both at the same time.

Welcome to the second edition of *American Educational Thought*. Our hope is that the book will cultivate conversation regardless of whether your work takes place in classrooms, boardrooms, or legislative chambers. Be sure to provide feedback to the editors if you have suggestions for future editions. May the journey toward universal education—begun by Comenius and extended by everyone in this book—continue throughout the twenty-first century and beyond.

—**Editors**
May 2009

Introduction to the First Edition, 2004

One hundred years ago, a prominent college professor and historian advised her students to "go to the sources." In making this recommendation, Lucy Maynard Salmon intended for her students to search primary source records to find historical artifacts and evidence. Not only would students learn the art of historical detection, but they also would discover untold historical narratives. This volume of primary source documents in American educational thought facilitates this task of going to the sources. The writings in this collection harbor myriad stories in the development of American education during the past several centuries. This book should serve as a useful primary or supplementary text for any undergraduate or graduate course in the history of American education, American educational thought, social foundations of education, philosophy of education, or curriculum theory. It is our hope that readers of this book will come to understand, and perhaps develop a desire to participate in, the "great conversation" that has taken place about education in America.

Importantly, the selected readings represent significant ideas and educational movements from Puritan times (early 1600s) to the more recent Progressive era (early 1900s). During this three-hundred-year time frame, American education witnessed significant changes. Early writings, such as those of John Cotton and Cotton Mather, shed light on the strong religious component of colonial education. In Europe, the church had preserved intellectual traditions, and in the colonies religious customs also served as a conveyer and source of knowledge. If a colonial family owned a book, the

American Educational Thought: Essays from 1640–1940, pages xv–xviii
Copyright © 2010 by Information Age Publishing
All rights of reproduction in any form reserved.

family Bible was first and foremost. The Bible was employed to help children learn to read and to facilitate the development of moral character.

The essays in this volume written by early American leaders —for example, Benjamin Franklin, Thomas Jefferson, and Benjamin Rush—demonstrate the significance of education to those who set forth the social and political principles that guide American society. These men sought to fashion a permanent education system in the newly formed country and solicited support for its establishment. They believed that an educated populace was critical to the success of their experiment with republican government, and realized that a robust school system was critical to the survival of the government. They also recognized that well-educated and properly trained teachers were the most central aspect of any educational institution or system. These patriots believed in the importance of educating Americans in America—rather than in Europe—and solicited support for the development of American education.

In the early 19th century, a burgeoning movement to include women in the arena of formal schooling developed. The women's education movement made possible the women's suffrage movement that began in Seneca Falls in 1848. In the early 1800s, Emma Willard, Mary Lyon, and Catharine Beecher were instrumental in establishing the first schools for young women. These schools were called female seminaries and they provided many new intellectual and social opportunities for women. Interestingly, the founders of the female seminaries often argued for women's education because of women's role in the domestic sphere. As women were most often charged with the primary responsibility for raising young children, they were viewed as preferable teachers for primary age students.

At the same time that the women's education movement began, the common school movement blossomed. Horace Mann, often referred to as the father of American education, is credited with the growth of common schools. Common schools were public, non-sectarian, tax-supported institutions that were to have common elements among the various schools throughout the state. Mann's influence ultimately extended beyond Massachusetts, where he served as the first Secretary of the Massachusetts Board of Education, and led to the growth of public schools throughout the country. As the common schools increased in number, so did the need for teachers. Mann also helped to establish the first normal school, an institution created specifically for the education of teachers, in 1839. Because women were often less expensive to hire as teachers than men, a major transition in the gender composition of the teaching workforce occurred in the late 19th century. Mann's work to establish non-sectarian public schools encountered some criticism, however, from groups that feared that a centralized system would ruin local autonomy, teacher initiative, and parental rights. At the same time, Catholics protested that the public schools were too oriented towards Protestant practices, such as having students reading from the King James Bible. The Catholic response was to establish a separate school system.

African Americans also had a separate school system, recognized by law in 1896, with the precedent established in *Plessy v. Ferguson*. Booker T. Washington and W.E.B. DuBois debated vigorously about the nature of the education that would serve to advance the social and economic status of African Americans. Washington founded Tuskegee Normal and Industrial Institute to teach agriculture and industrial trades to African American students. He believed that industrial education would benefit African Americans more than an education that strictly offered scholarly studies. Harvard-educated black activist W.E.B. DuBois, however, opposed Washington's educational philosophy. He sought education for African Americans that would challenge the established system and facilitate social advancement more rapidly.

In the late 19th and early 20th centuries, an increasing faith in science and the growth of an industrial economy had significant repercussions for American educational thought. America became an increasingly pluralistic society, as immigration increased from countries that had not heretofore populated America's shores. The children of these immigrants entered American schools and presented new challenges for the teaching workforce, similar to many issues teachers face today in classrooms. Faith in science led many educational researchers to turn to the science of psychology to provide answers to educational problems in the ever more complex society. G. Stanley Hall, William James, and E.L. Thorndike were prominent psychologists who sought to understand the human mind and apply emerging psychology to educational thought. These challenges and developments in modern America provoked a reevaluation of traditional approaches to education. Progressives, such as Francis Parker, Jane Addams, and John Dewey, envisioned an education that was "child-centered" and focused on the education of citizens for a rapidly changing democratic republic. Social Reconstructionists such as George Counts argued that education should provide a means for building a "new social order." The Progressive legacy is evident in current classrooms throughout the country. Progressive education was not without critics, however. The Essentialist movement, for example, sought to retain the laudable aspects of Progressive education, while at the same time emphasizing rigorous academics and the seriously important question of purpose, which many believed had been lost.

Because some of the primary source documents included in this volume were written many years ago, readers may notice inconsistencies in spelling. Three hundred years ago, authors did not have the benefits of Microsoft Word with a grammar and spell check function. Furthermore, the rules of the English language, much to Noah Webster's dismay, were not as standardized as is true today. Although reading "old English" occasionally presents comprehension challenges, such irregularities in original source materials hint at the novelty of minds in distant times. In the short descriptions before each of the documents, we have sought to explain why the authors included in this volume were prominent. These introductions also seek to introduce readers to the contributions these individuals have made to American educational thought. Hopefully, these writings will spark an interest in the minds of readers who seek to know more about educational ideas from the past. These ideas, in turn, should fuel interest and creativity in the minds and hearts of students in the future.

Photo Sources

1

Spiritual Milk for American Babes, Drawn out of the Breasts of Both Testaments for their Soul's Nourishment

John Cotton, c. 1641

John Cotton (1584–1652) immigrated to America in 1632 to escape arrest for his Puritan beliefs and practices. He eventually became one of the most influential leaders in the Massachusetts Bay Colony as a teacher in the First Church of Boston. His catechism for children, written around 1641, represents one of the earliest educational writings published in America. It also reflects the Puritan's desire for a literate Bible-reading populace, which they also enshrined in their early laws requiring education. The famous Massachusetts Education Laws of 1647 declared that every community of 50 households needed to collect money and hire a teacher, because it was the chief project of that "ould deluder Satan to keep men from the knowledge of ye Scriptures." The influence of Cotton's catechism reached even further when it was reprinted in one of the first school textbooks, the New England Primer, published in 1690. It is estimated that 3 million copies of the Primer were distributed in the eighteenth century, giving Cotton's essay a lasting and prominent influence among Colonial Americans. —PLG

American Educational Thought: Essays from 1640–1940, pages 1–7

Q. *What hath God done for you?*
A. God hath made me, he keepeth me, and he can save me.

Q. *Who is God?*
A. God is a Spirit of himself and for himself.

Q. *How many Gods be there?*
A. There is but one God in three Persons, the Father, and the Son, and the Holy Ghost.

Q. *How did God make you?*
A. In my first parents holy and righteous.

Q. *Are you then born holy and righteous?*
A. No, my first father sinned and I in him.

Q. *Are you then born a sinner?*
A. I was conceived in sin, and born in iniquity.

Q. *What is your birth sin?*
A. Adam's sin imputed to me, and a corrupt nature dwelling in me.

Q. *What is your corrupt nature?*
A. My corrupt nature is empty of grace, bent unto sin, only unto sin, and that continually.

Q. *What is sin?*
A. Sin is a transgression of the law.

Q. *How many commandments of the law be there?*
A. Ten.

Q. *What is the first commandment?*
A. Thou shalt have no other Gods before me.

Q. *What is the meaning of this commandment?*
A. That we should worship the only true God, and no other besides him.

Q. *What is the second commandment?*
A. Thou shalt not make to thyself any graven image, &c.

Q. *What is the meaning of this commandment?*
A. That we should worship the only true God, with true worship, such as he hath ordained, not such as man hath invented.

Q. *What is the third commandment?*
A. Thou shalt not take the name of the Lord thy God in vain.

Q. *What is meant by the name of God?*
A. God himself & the good things of God, whereby he is known as a man by his name, and his attributes, worship, word and works.

Q. *What is it not to take his name in vain?*
A. To make use of God & the good things of God to his glory, and our own good, not vainly, not irreverently, not unprofitably.

Q. *Which is the fourth commandment?*
A. Remember that thou keep holy the Sabbath day.

Q. *What is the meaning of this commandment?*
A. That we should rest from labor, and much more from play on the Lord's day, that we may draw nigh to God in holy duties.

Q. *What is the fifth commandment?*
A. Honor thy father and thy mother, that thy days may be long in the land which the Lord thy God giveth thee.

Q. *What are meant by father and mother?*
A. All our superiors whether in family, school, church and commonwealth.

Q. *What is the honor due unto them?*
A. Reverence, obedience, and (when I am able) recompense.

Q. *What is the sixth commandment?*
A. Thou shalt do no murder.

Q. *What is the meaning of this commandment?*
A. That we should not shorten the life or health of ourselves or others, but preserve both.

Q. *What is the seventh commandment?*
A. Thou shalt not commit adultery.

Q. *What is the sin here forbidden?*
A. To defile ourselves or others with unclean lusts.

Q. *What is the duty here commanded?*
A. Chastity to possess our vessels in holiness and honor.

Q. *What is the eighth commandment?*
A. Thou shalt not steal.

Q. *What is the stealth here forbidden?*
A. To take away another man's goods without his leave, or to spend our own without benefit to ourselves or others.

Q. *What is the duty here commanded?*
A. To get our goods honestly, to keep them safely, and spend them thriftily.

Q. *What is the ninth commandment?*
A. Thou shalt not bear false witness against thy neighbour.

Q. *What is the sin here forbidden?*
A. To lie falsely, to think or speak untruly of ourselves or others

Q. *What is the duty here required?*
A. Truth and faithfulness.

Q. *What is the tenth commandment?*
A. Thou shalt not covet, &c.

Q. *What is the coveting here forbidden?*
A. Lust after the things of other men, and want of contentment with our own.

Q. *Whether have you kept all these commandments?*
A. No, I and all men are sinners.

Q. *What are the wages of sin?*
A. Death and damnation.

Q. *How then look you to be saved?*
A. Only by Jesus Christ.

Q. *Who is Jesus Christ?*
A. The eternal Son of God, who for our sakes became man that he might redeem and save us.

Q. *How doth Christ redeem and save us?*
A. By his righteous life, and bitter death, and glorious resurrection to life again.

Q. *How do we come to have a part & fellowship with Christ in his death and resurrection?*
A. By the power of his word and spirit, which brings us to him, and keeps us in him.

Q. *What is the word?*
A. The Holy Scriptures of the prophets and apostles, the Old and New Testament, Law and Gospel.

Q. *How doth the Ministry of the Law bring you toward Christ?*
A. By bringing me to know my sin, and the wrath of God, against me for it.

Q. *What are you hereby the nearer to Christ?*
A. So I come to feel my cursed estate and need of a Saviour.

Q. *How doth the ministry of the Gospel help you in this cursed estate?*
A. By humbling me yet more, and then raising me out of this estate.

Q. *How doth the ministry of the Gospel humble you yet more?*
A. By revealing the grace of the Lord Jesus in dying to save sinners, and yet convincing me of my sin in not believing on him, and of my utter insufficiency to come to him, and so I feel myself utterly lost.

Q. *How doth the ministry of the gospel raise you up out of this lost estate to come to Christ?*
A. By teaching me the value and virtue of the death of Christ, and the riches of his grace to lost sinners by revealing the promise of grace to such, and by ministering the Spirit of grace to apply Christ, and his promise of grace unto myself, and to keep me in him.

Q. *How doth the Spirit of grace apply Christ and his promise of grace unto you and keep you in him?*
A. By begetting in me faith to receive him, prayer to call upon him, repentance to mourn after him, and new obedience to serve him.

Q. *What is faith?*
A. Faith is the grace of the Spirit, whereby I deny myself, and believe on Christ for righteousness and salvation.

Q. *What is prayer?*
A. It is calling upon God in the name of Christ by the help of the Holy Ghost, according to the will of God.

Q. *What is repentance?*
A. Repentance is a grace of the Spirit, whereby I loath my sins, and myself for them and confess them before the Lord, and mourn after Christ for the pardon of them, and for grace to serve him in newness of life.

Q. *What is the newness of life, or new obedience?*
A. Newness of life is a grace of the Spirit, whereby I forsake my former lust and vain company, and walk before the Lord in the light of his word, and in the communion of saints.

Q. *What is the communion of saints?*
A. It is the fellowship of the church in the blessings of the covenant of grace, and the seals thereof.

Q. *What is the church?*
A. It is a congregation of saints joined together in the bond of this covenant, to worship the Lord, and to edify one another in all his holy ordinances.

Q. *What is the bond of the covenant by which the church is joined together?*
A. It is the profession of that covenant which God has made with his faithful people, to be a God unto them, and to their seed.

Q. *What doth the Lord bind his people to in this covenant?*

A. To give up themselves and their seed first to the Lord to be his people, and then to the elders and brethren of the church to set forward the worship of God and their mutual edification.

Q. *How do they give up themselves and their seed to the Lord?*

A. By receiving through faith the Lord and his covenant to themselves, and to their seed and accordingly walking themselves and training up their children in the ways of the covenant.

Q. *How do they give up themselves and their seed to the elders and brethren of the church?*

A. By confessing of their sins, and profession of their faith, and of their subjection to the gospel of Christ; and so they and their seed are received into the fellowship of the church and the seals thereof.

Q. *What are the seals of the covenant now in the days of the gospel?*

A. Baptism and the Lord's Supper.

Q. *What is done for you in baptism?*

A. In baptism the washing with water is a sign and seal of my washing in the blood and spirit of Christ, and thereby of my ingrafting into Christ, of the pardon and cleansing of my sins, of my raising up out of afflictions, and also of my resurrection from the dead at the last day.

Q. *What is done for you in the Lord's supper?*

A. In the Lord's supper, the receiving of the bread broken and the wine poured out is a sign and seal of my receiving the communion of the body of Christ broken for me, and of his blood shed for me, and thereby of my growth in Christ, and the pardon and healing of my sins, of the fellowship of the Spirit, of my strengthening and quickening in grace, and of my sitting together with Christ on his throne of glory at the last judgment.

Q. *What was the resurrection from the dead, which was sealed up to you in baptism?*

A. When Christ shall come in his last judgment, all that are in their graves shall rise again, both the just and unjust.

Q. *What is the judgment, which is sealed up to you in the Lord's supper?*

A. At the last day we shall all appear before the judgment seat of Christ, to give an account of our works, and receive our reward according to them.

Q. *What is the reward that shall then be given?*
A. The righteous shall go into life eternal, and the wicked shall be cast into everlasting fire with the Devil and his angels.

2

Excerpts from Some Fruits of Solitude in Reflections and Maxims

William Penn, 1693

It is difficult to describe briefly William Penn's (1644–1718) wide-ranging background and accomplishments. He was the son of the naval hero Admiral Penn and thus knew kings (Charles II and James II) and famous philosophers (John Locke). Yet, despite this life of privilege, he would learn to identify with persecuted religious dissenters due to a unique conversion experience. While attending Oxford he converted to the pacifist Protestant sect known as the Quakers. Due to the persecution of the Quakers in England, Penn founded the colony of Pennsylvania to provide a haven for poor and oppressed people and religious dissenters. Like the Puritans in New England, he hoped his colony would be "an example…to the nations"; however, his vision of a colony without an established church proved quite different than that of Puritan New England. Penn's educational vision also differed from the Puritan vision. As these selections from his writings reveal, he emphasized the importance of studying nature and learning through experience rather than merely memorizing Scripture, a specific catechism, rules of grammar, and other systematic forms of knowledge. Instead of giving children the world already ordered and

American Educational Thought: Essays from 1640–1940, pages 9–14

explained, he suggested that children discover God's order and wisdom in nature themselves. —PLG

Ignorance

1. It is admirable to consider how many Millions of People come into, and go out of the World, Ignorant of themselves, and of the World they have lived in.

2. If one went to see Windsor-Castle, or Hampton-Court, it would be strange not to observe and remember the Situation, the Building, the Gardens, Fountains, &c. that make up the Beauty and Pleasure of such a Seat? And yet few People know themselves; No, not their own Bodies, the Houses of their Minds, the most curious Structure of the World; a living walking Tabernacle: Nor the World of which it was made, and out of which it is fed; which would be so much our Benefit, as well as our Pleasure, to know. We cannot doubt of this when we are told that the Invisible Things of God are brought to light by the Things that are seen; and consequently we read our Duty in them as often as we look upon them, to him that is the Great and Wise Author of them, if we look as we should do.

3. The World is certainly a great and stately Volume of natural Things; and may be not improperly styled the Hieroglyphicks of a better: But, alas! how very few Leaves of it do we seriously turn over! This ought to be the Subject of the Education of our Youth, who, at Twenty, when they should be fit for Business, know little or nothing of it.

Education

4. We are in Pain to make them Scholars, but not Men! To talk, rather than to know, which is true Canting.

5. The first Thing obvious to Children is what is sensible; and that we make no Part of their rudiments.

6. We press their Memory too soon, and puzzle, strain, and load them with Words and Rules; to know Grammer and Rhetorick, and a strange Tongue or two, that it is ten to one may never be useful to them; Leaving their natural Genius to Mechanical; and Physical, or natural Knowledge uncultivated and neglected; which would be of exceeding Use and Pleasure to them through the whole Course of their Life.

7. To be sure, Languages are not to be despised or neglected. But Things are still to be preferred.

8. Children had rather be making of Tools and Instruments of Play; Shaping, Drawing, Framing, and Building, &c. than getting some Rules of Propriety of Speech by Heart: And those also would follow with more Judgment, and less Trouble and Time.

9. It were Happy if we studied Nature more in natural Things; and acted according to Nature; whose rules are few, plain and most reasonable.

10. Let us begin where she begins, go her Pace, and close always where she ends, and we cannot miss of being good Naturalists.

11. The Creation would not be longer a Riddle to us: The Heavens, Earth, and Waters, with their respective, various and numerous Inhabitants: Their Productions, Natures, Seasons, Sympathies and Antipathies; their Use, Benefit and Pleasure, would be better understood by us: And an eternal Wisdom, Power, Majesty, and Goodness, very conspicuous to us, thro' those sensible and passing Forms: The World wearing the Mark of its Maker, whose Stamp is everywhere visible, and the Characters very legible to the Children of Wisdom.

12. And it would go a great way to caution and direct People in their Use of the World, that they were better studied and known in the Creation of it.

13. For how could Man find the Confidence to abuse it, while they should see the Great Creator stare them in the Face, in all and every part thereof?

14. Their Ignorance makes them insensible, and that Insensibility hardy in misusing this noble Creation, that has the Stamp and Voice of a Deity every where, and in every Thing to the Observing.

15. It is pity therefore that Books have not been composed for Youth, by some curious and careful Naturalists, and also Mechanicks, in the Latin Tongue, to be used in Schools, that they might learn Things with Words: Things obvious and familiar to them, and which would make the Tongue easier to be obtained by them.

16. Many able Gardiners and Husbandmen are yet Ignorant of the Reason of their Calling; as most Artificers are of the Reason of their own Rules that govern their excellent Workmanship. But a Naturalist and Mechanick of this sort is Master of the Reason of both, and might be of the Practice too, if his Industry kept pace with his Speculation; which were very commendable; and without which he cannot be said to be a complete Naturalist or Mechanick.

17. Finally, if Man be the Index or Epitomy of the World, as Philosophers tell us, we have only to read our selves well to be learned in it. But be-

cause there is nothing we less regard than the Characters of the Power that made us, which are so clearly written upon us and the World he has given us, and can best tell us what we are and should be, we are even Strangers to our own Genius: The Glass in which we should see that true instructing and agreeable Variety, which is to be observed in Nature, to the Admiration of that Wisdom and Adoration of that Power which made us all.

Pride

18. And yet we are very apt to be full of our selves, instead of Him that made what we so much value; and, but for whom we can have no Reason to value our selves. For we have nothing that we can call our own; no, not our selves: For we are all but Tenants, and at Will too, of the great Lord of our selves, and the rest of this great Farm, the World that we live upon.

19. But methinks we cannot answer it to our Selves as well as our Maker, that we should live and die ignorant of our Selves, and thereby of Him and the Obligations we are under to Him for our Selves.

20. If the worth of a Gift sets the Obligation, and directs the return of the Party that receives it; he that is ignorant of it, will be at a loss to value it and the Giver, for it.

21. Here is Man in his Ignorance of himself. He knows not how to estimate his Creator, because he knows not how to value his Creation. If we consider his Make, and lovely Compositure; the several Stories of his lovely Structure. His divers Members, their Order, Function and Dependency: The Instruments of Food, the Vessels of Digestion, the several Transmutations it passes. And how Nourishment is carried and diffused throughout the whole Body, by most innate and imperceptible Passages. How the Animal Spirit is thereby refreshed, and with an unspeakable Dexterity and Motion sets all Parts at work to feed themselves. And last of all, how the Rational Soul is seated in the Animal, as its proper House, as is the Animal in the Body: I say if this rare Fabrick alone were but considered by us, with all the rest by which it is fed and comforted, surely Man would have a more reverent Sense of the Power, Wisdom and Goodness of God, and of that Duty he owes to Him for it. But if he would be acquainted with his own Soul, its noble Faculties, its Union with the Body, its Nature and End, and the Providences by which the whole Frame of Humanity is preserved, he would Admire and Adore his Good and Great God. But Man is become a strange Contradiction to himself; but it is of himself; Not being by Constitution, but Corruption, such.

Knowledge

162. Knowledge is the Treasure, but Judgment the Treasurer of a Wise Man.

163. He that has more Knowledge than Judgment, is made for another Man's use more than his own.

164. It cannot be a good Constitution, where the Appetite is great and the Digestion is weak.

165. There are some Men like Dictionaries; to be lookt into upon occasions, but have no Connection, and are little entertaining.

166. Less Knowledge than Judgment will always have the advantage Upon the Injudicious knowing Man.

167. A Wise Man makes what he learns his own, 'tother shows he's but a Copy, or a Collection at most.

Wit

168. Wit is an happy and striking way of expressing a Thought.

169. 'Tis not often tho' it be lively and mantling, that it carries a great Body with it.

170. Wit therefore is fitter for Diversion than Business, being more grateful to Fancy than Judgment.

171. Less Judgment than Wit, is more Sale than Ballast.

172. Yet it must be confessed, that Wit gives an Edge to Sense, and recommends it extreamly.

173. Where Judgment has Wit to express it, there's the best Orator.

Obedience to Parents

174. If thou wouldest be obeyed, being a Father; being a Son, be Obedient.

175. He that begets thee, owns thee; and has a natural Right over thee.

176. Next to God, thy Parents; next them, the Magistrate.

177. Remember that thou are not more indebted to thy Parents for thy Nature, than for thy Love and Care.

178. Rebellion therefore in Children, was made Death by God's Law, and the next Sin to Idolatry, in the People; which is renouncing of God, the Parent of all.

179. Obedience to Parents is not only our Duty, but our Interest. If we received our Life from them, We prolong it by obeying them: For Obedience is the first Commandment with Promise.

180. The Obligation is as indissolvable as the Relation.

181. If we must not disobey God to obey them; at least we must let them see, that there is nothing else in our refusal. For some unjust commands cannot excuse the general Neglect of our Duty. They will be our Parents and we must be their Children still: And if we cannot act for them against God, neither can we act against them for ourselves or anything else.

3

An Essay Upon the Good Education of Children (An Essay Upon Well-Taught Children; And Upon an Able and Faithful Teacher of Them)

Cotton Mather, 1708

Cotton Mather (1662–1728) lived during a time of transition in the American colonies, and his life reflects the tension. In his more than 400 books, he vigorously defended the traditional Puritan way of life that was slowly losing influence to Enlightenment ways of thinking. Yet he also sought to find ways to reconcile the emerging scientific approach to knowledge with his Puritan theology. He advocated for the radical practice of inoculation, wrote treatises on the harmony of theology and science, and considered Sir Isaac Newton his scientific guide. Mather's treatise, "An Essay Upon the Good Education of Children," was actually delivered at the funeral of one of his own teachers. It clearly communicates the Puritan love for the Scriptures and education. It also provides an example of the reasons for their support for publicly funded forms of education. —PLG

American Educational Thought: Essays from 1640–1940, pages 15–31

2 Tim. 3:15. *From a child, thou hast known the Holy Scriptures, which are able to make thee wise unto salvation.*

It was a great case, which the parents to a son of great hope, once put unto a Messenger of Heaven; Judg. 13:12, *How shall we order the child and what shall we do unto him?* The education of our children is a point of inexpressible consequence: of unparalleled importance. Unworthy to be *parents*, most worthy to be esteemed rather *monsters* than parents, are they who are not follicituous to give their children an agreeable education. There is no serious religion in those parents, who are not follicitious, that their children should have a religious education. Our children are too numerous; the temptations which endanger the ruine of our children are so innumerable; that we ought frequently and earnestly to insist on this point; their agreeable and religious education. We will now therefore enquire; how shall we order the children, and what shall we do unto them?

I will answer in one word; let the children have such an education as Timothy had. We have before us a definition of that education; and a direction to give you this.

Doctrine

That saving wisdom is to be fetch'd from the knowledge of the Holy Scriptures; and the early knowledge of the Holy Scriptures, is the way to be betimes made wise unto salvation.

That we may more intelligibly prosecute this *doctrine*, we will first a little entertain our selves with the history of. *A child made wise unto salvation, by the knowledge of the Holy Scriptures.* A Timothy, and the *education* of a lovely *Timothy*, shall be first a little set before us.

Our *Timothy* is now address'd by the aged apostle *Paul*, at this time a prisoner at *Rome*, with an epistle written by him, a little before his martyrdom; an epistle, which *Chrysostom* ingeniously calls, *our Apostles last will and testament.* In this epistle, our Apostle exhorts his excellent and beloved *son Timothy*; [a *son*, he might well call him, having so many ways both *adopted* him, and instructed him:] he exhorts him to stedfastness in the faith and work of his glorious Lord. One argument, with which he inculcates this exhortation, is his *education.* For one educated in the *way of truth,* and in the *knowledge of the Holy Scriptures*, to forsake the *way of God*, is worse than for another to do so. From such as are *well* educated, there are *better things* expected than from others. Consider this, O apostates from a *new-english* education; *consider* it, you that *forget* how you have been *educated*, lest the *wrath of heaven tear you to peaces, and there be none to deliver you.* When the son and grandson perhaps, of those that have been faithful servants of God, shall first go off to an observable degree of bigotry for the *superstitions* against which his progenitors had born glorious *testimonies*; and then go on to a *malignity* against the people of God among whom he had his education; and publish his *malignity* with abhorred strains of *profaness* and *atheism*: 'tis not enough to call upon such an one, with the old Jewish rebuke, *O thou vinegar, the son of good wine!* It must be said, he is a *dreadful spectacle*. He has made himself so; and one may tremble to think, what the holy God will e'er long make of him. *Friend,* when the *goodness* of a young man, like the *morning cloud,* and the *early dew,* soon *passes away,* the justice of God is not long upon the deliberation, *what shall I do unto thee! What shall I do unto thee!*

Our Timothy was very happy in his education. It may be edifying for us, a little to reflect on the occasion of this education, and the influence of it.

Our Timothy had a godly mother, and a godly grandmother. He might suck in knowledge and goodness with his mothers milk. He might be taught the right wayes of the Lord, while his grandmother had him by his leading-strings, both of them were Jews; and probably they were early converts to Christianity. His father was a gentile! Whether a proselyte or no, we are not informed. But he also was converted unto Christianity at the same time with his desirable consort. They had before this, betimes begun to give their little son, the knowledge of the Holy Scriptures. An early tincture of Scriptural piety thus took the mind of the child. But when the parents were brought home to the blessed Jesus, they wholly committed, as it seems, their little son, unto the care of that venerable minister, who had been their spiritual father. Having themselves got good by a minister of God, they must have their child, in the way of getting the same good. They begg'd Paul, to take the tuition of him; oh! Happy child, in the hands of such a tutor!

Well; and what was the effect of this education? Our Timothy did himself prove. A Christian of the first rate; yea, and an admirable minister, his labours in the harvest of the Lord, were extraordinary; every one wondered, how any one man, could ever labour so abundantly. He was of a feeble constitution; and of such an abstemious temperance, that he was even blamed for it; but one of an active soul, one of a flaming zeal. The great Paul could give this testimony of him, that he did not know another man in the world, who so naturally took to the doing of good; who so readily and chearfully laid hold on all opportunities to be serviceable an angelical sort of a man; one highly esteemed by John, as well as by Paul; those angels in flesh loved him dearly. He was an angel in the church of Ephesus; the ancients agree to call him, An admirable young man. At last, he became an old man. And then, one day the votaries of Diana carrying their images about the town, and with masks and clubs, and dances, committing a thousand insipiencies, this brave man step'd out into the street, and would have perswaded them, to leave off their idolatries and impieties: whereat the enraged mob, fell upon him, and murdered him. He had the crown of martyrdom. He obtained a claim to a part in that resurrection, which his tutor once declared himself follicitous, by any means, to attain unto. What? And will the early knowledge of the Holy Scriptures make such a man?

I now with some enforcement, can tell my hearers over again;

That they who would be wise unto Salvation, must know the Holy Scriptures; And that for children to know the Holy Scriptures, is early wisdom, and saving wisdom.

I can demand their attention to several propositions; and such too, as it were to be wished, all our children were well acquainted with.

I. To yield obedience unto God, in the wayes and rules of his holy religion; this is to be, wise unto salvation.

There is an holy religion, wherewith we are to glorify God in this world. By doing so, we secure our title to an eternal glory with God in another and a better world. Now there never was a truer assertion, than that; Psal. 111:10, the beginning of wisdom, is the fear of the Lord, all they that give themselves to it, have a good understanding. It must needs be our truest wisdom, to glorify the God that made us; for by doing so, we answer the end for which he made us. There is nothing so reasonable as to be religious. It must needs be our truest wisdom; to make sure of eternal glory in another and better world; for we can be sure of nothing in this world; we are sure, that we shall shortly be strip't of every thing in this world. There is nothing so profitable, nothing so necessary, as to be religious. The rules of religion are prescribed by the only wise God; the God of whom we are assured, Psal. 145. 5. His understanding is infinite. They must needs be wise rules; it must needs be our wisdom to adhere unto them.

One main stroke in religion is, faith towards our Lord Jesus Christ. Faith is in the Bible often called by the name of, wisdom. 'tis most justly called so. It beholds, it receives, it enjoyes, that glorious Christ, in whom there is, the wisdom of God. And, the end of our faith will be the salvation of the soul.

Another main stroke in religion is, repentance towards God. Repentance is a resipiscence, or growing wise again. It must be wisdom, to abhor sin, to avoid sin; sin is always folly: to sin, is to do very foolishly. And, repentance, this will be unto salvation.

There is no man, but what will own, 'tis the wisdom of every man, to save his own soul: for, what is a man profited, if he gain the whole world, and lose his own soul? Now the issue of conformity to the rules of religion, will be the salvation of the soul. We read, Heb. 5:9. Christ, is the author of eternal salvation, unto all them that obey him.

II. Our knowledge of the Holy Scriptures, is that by which we come to know the rules of religion, and be religiously wise unto salvation. The rules of our holy religion, are all of them delivered in those oracles of God, which we call, the Holy Scriptures. If ever we come unto salvation, it must be by conversing with the Holy Scriptures. We are so called upon; Joh. 5:39. Search the Holy Scriptures, for in them ye think, ye have eternal life: and they are they who testify of me. It was very fit, that the will of God, giving us the rules of living unto him, should be contain'd in some writings or other. Those inspired writings which we have in our old and New Testament, are the only ones, that can pretend unto this dignity. In these Holy Scriptures we have the rules of religion, and the rules by the observation whereof we shall be wise unto salvation. Here, here is the gospel, whereof we are told; Eph. 1:13. It is the gospel of your salvation. If we lack the knowledge of this gospel, we shall miss of salvation, and be destroy'd for the lack of knowledge. If we do not know this gospel, we shall be a people of no understanding; of such a people, how terrible it thunders! He that made them will not have mercy on them; he that formed them, will show them no favour. What is all the learning in the world, without the knowledge of the Holy Scriptures! There were (they say) two hundred thousand books, in the library which Ptolomy erected at Alexandria; but it was the addition of the Holy Scriptures, which made it a truly learned library. And whatever we have learnt from all our books, 'tis the knowledge of the Holy Scriptures, that will bring us to the truest, and indeed the only learning. A dying Grotius, or Selden will tell you so?

But what sort of knowledge is requisite?

Be sure, a doctrinal knowledge of the Holy Scriptures is requisite, that we may be wise unto salvation. We read, 2 Cor. 4:3. If our gospel be hid, it is hid unto them that be lost. We must know doctrinally the main things that are communicated unto us in the Holy Scriptures. The creation of man by God; the confusion of man by sin; the redemption of man by Christ. These are the main things in the Holy Scriptures. If we are ignorant of these things our ignorance will plunge us into everlasting darkness: verily, it lays us in chains of darkness?

But then, a practical knowledge of the Holy Scriptures, is also requisite. We know to little purpose, except we do according to what we know. We read, Joh. 13:17. Since ye know these things, happy are ye, if you do them. Knowledge must be as John Baptist was to our Saviour, only a precursor to goodness; and we must say, that which comes after it is preferred before it. We must know the truth and walk in the truth. We must know God, and serve him. We must know Christ, and grow in grace. The lamp is without oyl; it will go out in everlasting darkness, if the knowledge be not soak'd and dip'd in love. It was the saying of Maximus Tyrius long ago, *scientia quis usus esse potest, nis ea agamus?* We must know and hear our duty, and we must be doers of the word, and not hearers only. Else we are not wise unto salvation. We foolishly deceive our selves, in our hope of salvation, if we do not know practically, our knowledge will not render us wise unto salvation. It will but aggravate our damnation; and there can be no wisdom in that. If we rebel against our light, it will not be saving wisdom. No, it will be a folly that will damn the rebellious. We read, Mat. 7:26. 'Tis the part of, a foolish man who builds his house on the sand, and great is the fall of it. It has been well enough sometimes thus expressed, one apple of the tree of life, in practice, is of more account than ten of the tree of knowledge. Thus Homer makes Phoenix, the tutor of Achilles, μυθων τε ρητεςα, πραχτηρα τε εργων. It is the sweet conjunction or the knowledge and practice, of the Holy Scriptures, that will gain our point. A conjunction that infallibly fore-tells a salvation to the uttermost.

III. The inference from hence is; that the early knowledge of the Holy Scriptures, is the way to be betimes made wise unto salvation.

And now there is a twofold application to be made of this observation. We will discourse on this observation, by applying it unto two sorts of persons.

I. It is the interest of all teachers to begin betimes, in teaching of children, the early knowledge of the Holy Scriptures, that so they may be wise unto salvation. It is to you, O teachers; unto you first, there must now come the word of the Lord. It must come, with an answer to divers enquires.

We will, first, enquire, and declare, when should we begin to teach our children, the knowledge of the Holy Scriptures?

Betimes! Betimes! Let the children have the early knowledge of the Holy Scriptures. That princely preacher, the Prince of Anbalt, would say; the Holy Scriptures, what are they but the swadling clothes of the holy child Jesus? He is to be found in every chapter. I will then say, let us teach our children the Holy Scriptures, as soon as we can after they come out of their swadling clothes. This is the direction of the Holy Scriptures, Deut. 6:7. Thou shalt teach them diligently unto thy children. And Eph. 6:4. Your children, bring them up in the nurture and admonition of the Lord. But the Holy

Scriptures have not expressly said, how early, we shall begin to teach our children, the knowledge of them. However, we may easily determine it.

First; how early do the children begin to be capable of knowing and minding what is in the Holy Scriptures? Most certainly we should begin as soon as we can. As soon as the children can know, so soon should we teach them, what they should know. So much there is to be learnt, it is pity any time should be lost. No doubt, they began so soon with Solomon; else he would not have said, Prov. 4:3, 4. I was my fathers son, a tender and only one in the sight of my mother, then he taught me.

Again; how early do the children begin to know other matters? Why should we not begin to teach them something from the Holy Scriptures, that may suit them, *lae capit hic infans,* as early as we teach them things less worthy, less useful! Can we teach them, what they owe to us? Methinks , we may then teach them, what they owe to the Lord, who made both us and them? Their little souls are precious cabinets. Why should not the best things be first put into them? We are so called upon; Matth. 6:33. Seek first the kingdom of God. Even so, with the first; let them learn the things that concern the kingdom of God.

Once more; how early do the children begin to know, and to do, what may be harmful to them? 'Tis very early, that they learn the things condemned in the Holy Scriptures. Why should they not as early learn the Holy Scriptures, which do condemn those pernicious and provoking evil? Why should they not know the precepts of God, as early as they know how to break the precepts? Why should they not be taught, that they must fear God, and love Christ, and hate sin, as early as they can learn to sin? Especially since this would be the way to preserve them from sin. A child no sooner begins to do any thing rational, but Satan begins to show it, how to do something that is criminal. Methinks, I see the image of it; Rev. 12:4. The dragon stood to devour the child as soon as it was born. Then say I; it becomes us to be aforehand with the dragon, if it be possible: To stand ready with the knowledge of the Holy Scriptures, to rescue the children from the venemous designs of the dragon upon them.

There is a plausible objection, against this early essay, to give our children the knowledge of the Holy Scriptures.

Will not this be to make the children, take the name of the Lord in vain? Would it not be more discretion, to stay till the children are themselves come to some years of discretion?

It is easily answered. Will you never teach the children, till you see them have the graces that will keep them from taking the name of the Lord in vain? Rather teach them, to keep them from it. And let our discretion teach us to manage the matter wisely, in teaching our children. Teach them with all possible gravity; and teach them to be grave, in every thing, that relates to God, and their souls. Consider also the capacity of the children: teach them, what shall be good for them; and forbear the rest, until they shall be more able to bear it.

We will, secondly, enquire, and declare, what is that knowledge of the Holy Scriptures, which we are to teach our children?

Truly, as much as ever we can help them to…all the knowledge, that they can take in, still as we find them able to take it in more particularly.

First, the histories of the Holy Scriptures; we are to teach them unto our children. Children are naturally taken with histories. Now, instead of corrupt stories, and idle fables, why should we not single out the histories in the Holy Scriptures for them? Only, it would be adviseable always to clench the histories, with some admonitions of piety, which are to be gathered from them. There are none of those histories, but it may be said upon them; Psal. 119.... Thy servant is warned by them.

Secondly; we are to teach our children the principles of the Holy Scriptures. Tell the children, what the Holy Scriptures have taught us to believe, about God, and his perfections, and his works: about the fall of man, and the method of his recovery out of that miserable fall; about the Lord Jesus Christ, who He is, & what He has done, and what He will do, for his chosen people. We read, that the principles of the doctrine of Christ are the milk for babes. That these things may be the better taught, an orthodox catechism, is to be employ'd. They should say their catechism, and be rewarded when they can say it. But then, we should put lesser questions unto them; unto which, their yes. Or no, will give us to perceive, whether they understand what they say. Canvase the matter with them. Ask them several things about it. Cause them to take much notice of it. See whether they have tak'n a right notion of it. We read, 2 Tim. 1:13. There is a form of sound words, which they must hear from us.

Thirdly; we are to teach our children the commandments of the Holy Scriptures. There are the Ten Commandments. The children should be made to know, what is implied in them, what is forbidden, what is required. How, as it has been of old noted the first table of the commandments, is a loadstone of the second; the second is a touchstone for the first. There are many lessons, which are to be inculcated on them, lessons by which their manners are to be regulated. Good lessons for children may be the title for them.

But there is one very great article, which is often to be insisted on. The children have, mostly, been baptised. O make 'em know the intent and meaning of their baptism. As soon as ever you can, inform them, that they have been baptised! And beget in them an awful sense of their baptismal obligations. Tell them, now, my child, you must be a servant of a glorious Christ. And be afraid of defiling your self with any sin, since you have been washed in the name, of the most holy Lord. Say to them; as....1 Chron. 28:9. My child, know thou the God of thy father and serve him with a perfect heart, and a willing mind; if thou seek him, he will be found of thee; but if thou forsake him, he will cast thee off for ever. You cannot imagine how much efficacy this teaching may have upon them.

Fourthly; the children should learn to read the Holy Scriptures; and this, as early as may be, to school therefore with them. Let them not be loitering at home, or playing abroad, when they should be at school. Be more concerned for their schooling, than for their cloathing. If there be any, as I suppose there cannot be many, so necessitous, as to call for it, let us in this town go on with our charity-schools. When the children can read, the Holy Scriptures, charge them, and cause them, every day to read that book of life. Hire them to remember what they read; to get select sentences of the Holy Scriptures into their memories. And then; show them, how to make prayers out of what they read. Help them to turn all into prayers, that they may be wise unto salvation. Oh, teach them to pray! When once it comes to be said, behold they pray! T'is likely that it may quickly be said, they are wise unto salvation. The Bible was well called, by one of the ancients, *epistola omnipotentis dei ad creaturam suam*, a letter from the Almighty God, unto his creatures, it should be considered as a letter from the Almighty God unto our children. They should be taught accordingly to read it, and reverence it, and answer it.

This it will be, for the children to know the Holy Scriptures.

We will, thirdly, enquire and declare, who it is, that is to teach the children, the knowledge of the Holy Scriptures. Come all hands to the work.

In particular; the pastors of the flock; they must not neglect the children of the flock. The charge of our Lord unto them, is that; Joh. 21:15. Feed my lambs. It seems proposed, as if it were, at least one third part of the pastoral charge. O men of God, how many ways may you devise good, in this great affair; to make the children under your charge, wise unto salvation! In the midst of many such devices, I will mention one, which the excellent Mr. White, in his manual for parents, has proposed;

That ministers would sometimes preach at the schools, as well as catechise; because as he says, the preaching of the word, is the converting ordinance. And when sermons are brought unto the schools, the children must needs hear with more attention, and hear of such things as do more immediately concern them, which in the publick assemblies, are not so much medled withal; and the ministers would condescend unto such expressions as might work most with them, which would not be so fit for a large congregation.

The master and mistress, in the school, may do much in this noble work. We read, the little ones have their angels. Truly, to teach the little ones, the knowledge of the Holy Scriptures, and make them wise unto salvation, it is a stately work; I had almost call'd it; a work for angels. It is an hard work to keep a school; and hardly ever duly recompensed. I suppose, it is easier to be at the plough all day, than in the school. But it is a good work: it is God's plough; and God speed it! I would not have you weary of it. Melchior Adam did well to call it, *molestissimam, fed deo longe gratissiman functionem;* a work, tho' very tiresome, and troublesome to the flesh, yet most highly acceptable to God. Go on with it chearfully; and often teach the children something of the Holy Scriptures; often drop some honey out of that rock upon them. Who can tell, but you may teach them the things that shall save their souls, and they shall bless God for you and with you, throughout eternal ages? Every time a new child comes to the school, oh! Why should you not think! Here my glorious Lord sends me another object, on which I may do something, to advance his kingdom in the world!

No, nor will we excuse the very servants in the family, from this blessed work; even the handmaids in the family, as they are dressing and feeding the children, O handmaids of the Lord how much may you do, to instill the knowledge of the Holy Scriptures into the children! If our servants would once come to take pleasure in such a thing, to keep teaching the children something from the Holy Scriptures, O my children, [for such servants are worthy to be called, children!] How much would you adorn the doctrine of God your Saviour! It was certainly a good speech, which I find written by a person of quality. It is certainly, the highest dignity, if not the greatest happiness, that humane nature is capable of, here in this vale below, to have a soul so far enlightened, as to become the mirror, or conduit or conveyer of Gods truth to others. Now, even a domestick servant, may arrive to this dignity, this happiness. Yea, let all ranks of men aspire after it.

But; lastly, and yet first of all, O parents arise; this matter chiefly belongs unto you; we also will be with you, none I say, none, are so much concerned, as parents to look after it, that their children be taught the knowledge of the Holy Scriptures. Our famous king Alfred, procured a law, that every man who had but as much as two hides of land, should bring up his children to learning, till fifteen years of age at least; that so they might know Christ, and live happily; else he said, they were but beasts and sots. I am to press it, that parents give their children all the learning they can; especially that which will bring them to know Christ, and live happily.

Parents, what motive can you desire more than this? 'Tis the way to make the children wise unto salvation. Certainly, you desire the salvation of your children. You have had your share among the causes of it, that they are by nature children of wrath. And would you not see them saved from that wrath? Did you duly teach your children the knowledge of the Holy Scriptures, there would be a likelihood of their being those children; I Joh. 2:13. Little children, ye have known the father. And oh! What would be the fruit of this knowledge? Truly, this is life eternal. You lodge in the little souls of your children, the seeds of life eternal, if God please to make them so. What a charming word is that? Gen. 18:19. He will command his children, and they shall keep the way of the Lord. But if the knowledge of the Holy Scriptures be withheld from the children, they perish, they perish dreadfully, if the understandings of the children be darkened, they will be alienated from the life of God; they will be slaves to the power of darkness; they are in the broad way to eternal darkness; if they know not God & the Lord Jesus Christ, their doom from the Lord will be, depart from me, I know you not. Oh, look upon the children, which you have so often set on your knees, which always ly so very near to your hearts; how can you bear to have them thrown into the place of dragons? They infallibly go thither, if by the knowledge of the Holy Scriptures, you do not save them from thence. Austin says of his excellent mother, *toties filios parturiebat, quoties a deo eos deviare cernebat;* she fell into travail for them, as often as she saw them fall into folly. Oh! Parents, be continually in travail for your children, that you may save them from all sinful folly. We read of a child; 2 King. 4:19. He said unto his father, my head, my head!

Parents, there are the cries, which the souls of your children make in your ears; 'My head, my head! Oh! 'That you would fill my head with the knowledge of the Holy Scriptures! My heart, my heart! It will be a very dungeon of wickedness, if you do not by the knowledge of the Holy Scriptures, purify it! It is a solemn expression of the martyr Cyprian. There are parents, who so neglect their children, that at the last day, their miserable children will cry out, *parentes sensimus parricidas;* our parents have been our murderers! Parents, beware of, coming under so bitter a condemnation. Let the command of God, and the promise of God, at last prevail with you. You have it in those terms; Prov. 22:4. Train up a child in the way he should go, and when he is old, he will not depart from it. God puts these children into your hands. He says, here, take this child; let it be taught the knowledge of the Holy Scriptures. I will reward all thy pains. Thy well-instructed child, shall be thy comfort, thy credit, a blessing to others in the world. If it miss of salvation, yet thou shalt have peace in thy mind, that thou didst thy endeavour to make it wise unto salvation. But if it want knowledge, and saving wisdom thro' any gross negligence of thine, thy punishment shall be terrible, in the day of the Lords pleading with thee.

Consider what I say, and the Lord give you understanding, to do your part, that your children may not want understanding, or die without instruction. 'Tis the wish of heaven over you; Deut. 32:29, O that they were wise that they understood this, that [so some render it] they would consider their posterity.

But then, it is the interest of all children, to learn the knowledge of the Holy Scriptures betimes, that so they may be wise unto salvation. We have many children in the auditory. I wish the little ones would now give a great attention.

This country once had a brave man in it, whose name was Mr. Giles Firmin. That man was pious, from his early childhood. And that which brought him to his piety was this. When he was a school boy, he with other lads went unto the lectures of the famous Rogers; where they could not get into the thronged auditory. The zealous preacher saw them in the porch, and lifting up his voice, he called unto them. Children, I hope you are come hither for a Christ; remember what I say unto you; if you will have a Christ for your Saviour, you shall have him. This word struck little Firmin to the heart; by this word, God quickened him; he became a godly child, and he dyed not long since, a very old man, and one of the best men in the world.

I will now say, children, I hope you are come hither that you may be made wise unto salvation. And if any of them are not attentive, I hope you that are their tutors, will afterwards repeat unto them the admonitions which are now provided for them.

Come, ye children, hearken to me, I will teach you, what you ought to do.

You ought, first, to be willing to be taught the fear of the Lord. When your teachers would learn you something of the Holy Scriptures, be willing to learn. Be not lothe to wait upon their teaching. Do not strive to get away from their teaching. Be not so set upon your childish & foolish play, as to count every minute a weary hour under their teaching. Rather come to your teachers, and beg it of them, I pray, teach me something. Oh! Count it a privilege, to be taught any things of the Holy Scriptures. Prize, prize the sincere milk of the word. Prize, prize the word of God, as being sweeter than the honey and the honey-comb. Count the knowledge of God, and Christ, and heavenly things, a more precious thing than any in the world.

Yea, secondly; you ought never to be satisfied. Know as much of the Holy Scriptures as ever you can; and never count that you know enough. Get your catechism exactly by heart. Become able to read the Bible. Read something of it every day. Ask abundance of questions about what you read. You are fond of ornaments; O despise all ornaments in comparison of this; to be adorned with the knowledge of the Holy Scriptures.

But, thirdly; be sure to do what you know from the Holy Scriptures that you ought to do. As now; do not you know from the Holy Scriptures, that you ought to keep holy the Lords-day, and to honour your parents, and rather suffer any thing than tell a lye: do not you know from the Holy Scriptures, that you ought to pray in secret every day, and pray without ceasing? Oh! Do these things, my children, be sure to do such things. What have the Holy Scriptures told you, concerning early religion? In them you have heard your Saviour say, Prov. 8:17. They that seek me early, shall find me. These the voice of your Saviour is, Matth. 19:14. Suffer little children to come unto me, for of such is the kingdom of heaven. Well then, betimes, now in your childhood, oh! Come to a glorious Christ; put your selves into his hands. Beg of him, I beseech, thee, O Lord, to deliver my soul, why, why, should your childhood be nothing but vanity! Nothing but a long step in the arms of death and darkness.

Remember, children; there have been many children in the world, who have in their early childhood, by the knowledge of the Holy Scriptures, been wise unto salvation. You have in your hands, the narratives of many such, that have been in our days. And such there were in the days of old. Origen was one; little Origen, when he was but a child, would rejoice the heart of his father, by his readiness to learn the Holy Scriptures, which he set him to learn. And while he was yet a child, he had so much of God in him, that as he lay asleep, his venerable father would lay his hand on the breast of the child, and say with unspeakable joy; here's a little temple of God! And there was a rare child at Antioch; one little more than seven years old; the lad was examined about what was in the Holy Scriptures, by bloody persecutors, who stood ready to murder him; he notably told them, there can be but one God, and our Christ is the true God; they ask'd him where he learn't this; he reply'd, I learn't it of my mother, it was with my mothers milk that I suck't it in. On this, they horribly scourg'd the lad, and then butchered him with hideous torments: he smiled under his torments, and he dyed a martyr of the Lord. Oh! That our children were so disposed!

The infant-children of the faithful, are the children of God. God calls them; Ezek. 16:21. My children. God forbid, that our children as soon as they come to act reasonably, should be so unreasonable, as to make themselves the children of Satan. Children, if you hate that which is good, if you disobey your parents, if you speak wicked words; and call wicked names, and lye, and curse, if you steal, and if you play on the Lords-day; whose children are you? Verily, your spot is, that you are not the children of God; you make Satan your father; you do like the children of Satan. How odious a spectacle are you! But serious, gracious, dutiful children, always breathing after the knowledge of the Holy Scriptures, how lovely a spectacle!

It was the speech of one that wise betimes; Psal. 119:147. I prevented the dawning of the morning, and I cried; I hoped in thy word. While you are yet children, you must have piety rectifying, sanctifying, purifying of your childhood. While reason is but upon the dawning with you, there is reason that you should mind religion. There was once an incomparable child, of whom we read, 1 Sam. 3:1. The child Samuel ministred unto the Lord. A child, which was visited & possessed by the spirit of God; a child, which quickly answered the calls of the Holy One; a child, that would leave his sleep, to hold communion with the Lord. O most amiable child!

Children, 'tis your dawning time. It may be your dying time. A child once grew very solid, and was more for his book than for his play, and pray'd, and pray'd unto God more than once every day. Being asked the cause, the child said, Why, I was in the burying-place a while-ago, and there I saw a grave shorter than my self! Children, go unto the burying-place; there you will see many a grave shorter than your selves. 'Tis now upon computation found, that more than half the children of men dy before they come to be seventeen years of age. And what needs any more be said for your awakening, to learn the Holy Scriptures!

We read of such a thing as that; Isa. 65:20. The child shalt dy an hundred years old. You may dy in your childhood: but you should be ambitious, that it should be for you may dy an hundred years old; have as much knowledge and vertue, as many men of an hundred years old. It was a brave stroke in an epitaph, on a child; *praterquain ataton nil puerile suit.* Some of you can construe it. I will do it for them that can't.

> *Except his age, the lovely lad*
> *Nothing that looked like childhood had.*

The small as well as the great, are to stand before the judgment-seat of God. Oh, that while you are yet small you would be greatly affected with the day of judgment. If you go on to do amiss, think, I know that for this, God will bring me into judgment. The Holy Scriptures give you the knowledge of such a thing.

Children. You may by your piety, approve your selves the regenerate children of God, while you are yet children cry unto, my father! Ah, children; be afraid of going prayerless to bed, lest the devil be your bed-fellow. Be afraid of playing on the Lords-day, lest the devil be your play-fellow. Be afraid of telling lies, or speaking wickedly, lest that evil tongue be one day tormented in the flames, where, a drop of water to cool the tongue, will be roared for.

We read. Matth. 18:10. The little ones have their angels. Dear children; behave your selves, as having the angels of God looking upon you; the angels of God looking after you!

Oh! That our glorious Lord, would set home such thoughts as these; upon the hearts of our children; and give perfect hearts unto them.

If they don't mind these things, in this more publick dispensation of them, will you that are their teachers, more privately inculcate such things upon them? I had the happiness of an education under a school-master who was exemplary for doing so! Before we part, I am to tell you more concerning him.

You shall give me leave to conclude with a very reasonable corollary.

Worthy of honour are the teachers that convey wisdom unto our children, worthy of double honour the happy instruments that convey saving wisdom to them! There are some whose peculiar profession it is, to assist the education of our children; and it is, therefore their endeavour to give them a religious education. Their employment is to bestow useful and various learning on our children; but they make their employment, a precious advantage to learn them the Holy Scriptures, and make them wise for eternity.

These our school masters, deserve a great encouragement; we are not wise for our children, if we do not greatly encourage them.

The particular persons, who have their children, in the tutelage of skilful and careful school-masters, ought to make them suitable recompences. Their stipends are generally far short of their deserts. They deserve additional compensations. Their pains are not small. What they do is very great. And surely our children are very dear to us; I need not quote Euripides to tell you, that they are as very life and soul, unto all mankind. I can't but observe it with a just indignation; to feed our children, to cloath our children, to do any thing for the bodies of our children; or perhaps to teach them some trise at a dancing school, scarcely worth their learning, we count no expence too much; at the same time to have the minds of our children enriched with the most valuable knowledge, here, to what purpose? Is the cry: A little expence, how heavily it goes off! My brethren, these things ought not so to be. Well-taught children are certainly very much to be accounted of. When the mother of the Gracchi was ask'd for the sight of her ornaments, how instructively did she present her two sons brought up in learning and vertue, as the brightest of all her ornaments! If we were duly sensible, how vast a comfort it is, how vast a concern, to have well-taught children, we should study all the ways imaginable, to express our thankfulness unto teachers of them. And it will not be complain'd, that a Mecanas is to be no where found but in Horace's poetry. The Christian emperour Gratian, one of the best men, that ever sway'd the Roman scepter conferr'd riches and honours on his master Ausonius, and he sent him that agreeable compliment with them; sir, I have paid what I ow'd, and I still owe, what I have paid. Language agreeable to the spirit of Christianity! Yea, a Zeno, that was a stranger to it, yet has this recorded in his commendation, that he would give his master, as much again, as the wages he ask'd of him. I hope, he won't be the only one, that shall have such a things spoken of him.

And the more liberal provision the publick does make for industrious, well-accomplished, well-disposed scholl-masters, the more is the publick wisdom testified & propagated. Ammianus Marcellinus, the historian, tho' a great admirer of Julian & of paganism, yet condemns his prohibition of school-masters unto the Christians: *illud autem inclemens obruendum perenni silentio, quod arcebat docere, magistros rhetoricos et grammaticos, ritus christiani cultores.* But, syrs, if you do not encourage your school-masters, you do a part of Julianism, and as bad as prohibit them. Certainly, if something of Julianism did not prevail too much among us (which among a people of our profession is highly scandalous,) we might ere now have seen, besides the petty schools of every town, a grammar-school at the head town of every county, and an able school-master with an ample salary, the shepherd in it; a thing so often, so often unsuccessfully petition'd for! We hear good words now and then spoken for the tribe of Levi. I desire, to speak one for the tribe of Simeon. The Simeonites were the school-masters that were scattered in Israel. I assure my self, than ours, do watch against the anger which is fierce and the wrath which is cruel; and that they use not instruments of cruelty in their habitations; but prudently study the tempers of the children, they have to deal withal. Tho' Moses left them out of his blessing; [the tribe not having them done any thing since Jacobs dying oracles, to signalize them.] Yet our glorious Jesus, has a blessing for them. They serve him wonderfully. His people will also bless them, and bless God for them....

School masters that have *used the office well, purchase to themselves, a good esteem* to out-live their *death,* as well as merit for themselves a good *support* while they *live.* 'Tis a justice to them, that they should be had in *everlasting remembrance;* . . .

4

Proposals Relating to the Youth
in Pensilvania

Benjamin Franklin, 1749

Benjamin Franklin (1706–1790) embodied the Age of Enlightenment. A printer, inventor, postmaster, newspaper editor, statesman, philosopher, scientist, and writer, Franklin was one of America's greatest 18th century figures. Franklin is most remembered for his role as politician. As a member of the second Continental Congress, he served on the committee that wrote the Declaration of Independence, and later he presided over the Constitutional Convention. He also procured French assistance in the American War for Independence and later negotiated peace with the British. In this essay, written twenty-five years before the Revolutionary War, Franklin writes about the importance of education. Although he addresses the youth of Pennsylvania in particular, his advice is applicable to all future Americans. Franklin suggests that education is the foundation of happiness, and therefore a

American Educational Thought: Essays from 1640–1940, pages 33–39

critical function of government. Because of the importance of education, Franklin advises that an academy be established in Pennsylvania and he makes recommendations for the students' course of study. Importantly, Franklin suggested the school "be furnished with a library." Franklin is credited with inventing the public lending library, which is absolutely fundamental to education. —CHB

The good Education of Youth has been esteemed by wise Men in all Ages, as the surest Foundation of the Happiness both of private Families and of Common-wealths. Almost all Governments have therefore made it a principal Object of their Attention, to establish and endow with proper Revenues, such Seminaries of Learning, as might supply the succeeding Age with Men qualified to serve the Publick with Honour to themselves, and to their Country.

Many of the first Settlers of these Provinces, were Men who had received a good Education in *Europe,* and to their Wisdom and good Management we owe much of our present Prosperity. But their Hands were full, and they could not do all Things. The present Race are not thought to be generally of equal Ability: For though the *American* Youth are allow'd not to want Capacity; yet the best Capacities require Cultivation, it being truly with them, as with the best Ground, which unless well tilled and sowed with profitable Seed, produces only ranker Weeds.

That we may obtain the Advantages arising from an Increase of Knowledge, and prevent as much as may be the mischievous Consequences that would attend a general Ignorance among us, the following *Hints* are offered towards forming a Plan for the Education of the Youth of *Pensilvania,* viz.

It is propos'd,

THAT some Persons of Leisure and publick Spirit, apply for a CHARTER, by which they may be incorporated, with Power to erect an ACADEMY for the Education of Youth, to govern the same, provide Masters, make Rules, receive Donations, purchase Lands, *&c.* and to add to their Number, from Time to Time such other Persons as they shall judge suitable.

That the Members of the Corporation make it their Pleasure, and in some Degree their Business, to visit the Academy often, encourage and countenance the Youth, countenance and assist the Masters, and by all Means in their Power advance the Usefulness and Reputation of the Design; that they look on the Students as in some Sort their Children, treat them with Familiarity and Affection, and when they have behav'd well, and gone through their Studies, and are to enter the World, zealously unite, and make all the Interest that can be made to establish them, whether in

Business, Offices, Marriages, or any other Thing for their Advantage, preferably to all other Persons whatsoever even of equal Merit.

And if Men may, and frequently do, catch such a Taste for cultivating Flowers, Planting, Grafting, Inoculating, and the like, as to despise all other Amusements for their Sake, why may not we expect they should acquire a Relish for that *more useful* Culture of young Minds. *Thompson* says,

> 'Tis Joy to see the human Blossoms blow,
> When infant Reason grows apace, and calls
> For the kind Hand of an assiduous Care;
> Delightful Task! to rear the tender Thought,
> To teach the young Idea how to shoot,
> To pour the fresh Instruction o'er the Mind,
> To breathe th' enliv'ning Spirit, and to fix
> The generous Purpose in the glowing Breast.

That a House be provided for the ACADEMY, if not in the Town, not many Miles from it; the Situation high and dry, and if it may be, not far from a River, having a Garden, Orchard, Meadow, and a Field or two.

That the House be furnished with a Library (if in the Country, if in the Town, the Town Libraries may serve) with Maps of all Countries, Globes, some mathematical Instruments, and Apparatus for Experiments in Natural Philosophy, and for Mechanics; Prints, of all Kinds, Prospects, Buildings, Machines, &c.

purpose That the RECTOR be a Man of good Understanding, good Morals, diligent and patient, learn'd in the Languages and Sciences, and a correct pure Speaker and Writer of the *English* Tongue; to have such Tutors under him as shall be necessary.

That the boarding Scholars diet together, plainly, temperately, and frugally.

That to keep them in Health, and to strengthen and render active their Bodies, they be frequently exercis'd in Running, Leaping, Wrestling, and Swimming &c.

That they have peculiar Habits to distinguish them from other Youth, if the Academy be in or near the Town; for this, among other Reasons, that their Behaviour may be the better observed.

As to their STUDIES, it would be well if they could be taught *every Thing* that is useful, and *every Thing* that is ornamental: But Art is long, and their Time is short. It is therefore propos'd that they learn those Things that are likely to be most useful and *most ornamental.* Regard being had to the several Professions for which they are intended.

All should be taught to write a *fair Hand,* and swift, as that is useful to All. And with it may be learnt something of *Drawing,* by Imitation of Prints, and some of the first Principles of Perspective.

Arithmetick, Accounts, and some of the first Principles of *Geometry,* and *Astronomy.*

The *English* Language might be taught by Grammar; in which some of our best Writers, as *Tillotson, Addison, Pope, Algernoon Sidney, Cato's* Letters, *&c.* should be Classicks: The *Stiles* principally to be cultivated, being the *clear* and the *concise.* Reading should also be taught, and pronouncing, properly, distinctly, emphatically; not with an even Tone, which *under-does,* nor a theatrical, which *over-does* Nature.

To form their Stile, they should be put on Writing Letters to each other, making Abstracts of what they read; or writing the same Things in their own Words; telling or writing Stories lately read, in their own Expressions. All to be revis'd and corrected by the Tutor, who should give his Reasons, explain the Force and Import of Words, *&c.*

To form their Pronunciation, they may be put on making Declamations, repeating Speeches, delivering Orations, *&c.* The Tutor assisting at the Rehearsals, teaching, advising, correcting their Accent, *&c.*

But if HISTORY be made a constant Part of their Reading, such as the Translations of the *Greek* and *Roman* Historians, and the modern Histories of antient *Greece* and *Rome,* &c. may not almost all Kinds of useful Knowledge be that Way introduc'd to Advantage, and with Pleasure to the Student? As

GEOGRAPHY, by reading with Maps, and being required to point out the Places *where* the greatest Actions were done, to give their old and new Names, with the Bounds, Situation, Extent of the Countries concern'd, *&c.*

CHRONOLOGY, by the Help of *Helvicus* or some other Writer of the Kind, who will enable them to tell *when* those Events happened; what Princes were Cotemporaries, what States or famous Men flourish'd about that Time, *&c.* The several principal Epochs to be first well fix'd in their Memories.

ANTIENT CUSTOMS, religious and civil, being frequently mentioned in History, will give Occasion for explaining them; in which the Prints of Medals, Basso Relievo's, and antient Monuments will greatly assist.

MORALITY, by descanting and making continual Observations on the Causes of the Rise or Fall of any Man's Character, Fortune, Power, &c. mention'd in History; the Advantages of Temperance, Order, Frugality,

curriculum

Industry, Perseverance, &c. &c. Indeed the general natural Tendency of Reading good History, must be, to fix in the Minds of Youth deep Impressions of the Beauty and Usefulness of Virtue of all Kinds, Publick Spirit, Fortitude, &c.

HISTORY will show the wonderful Effects of ORATORY, in governing, turning and leading great Bodies of Mankind, Armies, Cities, Nations. When the Minds of Youth are struck with Admiration at this, then is the Time to give them the Principles of that Art, which they will study with Taste and Application. Then they may be made acquainted with the best Models among the Antients, their Beauties being particularly pointed out to them. Modern Political Oratory being chiefly performed by the Pen and Press, its Advantages over the Antient in some Respects are to be shown; as that its Effects are more extensive, more lasting, &c.

History will also afford frequent Opportunities of showing the Necessity of a Publick Religion, from its Usefulness to the Publick; the Advantage of a Religious Character among private Persons; the Mischiefs of Superstition, &c. and the Excellency of the CHRISTIAN RELIGION above all others antient or modern.

History will also give Occasion to expatiate on the Advantage of Civil Orders and Constitutions, how Men and their Properties are protected by joining in Societies and establishing Government; their Industry encouraged and rewarded, Arts invented, and Life made more comfortable: The Advantages of Liberty, Mischiefs of Licentiousness, Benefits arising from good Laws and a due Execution of Justice, &c. Thus may the first Principles of sound Politicks be fix'd in the Minds of Youth.

On Historical Occasions, Questions of Right and Wrong, Justice and Injustice, will naturally arise, and may be put to Youth, which they may debate in Conversation and in Writing. When they ardently desire Victory, for the Sake of the Praise attending it, they will begin to feel the Want, and be sensible of the Use of Logic, or the Art of Reasoning to discover Truth, and of Arguing to defend it, and convince Adversaries. This would be the Time to acquaint them with the Principles of that Art. Grotius, Puffendorff, and some other Writers of the same Kind, may be used on these Occasions to decide their Disputes. Publick Disputes warm the Imagination, whet the Industry, and strengthen the natural Abilities.

When Youth are told, that the Great Men whose Lives and Actions they read in History, spoke two of the best Languages that ever were, the most expressive, copious, beautiful; and that the finest Writings, the most correct Compositions, the most perfect Productions of human Wit and Wisdom, are in those Languages, which have endured Ages, and will endure while there are Men; that no Translation can do them Justice, or give the Pleasure found in Reading the Originals; that those Languages contain all Science; that one of them is become almost universal, being the Language of Learned Men in all Countries; that to understand them is a distinguishing Ornament, &c. they may be thereby made desirous of learning those Languages, and their Industry sharpen'd in the Acquisition of them. All intended for Divinity should be taught the *Latin* and *Greek*; for Physick, the *Latin, Greek* and *French*; for Law, the *Latin* and *French*; Merchants, the *French, German,* and *Spanish*: And though all should not be compell'd to learn *Latin, Greek,* or the modern foreign Languages; yet none that have an ardent Desire to learn them should be refused; their *English,* Arithmetick, and other Studies absolutely necessary, being at the same Time not neglected.

If the new *Universal History* were also read, it would give a *connected* Idea of human Affairs, so far as it goes, which should be follow'd by the best modern Histories, particularly of our Mother Country; then of these Colonies; which should be accompanied with Observations on their Rise, Encrease, Use to *Great-Britain,* Encouragements, Discouragements, &c. the Means to make them flourish, secure their Liberties, &c.

With the History of Men, Times and Nations, should be read at proper Hours or Days, some of the best *Histories of Nature,* which would not only be delightful to Youth, and furnish them with Matter for their Letters, &c. as well as other History; but afterwards of great Use to them, whether they are Merchants, Handicrafts, or Divines; enabling the first the better to understand many Commodities, Drugs, &c. the second to improve his Trade or Handicraft by new Mixtures, Materials, &c. and the last to adorn his Discourses by beautiful Comparisons, and strengthen them by new Proofs of Divine Providence. The Conversation of all will be improved by it, as Occasions frequently occur of making Natural Observations, which are instructive, agreeable, and entertaining in almost all Companies. *Natural History* will also afford Opportunities of introducing many Observations, relating to the Preservation of Health, which may be afterwards of great Use. *Arbuthnot* on Air and Aliment, *Sanctorius* on Perspiration, *Lemery* on Foods, and some others, may now be read, and a very little Explanation will make them sufficiently intelligible to Youth.

While they are reading Natural History, might not a little *Gardening, Planting, Grafting, Inoculating,* &c. be taught and practised; and now and then Excursions made to the neighbouring Plantations of the best Farmers, their Methods observ'd and reason'd upon for the Information of Youth. The Improvement of Agriculture being useful to all, and Skill in it no Disparagement to any.

The History of *Commerce*, of the Invention of Arts, Rise of Manufactures, Progress of Trade, Change of its Seats, with the Reasons, Causes, *&c.* may also be made entertaining to Youth, and will be useful to all. And this, with the Accounts in other History of the prodigious Force and Effect of Engines and Machines used in War, will naturally introduce a Desire to be instructed in *Mechanicks*, and to be inform'd of the Principles of that Art by which weak Men perform such Wonders, Labour is sav'd, Manufactures expedited, *&c. &c.* This will be the Time to show them Prints of antient and modern Machines, to explain them, to let them be copied, and to give Lectures in Mechanical Philosophy.

With the whole should be constantly inculcated and cultivated, that *Benignity of Mind*, which shows itself in *searching for* and *seizing* every Opportunity *to serve* and *to oblige*, and is the Foundation of what is called GOOD BREEDING; highly useful to the Possessor, and most agreeable to all.

The Idea of what is *true Merit*, should also be often presented to Youth, explain'd and impress'd on their Minds, as consisting in an *Inclination* join'd with an *Ability* to serve Mankind, one's Country, Friends and Family; which *Ability* is (with the Blessing of God) to be acquir'd or greatly encreas'd by *true Learning*; and should indeed be the great *Aim* and *End* of all Learning.

5

Selected Writings of Thomas Jefferson

Thomas Jefferson (1743–1826), the author of the Declaration of Independence and the Virginia Statue for Religious Freedom, the founder of the University of Virginia, ambassador to France, and the third President of the United States, like Benjamin Franklin, embodied the ideals of the Age of Enlightenment. Jefferson believed in the importance of an educated populace, particularly in a democratic society where the people governed rather than monarchs. In 1778, two years after writing the Declaration of Independence, Jefferson proposed his Bill for the More General Diffusion of Knowledge to the Virginia legislature. The bill would have established a public system of elementary and secondary education throughout the state. It did not pass. Public education would not be firmly established in Virginia until after the Civil War. Unsuccessful in establishing an elementary and secondary system, later in life Jefferson turned his attention to founding a public university in his home state. Jefferson's commitment to education, particularly a system that rewarded those who excelled academically, remained steadfast throughout his life. —CHB

A Bill for the More General Diffusion of Knowledge, 1778

Whereas it appeareth that however certain forms of government are better calculated than others to protect individuals in the free exercise of

American Educational Thought: Essays from 1640–1940, pages 41–52
Copyright © 2010 by Information Age Publishing

41

their natural rights, and are at the same time themselves better guarded against degeneracy, yet experience hath shewn, that even under the best forms, those entrusted with power have, in time, and by slow operations, perverted it into tyranny; and it is believed that the most effectual means of preventing this would be, to illuminate, as far as practicable, the minds of the people at large, and more especially to give them knowledge of those facts, which history exhibiteth, that, possessed thereby of the experience of other ages and countries, they may be enabled to know ambition under all its shapes, and prompt to exert their natural powers to defeat its purposes; And whereas it is generally true that that people will be happiest whose laws are best, and are best administered, and that laws will be wisely formed, and honestly administered, in proportion as those who form and administer them are wise and honest; whence it becomes expedient for promoting the publick happiness that those persons, whom nature hath endowed with genius and virtue, should be rendered by liberal education worthy to receive, and able to guard the sacred deposit of the rights and liberties of their fellow citizens, and that they should be called to that charge without regard to wealth, birth or other accidental condition or circumstance; but the indigence of the greater number disabling them from so educating, at their own expence, those of their children whom nature hath fitly formed and disposed to become useful instruments for the public, it is better that such should be sought for and educated at the common expence of all, than that the happiness of all should be confided to the weak or wicked:

Be it therefore enacted by the General Assembly, that in every county within this commonwealth, there shall be chosen annually, by the electors qualified to vote for Delegates, three of the most honest and able men of their county, to be called the Aldermen of the county; and that the election of the said Aldermen shall be held at the same time and place, before the same persons, and notified and conducted in the same manner as by law is directed for the annual election of Delegates for the county.

The person before whom such election is holden shall certify to the court of the said county the names of the Aldermen chosen, in order that the same may be entered of record, and shall give notice of their election to the said Aldermen within a fortnight after such election.

The said Aldermen on the first Monday in October, if it be fair, and if not, then on the next fair day, excluding Sunday, shall meet at the courthouse of their county, and proceed to divide their said county into hundreds, bounding the same by water courses, mountains, or limits, to be run and marked, if they think necessary, by the county surveyor, and at the county expence, regulating the size of the said hundreds, according to the best of their discretion, so as that they may contain a convenient number of children to make up a school, and be of such convenient size that all the children within each hundred may daily attend the school to be established therein, distinguishing each hundred by a particular name; which division, with the names of the several hundreds, shall be returned to the court of the county and be entered of record, and shall remain unaltered until the increase or decrease of inhabitants shall render an alteration necessary, in the opinion of any succeeding Aldermen, and also in the opinion of the court of the county.

The electors aforesaid residing within every hundred shall meet on the third Monday in October after the first election of Aldermen, at such place, within their hundred, as the said Aldermen shall direct, notice thereof being previously given to them by such person residing within the hundred as the said Aldermen shall require who is hereby enjoined to obey such requisition, on pain of being punished by amercement and imprisonment. The electors being so assembled shall choose the most convenient place within their hundred for building a school-house. If two or more places, having a greater number of votes than any others, shall yet be equal between themselves, the Aldermen, or such of them as are not of the same hundred, on information thereof, shall decide between them. The said Aldermen shall forthwith proceed to have a school-house built at the said place, and shall see that the same be kept in repair, and, when necessary, that it be rebuilt; but whenever they shall think necessary that it be rebuilt, they shall give notice as before directed, to the electors of the hundred to meet at the said school-house, on such day as they shall appoint, to determine by vote, in the manner before directed, whether it shall be rebuilt at the same, or what other place in the hundred.

curriculum At every of these schools shall be taught reading, writing, and common arithmetick, and the books which shall be used therein for instructing the children to read shall be such as will at the same time make them acquainted with Graecian, Roman, English, and American history. At these schools all the free children, male and female, resident within the respective hundred, shall be intitled to receive tuition gratis, for the term of three years, and as much longer, at their private expence, as their parents, guardians or friends, shall think proper.

Over every ten of these schools (or such other number nearest thereto, as the number of hundreds in the county will admit, without fractional divisions) an overseer shall be appointed annually by the Aldermen at their first meeting, eminent for his learning, integrity, and fidelity to the commonwealth, whose business and duty it shall be, from time to time, to appoint a teacher to each school, who shall give assurance of fidelity to the commonwealth, and to remove him as he shall see cause; to visit every school once in every half year at the least; to examine the schollars; see that any general plan of reading and instruction recommended by the visiters of William and Mary College shall be observed; and to superintend the conduct of the teacher in every thing relative to his school.

Every teacher shall receive a salary of _____ by the year, which, with the expences of building and repairing the schoolhouses, shall be provided in such manner as other county expences are by law directed to be provided and shall also have his diet, lodging, and washing found him, to be levied in like manner, save only that such levy shall be on the inhabitants of each hundred for the board of their own teacher only.

And in order that grammar schools may be rendered convenient to the youth in every part of the commonwealth, Be it farther enacted, that on the first Monday in November, after the first appointment of overseers for the hundred schools, if fair, and if not, then on the next fair day, excluding Sunday, after the hour of one in the afternoon, the said overseers appointed for the schools in the counties of Princess Ann, Norfolk, Nansemond and Isle-of-Wight, shall meet at Nansemond court house; those for the counties of Southampton, Sussex, Surry and Prince George, shall meet at Sussex court-house; those for the counties of Brunswick, Mecklenburg and Lunenburg, shall meet at Lunenburg court-house; those for the counties of Dinwiddie, Amelia and Chesterfield, shall meet at Chesterfield court-house; those for the counties of Powhatan, Cumberland, Goochland, Henrico and Hanover, shall meet at Henrico court-house; those for the counties of Prince Edward, Charlotte and Halifax, shall meet at Charlotte court-house; those for the counties of Henry, Pittsylvania and Bedford, shall meet at Pittsylvania court-house; those for the counties of Buckingham, Amherst, Albemarle and Fluvanna, shall meet at Albemarle court-house; those for the counties of Botetourt, Rockbridge, Montgomery, Washington and Kentucky, shall meet at Botetourt court-house; those for the counties of Augusta, Rockingham and Greenbrier, shall meet at Augusta court-house; those for the counties of Accomack and Northampton, shall meet at Accomack court-house; those for the counties of Elizabeth City, Warwick, York, Gloucester, James City, Charles City and New-Kent, shall meet at James City court-house; those for the counties of Middlesex, Essex, King and Queen, King William and Caroline, shall meet at King and Queen court-house; those for the counties of Lancaster, Northumberland, Richmond and Westmoreland, shall meet at Richmond court-house; those for the counties of King George, Stafford, Spotsylvania, Prince William and Fairfax, shall meet at Spotsylvania court-house; those for the counties of Loudoun and Fauquier, shall meet at Loudoun court-house; those for the counties of Culpeper, Orange and Louisa, shall meet at Orange court-house; those for the counties of Shenandoah and Frederick, shall meet at Frederick court-house; those for the counties of Hampshire and Berkeley, shall meet at Berkeley court-house; and those for the counties of Yohogania, Monongalia and Ohio, shall meet at Monongalia court-house; and shall fix on such place in some one of the counties in their district as shall be most proper for situating a grammar school-house, endeavouring that the situation be as central as may be to the inhabitants of the said counties, that it be furnished with good water, convenient to plentiful supplies of provision and fuel, and more than all things that it be healthy. And if a majority of the overseers present should not concur in their choice of any one place proposed, the method of determining shall be as follows: If two places only were proposed, and the votes be divided, they shall decide between them by fair and equal lot; if more than two places were proposed, the question shall be put on those two which on the first division had the greater number of votes; or if no two places had a greater number of votes than the others, as where the votes shall have been equal between one or both of them and some other or others, then it shall be decided by fair and equal lot (unless it can be agreed by a majority of votes) which of the places having equal numbers shall be thrown out of the competition, so that the question shall be put on the remaining two, and if on this ultimate question the votes shall be equally divided, it shall then be decided finally by lot.

The said overseers having determined the place at which the grammar school for their district shall be built, shall forthwith (unless they can otherwise agree with the proprietors of the circumjacent lands as to location and price) make application to the clerk of the county in which the said house is to be situated, who shall thereupon issue a writ, in the nature of a writ of *ad quod damnum*, directed to the sheriff of the said county commanding him to summon and impannel twelve fit persons to meet at the place, so destined for the grammar school house, on a certain day, to be named in the said writ, not less than five, nor more than ten, days from the date thereof; and also to give notice of the same to the proprietors and tenants of the lands to be viewed, if they be to be found within the county, and if not, then to their agents therein if any they have. Which freeholders shall be charged by the said sheriff impartially, and to the best of their skill and judgment to view the lands round about the said place, and to locate and circumscribe, by certain metes and bounds, one hundred acres thereof, having regard therein principally to the benefit and convenience of the said school, but respecting in some measure also the convenience of the said proprietors, and to value and appraise the same in so many several and distinct parcels as shall be owned or held by several and distinct owners or tenants, and according to their respective interests and estates therein. And after such location and appraisement so made, the said sheriff shall forthwith return the same under the hands and seals of the said jurors, together with the writ, to the clerk's office of the said county and the right and property of the said proprietors and tenants in the said lands so circumscribed shall be immediately devested and be transferred to the commonwealth for the use of the said grammar school, in full and absolute dominion, any want of consent or disability to consent in the said owners or tenants notwithstanding. But it shall not be lawful for the said overseers so to situate the said grammar school-house, nor to the said jurors so to locate the said lands, as to include the mansion-house of the proprietor of the lands, nor the offices, curtilage, or garden, thereunto immediately belonging.

The said overseers shall forthwith proceed to have a house of brick or stone, for the said grammar school, with necessary offices, built on the said lands, which grammar school-house shall contain a room for the school, a hall to dine in, four rooms for a master and usher, and ten or twelve lodging rooms for the scholars.

To each of the said grammar schools shall be allowed out of the public treasury, the sum of pounds, out of which shall be paid by the Treasurer, on warrant from the Auditors, to the proprietors or tenants of the lands located, the value of their several interests as fixed by the jury, and the balance thereof shall be delivered to the said overseers to defray the expence of the said buildings.

In these grammar schools shall be taught the Latin and Greek languages, English grammar, geography, and the higher part of numerical arithmetick, to wit, vulgar and decimal fractions, and the extraction of the square and cube roots.

A visiter from each county constituting the district shall be appointed, by the overseers, for the county, in the month of October annually, either from their own body or from their county at large, which visiters or the greater part of them, meeting together at the said grammar school on the first Monday in November, if fair, and if not, then in the next fair day, excluding Sunday, shall have power to choose their own Rector, who shall call and preside at future meetings, to employ from time to time a master, and if necessary, an usher, for the said school, to remove them at their will, and to settle the price of tuition to be paid by the scholars. They shall also visit the school twice in every year at the least, either together or separately at their discretion, examine the scholars, and see that any general plan of instruction recommended by the visiters of William and Mary College shall be observed. The said masters and ushers, before they enter on the execution of their office, shall give assurance of fidelity to the commonwealth.

A steward shall be employed, and removed at will by the master, on such wages as the visiters shall direct; which steward shall see to the procuring provisions, fuel, servants for cooking, waiting, house cleaning, washing, mending, and gardening on the most reasonable terms; the expence of which, together with the steward's wages, shall be divided equally among all the scholars boarding either on the public or private expence. And the part of those who are on private expence, and also the price of their tuitions due to the master or usher, shall be paid quarterly by the respective scholars, their parents, or guardians, and shall be recoverable, if withheld, together with costs, on motion in any Court of Record, ten days notice thereof being previously given to the party, and a jury impannelled to try the issue joined, or enquire of the damages. The said steward shall also, under the direction of the visiters, see that the houses be kept in repair, and necessary enclosures be made and repaired, the accounts for which, shall, from time to time, be submitted to the Auditors, and on their warrant paid by the Treasurer.

Every overseer of the hundred schools shall, in the month of September annually, after the most diligent and impartial examination and enquiry, appoint from among the boys who shall have been two Years at the least at some one of the schools under his superintendance, and whose parents are too Poor to give them farther education, some one of the best and most promising genius and disposition, to Proceed to the grammar school of his district; which appointment shall be made in the court-house of the county, on the court day for that month if fair, and if not, then on the next fair day, excluding Sunday, in the presence of the Aldermen, or two of them at the least, assembled on the bench for that purpose, the said overseer being previously sworn by them to make such appointment, without favor or affection, according to the best of his skill and judgment, and being interrogated by the said Aldermen, either on their own motion, or on suggestions from the parents, guardians, friends, or teachers of the children, competitors for such appointment; which teachers shall attend for the information of the Aldermen. On which interrogatories the said Aldermen, if they be not satisfied with the appointment proposed, shall have right to negative it; whereupon the said visiter may proceed to make a new appointment, and the said Aldermen again to interrogate and negative, and so *toties quoties* until an appointment be approved.

Every boy so appointed shall be authorised to Proceed to the grammar school of his district, there to be educated and boarded during such time as is hereafter limited; and his quota of the expences of the house together with a compensation to the master or usher for his tuition, at the rate of twenty dollars by the year, shall be paid by the Treasurer quarterly on warrant from the Auditors.

A visitation shall be held, for the purpose of probation, annually at the said grammar school on the last Monday in September, if fair, and if not, then on the next fair day, excluding Sunday, at which one third of the boys sent thither by appointment of the said overseers, and who shall have been there one year only, shall be discontinued as public foundationers, being those who, on the most diligent examination and enquiry, shall be thought to be of the least promising genius and disposition; and of those who shall have been there two years, all shall be discontinued, save one only the best in genius and disposition, who shall be at liberty to continue there four years longer on the public foundation, and shall thence forward be deemed a senior.

The visiters for the districts which, or any part of which, be southward and westward of James river, as known by that name, or by the names of Fluvanna and Jackson's river, in every other year, to wit, at the probation meetings held in the years, distinguished in the Christian computation by odd numbers, and the visiters for all the other districts at their said meetings to be held in those years, distinguished by even numbers, after diligent examination and enquiry as before directed, shall chuse one among the said seniors, of the best learning and most hopeful genius and disposition, who shall be authorised by them to Proceed to William and Mary College, there to be educated, boarded, and clothed, three years; the expence of which annually shall be paid by the Treasurer on warrant From the Auditors.

Letter to John Banister: Advantages of an American Education, 1785

This is riveting and honest passage, written by Thomas Jefferson (1743–1826) about the differences in European and American education. At the time the passage was written, the Articles of Confederation were in place, but coming under intense scrutiny. Similarly, the topic of European and American education was controversial. Adopting a very patriotic position, Jefferson warns in this letter about the dangers of obtaining an education in Europe. An American, he suggests, loses in "his knowledge, in his morals, in his health, in his habits, and in his happiness," in seeking a European education. Jefferson even warns that a European education will produce changes in attitudes toward fidelity in marriage and towards soliciting whores. Clearly, Jefferson believes that an American education is preferable, and in his zeal he hopes to encourage the growth of American education. —CHB

I should sooner have answered the paragraph in your letter of September 19, respecting the best seminary for the education of youth in Europe, but that it was necessary for me to make inquiries on the subject. The result of these has been to consider the competition as resting between Geneva and Rome.

They are equally cheap and probably are equal in the course of education pursued. The advantage of Geneva is that students acquire there the habit of speaking French. The advantages of Rome are the acquiring a local knowledge of a spot so classical and so celebrated; the acquiring the true pronunciation of the Latin language; a just taste in the fine arts, more particularly those of painting, sculpture, architecture, and music; a familiarity with those objects and processes of agriculture, which experience has shown best adapted to a climate like ours; and lastly, the advantage of a fine climate for health. It is probable, too, that by being boarded in a French family, the habit of speaking that language may be obtained.

I do not count on any advantage to be derived in Geneva, from a familiar acquaintance with the principles of that government. The late revolution has rendered it a tyrannical aristocracy, more likely to give ill than good ideas to an American. I think the balance in favor of Rome. Pisa is sometimes spoken of as a place of education. But it does not offer the first and third of the advantages of Rome.

But why send an American youth to Europe for education? What are the objects of a useful American education? Classical knowledge; modern languages, chiefly French, Spanish, and Italian; mathematics; natural philosophy; natural history; civil history; and ethics. In natural philosophy, I mean to include chemistry and agriculture, and in natural history, to include botany, as well as the other branches of those departments. It is true that the habit of speaking the modern languages cannot be so well acquired in America; but every other article can be as well acquired at William and Mary College as at any place in Europe. When college education is done with and a young man is to prepare himself for public life, he must cast his eyes (for America) either on law or physic [medicine]. For the former, where can he apply so advantageously as to Mr. Wythe? For the latter, he must come to Europe. The medical class of students, therefore, is the only one which need come to Europe.

Let us view the disadvantages of sending a youth to Europe. To enumerate them all would require a volume. I will select a few. If he goes to England, he learns drinking, horse racing, and boxing. These are the peculiarities of English education. The following circumstances are common to education in that and the other countries of Europe. He acquires a fondness for European luxury and dissipation, and a contempt for the simplicity of his own country; he is fascinated with the privileges of the European aristocrats, and sees with abhorrence the lovely equality which the poor enjoy with the rich in his own country; he contracts a partiality for aristocracy or monarchy; he forms foreign friendships which will never be useful to him, and loses the seasons of life for forming in his own country those friendships which, of all others, are the most faithful and permanent. He is led by the strongest of all the human passions into a spirit for female intrigue, destructive of his own and others' happiness, or a passion for whores, destructive of his health; and, in both cases, learns to consider fidelity to the marriage bed as an ungentlemanly practice and inconsistent with happiness. He recollects the voluptuary dress and arts of the European women, and pities and despises the chaste affections and simplicity of those of his own country; he retains through life a fond recollection and a hankering after those places which were the scenes of his first pleasures and of his first connections.

He returns to his own country a foreigner, unacquainted with the practices of domestic economy necessary to preserve him from ruin, speaking and writing his native tongue as a foreigner, and therefore unqualified to obtain those distinctions which eloquence of the pen and tongue insures in a free country; for I would observe to you that what is called style in writing or speaking is formed very early in life, while the imagination is warm and impressions are permanent. I am of opinion that there never was an instance of a man's writing or speaking his native tongue with elegance who passed from fifteen to twenty years of age out of the country where it was spoken. Thus, no instance exists of a person's writing two languages perfectly. That will always appear to be his native language which was most familiar to him in his youth.

It appears to me, then, that an American coming to Europe for education loses in his knowledge, in his morals, in his health, in his habits, and in his happiness. I had entertained only doubts on this head before I came to Europe; what I see and hear since I came here proves more than I had even suspected. Cast your eye over America. Who are the men of most learning, of most eloquence, most beloved by their countrymen and most trusted and promoted by them? They are those who have been educated among them, and whose manners, morals, and habits are perfectly homogeneous with those of the country.

Did you expect by so short a question to draw such a sermon on yourself? I dare say you did not. But the consequences of foreign education are alarming to me as an American. I sin, therefore, through zeal, whenever I enter on the subject. You are sufficiently American to pardon me for it.

Letter to Nathaniel Burwell: Education of Women, 1818

In this letter written toward the end of his life, Thomas Jefferson (1743–1826) provides a brief explanation of his thoughts on female education. Jefferson, like many of his contemporaries, believed women's role was primarily domestic. Using words that may seem strange today, he noted that women's interest in novels was an obstacle to their education. Calling novels "a mass of trash," his remarks are similar to contemporary complaints about television. Jefferson preferred women to read works of literature, and to learn French, dancing, drawing, music, and of course, household economy. —CHB

Dear Sir,

Your letter of February 17th found me suffering under an attack of rheumatism, which has but now left me at sufficient ease to attend to the letters I have received. A plan of female education has never been a subject of systematic contemplation with me. It has occupied my attention so far only as the education of my own daughters occasionally required. Considering that they would be placed in a country situation, where little aid could be obtained from abroad, I thought it essential to give them a solid education, which might enable them, when become mothers, to educate their own daughters, and even to direct the course for sons, should their fathers be lost, or incapable, or inattentive. My surviving daughter accordingly, the mother of many daughters as well as sons, has made their education the object of her life, and being a better judge of the practical part than myself, it is with her aid and that of one of her *éleves* that I shall subjoin a catalogue of the books for such a course of reading as we have practised.

A great obstacle to good education is the inordinate passion prevalent for novels, and the time lost in that reading which should be instructively employed. When this poison infects the mind, it destroys its tone and revolts it against wholesome reading. Reason and fact, plain and unadorned, are rejected. Nothing can engage attention unless dressed in all the figments of fancy, and nothing so bedecked comes amiss. The result is a bloated imagination, sickly judgment, and disgust towards all the real businesses of life. This mass of trash, however, is not without some distinction; some few modeling their narratives, although fictitious, on the incidents of real life, have been able to make them interesting and useful vehicles of sound morality. Such, I think, are Marmontel's new moral tales, but not his old ones, which are really immoral. Such are the writings of Miss Edgeworth, and some of those of Madame Genlis. For a like reason, too, much poetry should not be indulged. Some is useful for forming style and taste. Pope, Dryden, Thompson, Shakspeare, and of the French, Molière, Racine, the Corneilles, may be read with pleasure and improvement.

The French language, become that of the general intercourse of nations, and from their extraordinary advances, now the depository of all science, is an indispensable part of education for both sexes. In the subjoined catalogue, therefore, I have placed the books of both languages indifferently, according as the one or the other offers what is best.

The ornaments, too, and the amusements of life, are entitled to their portion of attention.

These, for a female, are dancing, drawing, and music. The first is a healthy exercise, elegant and very attractive for young people. Every affectionate parent would be pleased to see his daughter qualified to participate with her companions, and without awkwardness at least, in the circles of festivity, of which she occasionally becomes a part. It is a necessary accomplishment, therefore, although of short use, for the French rule is wise, that no lady dances after marriage. This is founded in solid physical reasons, gestation and nursing leaving little time to a married lady when this exercise can be either safe or innocent. Drawing is thought less of in this country than in Europe. It is an innocent and engaging amusement, often useful, and a qualification not to be neglected in one who is to become a mother and an instructor. Music is invaluable where a person has an ear. Where they have not, it should not be attempted. It furnishes a delightful recreation for the hours of respite from the cares of the day, and lasts us through life. The taste of this country, too, calls for this accomplishment more strongly than for either of the others.

I need say nothing of household economy, in which the mothers of our country are generally skilled, and generally careful to instruct their daughters. We all know its value, and that diligence and dexterity in all its processes are inestimable treasures. The order and economy of a house are as honorable to the mistress as those of the farm to the master, and if either be neglected, ruin follows, and children destitute of the means of living.

This, Sir, is offered as a summary sketch on a subject on which I have not thought much. It probably contains nothing but what has already occurred to yourself, and claims your acceptance on no other ground than as a testimony of my respect for your wishes, and of my great esteem and respect.

6

Selected Writings of Benjamin Rush

Benjamin Rush (1745–1813), native of Philadelphia, was the only physician to sign the Declaration of Independence. In addition to a career as a doctor, he was an educator who taught college science courses, Treasurer of the U.S. Mint, Surgeon General of the Continental Army, and the author of the first chemistry textbook and the first psychiatric treatise in the United States. Rush's extensive correspondence, especially with friends John Adams and Thomas Jefferson, provides tremendous insight into the workings of a brilliant 18th century mind. While many of his medical practices, such as blood letting, have been long abandoned, his writing on female education was progressive for its time.

Although he favored a traditional role for women, in which females were educated for their future roles as wives and mothers, he stood in contrast to those who opposed female education entirely. Rush's curriculum for females was strictly pragmatic. Women were to learn the English language, be able to instruct their sons in principles of liberty and government, gain some knowledge of facts, figures, geography, vocal music, and dancing. He warned against the dangers of reading novels, remarked on the uselessness of teaching French to women, and cautioned about the significant expense of learning instrumental music. However, he supported instruction in Christianity. Clearly, for Rush the import of female education corresponded with domestic responsibilities, as wives and mothers, in Revolutionary America. —CHB

American Educational Thought: Essays from 1640–1940, pages 53–70

53

Thoughts upon Female Education, 1787

GENTLEMEN,

I have yielded with diffidence to the solicitations of the Principal of the Academy, in undertaking to express my regard for the prosperity of this seminary of learning by submitting to your candor a few thoughts upon female education.

The first remark that I shall make upon this subject is that female education should be accommodated to the state of society, manners, and government of the country in which it is conducted.

This remark leads me at once to add that the education of young ladies in this country should be conducted upon principles very different from what it is in Great Britain and in some respects different from what it was when we were a part of a monarchical empire.

There are several circumstances in the situation, employments, and duties of women in America which require a peculiar mode of education.

I. The early marriages of our women, by contracting the time allowed for education, renders it necessary to contract its plan and to confine it chiefly to the more useful branches of literature.

II. The state of property in America renders it necessary for the greatest part of our citizens to employ themselves in different occupations for the advancement of their fortunes. This cannot be done without the assistance of the female members of the community. They must be the stewards and guardians of their husbands' property. That education, therefore, will be most proper for our women which teaches them to discharge the duties of those offices with the most success and reputation.

III. From the numerous avocations to which a professional life exposes gentlemen in America from their families, a principal share of the instruction of children naturally devolves upon the women. It becomes us therefore to prepare them, by a suitable education, for the discharge of this most important duty of mothers.

IV. The equal share that every citizen has in the liberty and the possible share he may have in the government of our country make it necessary that our ladies should be qualified to a certain degree, by a peculiar and suitable education, to concur in instructing their sons in the principles of liberty and government.

V. In Great Britain the business of servants is a regular occupation, but in America this humble station is the usual retreat of unexpected indigence; hence the servants in this country possess less knowledge and subordination than are required from them; and hence our ladies are obliged to attend more to the private affairs of their families than ladies generally do of the same rank in Great Britain. "They are good servants," said an American lady of distinguished merit in a letter to a favorite daughter, "who will do well with good looking after." This circumstance should have great influence upon the nature and extent of female education in America.

The branches of literature most essential for a young lady in this country appear to be:

I. A knowledge of the English language. She should not only read but speak and spell it correctly. And to enable her to do this, she should be taught the English grammar and be frequently examined in applying its rules in common conversation.

Method

II. Pleasure and interest conspire to make the writing of a fair and legible hand a necessary branch of female education. For this purpose she should be taught not only to shape every letter properly but to pay the strictest regard to points and capitals.

I once heard of a man who professed to discover the temper and disposition of persons by looking at their handwriting. Without inquiring into the probability of this story, I shall only remark that there is one thing in which all mankind agree upon this subject, and that is in considering writing that is blotted, crooked, or illegible as a mark of a vulgar education. I know of few things more rude or illiberal than to obtrude a letter upon a person of rank or business which cannot be easily read. Peculiar care should be taken to avoid every kind of ambiguity and affectation in writing *names.*

I have now a letter in my possession upon business, from a gentleman of a liberal profession in a neighboring state, which I am unable to answer because I cannot discover the name which is subscribed to it. For obvious reasons I would recommend the writing of the first or Christian name at full length, where it does not consist of more than two syllables. Abbreviations of all kinds in letter writing, which always denote either haste or carelessness, should likewise be avoided. I have only to add under this head that the Italian and inverted hands, which are read with difficulty, are by no means accommodated to the active state of business in America or to the simplicity of the citizens of a republic.

III. Some knowledge of figures and bookkeeping is absolutely necessary to qualify a young lady for the duties which await her in this country. There are certain occupations in which she may assist her husband with this knowledge, and should she survive him and agreeably to the custom of our country be the executrix of his will, she cannot fail of deriving immense advantages from it.

IV. An acquaintance with geography and some instruction in chronology will enable a young lady to read history, biography, and travels, with advantage, and thereby qualify her not only for a general intercourse with the world but to be an agreeable companion for a sensible man. To these branches of knowledge may be added, in some instances, a general acquaintance with the first principles of astronomy and natural philosophy, particularly with such parts of them as are calculated to prevent superstition by explaining the causes or obviating the effects of natural evil.

V. Vocal music should never be neglected in the education of a young lady in this country. Besides preparing her to join in that part of public worship which consists in psalmody it will enable her to soothe the cares of domestic life. The distress and vexation of a husband, the noise of a nursery, and even the sorrows that will sometimes intrude into her own bosom may all be relieved by a song, where sound and sentiment unite to act upon the mind. I hope it will not be thought foreign to this part of our subject to introduce a fact here which has been suggested to me by my profession, and that is, that the exercise of the organs of the breast by singing contributes very much to defend them from those diseases to which our climate, and other causes have of late exposed them. Our German fellow citizens are seldom afflicted with consumptions, nor have I ever known but one instance of a spitting of blood among them. This, I believe, is in part occasioned by the strength which their lungs acquire by exercising them frequently in vocal music, for this constitutes an essential branch of their education. The music master of our academy has furnished me with an observation still more in favor of this opinion. He informed me that he had known several instances of persons who were strongly disposed to the consumption who were restored to health by the moderate exercise of their lungs in singing.

VI. Dancing is by no means an improper branch of education for an American lady. It promotes health and renders the figure and motions of the body easy and agreeable. I anticipate the time when the resources of conversation shall be so far multiplied that the amusement of dancing shall be wholly confined to children. But in our present state of society and knowledge, I conceive it to be an agreeable substitute for the ignoble pleasures of drinking and gaming in our assemblies of grown people.

VII. The attention of our young ladies should be directed as soon as they are prepared for it to the reading of history, travels, poetry, and moral essays. These studies are accommodated, in a peculiar manner, to the present state of society in America, and when a relish is excited for them in early life, they subdue that passion for reading novels which so generally prevails among the fair sex. I cannot dismiss this species of writing and reading without observing that the subjects of novels are by no means accommodated to our present manners. They hold up *life*, it is true, but it is not yet *life* in America. Our passions have not as yet "overstepped the modesty of nature," nor are they "torn to tatters," to use the expressions of the poet, by extravagant love, jealousy, ambition, or revenge. As yet the intrigues of a British novel are as foreign to our manners as the refinements of Asiatic vice. Let it not be said that the tales of distress which fill modern novels have a tendency to soften the female heart into acts of humanity. The fact is the reverse of this. The abortive sympathy which is excited by the recital of imaginary distress blunts the heart to that which is real; and, hence, we sometimes see instances of young ladies who weep away a whole forenoon over the criminal sorrows of a fictitious Charlotte or Werter, turning with disdain at two o'clock from the sight of a beggar who solicits in feeble accents or signs a small portion only of the crumbs which fall from their fathers' tables.

VIII. It will be necessary to connect all these branches of education with regular instruction in the Christian religion. For this purpose the principles of the different sects of Christians should be taught and explained, and our pupils should early be furnished with some of the most simple arguments in favor of the truth of Christianity. A portion of the Bible should be read by them every day and such questions should be asked, after reading it, as are calculated to imprint upon their minds the interesting stories contained in it.

Rousseau has asserted that the great secret of education consists in "wasting the time of children profitably." There is some truth in this observation. I believe that we often impair their health and weaken their capacities by imposing studies upon them which are not proportioned to their years. But this objection does not apply to religious instruction. There are certain simple propositions in the Christian religion that are suited in a peculiar manner to the infant state of reason and moral sensibility. A clergyman of long experience in the instruction of youth informed me that he always found children acquired religious knowledge more easily than knowledge upon other subjects, and that young girls acquired this kind of knowledge more readily than boys. The female breast is the natural soil of Christianity, and while our women are taught to believe its doctrines and obey its precepts, the wit of Voltaire and the style of Bolingbroke will never be able to destroy its influence upon our citizens.

I cannot help remarking in this place that Christianity exerts the most friendly influence upon science as well as upon the morals and manners of mankind. Whether this be occasioned by the unity of truth and the mutual assistance which truths upon different subjects afford each other, or whether the faculties of the mind be sharpened and corrected by embracing the truths of revelation and thereby prepared to investigate and perceive truths upon other subjects, I will not determine, but it is certain that the greatest discoveries in science have been made by Christian philosophers and that there is the most knowledge in those countries where there is the most Christianity. By knowledge I mean truth only; and by truth I mean the perception of things as they appear to the divine mind. If this remark be well founded, then those philosophers who reject Christianity and those Christians, whether parents or schoolmasters, who neglect the religious instruction of their children and pupils *reject* and *neglect* the most effectual means of promoting knowledge in our country.

IX. If the measures that have been recommended for inspiring our pupils with a sense of religious and moral obligation be adopted, the government of them will be easy and agreeable. I shall only remark under this head that *strictness* of discipline will always render *severity* unnecessary and that there will be the most instruction in that school where there is the most order.

I have said nothing in favor of the instrumental music as a branch of female education because I conceive it is by no means accommodated to the present state of society and manners in America. The price of musical instruments and the extravagant fees demanded by the teachers of the instrumental music form but a small part of my objections to it.

To perform well upon a musical instrument requires much time and long practice. From two to four hours in a day, for three or four years, appropriated to music are an immense deduction from that short period of time which is allowed by the peculiar circumstances of our country for the acquisition of the useful branches of literature that have been mentioned. How many useful ideas might be picked up in these hours from history, philosophy poetry, and the numerous moral essays with which our language abounds, and how much more would the knowledge acquired upon these subjects add to the consequence of a lady with her husband and with society than the best performed pieces of music upon a harpsichord or a guitar! Of the many ladies whom we have known who have spent the most important years of their lives in learning to play upon instruments of music, how few of them do we see amuse themselves or their friends with them after they become mistresses of families! Their harpsichords serve only as sideboards for their parlors and prove by their silence that necessity and circumstances will always prevail over fashion and false maxims of education.

Let it not be supposed from these observations that I am insensible of the charms of instrumental music or that I wish to exclude it from the education of a lady where a musical ear irresistibly disposes to it, and affluence at the same time affords a prospect of such an exemption from the usual cares and duties of the mistress of a family as will enable her to practice it. These circumstances form an exception to the general conduct that should arise upon this subject, from the present state of society and manners in America.

I beg leave further to bear a testimony against the practice of making the French language a part of female education in America. In Britain, where company and pleasure are the principal business of ladies, where the nursery and the kitchen form no part of their care, and where a daily intercourse is maintained with Frenchmen and other foreigners who speak the French language, a knowledge of it is absolutely necessary. But the case is widely different in this country. Of the many ladies who have applied to this language, how great a proportion of them have been hurried into the cares and duties of a family before they had acquired it; of those who have acquired it, how few have retained it after they were married; and of the few who have retained it, how seldom have they had occasion to speak it in the course of their lives! It certainly comports more with female delicacy, as well as the natural politeness of the French nation, to make it necessary for Frenchmen to learn to speak our language in order to converse with our ladies than for our ladies to learn their language in order to converse with them.

Let it not be said in defense of a knowledge of the French language that many elegant books are written in it. Those of them that are truly valuable are generally translated, but, if this were not the case, the English language certainly contains many more books of real utility and useful information than can be read without neglecting other duties by the daughter or wife of an American citizen.

It is with reluctance that I object to drawing as a branch of education for an American lady. To be the mistress of a family is one of the great ends of a woman's being, and while the peculiar state of society in America imposes this station so early and renders the duties of it so numerous and difficult, I conceive that little time can be spared for the acquisition of this elegant accomplishment.

It is agreeable to observe how differently modern writers and the inspired author of the *Proverbs* describe a fine woman. The former confine their praises chiefly to personal charms and ornamental accomplishments, while the latter celebrates only the virtues of a valuable mistress of a family and a useful member of society. The one is perfectly acquainted with all the fashionable languages of Europe; the other "opens her mouth with wisdom" and is perfectly acquainted with all the uses of the needle, the distaff, and the loom. The business of the one is pleasure; the pleasure of the other is business. The one is admired abroad; the other is honored and beloved at home. "Her children arise up and call her blessed, her husband also, and he praiseth her." There is no fame in the world equal to this, nor is there a note in music half so delightful as the respectful language with which a grateful son or daughter perpetuates the memory of a sensible and affectionate mother.

It should not surprise us that British customs with respect to female education have been transplanted into our American schools and families. We see marks of the same incongruity of time and place in many other things. We behold our houses accommodated to the climate of Great Britain by eastern and western directions. We behold our ladies panting in a heat of ninety degrees, under a hat and cushion which were calculated for the temperature of a British summer. We behold our citizens condemned and punished by a criminal law which was copied from a country where maturity in corruption renders public executions a part of the amusements of the nation. It is high time to awake from this servility— to study our own character— to examine the age of our country— and to adopt manners in everything that shall be accommodated to our state of society and to the forms of our government. In particular it is incumbent upon us to make ornamental accomplishments yield to principles and knowledge in the education of our women.

A philosopher once said, "let me make all the ballads of a country and I care not who makes its laws." He might with more propriety have said, let the ladies of a country be educated properly, and they will not only make and administer its laws, but form its manners and character. It would require a lively imagination to describe, or even to comprehend, the happiness of a country where knowledge and virtue were generally diffused among the female sex. Our young men would then be restrained from vice by the terror of being banished from their company. The loud laugh and the malignant smile, at the expense of innocence or of personal infirmities—the feats of successful mimicry and the low priced wit which is borrowed from a misapplication of scripture phrases—would no more be considered as recommendations to the society of the ladies. A *double-entendre* in their presence would then exclude a gentleman forever from the company of both sexes and probably oblige him to seek an asylum from contempt in a foreign country.

The influence of female education would be still more extensive and useful in domestic life. The obligations of gentlemen to qualify themselves by knowledge and industry to discharge the duties of benevolence would be increased by marriage; and the patriot—the hero—and the legislator would find the sweetest reward of their toils in the approbation and applause of their wives. Children would discover the marks of maternal prudence and wisdom in every station of life, for it has been remarked that there have been few great or good men who have not been blessed with wife and prudent mothers. Cyrus was taught to revere the gods by his mother Mandane; Samuel was devoted to his prophetic office before he was born by his mother Hannah; Constantine was rescued from paganism by his mother Constantia; and Edward the Sixth inherited those great and excellent qualities which made him the delight of the age in which he lived from his mother, Lady Jane Seymour. Many other instances might be mentioned, if necessary, from ancient and modern history, to establish the truth of this proposition.

I am not enthusiastic upon the subject of education. In the ordinary course of human affairs we shall probably too soon follow the footsteps of the nations of Europe in manners and vices. The first marks we shall perceive of our declension will appear among our women. Their idleness, ignorance, and profligacy will be the harbingers of our ruin. Then will the character and performance of a buffoon on the theater be the subject of more conversation and praise than the patriot or the minister of the gospel; then will our language and pronunciation be enfeebled and corrupted by a flood of French and Italian words; then will the history of romantic amours be preferred to the immortal writings of Addison, Hawkesworth, and Johnson; then will our churches be neglected and the name of the Supreme Being never be called upon but in profane exclamations; then will our Sundays be appropriated only to feasts and concerts; and then will begin all that train of domestic and political calamities.

But, I forbear. The prospect is so painful that I cannot help silently imploring the great Arbiter of human affairs to interpose his almighty goodness and to deliver us from these evil that, at least, one spot of the earth may be reserved as a monument of the effects of good education, in order to show in some degree what our species was before the fall and what it shall be after its restoration.

Thus, gentlemen, have I briefly finished what I proposed. If I am wrong in those opinions in which I have taken the liberty of departing from the general and fashionable habits of thinking I am sure you will discover and pardon my mistakes. But if I am right, I am equally sure you will adopt my opinions for to enlightened minds truth is alike acceptable, whether it comes from the lips of age or the hand of antiquity or whether it be obtruded by a person who has no other claim to attention than a desire of adding to the stock of human happiness.

I cannot dismiss the subject of female education without remarking that the city of Philadelphia first saw a number of gentlemen associated for the purpose of directing the education of young ladies. By means of this plan the power of teachers regulated and restrained and the objects of education are extended. By the separation of the sexes in the unformed state of their manners, female delicacy is cherished and preserved. Here the young ladies may enjoy all the literary advantages of boarding school and at the same time live under the protection of their parents. Here emulation may be excited without jealousy, ambition without envy, and competition without strife.

The attempt to establish this new mode of education for young ladies was an experiment, and the success of it hath answered our expectations. Too much praise cannot be given to our principal and his assistants, for the abilities and fidelity with which they have carried the plan into execution. The proficiency which the young ladies have discovered in reading, writing, spelling, arithmetic, grammar, geography, music, and their different catechisms since the last examination is a less equivocal mark of the merits of our teachers than anything I am able to express in their favor.

But the reputation of the academy must be suspended till the public are convinced by the future conduct and character of our pupils of the advantages of the institution. To you, therefore, YOUNG LADIES, an important problem is committed for solution; and that is, whether our present plan of education be a wise one and whether it be calculated to prepare you for the duties of social and domestic life. I know that the elevation of the female mind, by means of moral, physical, and religious truth, is considered by some men as unfriendly to the domestic character of a woman. But this is the prejudice of little minds and springs from the same spirit which opposes the general diffusion of knowledge among the citizens of our republics. If men believe that ignorance is favorable to the government of the female sex, they are certainly deceived, for a weak and ignorant woman will always be governed with the greatest difficulty.

I have sometimes been led to ascribe the invention of ridiculous and expensive fashions in female dress entirely to the gentlemen in order to divert the ladies from improving their minds and thereby to secure a more arbitrary and unlimited authority over them. It will be in your power LADIES, to correct the mistakes and practice of our sex upon these subjects by demonstrating that the female temper can only be governed by reason and that the cultivation of reason in women is alike friendly to the order of nature and to private as well as public happiness.

On the Mode of Education Proper in a Republic, 1798

> In this essay, Dr. Benjamin Rush (1745–1813) discusses the proper method of educating students in a republic. Rush wrote this essay in 1798, during John Adams' administration. Although the American experiment was still in its infancy at the time, clearly national pride and patriotism had begun to develop in America. Rush, in emphasizing utility, proposes a mode of education consistent with many ideas of other founding fathers. Students should be taught to serve their country, should study modern languages rather than wasting too much time on dead languages at too early an age, should be subjected to physical exercise, and should also study History, Eloquence, Commerce, and Chemistry. Strikingly, Rush also recommended that religion, particularly Christianity, should be the foundation of all education. In these beliefs, Rush stood apart from his friend Thomas Jefferson, who eliminated the professor of divinity position in establishing the University of Virginia. Rush believed that moral virtue was the foundation of all education. —CHB

The business of education has acquired a new complexion by the independence of our country. The form of government we have assumed, has created a new class of duties to every American. It becomes us, therefore, to examine our former habits upon this subject, and in laying the foundations for nurseries of wise and good men, to adapt our modes of teaching to the peculiar form of our government.

The first remark that I shall make upon this subject is, that an education in our own, is to be preferred to an education in a foreign country. The principle of patriotism stands in need of the reinforcement of prejudice. And it is well known that our strongest prejudices in favour of our country are formed in the first one and twenty years of our lives. The policy of the Lacedemonians is well worthy of our imitation. When Antipater demanded fifty of their children as hostages for the fulfillment of a distant engagement, those wise republicans refused to comply with his demand, but readily offered him double the number of their adult citizens, whose habits and prejudices could not be shaken by residing in a foreign country. Passing by, in this place, the advantages to the community from the early attachment of youth to the laws and constitution of their country, I shall only remark, that young men who have trodden the paths of science together, or have joined in the same sports, whether of swimming, skating, fishing, or hunting, generally feel, thro' life, such ties to each other, as add greatly to the obligations of mutual benevolence.

I conceive the education of our youth in this country to be peculiarly necessary in Pennsylvania, while our citizens are composed of the natives of so many different kingdoms in Europe. Our schools of learning, by producing one general, and uniform system of education, will render the mass of the people more homogeneous, and thereby fit them more easily for uniform and peaceable government.

I proceed in the next place, to enquire, what mode of education we shall adopt so as to secure to the state all the advantages that are to be derived from the proper instruction of youth; and here I beg leave to remark, that the only foundation for a useful education in a republic is to be laid in Religion. Without this there can be no virtue, and without virtue there can be no liberty, and liberty is the object and life of all republican governments.

Such is my veneration for every religion that reveals the attributes of the Deity, or a future state of rewards and punishments, that I had rather see the opinions of Confucius or Mohammed inculcated upon our youth than see them grow up wholly devoid of a system of religious principles. But the religion I mean to recommend in this place, is that of Jesus Christ.

It is foreign to my purpose to hint at the arguments which establish the truth of the Christian revelation. My only business is to declare, that all its doctrines and precepts are calculated to promote the happiness of society, and the safety and well being of civil government. A Christian cannot fail of being a republican. The history of the creation of man, and of the relation our species to each other by birth, which is recorded in the Old Testament, is the best refutation that can be given to the divine right of kings, and the strongest argument that can be used in favor of the original and natural equality of all mankind. A Christian, I say again, cannot fail of being a republican, for every precept of the Gospel inculcates those degrees of humility, self-denial, and brotherly kindness, which are directly opposed to the pride of monarchy and the pageantry of a court. A Christian cannot fail of being useful to the republic, for his religion teacheth him, that no man "liveth to himself." And lastly, a Christian cannot fail of being wholly inoffensive, for his religion teacheth him, in all things to do others what he would wish, in like circumstances, they should do to him.

I am aware that I dissent from one of those paradoxical opinions with which modern times abound; and that it is improper to fill the minds of youth with religious prejudices of any kind, and that they should be left to choose their own principles, after they have arrived at an age in which they are capable of judging for themselves. Could we preserve the mind in childhood and youth a perfect blank, this plan of education would have more to recommend it; but this we know to be impossible. The human mind runs as naturally into principles as it does after facts. It submits with difficulty to those restraints or partial discoveries which are imposed upon it in the infancy of reason. Hence the impatience of children to be informed upon all subjects that relate to the invisible world. But I beg leave to ask, why should we pursue a different plan of education with respect to religion, from that which we pursue in teaching the arts and sciences? Do we leave our youth to acquire systems of geography, philosophy, or politics, till they have arrived at an age in which they are capable of judging for themselves? We do not. I claim no more then for religion, than for the other sciences, and I add further, that if our youth are disposed after they are of age to think for themselves, a knowledge of *one* system, will be the best means of conducting them in a free enquiry into other systems of religion, just as an acquaintance with one system of philosophy is the best introduction to the study of all other systems in the world.

Next to the duty which young men owe to their Creator, I wish to see a regard to their country, inculcated upon them. When the Duke of Sully became prime minister to Henry the IVth of France, the first thing he did, he tells us, "Was to subdue and forget his own heart." The same duty is incumbent upon every citizen of a republic. Our country includes family, friends and property, and should be preferred to them all. Let our pupil be taught that he does not belong to himself, but that he is public property. Let him be taught to love his family, but let him be taught, at the same time, that he must forsake, and even forget them, when the welfare of his country requires it. He must watch for the state, as if its liberties depended upon his vigilance alone, but he must do this in such a manner as not to defraud his creditors, or neglect his family. He must love private life, but he must decline no station, however public or responsible it may be, when called to it by the suffrages of his fellow citizens. He must love popularity, but he must despise it when set in competition with the dictates of his judgement, or the real interest of his country. He must love character, and have a due sense of injuries, but he must be taught to appeal only to the laws of the state, to defend the one, and punish the other. He must love family honour, but must be taught that neither the rank nor antiquity of his ancestors, can command respect, without personal merit. He must avoid neutrality in all questions that divide the state, but he must shun the rage, and acrimony of party spirit. He must be taught to love his fellow creatures in every part of the world, but he must cherish with a more intense and peculiar affection, the citizens of Pennsylvania and of the United States. I do not wish to see our youth educated with a single prejudice against any nation our country;

but we impose a task upon human nature, repugnant alike to reason, revelation and the ordinary dimensions of the human heart, when we require him to embrace, with equal affection, the whole family of mankind. He must be taught to amass wealth, but it must be only to encrease his power of contributing to the wants and demands of the state. He must be indulged occasionally in amusements, but he must be taught that study and business should be his principal pursuits in life. Above all he must love life, and endeavour to acquire as many of its conveniences as possible by industry and economy, but he must be taught that this life "is not his own," when the safety of his country requires it. These are practicable lessons, and the history of the commonwealths of Greece and Rome show, that human nature, without the aids of Christianity, has attained these degrees of perfection.

While we inculcate these republican duties upon our pupil, we must not neglect, at the same time, to inspire him with republican principles. He must be taught that there can be no durable liberty but in a republic, and that government, like all other sciences, is of a progressive nature. The chains which have bound this science in Europe are happily unloosed in America. Here it is open to investigation and improvement. While philosophy has protected us by its discoveries from a thousand natural evils, government has unhappily followed with an unequal pace. It would be to dishonour human genius, only to name the many defects which still exist in the best systems of legislation. We daily see matter of a perishable nature rendered durable by certain chemical operations. In like manner, I conceive, that it is possible to combine power in such a way as not only to encrease the happiness, but to promote the duration of republican forms of government far beyond the terms limited for them by history, or the common opinions of mankind.

To assist in rendering religious, moral and political instructions more effectual upon the minds of our youth, it will be necessary to subject their bodies to physical discipline. To obviate the inconveniences of their studious and sedentary mode of life, they should live upon a temperate diet, consisting chiefly of broths, milk and vegetables. The black broth of Sparta, and the barley broth of Scotland, have been alike celebrated for their beneficial effects upon the minds of young people. They should avoid tasting Spirituous liquors. They should also be accustomed occasionally to work with their hands, in the intervals of Study, and in the busy seasons of the year in the country. Moderate sleep, silence, occasional solitude and cleanliness, should be inculcated upon them, and the utmost advantage should be taken of a proper direction of those great principles in human conduct, —sensibility, habit, imitations, and association.

The influence of these physical causes will be powerful upon the intellects, as well as upon the principles and morals of young people. To those who have studied human nature, it will not appear paradoxical to recommend, in this essay, a particular attention to vocal music. Its mechanical effects in civilizing the mind, and thereby preparing it for the influence of religion and government, have been so often felt and recorded, that it will be unnecessary to mention facts in favour of its usefulness, in order to excite a proper attention to it.

I cannot help bearing a testimony, in this place, against the custom, which prevails in some parts of America, (but which is daily falling into disuse in Europe) of crowding boys together under one roof for the purpose of education. The practice is the gloomy remains of monkish ignorance, and is as unfavorable to the improvements of the mind in useful learning, as monasteries are to the spirit of religion. I grant this mode of secluding boys from the intercourse of private families, has a tendency to make them scholars, but our business is to make them men, citizens, and Christians. The vices of young people are generally learned from each other. The vices of adults seldom infect them. By separating them from each other, therefore, in their hours of relaxation from study, we secure their morals from a principal source of corruption, while we improve their manners, by subjecting them to those restraints which the difference of age and sex, naturally produce in private families.

From the observations that have been made it is plain, that I consider it is possible to convert men into republican machines. This must be done, if we expect them to perform their parts properly, in the great machine of the government of the state. That republic is sophisticated with monarchy or aristocracy that does not revolve upon the wills of the people, and these must be fitted to each other by means of education before they can be made to produce regularity and unison in government.

Having pointed out those general principles, which should be inculcated alike in all the schools of the state, I proceed now to make a few remarks upon the method of conducting, what is commonly called, a liberal or learned education in a republic.

I shall begin this part of my subject, by bearing a testimony against the common practice of attempting to teach boys the learned languages, and the arts and sciences too early in life. The first twelve years of life are barely sufficient to instruct a boy in reading, writing and arithmetic. With these, he may be taught those modern languages which are necessary for him to speak. The state of memory, in early life, is favorable to the acquisition of languages, especially when they are conveyed to the mind, through the ear.

It is, moreover, in early life only, that the organs of speech yield in such a manner as to favour the just pronounciation of foreign languages.

Too much pains cannot be taken to teach our youth to read and write our American language with propriety and elegance. The study of the Greek language constituted a material part of the literature of the Athenians, hence the sublimity, purity and immortality of so many of their writings. The advantages of a perfect knowledge of our language to young men intended for the professions of law, physic, or divinity are too obvious to be mentioned, but in a state which boasts of the first commercial city in America, I wish to see it cultivated by young men, who are intended for the compting house, for many such, I hope, will be educated in our colleges. The time is past when an academical education was thought to be unnecessary to qualify a young man for merchandize. I conceive no profession is capable of receiving more embellishments from it. The French and German languages should likewise be carefully taught in all our Colleges. They abound with useful books upon all subjects. So important and necessary are those languages, that a degree should never be conferred upon a young man who cannot speak or translate them.

Connected with the study of language is the study of Eloquence. It is well known how great a part it constituted of the Roman education. It is the first accomplishment in a republic, and often sets the whole machine of government in motion. Let our youth, therefore, be instructed in this art. We do not extol it too highly when we attribute as much to the power of eloquence as to the sword, in bringing about American revolution.

With the usual arts and sciences that are taught in our American colleges, I wish to see a regular course of lectures given upon History and Chronology. The science of government, whether it related to constitutions or laws, can only be advanced by a careful selection of facts, and these are to be found chiefly in history. Above all, let our youth be instructed in the history of the ancient republics, and the progress of liberty and tyranny in the different states of Europe. I wish likewise to see the numerous facts that relate to the origin and present state of commerce, together with the nature and principles of Money, reduced to such a system, as to be intelligible and agreeable to a young man. If we consider the commerce of our metropolis only as the avenue of the wealth of the state, the study of it merits a place in a young man's education; but, I consider commerce in a much higher light when I recommend the study of it in republican seminaries. I view it as the best security against the influence of hereditary monopolies of land, and, therefore, the surest protection against aristocracy. I consider its effects as next to those of religion in humanizing mankind, and lastly, I view it as the means of uniting the different nations of the world together by the ties of mutual wants and obligations.

Chemistry by unfolding to us the effects of heat and mixture, enlarges our acquaintance with the wonders of nature and the mysteries of art; hence it has become, in most of the universities of Europe, a necessary branch of a gentleman's education. In a young country, where improvements in agriculture and manufactures are so much to be desired, the cultivation of this science, which explains the principles of both of them, should be considered as an object of the utmost importance.

Again, let your youth be instructed in all the means of promoting national prosperity and independence, whether they relate to improvements in agriculture, manufactures, or inland navigation. Let him be instructed further in the general principles of legislation, whether they relate to revenue, or to the preservation of life, liberty or property. Let him be directed frequently to attend the courts of justice, where he will have the best opportunities of acquiring habits of comparing, and arranging his ideas by observing the discovery of truth, in the examination of witnesses, and where he will hear the laws of the state explained, with all the advantages of that species of eloquence which belongs to the bar. Of so much importance do I conceive it to be, to a young man, to attend occasionally to the decisions of our courts of law, that I wish to see our colleges established, only in county towns.

But further, considering the nature of our connection with the United States, it will be necessary to make our pupil acquainted with all the prerogatives of the national government. He must be instructed in the nature and variety of treaties. He must know the difference in the powers and duties of the several species of ambassadors. He must be taught wherein the obligations of individuals and of states are the same, and wherein they differ. In short, he must acquire a general knowledge of all those laws and forms, which unite the sovereigns of the earth, or separate them from each other.

I beg pardon for having delayed so long to say any thing of the separate and peculiar mode of education proper for women in a republic. I am sensible that they must concur in all our plans of education for young men, or no laws will ever render them effectual. To qualify our women for this purpose, they should not only be instructed in the usual branches of female education, but they should be taught the principles of liberty and government; and the obligations of patriotism should be inculcated upon them. The opinions and conduct of men are often regulated by the women in the most arduous enterprises of life; and their approbation is frequently the principal reward of the hero's dangers, and the patriot's toils. Besides, the first impressions upon the minds of children are generally derived from the women. Of how much consequence, therefore, is it in a republic, that they should think justly upon the great subjects of liberty and government!

The complaints that have been made against religion, liberty and learning, have been, against each of them in a separate state. Perhaps like certain liquors, they should only be used in a state of mixture. They mutually assist in correcting the abuses, and in improving the good effects of each other. From the combined and reciprocal influence of religion, liberty and learning upon the morals, manners and knowledge of individuals, of these, upon government, and of government, upon individuals, it is impossible to measure the degrees of happiness and perfection to which mankind may be raised. For my part, I can form no ideas of the golden age, so much celebrated by the poets, more delightful, than the contemplation of that happiness which it is now in the power of the legislature of Pennsylvania to confer upon the citizens, by establishing proper modes and places of education in every part of the state.

7

On Education of Youth in America

Noah Webster, 1790

Noah Webster (1758–1843) is another important late 18th and early 19th century figure in American history. After serving in the Revolutionary War, he taught school and developed a dictionary, for which he is most well-known. In addition, Webster was a prolific author, and his brief History of the United States, was widely used as a school textbook. In this essay, Webster writes about the importance of educating the youth in public schools, especially in a republican form of government. Not surprisingly for a dictionary author, Webster emphasizes the benefits of studying the English language and of attending to rules of grammar and spelling. He also suggests that studies should have practical utility, and believes that Latin and Greek, the so-called dead languages, and the reading of the Bible were overemphasized in American education of his day. Webster believes that teachers ought to specialize in particular branches of learning and should be of upstanding moral character. His views on corporal punishment for students were typical of the time period, as were his views on education and domestic training for females. Similar to Thomas Jefferson, Webster favors educating the youth in America rather than Europe, in order to foster patriotism for the homeland. —CHB

American Educational Thought: Essays from 1640–1940, pages 71–95
Copyright © 2010 by Information Age Publishing

The education of youth is, in all governments, an object of the first consequence. The impressions received in early life usually form the characters of individuals, a union of which forms the general character of a nation.

The mode of education and the arts taught to youth have in every nation been adapted to its particular stage of society or local circumstances. In the martial ages of Greece the principal study of its legislators was to acquaint the young men with the use of arms, to inspire them with an undaunted courage, and to form in the hearts of both sexes an invincible attachment to their country. Such was the effect of their regulations for these purposes that the very women of Sparta and Athens would reproach their own sons for surviving their companions who fell in the field of battle. Among the warlike Scythians every male was not only taught to use arms for attack and defense but was obliged to sleep in the field, to carry heavy burdens, and to climb rocks and precipices, in order to habituate himself to hardships, fatigue, and danger. In Persia during the flourishing reign of the great Cyrus, the education of youth, according to Xenophon, formed a principal branch of the regulations of the empire. The young men were divided into classes, each of which had some particular duties to perform, for which they were qualified by previous instructions and exercise.

While nations are in a barbarous state, they have few wants and consequently few arts. Their principal objects are defense and subsistence; the education of a savage therefore extends little farther than to enable him to use with dexterity a bow and a tomahawk. But in the progress of manners and of arts, war ceases to be the employment of whole nations; it becomes the business of a few who are paid for defending their country. Artificial wants multiply the number of occupations, and these require a great diversity in the mode of education. Every youth must be instructed in the business by which he is to procure subsistence. Even the civilities of behavior in polished society become a science; a bow and a curtsy are taught with as much care and precision as the elements of mathematics. Education proceeds therefore by gradual advances, from simplicity to corruption. Its first object, among rude nations, is safety; its next, utility; it afterwards extends to convenience; and among the opulent part of civilized nations it is directed principally to show and amusement.

In despotic states education, like religion, is made subservient to government. In some of the vast empires of Asia children are always instructed in the occupation of their parents; thus the same arts are always continued in the same families. Such an institution cramps genius and limits the progress of national improvement; at the same time it is an almost immovable barrier against the introduction of vice, luxury, faction, and changes in government. This is one of the principal causes which have operated in combining numerous millions of the human race under one form of government and preserving national tranquility for incredible periods of time. The empire of China, whose government was founded on the patriarchical discipline, has not suffered a revolution in laws, manners, or language for many thousand years.

In the complicated systems of government which are established among the civilized nations of Europe education has less influence in forming a national character; but there is no state in which it has not an inseparable connection with morals and a consequential influence upon the peace and happiness of society.

Education is a subject which has been exhausted by the ablest writers, both among the ancients and moderns. I am not vain enough to suppose I can suggest any new ideas upon so trite a theme as education in general; but perhaps the manner of conducting the youth in America may be capable of some improvement. Our constitutions of civil government are not yet firmly established; our national character is not yet formed; and it is an object of vast magnitude that systems of education should be adopted and pursued which may not only diffuse a knowledge of the sciences but may implant in the minds of the American youth the principles of virtue and of liberty and inspire them with just and liberal ideas of government and with an inviolable attachment to their own country. It now becomes every American to examine the modes of education in Europe, to see how far they are applicable in this country and whether it is not possible to make some valuable alterations, adapted to our local and political circumstances. Let us examine the subject in two views. First, as it respects arts and sciences. Secondly, as it is connected with morals and government. In each of these articles let us see what errors may be found and what improvements suggested in our present practice.

The first error that I would mention is a too general attention to the dead languages, with a neglect of our own. This practice proceeds probably from the common use of the Greek and Roman tongues before the English was brought to perfection. There was a long period of time when these languages were almost the only repositories of science in Europe. Men who had a taste for learning were under a necessity of recurring to the sources, the Greek and Roman authors. These will ever be held in the highest estimation both for style and sentiment, but the most valuable of them have English translations, which, if they do not contain all the elegance, communicate all the ideas of the originals. The English language, perhaps, at this moment, is the repository of as much learning as one half the languages of Europe. In copiousness it exceeds all modern tongues, and though inferior to the Greek and French in softness and harmony, yet it exceeds the French in variety; it almost equals the Greek and Roman in energy and falls very little short of any language in the regularity of its construction.

In deliberating upon any plan of instruction, we should be attentive to its future influence and probable advantages. What advantage does a merchant, a mechanic, a farmer, derive from an acquaintance with the Greek and Roman tongues? It is true, the etymology of words cannot be well understood without a knowledge of the original languages of which ours is composed. But a very accurate knowledge of the meaning of words and of the true construction of sentences may be obtained by the help of dictionaries and good English writers, and this is all that is necessary in the common occupations of life. But suppose there is some advantage to be derived from an acquaintance with the dead languages, will this compensate for the loss of five or perhaps seven years of valuable time? Life is short, and every hour should be employed to good purposes. If there are no studies of more consequence to boys than those of Latin and Greek, let these languages employ their time, for idleness is the bane of youth. But when we have an elegant and copious language of our own, with innumerable writers upon ethics, geography, history, commerce, and government—subjects immediately interesting to every man, how can a parent be justified in keeping his son several years over rules of syntax, which he forgets when he shuts his book, or which, if remembered, can be of little or no use in any branch of business? This absurdity is the subject of common complaint; men see and feel the impropriety of the usual practice, and yet no arguments that have hitherto been used have been sufficient to change the system or to place an English school on a footing with a Latin one in point of reputation.

It is not my wish to discountenance totally the study of the dead languages. On the other hand, I should urge a more close attention to them among young men who are designed for the learned professions. The poets, the orators, the philosophers, and the historians of Greece and Rome furnish the most excellent models of style and the richest treasures of science. The slight attention given to a few of these authors in our usual nurse of education is rather calculated to make pedants than scholars, and the time employed in gaining superficial knowledge is really wasted.

> *A little learning is a dangerous thing,*
> *Drink deep, or taste not the Pierian spring.*

But my meaning is that the dead languages are not necessary for men of business, merchants, mechanics, planters, etc., nor of utility sufficient to indemnify them for the expense of time and money which is requisite to acquire a tolerable acquaintance with the Greek and Roman authors. Merchants often have occasion for a knowledge of some foreign living language as the French, the Italian, the Spanish, or the German, but men whose business is wholly domestic have little or no use for any language but their own, much less for languages known only in books.

There is one very necessary use of the Latin language which will always prevent it from falling into neglect; which is, that it serves as a common interpreter among the learned of all nations and ages. Epitaphs, inscriptions on monuments and medals, treaties, etc., designed for perpetuity, are written in Latin, which is everywhere understood by the learned and being a dead language is liable to no change.

But the high estimation in which the learned languages have been held has discouraged a due attention to our own. People find themselves able without much study to write and speak the English intelligibly and thus have been led to think rules of no utility. This opinion has produced various and arbitrary practices in the use of the language, even among men of the most information and accuracy; and this diversity has produced another opinion, both false and injurious to the language, that there are no rules or principles on which the pronunciation and construction can be settled.

This neglect is so general that there is scarcely an institution to be found in the country where the English tongue is taught regularly, from its elements to its true and elegant construction, in prose and verse. Perhaps in most schools boys are taught the definition of the parts of speech and a few hard names which they do not understand and which the teacher seldom attempts to explain; this is called *learning grammar*. This practice of learning questions and answers without acquiring any ideas has given rise to a common remark, *that grammar is a dry study;* and so is every other study which is prosecuted without improving the head or the heart. The study of geography is equally dry when the subject is not understood. But when grammar is taught by the help of visible objects, when children perceive that differences of words arise from differences in things, which they may learn at a very early period of life, the study becomes entertaining as well as improving. In general, when a study of any kind is tiresome to a person, it is a presumptive evidence that he does not make any proficiency in knowledge, and this is almost always the fault of the instructor.

In a few instances perhaps the study of English is thought an object of consequence, but here also there is a great error in the common practice, for the study of English is preceded by several years' attention to Latin and Greek. Nay, there are men who contend that the best way to become acquainted with English is to learn Latin first. Common sense may justly smile at such an opinion, but experience proves it to be false.

If language is to be taught mechanically or by rote, it is a matter of little consequence whether the rules are in English, Latin, or Greek, but if children are to acquire *ideas,* it is certainly easier to obtain them in a language which they understand than in a foreign tongue. The distinctions between the principal parts of speech are founded in nature and are within the capacity of a school boy. These distinctions should be explained in English, and when well understood will facilitate the acquisition of other languages. Without some preparation of this kind, boys will often find a foreign language extremely difficult and sometimes be discouraged. We often see young persons of both sexes puzzling their heads with French when they can hardly write two sentences of good English. They plod on for some months with much fatigue, little improvement, and less pleasure, and then relinquish the attempt.

The principles of any science afford pleasure to the student who comprehends them. In order to render the study of language agreeable, the distinctions between words should be illustrated by the differences in visible objects. Examples should be presented to the senses, which are the inlets of all our knowledge. That *nouns are the names of things and that adjectives express their qualities* are abstract definitions which a boy may repeat five years without comprehending the meaning. But that *table* is the name of an article and *hard* or *square* is its property is a distinction obvious to the senses and consequently within a child's capacity.

There is one general practice in schools which I censure with diffidence, not because I doubt the propriety of the censure, but because it is opposed to deep-rooted prejudices: this practice is the use of the Bible as a schoolbook. There are two reasons why this practice has so generally prevailed: the first is that families in the country are not generally supplied with any other book; the second, an opinion that the reading of the scriptures will impress upon the minds of youth the important truths of religion and morality. The first may be easily removed, and the purpose of the last is counteracted by the practice itself.

If people design the doctrines of the Bible as a system of religion, ought they to appropriate the book to purposes foreign to this design? Will not a familiarity, contracted by a careless disrespectful reading of the sacred volume, weaken the influence of its precepts upon the heart?

Let us attend to the effect of familiarity in other things.

The rigid Puritans who first settled the New England states often chose their burying ground in the center of their settlements. Convenience might have been a motive for the choice, but it is probable that a stronger reason was the influence which they supposed the frequent burials and constant sight of the tombs would have upon the lives of men. The choice, however, for the latter purpose was extremely injudicious, for it may be laid down as a general rule that those who live in a constant view of death will become hardened to its terrors.

No person has less sensibility than the surgeon who has been accustomed to the amputation of limbs. No person thinks less of death than the soldier who has frequently walked over the carcasses of his slain comrades or the sexton who lives among the tombs.

Objects that affect the mind strongly, whether the sensations they excite are painful or pleasurable, always lose their effect by a frequent repetition of their impressions. Those parts of the scripture, therefore, which are calculated to strike terror to the mind lose their influence by being too frequently brought into view. The same objection will not apply to the history and morality of the Bible, select passages of which may be read in schools to great advantage. In some countries the common people are not permitted to read the Bible at all. In ours, it is as common as a newspaper and in schools is read with nearly the same degree of respect. Both these practices appear to be extremes. My wish is not to see the Bible excluded from schools but to see it is used as a system of religion and morality.

These remarks suggest another error which is often committed in our inferior schools: I mean that of putting boys into difficult sciences while they are too young to exercise their reason upon abstract subjects. For example, boys are often put to the study of mathematics at the age of eight or ten years and before they can either read or write. In order to show the impropriety of such a practice, it is necessary to repeat what was just now observed, that our senses are the avenues of knowledge. This fact proves that the most natural course of education is that which employs, first the senses or powers of the body or those faculties of the mind which first acquire strength, and then proceeds to those studies which depend on the power of comparing and combining ideas. The art of writing is mechanical and imitative; this may therefore employ boys as soon as their fingers have strength sufficient to command a pen. A knowledge of letters requires the exercise of a mental power, memory, but this is coeval almost with the first operations of the human mind, and with respect to objects of sense, is almost perfect even in childhood. Children may therefore be taught reading as soon as their organs of speech have acquired strength sufficient to articulate the sounds of words.

But those sciences a knowledge of which is acquired principally by the reasoning faculties should be postponed to a more advanced period of life. In the course of an English education, mathematics should be perhaps the last study of youth in schools. Years of valuable time are sometimes thrown away in a fruitless application to sciences, the principles of which are above the comprehension of the students.

There is no particular age at which every boy is qualified to enter upon mathematics to advantage. The proper time can be best determined by the instructors, who are acquainted with the different capacities of their pupils.

Another error which is frequent in America is that a master undertakes to teach many different branches in the same school. In new settlements, where people are poor and live in scattered situations, the practice is often unavoidable, but in populous towns it must be considered as a defective plan of education. For suppose the teacher to be equally master of all the branches which he attempts to teach, which seldom happens, yet his attention must be distracted with a multiplicity of objects and consequently painful to himself and not useful to the pupils. Add to this the continual interruptions which the students of one branch suffer from those of another, which must retard the progress of the whole school. It is a much more eligible plan to appropriate an apartment to each branch of education, with a teacher who makes that branch his sole employment. The principal academies in Europe and America are on this plan, which both reason and experience prove to be the most useful.

With respect to literary institutions of the first rank, it appears to me that their local situations are an object of importance. It is a subject of controversy whether a large city or a country village is the most eligible situation for a college or university. But the arguments in favor of the latter appear to me decisive. Large cities are always scenes of dissipation and amusement, which have a tendency to corrupt the hearts of youth and divert their minds from their literary pursuits. Reason teaches this doctrine, and experience has uniformly confirmed the truth of it.

Strict discipline is essential to the prosperity of a public seminary of science, and this is established with more facility and supported with more uniformity in a small village where there are no great objects of curiosity to interrupt the studies of youth or to call their attention from the orders of the society.

That the morals of young men as well as their application to science depend much on retirement will be generally acknowledged, but it will be said also that the company in large towns will improve their manners. The question, then, is which shall be sacrificed—the advantage of an *uncorrupted heart* and an *improved head* or of polished manners. But this question supposes that the virtues of the heart and the polish of the gentleman are incompatible with each other, which is by no means true. The gentleman and the scholar are often united in the same person. But both are not formed by the same means. The improvement of the head requires close application to books; the refinement of manners rather attends some degree of dissipation or at least a relaxation of the mind. To preserve the purity of the heart, it is sometimes necessary, and always useful, to place a youth beyond the reach of bad examples, whereas a general knowledge of the world, of all kinds of company, is requisite to teach a universal propriety of behavior.

But youth is the time to form both the head and the heart. The understanding is indeed ever enlarging, but the seeds of knowledge should be planted in the mind while it is young and susceptible, and if the mind is not kept untainted in *youth,* there is little probability that the moral character of the *man* be unblemished. A genteel address, on the other hand, be acquired at any time of life and *must* be acquired, if ever, by mingling with good company. But were the cultivation of the understanding and of the heart inconsistent with genteel manners, still no rational person could hesitate which to prefer, goodness of a heart is of infinitely more consequence to society than an elegance of manners; nor will any superficial accomplishments repair the want of principle in the mind. It is always better to be *vulgarly right* than *politely wrong.*

But if the amusements, dissipation, and vicious examples in populous cities render them improper places for seats of learning, the monkish mode of sequestering boys from other society and confining them to the apartments of a college appears to me another fault. The human mind is like a rich field, which, without constant care, will ever be covered with a luxuriant growth of weeds. It is extremely dangerous to suffer young men to pass the most critical period of life, when the passions are strong, the judgment weak, and the heart susceptible and unsuspecting, in a situation where there is not the least restraint upon their inclinations. My own observations lead me to draw the veil of silence over the ill effects of this practice. But it is to be wished that youth might always be kept under the inspection of age and superior wisdom; that literary institutions might be so situated, that the students might live in decent families, be subject in some measure to their discipline, and even under the control of those whom they respect.

Perhaps it may also be numbered among the errors in our systems of education that in all our universities and colleges the students are all restricted to the same course of study and, by being classed, limited to the same progress. Classing is necessary, but whether students should not be

removable from the lower to the higher classes as a reward for their superior industry and improvements is submitted to those who know the effect
of emulation upon the human mind.

But young gentlemen are not all designed for the same line of business,
and why should they pursue the same studies? Why should a merchant trouble himself with the rules of Greek and Roman syntax or a planter puzzle
his head with conic sections? Life is too short to acquire, and the mind of
man too feeble to contain, the whole circle of sciences. The greatest genius
on earth, not even a Bacon, can be a perfect master of *every* branch, but any
moderate genius may, by suitable application, be perfect in any *one* branch.
By attempting therefore to teach imp gentlemen everything, we make the
most of them mere smatterers in science. In order to qualify persons to
figure in profession, it is necessary that they should attend closely to those
branches of learning which lead to it.

There are some arts and sciences which are necessary for every man.
Every man should be able to speak and write his native tongue with correctness and have some knowledge of mathematics. The rules of arithmetic are
indispensably requisite. But besides the learning which is of common utility, lads should be directed to pursue those branches which are connected
more immediately with the business for which they are destined.

It would be very useful for the farming part of the community to furnish
country schools with some easy system of practical husbandry. By repeatedly
reading some book of this kind, the mind would be stored with ideas which
might not indeed be understood in youth but which would be called into
practice in some subsequent period of life. This would lead the mind to the
subject of agriculture and pave the way for improvements.

Young gentlemen designed for the mercantile line, after having learned
to write and speak English correctly, might attend to French, Italian, or such
other living language as they will probably want in the course of business.
These languages should be learned early in youth, while the organs are
yet pliable; otherwise the pronunciation will probably be imperfect. These
studies might be succeeded by some attention to chronology, and a regular
application to geography, mathematics, history, the general regulations of
commercial nations, principles of advance in trade, of insurance, and to the
general principles of government.

It appears to me that such a course of education, which might be completed by the age of fifteen or sixteen, would have a tendency to make better merchants than the usual practice which confines boys to Lucian, Ovid,
and Tully till they are fourteen and then turns them into a store, without an

idea of their business or one article of education necessary for them except perhaps a knowledge of writing and figures.

Such a system of English education is also much preferable to a university education, even with the usual honors, for it might be finished so early as to leave young persons time to serve a regular apprenticeship, without which no person should enter upon business. But by the time a university education is completed, young men commonly commence *gentlemen;* their age and their pride will not suffer them to go through the drudgery of a counting house, and they enter upon business without the requisite accomplishments. Indeed it appears to me that what is now called a *liberal education* disqualifies a man for business. Habits are formed in youth and by practice, and as business is in some measure mechanical, every person should be exercised in his employment in an early period of life, that his habits may be formed by the time his apprenticeship expires. An education in a university interferes with the forming of these habits and perhaps forms opposite habits; the mind may contract a fondness for ease, for pleasure or for books, which no efforts can overcome. An academic education, which should furnish the youth with some ideas of men and things and leave time for an apprenticeship before the age of twenty-one years would in my opinion be the most eligible for young men who are designed for active employments.

The method pursued in our colleges is better calculated to fit youth for the learned professions than for business. But perhaps the period of study required as the condition of receiving the usual degrees is too short. Four years, with the most assiduous application, are a short time to furnish the mind with the necessary knowledge of the languages and of the several sciences. It might perhaps have been a period sufficiently long for an infant settlement, as America was, at the time when most of our colleges were founded. But as the country becomes populous, wealthy, and respectable, it may be worthy of consideration whether the period of academic life should not be extended to six or seven years.

But the principal defect in our plan of education in America is the want of good teachers in the academies and common schools. By good teachers I mean men of unblemished reputation and possessed of abilities competent to their stations. That a man should be master of what he undertakes to teach is a point that will not be disputed, and yet it is certain that abilities are often dispensed with, either through inattention or fear of expense.

To those who employ ignorant men to instruct their children, permit me to suggest one important idea: that it is better for youth to have *no* education than to have a bad one, for it is more difficult to eradicate habits than to impress new ideas. The tender shrub is easily bent to any figure, but the tree which has acquired its full growth resists all impressions.

Yet abilities are not the sole requisites. The instructors of youth ought, of all men, to be the most prudent, accomplished, agreeable, and respectable. What avail a man's parts, if, while he is the "wisest and brightest," he is the "meanest of mankind?" The pernicious effects of bad example on the *minds* of youth will probably be acknowledged, but with a view to *improvement* it is indispensably necessary that the teachers should possess good breeding and agreeable manners. In order to give full effect to instructions, it is requisite that they should proceed from a man who is loved and respected. But a low-bred clown or morose tyrant can command neither love nor respect, and that pupil who has no motive for application to books but the fear of a rod will not make a scholar.

The rod is often necessary in school, especially after the children have been accustomed to disobedience and a licentious behavior at home. All government originates in families, and if neglected there, it will hardly exist in society, but the want of it must be supplied by the rod in school, the penal laws of the state, and the terrors of divine wrath from the pulpit. The government both of families and schools should be absolute. There should in families be no appeal from one parent to another, with the prospect of pardon for offenses. The one should always vindicate, at least apparently, the conduct of the other. In schools the matter should be absolute in command, for it is utterly impossible for any man to support order and discipline among children who are indulged with an appeal to their parents. A proper subordination in families would generally supersede the necessity of severity in schools, and a strict discipline in both is the best foundation of good order in political society.

If parents should say, "We cannot give the instructors of our children unlimited authority over them, for it may be abused and our children injured," I would answer, they must not place them under the direction of any man in whose temper, judgment, and abilities they do not repose perfect confidence. The teacher should be, if such can be found, as judicious and reasonable a man as the parent.

There can be little improvement in schools without strict subordination; there can be no subordination without principles of esteem and respect in the pupils; and the pupils cannot esteem and respect a man who is not in himself respectable and who is not treated with respect by their parents. It may be laid down as an invariable maxim that a person is not fit to superintend the education of children who has not the qualifications which will command the esteem and respect of his pupils. This maxim is founded on a truth which every person may have observed—that children always *love* an *amiable* man and always *esteem a respectable* one. Men and women have their passions, which often rule their judgment and their conduct. They have their caprices, their interests, and their prejudices, which at times incline them to treat the most meritorious characters with disrespect. But children, artless and unsuspecting, resign their hearts to any person whose manners are agreeable and whose conduct is respectable. Whenever, therefore, pupils cease to respect their teacher, he should be instantly dismissed.

Respect for an instructor will often supply the place of a rod of correction. The pupil's attachment will lead him to close attention to his studies; he fears not the *rod* so much as the *displeasure* of his teacher; he waits for a smile or dreads a frown; he receives his instructions and copies his manners. This generous principle, the fear of offending, will prompt youth to exertions, and instead of severity on the one hand and of slavish fear with reluctant obedience on the other, mutual esteem, respect, and confidence strew flowers in the road to knowledge.

With respect to morals and civil society, the other view in which I proposed to treat this subject, the effects of education are so certain and extensive that it behooves every parent and guardian to be particularly attentive to the characters of the men whose province it is to form the minds of youth.

From a strange inversion of the order of nature, the cause of which it is not necessary to unfold, the most important business in civil society is in many parts of America committed to the most worthless characters. The education of youth, an employment of more consequence than making laws and preaching the gospel, because it lays the foundation on which both law and gospel rest for success, this education is sunk to a level with the most menial services. In most instances we find the higher seminaries of learning entrusted to men of good characters and possessed of the moral virtues of social affections. But many of our inferior schools, which, so far as the heart is concerned, are as important as colleges, are kept by men of no breeding, and many of them, by men infamous for the most detestable vices. Will this be denied? Will it be denied that before the war it was a frequent practice for gentlemen to purchase convicts who had been transported for their crimes and employ them as private tutors in their families?

Gracious Heavens! Must the wretches who have forfeited their lives and been pronounced unworthy to be inhabitants of a *foreign* country be entrusted with the education, the morals, the character of *American* youth?

Will it be denied that many of the instructors of youth, whose examples and precepts should form their minds for good men and useful citizens, are often found to sleep away in school the fumes of a debauch and to stun the ears of their pupils with frequent blasphemy? It is idle to suppress such truths; nay more, it is wicked. The practice of employing low and vicious characters to direct the studies of youth is in a high degree criminal; it is destructive of the order and peace of society; it is treason against morals and of course against government; it ought to be arraigned before the tribunal of reason and condemned by all intelligent beings. The practice is so exceedingly absurd that it is surprising it could ever have prevailed among rational people. Parents wish their children to be *well-bred,* yet place them under the care of *clowns.* They wish to secure their hearts from *vicious principles* and *habits,* yet commit them to the care of men of the most *profligate lives.* They wish to have their children taught *obedience* and *respect* for superiors, yet give them a master that both parents and children *despise.* A practice so glaringly absurd and irrational has no name in any language! Parents themselves will not associate with the men whose company they *oblige* their children to keep, even in that most important period when habits are forming for life.

Are parents and guardians ignorant that children always imitate those with whom they live or associate? That a boy, bred in the woods, will be a savage? That another, bred in the army, will have the manners of a soldier? That a third, bred in a kitchen, will speak the language and possess the ideas of servants? And that a fourth, bred in genteel company, will have the manners of a gentleman? We cannot believe that many people are ignorant of these truths. Their conduct therefore can be ascribed to nothing but inattention or fear of expense. It is perhaps literally true that a wild life among savages is preferable to an education in a kitchen or under a drunken tutor, for savages would leave the mind uncorrupted with the vices which reign among slaves and the depraved part of civilized nations. It is therefore a point of infinite importance to society that youth should not associate with persons whose manners they ought not to imitate; much less should they be doomed to pass the most susceptible period of life with clowns, profligates, and slaves.

There are people so ignorant of the constitution of our natures as to declare that young people should see vices and their consequences, that they may learn to detest and shun them. Such reasoning is like that of the novel writers, who attempt to defend their delineations of abandoned characters; and that of stage players, who would vindicate the obscene exhibitions of a theater; but the reasoning is totally false. Vice always spreads by being published; young people are taught many vices by fiction, books, or public exhibitions, vices which they never would have known had they never read such books or attended such public places. Crimes of all kinds, vices, judicial trials necessarily obscene, and infamous punishments should, if possible, be concealed from the young. An examination in a court of justice may teach the tricks of a knave, the arts of a thief, and the evasions of hackneyed offenders to a dozen young culprits and even tempt those who have never committed a crime to make a trial of their skill. A newspaper may spread crimes by communicating to a nation the knowledge of an ingenious trick of villainy which, had it been suppressed, might have died with its first inventor. It is not true that the effects of vice and crimes deter others from the practice except when rarely seen. On the other hand, frequent exhibitions either cease to make any impressions on the minds of spectators else reconcile them to a course of life which at first was disagreeable.

Vice is a monster of so frightful mein,
As to be hated, needs but to be seen;
Yet seen too oft, familiar with her face,
We first endure, then pity, then embrace.

For these reasons children should keep the best of company that they might have before them the best manners, the best breeding, and the best conversation. Their minds should be kept untainted till their reasoning faculties have acquired strength and the good principles which may be planted in their minds have taken deep root. They will then be able to make a firm and probably a successful resistance against the attacks of secret corruption and brazen libertinism.

Our legislators frame laws for the suppression of vice and immorality; our divines thunder from the pulpit the terrors of infinite wrath against the vices that stain the characters of men. And do laws and preaching effect a reformation of manners? Experience would not give a very favorable answer to this inquiry. The reason is obvious: the attempts are directed to the wrong objects. Laws can only check the public effects of vicious principles but can never reach the principles themselves, and preaching is not very intelligible to people till they arrive at an age when their principles are rooted or their habits firmly established. An attempt to eradicate old habits is as absurd as to lop off the branches of a huge oak in order to root it out of a rich soil. The most that such clipping will effect is to prevent a further growth.

The only practicable method to reform mankind is to begin with children, to banish, if possible, from their company every low-bred, drunken, immoral character. Virtue and vice will not grow together in a great degree, but they will grow where they are planted, and when one has taken root, it is not easily supplanted by the other. The great art of correcting mankind, therefore, consists in prepossessing the mind with good principles.

For this reason society requires that the education of youth should be watched with the most scrupulous attention. Education, in a great measure, forms the moral characters of men, and morals are the basis of government. Education should therefore be the first care of a legislature, not merely the institution of schools but the furnishing of them with the best men for teachers. A good system of education should be the first article in the code of political regulations, for it is much easier to introduce and establish an effectual system for preserving morals than to correct by penal statutes the ill effects of a bad system. I am so fully persuaded of this that I shall almost adore that great man who shall change our practice and opinions and make it respectable for the first and best men to superintend the education of youth.

Another defect in our schools, which, since the Revolution, is become inexcusable, is the want of proper books. The collections which are now used consist of essays that respect foreign and ancient nations. The minds of youth are perpetually led to the history of Greece and Rome or to Great Britain; boys are constantly repeating the declamations of Demosthenes and Cicero or debates upon some political question in the British Parliament. These are excellent specimens of good sense, polished style and perfect oratory, but they are not interesting to children. They cannot be very useful, except to young gentlemen who want them as models of reasoning and eloquence in the pulpit or at the bar.

But every child in America should be acquainted with his own country. He should read books that furnish him with ideas that will be useful to him in life and practice. As soon as he opens his lips, he should rehearse the history of his own country he should lisp the praise of liberty and of those illustrious heroes and statesmen who have wrought a revolution in her favor.

A selection of essays respecting the settlement and geography of America, the history of the late Revolution and of the most remarkable characters and events that distinguished it, and a compendium of the principles of the federal and provincial governments should be the principal schoolbook in the United States. These are interesting objects to every man; they call home the minds of youth and fix them upon the interests of their own country, and they assist in forming attachments to it, as well as in enlarging the understanding.

It is observed by the great Montesquieu that "the laws of education ought to be relative to the principles of the government."

In despotic governments the people should have little or no education, except what tends to inspire them with a servile fear. Information is fatal to despotism.

In monarchies education should be partial and adapted to the rank of each class of citizens. But "in a republican government," says the same writer, "the whole power of education is required." <u>Here every class of people should *know* and *love* the laws.</u> This knowledge should be diffused by means of schools and newspapers, and an attachment to the laws may be formed by early impressions upon the mind.

Two regulations are essential to the continuance of republican governments: 1. Such a distribution of lands and such principles of descent and alienation as shall give every citizen a power of acquiring what his industry merits. 2. Such a system of education as gives every citizen an opportunity of acquiring knowledge and fitting himself for places of trust. These are fundamental articles, the *sine qua non* of the existence of the American republics.

Hence the absurdity of our copying the manners and adopting the institutions of monarchies.

In several states we find laws passed establishing provision for colleges and academies where people of property may educate their sons, but no provision is made for instructing the poorer rank of people even in reading and writing. Yet in these same states every citizen who is worth a few shillings annually is entitled to vote for legislators. This appears to me a most glaring solecism in government. The constitutions are *republican* and the laws of education are *monarchical*. The *former* extend civil rights to every honest industrious man, the *latter* deprive a large proportion of the citizens of a most valuable privilege.

In our American republics, where government is in the hands of the people, knowledge should be universally diffused by means of public schools. Of such consequence is it to society that the people who make laws should be well informed that I conceive no legislature can be justified in neglecting proper establishments for this purpose.

When I speak of a diffusion of knowledge, I do not mean merely a knowledge of spelling books and the New Testament. An acquaintance with ethics and with the general principles of law, commerce, money, and government is necessary for the yeomanry of a republican state. This acquaintance they might obtain by means of books calculated for schools and read by the children during the winter months and by the circulation of public papers.

"In Rome it was the common exercise of boys at school to learn the laws of the twelve tables by heart, as they did their poets and classic authors." What an excellent practice this in a free government!

It is said, indeed by many, that our common people are already too well informed. Strange paradox! The truth is, they have too much knowledge and spirit to resign their share in government and are not sufficiently informed to govern themselves in all cases of difficulty.

There are some acts of the American legislatures which astonish men of information, and blunders in legislation are frequently ascribed to bad intentions. But if we examine the men who compose these legislatures, we shall find that wrong measures generally proceed from ignorance either in the men themselves or in their constituents. They often mistake their own interest, because they do not foresee the remote consequences of a measure.

It may be true that all men cannot be legislators, but the more generally knowledge is diffused among the substantial yeomanry, the more perfect will be the laws of a republican state.

Every small district should be furnished with a school, at least four months in a year, when boys are not otherwise employed. This school should be kept by the most reputable and well informed man in the district. Here children should be taught the usual branches of learning, submission to superiors and to laws, the moral or social duties, the history and transactions of their own country, the principles of liberty and government. Here the rough manners of the wilderness should be softened and the principles of virtue and good behavior inculcated. The *virtues* of men are of more consequence to society than their *abilities,* and for this reason the *heart* should be cultivated with more assiduity than the *head.*

Such a general system of education is neither impracticable nor difficult, and excepting the formation of a federal government that shall be efficient and permanent, it demands the first attention of American patriots. Until such a system shall be adopted and pursued, until the statesman and divine shall unite their efforts in *forming* the human mind, rather than in loping its excrescences after it has been neglected, until legislators discover that the only way to make good citizens and subjects is to nourish them from infancy, and until parents shall be convinced that the *worst* of men are not the proper teachers to make the *best,* mankind cannot know to what a degree of perfection society and government may be carried. America affords the fairest opportunities for making the experiment and opens the most encouraging prospect of success.

In a system of education that should embrace every part of the community the female sex claim no inconsiderable share of our attention.

The women in America (to their honor it is mentioned) are not generally above the care of educating their own children. Their own education should therefore enable them to implant in the tender mind such sentiments of virtue, propriety, and dignity as are suited to the freedom of our governments. Children should be treated as children, but as children that are in a future time to be men and women. By treating them as if they were always to remain children, we very often see their childishness adhere to them, even in middle life. The silly language called *baby talk,* in which most persons are initiated in infancy, often breaks out in discourse at the age of forty and makes a man appear very ridiculous. In the same manner, vulgar, obscene, and illiberal ideas imbibed in a nursery or a kitchen often give a tincture to the conduct through life. In order to prevent every evil bias, the ladies, whose province it is to direct the inclinations of children on their first appearance and to choose their nurses, should be possessed, not only of amiable manners, but of just sentiments and enlarged understandings.

But the influence of women in forming the dispositions of youth is not the sole reason why their education should be particularly guarded; their influence in controlling the manners of a nation is another powerful reason. Women, once abandoned, may be instrumental in corrupting society, but such is the delicacy of the sex and such the restraints which custom imposes upon them that they are generally the last to be corrupted. There are innumerable instances of men who have been restrained from a vicious life and even of very abandoned men who have been reclaimed by their attachment to ladies of virtue. A fondness for the company and conversation of ladies of character may be considered as a young man's best security against the attractives of a dissipated life. A man who is attached to *good* company seldom frequents that which is *bad.* For this reason, society requires that females should be well educated and extend their influence as far as possible over the other sex.

But a distinction is to be made between a *good* education and a *showy* one, for an education, merely superficial, is a proof of corruption of taste and has a mischievous influence on manners. The education of females, like that of males, should be adapted to the principles of the government and correspond with the stage of society. Education in Paris differs from that in Petersburg, and the education of females in London or Paris should not be a model for the Americans to copy.

In all nations a *good* education is that which renders the ladies correct in their manners, respectable in their families and agreeable in society. That education is always *wrong* which raises a woman above the duties of her station.

In America female education should have for its object what is *useful.* Young ladies should be taught to speak and write their own language with purity and elegance, an article in which they are often deficient. The French language is not necessary for ladies. In some cases it is convenient, but, in general, it may be considered as an article of luxury. As an accomplishment, it may be studied by those whose attention is not employed about more important concerns.

Some knowledge of arithmetic is necessary for every lady. Geography should never be neglected. *Belles-lettres* learning seems to correspond with the dispositions of most females. A taste for poetry and fine writing should be cultivated, for we expect the most delicate sentiments from the pens of that sex which is possessed of the finest feelings.

A course of reading can hardly be prescribed for all ladies. But it should be remarked that this sex cannot be too well acquainted with the writers upon human life and manners. The *Spectator* should fill the first place in every lady's library. Other volumes of periodical papers, though inferior to the *Spectator*, should be read, and some of the best histories.

With respect to novels, so much admired by the young and so generally condemned by the old, what shall I say? Perhaps it may be said with truth that some of them are useful, many of them pernicious, and most of them trifling. A hundred volumes of modern novels may be read without acquiring a new idea. Some of them contain entertaining stories, and where the descriptions are drawn from nature and from characters and events in themselves innocent, the perusal of them may be harmless.

Were novels written with a view to exhibit only one side of human nature, to paint the social virtues, the world would condemn them as defective, but I should think them more perfect. Young people, especially females, should not see the vicious part of mankind. At best, novels may be considered as the toys of youth, the rattle boxes of sixteen. The mechanic gets his pence for his toys, and the novel writer, for his books, and it would be happy for society if the latter were in all cases as innocent playthings as the former.

In the large towns in America music, drawing, and dancing constitute a part of female education. They, however, hold a subordinate rank, for my fair friends will pardon me when I declare that no man ever marries a woman for her performance on a harpsichord or her figure in a minuet. However ambitious a woman may be to command admiration *abroad*, her real merit is known only at *home*. Admiration is useless when it is not supported by domestic worth. But real honor and permanent esteem are always secured by those who preside over their own families with dignity.

Before I quit this subject, I beg leave to make some remarks on a practice which appears to be attended with important consequences; I mean that of sending boys to Europe for an education or sending to Europe for teachers. This was right before the Revolution, at least so far as national attachments were concerned, but the propriety of it ceased with our political relation to Great Britain.

In the first place, our honor as an independent nation is concerned in the establishment of literary institutions adequate to all our own purposes, without sending our youth abroad or depending on other nations for books and instructors. It is very little to the reputation of America to have it said abroad that after the heroic achievements of the late war these independent people are obliged to send to Europe for men and books to teach their children A B C.

But in another point of view, a foreign education is directly opposite to our political interests and ought to be discountenanced, if not prohibited.

Every person of common observation will grant that most men prefer the manners and the government of that country where they are educated. Let ten American youths be sent, each to a different European kingdom, and live there from the age of twelve to twenty, and each will give the preference to the country where he has resided.

The period from twelve to twenty is the most important in life. The impressions made before that period are commonly effaced; those that are made during that period *always* remain for many years and *generally* through life.

Ninety-nine persons of a hundred who pass that period in England or France will prefer the people, their manners, their laws, and their government to those of their native country. Such attachments are injurious, both to the happiness of the men and to the political interests of their own country. As to private happiness, it is universally known how much pain a man suffers by a change of habits in living. The customs of Europe are and ought to be different from ours, but when a man has been bred in one country, his attachments to its manners make them, in a great measure, necessary to his happiness. On changing his residence, he must therefore break his former habits, which is always a painful sacrifice; or the discordance between the manners of his own country and his habits must give him incessant uneasiness; or he must introduce into a circle of his friends the manners in which he was educated. These consequences may follow, and the last, which is inevitable, is a public injury. The refinement of manners in every country should keep pace exactly with the increase of its wealth, and perhaps the greatest evil America now feels is an improvement of taste and manners which its wealth cannot support.

A foreign education is the very source of this evil; it gives young gentlemen of fortune a relish for manners and amusements which are not suited to this country, which, however, when introduced by this class of people will always become fashionable.

But a corruption of manners is not the sole objection to a foreign education: an attachment to a *foreign* government, or rather a want of attachment to our *own*, is the natural effect of a residence abroad during the period of youth. It is recorded of one of the Greek cities that in a treaty with their conquerors it was required that they should give a certain number of *male children* as hostages for the fulfillment of their engagements. The Greeks absolutely refused, on the principle that these children would imbibe the ideas and embrace the manners of foreigners or lose their love for their own country, but they offered the same number of *old* men without hesitation. This anecdote is full of good sense. A man should always form his habits and attachments in the country where he is to reside for life. When these habits are formed, young men may travel without danger of losing their patriotism. A boy who lives in England from twelve to twenty will be an *Englishman* in his manners and his feelings, but let him remain at home till he is twenty and form his attachments, he may then be several years abroad and still be an *American*. There may be exceptions to this observation, but living examples may be mentioned to prove the truth of the general principle here advanced respecting the influence of habit.

It may be said that foreign universities furnish much better opportunities of improvement in the sciences than the American. This may be true and yet will not justify the practice of sending young lads from their own country. There are some branches of science which may be studied to much greater advantage in Europe than in America, particularly chemistry. When these are to be acquired, young gentlemen ought to spare no pains to attend the best professors. It may, therefore, be useful, in some cases, for students to cross the Atlantic to *complete* a course of studies, but it is not necessary for them to go early in life nor to continue a long time. Such instances need not be frequent even now, and the necessity for them will diminish in proportion to the future advancement of literature in America.

It is, however, much questioned whether in the ordinary course of study a young man can enjoy greater advantages in Europe than in America. Experience inclines me to raise a doubt whether the danger to which a youth must be exposed among the sons of dissipation abroad will not turn the scale in favor of our American colleges. Certain it is that four fifths of the great literary characters in America never crossed the Atlantic.

But if our universities and schools are not so good as the English or Scotch, it is the business of our rulers to improve them, not to endow them merely; for endowments alone will never make a flourishing seminary; but to furnish them with professors of the first abilities and most assiduous application and with a complete apparatus for establishing theories by experiments. Nature has been profuse to the Americans, in genius and in the advantages of climate and soil. If this country, therefore, should long be indebted to Europe for opportunities of acquiring any branch of science in perfection, it must be by means of a criminal neglect of its inhabitants.

The difference in the nature of the American and European governments is another objection to a foreign education. Men form modes of reasoning or habits of thinking on political subjects in the country where they are bred; these modes of reasoning may be founded on fact in all countries, but the same principles will not apply in all governments because of the infinite variety of national opinions and habits. Before a man can be a good legislator, he must be intimately acquainted with the temper of the people to be governed. No man can be thus acquainted with a people without residing among them and mingling with all companies. For want of this acquaintance, a Turgot and a Price may reason most absurdly upon the constitutions of the American states; and when any person has been long accustomed to believe in the propriety or impropriety of certain maxims or regulations of government, it is very difficult to change his opinions or to persuade him to adapt his reasoning to new and different circumstances.

One half the European Protestants will now contend that the Roman Catholic religion is subversive of civil government. Tradition, books, education have concurred to fix this belief in their minds, and they will not resign their opinions, even in America, where some of the highest civil offices are in the hands of Roman Catholics.

It is therefore of infinite importance that those who direct the councils of a nation should be educated in that nation. Not that they should restrict their personal acquaintance to their own country, but their first ideas, attachments, and habits should be acquired in the country which they are to govern and defend. When a knowledge of their own country is obtained and an attachment to its laws and interests deeply fixed in their hearts, then young gentlemen may travel with infinite advantage and perfect safety. I wish not therefore to discourage traveling, but, if possible, to render it more useful to individuals and to the community. My meaning is that *men* should travel and not *boys*.

It is time for the Americans to change their usual route and travel through a country which they never think of or think beneath their notice: I mean the United States.

While these states were a part of the British Empire, our interest, our feelings, were those of Englishmen; our dependence led us to respect and imitate their manners and to look up to them for our opinions. We little thought of arty national interest in America, and while our commerce and governments were in the hands of our parent country and we had no common interest, we little thought of improving our acquaintance with each other or of removing prejudices and reconciling the discordant feelings of the inhabitants of different provinces. But independence and union render it necessary that the citizens of different states should know each others' characters and circumstances, that all jealousies should be removed, that mutual respect and confidence should succeed and a harmony of views and interests be cultivated by a friendly intercourse.

A tour through the United States ought now to be considered as a necessary part of a liberal education. Instead of sending young gentlemen to Europe to view curiosities and learn vices and follies, let them spend twelve or eighteen months in examining the local situation of the different states—the rivers, the soil, the population, the improvements and commercial advantages of the whole—with an attention to the spirit and manners of the inhabitants, their laws, local customs, and institutions. Such a tour should at least precede a tour to Europe, for nothing can be more ridiculous than a man traveling in a foreign country for information when he can give no account of his own. When, therefore, young gentlemen have finished an academic education, let them travel through America, and afterwards to Europe if their time and fortunes will permit. But if they cannot make a tour through both, that in America is certainly to be preferred, for the people of America, with all their information, are yet extremely ignorant of the geography, policy, and manners of their neighboring states. Except a few gentlemen whose public employments in the army and in Congress have extended their knowledge of America, the people in this country, even of the higher classes, have not so correct information respecting the United States as they have respecting England or France. Such ignorance is not only disgraceful but is materially prejudicial to our political friendship and federal operations.

Americans, unshackle your minds and act like independent beings. You have been children long enough, subject to the control and subservient to the interest of a haughty parent. You have now an interest of your own to augment and defend: you have an empire to raise and support by your exertions and a national character to establish and extend by your wisdom and virtues. To effect these great objects, it is necessary to frame a liberal plan of policy and build it on a broad system of education. Before this system can be formed and embraced, the Americans must *believe* and *act* from the belief that it is dishonorable to waste life in mimicking the follies of other nations and basking in the sunshine of foreign glory.

8

An Address to the Public

Particularly to the Members of the Legislature
of New York, Proposing a Plan for Improving
Female Education

Emma Willard, 1819

Emma Willard (1787–1870) was a 19th century pioneer in the field of women's education. She established and directed several female seminaries, most notably Troy Female Seminary, which today is a secondary institution known as the Emma Willard School. Willard also published history textbooks and poems. In this essay, Willard discusses the benefits of establishing female seminaries. Her chief argument is that a seminary provides a superior and higher level of education to women than any previously offered. Another important reason for establishing seminaries is that she believes women are better teachers of children than men, and she argues that they also cost less to hire. Finally, Willard advances a logic similar to the founding fathers: Female education was critical in a republican form of government. —CHB

American Educational Thought: Essays from 1640–1940, pages 97–103
Copyright © 2010 by Information Age Publishing

In inquiring concerning the benefits of the plan proposed, I shall proceed upon the supposition that female seminaries will be patronized throughout our country. Nor is this altogether a visionary supposition. If one seminary should be well organized, its advantages would be found so great that others would soon be instituted; and that sufficient patronage can be found to put one in operation may be presumed from its reasonableness and from the public opinion with regard to the present mode of female education. It is from an intimate acquaintance with those parts of our country whose education is said to flourish most that the writer has drawn her picture of the present state of female instruction; and she knows that she is not alone in perceiving or deploring its faults. Her sentiments are shared by many an enlightened parent of a daughter who has received a boarding school education.

Counting on the promise of her childhood, the father had anticipated her maturity as combining what is excellent in mind with what is elegant in manners. He spared no expense that education might realize to him the image of his imagination. His daughter returned from her boarding school, improved in fashionable airs and expert in manufacturing fashionable toys; but, in her conversation, he sought in vain for that refined and fertile mind which he had fondly expected. Aware that his disappointment has its source in a defective education, he looks with anxiety on his other daughters, whose minds, like lovely buds, are beginning to open. Where shall he find a genial soil in which he may place them to expand? Shall he provide them male instructors? Then the graces of their persons and manners, and whatever forms the distinguishing charm of the feminine character, they cannot be expected to acquire. Shall he give them a private tutoress? She will have been educated at the boarding school, and his daughters will have the faults of its instruction second-handed. Such is now the dilemma of many parents; and it is one from which they cannot be extricated by their individual exertions. May not then the only plan which promises to relieve them expect their vigorous support?

Let us now proceed to inquire what benefits would result from the establishment of female seminaries.

They would constitute a grade of public education superior to any yet known in the history of our sex; and through them, the lower grades of female instruction might be controlled. The influence of public seminaries over these would operate in two ways: first by requiring certain qualifications for entrance; and second by furnishing instructresses initiated in these modes of teaching and imbued with their maxims. Female seminaries might be expected to have important and happy effects on common schools in general; and in the manner of operating on these would probably place the business of teaching children into hands now nearly useless to society; and take it from those whose services the state wants in many other ways.

That nature designed for our sex the care of children, she has made manifest by mental as well as physical indications. She has given us, in a greater degree than men, the gentle arts of insinuation to soften their minds and fit them to receive impressions; a greater quickness of invention to vary modes of teaching to different dispositions; and more patience to make repeated efforts. There are many females of ability to whom the business of instructing children is highly acceptable; and who would devote all their faculties to their occupation. For they would have no higher pecuniary object to engage their attention; and their reputation as instructors they would consider as important. Whereas, whenever able and enterprising men engage in this business, they consider it merely as a temporary employment to further some object, to the attainment of which their best thoughts and calculations are all directed. If, then, women were properly fitted by instruction, they would be likely to teach children better than the other sex; they could afford to do it cheaper; and those men who would otherwise be engaged in this employment might be at liberty to add to the wealth of the nation, by any of those thousand occupations from which women are necessarily debarred.

But the females who taught children would have been themselves instructed either immediately or indirectly by the seminaries. Hence through these, the government might exercise an intimate and most beneficial control over common schools. Anyone who has turned his attention to this subject must be aware that there is great room for improvement in these, both as to the modes of teaching and the things taught; and what method could be devised so likely to effect this improvement as to prepare by instruction a class of individuals whose interest, leisure, and natural talents would combine to make them pursue it with ardor! Such a class of individuals would be raised up by female seminaries. And therefore they would be likely to have highly important and happy effects on common schools.

T'is believed that such institutions would tend to prolong or perpetuate our excellent government.

An opinion too generally prevails that our present form of government, though good, cannot be permanent. Other republics have failed, and the historian and philosopher have told us that nations are like individuals; that at their birth, they receive the seeds of their decline and dissolution. Here, deceived by a false analogy, we receive an apt illustration of particular facts for a general truth. The existence of nations cannot, in strictness, be compared with the duration of animate life; for by the operation of physical causes, this, after a certain length of time, must cease. But the existence of nations is prolonged by the succession of one generation to another, and there is no physical cause to prevent this succession's going on, in a peaceable manner, under a good government, till the end of time. We must then look to other causes than necessity for the decline and fall of former republics. If we could discover these causes and seasonably prevent their operation, then might our latest posterity enjoy the same happy government with which we are blessed; or if but in part, then might the triumph of tyranny be delayed, and a few more generations be free.

Permit me, then, to ask the enlightened politician of any country whether, amid his researches for these causes, he cannot discover one in the neglect which free governments, in common with others, have shown to whatever regarded the formation of the female character.

In those great republics which have fallen of themselves, the loss of republican manners and virtues has been the invariable precursor of their loss of the republican form of government. But is it not the power of our sex to give society its tone, both as to manners and morals? And if such is the extent of female influence, is it wonderful that republics have failed when they calmly suffered that influence to become enlisted in favor of luxuries and follies wholly incompatible with the existence of freedom?

It may be said that the depravation of morals and manners can be traced to the introduction of wealth as its cause. But wealth will be introduced; even the iron laws of Lycurgus could not prevent it. Let us then inquire if means may not be devised to prevent its bringing with it the destruction of public virtue. May not these means be found in education? in implanting in early youth habits that may counteract the temptations to which, through the influence of wealth, mature age will be exposed? and in giving strength and expansion to the mind, that it may comprehend and prize those principles which teach the rigid performance of duty? Education, it may be said, has been tried as a preservative of national purity. But was it applied to every exposed part of the body politic? For if any part has been left within the pestilential atmosphere of wealth without this preservative, then that part, becoming corrupted, would communicate the contagion to the whole; and if so, then has the experiment, whether education may not preserve public virtue, never yet been fairly tried. Such a part has been left in all former experiments.

Females have been exposed to the contagion of wealth without the preservative of a good education; and they constitute that part of the body politic least endowed by nature to resist, most to communicate it. Nay, not merely have they been left without the defense of a good education, but their corruption has been accelerated by a bad one. The character of women of wealth has been, and in the old governments of Europe now is, all that this statement would lead us to expect. Not content with doing nothing to promote their country's welfare, like pampered children they revel in its prosperity and scatter it to the winds with a wanton profusion. And still worse, they empoison its source, by diffusing a contempt for useful labor. To court pleasure their business, within her temple in defiance of the laws of God and man, they have erected the idol fashion; and upon her altar they sacrifice, with shameless rites, whatever is sacred to virtue or religion. Not the strongest ties of nature, not even maternal love can restrain them! Like the worshiper of Moloch, the mother, while yet yearning over the newborn babe, tears it from the bosom which God has swelled with nutrition for its support, and casts it remorseless from her, the victim of her unhallowed devotion!

But while with an anguished heart I thus depict the crimes of my sex, let not the other stand by and smile. Reason declares that you are guiltier than we. You are our natural guardians, our brothers, our fathers, and our rulers. You know that our ductile minds readily take the impressions of education. Why then have you neglected our education? Why have you looked with lethargic indifference on circumstances ruinous to the formation of other characters which you might have controlled?

But it may be said the observations here made cannot be applied to any class of females in our country. True, they cannot yet; and if they could, it would be useless to make them; for when the females of any country have become thus debased, then is that country so corrupted that nothing but the awful judgments of heaven can arrest its career of vice. But it cannot be denied that our manners are verging toward those described; and the change, though gradual, has not been slow; already do our daughters listen with surprise when we tell them of the republican simplicity of our mothers. But our manners are not as yet so altered, but that throughout our country they are still marked with republican virtues.

The inquiry to which these remarks have conducted us is this: what is offered by the plan of female education here proposed, which may teach or preserve among females of wealthy families that purity of manners which is allowed to be so essential to national prosperity, and so necessary to the existence of a republican government?

1. Females, by having their understandings cultivated, their reasoning powers developed and strengthened, may be expected to act more from the dictates of reason and less from those of fashion and caprice.

2. With minds thus strengthened they would be taught systems of morality, enforced by the sanctions of religion; and they might be expected to acquire juster and more enlarged views of their duty, and stronger and higher motives to its performance.

3. This plan of education offers all that can be done to preserve female youth from a contempt of useful labor. The pupils would become accustomed to it in conjunction with the high objects of literature and the elegant pursuits of the fine arts; and it is to be hoped that, both from habit and association, they might in future life regard it as respectable.

To this it may be added that if housewifery could be raised to a regular art, and taught upon philosophical principles, it would become a higher and more interesting occupation; and ladies of fortune, like wealthy agriculturists, might find that to regulate their business was an agreeable employment.

4. The pupils might be expected to acquire a taste for moral and intellectual pleasures, which would buoy them above a passion for show and parade, and which would make them seek to gratify the natural love of superiority, by endeavoring to excel others in intrinsic merit, rather than in the extrinsic frivolities of dress, furniture, and equipage.

5. By being enlightened in moral philosophy and in that which teaches the operations of the mind, females would be enabled to perceive the nature and extent of that influence which they possess over their children, and the obligation which this lays them under, to watch the formation of their characters with unceasing vigilance, to become their instructors, to devise plans for their improvement, to weed out the vices from their minds, and to implant and foster the virtues. And surely, there is that in the maternal bosom which, when its pleadings shall be aided by education, will overcome the seductions of wealth and fashion, and will lead the mother to seek her happiness in communing with her children and promoting their welfare, rather than in a heartless intercourse with the votaries of pleasure: especially when, with an expanded mind, she extends her views to futurity, and sees her care to her offspring rewarded by peace of conscience, the blessings of her family, the prosperity of her country, and finally with everlasting pleasure to herself and to them.

Thus laudable objects and employments would be furnished for the great body of females who are not kept by poverty from excesses. But among these, as among the other sex, will be found master spirits who must have preeminence at whatever price they acquire it. Domestic life cannot hold these because they prefer to be infamous rather than obscure. To leave such without any virtuous road to eminence is unsafe to the community; for not unfrequently are the secret springs of revolution set in motion by their intrigues. Such aspiring minds we will regulate by education; we will remove obstructions to the course of literature which has heretofore been their only honorable way to distinction; and we offer them a new object, worthy of their ambition; to govern and improve the seminaries for their sex.

In calling on my patriotic countrymen to effect so noble an object, the consideration of national glory should not be overlooked. Ages have rolled away; barbarians have trodden the weaker sex beneath their feet; tyrants have robbed us of the present light of heaven, and fain would take its future. Nations calling themselves polite have made us the fancied idols of a ridiculous worship, and we have repaid them with ruin for their folly. But where is that wise and heroic country which has considered that our rights are sacred, though we cannot defend them? That though a weaker, we are an essential part of the body politic, whose corruption or improvement must effect the whole? And which, having thus considered, has sought to give us by education that rank in the scale of being to which our importance entitles us?

History shows not that country. It shows many whose legislatures have sought to improve their various vegetable productions and their breeds of useful brutes; but none whose public councils have made it an object of their deliberations to improve the character of their women. Yet though history lifts not her finger to such a one, anticipation does. She points to a nation which, having thrown off the shackles of authority and precedent, shrinks not from schemes of improvement because other nations have never attempted them; but which, in its pride of independence, would rather lead than follow in the march of human improvement: a nation, wise and magnanimous to plan, enterprising to undertake, and rich in resources to execute. Does not every American exult that this country is his own? And who knows how great and good a race of men may yet arise from the forming hand of mothers, enlightened by the bounty of that beloved country, to defend her liberties, to plan her future improvement, and to raise her to unparalleled glory.

9

The Character of Young Ladies

Mary Lyon, 1835

Mary Lyon (1797–1849) was an important figure in the advancement of education for women. She founded Mt. Holyoke Seminary in South Hadley, Massachusetts, and served as its president until her death. In the 19th century, seminaries offered a hybrid of secondary and collegiate education. Today, Mt. Holyoke is a selective liberal arts college for women. In this essay, which Lyon wrote two years before Mt. Holyoke formally opened, she argues that the character of young ladies was critical to the prosperity of the proposed institution. She also describes the rigorous proposed course of study for students. Although no established standard for female education existed at the time, Lyon hopes that students would advance before entering the seminary, so that the intellectual, religious, and social standards for women could be raised for the community of women at-large. —CHB

The character of the young ladies, who shall become members of this Seminary the first year, will be of great importance to the prosperity of the Institution itself, and to the cause of female education. Those, who use their influence in making out the number, will sustain no unimportant responsibility. It is very desirable, that the friends of this cause should carefully

American Educational Thought: Essays from 1640–1940, pages 105–114
Copyright © 2010 by Information Age Publishing
105

consider the real design of founding this Institution, before they use their influence to induce any of their friends and acquaintances to avail themselves of its privileges.

This institution is to be founded by the combined liberality of an enlarged benevolence, which seeks the greatest good on an extensive scale. Some minds seem to be cast in that peculiar mould, that the heart can be drawn forth only by individual want. Others seem best fitted for promoting public good. None can value too much the angel of mercy, that can fly as on the wings of the wind to the individual cry for help as it comes over in tender and melting strains. But who does not venerate those great souls—great by nature—great by education—or great by grace—or by all combined, whose plans and works of mercy are like a broad river swallowing up a thousand little rivulets. How do we stand in awe, when we look down, as on a map, upon their broad and noble plans, destined to give untold blessings to the great community in which they dwell—to their nation—to the world. As we see them urging their way forward, intent on advancing as fast as possible, the renovation of the whole human family—and on hastening the accomplishment of the glorious promises found on the page of inspiration, we are sometimes tempted to draw back their hand, and extend it forth in behalf of some traveller by the wayside, who seems to be overlooked. But we look again, and we behold the dearest personal interests of the traveller by the wayside, and those of a thousand other individuals, included in their large and warm embrace.

This is the class of benevolent men who will aid in founding this Seminary; these the men who are now contributing of their time and money to carry forward this enterprize.

It is ever considered a principle of sacred justice in the management of funds, to regard the wishes of the donors. The great object of those, who are enlisting in this cause, and contributing to it, as to the sacred treasury of the Lord, cannot be misunderstood. It is to meet public and not private wants. They value not individual good less, but the public good more. They have not been prompted to engage in this momentous work by a desire to provide for the wants of a few of the daughters of our land for their own sakes as individuals, but by a desire to provide for the urgent necessities of our country, and of the world, by enlisting in the great work of benevolence, the talents of many of our daughters of fairest promise. This Institution is expected to draw forth the talents of such, to give them a new direction, and to enlist them permanently in the cause of benevolence. We consider it is no more than a due regard to justice, to desire and pray, that a kind Providence may send as scholars to this Seminary, those who shall go forth, and by their deeds, do honor to the Institution, and to the wisdom and benevolence of its founders. The love of justice will also lead us to desire and pray, that the same kind of Providence may turn away the feet of those, who may in after life dishonor the Institution, or be simply harmless cumberers of the ground, though they should be our dearest friends, and those who for their own personal benefit, need its privileges more than almost any others.

The grand features of this Institution are to be an elevated standard of science, literature, and refinement, and a moderate standard of expense; all to be guided and modified by the spirit of the gospel. Here we trust will be found a delightful spot for those, 'whose heart has stirred them up' to use all their talents in the great work of serving their generation, and of advancing the Redeemer's kingdom.

In the same manner, we doubt not, that the atmosphere will be rendered uncongenial to those who are wrapped up in self, preparing simply to please, and to be pleased, whose highest ambition is, to be qualified to amuse a friend in a vacant hour.

The age of the scholars will aid in giving to the Institution a choice selection of pupils. This Seminary is to be for adult young ladies; at an age when they are called upon by their parents to judge for themselves to a very great degree, and when they can select a spot congenial to their taste. The great and ruling principle—an ardent desire to do the greatest possible good, will we hope, be the presiding spirit in many hearts, bringing together congenial souls. Like many institutions of charity, this does not hold out the prospect of providing for the personal relief of individual sufferers, nor for the direct instruction of the ignorant and degraded. But it does expect to collect, as in a focus, the sparks of benevolence, which are scattered in the hearts of many of our daughters, and after having multiplied them many fold and having kindled them to a flame, and given them a right direction, to send them out to warm and to cheer the world. Some of them may be the daughters of wealth, and the offering will be no less acceptable, because they have something besides themselves to offer to the great work. Others may be the daughters of mere competency, having been fitted for the service by an answer to Agur's petition. Others, again may struggle under the pressure of more moderate means, being called to surmount the greatest obstacles by persevering effort, and the aid of friends. But provided they have kindred spirits on the great essential principles, all can go forward together without a discordant note.

It has been stated, that the literary standard of this Institution will be high. This is a very indefinite term. There is no acknowledged standard of female education, by which an institution can be measured. A long list of branches to be taught, can be no standard at all. For if so, a contemplated manual labor school to be established in one of the less improved of the western states, whose prospectus we chanced to notice some two or three years since, would stand higher than most of our New England colleges. Whether the institution was ever established we know not, nor do we remember its name or exact location. But the list of branches to be taught as they appeared on paper, we do remember, as for the time, it served as a happy illustration of a general principle, relating to some of our attempts to advance the cause of education among us. In a seminary for females, we cannot as in the standard of education for the other sex, refer to established institutions, whose course of study and standard of mental discipline, are known to every literary man in the land. But it is believed, that our statement cannot be made more intelligible to the enlightened community, than by simply saying, that the course of study, and standard of mental culture will be the same as that of the Hartford Female Seminary—of the Ipswich Female Seminary—or of the Troy Female Seminary—or of some other institution that has stood as long, and ranked as high as these seminaries. Suffice it to say, that it is expected, that the Mount Holyoke Female Seminary will take the Ipswich Female Seminary for its literary standard. Of course there will be room for a continued advancement; as that institution has been raising its own standard from year to year. But at the commencement, the standard is to be as high as the present standard of that seminary. It is to adopt the same high standard of mental discipline—the same slow, thorough, and patient manner of study; the same systematic and extensive course of solid branches. Though this explanation will not be universally understood, yet it is believed that it will be understood by a great many in New England, and by many out of New England—by those, who have long been intimately acquainted with the character of that seminary, or who have witnessed its fruits in the lives of those whom it has sent forth to exert a power over society, which cannot be exerted by mere goodness, without intellectual strength. 'By their fruits ye shall know them.'

The following is an extract from the last catalogue the Ipswich Female Seminary.

Course of Study, &c.

The regular course will consist of primary studies, and a two years' course in the regular classes, denominated Junior and Senior.

It is not expected that all who enter the school, will pursue the regular course. Those among the more advanced pupils, who design to continue members of the school no more than one year, may either pursue an outline of the branches here taught, or make it an object to gain a thorough knowledge of such studies as seem best suited to promote their individual improvement. In recitations, the regular classes are not kept distinct; but all the pupils are arranged in temporary classes as may best promote the good of individuals.

Primary Studies

Mental Arithmetic,
Written Arithmetic,
English Grammar,
First Book of Euclid's Geometry,
Modern and Ancient Geography,
Government of the United States,
Modern and Ancient History,
Botany,
Watts on the Mind.

Studies of the Junior Class

Written Arithmetic completed,
English Grammar continued,
The Second, Third, and Fourth Books of Euclid's Geometry,
Natural Philosophy,
Chemistry,
Astronomy,
Intellectual Philosophy,
Rhetoric.

Studies of the Senior Class

Some of the preceding studies reviewed and continued,
Algebra,
Ecclesiastical History,
Natural Theology,
Philosophy of Natural History,
Analogy of Natural and Revealed Religion to the Constitution and Laws of Nature, Evidences of Christianity.
Reading, Composition, Calisthenics, Vocal Music, the Bible and several of the above branches of study, will receive attention through the course. Those who are deficient in spelling and writing will have exercises in these branches whatever may be.

Text Books

The Bible, Worcester's Abridgement of Webster or some other English Dictionary, the Eclectic Reader by B. B. Edwards, Porter's Rhetorical Reader, Colburn's First Lessons, Adams's Arithmetic, Smith's and Murray's Grammar, Simson's or Playfair's Euclid, Woodbridge's Larger Geography, Sullivan's Political Class Book, Goodrich's United States, Worcester's Elements of History, with Goldsmith's England, (Greece, and Rome, Mrs. Phelps's Botany, Olmstead's Natural Philosophy, Wilkins's Astronomy, Abercrombie on the Intellectual Powers, Newman's and Whately's Rhetoric, Baily's Algebra, Marsh's Ecclesiastical History, Paley's Natural Theology, Smellie's Philosophy of Natural History, Butler's Analogy, Alexander's Evidences of Christianity.

The time for admitting into the regular classes is near the close of the winter term. The pupils, who at that time have been members of the seminary a year, and in some cases only six months, on passing a thorough examination on the primary studies, or on such studies of the course as shall be equivalent to the primary studies, can be admitted into the Junior Class, and those who can pass a similar examination in such of the studies as shall equal all the primary studies, and those of the Junior Class, can be admitted into the Senior. Those who in addition are well acquainted with the studies of the Senior Class, receive at the close a testimonial of having completed with honor the course of study in this institution.

In order that this new institution may accomplish the greatest good to the cause of female education, it is desirable that the pupils should advance as far as possible in study before entering the Seminary. To many who are expecting to become members, it is a subject of deep regret that the commencement of operations should be delayed so long. To all, who are expecting to enter this seminary when it opens, it is earnestly recommended to spend as much of the intermediate time as possible in study. It is very desirable that the *least* improved of the pupils should have a thorough knowledge of arithmetic, geography, history of the United States and English grammar, though this may not be rigidly required of every individual the first year. These branches may be pursued privately without a regular teacher, or in the common district school, or in the young ladies' village school, or in any other situation, which may be convenient.

Those who wish to pursue these branches without a regular teacher to direct them, may derive advantage by pursuing something like the following order of study,

1. Colburn's First Lessons to the 11th Section;
2. A general course of Geography;

3. Adams' New Arithmetic to Fractions;
4. Rudiments and general principles of English Grammar;
5. Colburn's First Lessons completed;
6. Adams' Arithmetic to Proportion;
7. History of the United States;
8. Thorough course of Geography;
9. Thorough course of English Grammar.
10. Adams' Arithmetic completed.

Manner of Studying

Colburn's First Lessons

This book should be studied through so many times, and with such close attention, that all the difficult questions in every part of the book can be solved with great readiness, and the manner of solution described. In studying this, recitations are very important. In recitations, the book should not be opened by the learner. If the questions cannot be remembered, and all parts comprehended, as they are received from the lips of a teacher, it may be safely inferred, not that there is any deficiency in the ability of the learner, but that more hard study is still requisite. If a young lady attempts to gain a thorough knowledge of this book by private study at home, it is important for her to recite daily to a brother, or sister, or some other friend. In recitations, whether of a class, or of an individual, every answer, and every description should be given with great clearness, accuracy, and promptness. The effects of a continued practice of reciting in this way, both on the mind, and degree of intelligence, in the manner of an individual, can rarely be realized by those unaccustomed to observe them.

Adam's New Arithmetic (Some other book may be used as a substitute.)

In pursuing this branch of study, two things should be gained.

1. Perfect Accuracy. It should not be considered sufficient, that a question is finally solved correctly. No standard of accuracy is high enough, except that which will enable the learner to avoid all wrong steps in the statement, and all errors in every part of the process to be corrected by a second trial. Where a deficiency is observed in these respects, more close and careful study should be applied—the preceding parts of the book should be slowly and carefully reviewed—and every question should be solved the first time very slowly, and with an undivided attention, till accurate habits are acquired.

2. Readiness and Rapidity. These habits can be gained only by abundant practice. Reciting, that is, solving questions given out by another will be very useful. This study may be pursued without a regular teacher, but the learner should recite daily to some friend as recommended in Colburn's First Lessons. If any one is under the necessity of being her own teacher, of solving her own questions, and of overcoming her own difficulties, she will receive aid from observing the following rule. 'Whenever you are involved in difficulties, from which you know not how to extricate yourself, go back to the beginning, or nearly to the beginning of the book, and solve every question in course till you come to the point of difficulty.'

Most individuals will probably find it necessary to go through the whole book two or three times, in order to gain the needful accuracy and readiness.

English Grammar

But few succeed in studying this except with a regular teacher. Though the manner of pursuing this branch is very important, it is not easy to give short and specific directions. We will only say, be very thorough. Study every lesson closely and carefully.

Geography

The manner of studying this branch must depend much on the teacher. One direction may be given for the use of those who study it without a teacher. After studying regularly through some book, and reviewing it carefully once or twice, let the learner select a complete outline, embracing prominent facts relating to every part of the world. This outline should be reviewed weekly or monthly for months, or for a year or two, till the facts are so indelibly fixed on the memory, that the lady at any future time of life, could recall anything in this outline almost as readily as she could recollect the order of the letters of the alphabet. The learner is referred to a lecture delivered before the American Institute in 1833.

History of the United States

In studying history, some systematic method is very important. But very little dependence can be placed on mere reading. Here and there a mind can be found, which will by a regular reading of history, select and arrange its materials so systematically, that they can be laid up for future use. But such minds among young ladies in the present state of female education are rarely found. History furnishes to the teacher an almost boundless field for the exercise of the inventive powers. But the most successful parts of almost every system of teaching history, cannot be so described as to be used by a young lady without a teacher. An intelligent young lady might use the 'Topic System' as it has been called to a considerable advantage in the following manner. After gaining a general view of the book to be studied, let the young lady select a list of topics or subjects through the whole, to be learned and recited to some friend, like a connected narration. In learning these topics, it would not be well to charge the memory with every item which can be found, but with those which are the most important. In reciting, she should not attempt to state anything, of which she is not confident, but in what she does attempt to communicate, she should not allow herself the least indulgence for inaccuracy. She should charge herself with deficiency for the least inaccurate statement, even though she should correct it the next moment. The list of topics might with profit be recited through two or three times. If Goodrich's History of the United States is studied, Emerson's Questions may be used with advantage in connexion with the topics. Any one not accustomed to recite by the topic system, might use the Questions as a general guide in selecting items under each topic. Beginners have often found it useful in a few of the first lessons, to write out the items under each topic. But very soon, the mind will be able to collect and arrange its materials without consuming so much time. When topics are written, no use should be made of the notes during recitations.

If the whole of this course cannot be completed before entering the Seminary, let the first part be taken in order, and let what is done, be done thoroughly. After completing the preceding course in the manner described, young ladies can select for themselves from the regular course of study pursued at Ipswich. It is desirable to advance in study as far as possible before entering the seminary, provided that every branch taken up receives thorough attention. A superficial passing over any branch before commencing it regularly in school is always an injury instead of a benefit. But the greater the real capital, which any one possesses of improvement on entering the institution, the greater will be her proportionate income. Any who hope to be so far advanced as to enter the Senior Class at first, and complete the regular course of study in one year, may need some more specific directions and information relative to preparatory studies, to prevent disappointment. Such can obtain further information by directing a letter to Miss Mary Lyon, South Hadley, Mass. A thorough knowledge of a definite number of branches, is a term, which to different individuals has very different meanings. Some of the members of the Ipswich Female Seminary, who had gone through the regular course, except the studies of the Senior Class, have been successful teachers in some of the most important female seminaries in our country. The same high standard will be taken in this institution. But notwithstanding this, a few individuals, who are now making their arrangements with reference to a hope, that they shall be its members the first year, can be prepared to complete the course, and others there doubtless will be, who could do it by devoting all the time that they can command, before the institution commences, to pursuing the most important studies, and to reviewing those which they have gone over.

This institution will do much, we hope, to raise among the female part of the community a higher standard of science and literature, of economy and of refinement, of benevolence and religion. To accomplish this great end, we hope by the influence of the institution on the community, to lead many to discover and use the means within their reach, instead of mourning in indolence after those they can never enjoy. We hope to redeem from waste a great amount, of precious time, of noble intellect, and of moral power.

10

Selected Writings of Catharine Beecher

Catharine Esther Beecher (1800–1878) was an advocate for female higher education and an antisuffragist. She was the eldest daughter of Lyman Beecher, a prominent American clergyman. The Beechers were one of the most remarkable 19th century families. Among her thirteen siblings were many prominent and thoughtful individuals, including Harriet Beecher Stowe, Henry Ward Beecher, and Edward Beecher. Catharine Beecher, along with her sister Mary, founded Hartford Female Seminary. She moved with her father in 1832 to Cincinnati and founded the Western Female Institute, and devoted her life to establishing educational facilities in the Midwest. She helped to introduce domestic science into the school curriculum, and published several works. Although a reformer, Catharine Beecher opposed women's suffrage, as she believed it was detrimental to women's domestic sphere.

In this essay on the education of female teachers, Beecher explains why female education is important. Primarily, she believes that women need to be educated so they would be well qualified for their domestic roles in the home. In modern society, she argues, domestic roles are varied and demand intellect. As women have the primary responsibility for caring for young children, they are also well-suited for teaching. Furthermore, women are critical in helping to shape students' moral development. She believed women should teach before they assumed roles as wives and mothers. In sum, she hoped to garner support for female seminaries for teachers, a cause she devoted her life to achieving. —CHB

American Educational Thought: Essays from 1640–1940, pages 115–131
Copyright © 2010 by Information Age Publishing
115

An Essay on the Education of Female Teachers, 1835

Woman, whatever are her relations in life, is necessarily the guardian of the nursery, the companion of childhood, and the constant model of imitation. It is her hand that first stamps impressions on the immortal spirit, that must remain forever. And what demands such discretion, such energy, such patience, such tenderness, love, and wisdom, such perspicacity to discern, such versatility to modify, such efficiency to execute, such firmness to persevere, as the government and education of all the various characters and tempers that meet in the nursery and schoolroom? Woman also is the presiding genius who must regulate all those thousand minutiae of domestic business, that demand habits of industry, order, neatness, punctuality, and constant care. And it is for such varied duties that woman is to be trained. For this her warm sympathies, her lively imagination, her ready invention, her quick perceptions, all need to be cherished and improved; while at the same time those more foreign habits, of patient attention, calm judgment, steady efficiency, and habitual self-control, must be induced and sustained.

Is a weak, undisciplined, unregulated mind, fitted to encounter the responsibility, weariness, and watching of the nursery; to bear the incessant care and perplexity of governing young children; to accommodate with kindness and patience to the peculiarities and frailties of a husband; to control the indolence, waywardness, and neglect of servants; and to regulate all the variety of domestic cares? The superficial accomplishments of former periods were of little avail to fit a woman for such arduous duties; and for this reason it is, that as society has advanced in all other improvements, the course of female education has been gradually changing, and some portion of that mental discipline, once exclusively reserved for the other sex, is beginning to exert its invigorating influence upon the female character. At the same time the taste of the age is altered; and, instead of the fainting, weeping, vapid, pretty play-thing, once the model of female loveliness, those qualities of the head and heart that best qualify a woman for her duties, are demanded and admired.

None will deny the importance of having females properly fitted for their peculiar duties; and yet few are aware how much influence a teacher may exert in accomplishing this object. School is generally considered as a place where children are sent, not to form their habits, opinions, and character, but simply to learn from books. And yet, whatever may be the opinion of teachers and parents, children do, to a very great extent, form their character under influences bearing upon them at school. They are proverbially creatures of imitation, and accessible to powerful influences. Six hours every day are spent with teachers, whom they usually love and respect, and whose sentiments and opinions, in one way or another, they constantly discover. They are at the same time associate with companions of all varieties of temper, character, and habit. Is it possible that this can exist without involving constant and powerful influences, either good or bad? The simple fact that a teacher succeeds in making a child habitually accurate and thorough in all the lessons of school, may induce mental habits that will have a controlling influence through life. If the government of schools be so administered as to induce habits of cheerful and implicit obedience, if punctuality, neatness, and order in all school employments are preserved for a course of years, it must have some influence in forming useful habits. On the contrary, if a child is tolerated in disobedience and neglect, if school duties are performed in a careless, irregular, and deficient manner, pernicious habits may be formed that will operate disastrously through life. It is true that mismanagement and indulgence at home may counteract all the good influences of school; and the faithful discharge of parental duty may counteract, to some extent, the bad influences of school: but this does not lessen the force of these considerations.

Nor is the course of study and mental discipline of inferior consequence. The mere committing to memory of the facts contained in books is but a small portion of education. Certain portions of time should be devoted to fitting a woman for her practical duties: such, for example, as needlework. Other pursuits are designed for the cultivation of certain mental faculties, such as *attention, perseverance,* and *accuracy.* This, for example, is the influence of the study of the mathematics; while the conversation and efforts of a teacher, directed to this end, may induce habits of investigation and correct reasoning, not to be secured by any other method. Other pursuits are designed to cultivate the taste and imagination: such as rhetoric, poetry, and other branches of polite literature. Some studies are fitted to form correct moral principles, and strengthen religious obligation: such as mental and moral philosophy, the study of the evidences of Christianity, the study of the Bible, and of collateral subjects. Other studies are designed to store the mind with useful knowledge: such, for example, as geography, history, and the natural sciences. The proper selection and due proportion of these various pursuits, will have a decided influence in forming the mental habits and general character of the pupils.

When it is asserted that it is of more consequence that women be educated to be virtuous, useful, and pious, than that they become learned and accomplished, every one assents to the truth of the position. When it is said that it is the most important and most difficult duty of parents and teachers, to form the moral character, the principles and habits of children, no one will dissent. All allow it to be a labor demanding great watchfulness, great wisdom, and constant perseverance and care. For what comfort would parents find in the assurance, that their children are intelligent, learned, and accomplished, if all is to be perverted by indolence, vice, and irreligion? And what is the benefit to society, in increasing the power of intellect and learning, if they only add to the evils of contaminating example and ruinous vice? The necessity of *virtuous* intelligence in the mass of the community is peculiarly felt in a form of government like ours, where the people are not held in restraint by physical force, as in despotic governments, but where, if they do not voluntarily submit to the restraints of virtue and religion, they must inevitably run loose to wild misrule, anarchy, and crime. For a nation to be virtuous and religious, the females of that nation must be deeply imbued with these principles: for just as the wives and mothers sink or rise in the scale of virtue, intelligence, and piety, the husbands and the sons will rise or fall. These positions scarce any intelligent person will deny: so that it may be set down as one of the current truisms of society, that the formation of the moral and religious principles and habits is the most important part of education, even in reference to this life alone. To this is added the profession of all who reverence Christianity, that the interests of an immortal state of being are equally suspended on the same results.

In regard to education, the world is now making experiments, such as were never made before. Man is demanding disenthralment, alike from physical force, and intellectual slavery; and, by a slow and secret process, one nation after another is advancing in a sure, though silent progress. Man is bursting the chains of slavery, and the bonds of intellectual subserviency; and is learning to think, and reason, and act for himself. And the great crisis is hastening on, when it shall be decided whether disenthralled intellect and liberty shall voluntarily submit to the laws of virtue and of Heaven, or run wild to insubordination, anarchy, and crime. The great questions pending before the world, are simply these: Are liberty and intelligence, without the restraints of a moral and religious education, a blessing, or a curse? Without moral and religious restraints, is it best for man to receive the gift of liberty and intelligence, or to remain coerced by physical force, and the restraints of opinions and customs not his own?

The master-spirits of the age are watching the developments as they rise, and making their records for the instruction of mankind.

And what results are already gained? In England, the experiment has been made by the skeptical Brougham; and, at great expense, knowledge has gone forth with increasing liberty, and all who have witnessed the results are coming to the conviction, that increase of knowledge, without moral and religious influence, is only increase of vice and discontent. And

what are the results of the experiment in France? The statistics of education show, that the best educated departments are the most vicious, and the
most ignorant are the freest from crime. And, in that country, where the national representatives once declared that Christianity should be banished,
and the Bible burnt, and the Sabbath annihilated, we now find its most
distinguished statesmen and citizens uniting in the public declaration, that
moral and religious education must be the foundation of national instruction. Victor Cousin, one of the most distinguished philosophers of the age,
and appointed by the king of France to examine the various systems of
education in Europe, has reported, as the result of his investigations, that
education is a blessing, just in proportion as it is founded on moral and
religious principles.

Look, again, at Prussia! With its liberal and patriotic monarch, with a
system of education unequalled in the records of time, requiring by law that
all the children in the nation be sent to school, from the first day they are
seven years of age, till the last day they are fourteen, with a regular course
of literary and scientific instruction, instituted for every teacher required to
spend three years in preparing for such duties; while, on an average, one
teacher is furnished for every ten pupils through the nation. The effects of
merely intellectual culture soon convinced the monarch and his counselors
that moral and religious instruction must be the basis of all their efforts;
and now the Bible is placed in every school, and every teacher is required to
spend from one to two hours each day, in giving and enforcing instruction
in all the duties of man towards his Creator, towards constituted authorities,
and towards his fellow-men.

And what is the experience of our own country? Those portions of the
nation, most distinguished for the general diffusion of education, are those
in which moral and religious influences have been most extensively introduced into schools, and have pervaded all the institutions of society. But, in
those portions of our country the increase and jealousy of religious sects,
and other combining causes, have had an influence in banishing the Bible,
and moral and religious influence, more and more from public schools.
And now we hear the widely extended complaint, that common schools
are dangerous places for children; while parents, who are most regardful
of the moral influences exerted upon their children, are more and more
withdrawing them from what they deem such contaminating influence.

What patriot, what philanthropist, what Christian, does not see that all
that is sacred and dear in home, and country, and liberty, and religion, call
upon him to waken every energy, and put forth every effort?

Does the heart fail, and the courage sink, at the magnitude of the work, and the apparent destitution of means? We have the means—we have the power. There is wealth enough, and benevolence enough, and self-denying laborers enough. Nothing is wanting but a knowledge of our danger, our duty, and our means, and a willing mind in exerting our energies. Our difficulties and danger have been briefly noticed. It is the object of this essay to point out one important measure in the system of means that must be employed.

Men of patriotism and benevolence can commence by endowing two or three seminaries for female teachers in the most important stations in the nation, while to each of these seminaries shall be attached a model school, supported by the children of the place where it is located. In these seminaries can be collected those who have the highest estimate of the value of moral and religious influence, and the most talents and experience for both intellectual and moral education.

When these teachers shall have succeeded in training classes of teachers on the best system their united wisdom can devise, there will be instructors prepared for other seminaries for teachers, to be organized and conducted on the same plan; and thus a regular and systematic course of education can be disseminated through the nation.

And, as a system of right moral and religious education gains its appropriate influence, as women are more and more educated to understand and value the importance of their influence in society, and their peculiar duties, more young females will pursue their education with the expectation that, unless paramount private duties forbid, they are to employ their time and talents in the duties of a teacher, until they assume the responsibilities of domestic life. Females will cease to feel that they are educated just to enjoy themselves in future life, and realize the obligations imposed by Heaven to live to do good. And, when females are educated as they ought to be, every woman at the close of her school education, will be well qualified to act as a teacher.

Remedy for Wrongs to Women
(From: *The Evils Suffered by American Women and American Children*), 1846

This second essay in the volume by Catharine Beecher is a significant early writing about teaching being woman's "true" profession. Beecher hoped to encourage women to teach in the West, but more importantly she hoped to elevate the status of the teaching profession to be "the noblest of all professions." As the daughter of a minister, she also appealed to women's sense of mission to help educate destitute children. In addition, she believed that women's responsibilities in the domestic sphere gave them greater abilities to teach children. —CHB

Ladies and Friends:

The immediate object which has called us together is an enterprise now in progress, the design of which *is to educate destitute American children, by the agency of American women.* It is an effort which has engaged the exertions of a large number of ladies of various sects, and of all sections in our country, and one which, though commencing in a humble way and on a small scale, we believe is eventually to exert a most extensive and saving influence through the nation.

Permit me first to present some facts in regard to the situation of an immense number of young children in this land, for whom your sympathies at this time are sought. Few are aware of the deplorable destitution of our country in regard to the education of the rising generation, or of the long train of wrongs and sufferings endured by multitudes of young children from this neglect.

The last twelve years I have resided chiefly at the West, and my attention has been directed to the various interests of education. In five of the largest western states I have spent from several weeks to several months—I have traveled extensively and have corresponded or conversed with well-informed gentlemen and ladies on this subject in most of the western states. And I now have materials for presenting the real situation of vast multitudes of American children, which would "cause the ear that heareth it to tingle." But I dare not do it. It would be so revolting—so disgraceful—so heart-rending— so incredible— that in the first place, I should not be believed; and in the next place, such an outcry of odium and indignation would be aroused as would impede efforts to remedy the evil. The only thing I can safely do is to present some statistics, which cannot be disputed, because they are obtained from *official documents* submitted by civil officers to our national or state legislatures. Look then at the census, and by its data we shall find that now there are nearly a million adults who cannot read and write, and more than *two million* children utterly illiterate, and entirely without schools. Look at individual states, and we shall find Ohio and Kentucky, the two best supplied of our western states, demanding five thousand teachers each, to supply them in the same ration as Massachusetts is supplied. Ten thousand teachers are now needed in Ohio and Kentucky alone, to furnish schools for more than two hundred thousand children, who otherwise must grow up in utter ignorance.

To exhibit some faint idea of the results of such neglect, let me give an extract from a private letter of a Friend of mine, on a journey of observation in regard to education in one of these states, which was addressed to his children.

Could you, my dear daughters, see what I in my journeys so often see, the poor of your own sex and age, limited in wardrobe to one sordid cotton garment, without education to read a word, without skill to make or mend a garment, without a sufficient variety of proper food to unfold their forms to any perfection, lank as greyhounds, and their clothes hanging upon them like dresses upon a broomstick, and yet possessed of all your native love of dress, your quick capacity and your sprightliness, I do think you would behave better, be more humble, study harder, and feel more kindly to the poor than you ever have done. And yet what is all this to having the mind darkened, the feelings hardened, and the interests of the soul neglected, as is the case with many thousands around me! My heart bleeds at the irreligion, abject poverty, filth, and wretched vice which everywhere prevail. But my Heavenly Father enables me to hold on, and I am tolerably well; yet I cannot say that I am cheerful; it is too intolerable, and my spirits sink. The Methodist circuit riders are doing something, and have pitched upon the very plan I had thought of, that of having traveling schools among the most sparsely settled districts. Oh that our Heavenly Father may bless my mission, and that light may enter here!

This presents only a glance at the forlorn and degraded state of large portions of our country where education is totally neglected. A picture almost as melancholy is presented when we examine into the shocking abuse of young children in some of those states which are doing the most for education. The state of New York, for a few years, has been making exemplary efforts to raise her common schools from the low state in which they were found. In every county of the state a salaried officer devotes his whole time to the improvement of the common schools in his county, and every year he sends an account of them, to be presented to the legislature by the state superintendent.

The following is extracted from the general report made up by the general superintendent from the reports of the county superintendents for the year 1844.

The nakedness and deformity of the great majority of the schools, the comfortless and dilapidated buildings, the unhung doors, broken sashes, absent panes, stilted benches, yawning roofs, and muddy moldering floors, are faithfully portrayed, and many of the self-styled teachers, who lash and dogmatize in these miserable tenements of humanity, are shown to be low, vulgar, obscene, intemperate, and utterly incompetent to teach anything good. Thousands of the young are repelled from improvement, and contract a durable horror for books, by ignorant, injudicious, and even cruel modes of instruction. When the piteous moans and tears of the little pupils supplicate for exemption from the cold drudgery or the more pungent suffering of the school, let the humane parent be careful to ascertain the true cause of grief and lamentation.... No subject connected with the cause of elementary education affords a source for such humiliating reflection, as that of the condition of a large portion of the school-houses visited. Only one-third of the whole number were found in good repair, another third in only comfortable circumstances; while *three thousand, three hundred and nineteen* were unfit for the reception of either man or beast. Seven thousand we found destitute of any playground, nearly six thousand destitute of convenient seats and desks, and nearly eight thousand destitute of any proper facilities for ventilation, while six thousand were destitute of outdoor facilities for securing modesty and decency!

And it is in these miserable abodes of filth and dirt, deprived of wholesome air or exposed to the assaults of the elements, with no facilities for exercise or relaxation, with no conveniences for prosecuting their studies, crowded on to comfortless benches, and driven by dire necessity to violate the most common rules of decency and modesty, that upward of *six hundred thousand* children of this state are compelled to spend an average of eight months each year of their pupilage! Here the first lessons of human life, the incipient principles of morality, and the rules of social intercourse, are to be impressed upon the plastic mind. The boy is here to receive the permanent model of his character, and imbibe the elements of his future career. Here the instinctive delicacy of the young female, the characteristic ornament of her sex, is to be expanded into maturity by precept and example. Such are the temples of science, such the ministers under whose care susceptible childhood is to receive its earliest impressions! Great God! Shall man dare to charge to thy dispensations the vices, the crimes, the sickness, the sorrows, the miseries and brevity of human life, who sends his little children to a pest-house fraught with the deadly malaria of both moral and physical disease? Instead of impious murmurs, let him lay his hand upon his mouth, and his mouth in the dust, and cry unclean!

I wish now to point out that certain causes which have exerted a depressing influence upon our sex in this land; for we shall find that the very same effort, which aims to benefit the children of our country, will tend almost equally to benefit our own sex. The first cause that bears heavily on our sex is, the fact that in our country, the principle of caste, which is one of the strongest and most inveterate in our nature, is strongly arrayed against healthful and productive labor.

To understand the power of this principle, see what sacrifices men and women make, and what toils they endure, to save themselves from whatever sinks them in station and estimation. And this is a principle which is equally powerful in high and low, rich and poor. To observe how it bears against healthful and productive labor, let any woman, who esteems herself in the higher grades of society, put the case as her own, and imagine that her son, or brother, is about to marry a young lady, whose character and education are every way lovely and unexceptionable, but who, it appears, is a *seamstress*, or a *nurse*, or a *domestic*, and how few are there, who will not be conscious of the opposing principle of *caste*. But suppose the young lady to be one, who has been earning her livelihood by writing poetry and love stories, or who has lived all her days in utter idleness, and how suddenly the feelings are changed! Now, all the comfort and happiness of society depend upon having that work properly performed, which is done by nurses, seamstresses and chambermaids, and cooks; and so long as this kind of work is held to be degrading, and those who perform it are allowed to grow up ignorant and vulgar, and then are held down by the prejudices of caste, every woman will use the greatest efforts, and undergo the greatest privations, to escape from the degraded and discreditable position. And this state of society is now, by the natural course of things, bringing a just retribution on the classes who cherish it. Domestics are forsaking the kitchen, and thronging to the workshop and manufactory, and *mainly* under the influence of the principle of *caste*; while the family state suffers keenly from the loss. Meantime the daughters of wealth have their intellectual faculties and their sensibilities developed, while all the household labor, which would equally develop their physical powers, and save from ill-health, is turned off to hired domestics, or a slaving mother. The only remedy for this evil is, securing a proper education for all classes, and making productive labor honorable, by having all classes engage in it.

The next cause which bears severely on the welfare of our sex is the *excess of female population* in the older states from the disproportionate emigration of the other sex. By the census we find in only three of the small older states, *twenty thousand* more women than men, and a similar disproportion is found in other states. The consequence is that all branches of female employment in the older states are thronged, while in our new states, domestics, nurses, seamstresses, mantua-makers, and female teachers are in great demand. In consequence of this, women at the East become operatives in shops and mills, and at the West, men become teachers of little children, thus exchanging the appropriate labors of the sexes, in a manner injurious to all concerned.

Meantime, capitalists at the East avail themselves of this excess of female hands. Large establishments are set up in eastern cities to manufacture clothing. Work of all kinds is got from poor women, at prices that will not keep soul and body together, and then the articles thus made are sold for prices that give monstrous profits to the capitalist, who thus grows rich on the hard labors of our sex. Tales there are to be told of the sufferings of American women in our eastern cities, so shocking that they would scarcely be credited, and yet they are true beyond all dispute.

The following extracts, from some statistics recently obtained in New York City, verify what has been stated.

There are now in this city, according to close estimates, *ten thousand* women who live by the earnings of the needle. On an average, these women, by working twelve or fourteen hours a-day, can earn only *twelve and a half cents*, with which they are to pay for rent, fuel, clothes, and food.

Here follow the prices paid for various articles of women's work at the clothing stores, and then the following—

A great multitude of women are employed in making men's and boy's caps. We are told by an old lady, who lives by this work, that when she begins at sunrise and works till midnight, she earns *fourteen cents a-day!* That is, *eighty-four cents* a week, for incessant toil every waking hour, and this her sole income for every want! A large majority of these women are American born; some have been rich, many have enjoyed the ease of competence; some are young girls without homes; some are widows; some the wives of drunken husbands. . . .

Let us now turn to another class of our country women—the female operatives in our shops and mills. Unfortunately, this subject cannot be freely discussed without danger of collision with the vast pecuniary and party interests connected with it. I therefore, shall simply state facts, without expressing the impressions of my own mind.

Last year, I spent several days in Lowell, for the sole purpose of investigating this subject. I conversed with agents, overseers, clergymen, physicians, editors, ladies resident in the place, and a large number of the operatives themselves. All seemed disposed to present the most favorable side of the picture; and nothing unfavorable was said except as drawn forth by my questions.

In favor of this situation it was urged, that none were forced to go, or to stay in the mills, and therefore all must believe themselves better off there than in any other situation at command; that owners and agents incur great pains and expense to secure the physical comfort and intellectual and moral improvement of the operatives; that much care is used to exclude vicious persons; that great pains are taken to secure respectable women to keep the boarding-houses; that the board and lodging provided are at least comfortable; that the state of society and morals is good, and is superior to what many enjoy at home; that the *esprit du corps* of the community guards its morals; that there is much good society among the operatives, as is manifest from the great number who have been school teachers; that the bills of mortality show that there are fewer deaths in proportion than in other country places; and finally, that the night schools, Sunday schools, and faithful labors of the clergy secure great advantages and most favorable results....

Let me now present the facts I learned by observation or inquiry on the spot. I was there in mid-winter, and every morning I was wakened at *five*, by the bells calling to labor. The time allowed for dressing and breakfast was so short, as many told me, that both were performed hurriedly, and then the work at the mills was begun by lamp-light, and prosecuted without remission till twelve, and chiefly in a standing position. Then half an hour only allowed for dinner, from which the time for going and returning was deducted. Then back to the mills, to work till seven o'clock, the last part of the time by lamp-light. Then returning, washing, dressing, and supper occupied another hour. Thus ten hours only remained for recreation and sleep....

As to the *wages*, the average is found to be $1.75 a week; but they are paid by *the job* so that all are thus stimulated to work as much as possible every day, while prizes are given to such overseers as get the most work out of those they superintend. Thus everything goes under the stimulus of rivalry, ambition, and the excitement of gain, leading multitudes to sacrifice health for money. Thus it is said that the hours of labor are not more than the majority of the operatives desire, while sometimes even the regular hours are exceeded, to the great discontent of the over-worked and feeble minority. As to the large sums deposited in the Savings' bank, it is found that, of six thousand women, less than one thousand have made such deposits, and the average of such deposits do not amount to but about $100 for each depositor for three years of such hazardous toils....

Now, without expressing any opinion as to the influence, on health and morals, of taking women away from domestic habits and pursuits, to labor with men in shops and mills, I simply ask if it would not be better to put the thousands of men who are keeping school for young children into the mills, and employ the women to train the children?

Wherever education is most prosperous, there woman is employed more than man. In Massachusetts, where education is highest, five out of seven of the teachers are women, while in Kentucky, where education is so much lower, five out of six of the teachers are men.

Another cause of depression to our sex is found in the fact that there is no profession for women of education and high position, which, like law, medicine, and theology, opens the way to competence, influence, and honor, and presents motives for exertion. Woman ought never to be led to married life except under the promptings of pure affection. To marry for an establishment, for a position, or for something to do, is a deplorable wrong. But how many women, for want of a high and honorable profession to engage their time, are led to this melancholy course. This is not because Providence has not provided an ample place for such a profession for woman, but because custom or prejudice, or a low estimate of its honorable character, prevents her from entering it.

The educating of children, that is the true and noble profession of a woman—*that* is what is worthy the noblest powers and affections of the noblest minds.

Another cause which deeply affects the best interests of our sex is the contempt, or utter neglect and indifference, which has befallen this only noble profession open to woman. There is no employment, however disagreeable or however wicked, which custom and fashion cannot render elegant, interesting, and enthusiastically sought. A striking proof of this is seen in the military profession. This is the profession of *killing our fellow creatures,* and is attended with everything low, brutal, unchristian, and disgusting and yet what halos of glory have been hung around it, and how the young, the generous, and enthusiastic have been drawn into it! If one-half the poetry, fiction, oratory, and taste thus misemployed had been used to embellish and elevate the employment of training the mind of childhood, in what an altered position should we find this noblest of all professions!

As it is, the employment of teaching children is regarded as the most wearing drudgery, and few resort to it except from necessity; and one very reasonable cause of this aversion is the utter neglect of any arrangements for preparing teachers for this arduous and difficult profession. The mind of a young child is like a curious instrument, capable of exquisite harmony when touched by a skillful hand, but sending forth only annoying harshness when unskillfully addressed. To a teacher is committed a collection of these delicate contrivances; and, without experience, without instruction, it is required not only that each one should be tuned aright, but that all be combined in excellent harmony; as if a young girl were sent into a splendid orchestra, all, ignorant and unskillful, and required to draw melody from each instrument, and then to combine the whole in faultless harmony. And in each case there are, here and there, individual minds, who without instruction, are gifted by nature with aptness and skill in managing the music either of matter or of mind; but that does not lessen the folly, in either case, of expecting the whole profession, either of music or of teaching, to be pursued without preparatory training.

Look now into this small school-room, where are assembled a collection of children, with a teacher unskillful in her art. What noise and disorder! What indolence, and discontent, and misrule! The children hate school and all that belongs to it, and the teacher regards the children as little better than incarnate imps!

Look, again, into another, where the teacher, fitted by nature or trained by instruction and experience, is qualified for her office. See the little happy group around their best-beloved friend—their beau ideal of all that is good, and wise, and lovely! How their bright eyes sparkle as she opens the casket of knowledge and deals out its treasures! How their young hearts throb with generous and good emotions, as she touches the thrilling chords she has learned so skillfully to play! What neatness and order in all her little dominion! What ready obedience, what loving submission, what contrite confession, what generous aspirations after all that is good and holy! She spends the pleasant hours of school in the exercise of the noblest powers of intellect and feeling. She goes to rest at night, reviewing with gratitude the results of her toils; and as she sends up her daily thanks and petitions for her little ones, how does the world of peace and purity open to her vision, where, by the river of life, she shall gather her happy flock, and look back to earth, and on through endless years, to trace the sublime and never-ending results of her labors. Oh, beautiful office! Sublime employment! When will it attain its true honors and esteem?

There is another class of evils, endured by a large class of well-educated, unmarried women of the more wealthy classes, little understood or appreciated, but yet real and severe. It is the suffering that results from the *inactivity of cultivated intellect and feeling.*

The more a mind has its powers of feeling and action enlarged by cultivation, the greater the demand for noble objects to excite interest and effort. It is the entire withdrawal of stimulus from the mind and brain that makes solitary confinement so intolerable that reason is often destroyed by it. Medical men point out this want of worthy objects to excite, as the true cause of a large class of diseases of mind and body, that afflicts females of the higher classes, who are not necessitated to exertion for a support, especially those who have no families. And the greater the capacity and the nobler the affections, the keener is this suffering. It is only small and ignoble minds that can live contentedly without noble objects of pursuit.

Now, Providence ordains that, in most cases, a woman is to perform the duties of a mother. Oh, sacred and beautiful name! How many cares and responsibilities are connected with it! And yet what noble anticipations, what sublime hopes, we are given to animate and cheer! She is to train young minds, whose plastic texture will receive and retain each impress for eternal ages, who will imitate her tastes, habits, feelings, and opinions; who will transmit what they receive to their children, to pass again to the next generation, and then to the next, until a whole nation will have received its character and destiny from her hands. No imperial queen ever stood in a more sublime and responsible position, than that which every mother must occupy, in the eye of Him who reads the end from the beginning, and who, foreseeing those eternal results, denominates those of our race who fulfill their high calling "kings and priests unto God." Kings, to rule the destiny of all their descendants—priests, by sacrifices and suffering to work out such sublime results!

Now every woman whose intellect and affections are properly developed is furnished for just such an illustrious work as this. And when such large capacities and affections are pent up and confined to the trifling pursuits that ordinarily engage our best educated young women between school life and marriage, suffering, and often keen suffering, is the inevitable result. There is a restless, anxious longing for they know not what; while exciting amusements are vainly sought to fill the aching void. A teacher, like myself, who for years has been training multitudes of such minds, and learning their private history and secret griefs, knows, as no others can, the great amount of suffering among some of the loveliest and best of the youthful portion of our sex from this cause. True, every young lady *might*, the moment she leaves the schoolroom, commence the exulted labor of molding young minds for eternity, who again would transmit her handiwork from spirit to spirit, till thousands and thousands receive honor and glory from her hands. But the customs and prejudices of society forbid; and instead of this, a little working of muslin and worsted, a little light reading, a little calling and shopping, and a great deal of the high stimulus of fashionable amusement, are all the ailment her starving spirit finds. And alas! Christian parents find no way to remedy this evil!

The next topic I wish to present, and which has been brought to my observation very often during my extensive travels, is the *superior character* of my countrywomen and the great amount of influence that is placed in their hands.

It is the immediate object of this enterprise now presented, to engage American women to exert the great power and influence put into their hands, to remedy the evils which now oppress their countrywomen, and thus, at the same time, and by the same method, to secure a proper education to the vast multitude of neglected American Children all over our land.

The plan is, to begin on a small scale, and to take women already qualified intellectually to teach, and possessed of missionary zeal and benevolence, and, after some further training, to send them to the most ignorant portions of our land, to raise up schools, to instruct in morals and piety, and to teach the domestic arts and virtues. The commencement of this enterprise, until we gain confidence by experiment and experience, will be as the opening of a very small sluice. But so great is the number of educated and unemployed women at the East, and so great the necessity for teachers at the West, that as soon as the stream begins to move, it will grow wider and deeper and stronger, till it becomes as the river of life, carrying health and verdure to every part of our land.

If our success equals our hopes, soon, in all parts of our country, in each neglected village, or new settlement, the Christian female teacher will quietly take her station, collecting the ignorant children around her, teaching them habits of neatness, order, and thrift; opening the book of knowledge, inspiring the principles of morality, and awakening the hope of immortality. Soon her influence in the village will create a demand for new laborers, and then she will summon from among her friends at home, the nurse for the young and the sick, the seamstress and the mantua-maker, and these will prove her auxiliaries in good moral influences, and in sabbath school training. And often as the result of these labors, the Church will arise, and the minister of Christ be summoned to fill up the complement of domestic, moral, and religious blessing. Thus, the surplus of female population will gradually be drawn westward, and in consequence the value of female labor will rise at the East, so that capitalists can no longer use the power of wealth to oppress our sex. Thus, too, the profession of a teacher will gradually increase in honor and respectability, while endowed institutions will arise to qualify woman for her profession, as freely as they are provided for the other sex. Then it will be deemed honorable and praiseworthy for every young and well-educated woman, of whatever station, to enter this profession, and remain in it till pure affection leads her to another sphere. Then a woman of large affections and developed intellect will find full scope and happy exercise for all the cultivated energies conferred by heaven, alike for her own enjoyment and the good of others.

This will prove the true remedy for all those *wrongs of women* which her mistaken champions are seeking to cure by drawing her into professions and pursuits which belong to the other sex. . . .

11

Selected Writings of Horace Mann

Considered the father of American public education, Horace Mann (1796–1859) served as the first Secretary of the Massachusetts Board of Education (1837–1848), and in this role he helped establish common schools throughout the state. The common school movement spread across the United States eventually, and it revolutionized the organization, teaching, and structure of schools. Mann also established the first normal school in the United States. Normal schools were created to educate teachers, so they were precursors of modern colleges of education. Mann also served in the U.S. House of Representatives and at the end of his life became the President of Antioch College.

In this essay, written at the time that Mann became the Secretary of the Massachusetts Board of Education, Mann discusses the importance of common education throughout the state. He found that the provincialism that existed had hurt the cause of education. He found that there were educational principles which should be disseminated throughout the state, and the Massachusetts Board of Education was established to facilitate this purpose. Not only does Mann discuss in this writing important methods of education, such as the use of the senses, limiting the variety of textbooks, and bolstering the library, but he also addresses significant topics such as the architecture of schoolhouses, and the value of fresh air and ventilation in the process of learning. —CHB

American Educational Thought: Essays from 1640–1940, pages 133–175

Means and Objects of Common School Education, 1837

Gentlemen of the Convention:

In pursuance of notice, contained in a circular letter, lately addressed to the school committees and friends of Education, in this county, I now appear before you, as the Secretary of the Massachusetts Board of Education. That Board was constituted by an Act of the Legislature, passed April 20, 1837. It consists of the Governor and Lieutenant Governor of the Commonwealth, for the time being, who are members *ex officio,* and of eight other gentlemen, appointed by the Executive, with the advice and consent of the Council. The object of the Board is, by extensive correspondence, by personal interviews, by the development and discussion of principles, to collect such information, on the great subject of Education, as now lies scattered, buried and dormant; and after digesting, and, as far as possible, systematizing and perfecting it, to send it forth again to the extremest borders of the State; so that all improvements which are local, may be enlarged into universal; that what is now transitory and evanescent, may be established in permanency; and that correct views, on this all-important subject, may be multiplied by the number of minds capable of understanding them.

To accomplish the object of their creation, however, the Board are clothed with no power, either restraining or directory. If they know of better modes of education; they have no authority to enforce their adoption. Nor have they any funds at their disposal. Even the services of the members are gratuitously rendered. Without authority, then, to command, and without money to remunerate or reward, their only resources, the only sinews of their strength, are, their power of appealing to an enlightened community, to rally for the promotion of its dearest interests.

Unless, therefore, the friends of Education, in different parts of the State, shall proffer their cordial and strenuous cooperation, it is obvious, that the great purposes, for which the Board was constituted, can never be accomplished. Some persons, indeed, have suggested, that the Secretary of the Board should visit the schools, individually, and impart such counsel and encouragement as he might be able to do; not reflecting that such is their number and the shortness of the time during which they are kept, that, if he were to allow himself but one day for each school, to make specific examinations and to give detailed instructions, it would occupy something more than sixteen years to complete the circuit; —while the period, between the ages of four and sixteen, during which our children usually attend school, is but twelve years; so that, before the Secretary could come round upon his track again, one entire generation of scholars would have passed away, and one third of another. At his quickest speed, he would lose sight of one quarter of all the children in the State. The Board, therefore, have no voice, they have no organ, by which they can make themselves heard, in the distant villages and hamlets of this land, where those juvenile habits are now forming, where those processes of thought and feeling are, now, to-day, maturing; which, some twenty or thirty years hence, will find an arm, and become resistless might, and will uphold, or rend asunder, our social fabric. The Board may, I trust they will, be able to collect light and to radiate it; but upon the people, *upon the people,* will still rest the great and inspiring duty of prescribing to the next generation what their fortunes shall be, by determining in what manner they shall be educated. For it is the ancestors of a people, who prepare and predetermine all the great events in that people's history; their posterity only collect and read them. No just judge will ever decide upon the moral responsibility of an individual, without first ascertaining what kind of parents he had; nor will any just historian ever decide upon the honor or the infamy of a people, without placing the character of its ancestors in the judgment-balance. If the system of national instruction, devised and commenced by Charlemagne, had been continued, it would have changed the history of the French people. Such an event as the French Revolution never would have happened with free schools; any more than the American Revolution would have happened without them. The mobs, the riots, the burnings, the lynchings, perpetrated by the *men* of the present day, are perpetrated, because of their vicious or defective education, when children. We see, and feel, the havoc and the ravage of their tiger-passions, now, when they are full grown; but it was years ago that they were whelped and suckled. And so, too, if we are derelict from our duty, in this matter, our children, in their turn, will suffer. If we permit the vulture's eggs to be incubated and hatched, it will then be too late to take care of the lambs.

Some eulogize our system of Popular Education, as though worthy to be universally admired and imitated. Others pronounce it circumscribed in its action, and feeble, even where it acts. Let us waste no time in composing this strife. If good, let us improve it; if bad, let us reform it. It is of human institutions, as of men, not any one is so good that it cannot be made better; nor so bad, that it may not become worse. Our system of education is not to be compared with those of other states or countries, merely to determine whether it may be a little more or a little less perfect than they; but it is to be contrasted with our highest ideas of perfection itself, and then the pain of the contrast to be assuaged, by improving it, forthwith and continually. The love of excellence looks ever upward towards a higher standard; it is unimproving pride and arrogance only, that are satisfied with being superior to a lower. No community should rest contented with being superior to other communities, while it is inferior to its own capabilities. And such are the beneficent ordinations of Providence, that the very thought of improving is the germination of improvement.

The science and the art of Education, like every thing human, depend upon culture, for advancement. And they would be more cultivated, if the rewards for attention, and the penalties for neglect, were better understood. When effects follow causes, quick as thunder, lightning, even infants and idiots learn to beware; or they act, to enjoy. They have a glimmer of reason, sufficient, in such cases, for admonition, or impulse. Now, in this world, the entire succession of events, which fills time and makes up life, is nothing but causes and effects. These causes and effects are bound and linked together by an adamantine law. And the Deity has given us power over the effects, by giving us power over the causes. This power consists in a knowledge of the connection established between causes and effects, enabling us to foresee the future consequences of present conduct. If you show to me a handful of perfect seeds, I know, that, with appropriate culture, those seeds will produce a growth after their kind; whether it be of pulse, which is ripened for human use in a month, or of oaks, whose lifetime is centuries. So, in some of the actions of men, consequences follow conduct with a lock-step; in others, the effects of youthful actions first burst forth as from a subterranean current, in advanced life. In those great relations which subsist between different generations, between ancestors and posterity, effects are usually separated from their causes, by long intervals of time. The pulsations of a nation's heart are to be counted, not by seconds, but by years. Now, it is in this class of cases, where there are long intervals lying between our conduct and its consequences; where one generation sows, and another generation reaps; it is in this class of cases, that the greatest and most sorrowful of human errors originate. Yet, even for these, a benevolent Creator has supplied us with an antidote. He has given us the faculty of reason, whose especial office and function it is, to discover the connection between causes and effects; and thereby to enable us so to regulate the causes of to-day, as to predestinate the effects of to-morrow. In the eye of reason, causes and effects exist in proximity, in juxtaposition. They lie side by side, whatever length of time, or distance of space, comes in between them. If I am guilty of an act or a neglect, to-day, which will certainly cause the infliction of a wrong, it matters not whether that wrong happens, on the other side of the globe, or in the next century. Whenever or wherever it happens, it is mine; it belongs to me; my conscience owns it, and no sophistry can give me absolution. Who would think of acquitting an incendiary, because the train which he had laid and lighted, first circuited the globe before it reached and consumed his neighbor's dwelling? From the nature of the case, in education, the effects are widely separated from the causes. They happen so long afterwards, that the reason of the community loses sight of the connection between them. It does not bring the cause and the effect together, and lay them, and look at them, side by side.

If, instead of twenty-one *years,* the course of Nature allowed but twenty-one *days,* to rear an infant to the full stature of manhood, and to sow in his bosom, the seeds of unbounded happiness or of unspeakable misery, I suppose, in that case, the merchant would abandon his bargains, and the farmer would leave the in-gathering of his harvest, and even the drunkard would head homeward from the midst of his revel, and *that* twenty-one days would be spent, without much sleep, and with many prayers. And yet, it cannot be denied, that the consequences of a vicious education, inflicted upon a child, are now precisely the same as they would be, if, at the end of twenty-one days after an infant's birth, his tongue were already roughened with oaths and blasphemy; or he were seen skulking through society, obtaining credit upon false pretences, or with rolls of counterfeit bills in his pocket; or were already expiating his offences in the bondage and infamy of a prison. And the consequences of a virtuous education, at the end of twenty-one years, are now precisely the same as they would be, if, at the end of twenty-one days after his birth, the infant had risen from his cradle into the majestic form of manhood, and were possessed of all those qualities and attributes, which a being created in the image of God *ought to have;* with a power of fifty years of beneficent labor compacted into his frame; with nerves of sympathy, reaching out from his own heart and twining around the heart of society, so that the great social wants of men should be a part of his consciousness; and with a mind able to perceive what is right, prompt to defend it, or, if need be, to die for it. It ought to be understood, that none of these consequences become any the less certain, because they are more remote. It ought to be universally understood and intimately felt, that, in regard to children, all precept and example; all kindness and harshness; all rebuke and commendation; all forms, indeed, of direct or indirect education, affect mental growth, just as dew, and sun, and shower, or untimely frost, affect vegetable growth. Their influences are integrated and made one with the soul. They enter into spiritual combination with it, never afterwards to be wholly decompounded. They are like the daily food eaten by wild game, so pungent and saporific in its nature, that it flavors every fibre of their flesh, and colors every bone in their body. Indeed, so pervading and enduring is the effect of education upon the youthful soul, that it may well be compared to a certain species of writing-ink, whose color, at first, is scarcely perceptible, but which penetrates deeper and grows blacker by age, until, if you consume the scroll over a coal-fire, the character will still be legible in the cinders. It ought to be understood and felt, that, however it may be in a social or jurisprudential sense, it is nevertheless true, in the most solemn and dread-inspiring sense, that, by an irrepealable law of Nature, the iniquities of the fathers are still visited upon the children, unto the third and fourth generation. Nor do the children suffer for the iniquities only, of their parents; they suffer for their neglect and even for their ignorance. Hence, I have always admired that law of the Icelanders, by which, when a minor child commits an offence, the courts first make judicial inquiry, whether his parents have given him a good education; and, if it be proved they have not, the child is acquitted and the parents are punished. In both the old Colonies of Plymouth, and of Massachusetts Bay, if a child, over sixteen, and under twenty-one years of age, committed a certain capital offence against father or mother, he was allowed to arrest judgment of death upon himself, by showing that his parents, in the language of the law, "had been very unchristianly negligent in his education."

How, then, are the purposes of education to be accomplished? However other worlds may be, this world of ours is evidently constructed on the plan of producing ends by using means. Even the Deity, with his Omniscience and his Omnipotence, carries forward our system, by processes so minute, and movements so subtile, as generally to elude our keenest inspection. He might speak all the harvests of the earth and all the races of animals and of men, into full-formed existence, at a word; and yet the tree is elaborated from the kernel, and the wing from the chrysalis, by a series of processes, which occupies years, and sometimes centuries, for its completion. Education, more than any thing else, demands not only a scientific acquaintance with mental laws, but the nicest art in the detail and the application of means, for its successful prosecution; because influences, imperceptible in childhood, work out more and more broadly into beauty or deformity, in after-life. No unskilful hand should ever play upon a harp, where the tones are left, forever, in the strings. In the first place, the best methods should be well ascertained; in the second, they should be universally diffused. In this Commonwealth, there are about three thousand Public Schools, in all of which the rudiments of knowledge are taught. These schools, at the present time, are so many distinct, independent communities; each being governed by its own habits, traditions, and local customs. There is no common, superintending power over them; there is no bond of brotherhood or family between them. They are strangers and aliens to each other. The teachers are, as it were, imbedded, each in his own school district; and they are yet to be excavated and brought together, and to be established, each as a polished pillar of a holy temple. As the system is now administered, if any improvement in principles or modes of teaching is discovered by talent or accident, in one school, instead of being published to the world, it dies with the discoverer. No means exist for multiplying new truths, or even for preserving old ones. A gentleman, filling one of the highest civil offices in this Commonwealth, a resident in one of the oldest counties and in one of the largest towns in the State, a sincere friend of the cause of education, recently put into my hands a printed report, drawn up by a clergyman of high repute, which described, as was supposed, an important improvement in relation to our Common Schools, and earnestly enjoined its general adoption; when it happened to be within my own knowledge, that the supposed new discovery had been in successful operation for sixteen years, in a town but little more than sixteen miles distant. Now in other things, we act otherwise. If a manufacturer discovers a new combination of wheels, or a new mode of applying water or steam-power, by which stock can be economized, or the value of fabrics enhanced ten per cent, the information flies over the country at once; the old machinery is discarded, the new is substituted. Nay, it is difficult for an inventor to preserve the secret of his invention, until he can secure it by letters-patent. Our mechanics seem to possess a sort of keen, greyhound faculty, by which they can scent an improvement afar off. They will sometimes go, in disguise, to the inventor, and offer themselves as workmen; and instances have been known of their breaking into his workshop, by night, and purloining the invention. And hence that progress in the mechanic arts, which has given a name to the age in which we live, and made it a common wonder. Improvements in useful, and often in useless, arts, command solid prices, twenty, fifty, or even a hundred thousand dollars, while improvements in education, in the means of obtaining new guaranties for the permanence of all we hold dear, and for making our children and our children's children wiser and happier, these are scarcely topics of conversation or inquiry. Do we not need, then, some new and living institution, some animate organization, which shall at least embody and diffuse all that is now known on this subject, and thereby save, every year, hundreds of children from being sacrificed to experiments which have been a hundred times exploded.

Before noticing some particulars, in which a common channel for receiving and for disseminating information, may subserve the prosperity of our Common Schools, allow me to premise, that there is one rule, which, in all places, and in all forms of education, should be held as primary, paramount, and, as far as possible, exclusive. Acquirement and pleasure should go hand in hand. They should never part company. The pleasure of acquiring should be the incitement to acquire. A child is wholly incapable of appreciating the ultimate value or uses of knowledge. In its early beginnings, the motive of general, future utility will be urged in vain. Tell an abecedarian, as an inducement to learn his letters, of the sublimities of poetry and eloquence, that may be wrought out of the alphabet; and to him it is not so good as moonshine. Let me ask any man, whether he ever had, when a child, any just conception of the uses, to which he is now, as a man, daily applying his knowledge. How vain is it, then, to urge upon a child, as a motive to study, that which he cannot possibly understand! Nor is the motive of fear preferable. Fear is one of the most debasing and dementalizing of all the passions. The sentiment of fear was given us, that it might be roused into action, by whatever should be shunned, scorned, abhorred. The emotion should never be associated with what is to be desired, toiled for, and loved. If a child appetizes his books, then, lesson-getting is free labor. If he revolts at them, then, it is slave-labor. Less is done, and the little is not so well done. Nature has implanted a feeling of curiosity in the breast of every child, as if to make herself certain of his activity and progress. The desire of learning alternates with the desire of food; the mental with the bodily appetite. The former is even more craving and exigent, in its nature, than the latter, and acts longer without satiety. Men sit with folded arms, even while they are surrounded by objects of which they know nothing. Who ever saw that done by a child? But we cloy, disgust, half-extirpate, this appetite for knowledge, and then deny its existence. Mark a child, when a clear, well-defined, vivid conception seizes it. The whole nervous tissue vibrates. Every muscle leaps. Every joint plays. The face becomes auroral. The spirit flashes through the body, like lightning through a cloud. Tell a child the simplest story, which is adapted to his present state of mental advancement, and therefore intelligible, and he will forget sleep, leave food untasted, nor would he be enticed from hearing it, though yon should give him for play-things, shining fragments broken off from the sun. Observe the blind, and the deaf and dumb. So strong is their inborn desire for knowledge, such are the amazing attractive forces of their minds for it, that, although those natural inlets, the eye and the ear, are closed, yet they will draw it inward, through the solid walls and encasements of the body. If the eye be curtained with darkness, it will enter through the ear. If the ear be closed in silence, it will ascend along the nerves of touch. Every new idea, that enters into the presence of the sovereign mind, carries offerings of delight with it, to make its coming welcome. Indeed, our Maker created us in blank ignorance, for the very purpose of giving us the boundless, endless pleasure of learning new things; and the true path for the human intellect leads onward and upward from ignorance towards omniscience, ascending by an infinity of steps, each novel and delightful.

The voice of Nature, therefore, forbids the infliction of annoyance, discomfort, pain, upon a child, while engaged in study. If he actually suffers

from position, or heat, or cold, or fear, not only is a portion of the energy
of his mind withdrawn from his lesson, all of which should be concentrated upon it; but, at that undiscriminating age, the pain blends itself with
the study, makes part of the remembrance of it, and thus curiosity and the
love of learning are deadened, or turned away towards vicious objects. This
is the philosophy of children's hating study. We insulate them by fear; we
touch them with nonconductors; and then, because they emit no spark, we
gravely aver that they are non-electric bodies. If possible, pleasure should
be made to flow like a sweet atmosphere around the early learner, and pain
be kept beyond the association of ideas. You cannot open blossoms with
a northeast storm. The buds of the hardiest plants will wait for the genial
influences of the sun, though they perish, while waiting.

The first practical application of these truths, in relation to our Common Schools, is to School-house Architecture, a subject so little regarded,
yet so vitally important. The construction of schoolhouses involves, not the
love of study and proficiency, only, but health and length of life. I have the
testimony of many eminent physicians to this fact. They assure me that it
is within their own personal knowledge, that there is, annually, loss of life,
destruction of health, and such anatomical distortion as renders life hardly
worth possessing, growing out of the bad construction of our schoolhouses.
Nor is this evil confined to a few of them, only. It is a very general calamity.
I have seen many schoolhouses, in central districts of rich and populous
towns, where each seat connected with a desk, consisted only of an upright
post or pedestal, jutting up out of the floor, the upper end of which was
only about eight or ten inches square, without side-arms or backboard; and
some of them so high that the feet of the children in vain sought after the
floor. They were beyond soundings. Yet, on the hard top of these stumps,
the masters and misses of the school must balance themselves, as well as
they can, for six hours in a day. All attempts to preserve silence in such a
house are not only vain, but cruel. Nothing but absolute empalement could
keep a live child still, on such a seat; and you would hardly think him worth
living, if it could. The pupils will resort to every possible bodily evolution
for relief; and, after all, though they may *change the place, they keep the pain.* I
have good reasons for remembering one of another class of schoolhouses,
which the scientific would probably call the *sixth,* order of architecture,
the wicker-work order, summer-houses for winter residence, where there
never was a severely cold day, without the ink's freezing in the pens of the
scholars while they were writing; and the teacher was literally obliged to
compromise between the sufferings of those who were exposed to the cold
of the windows and those exposed to the heat of the fire, by not raising the
thermometer of the latter above ninety degrees, until that of the former

fell below thirty. A part of the children suffered the Arctic cold of Captains Ross and Parry, and a part, the torrid heat of the Landers, without, in either case, winning the honors of a discoverer. It was an excellent place for the teacher to illustrate one of the facts in geography; for five steps would have carried him through the five zones. Just before my present circuit, I passed a school-house, the roof of which, on one side, was trough-like; and down towards the eaves there was a large hole; so that the whole operated like a tunnel to catch all the rain and pour it into the schoolroom. At first, I did not know but it might be some apparatus designed to explain the Deluge. I called and inquired of the mistress, if she and her little ones were not sometimes drowned out. She said she should be, only that the floor leaked as badly as the roof, and drained off the water. And yet a healthful, comfortable schoolhouse can be erected as cheaply as one, which, judging from its construction, you would say, had been dedicated to the evil genius of deformity and suffering.

There is another evil in the construction of our schoolhouses, whose *immediate* consequences are not so bad, though their *remote* ones are indefinitely worse. No fact is now better established, than that a man cannot live, without a supply of about a gallon of fresh air, every minute; nor enjoy good health, indeed, without much more. The common air, as is now well known, is mainly composed of two ingredients, one only of which can sustain life. The action of the lungs upon the vital portion of the air, changes its very nature, converting it from a life-sustaining to a life-destroying element. As we inhale a portion of the atmosphere, it is healthful; the same portion, as we exhale it, is poisonous. Hence, ventilation in rooms, especially where large numbers are collected, is a condition of health and life. Privation admits of no excuse. To deprive a child of comfortable clothes, or wholesome food, or fuel, may sometimes, possibly, be palliated. These cost money, and often draw hardly upon the scanty resources of the poor. But what shall we say of stinting and starving a child, in regard to this prime necessary of life, fresh air? of holding his mouth, as it were, lest he should obtain a sufficiency of that vital element, which God, in His munificence, has poured out, a hundred miles deep, all around the globe? Of productions, reared or transported by human toil, there may be a dearth. At any rate, frugality in such things is commendable. But to put a child on short allowances out of this sky-full of air, is enough to make a miser weep. It is as absurd, as it would have been for Noah, while the torrents of rain were still descending, to have put his family upon short allowances of water. This vast quantity of air was given us to supersede the necessity of ever using it at second-hand. Heaven has ordained this matter with adorable wisdom. That very portion of the air which we turn into poison, by respiring it, becomes the aliment of vegetation. What is death to us is life to all verdure and flowerage. And again, vegetation rejects the ingredient which is life to us. Thus the equilibrium is forever restored; or rather, it is never destroyed. In this perpetual circuit, the atmosphere is forever renovated, and made the sustainer of life, both for the animal and vegetable worlds.

A simple contrivance for ventilating the schoolroom, unattended with any perceptible expense, would rescue children from this fatal, though unseen evil. It is an indisputable fact, that, for years past, far more attention has been paid, in this respect, to the construction of jails and prisons, than to that of schoolhouses. Yet, why should we treat our felons better than our children? I have observed in all our cities and populous towns, that, wherever stables have been recently built, provision has been made for their ventilation. This is encouraging, for I hope the children's turn will come, when gentlemen shall have taken care of their horses. I implore physicians to act upon this evil. Let it be removed, extirpated, cut off, surgically.

I cannot here stop to give even an index of the advantages of an agreeable site for a schoolhouse; of attractive, external appearance; of internal finish, neatness, and adaptation; nor of the still more important subject of having two rooms for all large schools, both on the same floor, or one over the other, so as to allow a separation of the large from the small scholars, for the purpose of placing the latter, at least, under the care of a female teacher. Each of these topics, and especially the last, is worthy of a separate essay. Allow me, however, to remark, in passing, that I regard it as one of the clearest ordinances of nature, that woman is the appointed guide and guardian of children of a tender age. And she does not forego, but, in the eye of prophetic vision, she anticipates and makes her own, all the immortal honors of the academy, the forum, and the senate, when she lays their deep foundations, by training up children in the way they should go.

A great mischief, I use the word *mischief*, because it implies a certain degree of wickedness, a great mischief is suffered in the diversity and multiplicity of our school books. Not more than twenty or thirty different kinds of books, exclusive of a school library, are needed in our Common Schools; and yet, though I should not dare state the fact, if I had not personally sought out the information from most authentic sources, there are now, in actual use in the schools of this State, more than three hundred different kinds of books; and, in the markets of this and the neighboring States, seeking for our adoption, I know not how many hundreds more. The standards, in spelling, pronunciation, and writing; in rules of grammar and in processes in arithmetic, are as various as the books. Correct language, in one place, is provincialism in another. While we agree in regarding the confusion of

Babel as a judgment, we unite in confounding it more, as though it were a blessing. But is not uniformity on these subjects desirable? Are there not some of these books, to which all good judges, on comparison, would award the preference? Could they not be afforded much cheaper for the great market which uniformity would open; thus furnishing better books at lower prices? And why not teach children aright, the first time? It is much harder to unlearn than to learn. Why go through three processes instead of one, by first learning, then unlearning, and then learning, again? This mischief grew out of the immense profits formerly realized from the manufacture of school books. There seems never to have been any difficulty in procuring reams of recommendations, because patrons have acted under no responsibility. An edition once published must be sold; for the date has become almost as important in school books, as in almanacs. All manner of devices are daily used to displace the old books, and to foist in new ones. The compiler has a cousin in the town of A, who will decry the old and recommend the new; or a literary gentleman in the city of B has just published some book on a different subject, and is willing to exchange recommendations, even; or the author has a mechanical friend, in a neighboring town, who has just patented some new tool, and who will recommend the author's book, if the author will recommend his tool? Publishers often employ agents to hawk their books about the country; and I have known several instances where such a pedlar, or picaroon, has taken all the old books of a whole class in school, in exchange for his new ones, book for book, looking, of course, to his chance of making sales after the book had been established in the school, for reimbursement and profits; so that at last, the children have to pay for what they supposed was given them. On this subject, too, cannot the mature views of competent and disinterested men, residing, respectively, in all parts of the State, be the means of effecting a much-needed reform?

There is another point, where, as it seems to me, a united effort among the friends of education would, in certain branches of instruction, increase tenfold the efficiency of our Common Schools. I mean, the use of some simple apparatus, so as to employ the eye, more than the ear, in the acquisition of knowledge. After the earliest years of childhood, the superiority of the eye over the other senses, in quickness, in precision, in the vastness of its field of operations, and in its power of penetrating, like a flash, into any interstices, where light can go and come, is almost infinite. The senses of taste, and smell, and touch, seem to be more the servants of the body than of the soul; and, amongst the infinite variety of objects in the external world, hearing takes notice of sounds only. Close your eyes, and then, with the aid of the other senses, examine a watch, an artisan's workshop, a manufactory, a ship, a steam-engine; and how meagre and formless are all the ideas they present to you. But the eye is the great thoroughfare between the outward and material infinite, and the inward and spiritual infinite. The mind often acquires, by a glance of the eye, what volumes of books and months of study could not reveal so livingly through the ear. Every thing that comes through the eye, too, has a vividness, a clear outline, a just collocation of parts, each in its proper place, which the other senses can never communicate. Ideas or impressions acquired through vision are long-lived. Those acquired through the agency of the other senses often die young. Hence, the immeasurable superiority of this organ is founded in Nature. There is a fund of truth in the old saying, that "seeing is believing." There never will be any such maxim, in regard to the other senses. To use the ear instead of the eye, in any case where the latter is available, is as preposterous, as it would be for our migratory birds, in their overland passage, to walk rather than to fly. We laugh at the Germans, because in using their oxen, they attach the load to the horns, instead of the neck; but do we not commit a much greater absurdity, in communicating knowledge through the narrow fissure of the ear, which holds communication only with a small circle of things, and in that circle, only with things that utter a sound, instead of conveying it through the broad portals of the earth and heaven surveying eye?

Nine tenths, may I not say ninety-nine hundredths, of all our Common School instruction are conveyed through the ear; or, which is the same thing, through the medium of written instead of spoken *words*, where the eye has been taught to do the work of the ear. In teaching those parts of geography which comprise the outlines and natural features of the earth, and in astronomy, the use of the globe and the planetarium would reduce the labor of months to as many hours. Ocular evidence, also, is often indispensable for correcting the imperfections of language, as it is understood by a child. For instance, (and I take this illustration from fact and not from imagination,) a child, born in the interior, and who has never seen the ocean, is taught that the earth is *surrounded* by an elastic medium, called the atmosphere. He thereby gets the idea of perfect circumfusion and envelopment. In the next lesson, he is taught that an island is a small body of land *surrounded* by water. If he has a quick mind, he may get the idea that an island is land, enveloped in water, as the earth is in air. Mature minds always modify the meaning of words and sentences by numerous rules, of which a child knows nothing. If, when speaking of the Deity to a man of common intelligence, I use the word "power," he understands omnipotence; and if I use the same word when speaking of an ant, he understands that I mean strength enough to lift a grain; but a child would require explanations, limiting the meaning of the word in the one case, and extending it in the other.

Other things being equal, the pleasure which a child enjoys, in studying or contemplating, is proportioned to the liveliness of his perceptions and ideas. A child who spurns books, will be attracted and delighted by visible objects of well-defined forms and striking colors. In the one case, he sees things through a haze; in the other, by sunlight. A contemplative child, whose mind gets as vivid images from reading as from gazing, always prefers reading. Although it is undoubtedly true, that taste and predilection, in regard to any subject, will give brightness and distinctness to ideas; yet it is also true that bright and distinct ideas will greatly modify tastes and predilections. Now the eye may be employed much more extensively than it ever has been, in giving what I will venture to call the geography of ideas, that is, a perception, where one idea bounds on another, where the province of one idea ends, and that of the adjacent ideas begins. Could children be habituated to fixing these lines of demarcation, to seeing and feeling ideas as distinctly as though they were geometrical solids, they would then experience an insupportable uneasiness, whenever they were lost in fog-land and among the Isles of the Mist; and this uneasiness would enforce investigation, survey, and perpetual outlook; and in after-life, a power would exist of applying luminous and exact thought to extensive combinations of facts and principles, and we should have the materials of philosophers, statesmen and chief-justices. The pleasure which children enjoy in visiting our miserable toy-shop collections—the dreams of crazy brains, *done* into wood and pewter, comes mainly from the vividness, the oneness, wholeness, completeness, of their perceptions. The gewgaws do not give delight, because of their grotesqueness, but in spite of it. Natural ideas derived through a microscope, or from any mechanism which would stamp as deep an imprint and glow with as quick a vitality, would give them far greater delight. And how different, as to attainments in useful knowledge, would children be, at the end of eight or ten years, accordingly as they had sought their gratification from one or the other of these sources.

And what higher delight, what reward, at once so innocent and so elevating, as to explain by means of suitable apparatus, to the larger scholars in a school, the cause and manner of an eclipse of the sun or moon! And when those impressive phenomena occur, how beautiful to witness the manifestations of wonder and of reverence for God, which spring spontaneously from the intelligent observation of such sublime spectacles; instead of their being regarded with the horrible imaginings of superstition, or with such stupid amazement, as belongs only to the brutes that perish! If a model were given, every ingenious boy, with a few broken window panes and a pocket-knife, could make a prism. With this, the rainbow, the changing colors of the dew-drop, the gorgeous light of the sunset sky, could be explained; and thus might the minds of children be early imbued with a love of pure and beautiful things, and led upward towards the angel, instead of downward towards the brute, from this middle ground of humanity. Imbue the young mind with these sacred influences, and they will forever constitute a part of its moral being; they will abide with it and tend to uphold and purify it, wherever it may be cast by fortune, in this tumultuous arena of life. A spirit so softened and penetrated, will be

> *Like the vase in which roses have once been distilled;*
> *You may break, you may ruin the vase, if you will,*
> *But the scent of the roses will hang round it still.*

At the last session of the Legislature, a law was enacted, authorizing school districts to raise money for the purchase of apparatus and Common School libraries, for the use of the children, to be expended in sums not exceeding thirty dollars, for the first year, and ten dollars, for any succeeding year. Trifling as this may appear, yet I regard the law as hardly second in importance to any which has been passed since the year 1647, when Common Schools were established. Every district can find some secure place for preserving them, until, in repairing or rebuilding schoolhouses, a separate apartment can be provided for their safe-keeping. As soon as one half the benefits of these instruments of learning shall be understood, I doubt not that public-spirited individuals will be found, in most towns, who will contribute something to the library; and artisans, too, who will feel an honorable pleasure in adding something to the apparatus, wrought by their own hands, perhaps devised by their own ingenuity. "Build dove-holes," says the proverb, "and the doves will come." And what purer satisfaction, what more sacred object of ambition, can any man propose to himself, than to give the first impulse to an improvement, which will go on increasing in value, forever! It may be said, that mischievous children will destroy or mutilate whatever is obtained for this purpose. But children will not destroy or injure what gives them pleasure. Indeed, the love of malicious mischief, the proneness to deface whatever is beautiful, this vile ingredient in the old Saxon blood, wherever it flows, originated, and it is aggravated, by the almost total want, amongst us, of objects of beauty, taste, and elegance, for our children to grow up with, to admire, and to protect.

The expediency of having District School Libraries is fast becoming a necessity. It is too late to stop the art of printing, or to arrest the general circulation of books. Reading of some kind, the children will have; and the question is, whether it is best, that this reading should be supplied to them by the choice of men, whose sole object is gain; or whether it shall be prepared by wise and benevolent men, whose object is to do good. Probably, not one child in ten, in this State, has free access to any library of useful and entertaining knowledge. Where there are town, parish, or social libraries, they either do not consist of suitable books, or they are burdened with restrictions which exclude more than are admitted. A District School Library would be open to all the children in the district. They would enter it independently. Wherever there is genius, the library would nourish it. Talents would not die of inaction, for want of some sphere for exercise. Habits of reading and reflection would be formed, instead of habits of idleness and malicious mischief. The wealth and prosperity of Massachusetts are not owing to natural position or resources. They exist, in despite of a sterile soil and an inhospitable clime. They do not come from the earth, but from the ingenuity and frugality of the people. Their origin is good thinking, carried out into good action; and intelligent reading in a child will result in good thinking in the man or woman. But there is danger, it is said, of reading bad books. So there is danger of eating bad food; shall we therefore have no harvests? No! It was the kindling excitement of a few books, by which those Massachusetts boys, John Adams and Benjamin Franklin, first struck out an intellectual spark, which broadened into magnitude and brightened into splendor, until it became a mighty luminary, which now stands, and shall forever stand, among the greater lights in the firmament of glory.

But in the selection of books for school libraries, let every man stand upon his honor, and never ask for the introduction of any book, because it favors the distinctive views of his sect or party. A wise man prizes only the free and intelligent assent of unprejudiced minds; he disdains a slavish and non-compos echo, even to his best-loved opinions. In striving together for a common end, peculiar ends must neither be advocated nor assailed. Strengthen the intellect of children, by exercise upon the objects and laws of Nature; train their feelings to habits of order, industry, temperance, justice; to the love of man, because of his wants, and to the love of God, because of his universally-acknowledged perfections; and, so far as public measures, applicable to all, can reach, you have the highest human assurance, that, when they grow up, they will adopt your favorite opinions, if they are right, or discover the true reasons for discarding them, if they are wrong.

An advantage altogether invaluable, of supplying a child, by means of a library and of apparatus, with vivid ideas and illustrations, is, that he may always be possessed, in his own mind, of correct standards and types with which to compare whatever objects he may see in his excursions abroad; and that he may also have useful subjects of reflection, whenever his attention is not engrossed by external things. A boy who is made clearly to understand the philosophical principle on which he flies his kite, and then to recognize the same principle in a wind or a water-wheel, and in the sailing of a ship; wherever business or pleasure may afterwards lead him, if he sees that principle in operation, he will mentally refer to it, and think out its applications, when, otherwise, he would be singing or whistling. Twenty years would work out immense results from such daily observation and reflection. Dr. Franklin attributed much of his practical turn of mind, which was the salient point of his immortality, to the fact, that his father, in his conversations before the family, always discussed some useful subject, or developed some just principle of individual or social action, instead of talking forever about trout-catching or grouse-shooting; about dogs, dinners, dice, or trumps. In its moral bearings this subject grows into immense importance. How many months, may I not say years, in a child's life, when, with spontaneous activity, his mind hovers and floats wherever it listeth! As he sits at home, amid familiar objects, or walks frequented paths, or lies listlessly in his bed, if his mind be not preoccupied with some substantial subjects of thought, the best that you can hope is, that it will wander through dream-land, and expend its activity in chasing shadows. Far more probable is it, especially if the child is exposed to the contamination of profane or obscene minds, that in these seasons of solitude and reverie, the cockatrice's eggs of impure thoughts and desires will be hatched. And what *boy*, at least, is there who is not in daily peril of being corrupted by the evil communications of his elders? We all know, that there are self-styled gentlemen amongst us, *self-styled gentlemen*, who daily, and hourly, lap their tongues in the foulness of profanity; and though, through a morally-insane perversion, they may restrain themselves, in the presence of ladies and of clergymen, yet it is only for the passing hour, when they hesitate not to pour out the pent-up flood, to deluge and defile the spotless purity of childhood, and this, too, at an age, when these polluting stains sink, centre-deep, into their young and tender hearts, so that no moral bleachery can ever afterwards wholly cleanse and purify them. No parent, no teacher, can ever feel any rational security about the growth of the moral nature of his child, unless he contrives in some way to learn the tenor of his secret, silent meditations, or prepares the means, beforehand, of determining what those meditations shall be. A child may soon find it no difficult thing, to converse and act by a set of approved rules, and then to retire into the secret chambers of his own soul, and there to riot and gloat upon guilty pleasures, whose act would be perdition, and would turn the fondest home into a hell. But there is an antidote, I do not say for all, but for most, of this peril. The mind of children can be supplied with vivid illustrations of the works of Nature and of

Art; its chambers can be hung round with picture-thoughts and images of truth, and charity, and justice, and affection, which will be companions to the soul, when no earthly friend can accompany it.

It is only a further development of this topic, to consider the inaptitude of many of our educational processes, for making accurately-thinking minds. It has been said by some one, that the good sense, and sound judgment, which we find in the community, are only what have escaped the general ravage of a bad education. School studies ought to be so arranged, as to promote a harmonious development of the faculties. In despotic Prussia, a special science is cultivated, under the name of *methodik*, the scope of which is to arrange and adapt studies, so as to meet the wants and exercise the powers of the opening mind. In free America, we have not the name; indeed, we can scarcely be said to have the idea. Surely, the farmer, the gardener, the florist, who have established rules for cultivating every species of grain, and fruit, and flower, cannot doubt, that, in the unfolding and expanding of the young mind, some processes will be congenial, others fatal. Those whose business it is to compound ingredients, in any art, weigh them with the nicest exactness, and watch the precise moments of their chemical combinations. The mechanic selects all his materials with the nicest care, and measures all their dimensions to a hair's breadth; and he knows that if he fails in aught, he will produce a weak, loose, irregular fabric. Indeed, can you name any business, avocation, profession, or employment, whatever,—even to the making of hobnails or wooden skewers, where chance, ignorance, or accident, is ever rewarded with a perfect product? But in no calling is there such a diversity as in education, diversity in principles, diversity in the application of those principles. Discussion, elucidation, the light of a thousand minds brought to a focus, would result in discarding the worst and in improving even the best. Under this head are included the great questions respecting the order and succession of studies; the periods of alternation between them; the proportion between the exact and the approximate sciences; and what is principal and what is subsidiary, in pursuing them.

There is a natural order and progression in the development of the faculties: "First the blade, then the ear, afterwards the full corn in the ear." And in the mind, as in the grain, the blade may be so treated that the full corn will never appear. For instance, if any faculty is brooded upon and warmed into life before the period of its natural development, it will have a precocious growth, to be followed by weakness, or by a want of symmetry and proportion in the whole character. Consequences still worse will follow, where faculties are cultivated in the reverse order of their natural development. Again, if collective ideas are forced into a child's mind, without his being made to analyze them, and understand the individual ideas of which they are composed, the probability is, that the collective idea will never be comprehended. Let me illustrate this position by a case where it is least likely to happen, that we may form some idea of its frequency in other things. A child is taught to count *ten*. He is taught to repeat the words, *one, two,* &c., as words, merely; and if care be not taken, he will attach no more comprehensive idea to the word *ten,* than he did to the word *one.* He will not think often ones, as he uses it. In the same way, he proceeds to use the words, hundred, thousand, million, &c., the idea in his mind, not keeping within hailing distance of the signification of the words used. Hence there is generated a habit of using words, not as the representatives of ideas, but as sounds, merely. How few children there are of the age of sixteen years, an age at which almost all of them have ceased to attend upon our schools, who have any adequate conception of the power of the signs they have been using. How few of them know even so simple a truth as this, that, if they were to count one, every second, for ten hours in a day, without intermission, it would take about twenty-eight days to count a million. Yet they have been talking of millions, and hundreds of millions, as though they were units. Now, suppose you speak to such a person of millions of children, growing up under a highly elaborated system of vicious education, unbalanced by any good influences; or suppose you appeal to him, in behalf of a million of people wailing beneath the smitings of the oppressor's rod, he gets no distinct idea of so many as fifty; and therefore he has no intellectual substratum, upon which to found an appropriate feeling, or by which to graduate its intensity.

Again; in geography, we put a quarto-sized map, or perhaps a globe no larger than a goose's egg, into a child's hands, and we invite him to spread out his mind over continents, oceans, and archipelagoes, at once. This process does not expand the mind of the child to the dimensions of the objects, but it belittles the objects to the nutshell capacity of the mind. Such a course of instruction may make precocious, green-house children; but you will invariably find, that, when boys are prematurely turned into little men, they remain little men, always. Physical geography should be commenced by making a child describe and plot a loom with its fixtures, a house with its apartments, the adjoining yards, fields, roads or streets, hills, waters, &c. Then embracing, if possible, the occasion of a visit to a neighboring town, or county, that should be included. Here, perpetual reference must be had to the points of the compass. After a just extension has been given to his ideas of a county, or a state, then that county or state should be shown to him on a globe; and, cost what labor or time it may, his mind must be expanded to it comprehension of relative magnitudes, so that his idea of the earth shall be as adequate to the size of the earth, as his idea of the house or the field was to the size of the house or the field. Thus the pupil founds his knowledge of unseen things upon the distinct notions of eyesight, in regard to familiar objects. Yet I believe it is not very uncommon to give the mind of the young learner a continent, for a single intellectual meal, and an ocean to wash it down with. It recently happened, in a school within my own knowledge, that a class of small scholars in geography, on being examined respecting the natural divisions of the earth, its continents, oceans islands, gulfs, &c., answered all the questions with admirable precision and promptness. They were then asked, by a visiter, some general questions respecting their lesson, and, amongst others, whether they had ever seen the earth about which they had been reciting; and they unanimously declared, in good faith, that they never had. Do we not find here an explanation, why there are so many men whose conceptions on all subjects are laid down on so small a scale of miles, so many thousand leagues to a hair's breadth? By such absurd processes, no vivid ideas can be gained, and therefore no pleasure is enjoyed. A capacity of wonder is destroyed in a day, sufficient to keep alive the flame of curiosity for years. The subjects of the lessons cease to be new, and yet are not understood. Curiosity, which is the hunger and thirst of the mind, is forever cheated and balked; for nothing but a real idea can give real, true, intellectual gratification. A habit, too, is inevitably formed of reciting, without thinking. At length, the most glib recitation becomes the best; and the less the scholars are delayed by thought, the faster they can prate, as a mill clacks quicker when there is no grist in the hopper. Thoroughness, therefore, thoroughness, and again I say, *thoroughness*, for the sake of the knowledge and still more for the sake of the habit, should, at all events, be enforced; and a pupil should never be suffered to leave any subject, until he can reach his arms quite around it, and clench his hands upon the opposite side. Those persons, who know a little of everything but nothing well, have been aptly compared to a certain sort of pocket-knife, which some over-curious people carry about with them, which, in addition to a common knife, contains a file, a chisel, a saw, a gimlet, a screw-driver, and a pair of scissors, but all so diminutive, that the moment they are needed for use, they are found useless.

It seems to me that one of the greatest errors in education, at the present time, is the desire and ambition, at single lessons, to teach complex truths, whole systems, doctrines, theorems, which years of analysis are scarcely sufficient to unfold; instead of commencing with simple elements, and then rising, by gradations, to combined results. All is administered in a mass. We strive to introduce knowledge into the child's mind, the great end first. When lessons are given in this way, the pupil, being unable to comprehend the ideas, tries to remember the words, and thus, at best, is sent away with a single fact, instead of a principle, explanatory of whole classes of facts. The lessons are learned by rote; and when a teacher practises upon the rote system, he uses the minds of the pupils, just as they use their own slates, in working arithmetical questions; whenever a second question is to be wrought, the first is sponged out, to make room for it. What would be thought of a teacher of music, who should give his pupils the most complicated exercises, before they had learned to sound simple notes? It is said of the athlete, Milo of Crotona, that he began by lifting a calf, and, continuing to lift it daily, he gained strength as fast as the animal gained weight; so that he was able to lift it, when it became an ox. Had he begun by straining to lift an ox, he would probably have broken down, and been afterwards unable to lift even a calf. The point to which I would invite the regards of the whole community, is, whether greater attention should not be paid to gradation, to progression in a natural order, to adjustment, to the preparation of a child's mind for receiving the higher forms of truth, by first making it thoroughly acquainted with their elements. The temptation to this error is perhaps the most seductive, that ever beguiles a teacher from his duty. He desires to make his pupils *appear* well. He forgets that the great objects of their education lie in the power, and dignity, and virtue of life, and not in their recitations, at the end of the quarter. Hence he strives to prepare them for the hastening day of exhibition. They must be able to state, in words, the great results, in science, which human reason has achieved, after almost sixty centuries of labor. For this purpose, in which they also are tempted to conspire, he loads their memories with burden after burden of definitions and formulas; which is about as useful a process, and is it not also about as honest? —as it would be for the rearer of nursery trees to buy golden pippins in the market, and, tying them upon the branches of his young trees, to palm them off upon purchasers, as though the delicious fruit had been elaborated from the succulence of the stock he sells.

Another question of method, to which I most earnestly solicit the attention of teachers and of the whole public, is, whether there is not too much teaching of words, instead of things. Never was a severer satire uttered against human reason, than that of Mirabeau, when he said, "words are things." That single phrase explains the whole French Revolution. Such a revolution never could have occurred amongst a people who spoke things, instead of words. Just so far as words are things, just so far the infinite contexture of realities pertaining to body and soul, to earth and heaven, to time and eternity, is nothing. The ashes, and shreds, and wrecks of every thing else are of some value; but of words not freighted with ideas, there is no salvage. It is not *words,* but words *fitly spoken,* that are like apples of gold in pictures of silver. Words are but purses; things, the shining coin within them. Why buy seventy or eighty thousand purses, for it is said we have about that number of untechnical words in the language, without a copper for deposit? I believe it is almost universally true, that young students desire to be composers; and as universally true, that they dread composition. When they would compose, of what service, then, are those columns of spelling-book words, which they have committed to memory by the furlong? Where then, too, are the rich mines of thought contained in their Readers, their First-Class Books, and their little libraries? These they have been accustomed to consider merely as instruments, to practise pronunciation, emphasis, and cadence, upon. They have moved, for years, in the midst of ideas, like blind men in picture-galleries. Hence they have no knowledge of *things,* and their relations; and, when called upon for composition, they have nothing to compound. But, as the outward and visible sign of composition is a sheet-full of words, a sheet is filled, though more from the dictionary than from the head. This practice comes at last, to make them a kind of sportsmen or warriors, who think their whole business is to fire, not to hit. Some, who have a strong verbal memory, become dexterous in the use of language; so that, if they can have two ideas, on any subject, to set up at the ends, as termini, they will fill up with words any distance of space between them. Those who have not this verbal memory, become the wind-driven hubbies of those who have. When the habit is confirmed, of relying on the verbal faculty, the rest of the mind dies out. The dogma taught by Aristotle, that Nature abhors a vacuum, is experimentally refuted. I know of but one compensation for these word-men; I believe they never become insane. Insanity requires some mind, for a basis.

The subject of penal discipline, I hardly dare to mention; especially discipline by corporal punishment. In this department, extremes both of doctrine and of practice prevail. The public have taken sides, and parties are arrayed against each other. Some repudiate and condemn it, altogether. With others, it is the great motive-power; and they consider it as, at least, the first and second, if not the three estates in the realm of school-keeping. Generally speaking, I fear that but little judgment and forethought are brought to the decision of its momentous questions. It cannot be discussed, alone. It is closely connected with intellectual progress; its influences pervade the whole moral nature; and it must be looked at, in its relations to them. The justifiable occasions, if any, for inflicting it; the mode, and emphatically, the spirit, of its administration; its instruments; its extent; the conduct that should precede and should follow it, are questions worthy of the deepest attention. That corporal punishment, considered by itself, and without reference to its ultimate object, is an evil, probably none will deny. Yet, with almost three thousand public schools in this State, composed of all kinds of children, with more than five thousand teachers, of all grades of qualification, to govern them, probably the evils of corporal punishment must be endured, or the greater ones of insubordination and mutiny be incurred. I hesitate also to speak so fully of the magnitude of these evils, as I would wish to do; because there are some excellent teachers, who manage schools without resorting to it; while others, ambitious for the same honor, but destitute of skill and of the divine qualities of love, patience, sympathy, by which alone it can be won, have discarded what they call corporal punishment, but have resorted to other modes of discipline, which, though they may bear a milder name, are, in reality, more severe. To imprison timid children in a dark and solitary place; to brace open the jaws with a piece of wood; to torture the muscles and bones, by the strain of an unnatural position, or of holding an enormous weight; to inflict a wound upon the instinctive feelings of modesty and delicacy, by making a girl sit with the boys, or go out with them, at recess; to bring a whole class around a fellow-pupil, to ridicule and shame him; to break down the spirit of self-respect, by enforcing some ignominious compliance; to give a nick-name; these, and such as these, are the gentle appliances, by which some teachers, who profess to discard corporal punishment, maintain the empire of the schoolroom; as though the muscles and bones were less corporeal than the skin; as though a wound of the spirit were of less moment than one of the flesh; and the body's blood more sacred than the soul's purity. But of these solemn topics, it is impossible here to speak. I cannot, however, forbear to express the opinion, that punishment should never be inflicted, except in cases of the extremest necessity; while the experiment of sympathy, confidence, persuasion, encouragement, should be repeated, for ever and ever. The fear of bodily pain is a degrading motive; but we have authority for saying, that where there is perfect love, every known law will be fulfilled. Parents and teachers often create that disgust at study, and that incorrigibleness and obstinacy of disposition, which they deplore. It is a sad exchange, if the very blows, which beat arithmetic and grammar into a boy, should beat confidence and manliness out. So it is quite as important to consider what feelings are excited, in the mind, as what are subdued, by the punishment. Which side gains, though the evil spirit of roguery or wantonness be driven out, if seven other evil spirits, worse than the first, sullenness, irreverence, fraud, lying, hatred, malice, revenge, are allowed to come in? The motive from which the offence emanated, and the motives with which the culprit leaves the bar of his judge and executioner, are everything. If these are not regarded, the offender may go away worse than he came, in addition to a gratuitous flagellation. To say a child knows better, is nothing; if he knows better, why does he not do better? The answer to this question reveals the difficulty; and whoever has not patience and sagacity to solve that inquiry, is as unworthy of the parental trust, as is the physician, of administering to the sick, who prescribes a fatal nostrum, and says, in justification, that he knew nothing of the disease. In fine, if anything, in the wide range of education, demands patience, forethought, judgment, and the all-subduing spirit of love, it is this; and though it may be too much to say, that corporal punishment can be disused by all teachers, with regard to all scholars, in all schools, yet it may be averred, without exception, that it is never inflicted with the right spirit, nor in the right measure, when it is not more painful to him who imposes, than to him who receives it.

Of emulation in school, as an incitement to effort, I can here say but a word; but I entreat all intelligent men to give to this subject a most careful consideration. And let those who use it, as a quickener of the intellect, beware, lest it prove a depraver of the social affections. There is no necessary incompatibility between the upward progress of one portion of our nature, and the lower and lower debasement of another. The intellect may grow wise, while the passions grow wicked. No cruelty towards a child can be so great as that which barters morals for attainment. If, under the fiery stimulus of emulation, the pupil comes to regard a successful rival with envy or malevolence, or an unsuccessful one with arrogance or disdain; if, in aiming at the goal of precedence, he loses sight of the goal of perfection; if, to gain his prize, he becomes the hypocrite instead of the reverer of virtue;— then, though his intellect should enter upon the stage of life with all the honors of an early triumph; yet the noblest parts of his nature, his moral and social affections, will be the victims, led captive in the retinue. Suppose, in some Theological Seminary, a prize were offered for the best exposition of the commandment, *"Thou shall love thy neighbor as thyself,"* and two known competitors were to task their intellects, to win it; and, on the day of trial, one of these neighbor-loving rivals, with dilated nostril and expanded frame, should clutch the honor; while the other neighbor-loving rival, with quivering lip and livid countenance, stood by, the vulture of envy, all the while, forking her talons into his heart; —would it not be that very mixture of the ludicrous and the horrible, which demons would choose for the subject of an epigram! Paint, or chisel the whole group of *neighbor-loving* rivals, and pious doctors sitting around and mingling, in one chalice, the helle-bore of pride, and in another, the wormwood of defeat, to be administered to those who should be brothers, and can aught be found more worthy to fill a niche in the council-hall of Pandemonium! Who has not seen winter, with its deepest congelations, come in between ingenuous-minded and loving fellow-students, whose hearts would otherwise have run together, like kindred drops of water? Who has not witnessed a consumption, not of the lungs, but of the heart; nay, both of lungs and heart, —wasting its victims with the smothered frenzy of emulation? It surely is within the equity of the prayer, "lead *us* not into temptation," not to lead others into it. And ought not the teacher, who, as a general and prevalent, I do not say a universal rule, cannot sustain order and insure proficiency, in a school, without resorting to fear and emulation, to consider, whether the fault be in human nature or in himself? And will there ever be any more of that secret, silent beneficence amongst us, where the left hand knows not of the blessings scattered by the right? —will there ever be any less of this deadly strife for the ostensible signs of precedence, in the social and political arena, while the germs of emulation are so assiduously cultivated in the schoolroom, the academy, and the college? The pale ambition of men, ready to, sacrifice country and kind for self, is only the fire of youthful emulation, heated to a white heat. Yet, there is an inborn sentiment of emulation, in all minds, and there are external related objects of that sentiment. The excellent, who may be present with us, but who are advanced in life; the great and good, who are absent, but whose fame is every where; the illustrious dead; these are the objects of emulation. A rivalry with these yields sacred love, not consuming envy. On these, therefore, let the emulous and aspiring gaze, until their eyes overflow with tears, and every tear will be the baptism of honor and of purity.

Such are some of the most obvious topics, belonging to that sacred work, the education of children. The science, or philosophical principles on which this work is to be conducted; the art, or manner in which those principles are to be applied, must all be rightly settled and generally understood, before any system of Public Instruction can operate with efficiency. Yet all this has been mainly left to chance. Compared with its deserts, how disproportionate, how little, the labor, cost and talent, devoted to it. We have a Congress, convening annually, at almost incredible expense, to decide upon questions of tariff, internal improvement, and currency. We have a State Legislature, continuing in session more than a fourth part of every year, to regulate our internal polity. We have Courts, making continual circuits through the Commonwealth to adjudicate upon doubtful rights of person or property, however trivial. Every great department of literature and of business has its Periodical. Every party, political, religious and social, has its Press. Yet Education, that vast cause, of which all other causes are only constituent parts; that cause, on which all other causes are dependent, for their vitality and usefulness, if I except the American Institute of Instruction, and a few local, feeble, unpatronized, though worthy associations, Education has literally nothing, in the way of comprehensive organization and of united effort, acting for a common end and under the focal light of a common intelligence. It is under these circumstances; it is in view of these great public wants, that the Board of Education has been established, not to legislate, not to enforce, but to collect facts, to educe principles, to diffuse a knowledge of improvements; in fine, to submit the views of men who have thought much upon this subject to men who have thought but little.

To specify the labors which education has yet to perform, would be only to pass in review the varied interests of humanity. Its general purposes are to preserve the good and to repudiate the evil which now exist, and to give scope to the sublime law of progression. It is its duty to take the accumulations in knowledge, of almost six thousand years, and to transfer the vast treasure to posterity. Suspend its functions for but one generation, and the experience and the achievements of the past are lost. The race must commence its fortunes anew, and must again spend six thousand years, before it can grope its way upward from barbarism to the present point of civilization. With the wisdom, education must also teach something of the follies, of the past, for admonition and warning: for it has been well said, that mankind have seldom arrived at truth, on any subject, until they had first exhausted its errors.

Education is to instruct the whole people in the proper care of the body, in order to augment the powers of that wonderful machine, and to prevent so much of disease, of suffering, and of premature death. The body is the mind's instrument; and the powers of the mind, like the skill of an artisan, may all be baffled, through the imperfection of their utensils. The happiness and the usefulness of thousands and tens of thousands of men and women have been destroyed, from not knowing a few of the simple laws of health, which they might have learned in a few months; nay, which might have been so impressed upon them, as habits, in childhood, that they would never think there was any other way. I do not speak of the ruin that comes from slavery to throned appetites, where the bondage might continue in defiance of knowledge; but I speak of cases, where the prostration of noble powers and the suffering of terrible maladies result from sheer ignorance and false views of the wise laws to which God has subjected our physical nature. No doubt, Voltaire said truly, that the fate of many a nation had depended upon the good or bad digestion of its minister; and how much more extensively true would the remark be, if applied to individuals? How many men perfectly understand the observances by which their horses and cattle are made healthy and strong; while their children are puny, distempered, and have chronic diseases, at the very earliest age, at which so highly-finished an article as a chronic disease can be prepared. There is a higher art than the art of the physician; the art, not of *restoring,* but of *making* health. Health is a product. Health is a manufactured article, as much so as any fabric of the loom or the workshop; and, except in some few cases of hereditary taint or of organic lesion from accident or violence, the how much, or the how little, health any man shall enjoy, depends upon his treatment of himself; or rather, upon the treatment of those who manage his infancy and childhood, and create his habits for him. Situated, as we are, in a high latitude, with the Atlantic ocean on one side and a range of mountains on the other, we cannot escape frequent and great transitions, in the temperature of our weather. Our region is the perpetual battle-ground of the torrid and the arctic, where they alternately prevail; and it is only by a sort of average that we call it *temperate.* Yet to this natural position we must adapt ourselves, or abandon it, or suffer. Hence the necessity of *making* health, in order to endure natural inclemencies; and hence also the necessity of including the simple and benign laws on which it depends, in all our plans of education. Certainly, our hearts should glow with gratitude to Heaven, for all the means of health; but every expression indicating that health is a Divine gift, in any other sense than all our blessings are a Divine gift, should be discarded from the language; and it should be incorporated into the forms of speech, that a man prepares his own health, as he does his own house.

Education is to inspire the love of truth, as the supremest good, and to clarify the vision of the intellect to discern it. We want a generation of men above deciding great and eternal principles, upon narrow and selfish grounds. Our advanced state of civilization has evolved many complicated questions respecting social duties. We want a generation of men capable of taking up these complex questions, and of turning all sides of them towards the sun, and of examining them by the white light of reason, and not under the false colors which sophistry may throw upon them. We want no men who will change, like the vanes of our steeples, with the course of the popular wind; but we want men who, like mountains, will change the course of the wind. We want no more of those patriots who exhaust their patriotism, in lauding the past; but we want patriots who will do for the future what the past has done for us. We want men capable of deciding, not merely what is right, in principle, *that* is often the smallest part of the case; but we want men capable of deciding what is right in means, to accomplish what is right in principle. We want men who will speak to this great people in counsel, and not in flattery. We want godlike men who can tame the madness of the times, and, speaking divine words in a divine spirit, can say to the raging of human passions, "Peace, be still;" and usher in the calm of enlightened reason and conscience. Look at our community, divided into so many parties and factions, and these again subdivided, on all questions of social, national, and international, duty; while, over all, stands, almost unheeded, the sublime form of Truth, eternally and indissolubly *One!* Nay, further, those do not agree in thought who agree in words. Their unanimity is a delusion. It arises from the imperfection of language. Could men, who subscribe to the same forms of words, but look into each other's minds, and see, there, what features their own idolized doctrines wear, friends would often start back from the friends they have loved, with as much abhorrence as from the enemies they have persecuted. Now, what can save us from endless contention, but the love of "truth"? What can save us, and our children after us, from eternal, implacable, universal war, but the greatest of all human powers, the power of impartial thought? Many, may I not say most, of those great questions, which make the present age boil and seethe, like a cauldron, will never be settled, until we have a generation of men who were educated, from childhood, to seek for truth and to revere justice. In the middle of the last century, a great dispute arose among astronomers, respecting one of the planets. Some, in their folly, commenced a war of words, and wrote hot books against each other; others, in their wisdom, improved their telescopes, and soon settled the question forever. Education should imitate the latter. If there are momentous questions which, with present lights, we cannot demonstrate and determine, let us rear up stronger, and purer, and more impartial, minds, for the solemn arbitrament. Let it be for ever and ever inculcated, that no bodily wounds or maim, no deformity of person, nor disease of brain, or lungs, or heart, can be so disabling or so painful, as error; and that he who heals us of our prejudices is a thousand fold more our benefactor, than he who heals us of mortal maladies. Teach children, if you will, to beware of the bite of a mad dog; but teach them still more faithfully, that no horror of water is so fatal as a horror of truth, because it does not come from our leader or our party. Then shall we have more men who will think, as it were, under oath; not thousandth and ten thousandth transmitters of falsity; not copyists of copyists, and blind followers of blind followers; but men who can track the Deity in his ways of wisdom. A love of truth, *a love of truth;* this is the pool of a moral Bethesda, whose waters have miraculous healing. And though we lament that we cannot bequeath to posterity this precious boon, in its perfectness, as the greatest of all patrimonies, yet let us rejoice that we can inspire a love of it, a reverence for it, a devotion to it; and thus circumscribe and weaken whatever is wrong, and enlarge and strengthen whatever is right, in that mixed inheritance of good and evil, which, in the order of Providence, one generation transmits to another.

If we contemplate the subject with the eye of a statesman, what resources are there, in the whole domain of Nature, at all comparable to that vast influx of power which comes into the world with every incoming generation of children? Each embryo life is more wonderful than the globe it is sent to inhabit, and more glorious than the sun upon which it first opens its eyes. Each one of these millions, with a fitting education, is capable of adding something to the sum of human happiness, and of subtracting something from the sum of human misery; and many great souls amongst them there are, who may become instruments for turning the course of nations, as the rivers of water are turned. It is the duty of moral and religious education to employ and administer all these capacities of good, for lofty purposes of human beneficence, as a wise minister employs the resources of a great empire. "*Suffer little children to come unto me,*" said the Savior, "*and forbid them not, for of such is the kingdom of Heaven.*" And who shall dare say, that philanthropy and religion cannot make a better world than the present, from beings like those in the kingdom of Heaven!

Education must be universal. It is well, when the wise and the learned discover new truths; but how much better to diffuse the truths already discovered, amongst the multitude! Every addition to true knowledge is an addition to human power; and while a philosopher is discovering one new truth, millions may be propagated amongst the people. Diffusion, then, rather than discovery, is the duty of our government. With us, the qualification of voters is as important as the qualification of governors, and even comes first, in the natural order. Yet there is no Sabbath of rest, in our contests about the latter, while so little is done to qualify the former. The theory of our government is, not that all men, however unfit, shall be voters, but that every man, by the power of reason and the sense of, duty, shall become fit to be a voter. Education must bring the practice as nearly as possible to the theory. As the children now are, so will the sovereigns soon be. How can we expect the fabric of the government to stand, if vicious materials are daily wrought into its frame-work? Education must prepare our citizens to become municipal officers, intelligent jurors, honest witnesses, legislators, or competent judges of legislation, in fine, to fill all the manifold relations of life. For this end, it must be universal. The whole land must be watered with the streams of knowledge. It is not enough to have, here and there, a beautiful fountain playing in palace-gardens; but let it come like the abundant fatness of the clouds upon the thirsting earth.

Finally, education, alone, can conduct us to that enjoyment which is, at once, best in quality and infinite in quantity. God has revealed to us, not by ambiguous signs, but by His mighty works; not in the disputable language of human invention, but by the solid substance and reality of things, what He holds to be valuable, and what He regards as of little account. The latter He has created sparingly, as though it were nothing worth; while the former He has poured forth with immeasurable munificence. I suppose, all the diamonds ever found, could be hid under a bushel. Their quantity is little, because their value is small. But iron ore, without which mankind would always have been barbarians; without which they would now relapse into barbarism, he has strewed profusely all over the earth. Compare the scantiness of pearl, with the extent of forests and coal-fields. Of one, little has been created, because it is worth little; of the others, much, because they are worth much. His fountains of naphtha, how few, and myrrh and frankincense, how exiguous; but who can fathom His reservoirs of water, or measure the light and the air! This principle pervades every realm of Nature. Creation seems to have been projected upon the plan of increasing the quantity, in the ratio of the intrinsic value. Emphatically is this plan manifested, when we come to that part of creation we call *ourselves*. Enough of the materials of worldly good has been created to answer this great principle, that, up to the point of competence, up to the point of independence and self-respect, few things are more valuable than property; beyond that point, few things are of less. And hence it is, that all acquisitions of property, beyond that point, considered and used as mere property, confer an inferior sort of pleasure, in inferior quantities. However rich a man may be, a certain number of thicknesses of woollens or of silks is all he can comfortably wear. Give him a dozen palaces, he can live in but one at a time. Though the commander be worth the whole regiment, or ship's company, he can have the animal pleasure of eating only his own rations; and any other animal eats, with as much relish as he. Hence the wealthiest, with all their wealth, are driven back to a cultivated mind, to beneficent uses and appropriations; and it is then, and then only, that a glorious vista of happiness opens out into immensity and immortality.

Education, then, is to show to our youth, in early life, this broad line of demarcation between the value of those things which can be owned and enjoyed by but one, and those which can be owned and enjoyed by all. If I own a ship, a house, a farm, or a mass of the metals called precious, my right to them is, in its nature, sole and exclusive. No other man has a right to trade with my ship, to occupy my house, to gather my harvests, or to appropriate my treasures to his use. They are mine, and are incapable, both of a sole and of a joint possession. But not so of the treasures of knowledge, which it is the duty of education to diffuse. The same truth may enrich and ennoble all intelligences at once. Infinite diffusion subtracts nothing from depth. None are made poor because others are made rich. In this part of the Divine economy, the privilege of primogeniture attaches to all; and every son and daughter of Adam are heirs to an infinite patrimony. If I own an exquisite picture or statue, it is mine, exclusively. Even though publicly exhibited, but few could be charmed by its beauties, at the same time. It is incapable of bestowing a pleasure, simultaneous and universal. But not so of the beauty of a moral sentiment; not so of the glow of sublime emotion; not so of the feelings of conscious purity and rectitude. These may shed rapture upon all, without deprivation of any; be imparted, and still possessed; transferred to millions, yet never surrendered; carried out of the world, and still left in it. These may imparadise mankind, and, undiluted, unattenuated, be sent round the whole orb of being. Let education, then, teach children this great truth, written as it is on the fore-front of the universe, that God has so constituted this world, into which He has sent them, that whatever is really and truly valuable may be possessed by all, and possessed in exhaustless abundance.

And now, you, my friends! who feel that you are patriots and lovers of mankind, what bulwarks, what ramparts for freedom can you devise, so enduring and impregnable, as intelligence and virtue! Parents! among the happy groups of children whom you have at home, more dear to you than the blood in the fountain of life, you have not a son nor a daughter who, in this world of temptation, is not destined to encounter perils more dangerous than to walk a bridge of a single plank over a dark and sweeping torrent, beneath. But it is in your power and at your option, with the means which Providence will graciously vouchsafe, to give them that firmness of intellectual movement and that keenness of moral vision, that light of knowledge and that omnipotence of virtue, by which, in the hour of trial, they will be able to walk, with unfaltering step, over the deep and yawning abyss, below, and to reach the opposite shore, in safety, and honor, and happiness.

Twelfth Annual Report of the Secretary of the Massachusetts School Board, 1848

Horace Mann (1796–1859) wrote twelve annual reports in support of public education to the Massachusetts Board of Education during the years that he served as its First Secretary (1837–1848). His reports became famous and helped establish the common school movement. Mann campaigned tirelessly for education, and ultimately his influence extended beyond Massachusetts. In the last report he wrote, he presented an argument for the support of public education through a system of taxation. He believed that society benefited and improved by having an educated public. In a more controversial stance, Mann also argued for non-sectarian schools. He had converted from orthodox Calvinism to Unitarianism as a young person, and believed that common ethical principles across Christianity should be taught, but not doctrines about which different sects disagreed. In advancing non-sectarian schools, the taxpayer would not have to support religious tenets with which she might disagree. —CHB

Without undervaluing any other human agency, it may be safely affirmed that the Common School, improved and energized, as it can easily be, may become the most effective and benignant of all the forces of civilization. Two reasons sustain this position. In the first place, there is a universality in its operation, which can be affirmed of no other institution whatever. If administered in the spirit of justice and conciliation, all the rising generation may be brought within the circle of its reformatory and elevating influences. And, in the second place, the materials upon which it operates are so pliant and ductile as to be susceptible of assuming a greater variety of forms than any other earthly work of the Creator. The inflexibility and ruggedness of the oak, when compared with the lithe sapling or the tender germ, are but feeble emblems to typify the docility of childhood, when contrasted with the obduracy and intractableness of man. It is these inherent advantages of the Common School, which, in our own State, have produced results so striking, from a system so imperfect, and an administration so feeble. In teaching the blind, and the deaf and dumb, in kindling the latent spark of intelligence that lurks in an idiot's mind, and in the more holy work of reforming abandoned and outcast children, education has proved what it can do, by glorious experiments. These wonders, it has done in its infancy, and with the lights of a limited experience; but, when its faculties shall be fully developed, when it shall be trained to wield its mighty energies for the protection of society against the giant vices which now invade and torment it; against intemperance, avarice, war, slavery, bigotry, the woes of want and the wickedness of waste, —then, there will not be a height to which these enemies of the race can escape, which it will not scale, nor a Titan among them all, whom it will not slay.

Now I proceed, then, in endeavoring to show how the true business of the schoolroom connects itself, and becomes identical, with the great interests of society. The former is the infant, immature state of those interests; the latter, their developed, adult state. As "the child is father to the man," so may the training of the schoolroom expand into the institutions and fortunes of the State.

Physical Education

In the worldly, prosperity of mankind, Health and Strength are indispensable ingredients. Reflect, for a moment, what an inroad upon the comfort of a family and its means of support, is a case of chronic sickness or debility, in a single one of its members. Should a farmer contract to support, and to continue to pay his laborer, or a manufacturer his operative, whether able or unable to work, they would demand a serious abatement of wages, as a premium for the risk. But, whatever drawback a sick member would be to the pecuniary prosperity of a family, or a sick laborer to that of an employer bound to support him, just such a drawback is a sick or disabled member of the community to the financial prosperity of the State to which he belongs. The amount of loss consequent upon such sickness or disability may not be drawn out of the public treasury, but it is subtracted from the common property of the State, in a way still more injurious than if the same amount of gold were taken from the public coffers by warrant of the executive. Money, so taken, would be transferred to another hand. It would still exist. But the want of health and strength is a dead loss to the community; and, whenever the next valuation is taken, there wilt be a corresponding deficit in the aggregate of national property. Hence, every citizen, as such, is pecuniarily interested in the health and strength of all his fellow-citizens...

Now modern science has made nothing more certain, than that both good and ill health are the direct result of causes, mainly within our own control. In other words, the health of the race is dependent upon the conduct of the race. The health of the individual is determined primarily by his parents; secondarily, by himself. The vigorous growth of the body, its strength and its activity, its powers of endurance, and its length of life, on the one hand; and dwarfish-ness, sluggishness, infirmity, and premature death, on the other, are all the subjects of unchangeable laws. These laws are ordained of God; but the knowledge of them is left to our diligence, and the observance of them to our free agency. These laws are very few; they are so simple that all can understand them, and so beautiful that the pleasure of contemplating them, even independent of their utility, is a tenfold reward for all the labor of their acquisition. The laws, I repeat, are few. The circumstances, however, under which they are to be applied, are exceedingly various and complicated. These circumstances embrace the almost infinite varieties of our daily life; exercise and rest; sleeping and watching; eating, drinking, and abstinence; the affections and passions; exposure to vicissitudes of temperature, to dryness and humidity, to the effluvia and exhalations of dead animal or decaying vegetable matter; in fine, they embrace all cases where excesses, indiscretions, or exposures, may induce disease; or where exercise, temperance, cleanliness, and pure air, may avert it. Hence it would be wholly impossible to write out any code of "Rules and Regulations," applicable to all cases. So, too, the occasions for applying the laws to new circumstances recur so continually that no man can have a Mentor at his side, in the form of a physician or physiologist, to direct his conduct in new emergencies. Even the most favored individual, in ninety-nine cases in a hundred, must prescribe for himself. And hence the uncompromising necessity that all children should be instructed in these laws; and not only instructed, but that they should receive such a *training*, during the whole course of pupilage, as to enlist the mighty forces of habit on the side of obedience; and that their judgment also should be so developed and matured that they will be able to discriminate between different combinations of circumstances, and to adapt, in each case, the regimen to the exigency . . .

My general conclusion, then, under this head, is, that it is the duty of all the governing minds in society—whether in office or out of it, to diffuse a knowledge of these beautiful and beneficent laws of health and life, throughout the length and breadth of the State; to popularize them; to make them, in the first place, the common acquisition of all, and, through education and custom, the common inheritance of all; so that the healthful habits naturally growing out of their observance, shall be inbred in the people; exemplified in the personal regimen of each individual; incorporated into the economy of every household; observable in all private dwellings, and in all public edifices, especially in those buildings which are erected by capitalists for the residence of their work-people, or for renting to the poorer classes; obeyed, by supplying cities with pure water; by providing public baths, public walks, and public squares; by rural cemeteries; by the drainage and sewerage of populous towns, and in whatever else may promote the general salubrity of the atmosphere; in fine, by a religious observance of all those sanitary regulations with which modern science has blessed the world.

For this thorough diffusion of sanitary intelligence, the Common School is the only agency.

Intellectual Education As a Means of Removing Poverty, and Securing Abundance

Another cardinal object which the government of Massachusetts, and all the influential men in the State should propose to themselves, is the physical well-being of all the people, the sufficiency, comfort, competence, of every individual, in regard to food, raiment, and shelter. And these necessaries and conveniences of life should be obtained by each individual for himself, or by each family for themselves, rather than accepted from the hand of charity, or extorted by poor-laws. It is not averred that this most desirable result can, in all instances, be obtained; but it is, nevertheless, the end to be aimed at. True statesmanship and true political economy, not less than true philanthropy, present this perfect theory as the goal, to be more and more closely approximated by our imperfect practice. The desire to achieve such a result cannot be regarded as an unreasonable ambition; for, though all mankind were well-fed, well-clothed, and well-housed, they might still be but half-civilized.

Poverty is a public as well as a private evil. There is no physical law necessitating its existence. The earth contains abundant resources for ten times, doubtless for twenty times, its present inhabitants. Cold, hunger, and nakedness, are not, like death, an inevitable lot...

According to the European theory, men are divided into classes, some to toil and earn, others to seize and enjoy. According to the Massachusetts theory, all are to have an equal chance for earning, and equal security in the enjoyment of what they earn. The latter tends to equality of condition; the former to the grossest inequalities. Tried by any Christian standard of morals, or even by any of the better sort of heathen standards, can any one hesitate, for a moment, in declaring which of the two will produce the greater amount of human welfare; and which, therefore, is the more conformable to the Divine will? The European theory is blind to what constitutes the highest glory, as well as the highest duty, of a State. Its advocates and admirers are forgetful of that which should be their highest ambition, and proud of that which constitutes their shame. How can any one, possessed of the attributes of humanity, look with satisfaction upon the splendid treasures, the golden regalia, deposited in the Tower of London, or in Windsor Palace, each "an India in itself," while thousands around are dying of starvation; or have been made criminals by the combined forces of temptation and neglect? The present condition of Ireland cancels all the glories of the British crown. The brilliant conception which symbolizes the nationality of Great Britain as a superb temple, whose massive and grand proportions are upheld and adorned by the four hundred and thirty Corinthian columns of the aristocracy, is turned into a loathing and a scorn, when we behold the five millions of paupers that cower and shiver at its base. The galleries and fountains of Versailles, the Louvre of Paris, her Notre Dame, and her Madeleine, though multiplied by thousands in number and in brilliancy, would be no atonement for the hundred thousand Parisian *ouvriers*, without bread and without work. The galleries of painting and of sculpture, at Rome, at Munich, or at Dresden, which body forth the divinest ideals ever executed or ever conceived, are but an abomination in the sight of Heaven and of all good men, while actual, living beings, beings that have hearts to palpitate, and nerves to agonize, and affections to be crushed or corrupted, are experimenting, all around them, upon the capacities of human nature for suffering and for sin...

If one class possesses all the wealth and the education, while the residue of society is ignorant and poor, it matters not by what name the relation between them may be called; the latter, in fact and in truth, will be the servile dependants and subjects of the former. But if education be equably diffused, it will draw property after it, by the strongest of all attractions; for such a thing never did happen, and never can happen, as that an intelligent and practical body of men should be permanently poor. Property and labor, in different classes, are essentially antagonistic; but property and labor, in the same class, are essentially fraternal. The people of Massachusetts have, in some degree, appreciated the truth, that the unexampled prosperity of the State, its comfort, its competence, its general intelligence and virtue, is attributable to the education, more or less perfect, which all its people have received; but are they sensible of a fact equally important?—namely, that it is to this same education that two thirds of the people are indebted for not being, to-day, the vassals of as severe a tyranny, in the form of capital, as the lower classes of Europe are bound to in the form of brute force.

Education, then, beyond all other devices of human origin, is the great equalizer of the conditions of men—the balance-wheel of the social machinery. I do not here mean that it so elevates the moral nature as to make men disdain and abhor the oppression of their fellow-men. This idea pertains to another of its attributes. But I mean that it gives each man the independence and the means, by which he can resist the selfishness of other men. It does better than to disarm the poor of their hostility towards the rich; it prevents being poor. Agrarianism is the revenge of poverty against wealth. The wanton destruction of the property of others, the burning of hay-ricks and corn-ricks, the demolition of machinery, because it supersedes hand-labor, the sprinkling of vitriol on rich dresses, is only agrarianism run mad. Education prevents both the revenge and the madness. On the other hand, a fellow-feeling for one's class or caste is the common instinct of hearts not wholly sunk in selfish regards for person, or for family. The spread of education, by enlarging the cultivated class or caste, will open a wider area over which the social feelings will expand; and, if this education should be universal and complete, it would do more than all things else to obliterate factitious distinctions in society.

The main idea set forth in the creeds of some political reformers, or revolutionizers, is that some people are poor *because* others are rich. This idea supposes a fixed amount of property in the community, which, by fraud or force, or arbitrary law, is unequally divided among men; and the problem presented for solution is, how to transfer a portion of this property from those who are supposed to have too much, to those who feel and know that they have too little. At this point, both their theory and their expectation of reform stop. But the beneficent power of education would not be exhausted, even though it should peaceably abolish all the miseries that spring from the coexistence, side by side, of enormous wealth and squalid want. It has a higher function. Beyond the power of diffusing old wealth, it has the prerogative of creating new. It is a thousand times more lucrative than fraud; and adds a thousandfold more to a nation's resources than the most successful conquests. Knaves and robbers can obtain only what was before possessed by others. But education creates or develops new treasures, treasures not before possessed or dreamed of by any one. . . .

For the creation of wealth, then, for the existence of a wealthy people and a wealthy nation, intelligence is the grand condition. The number of improvers will increase, as the intellectual constituency, if I may so call it, increases. In former times, and in most parts of the world even at the present day, not one man in a million has ever had such a development of mind, as made it possible for him to become a contributor to art or science. Let this development precede, and contributions, numberless, and of inestimable value, will be sure to follow. That Political Economy, therefore, which busies itself about capital and labor, supply and demand, interest and rents, favorable and unfavorable balances of trade; but leaves out of account the element of a wide-spread mental development, is nought but stupendous folly. The greatest of all the arts in political economy is, to change a consumer into a producer; and the next greatest is to increase the producer's producing power; an end to be directly attained, by increasing his intelligence.

Political Education

The necessity of general intelligence, that is, of education, (for I use the terms as substantially synonymous; because general intelligence can never exist without general education, and general education will be sure to produce general intelligence,)—the necessity of general intelligence, under a republican form of government, like most other very important truths, has become a very trite one. It is so trite, indeed, as to have lost much of its force by its familiarity. Almost all the champions of education seize upon this argument, first of all; because it is so simple as to be understood by the ignorant, and so strong as to convince the skeptical. Nothing would be easier than to follow in the train of so many writers, and to demonstrate, by logic, by history, and by the nature of the case, that a republican form of government, without intelligence in the people, must be, on a vast scale, what a madhouse, without superintendent or keepers, would be, on a small one. . . .

However elevated the moral character of a constituency may be; however well informed in matters of general science or history, yet they must, if citizens of a Republic understand something of the true nature and functions of the government under which they live. That any one who is to participate in the government of a country, when he becomes a man, should receive no instruction respecting the nature and functions of the government he is afterwards to administer, is a political solecism. In all nations, hardly excepting the most rude and barbarous, the future sovereign receives some training which is supposed to fit him for the exercise of the powers and duties of his anticipated station.... Hence, the constitution of the United States, and of our own State, should be made a study in our Public Schools. The partition of the powers of government into the three co-ordinate branches, legislative, judicial, and executive, with the duties appropriately devolving upon each; the mode of electing or of appointing all officers, with the reason on which it was founded; and, especially, the duty of every citizen, in a government of laws, to appeal to the courts for redress, in all cases of alleged wrong, instead of undertaking to vindicate his own rights by his own arm; and, in a government where the people are the acknowledged sources of power, the duty of changing laws and rulers by an appeal to the ballot, and not by rebellion, should be taught to all the children until they are fully understood.

Moral Education

Moral education is a primal necessity of social existence. The unrestrained passions of men are not only homicidal, but suicidal; and a community without a conscience would soon extinguish itself. Even with a natural conscience, how often has Evil triumphed over Good! From the beginning of time, Wrong has followed Right, as the shadow the substance.... The government sees the evils that come from the use of intoxicating drinks, and prohibits their sale; but unprincipled men pander to depraved appetites, and gather a harvest of dishonest profits. Instead of licensing lotteries, and deriving a revenue from the sale of tickets, the State forbids the mischievous traffic; but while law-abiding men disdain to practise an illicit trade, knavish brokers, by means of the prohibition itself, secure a monopoly of the sales, and pocket the infamous gain. The government imposes duties on imported goods; smugglers evade the law, and bring goods into the country clandestinely; or perjurers swear to false invoices, and escape the payment of duty, and thus secure to themselves the double advantage of increased sales, and enhanced profits upon what is sold. Science prepares a new medicine to heal or alleviate the diseases of men; crime adulterates it, or prepares, as a substitute, some cheap poison that resembles it, and can be sold instead of it. A benefactor of the race discovers an agent which has the marvellous power to suspend consciousness, and take away the susceptibility of pain; a villain uses it to rob men or pollute women. Houses are built; the incendiary burns them, that he may purloin the smallest portion of their goods. The press is invented to spread intelligence; but libellers use it to give wings to slander. And, so, throughout all the infinitely complex and ramified relations of society, wherever there is a right there may be a wrong; and wherever a law is made to repress the wrong, it may be evaded by artifice or overborne by violence. In fine, all means and laws designed to repress injustice and crime, give occasion to new injustice and crime. For every lock that is made, a false key is made to pick it; and for every Paradise that is created, there is a Satan who would scale its walls . . .

Education has never yet been brought to bear with one hundredth part of its potential force, upon the natures of children, and, through them, upon the character of men, and of the race. In all the attempts to reform mankind which have hitherto been made, whether by changing the frame of government, by aggravating or softening the severity of the penal code, or by substituting a government-created, for a God-created religion; in all these attempts, the infantile and youthful mind, its amenability to influences, and the enduring and self-operating character of the influences it receives, have been almost wholly unrecognized. Here, then, is a new agency, whose powers are but just beginning to be understood, and whose mighty energies, hitherto, have been but feebly invoked; and yet, from our experience, limited and imperfect as it is, we do know that, far beyond any other earthly instrumentality, it is comprehensive and decisive.

Religious Education

. . . On this subject, I propose to speak with freedom and plainness, and more at length than I should feel required to do, but for the peculiar circumstances in which I have been placed. It is matter of notoriety, that the views of the Board of Education, and my own, perhaps still more than those of the Board, on the subject of religious instruction in our Public Schools, have been subjected to animadversion. Grave charges have been made against us, that our purpose was to exclude religion; and to exclude that, too, which is the common exponent of religion, the Bible, from the Common Schools of the State; or, at least, to derogate from its authority, and destroy its influence in them. Whatever prevalence a suspicion of the truth of these imputations may heretofore had, I have reason to believe that further inquiry and examination have done much to disabuse the too credulous recipients of so groundless a charge. Still, amongst a people so commendably sensitive on the subject of religion, as are the people of Massachusetts, any suspicion of irreligious tendencies, will greatly prejudice any cause, and, so far as any cause may otherwise have the power of doing good, will greatly impair that power.

It is known, too, that our noble system of Free Schools for the whole people, is strenuously opposed; by a few persons in our own State, and by no inconsiderable numbers in some of the other states of this Union; and that a rival system of "Parochial" or "Sectarian Schools," is now urged upon the public by a numerous, a powerful, and a well-organized body of men.

It has pleased the advocates of this rival system, in various public addresses, in reports, and through periodicals devoted to their cause, to denounce our system as irreligious and anti-Christian. They do not trouble themselves to describe what our system is, but adopt a more summary way to forestall public opinion against it, by using general epithets of reproach, and signals of alarm . . .

All the schemes ever devised by governments, to secure the prevalence and permanence of religion among the people, however variant in form they may have been, are substantially resolvable into two systems. One of these systems holds the regulation and control of the religious belief of the people to be one of the functions of government, like the command of the army or the navy, or the establishment of courts, or the collection of revenues. According to the other system, religious belief is a matter of individual and parental concern; and, while the government furnishes all practicable facilities for the independent formation of that belief, it exercises no authority to prescribe, or coercion to enforce it. The former is the system, which, with very few exceptions, has prevailed throughout Christendom, for fifteen hundred years. Our own government is almost a solitary example among the nations of the earth, where freedom of opinion and the inviolability of conscience have been even theoretically recognized by the law . . .

The very terms, *Public School,* and *Common School,* bear upon their face, that they are schools which the children of the entire community may attend. Every man, not on the pauper list, is taxed for their support. But he is not taxed to support them as special religious institutions; if he were, it would satisfy, at once, the largest definition of a Religious Establishment. But he is taxed to support them, as a *preventive* means against dishonesty, against fraud, and against violence; on the same principle that he is taxed to support criminal courts as a *punitive* means against the same offences. He is taxed to support schools, on the same principle that he is taxed to support paupers; because a child without education is poorer and more wretched than a man without bread. He is taxed to support schools, on the same principle that he would be taxed to defend the nation against foreign invasion, or against rapine committed by a foreign foe: because the general prevalence of ignorance, superstition, and vice, will breed Goth and Vandal at home, more fatal to the public well-being, than any Goth or Vandal from abroad. And, finally, he is taxed to support schools, because they are the most effective means of developing and training those powers and faculties in a child, by which, when he becomes a man, he may understand what his highest interests and his highest duties are; and may be, in fact, and not in name only, a free agent . . .

If, then, a government would recognize and protect the rights of religious freedom, it must abstain from subjugating the capacities of its children to any legal standard of religious faith, with as great fidelity as it abstains from controlling the opinions of men. It must meet the unquestionable fact, that the old spirit of religious domination is adopting new measures to accomplish its work, measures, which, if successful, will be as fatal to the liberties of mankind, as those which were practised in by-gone days of violence and terror. These new measures are aimed at children instead of men. They propose to supersede the necessity of subduing free thought, *in the mind of the adult,* by forestalling the development of any capacity of free thought, *in the mind of the child.* They expect to find it easier to subdue the free agency of children, by binding them in fetters of bigotry, than to subdue the free agency of men, by binding them in fetters of iron. For this purpose, some are attempting to deprive children of their right to labor, and, of course, of their daily bread, unless they will attend a government school, and receive its sectarian instruction. Some are attempting to withhold all means, even of secular education, from the poor, and thus punish them with ignorance, unless, with the secular knowledge which they desire, they will accept theological knowledge which they condemn. Others, still, are striving to break down all free Public School systems, where they exist, and to prevent their establishment, where they do not exist, in the hope, that on the downfall of these, their system will succeed. The sovereign antidote against these machinations, is, Free Schools for all, and the right of every parent to determine the religious education of his children.

This topic invites far more extended exposition; but this must suffice. In bidding an official Farewell to a system, with which I have been so long connected, to which I have devoted my means, my strength, my health, twelve years of time, and, doubtless, twice that number of years from what might otherwise have been my term of life, I have felt bound to submit these brief views in its defence. In justice to my own name and memory; in justice to the Board of which I was originally a member, and from which I have always sought counsel and guidance; and in justice to thousands of the most wise, upright, and religious-minded men in Massachusetts, who have been my fellow-laborers in advancing the great cause of Popular Education, under the auspices of this system, I have felt bound to vindicate it from the aspersions cast upon it, and to show its consonance with the eternal principles of equity and justice. I have felt bound to show, that, so far from its being an irreligious, an anti-Christian, or an un-Christian system, it is a system which recognizes religious obligations in their fullest extent; that it is a system which invokes a religious spirit, and can never be fitly administered without such a spirit; that it inculcates the great commands, upon which hang all the law and the prophets; that it welcomes the Bible, and therefore welcomes all the doctrines which the Bible really contains, and that it listens to these doctrines so reverently, that, for the time being, it will not suffer any rash mortal to thrust in his interpolations of their meaning, or overlay the text with any of the "many inventions" which the heart of man has sought out. It is a system, however, which leaves open all other means of instruction, the pulpits, the Sunday schools, the Bible classes, the catechisms, of all denominations, to be employed according to the preferences of individual parents. It is a system which restrains itself from teaching, that what it does teach is all that needs to be taught, or that should be taught; but leaves this to be decided by each man for himself, according to the light of his reason and conscience; and on his responsibility to that Great Being, who, in holding him to an account for the things done in the body, will hold him to the strictest account for the manner in which he has "trained up" his children.

Such, then, in a religious point of view, is the Massachusetts system of Common Schools. Reverently, it recognizes and affirms the sovereign rights of the Creator; sedulously and sacredly it guards the religious rights of the creature; while it seeks to remove all hinderances, and to supply all furtherances to a filial and paternal communion between man and his Maker, in a social and political sense, it is a *Free* school system. It knows no distinction of rich and poor, of bond and free, or between those who, in the imperfect light of this world, are seeking, through different avenues, to reach the gate of heaven. Without money and without price, it throws open its doors, and spreads the table of its bounty, for all the children of the State. Like the sun, it shines, not only upon the good, but upon the evil, that they may become good; and, like the rain, its blessings descend, not only upon the just, but upon the unjust, that their injustice may depart from them and be known no more.

To the great founders of this system, we look back with filial reverence and love. Amid the barrenness of the land, and in utter destitution of wealth, they coined the rude comforts, and even the necessaries of life, into means for its generous support. Though, as laborers by day, they subdued the wilderness, and, as sentinels by night, they guarded the camp, yet they found time for the vigilant administration and oversight of the schools, in the day of their infancy and weakness. But for this single institution, into which they transfused so much of their means and of their strength, and of which they have made us the inheritors, how different would our lot and our life have been! Upon us, its accumulated blessings have descended. It has saved us from innumerable pains and perils, that would otherwise have been our fate; from the physical wretchedness, that is impotent to work out its own relief; from the darkness of the intellect, whose wanderings after light so often plunge it into deeper gloom; and from the moral debasement, whose pleasures are vices and crimes. It has surrounded us with a profusion of comforts and blessings, of which the most poetic imagination would never otherwise have conceived. It has found, not mythologic goddesses, but gigantic and tireless laborers in every stream; not evil and vindictive spirits, but beneficent and helping ones, in all the elements; and, by a pro-founder alchemy than the schoolmen ever dreamed of, it transmutes quarries and ice fields into gold. It has given cunning to the hand of the mechanic, keenness to the artisan's eye, and made a sterile soil grow grateful beneath the skill of the husbandman. Hence, the absence of poverty among our native population; hence, a competency for the whole people, the means for mental and moral improvement, and for giving embellishment and dignity to life, such as the world has never known before, and such as no where else can be found upon the face of the earth . . .

But not the fortunes of our children alone, or of our children's children, are dependant upon us. The influences of our conduct extend outward in space, as well as onward in time. We are part of a mighty nation, which has just embarked upon the grandest experiment ever yet attempted upon earth; the experiment of the capacity of mankind for the wise and righteous government of themselves.

12

Report of the Committee on Education of the House of Representatives

Allen Dodge, 1840

Today we often take the current public school system for granted. Yet, Horace Mann's arguments for a nonsectarian public school system were hotly contested during his time. The following report concerning the establishment of a Board of Education in Massachusetts reveals a number of concerns with the emerging centralized system of public education. A significant group of Americans believed the growing public school system might undermine voluntary teacher initiative, local control, religious freedom, and parental rights—issues that still plague public education today. Overall, they considered the new public school system to be a threat rather than an aid to American democracy. —PLG

House of Representatives, March 7th, 1840.

The Committee on Education having been directed by an order of the House of the 3d inst., to consider the expediency of abolishing the Board of Education and the Normal Schools, and to report by bill or otherwise, have attended to that duty, and respectfully submit the following REPORT:

American Educational Thought: Essays from 1640–1940, pages 177–185
Copyright © 2010 by Information Age Publishing

In entering upon the duties entrusted to them, your Committee were fully aware of the difficulties with which it is encompassed. Their inquiry extends to the principles, operation and probable effects of an institution, organized by a former Legislature, to promote the great interest of common schools. A period of nearly three years has elapsed, since the act of the Legislature which established the Board of Education; two successive legislatures have acquiesced in its existence, and the three annual reports of the Board and their Secretary, have borne strong testimony to its beneficial influence. Under these circumstances, for your Committee to give an opposite testimony, might seem to savor of temerity—not to say, of presumption. But your Committee, in the faithful performance of their duty, do not shrink from encountering this charge; —they cannot allow themselves to be deterred from expressing the deliberate conclusions of their judgment, by the fear of this or any other imputation. Their apprehensions spring from a different source. An attempt may be made to identify the interests of common schools with the existence of the Board of Education, and any objections to that Board, may, perhaps, be regarded by some, as a covert assault upon our long established system of public instruction. But since our system of public schools did not owe its origin to the Board of Education, but was in existence for two centuries before that Board was established, a proposal to dispense with its further services cannot be reasonably considered as indicating any feelings of hostility or of indifference, towards our system of common schools. It is, indeed, the attachment of your Committee to that system, which has induced them to investigate, with care and attention, the tendencies of the Board of Education. And it is the conclusion to which they have arrived, that the operations of that Board are incompatible with those principles upon which our common schools have been founded and maintained, that leads them to make this report.

The first question to be considered, is, what is the power of the Board of Education? Upon this point very great differences of opinion appear to prevail. By the terms of the act, the board seems to have only a power of recommending, but it is the opinion of many that this power of recommendation, exercised by such a board, must of necessity be soon converted into a power of regulation; and even if it were not, the vantage ground which such a board occupies, must obviously give it, for all practical purposes, an equivalent power. One manifest means by which this power of recommending measures, may become, and, in several instances, has already become equivalent to a power of regulation, is to be found in the circumstance that the Legislature will naturally lend a ready ear to the suggestions of the board, and will be apt, without much examination, to clothe with a legal sanction such rules and regulations, as the board may recommend. It would thus appear that the board has a tendency, and a strong tendency, to engross to itself the entire regulation of our common schools, and practically to convert the Legislature into a mere instrument for carrying its plans into execution. If, however, this result should be disclaimed, and the Legislature is left as independent as before, and with the same feeling of responsibility for all enactments on the subject of schools, the Board seems to be useless, for the Legislature will not lack suggestions from a variety of other quarters, equally well adapted to furnish them. If, then, the board has any actual power, it is a dangerous power, trenching directly upon the rights and duties of the Legislature; if it has no power, why continue its existence, at an annual expense to the Commonwealth?

As a mere organ for the collection and diffusion of information on the subject of education, the Board seems to your Committee to be, in several respects, very much inferior to those voluntary associations of teachers, which preceded the existence of the board, and which, perhaps, suggested the idea of it. In these voluntary associations a vast number of persons are interested; a spirit of emulation exists, and each member is anxious to distinguish himself by his contributions to the common cause. Indeed the Board of Education has found itself obliged to have recourse to these very associations, as a principal means for carrying out its plans. But it is obvious to your Committee, that conventions of teachers called by authority, and subjected to a foreign control, will not feel themselves free to act, they will not feel a due responsibility, and will not share the zeal and emulation to be expected in associations purely voluntary. As your Committee have already stated, these associations of teachers were in existence before the Board was established, and, from the best information your Committee have been able to obtain, instead of increasing they have, in some places, declined in interest and utility, since they were taken under the patronage of the Board.

Considering the degree of interest which pervades this community on the subject of education, and the large number of intelligent persons whose lives are devoted to that profession, your Committee do not apprehend that any discoveries, which may be made in the art or science of teaching, will remain undisseminated, through want of zeal to spread information or of disposition to acquire it. Your Committee can well imagine that in a different state of society,—such as is to be found in the newly settled States,—where common schools are a novelty and teachers are generally ill qualified for their office, some artificial means, such as a Board of Education, might be useful, in stimulating a spirit of inquiry and in disseminating knowledge. But among us, with so many accomplished teachers, a public Board, established for the benefit of the profession of teaching, seems as little needed as a public Board for the benefit of Divinity, Medicine, or the Law. Undoubtedly, in all these professions, great improvements might be made, but it is better to leave them to private industry and free competition, than for the Legislature to put them under the superintendence of an official Board.

The true way to judge of the practical operations of the Board of Education, is not merely to consult the statutes by which the Board is established, but also to examine its own reports. They will furnish an unquestionable means of discovering what are the objects, which the Board actually proposes for itself. A very cursory examination of these documents, will suffice to show that, so far from continuing our system of public instruction, upon the plan upon which it was founded, and according to which it has been so long and so successfully carried on, the aim of the Board appears to be, to re-model it altogether after the example of the French and Prussian systems.

These systems have a Central Board, which supplies the ignorance and incapacity of the administrators of local affairs, and which models the schools of France and Prussia, all upon one plan, as uniform and exact as the discipline of an army. On the other hand, our system of public instruction has proceeded upon the idea, that the local administrators of affairs, that is to say, the school committees of the several towns and districts, are qualified to superintend the schools, and might best be trusted with that superintendence. This different method of operating is not confined to public schools, but extends to every other department of life. In France or Prussia, the smallest bridge cannot be built, or any village road repaired, until a Central Board has been consulted,—a plan, which, in its practical operations, and notwithstanding the science of the Central Board, and the skill of the engineers whom it has at command, is found not at all comparable with our system of local authority.

De Tocqueville, whose work upon America has been so much admired, dwells at great length and with great emphasis, upon the advantages which New England derives from its excellent system of local authority; while he points out the want of local public spirit in the countries of Europe, and the deficiency of interest in local affairs, as the greatest obstacle in the way of public improvements. This system of local authority is as beneficial to the schools, as to any thing else. It interests a vast number of people in their welfare, whose zeal and activity, if they find themselves likely to be overshadowed by the controlling power of a Central Board, will be apt to grow faint. Improvements, which a teacher or school committee have themselves hit upon, will be likely to be pushed with much more spirit, than those which are suggested, or, as it were, commanded, by a foreign and distant power.

After all that has been said about the French and Prussian systems, they appear to your Committee to be much more admirable as a means of political influence, and of strengthening the hands of the government, than as a mere means for the diffusion of knowledge. For the latter purpose, the system of public common schools, under the control of persons most interested in their flourishing condition, who pay taxes to support them, appears to your Committee much superior. The establishment of the Board of Education, seems to be the commencement of a system of centralization and of monopoly of power in a few hands, contrary, in every respect, to the true spirit of our democratical institutions, and which, unless speedily checked, may lead to unlooked for and dangerous results.

As to the practical operation of this centralizing system, your Committee would observe, that some of the rules and regulations already devised by the Board of Education, and, doubtless, considered by it as of a very useful tendency, have proved, when carried into execution in the schools, very embarrassing, and have engrossed much of the time and attention of the teachers, which might better have been bestowed upon the instruction of their pupils, than in making out minute and complicated registers of statistics. The Board passes new regulations respecting the returns to be made out by the school committees, and sends forth its blanks; the school committees are abruptly notified of them, without being informed of the reasons upon which they are founded. The rules and regulations become so numerous and complicated, as to be difficult of apprehension as well as of execution. Indeed, a periodical commentary seems necessary, from the secretary of the board, in order to enable school committees to discharge their duties. Your committee are strongly of opinion, that nothing but a prevailing impression, well or ill founded, that a compliance with the rules and regulations of the Board, is necessary to secure to towns their annual share of the school fund, has enabled those rules and regulations to be at all regarded. The multiplicity and complexity of laws, with respect to any subject, are matter of just complaint; and this is especially the case with respect to common schools, the teachers of which have a great variety of arduous duties, which must, of necessity, be performed, and which ought not to be aggravated by any requirements, not essential to the welfare of the schools. A Central Board, the members of which are not practical teachers, will be easily led to imagine, that minute statistical facts and other like information, may be obtained at a much less expense of valuable time, than is actually needed for procuring them.

Your Committee have already stated that the French and Prussian system of public schools appears to have been devised more for the purpose of modifying the sentiments and opinions of the rising generation, according to a certain government standard, than as a mere means of diffusing elementary knowledge. Undoubtedly, common schools may be used as a potent means of engrafting into the minds of children, political, religious and moral opinions;—but, in a country like this, where such diversity of sentiments exists, especially upon theological subjects, and where morality is considered a part of religion, and is, to some extent, modified by sectarian views, the difficulty and danger of attempting to introduce these subjects into our schools, according to one fixed and settled plan, to be devised by a Central Board, must be obvious. The right to mould the political, moral and religious opinions of his children, is a right exclusively and jealously reserved by our own laws to every parent; and for the government to attempt, directly or indirectly, as to these matters, to stand in the parent's place, is an undertaking of very questionable policy. Such an attempt cannot fail to excite a feeling of jealousy, with respect to our public schools, the results of which could not but be disastrous.

A prominent measure, already brought forward by the Board of Education, as a means of moulding the sentiments of the rising generation, is the project of furnishing, under the sanction of the Board, a school library for each district in the Commonwealth. It is professed, indeed, that the matter selected for this library, will be free both from sectarian and political objections. Unquestionably, the board will endeavor to render it so. Since, however, religion and politics, in this free country, are so intimately connected with every other subject, the accomplishment of that object is utterly impossible, nor would it be desirable, if possible. That must, indeed, be an uninteresting course of reading, which would leave untouched either of these subjects; and he must be a heartless writer, who can treat religious or political subjects, without affording any indication of his political or religious opinions. Books, which confine themselves to the mere statement of undisputed propositions, whether in politics, religion, or morals, must be meagre indeed; nor is it possible to abstract, from treatises on these subjects, all that would give offence, without abstracting, at the same time, the whole substance of the matter. Mere abstract propositions are of very little interest—it is their practical application to particular cases, in which all readers, and especially young readers, are principally interested. It is not sufficient, and it ought not to be, that a book contains nothing which we believe to be false. If it omit to state what we believe to be true; if it founds itself upon vague generalities, which will equally serve the purpose of all reasoners alike, this very omission to state what we believe to be the truth, becomes, in our eyes, a fault of the most serious character. A book, upon politics, morals, or religion, containing no party or sectarian views, will be apt to contain no distinct views of any kind, and will be likely to leave the mind in a state of doubt and skepticism, much more to be deplored than any party or sectarian bias.

If a taste for reading exist in our common schools, considering the cheapness and multiplicity of books, and the vast number of pens devoted to the supply of intellectual wants, it cannot be doubted that, according to the ordinary rules of demand and supply, books adapted for the purpose of a school library will be furnished, as fast as they are needed; and out of the books, thus produced, every school committee would be at liberty to make a selection, adapted to the wants and wishes of their district. The question whether the public money should be appropriated to aid the school districts in providing themselves with books, is a question as to which your Committee do not feel themselves called upon to express any opinion. That question, however, is very different from the question whether the Commonwealth shall aid, by an appropriation of the public money, and by lending its countenance and patronage to give an artificial circulation, to a particular set of books. Your Committee have no doubts as to the inexpediency of such a proceeding.

Another project, imitated from France and Prussia, and set on foot under the superintendence of the Board of Education, is the establishment of Normal schools. Your Committee approach this subject with some delicacy, inasmuch as one half the expense of the two Normal schools already established, has been sustained by private munificence. If, however, no benefit in proportion to the money spent, is derived from these schools, it is our duty, as legislators, in justice not only to the Commonwealth but to the private donor, to discontinue the project. Comparing the two Normal Schools already established with the Academies and High Schools of the Commonwealth, they do not appear to your Committee to present any peculiar or distinguishing advantages.

Academies and High Schools, cost the Commonwealth nothing, and they are fully adequate, in the opinion of your Committee, to furnish a competent supply of teachers. In years past, they have not only supplied our own schools with competent teachers, but have annually furnished hundreds to the west and the south. There is a high degree of competition existing between these Academies, which is the best guaranty for excellence. It is insisted by the Board, however, that the art of teaching is a peculiar art, which is particularly and exclusively taught at Normal Schools; but it appears to your Committee, that every person, who has himself undergone a process of instruction, must acquire, by that very process, the art of instructing others. This certainly will be the case with every person of intelligence;—if intelligence be wanting, no system of instruction can supply its place. An intelligent mechanic, who has learned his trade, is competent, by that very fact, to instruct others in it, and needs no Normal School to teach him the art of teaching his apprentices.

Considering that our District Schools are kept, on an average, for only three or four months in the year, it is obviously impossible, and, perhaps, it is not desirable, that the business of keeping these schools should become a distinct and separate profession, which the establishment of Normal Schools seems to anticipate.

Even if these schools did furnish any peculiar and distinguishing advantages, we have no adequate security that the teachers, thus taught at the public expense, will remain in the Commonwealth; and it seems hardly just that Massachusetts, in the present state of her finances, should be called upon to educate, at her own cost, teachers for the rest of the Union.

If it be true, that the teachers of any of our District Schools, are insufficiently qualified for the task, the difficulty originates, as it appears to your Committee, not in any deficiency of the means of obtaining ample qualifications, but in insufficiency of compensation. Those districts which are inclined to pay competent wages, can at all times be supplied with competent teachers; and the want of means or inclination to pay an adequate salary, is not a want which Normal Schools have any tendency to supply.

From the number of scholars who have hitherto attended the Normal Schools, established by the Board of Education, it does not appear, that any want of such institutions, is seriously felt. The number of pupils falls far short of the average number in our Academies and High Schools.

It may be suggested, that to abolish these Normal Schools, when they have been in operation for so short a time, is not to give the experiment a fair trial. But the objections of your Committee, as will appear from the considerations above submitted, are of a general and fundamental nature, and they do not consider it advisable to persevere in an experiment, of the inutility of which they are perfectly satisfied. In fact, these schools do not appear to your Committee, to have any stronger claims on the public treasury, for an appropriation of two thousand dollars a year, than many of our Academies and High Schools.

Should the Normal Schools be discontinued by the Legislature, it is but just and reasonable, in the opinion of your Committee, that the sums advanced by the individual, who has generously contributed to the support of those schools, should be refunded; which might be done, by an appropriation of probably five or six hundred dollars, in addition to the money not yet expended, in the hands of the treasurer of the fund.

The Secretary of the Board of Education, stated, in his argument before your Committee on the subject of Normal Schools, that engagements with the teachers of those schools and other parties interested, had been entered into for a term of three years; and he argued, that it would be improper for the Legislature to disturb these contracts. With respect to these contracts, your Committee are decidedly of opinion, that they ought never to have been made, except with the express understanding of a liability to be rescinded or modified, at the pleasure of the Legislature. If, however, they have been otherwise made, and if any individuals shall appear to have any reasonable claim to be remunerated for any disappointment, occasioned by discontinuing the schools, the Legislature have the power to make such remuneration; and your Committee believe, that the sooner such a settlement is made, the better,—inasmuch as an increase in the number of the schools, as contemplated by the board, would increase the difficulty and cost of such a settlement.

In conclusion, the idea of the State controlling Education, whether by establishing a Central Board, by allowing that Board to sanction a particular Library, or by organizing Normal Schools, seems to your Committee a great departure from the uniform spirit of our institutions,—a dangerous precedent and an interference with a matter more properly belonging to those hands, to which our ancestors wisely entrusted it. It is greatly to be feared, that any attempt to form all our schools and all our teachers, upon one model, would destroy all competition,—all emulation, and even the spirit of improvement itself. When a large number of teachers and school committees, are all aiming at improvement, as is doubtless the case to a great extent in this Commonwealth, improvements seem much more likely to be found out and carried into practice, than when the chief right of experimenting is vested in a Central Board.

With these views, your Committee have come to the conclusion, that the interests of our common schools would rest upon a safer and more solid foundation, if the Board of Education and the Normal Schools were abolished. Your Committee would, therefore, recommend the passage of the following bill.

For the committee,
ALLEN W. DODGE

13

The Catholic Response to Protestantism in Public Schools

Various Documents, 1840

The Protestant nature of the emerging public school system often came in conflict with the growing Catholic population. Catholics opposed the prevalent practice of reading from the King James Version of the Bible without comment, because they felt it fostered the Protestant doctrine of the private interpretation of Scripture. In addition, Catholics complained about the recitation of Protestant hymns and prayers, and the anti-Catholicism evident in public school textbooks. The Catholic hierarchy attempted to protect Catholic children from Protestant influence by creating their own school system. Due to the financial burden of such an enterprise, they often requested government aid for their schools. The following documents are an example of one of the most famous of these incidents. Bishop John Hughes attempted to obtain state aid in New York for Catholic parochial schools. However, even with the support of the governor, the state senate voted down Hughes' proposals. In fact, as the last document illustrates, Catholic pleas for state aid only galvanized the Protestant opposition to government monetary support for parochial schools. —PLG

American Educational Thought: Essays from 1640–1940, pages 187–202
Copyright © 2010 by Information Age Publishing

Petition of the Catholics of the City of New York
Thomas O' Connor, 1840

To the Honorable the Board of Aldermen of the City of New York:
The Petition of the Catholics of New York Respectfully Presents:

That your petitioners yield to no class in their performance of, and disposition to perform, all the duties of citizens. They bear, and are willing to bear their portion of every common burden; and feel themselves entitled to a participation in every common benefit.

This participation, they regret to say, has been denied them for years back, in reference to common school education in the City of New York, except on conditions with which their conscience, and, as they believe, their duty to God, did not, and does not leave them at liberty to comply.

The rights of conscience, in this country, are held by both the Constitution and universal consent, to be sacred and inviolable. No stronger evidence of this need be adduced than the fact, that one class of citizens are exempted from the duty or obligation of defending their country against an invading foe, out of delicacy and deference to the rights of conscience which forbids them to take up arms for any purpose.

Your petitioners only claim the benefit of this principle, in regard to the public education of their children. They regard the public education which the State has provided as a common benefit, in which they are most desirous, and feel that they are entitled, to participate; and therefore they pray your Honorable Body that they may be permitted to do so, without violating their conscience.

But your petitioners do not ask that this prayer be granted without assigning their reasons for preferring it. In ordinary cases men are not required to assign the motives of conscientious scruples in matters of this kind. But your petitioners are aware that a large, wealthy, and concentrated influence is directed against their claim by the corporation called the Public School Society. And that this influence, acting on a public opinion already but too much predisposed to judge unfavorably of the claims of your petitioners, requires to be met by facts which justify them in thus appealing to your Honorable Body, and which may, at the same time, convey a more correct impression to the public mind. Your petitioners adopt this course the more willingly, because the justice, and impartiality which distinguish the decisions of public men, in this country, inspire them with the confidence that your Honorable Body will maintain, in their regard, the principle of the rights of conscience, if it can be done without violating the rights of others, and on no other condition is the claim solicited.

It is not deemed necessary to trouble your Honorable Body with a detail of the circumstances by which the monopoly of the public education of children in the City of New York, and of the funds provided for that purpose at the expense of the State, have passed into the hands of a private corporation, styled in its act of charter, "The Public School Society of the City of New York." It is composed of men of different sects or denominations. But that denomination, Friends [Quakers], which is believed to have the controlling influence, both by its numbers and otherwise, holds as a peculiar *sectarian principle* that any formal or official teaching of religion is, at best, unprofitable. And your petitioners have discovered that such of *their* children as have attended the public schools, are generally, and at an early age, imbued with the same principle—that they become intractable, disobedient, and even contemptuous towards their parents—unwilling to learn any thing of religion—as if they had become illuminated, and could receive all the knowledge of religion necessary for them, by instinct or inspiration. Your petitioners do not pretend to assign the cause of this change in their children: they only attest the fact, as resulting from their attendance at the public schools of the Public School Society.

This society, however, is composed of gentlemen of various sects, including even one or two Catholics. But they profess to exclude all sectarianism from their schools. If they do not exclude sectarianism, they are avowedly no more entitled to the school funds than your petitioners, or any other denomination of professing Christians. If they do, as they profess, exclude sectarianism, then your petitioners contend that they exclude Christianity; and leave to the advantage of infidelity the tendencies which are given to the minds of youth by the influence of this feature and pretension of their system.

If they could accomplish what they profess, other denominations would join your petitioners in remonstrating against their schools. But they do not accomplish it. Your petitioners will show your Honorable Body that they do admit what Catholics call sectarianism, (although others may call it only religion,) in a great variety of ways.

In their 22d report, as far back as the year 1827, they tell us, page 14, that they *"are aware of the importance of early Religious Instruction"*—and that none but what is "exclusively general and scriptural in its character should be introduced into the schools under their charge." Here, then, is their own testimony that they did introduce and authorize "religious instruction" in their schools. And that they solved, with the utmost composure, the difficult question on which the sects disagree, by determining *what kind* of *"religious instruction"* is *"exclusively general and scriptural in its character."* Neither could they impart this "early religious instruction" themselves. They must have left it to their teachers—and these, armed with official influence, could impress those "early religious instructions" on the susceptible minds of the children, with the authority of dictators.

The Public School Society, in their report for the year 1832, page 10, describe the effect of these "early religious instructions," without, perhaps, intending to do so; but yet precisely as your petitioners have witnessed it, in such of their children as attended those schools. "The age at which children are usually sent to school, affords a much better opportunity to mould their minds to peculiar and exclusive forms of faith than any subsequent period of life." In page 11, of the same report, they protest against the injustice of supporting "religion in any shape" by public money: as if the "early religious instruction" which they had themselves authorized in their schools, five years before, was not "religion in some shape," and was not supported by public taxation. They tell us again, in more guarded language, "The Trustees are deeply impressed with the importance of imbuing the youthful mind with religious impressions, and they have endeavoured to attain this object, as far as the nature of the institution will admit."

In their 33d Annual Report they tell us, that "they would not be understood as regarding religious impressions in early youth as unimportant; on the contrary, they desire to do all which may with propriety be done, to give a right direction to the minds of the children entrusted to their care. Their schools are uniformly opened with the reading of the Scriptures, and the class books are such as recognise and enforce the great and generally acknowledged principles of Christianity."

In their 34th Annual Report, for the year 1839, they pay a high compliment to a deceased teacher for "the moral and religious influence exerted by her over the three hundred girls daily attending her school," and tell us that "it could not but have had a lasting effect on many of their susceptible minds." And yet in all these "early religious instructions, religious impressions, and religious influence," essentially anti-catholic, your petitioners are to see nothing sectarian; but if in giving the education which the State requires, they were to bring the same influences to bear on the "susceptible minds" of their *own* children, in favor, and not against, their *own* religion, then this society contends that it would be sectarian!!

Your petitioners regret that there is no means of ascertaining to what extent the teachers in the schools of this society carried out the views of their principals on the importance of conveying "early religious instructions" to the "susceptible minds" of the children. But they believe it is in their power to prove, that, in some instances, the Scriptures have been explained, as well as read, to the pupils.

Even the reading of the Scriptures in those schools your petitioners cannot regard otherwise than as sectarian; because Protestants would certainly consider as such the introduction of the Catholic Scriptures, which are different from theirs; and the Catholics have the same ground of objection when the Protestant version is made use of.

Your petitioners have to state further, as grounds of their conscientious objections to those schools, that many of the selections in their elementary reading lessons contain matter prejudicial to the Catholic name and character. The term "Popery" is repeatedly found in them. This term is known and employed as one of insult and contempt towards the Catholic religion, and it passes into the minds of children with the feeling of which it is the outward expression. Both the historical and religious portions of the reading lessons are selected from Protestant writers, whose prejudices against the Catholic religion render them unworthy of confidence in the mind of your petitioners, at least so far as their own children are concerned.

The Public School Society have heretofore denied that their books contained any thing reasonably objectionable to Catholics. Proofs of the contrary could be multiplied, but it is unnecessary, as they have recently retracted their denial, and discovered, after fifteen years enjoyment of their monopoly, that their books do contain objectionable passages. But they allege that they have proffered repeatedly to make such corrections as the Catholic Clergy might require. Your petitioners conceive that such a proposal could not be carried into effect by the Public School Society without giving just ground for exception to other denominations. Neither can they see with what consistency that society can insist, as it has done, on the perpetuation of its monopoly, when the Trustees thus avow their incompetency to present unexceptionable books, without the aid of the Catholic, or any other Clergy. They allege, indeed, that with the best intentions they have been unable to ascertain the passages which might be offensive to Catholics. With their intentions, your petitioners cannot enter into any question. Nevertheless, they submit to your Honorable Body, that this society is eminently incompetent for the superintendence of public education, if they could not see that the following passage was unfit for the public schools, and especially unfit to be placed in the hands of Catholic children.

They will quote the passage as one instance, taken from Putnam's Sequel, page 296:

"HUSS, John — a zealous reformer from Popery, who lived in Bohemia, towards the close of the fourteenth, and the beginning of the fifteenth centuries. He was bold and persevering; but at length, trusting himself to the deceitful Catholics, he was by them brought to trial, condemned as a heretic, and burnt at the stake."

The Public School Society may be excused for not knowing the historical inaccuracies of this passage; but surely assistance of the Catholic Clergy could not have been necessary to an understanding of the word "deceitful," as applied to all who profess the religion of your petitioners.

For these reasons, and others of the same kind, your petitioners cannot, in conscience, and consistently with their sense of duty to God, and to their offspring, entrust the Public School Society with the office of giving "a right direction to the minds of their children." And yet this society claims that office, and claims for the discharge of it the Common School Funds, to which your petitioners, in common with other citizens are contributors. In so far as they are contributors, they are not only deprived of any benefit in return, but their money is employed to the damage and detriment of their religion, in the minds of their own children, and of the rising generation of the community at large. The contest is between the *guarantied* rights, civil and religious, of the citizen on the one hand, and the pretensions of the Public School Society on the other: and whilst it has been silently going on for years, your petitioners would call the attention of your Honorable Body to its consequences on that class for whom the benefits of public education are most essential—the children of the poor.

This class (your petitioners speak only so far as relates to their own denomination) after a brief experience of the schools of the Public School Society, naturally and deservedly withdrew all confidence from it. Hence the establishment by your petitioners of schools for the education of the poor. The expense necessary for this, was a second taxation, required, not by the laws of the land, but by the no less imperious demands of their conscience.

They were reduced to the alternative of seeing their children growing up in entire ignorance, or else taxing themselves anew for private schools, whilst the funds provided for education, and contributed in part by themselves, were given over to the Public School Society, and by them employed as has been stated above.

Now your petitioners respectfully submit, that without this confidence, no body of men can discharge the duties of education as intended by the State, and required by the people. The Public School Society are, and have been at all times, conscious that they had not the confidence of the poor. In their twenty-eighth report, they appeal to the ladies of New York to create or procure it, by the "persuasive eloquence of female kindness;" page 5. And from this they pass, on the next page, to the more efficient eloquence of coercion, under penalties and privations to be visited on all persons "whether emigrants or otherwise," who being in the circumstances of poverty referred to, should not send their children to some "public or other daily school." In their twenty-seventh report, pages 15 and 16, they plead for the doctrine, and recommend it to public favor by the circumstance that it will affect but "few natives." But why should it be necessary at all, if they possessed that confidence of the poor, without which they need never hope to succeed. So well are they convinced of this, that no longer ago than last year, they gave up all hope of inspiring it, and loudly call for coercion by *"the strong arm of the civil power"* to supply its deficiency. Your petitioners will close this part of their statement with the expression of their surprise and regret that gentlemen who are themselves indebted much to the respect which is properly cherished for the rights of conscience, should be so unmindful of the same rights in the case of your petitioners. Many of them are by religious principle so pacific that they would not take up arms in the defence of the liberties of their country, though she should call them to her aid; and yet, they do not hesitate to invoke the "strong arm of the civil power" for the purpose of abridging the private liberties of their fellow citizens, who may feel equally conscientious.

Your petitioners have to deplore, as a consequence of this state of things, the ignorance and vice, to which hundreds, nay, thousands of their children are exposed. They have to regret, also, that the education which they can provide, under the disadvantages to which they have been subjected, is not as efficient as it should be. But should your Honorable Body be pleased to designate their schools as entitled to receive a just proportion of the Public Funds, which belong to your petitioners, in common with other citizens, their schools could be improved, for those who attend; others now growing up in ignorance, could be received, and the ends of the Legislature could be accomplished—a result which is manifestly hopeless, under the present system.

Your petitioners will now invite the attention of your Honorable Body, to the objections and misrepresentations that have been urged by the Public School Society, to granting the claim of your petitioners. It is urged by them, that it would be appropriating money raised by general taxation, to the support of the Catholic religion. Your petitioners join issue with them, and declare unhesitatingly, that if this objection can be established, the claim shall be forthwith abandoned. It is objected, that though we are taxed as citizens, we apply for the benefits of education, as "Catholics." Your petitioners, to remove this difficulty, beg to be considered in their application in the identical capacity in which they are taxed, viz: as citizens of the Commonwealth. It has been contended by the Public School Society, that the law disqualifies schools, which admit any profession of religion, from receiving any encouragements from the School Fund. Your petitioners have two solutions for this pretended difficulty. *First*—Your petitioners are unable to discover any such disqualification in the law, which merely delegates to your Honorable Body, the authority and discretion of determining what schools or societies shall be entitled to its bounty. *Second*—Your petitioners are willing to fulfill the conditions of the law, so far as religious teaching is proscribed, during school hours. In fine, your petitioners, to remove all objection, are willing that the material organization of their schools, and the disbursements of the funds allowed for them, shall be conducted, and made, by persons unconnected with the religion of your petitioners; even the Public School Society, if it should please your Honorable Body to appoint them for that purpose. The public may then be assured, that the money will not be applied to the support of the Catholic religion.

It is deemed necessary by your petitioners, to save the Public School Society the necessity of future misconception, thus to state the things which are *not* petitioned for. The members of that society, who have shown themselves so impressed with the importance of conveying *their* notions of "early religious instruction" to the "susceptible minds" of Catholic children, can have no objection that the parents of the children, and teachers in whom the parents have confidence, should do the same: provided, no law is violated thereby, and no disposition evinced to bring the children of other denominations within its influence.

Your petitioners, therefore, pray that your Honorable Body, will be pleased to designate, as among the schools entitled to participate in the Common School Fund, upon complying with the requirements of the law, the ordinances of the Corporation of the city, or for such other relief, as to your Honorable Body shall seem meet—St. Patrick's School, St. Peter's School, St. Mary's School, St. Joseph's School, St. James' School, St. Nicholas' School, Transfiguration Church School, and St. John's School.

And your petitioners further request, in the event of your Honorable Body's determining to hear your petitioners, on the subject of their petition, that such time may be appointed, as may be most agreeable to your Honorable Body, and that a full session of your Honorable Board be convened for that purpose.

And your petitioners, &c.
THOMAS O'CONNOR, *Chairman,*
GREGORY DILLON, ANDREW CARRIGAN, PETER DUFFY, *Vice Chairmen,*
B. O'CONNOR, JAMES KELLY, J. McLOUGHLIN, *Secretaries.*

Of a general meeting of the Catholics of the City of N. York, convened in the schoolroom of St. James' Church, 21st September 1840.

Report of the Special Committee of the Board of Aldermen, 1840

The Special Committee, to whom were referred the petition of the Catholics of New York, relative to the distribution of the School Fund, the several remonstrances and other documents connected with the subject, together with the above resolution of instructions, respectfully submit the following REPORT:

In pursuance of the instructions contained in the resolution, they employed two entire days in visiting the public schools, accompanied by a Committee of the petitioners, and also of the Public School Society, with a view to ascertain if any defects exist in their organization; and after a thorough scrutiny, in which all parties participated, your Committee not only failed to discover anything strikingly defective in the system, but became strongly impressed with a conviction that the public schools under their present organization, are admirably adapted to afford precisely the kind of instruction for which they were instituted [sic]. It is deemed essential to the welfare and security of our government, that the means of mental cultivation should be extended to every child in the community. The rising generation are destined to be the future rulers of the land, and their happiness can only be secured by such an education as will constitute them an intelligent community, prepare them to guard against the machinations of demagogues, and so to exercise the rights and franchises of citizens as not to deprive themselves of the invaluable privileges which are their birthright. That the public school system, as now organized, is calculated to effect these objects, your Committee do not entertain a doubt; but, though they regard it as an incalculable public blessing, if they could be persuaded that it trespassed upon the conscientious rights of any portion of our citizens, they would begin to doubt the propriety of its continuance: they cannot, however, conceive that it is justly amenable to such a charge, so long as sectarian dogmas and peculiarities are excluded from the schools, and no pupils are either admitted into them, or excluded from them, against the consent of their natural or legal guardians. The system has grown up under the auspices of a voluntary association of individuals usually known as "The Public School Society," formed for the purpose of promoting education, and admitting to membership any citizen of good moral character, who is not a clergyman, upon a contribution of ten dollars to its funds. This society has watched with indefatigable vigilance and untiring assiduity over the rise and progress of the system, and by their unrequited labors it has been nurtured into maturity. In its present aspect, it is a monument of disinterestedness and public spirit, of which our city has reason to be proud. Your

Committee hereby acknowledge their indebtedness to the members of that society, for the prompt manner in which they responded to every call made upon them, and they cannot but hope that the spirit of candor which they have displayed, and which the petitioners in the same spirit acknowledge, will ultimately remove every barrier, which, through misapprehension, as your Committee believe, has hitherto retarded the entire success of their benevolent and patriotic exertions. It has been objected on the part of the petitioners, that the books used in the public schools contain passages that are calculated to prejudice the minds of children against the Catholic faith. This objection, your Committee discovered to be not wholly unfounded; but we are happy to have it in our power to add, that the School Society fully agree with us in the opinion that nothing in the books or usages of the schools should be continued that is calculated in the remotest degree to wound the feelings or prejudice the minds of children in favor of or against any religious sect whatever; that they have expunged such passages in the books as they have been able to discover in any way objectionable; that they desire to continue, and earnestly solicit the aid and co-operation of the petitioners, in the work of expurgation, until every really objectionable feature shall be entirely obliterated. The extreme difficulty of this under-taking, is illustrated by the fact that some of the very same passages quoted by the petitioners as particularly objectionable, and which have been oblit-erated in the public school books, were found by your Committee entirely unobscured in the books used in one of the Catholic schools. It is a mel-ancholy fact, that in neighborhoods where Catholic children are numer-ous, the public schools number but few children whose parents profess the Catholic faith; but after the arduous task of expurgation shall have been completed, and every well grounded objection removed, your Committee fondly hope that the school houses will be filled with children, and that no parents or guardians, be their religious feelings what they may, will refuse to avail themselves of the benefits of the public schools for the Education of their children, being fully persuaded that many years would elapse before any new system of instruction could be organized, with advantages equal to the one now equally available to every child in the community. If, with such a system, any portion of the children should be left uneducated, it cannot be justly chargeable to a want of comprehensiveness in the system, but is more fairly attributable to imperfections which human legislation cannot remedy. The general objections to sectarian public schools, do not apply to cases where children are supported by charity, and necessarily confined to a particular locality, and not open to all children. Your Committee think that all such establishments might enjoy the benefits of education, at public expense, without an infringement of the principles contended for; and the rule being made general, their participation in the benefits of the School Fund would not necessarily constitute a public recognition of their religious sectarian character. No school system can be perfect which does not place the means of education within the reach of every child who is capable of receiving instruction; and such, your Committee believe, to be the design and capacity of the system now in use in this city.

The Public School buildings are constructed upon a uniform model; the books used are the same in all the schools, and the classes and departments in each are so similarly constituted and provided, that the removal of a pupil from one school to another, will not interrupt his studies or retard his progress. Though religion constitutes no specific part of the system of instruction, yet the discipline of the schools, and the well arranged and selected essays and maxims which abound in their reading books, are well calculated to impress upon the minds of children, a distinct idea of the value of religion; the importance of the domestic and social duties; the existence of God, the creator of all things; the immortality of the soul; man's future accountability; present dependence upon a superintending providence; and other moral sentiments, which do not conflict with sectarian views and peculiarities.

The different classes examined in several schools by your Committee, exhibited an astonishing progress in geography, astronomy, arithmetic, reading, writing, &c.; and indicated a capacity in the system for imparting instruction, far beyond our expectations; and, though the order and arrangement of each school would challenge comparison with a camp under a rigid disciplinarian, yet the accustomed buoyancy and cheerfulness of youth and childhood, did not appear to be destroyed, in any one of them: such were the favorable impressions forced upon our minds by a careful examination of the public schools. It is due to the Trustees, to add, that not one of our visits was anticipated, and no opportunity was afforded to any of the teachers, for even a momentary preparation. In the course of our investigations, we also visited three of the schools established by the petitioners, and for the benefit of which, a portion of the School Fund is solicited. We found them, as represented by the petitioners, lamentably deficient in accommodations, and supplies of books and teachers: the rooms were all excessively crowded and poorly ventilated; the books much worn as well as deficient in numbers, and the teachers not sufficiently numerous; yet, with all these disadvantages, though not able to compete successfully with the public schools, they exhibited a progress, which was truly creditable; and with the same means at their disposal, they would doubtless soon be able, under suitable direction, greatly to improve their condition. The object of the petitioners, is to supply these deficiencies from the fund provided by the bounty of the State, for the purposes of common school education. But however strongly our sympathies may be excited in behalf of the poor children assembled in these schools, such is the state of the public mind on this subject, that if one religious sect should obtain a portion of the School Fund, every other one would present a similar claim, and it would be a signal for the total demolition of the system, which has grown up under the guidance of many years of toilsome experience; attaining a greater degree of perfection, than has perhaps, ever before been achieved, and which is probably extending a greater amount of instruction at smaller expense than can possibly be imparted by any other school system, that has been devised. This result of such a disposal of the School Funds, would most probably, be followed by a counteraction in the public mind, which would lead to a revocation of the Act, by a succeeding Common Council, and the awakening of a spirit of intolerance, which, in our country, is of all calamities, the one most to be dreaded. Political intolerance, is an unmitigated evil; but the experience of past ages ought to admonish us to guard, with unceasing vigilance, against religious intolerance, as an evil greater in magnitude, in proportion as eternal consequences exceed those of time. So long as government refuses to recognise religious sectarian differences, no danger need be apprehended from this source; but when it begins to legislate with particular reference to any particular denomination of Christians, in any manner which recognises their religious peculiarities, it oversteps a boundary which public opinion has established; violates a principle which breath[e]s in all our Constitutions; and opens a door to that unholy connection of politics with religion, which has so often cursed and desolated Europe. Under these impressions of the impossibility of granting the prayer of the petitioners, without producing the most fatal consequences, and impressed, at the same time, with an anxious desire to remove every obstacle out of the way of the public education of their children, if it could be done without sacrifising any fundamental principle, your Committee invited the School Society and the petitioners, to appoint delegates to meet them, with a view to effect a compromise, if possible. The invitation was promptly responded to, and several meetings were held, at which the subject was fully and very courteously discussed, in all its bearings, and though we extremely regret to report, that the conferences did not result as favorably as we had hoped, yet the spirit and tenor of the following propositions, submitted at our request, by both the School Society and the petitioners, encourage a belief, that our labor may not have been entirely in vain.

Memorial of a Committee of the Methodist Episcopal Church

N. Bangs, Thomas E. Bond, & George Peck, 1840

To the Honorable the Common Council of the City of New York.

The undersigned Committee, appointed by the Pastors of the Methodist Episcopal Church in this City, on the part of said pastors and churches, do most respectfully represent:

That they have heard with surprise and alarm, that the Roman Catholics have renewed their application to the Common Council, for an appropriation from the Common School Fund, for the support of the schools under their own direction; in which they teach, and propose still to teach, their own sectarian dogmas; not only to their own children, but to such Protestant children as they may find means to get into their schools.

Your memorialists had hoped that the clear, cogent, and unanswerable arguments, by which the former application for this purpose was resisted, would have saved the Common Council from further importunity.

It was clearly shown that the Council could not legally make any sectarian appropriation of the public funds; and it was as clearly shown, that it would be utterly destructive of the whole scheme of public school instruction to do so, even if it could be legally done. But it seems that neither the Constitution of the State, nor the public welfare, are to be regarded, when they stand in the way of Roman Catholic sectarianism and exclusiveness.

It must be manifest to the Common Council, that if the Roman Catholic claims are granted, all the other Christian denominations will urge their claims for a similar appropriation; and that the money raised for education by a general tax, will be solely applied to the purposes of proselytism through the medium of sectarian schools. But if this were done, would it be the price of peace? or would it not throw the apple of discord into the whole Christian community? Should we agree in the division of the spoils? Would each sect be satisfied with the portion allotted to it? We venture to say that the sturdy claimants who now beset the Council, would not be satisfied with much less than the lion's share; and we are sure that there are other Protestant denominations, besides ourselves, who would not patiently submit to the exaction. But when all the Christian sects shall be satisfied with their individual share of the public fund, what is to become of those children whose parents belong to none of these sects, and who cannot conscientiously allow them to be educated in the peculiar dogmas of any one of them? The different Committees who on a former occasion approached your Honorable Body, have shown that to provide schools for these only, would require little less than is now expended; and it requires little arithmetic to show that when the religious sects have taken all, nothing will remain for those who have not yet been able to decide, which of the Christian denominations to prefer. It must be plain to every impartial observer, that the applicants are opposed to the whole system of public school instruction; and it will be found, that the uncharitable exclusiveness of their creed, must ever be opposed to all public instruction, which is not under the direction of their own priesthood. They may be conscientious in all this; but though it be no new claim on their part, we cannot yet allow them to guide and control the consciences of all the rest of the community. We are sorry that the reading of the Bible, in the public schools, without note or commentary, is offensive to them; but we cannot allow the holy scriptures to be accompanied with *their* notes and commentaries, and to be put into the hands of the children, who may hereafter be the rulers and legislators of our beloved country; because, among other bad things taught in these commentaries, is to be found the lawfulness of murdering heretics; and the unqualified submission in all matters of conscience to the Roman Catholic Church.

But if the principle on which this application is based should be admitted, it must be carried far beyond the present purpose.

If all are to be released from taxation when they cannot conscientiously derive any benefit from the disbursement of the money collected, what will be done for the Society of Friends, and other sects, who are opposed to war, under all circumstances. Many of these, beside the tax paid on all the foreign goods they consume, pay direct duties at the Custom House, which go to the payment of the army and to purchase the munitions of war. And even when the Government finds it necessary to lay direct war taxes, these conscientious sects are compelled to pay their proportion, on the ground that the public defence requires it. So it is believed the public interest requires the education of the whole rising generation; because it would be unsafe to commit the public liberty, and the perpetuation of our republican institutions, to those whose ignorance of their nature and value would render them careless of their preservation, or the easy dupes of artful innovators; and hence every citizen is required to contribute in proportion to his means to the public purpose of universal education.

The Roman Catholics complain that books have been introduced into the public schools, which are injurious to them as a body. It is allowed, however, that the passages in these books, to which such reference is made, are chiefly, if not entirely, historical; and we put it to the candour of the Common Council to say, whether any history of Europe, for the last ten centuries, could be written, which could either omit to mention the Roman Catholic Church, or mention it without recording historical facts unfavorable to that church? We assert that if all the historical facts in which the Church of Rome has taken a prominent part, could be taken from writers of her own communion, only, the incidents might be made more objectionable to the complainants, than any book to which they now object. History itself, then, must be falsified for their accommodation; and yet they complain that the system of education adopted in the Public Schools does not teach the sinfulness of lying! They complain that no religion is taught in these schools, and declare that any, even the worst form of Christianity, would be better than none; and yet they object to the reading of the Holy Scriptures, which are the only foundation of all true religion. Is it not plain, then, that they will not be satisfied with any thing short of the total abandonment of public school instruction, or the appropriation of such portion of the public fund as they may claim, to their own sectarian purposes.

But this is not all. They have been most complaisantly offered the censorship of the books to be used in the Public Schools. The Committee to whom has been confided the management of these schools, in this city, offered to allow the Roman Catholic Bishop to expurgate from these books any thing offensive to him.

But the office was not accepted; perhaps, for the same reason that he declined to decide on the admissibility of a book of extracts from the Bible, which had been sanctioned by certain Roman Catholic Bishops in Ireland. An appeal, it seems, had gone to the Pope on the subject, and nothing could be said or done in the matter until his Holiness had decided. The Common Council of New York will therefore find that when they shall have conceded to the Roman Catholics of this city, the selection of books for the use of the Public Schools, that these books must undergo the censorship of a foreign potentate. We hope the time is far distant when the citizens of this country will allow any foreign power to dictate to them in matters relating to either general or municipal law.

We cannot conclude this memorial without noticing one other ground on which the Roman Catholics, in their late appeal to their fellow citizens, urged their sectarian claims, and excused their conscientious objections to the Public Schools. Their creed is dear to them, it seems, because some of their ancestors have been martyrs to their faith. This was an unfortunate allusion. Did not the Roman Catholics know that they addressed many of their fellow citizens who could not recur to the memories of their own ancestors, without being reminded of the revocation of the Edict of Nantz; the massacre of Saint Bartholomew's day; the fires of Smithfield; or the crusade against the Waldenses?

We would willingly cover these scenes with the mantle of charity; and hope that our Roman Catholic fellow citizens will, in future, avoid whatever has a tendency to revive the painful remembrance.

Your memorialists had hoped that the intolerance and exclusiveness which had characterized the Roman Catholic Church in Europe, had been greatly softened under the benign influences of our civil institutions. The pertinacity with which their sectarian interests are now urged, has dissipated the illusion. We were content with their having excluded us, "ex cathedra," from all claim to heaven, for we were sure they did not possess the keys, notwithstanding their confident pretensions; nor did we complain that they would not allow us any participation in the benefits of Pugatory; for it is a place they have made for themselves, and of which they may claim the exclusive propriety; but we do protest against any appropriation of the Public School Fund for their exclusive benefit, or for any other sectarian purposes whatever.

Assured that the Common Council will do, what it is right to do in the premises, we are, gentlemen, with great respect,

Your most obedient servants,
N. BANGS, THOMAS E. BOND, GEORGE PECK

14

The Declaration of Sentiments, Seneca Falls

Elizabeth Cady Stanton, 1848

Elizabeth Cady Stanton lived from 1815–1902. The world for American women in the 19th century was very different from contemporary times. Laws denied women many rights, including the right to own property and the right to vote. Indeed, women's mental and physical capacities were viewed as deficient in comparison to men. Stanton dedicated her life to changing the laws and the views of women's abilities. Stanton was one of a small number of women who earned a formal education, as she attended Troy Seminary, founded by Emma Willard. Nonetheless, she did not attend Union College, like her brother, as it was only open to men, like most colleges in the 1800s. Despite her challenges to traditional views of women, Stanton had seven children with her husband, abolitionist and lawyer, Henry Stanton. Elizabeth Cady Stanton was the principal author of the Declaration of Rights and Sentiments signed at the Seneca Falls Convention. She modeled the Declaration of Rights and Sentiments after the U.S. Declaration of Independence. At the time, the document was considered radical, particularly because of the statements supporting women's suffrage. Along with Susan B. Anthony, her lifelong friend, Stanton is considered a founder of the women's suffrage movement. —CHB

American Educational Thought: Essays from 1640–1940, pages 203–206
Copyright © 2010 by Information Age Publishing

When, in the course of human events, it becomes necessary for one portion of the family of man to assume among the people of the earth a position different from that which they have hitherto occupied, but one to which the laws of nature and of nature's God entitle them, a decent respect to the opinions of mankind requires that they should declare the causes that impel them to such a course.

We hold these truths to be self-evident: that all men and women are created equal; that they are endowed by their Creator with certain inalienable rights; that among these are life, liberty, and the pursuit of happiness; that to secure these rights governments are instituted, deriving their just powers from the consent of the governed. Whenever any form of government becomes destructive of these ends, it is the right of those who suffer from it to refuse allegiance to it, and to insist upon the institution of a new government, laying its foundation on such principles, and organizing its powers in such form, as to them shall seem most likely to effect their safety and happiness.

Prudence, indeed, will dictate that governments long established should not be changed for light and transient causes; and accordingly all experience hath shown that mankind are more disposed to suffer, while evils are sufferable, than to right themselves by abolishing the forms to which they are accustomed. But when a long train of abuses and usurpations, pursuing invariably the same object, evinces a design to reduce them under absolute despotism, it is their duty to throw off such government, and to provide new guards for their future security. Such has been the patient sufferance of the women under this government, and such is now the necessity which constrains them to demand the equal station to which they are entitled.

The history of mankind is a history of repeated injuries and usurpations on the part of man toward woman, having in direct object the establishment of an absolute tyranny over her. To prove this, let facts be submitted to a candid world.

He has never permitted her to exercise her inalienable right to the elective franchise.

He has compelled her to submit to laws, in the formation of which she had no voice.

He has withheld from her rights which are given to the most ignorant and degraded men—both natives and foreigners.

. Having deprived her of this first right of a citizen, the elective franchise, thereby leaving her without representation in the halls of legislation, he has oppressed her on all sides.

He has made her, if married, in the eye of the law, civilly dead.

He has taken from her all right in property, even to the wages she earns.

He has made her, morally, an irresponsible being, as she can commit many crimes with impunity, provided they be done in the presence of her husband. In the covenant of marriage, she is compelled to promise obedience to her husband, he becoming, to all intents and purposes, her master—the law giving him power to deprive her of her liberty, and to administer chastisement. He has so framed the laws of divorce, as to what shall be the proper causes, and in case of separation, to whom the guardianship of the children shall be given, as to be wholly regardless of the happiness of women—the law, in all cases, going upon a false supposition of the supremacy of man, and giving all power into his hands.

After depriving her of all rights as a married woman, if single, and the owner of property, he has taxed her to support a government which recognizes her only when her property can be made profitable to it.

He has monopolized nearly all the profitable employments, and from those she is permitted to follow, she receives but a scanty remuneration. He closes against her all the avenues to wealth and distinction which he considers most honorable to himself. As a teacher of theology, medicine, or law, she is not known.

He has denied her the facilities for obtaining a thorough education, all colleges being closed against her.

He allows her in church, as well as state, but a subordinate position, claiming apostolic authority for her exclusion from the ministry, and, with some exceptions, from any public participation in the affairs of the church.

He has created a false public sentiment by giving to the world a different code of morals for men and women, by which moral delinquencies which exclude women from society, are not only tolerated, but deemed of little account in man.

He has usurped the prerogative of Jehovah himself, claiming it as his right to assign for her a sphere of action, when that belongs to her conscience and to her God.

He has endeavored, in every way that he could, to destroy her confidence in her own powers, to lessen her self-respect, and to make her willing to lead a dependent and abject life.

Now, in view of this entire disfranchisement of one-half the people of this country, their social and religious degradation—in view of the unjust laws above mentioned, and because women do feel themselves aggrieved, oppressed, and fraudulently deprived of their most sacred rights, we insist that they have immediate admission to all the rights and privileges which belong to them as citizens of the United States.

15

Common Schools

Horace Bushnell, 1853

Horace Bushnell (1802–1876) was a teacher early in his life, but he eventually went to Divinity School and became a well-known preacher. Nonetheless, he always maintained an interest in the education of children. His various writings and ideas about this topic provide examples of the conflicts and contradictions of his time. In his theology, Bushnell attempted to be progressive by presenting an alternative to the Puritan doctrine of original sin. Yet, with regard to emerging social issues, he opposed more conservative Northern Evangelicals through his opposition to the abolition of slavery and women's rights. When it came to the public education system though, Bushnell's arguments reflected the opinion of the majority of American Protestants. Clearly anti-Catholic, he saw public schools as a major way the United States could educate immigrants into America's democratic culture. As a liberal Protestant, he also disdained more sectarian Protestants concerned about the lack of theological teaching in public schools. Nonetheless, he still believed that common schools should be Christian "in the recognition of God and Christ and providence and the Bible." Ironically, what Bushnell understood as "common" in the 1850s would eventually change in the increasingly pluralistic America. —PLG

American Educational Thought: Essays from 1640–1940, pages 207–224
Copyright © 2010 by Information Age Publishing
All rights of reproduction in any form reserved.

Lev. 24:22. Ye shall have one manner of law, as well for the stranger, as for one of your own country: for I am the Lord your God.

It is my very uncommon privilege and pleasure to speak to you, for once, from a text already fulfilled, and more than fulfilled in the observance. For we, as a people, or nation, have not only abstained from passing laws that are unequal, or hard upon strangers, which is what the rule of the text forbids, but we have invited them to become fellow-citizens with us in our privileges, and bestowed upon them all the rights and immunities of citizens. We have said to the strangers from Germany, France, Switzerland, Norway, Ireland, and indeed of every land, "Come and be Americans with us, you and your children; and whatsoever right or benefit we have, in our free institutions and our vast and fertile domain, shall be yours."

Thus invited, thus admitted to an equal footing with us, they are not content, but are just now returning our generosity by insisting that we must excuse them and their children from being wholly and properly American. They will not have one law for us and for themselves, but they demand immunities that are peculiar to themselves, and before unheard of by us; or else that we wholly give up institutions for their sake that are the dearest privileges of our birthright. They accept the common rights of the law, the common powers of voting, the common terms of property, a common privilege in the new lands and the mines of gold, but when they come to the matter of common schools, they will not be common with us there— they require of us, instead, either to give up our common schools, or else, which in fact amounts to the same thing, to hand over their proportion of the public money, and let them use it for such kind of schools as they happen to like best; ecclesiastical schools, whether German, French, or Irish; any kind of schools but such as are American, and will make Americans of their children.

It has been clear for some years past, from the demonstrations of our Catholic clergy and their people, and particularly of the clergy, that they were preparing for an assault upon the common school system, hitherto in so great favor with our countrymen; complaining, first, of the Bible as a sectarian book in the schools, and then, as their complaints have begun to be accommodated by modifications that amount to a discontinuance, more or less complete, of religious instruction itself, of our "godless scheme of education;" to which (as godless only as they have required it to be) they say they can not surrender their children without a virtual sacrifice of all religion. Growing more hopeful of their ability, by the heavy vote they can wield, to turn the scale of an election one way or the other between opposing parties, and counting on the sway they can thus exert over the popular leaders and candidates, they have lately attempted a revolution of the school system of Michigan, and are now memorializing the legislatures of Pennsylvania and Ohio, and urging it on the people of these states to allow a change or modification of theirs that amounts to a real discontinuance; viz., to make a distribution of the public school money to all existing schools, of whatever description, according to the number of their scholars; and the moment this is done, plainly nothing will be left of the common school system but a common fund, gathered by a common tax on property, to support private schools.

Evidently the time has now come, and the issue of life or death to common schools is joined for trial. The ground is taken, the flag is raised, and there is to be no cessation, till the question is forever decided, whether we are to have common schools in our country or not. And accordingly, it is time for us all, citizens, public men and Christians, to be finding the ground on which we expect and may be able to stand. In one view the question is wholly a religious question; in another it is more immediately a civil or political question. And yet the lines cross each other in so many ways that any proper discussion of the topic must cover both aspects or departments, the religious and the political. I take up the question at this early period, before it has become, in any sense, a party question, that I may have the advantage of greater freedom, and that I may suffer no imputation of a party bias, to detain me from saying any thing which pertains to a complete view of the subject.

As this day of fasting is itself a civil appointment, I have always made it a point to occupy the day, in part, with some subject that pertains to the public duties and religious concerns of the state or nation. I propose, therefore, now to anticipate, as it were, the pressure of this great subject, and discharge myself, once for all, of my whole duty concerning it; and I hope to speak of it under that sense of responsibility, as well as in that freedom from prejudice, which one of the greatest and most serious of all American subjects requires. I wish I might also speak in a manner to exclude any narrow and partial or sectarian views of it, such as time and the further consideration of years might induce a wish to qualify or amend.

I will not undertake to say that our Catholic friends have, in no case, any just reason for uneasiness or complaint. A great many persons and even communities will very naturally act, for a time, as power is able to act, and will rather take counsel of their prejudices than of reason, or of the great principles that underlie our American institutions. Consideration, as a rectifying power, is often tardy in its coming, and of course there will be something unrectified, for so long a time, in the matter that waits for its arrival.

Meantime the subject itself is one of some inherent difficulty, and can not be expected to settle itself upon its right foundation, without some delay or some agitation, more or less protracted, of its opposing interests and reasons. We began our history in all but the single colony of Baltimore, as Protestant communities; and, in those especially of New England, we have had the common school as a fundamental institution from the first—in our view a Protestant institution—associated with all our religious convictions, opinions, and the public sentiment of our Protestant society. We are still, as Americans, a Protestant people, and many are entirely ignorant, as yet, of the fact that we are not still Protestant states also, as at the first; Protestant, that is, in our civil order, and the political fabric of our government. And yet we very plainly are not. We have made a great transition; made it silently and imperceptibly, and scarcely know as yet that it is made. Occupied wholly with a historic view of the case, considering how the country and its institutions are, historically speaking, ours; the liberality and kindness we have shown to those who have come more recently to join us, and are even now heard speaking in a foreign accent among us; the asylum we have generously opened for them and their children; the immense political trust we have committed to them, in setting them on a common footing, as voters, with ourselves; and that now we offer to give a free education to their children, at the public expense, or by a tax on all the property of the state—considering all this, and that we and our fathers are Protestants, it seems to be quite natural and right, or even a matter of course, that our common schools should remain Protestant, and retain their ancient footing undisturbed.

But we shall find, on a second consideration, that we have really agreed for something different, and that now we have none to complain of but ourselves, if we have engaged for more than it is altogether pleasant to yield. Our engagement, in the large view of it, is to make the state or political order a platform of equal right to all sects and denominations of Christians. We have slid off, imperceptibly, from the old Puritan, upon an American basis, and have undertaken to inaugurate a form of political order that holds no formal church connexion. The properly Puritan common school is already quite gone by; the intermixture of Methodists, Quakers, Unitarians, Episcopalians, and diverse other names of Christians, called Protestants, has burst the capsule of Puritanism, and, as far as the schools are concerned, it is quite passed away; even the Westminster catechism is gone by, to be taught in the schools no more. In precisely the same manner, have we undertaken also to loosen the bonds of Protestantism in the schools, when the time demanding it arrives. To this we are mortgaged by our great American doctrine itself, and there is no way to escape the obligation but to renounce the doctrine, and resume, if we can, the forms and lost prerogatives of a state religion.

But there is one thing, and a very great thing, that we have not lost, nor agreed to yield; viz., *common schools.* Here we may take our stand, and upon this we may insist as being a great American institution; one that has its beginnings with our history itself; one that is inseparably joined to the fortunes of the republic; and one that can never wax old, or be discontinued in its rights and reasons, till the pillars of the state are themselves cloven down forever. We can not have Puritan common schools—these are gone already—we can not have Protestant common schools, or those which are distinctively so; but we can have common schools, and these we must agree to have and maintain, till the last or latest day of our liberties. These are American, as our liberties themselves are American, and whoever requires of us, whether directly or by implication, to give them up, requires what is more than our bond promises, and what is, in fact, a real affront to our name and birthright as a people.

I mean, of course, by common schools, when I thus speak, schools for the children of all classes, sects and denominations of the people; so far perfected in their range of culture and mental and moral discipline, that it shall be the interest of all to attend, as being the best schools which can be found; clear too, of any such objections as may furnish a just ground of offense to the conscience or the religious scruples of any Christian body of our people. I mean, too, schools that are established by the public law of the state, supported at the public expense, organized and superintended by public authority. Of course it is implied that the schools shall be under laws that are general, in the same way as the laws of roads, records, and military service; that no distribution shall be made, in a way of exception, to schools that are private, ecclesiastical or parochial; that whatever accommodations are made to different forms of religion, shall be so made as to be equally available to all; that the right of separate religious instruction, the supervision, the choice of teachers, the selection of books, shall be provided for under fixed conditions, and so as to maintain the fixed rule of majorities, in all questions left for the decision of districts. The schools, in other words, shall be common, in just the same sense that all the laws are common, so that the experience of families and of children under them, shall be an experience of the great republican rule of majorities—an exercise for majorities, of obedience to fixed statutes, and of moderation and impartial respect to the rights and feelings of minorities—an exercise for minorities of patience and of loyal assent to the will of majorities—a schooling, in that manner, which begins at the earliest moment possible, in the rules of American law, and the duties of an American citizen.

And this, I undertake to say, is the institution which we are not for any reason to surrender, but to hold fast as being a necessary and fixed element of the public order, one without which our American laws and liberties are scarcely American longer; or, if we call them by that name, have no ground longer of security and consolidated public unity.

In the first place, it will be found, if we closely inspect our institutions, that the common school is, in fact, an integral part of the civil order. It is no eleemosynary institution, erected outside of the state, but is itself a part of the public law, as truly so as the legislatures and judicial courts. The school-houses are a public property, the district committees are civil officers, the teachers are as truly functionaries of the law as the constables, prison-keepers, inspectors and coroners. We perceive then, if we understand the question rightly, that an application against common schools, is so far an application for the dismemberment and reorganization of the civil order of the state. Certain religionists appear, in the name of religion, demanding that the state shall be otherwise constructed. Or, if it be said that they do not ask for the discontinuance of the common schools, but only to have a part of the funds bestowed upon their ecclesiastical schools, the case is not mended but rather made worse by the qualification; for in that view they are asking that a part of the funds which belong to the civil organization shall be paid over to their religion, or to the *imperium in imperio*, their religion so far substitutes for the civil order. It is as if they were to ask that the health wardens should so far be substituted by their church wardens, or the coroner's inquest by their confessional, and that the state, acknowledging their right to the substitution demanded, should fee the church wardens and confessors, in their behalf. If an application that infringes on the civil polity of our states, in a manner so odious, is to be heard, the civil order may as well be disbanded, and the people given over to their ecclesiastics, to be ruled by them in as many clans of religion as they see fit to make. Are we ready, as Americans, to yield our institutions up in this manner, or to make them paymasters to a sect who will so far dismember their integrity?

This great institution, too, of common schools, is not only a part of the state, but is imperiously wanted as such, for the common training of so many classes and conditions of people. There needs to be some place where, in early childhood, they may be brought together and made acquainted with each other; thus to wear away the sense of distance, otherwise certain to become an established animosity of orders; to form friendships; to be exercised together on a common footing of ingenuous rivalry; the children of the rich to feel the power and do honor to the struggles of merit in the lowly, when it rises above them; the children of the poor to learn the force of merit, and feel the benign encouragement yielded by its blameless victories. Indeed, no child can be said to be well trained, especially no male child, who has not met the people as they are, above him or below, in the seatings, plays and studies of the common school. Without this he can never be a fully qualified citizen, or prepared to act his part wisely as a citizen. Confined to a select school, where only the children of wealth and distinction are gathered, he will not know the merit there is in the real virtues of the poor, or the power that slumbers in their talent. He will take his better dress as a token of his better quality, look down upon the children of the lowly with an educated contempt, prepare to take on lofty airs of confidence and presumption afterward; finally, to make the discovery when it is too late, that poverty has been the sturdy nurse of talent in some unhonored youth who comes up to affront him by an equal, or mortify and crush him by an overmastering force. So also the children of the poor and lowly, if they should be privately educated, in some inferior degree, by the honest and faithful exertion of their parents; secreted as it were, in some back alley or obscure corner of the town, will either grow up in a fierce, inbred hatred of the wealthier classes, or else in a mind cowed by undue modesty, as being of another and inferior quality, unable, therefore, to fight the great battle of life hopefully, and counting it a kind of presumption to think that they can force their way upward, even by merit itself.

Without common schools, the disadvantage falls both ways in about equal degrees, and the disadvantage that accrues to the state, in the loss of so much character, and so many cross ties of mutual respect and generous appreciation, the embittering so fatally of all outward distinctions, and the propagation of so many misunderstandings, (righted only by the immense public mischiefs that follow)—this, I say, is greater even than the disadvantages accruing to the classes themselves; a disadvantage that weakens immensely, the security of the state, and even of its liberties. Indeed, I seriously doubt whether any system of popular government can stand the shock, for any length of time, of that fierce animosity, that is certain to be gendered, where the children are trained up wholly in their classes, and never brought together to feel, understand, appreciate and respect each other, on the common footing of merit and of native talent, in a common school. Falling back thus on the test of merit and of native force, at an early period of life, moderates immensely their valuation of mere conventionalities and of the accidents of fortune, and puts them in a way of deference that is genuine as well as necessary to their common peace in the state. Common schools are nurseries thus of a free republic, private schools of factions, cabals, agrarian laws and contests of force. Therefore, I say, we must have common schools; they are American, indispensable to our American institutions, and must not be yielded for any consideration smaller than the price of our liberties.

Nor is it only in this manner that they are seen to be necessary. The same argument holds, with even greater force, when applied to the religious distinctions of our country. It is very plain that we can not have common schools for the purposes above named, if we make distributions, whether of schools or of funds, under sectarian or ecclesiastical distinctions. At that moment the charm and very much of the reality of common schools vanish. Besides, the ecclesiastical distinctions are themselves distinctions also of classes, in another form, and such too as are much more dangerous than any distinctions of wealth. Let the Catholic children, for example, be driven out of our schools by unjust trespasses on their religion, or be withdrawn for mere pretexts that have no foundation, and just there commences a training in religious antipathies bitter as the grave. Never brought close enough to know each other, the children, subject to the great well known principle that whatever is unknown is magnified by the darkness it is under, have all their prejudices and repugnances magnified a thousand fold. They grow up in the conviction that there is nothing but evil in each other, and close to that lies the inference that they are right in doing what evil to each other they please. I complain not of the fact that they are not assimilated, but of what is far more dishonest and wicked, that they are not allowed to understand each other. They are brought up, in fact, for misunderstanding; separated that they may misunderstand each other; kept apart, walled up to heaven in the inclosures of their sects, that they may be as ignorant of each other, as inimical, as incapable of love and cordial good citizenship as possible. The arrangement is not only unchristian, but it is thoroughly un-American, hostile at every point, to our institutions themselves. No bitterness is so bitter, no seed of faction so rank, no division so irreconcilable, as that which grows out of religious distinctions, sharpened to religious animosities, and softened by no terms of intercourse; the more bitter when it begins with childhood; and yet more bitter when it is exasperated also by distinctions of property and social life that correspond; and yet more bitter still, when it is aggravated also by distinctions of stock or nation.

In this latter view, the withdrawing of our Catholic children from the common schools, unless for some real breach upon their religion, and the distribution demanded of public moneys to them in schools apart by themselves, is a bitter cruelty to the children, and a very unjust affront to our institutions. We bid them welcome as they come, and open to their free possession, all the rights of our American citizenship. They, in return, forbid their children to be Americans, pen them as foreigners to keep them so, and train them up in the speech of Ashdod among us. And then, to complete the affront, they come to our legislatures demanding it, as their right, to share in funds collected by a taxing of the whole people, and to have these funds applied to the purpose of keeping their children from being Americans.

Our only answer to such demands is, "No! take your place with us in our common schools, and consent to be Americans, or else go back to Turkey, where Mohammedans, Greeks, Armenians, Jews are walled up by the laws themselves, forbidding them ever to pass over or to change their superstitions; there to take your chances of liberty, such as a people are capable of when they are trained up, as regards each other, to be foreigners for all coming time, in blood and religion." I said go back to Turkey—that is unnecessary. If we do not soon prepare a state of Turkish order and felicity here, by separating and folding our children thus, in the stringent limits of religious non-acquaintance and consequent animosity, it will be because the laws of human nature and society have failed.

Besides, there are other consequences of such a breach upon the common school system, implied in yielding this demand, which are not to be suffered. A very great part of the children, thus educated, will have very inferior advantages. They will be shut up in schools that do not teach them what, as Americans, they most of all need to know, the political geography and political history of the world, the rights of humanity, the struggles by which those rights are vindicated, and the glorious rewards of liberty and social advancement that follow. They will be instructed mainly into the foreign prejudices and superstitions of their fathers, and the state, which proposes to be clear of all sectarian affinities in religion, will pay the bills!

It will also be demanded, next, that the state shall hold the purse for the followers of Tom Paine, and all other infidels, discharging the bills of schools where Paine's Age of Reason, or the Mormon Bible, or Davis' Revelations are the reading books of the children.

The old school Presbyterian church took ground, six years ago, in their General Assembly, at the crisis of their high church zeal, against common and in favor of parochial schools. Hitherto their agitation has yielded little more than a degree of discouragement and disrespect to the schools of their country; but if the Catholics prevail in their attempt, they also will be forward in demanding the same rights, upon the same grounds, and their claim also must be granted. By that time the whole system of common schools is fatally shaken. For, since education is thrown thus far upon the care of individual parents, still another result is certain to follow in close proximity, viz., the discontinuance of all common schools, and of all public care of education; and then we shall have large masses of children growing up in neglect, with no school at all provided to which they can be sent; ignorant, hopeless and debased creatures; banditti of the street; wild men of anarchy, waiting for their leaders, and the guerilla practice of the mountains; at first the pest of society, and finally its end or overthrow. A result that will be further expedited, by the fact that many children, now in our public schools, will be gathered into schools of an atheistic or half pagan character, where they will be educated in a contempt of all order and decency, to be leaders of the ignorance and brutality supplied by the uneducated. How different the picture from that which is now presented by our beautiful system of common schools—every child provided with a good school, all classes and conditions brought together on an equal footing of respect and merit, the state their foster-mother, all property a willing and glad contributor for their outfit in life, and their success in the ways of intelligence and virtue!

Take it then for a point established, that common schools are to remain as common schools, and that these are to be maintained by the state as carefully as the arsenals and armed defenses of the country—these and no other. Just here, then, comes the difficult question, what we are to do, how to accommodate the religious distinctions of the people, so as to make their union in any common system of schools, possible— how the Catholics, in particular, are to be accommodated in their religion, in those societies and districts where Protestants are the majority; how Protestants, where Catholics are the majority?

The question how Pagans, Mohammedans, and Atheists are to be accommodated is, in my view, a different question, and one, I think, which is to be answered in a different manner. They are to be tolerated, or suffered, but in no case to be assisted or accommodated, by acts of public conformity. I can not agree to the sentiment sometimes advanced, that we are not a Christian nation, in distinction from a Pagan, Mohammedan or Infidel. Indeed I will go further, assuming the fact of God's existence, I will say that no government can write a legitimate enactment or pass a valid decree of separation from God. Still, after the act is done, God exists, God is the only foundation it has of public right or authority. The state, indeed, is a fiction, a lie, and no state, save as it stands in him. And then as Christianity is only the complete revelation of God, otherwise only partially revealed, it follows that the state can not be less than a Christian state, can not any more disown or throw off its obligations to be Christian, than an individual can. Nor in fact has our government ever attempted to shake off Christianity, but has always, from the first day till now, taken the attitude and character of a Christian commonwealth—accepting the Christian Sabbath, appointing fasts and thanksgivings, employing military and legislative chaplains, and acknowledging God by manifold other tokens. Accordingly our schools are, to the same extent, and are to be Christian schools. This is the American principle, and as we have never disowned God and Christ, as a point of liberty in the state, or to accommodate unbelievers, so we are required by no principle of American right or law to make our schools unchristian, to accommodate Turks and Pagans, or rejectors and infidels.

Common schools, then, are to be Christian schools—how Christian? In the same sense, I answer, that Catholics and Protestants are Christians, in the same sense that our government is Christian, in the same that Christendom is Christian, that is, in the recognition of God and Christ and providence and the Bible. I fully agree with our Catholic friends regarding what they say in deprecation of a godless system of education. Dr. Chalmers, engaged in a society to establish Catholic schools in Glasgow, went so far as to say that if he had not been able to obtain "favorable terms from the priest, that is, the liberty of making the Bible a school-book," he would still have persevered, "on the principle that a Catholic population, with the capacity of reading, are a more hopeful subject than without it." Perhaps he was right, but the statistics reported in France, a few years ago, showing that public crimes, in the different departments, were very nearly in the ratio of education, increasing too in the ratio of the increase of education, are sufficient to throw a heavy shade of doubt on the value of all attempts to educate, that increase the power of men, and add no regulative force of principle and character. It is, to say the least, a most perilous kind of beneficence. The chances are far too great that knowledge, without principle, will turn out to be only the equipment of knaves and felons.

The greater reason is there that our Catholic fellow-citizens should not do what they can to separate all the schools of the nation from Christian truth and influence, by requiring a surrender of every thing Christian in the schools, to accommodate their sectarian position. Or, if they reply that they would wholly supplant the common schools, leaving only parochial and sectarian schools in their place, on the ground that our government can not, without some infringement on religion, be made to coalesce with any thing Christian, then is it seen they are endeavoring to make the state "godless" in order to make the school Christian. Exactly this, indeed, one of their most distinguished and capable teachers in Pennsylvania is just now engaged to effect; insisting that the civil state has no right to educate children at all; not only controverting a constituent element of our civil order, but claiming it as a Christian right that the state shall exercise no Christian function. Which then is better, a godless government or a godless school? And if his own church will not suffer a godless school, what has it more earnestly insisted on than the horrible impiety of a state separated from God and religion, and the consequent duty of all kings and magistrates to be servants and defenders of the church? The Catholic doctrine is plainly in a dilemma here, and can no way be accommodated. If the state is godless, then it should as certainly withdraw from that as from the school, which, if it persists in doing, it as certainly does what it can, under the pretext of religion, to empty both the state and the schools of all religion.

The true ideal state manifestly is one school and one Christianity. But it does not follow that we are to have as many schools as we have distinct views of Christianity, because we have not so many distinct Christianities. Nor is any thing more cruel and abominable than to take the little children apart, whom Christ embraced so freely, and make them parties to all our grown up discords whom Christ made one with himself and each other, in their lovelier and, God forgive us if perchance it also be, their wiser age. Let us draw near rather to the common Christ we profess, doing it through them and for their sake, and see if we can not find how to set them together under Christ, as his common flock.

In most of our American communities, especially those which are older and more homogeneous, we have no difficulty in retaining the Bible in the schools and doing every thing necessary to a sound Christian training. Nor, in the larger cities, and the more recent settlements, where the population is partly Catholic, is there any, the least difficulty in arranging a plan so as to yield the accommodation they need, if only there were a real disposition on both sides to have the arrangement. And precisely here, I suspect, is the main difficulty. There may have been a want of consideration sometimes manifested on the Protestant side, or a willingness to thrust our own forms of religious teaching on the children of Catholics. Wherever we have insisted on retaining the Protestant Bible as a school book, and making the use of it by the children of Catholic families, compulsory, there has been good reason for complaining of our intolerance. But there is a much greater difficulty, I fear, and more invincible, on the other side. In New York the Catholics complained of the reading of the Protestant Scriptures in the schools, and of the text-books employed, some of which contained hard expressions against the Catholic church. The Bible was accordingly withdrawn from the schools and all religious instruction discontinued. The text-books of the schools were sent directly to Archbishop Hughes, in person, to receive exactly such expurgations as he and his clergy would direct. They declined the offer, by a very slender evasion, and it was afterward found that some of the books complained of were in actual use, in their own church schools, though already removed from the schools of the city. Meantime the immense and very questionable sacrifice thus made, to accommodate the complaints of the Catholics, resulted in no discontinuance of their schools, neither in any important accession to the common schools of the city, from the children of Catholic families. On the contrary, the priests now change their note and begin to complain that the schools are "godless" or "atheistical"—just as they have required them to be. In facts like these, fortified by the fact that some of the priests are even denying, in public lectures, the right of the state to educate children at all, we seem to discover an absolute determination that the children shall be withdrawn, at whatever cost, and that no terms of accommodation shall be satisfactory. It is not that satisfaction is impossible, but that there is really no desire for it. Were there any desire, the ways in which it may be accomplished are many and various.

1. Make the use of the Bible in the Protestant or Don version, optional.
2. Compile a book of Scripture reading lessons, by agreement from both versions.
3. Provide for religious instruction, at given hours, or a given day, by the clergy, or by qualified teachers such parents may choose.
4. Prepare a book of Christian morality, distinctive doctrine of religion or a faith, which shall be taught indiscriminately to all the scholars.

Out of these and other elements like these, it is not difficult to construct, by agreement, such a plan as will be Christian, and will not infringe, in the least, upon the tenets either party, the Protestant or the Catholic. It has been done in Holland and, where it was much more difficult, in Ireland. The British government, undertaking at last, in good faith, construct a plan of national education for Ireland, appoint Archbishop Whately and the Catholic Archbishop of Dublin with five others, one a Presbyterian and one a Unitarian, to be a board or committee of superintendence. They agreed upon selection of reading lessons from both translations of the Scriptures, and, by means of a system of restrictions and qualifications, carefully arranged, providing for distinct methods and times of religious instruction, they were able to construct a union, not godless or negative, but thoroughly Christian in its character, and so to draw as many as 500,000 of the children into the public schools; conferring thus upon the poor neglected and hitherto oppressed Irish, greater benefits than they have before received from any and all public measures since the conquest.

I can not go into the particulars of this adjustment, neither is it necessary. Whoever will take pains to trace out the particular features of the plan, will see that such an adjustment is possible. Enough is it for the present to say, that what has been can be, and that if there is a real and true desire in the two parties to this coming controversy, to settle any plan that will unite and satisfy them both, it will be done. It may never be done in such a manner as to silence all opposition or attack from the ultra Protestant party on one side, and the ultra Catholic on the other. Bigotry will have its way, and will assuredly act in character here, as it has in all ages past and does in Ireland now. The cry will be raised on one side, that the Bible is given up because it is read only at the option of the parents, or because only extracts from it are read, though the extracts amount to nearly the whole book, or because they are, some of them, made from the Catholic and some from the Protestant version; whereas, if only this or that catechism were taught, with not a word of Scripture, no complaint of a loss of the Bible would be heard of, or if the Psalter translation were read, instead of the Psalms, it would be regarded as no subject of complaint at all. On the other, the Catholic side, it will be insisted that the church authority is given up, though every word and teaching is by and from it, or that religion itself is corrupted by the profane mixtures of a Protestant proximity and intercourse. Probably the bigots, on both sides, will have much to say, in deprecation of the "godless system of education," and yet there will be more religious teaching, and more impression made of true religion, by that cordial and Christian adjustment of differences, which brings the children of two hostile bands together, in this manner, than by whole days and weeks of drill and catechism in separate schools.

There is a great deal of cant in this complaint of godless education, or the defect of religious instruction in schools, as Baptist Noel, Dr. Vaughan, and other distinguished English writers, have abundantly shown. It is not, of course, religious instruction for a child to be drilled, year upon year, in spelling out the words of the Bible, as a reading book—it may be only an exercise that answers the problem how to dull the mind most effectually to all sense of the Scripture words, and communicate least of their meaning. Nay, if the Scriptures were entirely excluded from the schools, and all formal teaching of religious doctrine, I would yet undertake, if I could have my liberty as a teacher, to communicate more of real Christian truth to a Catholic and a Protestant boy, seated side by side, in the regulation of their treatment of each other, as related in terms of justice and charity, and their government as members of the school community, (where truth, order, industry and obedience are duties laid upon the conscience, under God,) than they will ever draw from any catechism, or have worn into their brain by the dull and stammering exercise of a Scripture reading lesson. The Irish schools have a distinct Christian character, only not as distinctly sectarian as if they were wholly Protestant or wholly Catholic. They are Christian schools, such as ours may be and ought to be, and, I trust, will be, to the latest generations, nor any the less so that they are common schools.

Neither is it to be imagined or felt that religion has lost its place in the scheme of education, because the Scriptures are not read as a stated and compulsory exercise, or because the higher mysteries of Christianity as a faith or doctrine of salvation, are not generally taught, but only the Christian rules of conduct, as pertaining to the common relations of duty under God. What is wanting may still be provided for, only less adequately, in other places; at home, in the church, or in lessons given by the clergy. It is not as when children are committed to a given school, like the Girard College, for example, there to receive their whole training, and where, if it excludes religion, they have no religious training at all.

I do then take the ground, and upon this I insist, as the true American ground, that we are to have common schools, and never to give them up, for any purpose, or in obedience to any demand whatever—never to give them up, either by formal surrender, or by implication; as by a distribution of moneys to ecclesiastical and sectarian schools. The state can not distribute funds, in this manner, without renouncing even a first principle of our American institutions, and becoming the supporter of a sect in religion. It may as well support the priests of a church, as support the schools of a church, separated from other schools, for the very purpose of being subjected to the priests.

But while we are firm in this attitude, and hold it as a point immovable, we must, for that very reason, be the more ready to do justice to the religious convictions of all parties or sects, and to yield them such concessions, or enter into such arrangements as will accommodate their peculiar principles and clear them of any infringement.

But it will be objected by some, that while this should be done, if there were any thing to hope from it, there is really no hope that our concessions or modifications will be of any avail, and therefore that they should not be made at all; for they will only so far abridge the value of our schools without yielding any recompense for the loss. Then let us offer the modifications, offer any terms of union that can be offered without a virtual destruction or renunciation of the system; and then if they are not accepted it will not be our fault. I very much fear they will not be, that an absolute separation of the Catholic children from our schools is already determined, and that no revision of the sentence can be had. Still it is much for us to take away every excuse for such a determination, and every complaint or pretext by which it is justified.

Then, having done it, we can take the ground explicitly, and clear of all ambiguity, that they who exclude themselves are not Americans, and are not acting in their complaints or agitations, on any principle that meets the tenor of our American institutions. Nothing will be more evident, and they should be made to bear the whole odium of it. If to keep their people apart from the dreaded influence of Protestant Christianity, they were to buy townships of land, or large quarters in our cities, to be occupied only by Catholics, walled in by their own by-laws, and allowing no Protestant family, or tradesman, or publican, to reside in the precinct—no one to enter it without a pass; and then to come before our legislatures in petition that we will distribute moneys to support their roads, and pay their constables and gate-keepers; they would scarcely do a greater insult to our American society than they do in these separations from our common schools, and the petitions they are offering to be justified and rewarded in the separation.

But we tax them, it will be said, for the support of the common schools, and then, receiving no benefit from the tax they pay, they are obliged to tax themselves again, for schools of their own. It is even so, and for one, apart from all resentment, I rejoice in it; unless they have grievances put upon them by the organization of our schools, such as justify their withdrawal. We tax the Quakers for defect of military service, and bachelors who have no children, and we ought, much more, to tax the refractory un-American position taken by these Catholic strangers, after we have greeted them with so great hospitality, and loaded them with so many American privileges. If now they will not enter into the great American institution, so fundamental to our very laws and liberties, let them pay for it, and measure their deserts by their dissatisfactions. If they will be foreigners still among our people, let them have remembrances that interpret their conduct to them in a way of just emphasis.

Meantime let us be sure also of this, that a day is at hand when they will weary of this kind of separation, and will visit on their priests, who have required it, a just retribution. One generation, or possibly two, may bear this separation, this burden of double taxation, this withdrawal of their children from society and its higher advantages, to be shut up or penned as foreign tribes in the state, thus to save the prejudices of a discarded and worthless nationality; but another generation is to come who will have drunk more deeply into the spirit of our institutions, and attained to a more sufficient understanding of the hard lot put upon them, in this manner, by a jealous and overbearing priesthood. Then comes a reaction, both against them and their religion; then a flocking back to the schools to reap their advantages; and it will be strange if the very measure now counted on as the means of their preservation, does not, of itself, become one of the strongest reasons for the alienation of their children from it. Of this we may be quite sure, and it ought not to be any secret to them, that their children of the coming time will at last find a way to be Americans; if not under the Pope and by the altars, then without them.

Neither let it be said that this is a matter which lies at the disposal of politics, and that our political demagogues will sell any thing, even our birthright as a people, to carry the vote of a campaign. The experiment has just been tried in Detroit, with a most signal and disastrous failure. In cases where the issue touches no religious interest or feeling of the Protestants, and the Catholics can be gained to throw a casting vote on one side or the other, the politicians will not deal so absurdly, if they consent to buy that vote by some great promise, and I have so little confidence in many of them, under the prodigious temptations of a canvass, as to have it for granted, that they will stick at nothing which is possible. But here, thank God, is one thing that is impossible, and whatever politician ventures on the experiment, will find that he has not worked his problem rightly—that if Catholics can be often united and led in masses to the vote, so Protestants will sometimes go in masses where they are not led, save by their principles. That our legislatures can not and will not be gained to allow the ruling out of the Scriptures, and all religious instruction from the schools, as in New York city, I am by no means certain—I very much fear that they will—but that they can ever become supporters and fund-holders to ecclesiastical schools, or be induced to give up common schools, I do not believe. Whatever politician or political party ventures on that experiment, will find that he has rallied a force manifold greater against him than he has drawn to his aid. A point so thoroughly un-American, so directly opposite also to the deepest convictions of the great Protestant majorities of the country, can not be carried, and, if pressed, will suffice to fix a stigma that is immovable upon any leader who is desperate enough to try the experiment.

Here I will close. The subject is a painful one, and not any the less so that the line of our duty is plain. It can not be said by any, the most prejudiced critic, that our conduct as a people, to strangers and men of another religion, has not been generous and free beyond any former example in the history of mankind. We have used hospitality without grudging. In one view it seems to be a dark and rather mysterious providence, that we have thrown upon us, to be our fellow-citizens, such multitudes of people, depressed, for the most part, in character, instigated by prejudices so intense against our religion. But there is a brighter and more hopeful side to the picture. These Irish prejudices, embittered by the crushing tyranny of England, for three whole centuries and more, will gradually yield to the kindness of our hospitality, and to the discovery that it is not so much the Protestant religion that has been their enemy, as the jealousy and harsh dominion of conquest. God knows exactly what is wanting, both in us and them, and God has thrown us together that, in terms of good citizenship, and acts of love, we may be gradually melted into one homogeneous people. Probably no existing form of Christianity is perfect—the Romish we are sure is not—the Puritan was not, else why should it so soon have lost its rigors? The Protestant, more generally viewed, contains a wider variety of elements, but these too seem to be waiting for some process of assimilation that shall weld them finally together. Therefore God, we may suppose, throws all these diverse multitudes, Protestant and Catholic, together, in crossings so various, and a ferment of experience so manifold, that he may wear us into some other and higher and more complete unity, than we are able, of ourselves and by our own wisdom, to settle. Let us look for this, proving all things, and holding fast that which is good, until the glorious result of a perfected and comprehensive Christianity is made to appear, and is set up here for a sign to all nations. Let us draw our strange friends as close to us as possible, not in any party scramble for power, but in a solemn reference of duty to the nation and to God. I can not quite renounce the hope that a right and cordial advance on our part—one that, duly careful to preserve the honors of Christianity, concedes every thing required by our great principle of equal right to all, and as firmly refuses to yield any thing so distinctively American as this noble institution, identified with our history as the blood with the growth of our bodies—will command the respect and finally the assent of our Catholic friends themselves. And since God has better things in store even for religion, than the repugnant attitudes of its professed disciples can at present permit, I would even hope that he may use an institution so far external to the church, as a means of cementing the generations to come in a closer unity, and a more truly catholic peace; that, as being fellow-citizens with each other, under the state, in the ingenuous days of youth and youthful discipline, they may learn how also to be no more strangers and foreigners, but fellow-citizens with the saints and of the household of God.

16

Education

Ralph Waldo Emerson, 1876

Ralph Waldo Emerson (1803–1882) is widely regarded as one of America's most influential writers, thinkers, and philosophers. He was one of the central founders of Transcendentalism, a philosophy that sought to transcend the empirical realm by relying upon intuition as a source of knowledge. Emerson was born on May 25, 1803, in Boston, Massachusetts. After graduation from high school in 1821, he taught school for two years in Waltham, Massachusetts. The son of a minister, Emerson soon followed his father's footsteps and began preparation as a minister. In 1825, he entered Harvard University's Divinity School. In 1830, he became a minister at the Second Unitarian Church of Boston. Only a few years later, however, he began to question his faith. Eventually, he left his pastoral role for other pursuits. He spent the rest of his life as a lecturer and writer.

In general, the philosophy that Emerson developed rejected traditional hierarchical roles in society in favor of an individualistic approach. His work also emphasized the need for man to connect with nature in order to reach his full potential. He developed famous lectures such as "The American Scholar" and "The Divinity School Address," which challenged traditional understandings of theology. His writings were quite radical at the time. Throughout his

American Educational Thought: Essays from 1640–1940, pages 225–233
Copyright © 2010 by Information Age Publishing

remarkable career, Emerson published hundreds of books, articles, lectures, addresses, and poems. He remains one of the most influential intellectual figures in American history. —JWN

With the key of the secret he marches faster
From strength to strength, and for night brings day,
While classes or tribes too weak to master
The flowing conditions of life, give way.

There comes the period of the imagination to each, a later youth; the power of beauty, the power of books, of poetry. Culture makes his books realities to him, their characters more brilliant, more effective on his mind, than his actual mates. Do not spare to put novels into the hands of young people as an occasional holiday and experiment; but, above all, good poetry in all kinds, epic, tragedy, lyric. If we can touch the imagination, we serve them, they will never forget it. Let him read "Tom Brown at Rugby," read "Tom Brown at Oxford,"—better yet, read "Hodson's Life"—Hodson who took prisoner the king of Delhi. They teach the same truth, —a trust, against all appearances, against all privations, in your own worth, and not in tricks, plotting, or patronage.

I believe that our own experience instructs us that the secret of Education lies in respecting the pupil. It is not for you to choose what he shall know, what he shall do. It is chosen and foreordained, and he only holds the key to his own secret. By your tampering and thwarting and too much governing he may be hindered from his end and kept out of his own. Respect the child. Wait and see the new product of Nature. Nature loves analogies, but not repetitions. Respect the child. Be not too much his parent. Trespass not on his solitude.

But I hear the outcry which replies to this suggestion: —Would you verily throw up the reins of public and private discipline; would you leave the young child to the mad career of his own passions and whimsies, and call this anarchy a respect for the child's nature? I answer, —Respect the child, respect him to the end, but also respect yourself. Be the companion of his thought, the friend of his friendship, the lover of his virtue, —but no kinsman of his sin. Let him find you so true to yourself that you are the irreconcilable hater of his vice and imperturbable slighter of his trifling.

The two points in a boy's training are, to keep his *nature* and train off all but that—to keep his *nature*, but stop off his uproar, fooling and horseplay—keep his nature and arm it with knowledge in the very direction in which it points. Here are the two capital facts, Genius and Drill. The first is the inspiration in the well-born healthy child, the new perception he has of nature. Somewhat he sees in forms or hears in music or apprehends in mathematics, or believes practicable in mechanics or possible in political society, which no one else sees or hears or believes. This is the perpetual romance of new life, the invasion of God into the old dead world, when he sends into quiet houses a young soul with a thought which is not met, looking for something which is not there, but which ought to be there: the thought is dim but it is sure, and he casts about restless for means and masters to verify it; he makes wild attempts to explain himself and invoke the aid and consent of the bystanders. Baffled for want of language and methods to convey his meaning, not yet clear to himself, he conceives that though not in this house or town, yet in some other house or town is the wise master who can put him in possession of the rules and instruments to execute his will. Happy this child with a bias, with a thought which entrances him, leads him, now into deserts now into cities, the fool of an idea. Let him follow it in good and in evil report, in good or bad company; it will justify itself; it will lead him at last into the illustrious society of the lovers of truth.

In London, in a private company, I became acquainted with a gentleman, Sir Charles Fellowes, who, being at Xanthus, in the Aegean Sea, had seen a Turk point with his staff to some carved work on the corner of a stone almost buried in the soil. Fellowes scraped away the dirt, was struck with the beauty of the sculptured ornaments, and, looking about him, observed more blocks and fragments like this. He returned to the spot, procured laborers and uncovered many blocks. He went back to England, bought a Greek grammar and learned the language; he read history and studied ancient art to explain his stones; he interested Gibson the sculptor; he invoked the assistance of the English Government; he called in the succor of Sir Humphry Davy to analyze the pigments; of experts in coins, of scholars and connoisseurs; and at last in his third visit brought home to England such statues and marble reliefs and such careful plans that he was able to reconstruct, in the British Museum where it now stands, the perfect model of the Ionic trophy-monument, fifty years older than the Parthenon of Athens, and which had been destroyed by earthquakes, then by iconoclast Christians, then by savage Turks. But mark that in the task he had achieved an excellent education, and become associated with distinguished scholars whom he had interested in his pursuit; in short, had formed a college for himself; the enthusiast had found the master, the masters, whom he sought. Always genius seeks genius, desires nothing so much as to be a pupil and to find those who can lend it aid to perfect itself.

Nor are the two elements, enthusiasm and chill, incompatible. Accuracy is essential to beauty. The very definition of the intellect is Aristotle's:

"that by which we know terms or boundaries." Give a boy accurate perceptions. Teach him the difference between the similar and the same. Make
him call things by their right names. Pardon in him no blunder. Then he
will give you solid satisfaction as long as he lives. It is better to teach the
child arithmetic and Latin grammar than rhetoric or moral philosophy,
because they require exactitude of performance; it is made certain that the
lesson is mastered, and that power of performance is worth more than the
knowledge. He can learn anything which is important to him now that the
power to learn is secured: as mechanics say, when one has learned the use
of tools, it is easy to work at a new craft.

Letter by letter, syllable by syllable, the child learns to read, and in good
time can convey to all the domestic circle the sense of Shakespeare. By
many steps each just as short, the stammering boy and the hesitating colle-
gian, in the school debate, in college clubs, in mock court, comes at last to
full, secure, triumphant unfolding of his thought in the popular assembly,
with a fullness of power that makes all the steps forgotten.

But this function of opening and feeding the human mind is not to be
fulfilled by any mechanical or military method; is not to be trusted to any
skill less large than Nature itself. You must not neglect the form, but you
must secure the essentials. It is curious how perverse and intermeddling we
are, and what vast pains and cost we incur to do wrong. Whilst we all know
in our own experience and apply natural methods in our own business,
—in education our common sense fails us, and we are continually trying
costly machinery against nature, in patent schools and academies and in
great colleges and universities.

The natural method forever confutes our experiments, and we must
still come back to it. The whole theory of the school is on the nurse's or
mother's knee. The child is as hot to learn as the mother is to impart. There
is mutual delight. The joy of our childhood in hearing beautiful stories
from some skilful aunt who loves to tell them, must be repeated in youth.
The boy wishes to learn to skate, to coast, to catch a fish in the brook, to
hit a mark with a snowball or a stone; and a boy a little older is just as well
pleased to teach him these sciences. Not less delightful is the mutual pleasure of teaching and learning the secret of algebra, or of chemistry, or of
good reading and good recitation of poetry or of prose, or of chosen facts
in history or in biography.

Nature provided for the communication of thought, by planting with
it in the receiving mind a fury to impart it. T'is so in every art, in every science. One burns to tell the new fact, the other burns to hear it. See how far
a young doctor will ride or walk to witness a new surgical operation. I have

seen a carriage-maker's shop emptied of all its workmen into the street, to scrutinize a new pattern from New York. So in literature, the young man who has taste for poetry, for fine images, for noble thoughts, is insatiable for this nourishment, and forgets all the world for the more learned friend, —who finds equal joy in dealing out his treasures.

Happy the natural college thus self-instituted around every natural teacher; the young men of Athens around Socrates; of Alexandria around Plotinus; of Paris around Abelard; of Germany around Fichte, or Niebuhr, or Goethe: in short the natural sphere of every leading mind. But the moment this is organized, difficulties begin. The college was to be the nurse and home of genius; but, though every young man is born with some determination in his nature, and is a potential genius; is at last to be one; it is, in the most, obstructed and delayed, and, whatever they may hereafter be, their senses are now opened in advance of their minds. They are more sensual than intellectual. Appetite and indolence they have, but no enthusiasm. These come in numbers to the college: few geniuses: and the teaching comes to be arranged for these many, and not for those few. Hence the instruction seems to require skilful tutors, of accurate and systematic mind, rather than ardent and inventive masters. Besides, the youth of genius are eccentric, won't drill, are irritable, uncertain, explosive, solitary, not men of the world, not good for every-day association. You have to work for huge classes instead of individuals; you must lower your flag and reef your sails to wait for the dull sailors; you grow departmental, routinary, military almost with your discipline and college police. But what doth such a school to form a great and heroic character? What abiding Hope can it inspire? What Reformer will it nurse? What poet will it breed to sing to the human race? What discoverer of Nature's laws will it prompt to enrich us by disclosing in the mind the statute which all matter must obey? What fiery soul will it send out to warm a nation with his charity? What tranquil mind will it have fortified to walk with meekness in private and obscure duties, to wait and to suffer? Is it not manifest that our academic institutions should have a wider scope; that they should not be timid and keep the ruts of the last generation, but that wise men thinking for themselves and heartily seeking the good of mankind, and counting the cost of innovation, should dare to arouse the young to a just and heroic life; that the moral nature should be addressed in the school-room, and children should be treated as the highborn candidates of truth and virtue?

So to regard the young child, the young man, requires, no doubt, rare patience: a patience that nothing but faith in the remedial forces of the soul can give. You see his sensualism; you see his want of those tastes and perceptions which make the power and safety of your character. Very likely. But he has something else. If he has his own vice, he has its correlative virtue. Every mind should be allowed to make its own statement in action, and its balance will appear. In these judgments one needs that foresight which was attributed to an eminent reformer, of whom it was said "his patience could see in the bud of the aloe the blossom at the end of a hundred years." Alas for the cripple Practice when it seeks to come up with the bird Theory, which flies before it. Try your design on the best school. The scholars are of all ages and temperaments and capacities. It is difficult to class them, some are too young, some are slow, some perverse. Each requires so much consideration, that the morning hope of the teacher, of a day of love and progress, is often closed at evening by despair. Each single case, the more it is considered, shows more to be done; and the strict conditions of the hours, on one side, and the number of tasks, on the other. Whatever becomes of our method, the conditions stand fast, —six hours, and thirty, fifty, or a hundred and fifty pupils. Something must he done, and done speedily, and in this distress the wisest are tempted to adopt violent means, to proclaim martial law, corporal punishment, mechanical arrangement, bribes, spies, wrath, main strength and ignorance, in lieu of that wise genial providential influence they had hoped, and yet hope at some future day to adopt. Of course the devotion to details reacts injuriously on the teacher. He cannot indulge his genius, he cannot delight in personal relations with young friends, when his eye is always on the clock, and twenty classes are to be dealt with before the day is done. Besides, how can he please himself with genius, and foster modest virtue? A sure proportion of rogue and dunce finds its way into every school and requires a cruel share of time, and the gentle teacher, who wished to be a Providence to youth, is grown a martinet, sore with suspicions; knows as much vice as the judge of a police court, and his love of learning is lost in the routine of grammars and books of elements.

A rule is so easy that it does not need a man to apply it; an automaton, a machine, can be made to keep a school so. It facilitates labor and thought so much that there is always the temptation in large schools to omit the end-less task of meeting the wants of each single mind, and to govern by steam. But it is at frightful cost. Our modes of Education aim to expedite, to save labor; to do for masses what cannot be done for masses, what must be done reverently, one by one: say rather, the whole world is needed for the tuition of each pupil. The advantages of this system of emulation and display are so prompt and obvious, it is such a time-saver, it is so energetic on slow and on bad natures, and is of so easy application, needing no sage or poet, but any tutor or schoolmaster in his first term can apply it, —that it is not strange that this calomel of culture should be a popular medicine. On the other hand, total abstinence from this drug, and the adoption of simple discipline and the following of nature, involves at once immense claims on the time, the thoughts, on the life of the teacher. It requires time, use, insight, event, all the great lessons and assistances of God; and only to think of using it implies character and profoundness; to enter on this course of discipline is to be good and great. It is precisely analogous to the difference between the use of corporal punishment and the methods of love. It is so easy to bestow on a bad boy a blow, overpower him, and get obedience without words, that in this world of hurry and distraction, who can wait for the returns of reason and the conquest of self; in the uncertainty too whether that will ever come? And yet the familiar observation of the universal compensations might suggest the fear that so summary a stop of a bad humor was more jeopardous than its continuance.

Now the correction of this quack practice is to import into Education the wisdom of life. Leave this military hurry and adopt the pace of Nature. Her secret is patience. Do you know how the naturalist learns all the secrets of the forest, of plants, of birds, of beasts, of reptiles, of fishes, of the rivers and the sea? When he goes into the woods the birds fly before him and he finds none; when he goes to the river bank, the fish and the reptile swim away and leave him alone. His secret is patience; he sits down, and sits still; he is a statue; he is a log. These creatures have no value for their time, and he must put as low a rate on his. By dint of obstinate sitting still, reptile, fish, bird and beast, which all wish to return to their haunts, begin to return. He sits still; if they approach, he remains passive as the stone he sits upon. They lose their fear. They have curiosity too about him. By and by the curiosity masters the fear, and they come swimming, creeping and flying towards him; and as he is still immovable, they not only resume their haunts and their ordinary labors and manners, show themselves to him in their work-day trim, but also volunteer some degree of advances towards fellowship and good understanding with a biped who behaves so civilly and well. Can you not baffle the impatience and passion of the child by your tranquility? Can you not wait for him, as Nature and Providence do? Can you not keep for his mind and ways, for his secret, the same curiosity you give to the squirrel, snake, rabbit, and the sheldrake and the deer? He has a secret; wonderful methods in him; he is, —every child, —a new style of man; give him time and opportunity. Talk of Columbus and Newton! I tell you the child just born in yonder hovel is the beginning of a revolution as great as theirs. But you must have the believing and prophetic eye. Have the self-command you wish to inspire. Your teaching and discipline must have the reserve and taciturnity of Nature. Teach them to hold their tongues by holding your own. Say little; do not snarl; do not chide; but govern by the eye. See what they need, and that the right thing is done.

I confess myself utterly at a loss in suggesting particular reforms in our ways of teaching. No discretion that can be lodged with a school-committee, with the overseers or visitors of an academy, of a college, can at all avail to reach these difficulties and perplexities, but they solve themselves when we leave institutions and address individuals. The will, the male power, organizes, imposes its own thought and wish on others, and makes that military eye which controls boys as it controls men; admirable in its results, a fortune to him who has it, and only dangerous when it leads the workman to overvalue and overuse it and precludes him from finer means. Sympathy, the female force, —which they must use who have not the first, —deficient in instant control and the breaking down of resistance, is more subtle and lasting and creative. I advise teachers to cherish mother-wit. I assume that you will keep the grammar, reading, writing and arithmetic in order; 'tis easy and of course you will. But smuggle in a little contraband wit, fancy, imagination, thought. If you have a taste which you have suppressed because it is not shared by those about you, tell them that. Set this law up, whatever becomes of the rules of the school: they must not whisper, much less talk; but if one of the young people says a wise thing, greet it, and let all the children clap their hands. They shall have no book but school-books in the room; but if one has brought in a Plutarch or Shakespeare or Don Quixote or Goldsmith or any other good book, and understands what he reads, put him at once at the head of the class. Nobody shall be disorderly, or leave his desk without permission, but if a boy runs from his bench, or a girl, because the fire falls, or to check some injury that a little dastard is inflicting behind his desk on some helpless sufferer, take away the medal from the head of the class and give it on the instant to the brave rescuer. If a child happens to show that he knows any fact about astronomy, or plants, or birds, or rocks, or history, that interests him and you, hush all the classes and encourage him to tell it so that all may hear. Then you have made your school-room like the world. Of course you will insist on modesty in the children, and respect to their teachers, but if the boy stops you in your speech, cries out that you are wrong and sets you right, hug him!

To whatsoever upright mind, to whatsoever beating heart I speak, to you it is committed to educate men. By simple living, by an illimitable soul, you inspire, you correct, you instruct, you raise, you embellish all. By your own act you teach the beholder how to do the practicable. According to the depth from which you draw your life, such is the depth not only of your strenuous effort, but of your manners and presence.

The beautiful nature of the world has here blended your happiness with your power. Work straight on in absolute duty, and you lend an arm and an encouragement to all the youth of the universe. Consent yourself to be an organ of your highest thought, and lo! suddenly you put all men in your debt, and are the fountain of an energy that goes pulsing on with waves of benefit to the borders of society, to the circumference of things.

17

Secularized Education

Robert Louis Dabney, 1879

Born to parents who were friends with the likes of Patrick Henry and Thomas
Jefferson, Robert Louis Dabney (1820–1898) grew up with family connections
to the plantation aristocracy of Virginia. He underwent an education common to those on smaller southern plantations, which included both individual tutoring by his elder brother and attendance at an "old field school"—a
situation where classes were held in abandoned old fields or small log cabins
by a teacher who was voluntarily paid by the parents.

Dabney's father died when he was fourteen, but he still managed to matriculate at the age of sixteen at Hampden-Sydney College. He went on to complete his master's degree at the University of Virginia, after which he taught
school for a short period of time while helping run the family farm. He later
attended United Theological Seminary and after graduating served as pastor
for seven years in two different communities. In one of these communities,
he also started a classical school. Later, he taught theology at the seminary for
twenty-four years while co-pastoring the college church in Hampden Sydney.
At the end of his life he taught for eleven years at the University of Texas at
Austin.

American Educational Thought: Essays from 1640–1940, pages 235–254
Copyright © 2010 by Information Age Publishing
235

A well-known intellectual leader among southern Presbyterians, when he died he was eulogized as a "lover of the South." A staunch defender of states' rights and slavery, Dabney served in the Civil War as an officer under his brother-in-law, Stonewall Jackson. In education Dabney argued against what he saw as the Northern idea of state-supported public schooling. In this essay, he sets forth his difficulties with this option and his own alternative by asking and answering two critical questions: "Who is the agent entitled to control education?" and "What is right education?" —PLG

Who is the agent entitled to control education? What is right education? These questions are interdependent. Two answers have been proposed to the first in history: The State, the Church. In Europe, Liberalism says the State, and insists on secularizing education, by which it means its release from the control of popery. Liberals see clearly that, under that control, there will be no true freedom. But, as they also insist on secularizing the State, their idea of a free education is of one devoid of religion, separating the mental from the spiritual culture. Thus they conclude that education must be Godless, in order to be free. Rome has herself to blame for this error, as for most of European skepticism. She claims that she alone is Christian: independent minds reply, "Then Christianity is evil." So if her education were the only Christian, freemen would have to reject Christian education. If private judgment is sin; if the hierarchy is the church; if the teacher is a real priest and essential "proxy" between men and salvation; if his teaching is infallible; if the real end of the culture is to enslave the soul to a priesthood with a foreign head; if that head is absolutely superior to the secular sovereignty, such ecclesiastical education will be civil slavery. It is not strange that men seeking civil liberty spurn it.

The mistake is in confounding ecclesiastical with Christian education. Let the Scripture be heard: "The kingdom of God is within you," consisting, not in a greedy hierarchy, but in the rule of Truth; the clergy are not lords over God's heritage, but only "ministers by whom we believe"; it has no penalties but the spiritual, reaching no man's civil rights; its only other function is didactic, and its teaching only binds so far as the layman's own conscience responds; it is the Church's duty to instruct parents how God would have them rear their children, and enforce the duty by spiritual sanctions; but there its official power ends. It does not usurp the doing of the important task it inculcates. As a Christian private man the minister lends other parents his knowledge and virtues to co-operate in their work. But all this implies no danger either to spiritual or religious liberty.

But it will be well for the modern Liberal to pause and ask whether he secures anything by this transfer of the educating function from Church to State? Does he point to the results of Jesuit teaching, spurious, shallow scholarship, an enslaved and morbid conscience, which dares not even wish to break its fetters, the insatiable greed of the hierarchy for influence and money, the hateful perversion of the sacred task to inspire falsehood and prejudice for this end? The picture is sufficiently repulsive. But are only ecclesiastics grasping? Is human nature depraved? Is it essentially the same in all men? Then why are they not to be expected to act in similar ways, when subjected to the same temptations? And the modern Liberal is the last man to overlook this truth; since he is sceptical of all professions of spiritual principles in clergymen, and prone to ascribe secular motives. He should, then, expect the demagogue to show a misguided ambition exactly like the priests. What is the hierarch but a ghostly demagogue? The demagogue is but the hierarch of Mammon's altar. Does he not, for instance, pervert that other educating agency, the press, just as violently as the Jesuit the school? Now, let him become ruler in the State and the State become educator; and there is just the same risk that the education of youth will be perverted to subserve a faction, and that, by the hateful means of imbuing their minds with error and passion in place of truth and right. The result is despotism of a party instead of pope. One may be as bad as the other.

But if the State is the educator, in America, at least, education must be secularized totally. In theory our State is the institute for realizing secular justice. It has absolutely severed itself from all religions equally; has pledged itself that no man's civil rights shall be modified or equality diminished by any religion or the lack of any; and has forbidden the establishment of any religion by law, and the imposition of any burden for a religious pretext on any. But the State school teacher is her official, and teaches by her authority. All school-officials derive their authority from State laws, hence all their functions are as truly State actions as those of the sheriff in hanging, or the judge in sentencing a murderer. Especially is the school fund, raised by taxation, the common and equal property of the people.

But as our people are divided among many religions, that money ought no more to be used in schools to teach one religion in preference to the others, than in a church establishment. Once the people of a small State, like Connecticut, were so homogeneous, that any dissentient minority was minute, and the dominant religion was taught "on State account," without any protest loud enough to be inconvenient. But the mixture of our people, and especially the strength and audacity of popery, now makes all this different. Papists make an effective issue, arguing that the State must not use the people's money to teach King James's version, which they, a part of the people, believe heretical. Zealous Protestants, usually zealous State school men, try to flout this plea. But would they assent to the State's teaching their children, with their money, the version which says: "Except ye do penance ye shall all likewise perish?" They exclaim: "That is an erroneous version, while King James's is faithful." Theologically that is doubtless true. But the very point of the State's covenant with the people is, that the State shall not judge, either way, of that proposition. It has been bargained that, in the State arena, we shall respect papists' religious views, precisely as we require them to respect ours. Suppose them, some day, in as large a majority in some State as Protestants are in New England, would we acquiesce in their forcing the study of the Douay version in State schools? So, unless we admit that our might makes our right, we ought not to inflict the parallel wrongs on the Jews, Mohammedans, Atheists, and Buddhists among us, because they are still few.

It is sought to parry this conclusion thus: While all religions are equal, and no one established, the State is not an atheistic institute, but must ground itself in the will of God, which is the standard of all rights. That the State is an ethical institute and for ethical ends. That hence it enjoins the Sabbath, punishes blasphemy, etc. That equally the State, while not establishing one religion to the prejudice of others, ought to teach the divine truths common to all, by the unsectarian use of the Bible. But whether this be the just basis of a commonwealth or not, our States do not avow it. And second, the question is not of the original Scripture in common schools, but of some one version, among other competing ones, which even Protestants do not claim to be infallible. Hence the question, Which version? raises sectarian issues. Third, we do not believe, any more than these reasoners, that the State can be atheistic, because it is an ethical institute, and the divine will is the only valid ethical rule. But the State finds the theistic basis in natural theology. The proof is, that pagan States, resting only on natural theism, were valid, and rightfully (Rom.13:5) possessed the allegiance even of Christians. The evasion therefore is futile.

But be the logic of this question what it may, the actual result is certain. The papists will inevitably carry the point, as they have already done in many places. That they will triumph everywhere else that they care to try, is plain from the growing timidity of the Bible advocates, the poverty of the compromises they offer, and the spreading indifference of the masses to the value of biblical teaching. In fact, on American premises, the Bible advocates have no plea but a pious predilection, and sooner or later logical considerations, when so clear, must assert their force. The difficulty of the problem appears thus: That it agitates other free governments than ours, as the British and Holland, at this day.

For the solution there are, on the theory of State education, four suggestions. The first is the unjust one of forcing the religion of the majority on the minority. The second is what is called in Great Britain the plan of "concurrent endowments." Each denomination may have its own schools endowed by the State, and teach its own religion in it along with secular learning. This is virtually the plan by which New York papists have been partially appeased. It is justly rejected by Protestants everywhere. First, because it offers no solution save where the several denominations are populous enough to sustain a school for each in the same vicinage. Second, because the State has no right thus virtually to assert the co-ordinate and equal value of opposing creeds, the truth of one of which may imply the positive falsehood of another. Third, because the State has no right to indicate of either of the creeds that it is, or is not, true and valuable. Fourth, because Protestantism is more promotive of thrift and wealth than the erroneous creeds; whence a given number of Protestants will pay more school-tax then the same number of errorists, so that this plan uses a part of their money to foster creeds they conscientiously believe mischievous. Fifth, it gives to error a pecuniary and moral support beyond what it would receive from the spontaneous zeal of its votaries. And last, it disunites the population by training youth in hostile religious camps. Irish and American papists have professed to approve because they gain by the plan. But who dreams that if they were in the majority they would be willing to see "good Catholic money" expended in teaching Protestant heresy?

The third plan proposes to give "unsectarian" religious instruction in the first hour of the day, while parents who dissent from it are allowed to detain their children from school until that hour is passed. This amounts to the State's establishing a religion and using the people's money to teach it, but permitting dissent without any other penalty than the taxation for a religious object which the taxpayer condemns. That is to say, it places the matter where England places her established religion, since the "Toleration Act" of William and Mary relieved dissenters of penal pains for absence from the Anglican churches. But the thing Americans claim is liberty and not toleration. They deny the State's right to select a religion, as the true and useful one, for anybody, willing or unwilling. Those who dissent from the selected religion deny that the State may thus expend the people's money as a bait to careless or erroneous parents to submit their children to the inculcation of error.

The only other alternative is to secularize the State's teaching absolutely, limiting it to matters merely secular, and leaving parents or the Church to supplement it with such religious teaching as they may please, or none. Some Christians, driven by the difficulty which has been disclosed, adopt this conclusion. The largest number, notwithstanding the difficulty, reject it with energy. Let us see whether this plan is either possible or admissible.

This is really the vital question. It cannot be discussed until we agree what education is, and disperse deceptive misconceptions of it. It is properly the whole man or person that is educated; but the main subject of the work is the spirit. Education is the nurture and development of the whole man for his proper end. The end must be conceived aright in order to understand the process. Even man's earthly end is predominantly moral. Now, if dexterity in any art, as in the handling of printer's type, a musket, a burin, a power-loom, were education, its secularization might be both possible and proper. Is not a confusion here the source of most of the argument in defence of that theory? For instance, "Why may not the State teach reading and writing without any religious adjuncts, as legitimately as the mechanic thus teaches his apprentices filing, planing, or hammering?" Because dexterity in an art is not education. The latter nurtures a soul, the other only drills a sense-organ or muscle; the one has a mechanical end, the other a moral. And this answer cannot be met by saying, "let it then be agreed that the State is only teaching an art, a dexterity that, for instance, of letters." For the State refuses to be understood thus: it claims to educate; as is witnessed by the universal argument of the advocates of this State function, that she has the right and duty of providing that the young citizens shall be competent to their responsibility as citizens. But these are ethical. Again, if the State professed to bestow, not an education, but a dexterity, equity would require her bestowing not only the arts of letters, but all other useful arts. For only the minority can ever live by literary arts; the great majority of children have equal rights to be taught the other bread-winning arts. Thus government would become the wildest communism. No, the State cannot adopt this evasion; unless she says that she educates, she can say nothing.

It should also be remarked here that the arts of reading and writing are rather means of education than education itself, and not the only nor the most effective means. As Macaulay showed, against Dr. S. Johnson, the unlettered part of Athenians were, in some respects, highly educated, while we see many minds, with these arts, really underdeveloped.

But is a really secularized education either possible or admissible?

First, No people of any age, religion, or civilization, before ours, has ever thought so. Against the present attempt, right or wrong, stands the whole common sense of mankind. Pagan, Papist, Mohammedan, Greek, Protestant, have all hitherto rejected any other education than one grounded in religion, as absurd and wicked. Let Mr. Webster be heard against the Girard will, which enjoined, in order to exclude Christianity from his college, that no minister should ever enter its walls. The argument against the will here was, that the trust it proposed to create was, in this, so opposed to all civilized jurisprudence, as to make it outside the law, and so void. So formidable did the point seem to lawyers, that Mr. Horace Binney, of the defence, went to England to ransack the British laws of trusts. It was in urging this point that Mr. Webster uttered the memorable words:

"In what age, by what sect, where, when, by whom, has religious truth been excluded from the education of youth? Nowhere. Never! Everywhere, and at all times, it has been regarded as essential. It is of the essence, the vitality of useful instruction."

And this was not the assertion of Mr. Webster, the politician, but of the learned lawyer, face to face with able opponents, and making one of the most responsible forensic efforts of his life. He knew that he was uttering the weighty voice of history and jurisprudence.

Let another witness be heard of equal learning, and superior character. "It must be acknowledged to be one of the most remarkable phenomena of our perverted humanity, that among a Christian people, and in a Protestant land, such a discussion should not seem as absurd as to inquire whether school-rooms should be located under water or in darksome caverns! The Jew, the Mohammedan, the follower of Confucius, and of Brahma, each and all are careful to instruct the youth of their people in the tenets of the religions they profess, and are not content until, by direct and reiterated teaching, they have been made acquainted with at least the outline of the books which contain, as they believe, the revealed will of Deity. Whence comes it that Christians are so indifferent to a duty so obvious and so obviously recognized by Jew and Pagan?"

We are attempting then an absolute novelty. But may not the tree be already known by its fruits? State education among Americans tends to be entirely secularized. What is the result? Whence this general revolt from the Christian faith in this country, so full of churches, preachers, and a redundant Christian literature, so boastful of its Sabbaths and its evangelism? What has prepared so many for the dreary absurdities of materialism? Why do the journals which seek a national circulation think it their interest to affect irreligion? Why so many lamentations over public and popular corruptions? He who notes the current of opinion sees that the wisest are full of misgivings as to the fruits of present methods. As a specimen, let these words, from the Governor of Massachusetts, at a recent anniversary, be taken: "He" (Gov. Rice) "lifted up a warning voice, with respect to the inadequacy and perils of our modern system of one-sided education, which supposed it could develop manhood and good citizenship out of mere brain culture."

Second, True education is, in a sense, a spiritual process, the nurture of a soul. By spiritual, the divines mean the acts and states produced by the Holy Ghost, as distinguished from the merely ethical. The nurture of these is not human education, but sanctification. Yet education is the nurture of a spirit which is rational and moral, in which conscience is the regulative and imperative faculty; whose proper end, even in this world is moral. But God is the only Lord of the conscience; this soul is his miniature likeness; his will is the source of obligation to it; likeness to him is its perfection, and religion is the science of the soul's relations to God. Let these statements be placed together, and the theological and educational processes appear so cognate that they cannot be separated. Hence it is that the common sense of mankind has ever invoked the guidance of the minister of religion for the education of youth; in India the Brahmin, in Turkey the Imam, in Jewry the Rabbi, and in Christian lands the pastor. So, everywhere, the sacred books have always been the prime text-books. The only exception in the world is that which Rome has made for herself by her intolerable abuse of her powers. Does the secularist answer that this sacerdotal education results in a Boeotian character and puerile culture? Yes, where the sacred books are false Scriptures, but not where it is the Bible which is the text-book. So that these instances prove that the common sense of mankind has been at bottom correct, and has only been abused in some instances, by imposture.

The soul is a spiritual monad, an indivisible, spiritual unit, without parts, as without extension. Those powers, which we name as separate faculties, are only modes of function with which this unit is qualified, differentiated by the distinctions of the objects on which they operate. The central power is still one. From these truths it would appear that it cannot be successfully cultivated by patches. We cannot have the intellectual workman polish it at one place, and the spiritual at another. A succession of objects may be presented to the soul, to evoke and discipline its several powers; yet the unity of the being would seem to necessitate a unity in its successful culture.

It is the Christian ideas which are most stimulating and ennobling to the soul. He who must needs omit them from his teaching is robbed of the right arm of his strength. Where shall he get such a definition of virtue as is presented in the revealed character of God? Where so ennobling a picture of benevolence as that presented in Christ's sacrifice for his enemies? Can the conception of the inter-stellar spaces so expand the mind as the thought of an infinite God, an eternal existence, and an everlasting destiny?

Every line of true knowledge must find its completeness in its convergency to God, even as every beam of daylight leads the eye to the sun. If religion be excluded from our study, every process of thought will be arrested before it reaches its proper goal. The structure of thought must remain a truncated cone, with its proper apex lacking. Richard Baxter has nervously expressed this truth.

Third, If secular education is to be made consistently and honestly non-Christian, then all its more important branches must be omitted, or they must submit to a mutilation and falsification, far worse than absolute omission. It is hard to conceive how a teacher is to keep his covenant faithfully with the State so to teach history, cosmogony, psychology, ethics, the laws of nations, as to insinuate nothing favourable or unfavourable touching the preferred beliefs of either the evangelical Christians, Papists, Socinians, Deists, Pantheists, Materialists, or Fetish worshippers, who claim equal rights under American institutions. His pedagogics must indeed be "the play of Hamlet, with the part of Hamlet omitted." Shall the secular education leave the young citizen totally ignorant of his own ancestry? But how shall he learn the story of those struggles, through which Englishmen achieved those liberties which the colonies inherited, without understanding the fiery persecutions of the Protestants under "Bloody Mary ," over which the Pope's own legate, Cardinal Pole, was sent to preside? How shall the sons of Huguenot sires in New York, Virginia, or Carolina know for what their fathers forsook beautiful France, to hide themselves in the Northern snows or the malarious woods of the South, and read nothing of the violation of the "Edict of Nantes ," the "Dragonnades," and the wholesale assassination of St. Bartholomew's day, in honour of which an "infallible" predecessor of the Pope sang Te Deums and struck medals? Or, if the physicist attempt to ascend farther in man's history, can he give the genesis of earth and man, without intimating whether Moses or Huxley is his prophet? Or can the science of moral obligation be established in impartial oversight of God's relation to it, and of the question whether or not his will defines and grounds all human duty? Or can a Grotius or a Vattel settle the rights of nature and nations without either affirming along with the Apostles that "God hath made of one blood all nations of men for to dwell on all the face of the earth, and hath determined the times before appointed and the bounds of their habitation," or else denying it with the infidel ethnologist? How much of the noblest literature must be ostracized, if this plan is to be honestly carried out? The State teacher must not mention to his pupil Shakespeare, nor Bacon, nor Milton, nor Macaulay. The Expurgatorious of free democracy will be far more stringent than that of despotic Rome! But it is not necessary to multiply these instances. They show that Christian truths and facts are so woven into the very warp and woof of the knowledge of Americans, and constitute so beneficial and essential a part of our civilization, that the secular teacher, who impartially avoids either the affirmation or denial of them, must reduce his teaching to the bare giving of those scanty rudiments, which are, as we have seen, not knowledge, but the mere signs of knowledge.

Does some one say that practically this showing is exaggerated, for he is teaching some purely secular course, without any such maiming of his subjects or prejudicing of Christianity? If his teaching is more than a temporary dealing with some corner of education, the fact will be found to be that it is tacitly anti-Christian; overt assaults are not made; but there is a studied avoidance which is in effect hostile. There can be no neutral position between two extremes, where there is no middle ground, but "a great gulf fixed."

Fourth, Of all rightful human action the will is the executive and the conscience the directive faculty. Unless these be purified and enlightened, to enhance the vigour of the soul's other actions by training is but superfluous mischief. If in a ship the compass be lost and the pilot blind, it is better that there should not be a great force to move her machinery. The more energetic its motion, the greater is the likelihood the ship will speedily be upon the breakers. Surely this is sufficient to show to the reflecting mind that right moral inculcation cannot be separated at any point or for any time from the intellectual, without mischief.

One very obvious and yet not the weightiest application of this truth is to the discipline of the school itself. No training of any faculty takes place without some government. On what moral basis shall the teacher who wholly suppresses all appeal to religion rest that authority which he must exercise in the school-room? He will find it necessary to say to the pupil, "Be diligent. Be obedient. Lie not. Defraud not," in order that he may learn his secular knowledge. But on whose authority? There is but one ground of moral obligation, the will of God, and among the people of this country he who does not find the disclosure of that will in the Scriptures, most often finds it nowhere. But this teacher must not inculcate this Bible. Then his mere might must make his right, or else the might of the parent, or of the magistrate, to whose delegated authority he points back. Or his appeal may be to mere self-interest!

Will this government be wholesome for a youth's soul?

But from a pupil the youth becomes a citizen. He passes under wider and more complex obligations. The end of the State schooling is to fit him for this. The same question recurs, with transcendent moment, On what basis of right shall these duties rest? As a man, it is presumable he will act as he was taught while a boy. Of course then the grounds of obligation employed with him in school should be the ones he is to recognize in adult life. In the State school a non-Christian standard alone could be given him. He cannot be expected now to rise to any better; he may sink lower, seeing the ground then given him had no foundation under it.

That is to say, young Americans are to assume their responsibilities with pagan morals, for these are just what human reason attains from the non-Christian standard. Will this suffice to sustain American institutions? One may say: Natural theism may deduce quite a high ethical code, as witness the Greek philosophy. So could a man who rightly construed the data of his consciousness be an atheist; even the atheist might find in them proof that conscience ought to govern. But he does not, nor does the pagan reason act as Epictetus speculated. Let us begin to legislate for the people as they ought to be, and we shall have a fine card-castle. In fact, Americans, taken as we find them, who do not get their moral restraints from the Bible, have none. If, in our moral training of the young, we let go the "Thus saith the Lord," we shall have no hold left. The training which does not base duty on Christianity is, for us, practically immoral. If testimony to this truth is needed, let the venerable Dr. Griffin, of a former generation, be heard. "To educate the mind of a bad man without correcting his morals is to put a sword into the hands of a maniac." Let John Locke be heard. "It is virtue, then, direct virtue, which is the hard and valuable part to be aimed at in education. . . . If virtue and a well-tempered soul be not got and settled so as to keep out ill and vicious habits, languages and science, and all the other accomplishments of education, will be to no purpose but to make the worse or more dangerous man." Let Dr. Francis Wayland be heard. "Intellectual cultivation may easily exist without the existence of virtue or love of right. In this case its only effect is to stimulate desire; and this, unrestrained by the love of right, must eventually overturn the social fabric which it at first erected." Last, let Washington be heard, in his farewell address, where he teaches that the virtue of the citizens is the only basis for social safety, and that the Christian religion is the only adequate basis for that virtue.

But, is not mental culture per se elevating? It is hard for us to give up this flattery, because hitherto education has been more or less Christian. The minister has been the American school-master. But are not the educated the more elevated? Yes. For the reason just given, and for another; not that their mental culture made them seek higher morals, but their (and their parents') higher morals made them seek mental culture! We are prone to put the cart before the horse. Again I cite evidence. James Anthony Froude, a witness by no means friendly to orthodoxy, quoting Miss Florence Nightingale, emphatically endorses her opinion, that the ordinary, as the natural effect of the mere communication of secular knowledge to youths, is only to suggest the desire for more numerous, and, for the bulk of men whose destiny is inevitably narrow, illicit objects of desire. But they plead: In teaching the youth to know of more objects of desire you also teach him to know more restraining considerations. The fatal answer is that knowledge does not rule the heart, but conscience (if anything does); mere knowledge, without God's fear, makes desire grow faster than discretion. Says Sir Henry Bulwer: "I do not place much confidence in the philosopher who pretends that the knowledge which develops the passions is an instrument for their suppression, or that where there are the most desires there is likely to be the most order, and the most abstinence in their gratification." Again, the soul should grow symmetrically. Let the boughs of a tree grow, while the roots (without actual disease) stand still; the first gale would blow it over, because of the disproportion of its parts.

Fifth, We need the best men to teach our Children. The best are true Christians, who carry their religion into everything. Such men neither can nor will bind themselves to hold so influential a relation to precious souls for whom Christ died, and make no effort to save them. So the tendency must be towards throwing State schools into the hands of half-hearted Christians or of contemptuous unbelievers. Can such be even trusted with an important secular task? Railroads persist in breaking the Sabbath; so they must be served on the track exclusively by profane Sabbath-breakers or truckling professors of religion. The consequence is, they are scourged with negligent officials, drunken engineers, and defaulting cashiers. So the State will fall into the hands of teachers who will not even teach secular learning honestly; money will be wasted, and the schools will become corrupting examples to their own pupils of slighted work and abused trusts.

Sixth, to every Christian citizen, the most conclusive argument against a secularized education is contained in his own creed touching human responsibility. According to this, obligation to God covers all of every man's being and actions. Even if the act be correct in outward form, which is done without any reference to his will, he will judge it a shortcoming. "The ploughing of the wicked is sin." The intentional end to which our action is directed determines its moral complexion supremely. Second, Our Saviour has declared that there is no moral neutrality; "He that is not with him is against him, and he that gathereth not with him scattereth abroad." Add now the third fact, that every man is born in a state of alienation from God; that practical enmity and atheism are the natural outgrowth of this disposition; that the only remedy for this natural disease of man's spirit is gospel truth. The comparison of these truths will make it perfectly plain that a non-Christian training is literally an anti-Christian training.

This is the conclusive argument. The rejoinder is attempted; that Christians hold this theology as church members, and not as citizens; and that we have ourselves urged that the State is not an evangelical agent, and its proper business is not to convert souls from original sin. True, but neither has it a right to become an antievangelical agency, and resist the work of the spiritual commonwealth. While the State does not authorize the theological beliefs of the Christian citizens, neither has it a right to war against them. While we have no right to ask the State to propagate our theology, we have a right to demand that it shall not oppose it. But to educate souls thus is to oppose it, because a non-Christian training is an anti-Christian training. It may be urged again, that this result, if evil, will not be lessened by the State's ceasing to teach at all, for then the training of youth will be, so far as she is concerned, equally non-Christian. The answer is, that it is one thing to tolerate a wrong as done by a party over whom we have not lawful control, but wholly another to perpetrate that wrong ourselves. For the State thus to do what she ought to condemn in the godless parent, though she be not authorized to interfere would be the sin of "framing mischief by a law," the very trait of that "throne of iniquity" with which the Lord cannot have fellowship.

It is objected again, that if the State may govern and punish, which are moral functions, she may also teach. If we are prepared for the theocratic idea of the State, which makes it the universal human association, To Pan of human organisms, bound to do everything for society from mending a road or draining a marsh up to supporting a religion, then we can conclude thus. But then consistency will add to State schools a State religion, a beneficed clergy, a religious test for office, and State power wielded to suppress theological as well as social error. Again, while secular ruling and punishing are ethical functions, they are sufficiently grounded in the light of natural theism. But teaching is a spiritual function in the sense defined and for teaching beings fallen, and in moral ruin, natural theism is wholly inadequate, as witness the state of pagan society. Christian citizens are entitled (not by the State, but one higher, God) to hold that the only teaching adequate for this fallen soul is redemption. But of this the State, as such, knows nothing. As God's institute for realizing secular justice, she does know enough of moral right to be a praise to them that do well and a terror to evil-doers.

The most plausible evasion is this: "Since education is so comprehensive a work, why may there not be a division of labour?" Let the State train the intellect and the Christian parent and the Church train the conscience and heart in the home and the house of worship. With this solution some Christians profess themselves satisfied. Of course such an arrangement would not be so bad as the neglect of the heart by both State and parent.

Points already made contain fatal answers. Since conscience is the regulative faculty of all, he who must not deal with conscience cannot deal well with any. Since the soul is a monad, it cannot be equipped as to different parts at different times and places, as a man might get his hat at one shop and his boots at another; it has no parts. Since all truths converge towards God, he who is not to name God, must have all his teachings fragmentary; he can only construct a truncated figure. In history, ethics, philosophy, jurisprudence, religious facts and propositions are absolutely inseparable. The necessary discipline of a school-room and secular fidelity of teachers call for religion, or we miss of them. And no person nor organism has a right to seem to say to a responsible, immortal soul, "In this large and intelligent and even ethical segment of your doings you are entitled to be godless." For this teaching State must not venture to disclaim that construction of its own proceeding to its own pupil. That disclaimer would be a religious inculcation!

But farther: Why do people wish the State to interfere in educating? Because she has the power, the revenues to do it better. Then, unless her intervention is to be a cheat, her secularized teaching must be some very impressive thing. Then its impression, which is to be non-Christian, according to the theory, will be too preponderant in the youth's soul, to be counterpoised by the feebler inculcation of the seventh day. The natural heart is carnal, and leans to the secular and away from the gospel truths. To the ingenuous youth, quickened by animating studies, his teacher is Magnus Apollo, and according to this plan he must be to his ardent young votary wholly a heathen deity. The Christian side of the luminary, if there is one, must not be revealed to the worshipper! Then how pale and cold will the infrequent ray of gospel truth appear when it falls on him upon the seventh day! In a word, to the successful pupil under an efficient teacher, the school is his world. Make that godless, and his life is made godless.

If it be asked again: Why may not the State save itself trouble by leaving all education to parents? The answer is, because so many parents are too incapable or careless to be trusted with the task. Evidently, if most parents did the work well enough, the State would have no motive to meddle. Then the very *raison d'etre* of the State school is in this large class of negligent parents. But man is a carnal being, alienated from godliness, whence all these who neglect their children's mental, will, *a fortiori*, neglect their spiritual, culture. Hence we must expect that, as to the very class which constitutes the pretext for the State's interposition, the fatally one-sided culture she gives will remain one-sided. She has no right to presume anything else. But, it may be asked: Is not there the church to take up this part, neglected by both secularized State and godless parent? The answer is, The State, thus secularized, cannot claim to know the Church as an ally. Besides, if the Church be found sufficiently omnipresent, willing, and efficient, through the commonwealth, to be thus relied on, why will she not inspire in parents and individual philanthropists zeal enough to care for the whole education of youth? Thus again, the whole *raison d'etre* for the State's intervention would be gone. In fact the Church does not and cannot repair the mischief which her more powerful, rich, and ubiquitous rival, the secularized State, is doing in thus giving, under the guise of a non-Christian, an anti-Christian training. It is also well known to practical men that State common schools obstruct parental and philanthropic effort. Thus, parents who, if not meddled with, would follow the impulse of enlightened Christian neighbours, their natural guides, in creating a private school for their children, to make it both primary and classical, now always stop at the primary. "The school tax must be paid anyhow, which is heavy, and that is all they can do." Next, children of poor parents who showed aspiration for learning found their opportunity for classical tuition near their homes, in the innumerable private schools created by parental interest and public spirit, and kindly neighbourhood charity never suffered such deserving youths to be arrested for the mere lack of tuition. Now, in country places not populous enough to sustain "State High Schools," all such youths must stop at the rudiments. Thus the country loses a multitude of the most useful educated men. Next, the best men being the natural leaders of their neighbours, would draw a large part of the children of the children of the class next them upward into the private schools created for their own families, which, for the same reason, were sure to be Christian schools. The result is, that while a larger number of children are brought into primary schools, and while the statistics of the illiterate are somewhat changed, to the great delectation of shallow philanthropists, the number of youths well educated in branches above mere rudiments, and especially of these brought under daily Christian training, is diminished. In cities, (where public opinion is chiefly manufactured) high schools may be sustained, and this evil obviated so far as secular tuition goes. But in the vast country regions, literary culture is lowered just as it is extended. It is chiefly the country which fills the useful professions town youths go into trade.

The actual and consistent secularization of education is inadmissible.

But nearly all public men and divines declare that the State schools are the glory of America, that they are a finality, and in no event to be surrendered. And we have seen that their complete secularization is logically inevitable. Christians must prepare themselves then, for the following results: All prayers, catechisms, and Bibles will ultimately be driven out of the schools. But this will not satisfy Papists, who obstinately and correctly were their religion correct insist that education shall be Christian for their children. This power over the hopes and fears of the demagogues will secure, what Protestants cannot consistently ask for, a separate endowment out of the common funds. Rome will enjoy, relatively to Protestantism, a grand advantage in the race of propagandism; for humanity always finds out, sooner or later, that it cannot get on without a religion, and it will take a false one in preference to none. Infidelity and practical ungodliness will become increasingly prevalent among Protestant youth, and our churches will have a more arduous contest for growth if not for existence.

Perhaps American Protestants might be led, not to abandon but to revise their opinions touching education, by recalling the conditions under which the theory of State education came to be first accepted in this country. This came about in the colonies which at the same time held firmly to a union of Church and State. The Massachusetts and Connecticut colonies, for instance, honourable pioneers in State education in this country, were decidedly theoretic in their constitution. The Reformed religion was intimately interwoven. So all the Protestant States of Europe, whose successful example is cited, as Scotland and Prussia, have the Protestant as an established religion. This and State primary education have always been parts of one consistent system in the minds of their rulers in Church and State. A secularized education, such as that which is rapidly becoming the result of our State school system, would have been indignantly reprobated by the Winthrops and Mathers, the Knoxs, Melvilles, and Chalmers, and it is presumed, by the Tholucks and even Bismarcks of those commonwealths, which are pointed to as precedents and models. It is submitted, whether it is exactly candid to quote the opinions and acts of all these great men, for what is, in fact, another thing from what they advocated? Knox, for instance, urged the primary education of every child in Scotland by the State. But it was because the State he had helped to reconstruct there was clothed with a recognized power of teaching the Reformed religion, (through the allied Church), and because it was therefore able, in teaching the child to read, also to teach it the Scriptures and the Assembly's Catechism. Had Knox seen himself compelled to a severance of Church and State, (which he would have denounced as wicked and paganish), and therefore to the giving by the State of a secularized education, which trained the intellect without the conscience or heart, his heroic tongue would have given no uncertain sound. Seeing then that the wise and good men in adopting and successfully working this system, did so only for communities which united Church and State, and mental and spiritual training, the question for candid consideration is: What modifications the theory should receive, when it is imported into commonwealths whose civil governments have absolutely secularized themselves and made the union of the secular and spiritual powers illegal and impossible?

The answer may, perhaps, be found by going back to a first principle hinted in the outset of this discussion. Is the direction of the education of children either a civic or an ecclesiastical function? Is it not properly a domestic and parental function? First, we read in holy writ that God ordained the family by the union of one woman to one man, in one flesh, for life, for the declared end of "seeking a godly seed." Does not this imply that he looks to parents, in whom the family is founded, as the responsible agents of this result? He has also in the fifth Commandment connected the child proximately, not with either presbyter or magistrate, but with the parents, which, of course, confers on them the adequate and the prior authority. This argument appears again in the very order of the historical genesis of the family and State, as well as of the visible Church. The family was first. Parents at the outset were the only social heads existing. The right rearing of children by them was in order to the right creation of the other two institutes. It thus appears that naturally the parents' authority over their children could not have come by deputation from either State or visible Church, any more than the water in a fountain by derivation from it's reservoir below. Second, the dispensation of Divine Providence in the course of nature shows where the power and duty of education are deposited. That ordering is that the parents decide in what status the child shall begin his adult career. The son inherits the fortune, the social position, the responsibility, or the ill-fame of his father. Third, God has provided for the parents social and moral influences so unique, so extensive, that no other earthly power, or all others together, can substitute them in fashioning the child's character. The home example, armed with the venerable authority of the father and the mother, repeated amidst the constant intimacies of the fireside, seconded by filial reverence, ought to have the most potent plastic force over character. And this unique power God has guarded by an affection, the strongest, most deathless, and most unselfish, which remains in the breast of fallen man. Until the magistrate can feel a love, and be nerved by it to a self-denying care and toil, equal to that of a father and a mother, he can show no pretext for assuming any parental function.

But the best argument here is the heart's own instinct. No parent can fail to resent, with a righteous indignation, the intrusion of any authority between his conscience and convictions and the soul of his child. If the father conscientiously believes that his own creed is true and righteous and obligatory before God, then he must intuitively regard the intrusion of any other power between him and his minor child, to cause the rejection of that creed, as a usurpation. The freedom of mind of the child alone, when become an adult, and his father's equal, can justly interpose. If this usurpation is made by the visible church, it is felt to be in the direction of popery, if by the magistrate, in the direction of despotism.

It may be said that this theory makes the parent sovereign, during the child's mental and moral minority, in the moulding of his opinions and character, whereas, seeing the parent is fallible, and may form his child amiss, there ought to be a superior authority to superintend and intervene. But the complete answer is, that inasmuch as the supreme authority must be placed somewhere, God has indicated that, on the whole, no place is so safe for it as the hands of the parent, who has the supreme love for the child and the superior opportunity. But many parents nevertheless neglect or pervert the power? Yes, and does the State never neglect and pervert its powers? With the lessons of history to teach us the horrible and almost universal abuses of power in the hands of civil rulers, that question is conclusive. In the case of an unjust or godless State, the evil would be universal and sweeping. Doubtless God has deposited the duty in the safest place.

The competitions of the State and the Church for the educating power have been so engrossing that we have almost forgotten the parent, as the third and the rightful competitor. And now many look at his claim almost contemptuously. Because the civic and the ecclesiastical spheres are so much wider and more populous than his, they are prone to regard it as every way inferior. Have we not seen that the smaller circle is, in fact, the most original and best authorized of the three? Will any thinking man admit that he derives his right to marry, to be a father, from the permission of the State? Yet there is an illusion here, because civic constitutions confer on the State certain police functions, so to speak, concerning marriage and families. So there are State laws concerning certain ecclesiastical belongings. But what Protestant concedes therefrom that his religious rights were either conferred, or can be rightfully taken away, by civil authority? The truth is, that God has immediately and authoritatively instituted three organisms for man on earth, the State, the visible Church, and the Family, and these are co-ordinate in rights and mutual independence. The State or Church has no more right to invade the parental sphere than the parent to invade theirs. The right distribution of all duties and power between the three circles would be the complete solution of that problem of good government which has never yet been solved with full success. It is vital to a true theory of human rights, that the real independence of the smallest yet highest realm, that of the parent, be respected. Has it not been proved that the direction of education is one of its prerogatives?

But does not the State's right to exist imply the right to secure all the conditions of its existence? And as parents may so pervert or neglect education as to rear a generation incompetent to preserve their civil institutions, does not this give the State control over education? I answer, first, it is not even a pretext for the State's invading the parental sphere any farther than the destructive negligence exists, that is, to stimulate, or help, or compel the neglectful parents alone. Second, precisely the same argument may authorize the State to intrude into the spiritual circle and establish and teach a religion. But the sophism is here: It is assumed that a particular form of civil institutions has a prescriptive right to perpetuate itself. It has none. So the American theory teaches, in asserting for the people the inherent right to change their institutions. Did our republican fathers hold that any people have ever the right to subvert the moral order of society ordained by God and nature? Surely not. Here then is disclosed that distinction between the moral order and any particular civil order, so often overlooked, but so eloquently drawn by Cousin. So far is it from being true that the civil authority is entitled to shape a people to suit itself; the opposite is true, the people should shape the civil authority.

It is a maxim in political philosophy, as in mechanics, that when an organism is applied to a function for which it was not designed, it is injured and the function is ill done. Here is a farmer who has a mill designed and well fitted to grind his meal. He resolves that it shall also thresh his sheaves. The consequence is that he has wretched threshing and a crippled mill. I repeat, God designed the State to be the organ for securing secular justice. When it turns to teaching or preaching it repeats the farmers' experience. The Chinese Government and people are an example in point. The Government has been for a thousand years educating the people for its own ends. The result is what we see.

Government powerfully affects national character by the mode in which it performs its proper functions, and if the administration is equitable, pure and free, it exalts the people. But it is by the indirect influence. This is all it can do well. As for the other part of the national elevation (an object which every good man must desire), it must come from other agencies; from the dispensation of Almighty Providence; from fruitful ideas and heroic acts with which he inspires the great men whom he sovereignly gives to the nations he designs to bless; chiefly from the energy of divine Truth and the Christian virtues, first in individuals, next in families, and last in visible churches.

Let us suppose, then, that both State and Church recognize the parent as the educating power; that they assume towards him an ancillary instead of a dominating attitude; that the State shall encourage individual and voluntary efforts by holding the impartial shield of legal protection over all property which may be devoted to education; that it shall encourage all private efforts; and that in its eleemosynary character it shall aid those whose poverty and misfortunes disable them from properly rearing their own children. Thus the insoluble problems touching religion in State schools would be solved, because the State was not the responsible creator of the schools, but the parents. Our educational system might present less mechanical symmetry, but it would be more flexible, more practical, and more useful.

18

Selected Writings of William Torrey Harris

William Torrey Harris (1835–1909) was perhaps America's most leading philosopher of education during the late 19th and early 20th centuries. He was born in North Killingly, Connecticut, on September 10, 1835. He attended school at Phillips Andover Academy in Andover, Massachusetts, and later Yale University. He departed Yale before graduating, however, to accept a position teaching shorthand in the St. Louis public schools.

While teaching in St. Louis, Harris became increasingly interested in German philosophy, specifically the work of G. W. F. Hegel. He helped to found the St. Louis Philosophical Society in 1866. From 1867 to 1893, he edited *The Journal of Speculative Philosophy*. This journal served as the primary outlet for Hegelian philosophy in the United States during this time period. Harris published numerous books and articles that described his ideas on curriculum, pedagogy, and educational philosophy at all levels.

Harris served as superintendent of the St. Louis Public schools from 1868 to 1880. In St. Louis, he established the first public school kindergarten in the U.S. During his twelve years as superintendent, he developed the St. Louis public school system to such an extent that it became well known for its quality throughout the U.S. Late in his career, from 1889 to 1906, he served as U.S. Commissioner of Education. All of these roles helped Harris to spread his educational philosophy in both theoretic and practical ways. —JWN

American Educational Thought: Essays from 1640–1940, pages 255–268
Copyright © 2010 by Information Age Publishing

Compulsory Education in Relation to Crime and Social Morals, 1885

What is the training which develops in the child a respect for the social whole, a feeling that society embodies his substantial good, —a feeling of preference for the good of his fellow-man over his own whim or caprice?

Certainly, that training is the training which is given by bringing up the child in the society of others, and causing him to practise perpetually those customs which respect persons and property. A due sense of public opinion, a respect for the ideal standard of right and wrong set up in the community, is the primary requisite.

It is clear that man can live in society and constitute a social whole only so far as individuals are educated out of their natural animal condition, and made to respect social forms more highly than mere animal impulses. Hence, it is clear that society itself rests upon education, in this broad sense of the word.

But what has this to do with school education? Much of the education into a respect for social forms and usages is given by the family, and before the age proper for schooling. Then, again, it must be admitted that another part of this education comes later, and is learned in the pursuit of one's vocation in life, —the education that comes from bending one's energies into a special channel for the purpose of earning a living. Another form of education is to be found in the part that one bears in politics, within one's party, or in the exercise of functions conferred by the State, or still farther in the exercise of patriotic feeling. Lastly, there is the Church, which furnishes a form of education most important, because it lays fullest stress on human duty, basing it on divine commands. The Church educates the individual into the sense of his existence as a mere unsubstantial creature when living in neglect of the divine ideal manhood, but as a substantial and eternally blessed life when lived according to the forms prescribed in religion. These forms are forms that respect the welfare of the whole, and measure the conduct of the individual by his preference of that welfare over his own selfish impulses.

The family, the vocation, the State, the Church, are the four great cardinal institutions of education. The school is only a device brought in to re-enforce these substantial institutions; but it is a very important device, notwithstanding its supplementary character. It may re-enforce the family by giving to the youth the command of such conventionalities as reading and writing and moral behavior; or it may re-enforce the vocation by giving instruction in arts and trades or professions; or it may re-enforce the Church as a Sunday-school, giving instruction in religion; the military school or the naval school may re-enforce the education of the State.

Our question deals directly with the education of the school; but we must carefully bear in mind the several educational functions of these institutions, so as not to overestimate the functions of the school or in any way confound its province with what belongs to the great social institutions.

Family education must furnish that indispensable preliminary education in personal habits, such as cleanliness, care of the person and clothing, respectful treatment of elders and superiors, obedience to authority the sense of shame, religious observances, and the use of the mother tongue. The school must presuppose that these are already taught by the family; but the school must not neglect them, although it does not make them its special aim. The family does more, in fact, than educate the child in those indispensable things just recited. It builds up within the child's mind the structure of his moral character, making for him a second nature of moral habit and custom, whose limits and boundaries he regards as of supreme moment. This second nature, or moral nature, is secured by daily sacrifice; and all forms of education lay stress upon self-sacrifice as the foundation of their disciplines.

This process which we call education is, in short, essentially the shaping of man by habit into an ideal or spiritual type of being, —a realization of what we call human nature in contradistinction to mere animal nature. It is an artificial life, a conventional form of living; but it is far more substantial and divine than the life of the mere animal man. Man as an animal is a savage: as civilized, he is an ethical being, who has set up within himself a system of duties and obligations which he observes at the expense of neglecting the impulses of his merely animal nature.

To what end is all this? Is it not because man, as an individual, wills to combine with his fellow-men in such a way as to avail himself of the united endeavor of all? By the organization of social institutions, law converts a multitude of atomic individuals into a social unity. The individuals do not get lost in this social unity, like the waves of the sea. But the social unity is of that wonderful character that it re-enforces the might of each individual by the might of the whole. Speaking technically, the individual becomes the species; or, in giving up by self-sacrifice his selfish peculiarities and devoting himself to the service of others, he gains for himself the service of all mankind. The individuals are transmuted into one grand individual, of which each individual is the head, and each individual is also the foot. According to Kant's definition, a living organism is such that every part of it is alike means and end to all the other parts. So, in this social body, every individual human being is alike the means and the end for all others. Hence there is a "Grand Man," as Swedenborgians say.

In the matter of food, clothing, and shelter, the individual toils in his vocation to produce a special product, —something useful to the rest, and demanded in the market of the world. In return for this gift of his day's labor, he is permitted to draw from the market of the world his share of all the productions collected from all climes, brought hither by the commerce of nations. This is a perpetual process of united human endeavor, in which by self-sacrifice the individual re-enforces himself by the race.

So, too, the family, the most embryonic of human institutions,—the family enables the elder to assist the younger, the mature the immature, the well and strong to assist the sick and weak. It equalizes age and bodily condition, re-enforcing each condition by the aid of all others.

The great object, then, of education is the preparation of the individual for a life in institutions, the preparation of each individual for social combination. Education inculcates sacrifice of animal proclivities, in order to secure a higher well-being in the life of the community.

Crime is, therefore, a reaction on the part of the individual against the very object of education. It attacks the necessary forms of social life, and asserts for itself the right to persist in the form of the non-social individual. Society must defend itself, and reduce the rebellious individual to harmony with itself. Inasmuch as the social form is such that the individual who puts it on and becomes a member of the family, the community, or the State, does not act directly for himself, but works for others and accepts the service of others in return for his own deed, so, too, punishment for crime takes on the same form: the criminal is made to receive for his deed an equivalent reflected back from society. As his deed injures society, it is returned upon him by society and injures him. If he attacks his neighbors by personal violence, his deed is made to come back to him by physical constraint or even by violent death on the gallows. If he attacks the property of his fellow-men, he is made to suffer in property, in the possession of personal freedom and the right to the products of his own labor. Thus, society treats the criminal who rebels against it just as though he, the criminal, had intended to do a social deed, and not a selfish one. It is a piece of irony. The State says to the criminal: "Of course, you recognize society, and expect to reap what you sow. You have an undoubted right to possess and enjoy the fruits of your own deeds. I will see that they are returned upon you. Your deed of violence on your neighbor shall therefore return upon you. Whatever you do you shall do to yourself."

Turning now from this view of the general educative character of the institutions of society, and the end and aim of all society to aid the individual by the might of the whole, and from this study of crime, let us define for ourselves the place of the school in education, and try to discover its relation to the prevention of crime.

The school, as we have seen, is a means of education auxiliary to each of the four cardinal institutions; and, as such, the school in all of its forms is ethical and preventive of crime. The ordinary type of school—the so-called "common school"—receives the child from the family at the age of five or six years. It receives him into a social body (for the school is a community), and educates him by "discipline" and "instruction," as they are technically called. By "discipline" is meant the training in behavior, a training of the will, moral training. It consists in imposing upon the child a set of forms of behavior rendered necessary in order to secure concert of action, —such forms as regularity, punctuality, silence, and industry. These are the four cardinal duties of the school pupil. Without them, the school cannot act as a unit, instruction cannot be given in classes, and no good result achieved. We call these duties mechanical duties, but they underlie all higher ethics. Without silence in the school, without self-sacrifice on the part of each pupil, restraining his impulse to prate and chatter and occupy the attention of his fellow-pupils, there could be no work done. Each pupil would interfere with the work of every other pupil; and the result would be chaos or worse, —because anarchy is chaos made active and hostile to heaven's first law.

Order is not only the first celestial law, but it is the first law of all social combination. The school could not possibly undertake a more direct and efficient training of the child for social combination than it does undertake in its four cardinal phases of discipline, —regularity, punctuality, silence, and industry.

Its method of securing these items of discipline may be good, bad, or indifferent, according to the pains it takes to convert external constraint into willing obedience and unconscious habit. The good school unquestionably shows us the constant spectacle of good behavior become or becoming a second nature to the pupils, so that there is a maximum of regularity, punctuality, silence, and industry with a minimum of self-consciousness in regard to it, although there is an insight into the necessity of such conformity to rule, and a conscious conviction in favor of it whenever any untoward occasion brings up the question. Consequently there is a minimum of corporal punishment in the good school. Necessary as it is in dealing with crude depravity, the school must have got far beyond that stage of discipline before it can be called "good."

This training of the will, we observe, is a training of each pupil to behave in such a form of artificial or conventional restraint that he may combine in the best manner with his fellow pupils, and be in a condition to give to and receive from them school instruction. Is it not clear that, once trained to observe set forms of behavior in the school it becomes a second nature to observe such forms everywhere, and the individual has solved the problem of life so far as the prevention of crime is concerned?

The Philosophy of Education, 1893

Lecture I — January 7th, 1893

The Literature of Education

The first and most important of all educational literature is that showing the ideals of a people—the literature on which they are brought up—generally the sacred books which reveal what the people regard as divine; consequently what is the highest ideal to be realized. China, for example, has Confucius and Mencius, showing the family as the type of the social whole. These writings furnish the contents of the mind of the Chinese —minute observances of etiquette; how to behave towards one's elders and superiors in rank; towards one's inferiors or juniors; towards one's equals. Chinese schools are almost exclusively devoted to filling the memory of the pupil with the ethical maxims of these sacred books, so that the mind shall be full of family etiquette. The aim of Chinese education was to teach the young how to behave; that of the Persians, how to ride, shoot, and speak the truth—a faculty not much thought of by the Hindus. The Persian differs from the Buddhist in that the latter wishes to get rid of the world, while the former attempts to conquer the real. The Phoenicians, again, furnish a contrast to Chinese education. Their object was to wean the child from the family; whereas the Chinese endeavor to educate the young so that they will become submerged in the family. The Phoenicians aimed to create a love of adventure. Their children were educated in myths. The stories in Homer's "Odyssey" must have been derived from the tales of the Phoenician sailors, which were calculated to engender a hunger and thirst for adventure, so that the young Phoenician would gladly get on board ship and go to the ends of the world in the interests of trade. The Greeks were imbued with the new world-principle of a spiritual and beautiful individuality. They thought more of the games which they practised in the evenings on the village green than of the tasks by which they earned their bread. They learned history and geography from the second book of Homer's "Iliad." They thought not of commercial education, like the Phoenicians, but of that heroic individual who furnished a beautiful ideal. Later on, Greek education became more scientific and more reflective. The Roman concentrated his whole mind on the will. He went beyond the circle of his city, and studied to cause even foreigners to live under the same laws with himself. Freedom meant more to him than to any of the Asiatic nations. It meant the power of the individual to hold, alienate, and devise property. This was an enormous step upward in educational progress. Hitherto, property could only be held by the family. Contract is the supreme idea of the Roman. He even carries it into his religion. Thus he prays to one of his deities to help him in some extremity or to give him his desire, and he promises, in turn, to build the god a temple. The Roman wants to conquer all peoples and to make them free under the law. But the greatest educational lesson is derived from the Hebrew people. They teach the personality of the Divine apart from Nature. This Divine Person creates Nature in order that He shall have something to recognize Him. The Divine Being does not efface man simply, but is the embodiment of goodness and righteousness—the righteousness that breathes the spirit of loving kindness, holding his creatures responsible only in so far as they know the right, and returning their deeds upon them. Art education ranked first in the Greek mind, for he worshipped the beautiful. Then came science and philosophy. From the Greeks we get these elements of our educational curriculum. From the Romans we get the principle of organization. Whether or not a person is educated reflectingly into civilization, he finds himself in the great network of usages that go to make up civilization. Education is meant to give one an insight into the genesis of these things, so that he can detect an element of each in the threads of his civilization. Ninety-nine out of a hundred people in every civilized nation are automata, careful to walk in the prescribed paths, careful to follow prescribed custom. This is the result of substantial education, which, scientifically defined, is the subsumption of the individual under his species. The other educational principle is the emancipation from this subsumption. This is subordinate, and yet, in our time, we lay more stress upon it than the other. Look at the French Revolution. What a prodigious emancipation that was. It was predicted by Rousseau; but those who read him only superficially, without first studying his genesis, will find that their minds are poisoned by his doctrine of the supremacy of nature. Comenius taught the emancipation of the individual from the printed page. Spencer says that the modern school system is all wrong, and has a tendency to get away from science and cause students to waste time over the dead languages. Emancipation has now become the important side of the educational question. But the student of advanced education must first avail himself of the wisdom of the race, and learn how not to be limited by it. He cannot progress unless he is a free man, for he must not be so much subsumed that he cannot investigate scientifically, and with safety to himself, all problems that present themselves.

Lecture II — Saturday, January 14th, 1893

Problems Peculiar to American Education

There are two kinds of education. The first may be called substantial education—the education by means of the memory; the education which gives to the individual, methods and habits and the fundamentals of knowledge. It is this education which the child begins to receive from its birth. This sort of education is education by authority—that is, the individual accepts the authority of the teacher for the truth of what he is told, and does not question it or seek to obtain insight into the reason for its being so. It is this education by authority—the education of the past—that the modern or second kind of education seeks to supersede. This second kind may be called individual or scientific education; it is the education of insight as opposed to that of authority. When this kind of education is acquired, it frees the individual from the authority of the other. Under the system of education by authority when told, for instance, that the sum of three angles of a triangle are equal to two right angles, this will be blindly believed only as long as authority sanctions this belief; but when an insight into the reason for this geometrical truth is obtained, no change of authority is able to make the individual doubt. But there is this danger in the system of education by insight, if begun too early, that the individual tends to become so self-conceited with what he considers knowledge gotten by his own personal thought and research, that he drifts toward empty agnosticism with the casting overboard of all authority. It is, therefore, necessary that this excessive conceit of self which this modern scientific method of education fosters, be lessened by building on the safe foundations of what has been described as the education of authority. The problems of the reform movement centre, therefore, on the proper method of replacing this authoritative or passive method of education by education through self-activity.

There is another problem—that of the method of study. Germany advises us to teach by oral methods, by giving pieces of information and insight orally by word of mouth. But the American educators have blundered upon what may be defended as the correct method, namely, the text-book method. It was merely the outcome of an unconscious trend. The method is of course liable to very serious abuse, but the good points greatly outweigh the bad. It has the advantage of making one independent of his teacher; you can take your book wherever you please. You cannot do that with the great lecturer, neither can you question him as you can the book, nor can you select the time for hearing the great teacher talk as you can for reading the book. And it is true that nearly all the great teachers have embodied their ideas in books. The greatest danger of text-book education is verbatim, parrot-like recitation; but even then from the poorest text-book a great deal of knowledge can be gleaned. Then there is the alertness which in any large class will necessarily be engendered by an intelligent understanding and criticism of the results arrived at by different pupils in discussing a certain piece of work given in his own words. And then there is the advantage to be found in the fact that with the text-book the child can be busy by itself. Lastly, there is the problem of discipline. There should be very little corporal punishment; the milder forms of restraint should be used. The child that is brought up accustomed to the rod loses his self-respect, and may become the man who must have police surveillance. Silence, punctuality, regularity and industry are fundamental parts of a "substantial education" as much as the critical study of mathematics, literature, science and history is a part of the "education of insight." These two kinds of education, that of authority and that of self-activity, should be made complementary.

Lecture III — January 21st, 1893

Opposition between Pestalozzi and Herbart
as Educational Leaders

Pestalozzi laid great stress on sense-perception as the foundation of all school education. Herbart lays stress on the elaboration of sense-perception or rather upon the mental reaction against the impressions made on our senses. Thought goes back of the object to understand and explain its origin, how it became to be what it is, what purpose it is to serve. Thought sees objects in the perspective of their history. It studies causes and purposes. Thus thought is not as the disciples of Pestalozzi hold, a continued and elevated sort of sense-perception, but rather a reaction against it. It is a discovery of the subordinate place held by objects in the world; they are seen to be mere steps in a process of manifestation—the manifestation of causal energies. A new perception is received into the mind by adjusting it to our previous knowledge; we explain it in terms of the old; we classify it, identify it; reconcile what is strange and unfamiliar in it with previous experience; we interpret the object and comprehend it; we translate the unknown into the known. This process of adjusting, explaining, classifying, identifying, reconciling, interpreting and translating, is called apperception. We must not only perceive, but we must apperceive; not only see and hear, but digest or assimilate what we hear and see. Herbart's "apperception" is far more important for education than Pestalozzi's "perception." At first the memory was the chief faculty cultivated in education; then Pestalozzi reformed it by making the culture of sense-perception chief aim;

now with Herbart the chief aim would be apperception or the mental digestion of what is received by perception or memory. Illustrations of the power of apperception to strengthen perception: Cuvier could reconstruct the entire skeleton from a single bone; Agassiz the entire fish from one of its scales; Winckelman the entire statue from a fragment of the face; Lyell could see its history in a pebble; Asa Gray the history of a tree by a glance. Apperception adds to the perceived object its process of becoming. Noire has illustrated apperception by showing the two series of ideas called up by the perception of a piece of bread. First the regressive series—dough, flour, rye; and the processes—baking, kneading, grinding, threshing, harvesting, planting, &c. Each one of these has collateral series, as for example, planting has plowing, plow, oxen, yoke, furrow, harrowing, sowing seeds, covering it, etc. The second series is progressive—bread suggests its uses and functions; food, eating, digesting, organic tissue, life, nourishing strength, supply of heat, bodily labor, &c. The course of study in schools must be arranged so as to prepare the mind for quick apperception of what is studied. The Pestalozzian makes form, number, and language the elements of all knowledge. He unfortunately omits causal ideas, which are the chief factors of apperception; we build our series on causality. Accidental association satisfies only the simple-minded and empty-headed.

LECTURE IV — *January 28th, 1893*

Rousseau and the Return to Nature—Revolutionary Protest

The time of Louis XIV: the nobles attracted to Court and to a life of gayety, neglecting their estates and wasting the fruits of toil in riotous living; the laborers deprived of the advantage of the directive power of the nobility fail in power of production. The French Revolution is the result. Rousseau its prophet; he proclaims a return to nature. "Nature," a word of ambiguous meaning; human nature versus physical nature; human history the revelation of man's nature; it is realized in institutions and not by man as an isolated individual. Nature in time and space is under the dominion of necessity; everything constrained to be what it is by outside forces. Human nature is an ideal, and when realized it has the form of freedom and self-determination, each man a law unto himself and each one engaged in helping every other one, for by this each one helps himself. Rousseau appealed to nature in everything. What we call civilization was to him a mere artificial form. His plea was to be natural, come back to the point where nature leaves you. Rousseau came from Switzerland to France, and at an opportune time for him; for there was a great ferment of ideas at this epoch. He was struggling along in Paris, barely securing a livelihood, when there came the offer from the Academy of Dijon of a prize for an essay on the progress of the arts and sciences, whether it has tended towards the purification of morals and manners. The negative side suggested itself more forcibly to him, as he was better fitted for it by his mode of living and morals, and by his literary style, and he found himself at once a "censor of civilization." This essay was soon followed (1752) by one on the origin of the inequality among men. The great tension produced by the artificiality of the civilization of the Court life of the time had caused men to become anxious to get back to a simplicity of living, and Chateaubriand painted the charms of the forest life of the Indians. In this reaction the meaning of civilization is ignored. Man emancipates himself from drudgery and compels nature by the forces of his intellect to feed and clothe him. The "Social Contract" followed (1762) this with an attack on the authority of the State; and in the same year his *Emile* undermined the School and the Church; and so he attacked all the social institutions one after another—the family, civil society, the Church and State. He proposed to sweep all away by summoning them before the bar of his individual judgment and condemning all. In the opening paragraph of his *Emile* he declares that everything which comes from nature is good, while everything degenerates in the hands of man. The antithesis of civilization is savagery, and Voltaire wittily exposed the fallacy of Rousseau's teaching in his letter accepting the book. He said —"never has anyone employed so much genius to make us into beasts. When one reads your book he is seized at once with a desire to go down on all fours." External authority is a perennial necessity for man in his immaturity. An appeal to nature is always a piece of jugglery with words. In mere nature we have matter and force. Everything inorganic is made by some external influence. But organic nature is the opposite of inorganic. The plant has the power of assimilation, and the animal the further powers of locomotion and feeling, or ability to select or choose its surroundings. In man this is still further increased by recollection and memory, by which the mind makes over its impressions. To do his duty properly he must look to higher things, and in ethical ideas the human becomes transcendental. The moral man acts as though the sole being in the world is humanity. No natural instinct is admitted as having validity against the moral law. If we adopt the doctrines of material nature and yield to our feelings and impulses, we remain animals. But if we take nature in the sense of our ideal, divine possibility, and realize it by education, we attain to human nature properly so-called, which is not something given us without effort, but only the product of culture.

LECTURE V — February 4th, 1893

Herbert Spencer and What Knowledge is of Most Worth

In Herbert Spencer, the return to nature means the study of natural science, and this becomes the great thing. But natural science is only the instrument with which we conquer nature. Everybody becomes filled with the idea of progress by it, for we see that nature as it is, existing in time and space, is conquered by inventions and made to serve man. There was never a more unscientific book made than Spencer's essay on education; for while he praises science, he does not apply it to a study of education as it is and has been. To do this he ought to study the genesis of the course of study and explain its functions. The unscientific person takes things as they are and cares not for their origin. To study things from a scientific standpoint means to take an inventory of them—to find the process in which they are being produced; to connect them with other things; to see things in their causal process. He does not understand the system of education as it exists, because he does not know the educational value of its branches. The education he proposes for us is for the purpose of complete living; but what is Spencer's definition of this complete living? Spencer does not take education as the genesis of man's spiritual life, but merely as something useful for showing how to care for the body and perform the lower social functions as the tool of life, the instrument by which life is preserved. Now suppose the definition of complete living to be, to elevate each individual so that he can take advantage of the life and experience of his race. Then he would find complete living to involve the initiation into the civilizations of the past that furnish the elements out of which our own civilization is formed. Spencer thinks that the first business of the child is to know physiology; the next is the selection of a vocation or trade, which leads to training for citizenship; and last of all he puts relaxation and amusement, in which he includes literature and art. Now, Aristotle characterized man as the symbol-making animal. Human nature has to be expressed by symbols. The poets of a people first paint the ideal, which makes civilization possible. Literature furnishes the most essential branch of education, so far as its function is to help the child into civilization. Man sits in the theatre of the world (as Plato tells us) and sees the shadows of men and events thrown on the curtain before him. Behind him and out of his sight is the Great Leader, who is making these shadows. From them he draws his ideals, but ideals are potentialities, not realities. Self-activity, the freedom of the soul, is made possible by the institutions of society, the family, civil society, State and Church. We must not confound the mere school with these other great institutions of civilization. In the family are learned the mother tongue, habits, and nurture. Civil society teaches him his vocation; the State, his duties as citizen;

and the Church shows him his place in the divine plan of the universe. Spencer calls education the subject which involves all other subjects, and the one in which they should all culminate. But some one has better said that school education is the giving to man the possession of the instrumentalities of intelligence. By his school education he does not attain all education, but he gets the tools of thought by which to master the wisdom of the race. There are, then, three epochs of school education—elementary, secondary and higher. The first or elementary stage is the opening of the five windows of the soul. (1) Arithmetic is the foundation of our knowledge of nature, by which we measure and count all things inorganic. When its first principles are mastered the child begins to want to combine the organic with the inorganic, and then we come to another window, (2), that of elementary geography. The distribution of animal and plant life is learned, and the child begins to peep into the organization of things, the growth of plants, and the formation of the continents and the earth. Thirdly, he learns to read and write, and gets a glimpse into literature. The original colloquial vocabulary learned at home, variously estimated at from 300 or 400 to 3,000 or 4,000 words, deals only with commonplace things. But the school takes this colloquial vocabulary as a key and opens up the great reservoir of literature in books, initiating him into a higher class of words, expressive of fine shades of feeling and thought. Thus, to his own vocabulary are added those of great writers, who have seen nature from a different point of view, and presented their thoughts in gems of literary style. Literature lifts up the pupil into the realms of human nature and discloses the motives which govern the actions of men. Yet Spencer puts this last in his course of study. After learning all science has to give, after learning one's trade and the care of his body, he would then, if there is leisure, permit literature and art. But literature is the greatest educator we have. It has made possible newspapers and periodicals and books, with pictures of human life and of the motives governing our actions. The fourth window of the soul is grammar, wherein we have a glimpse of the logical structure of the intellect as revealed in language. The fifth window is history (that of his own country), wherein he sees revealed the aspirations of his countrymen, his own nature, written out in colossal letters; and these five studies should make the elementary education of the student. The secondary education takes up human learning and continues it along the same lines, namely: 1, inorganic nature; 2, organic nature; 3, literature (the heart); 4, grammar and logic (the intellect); and 5, history (the will). Algebra deals with general numbers, while Arithmetic has definite numbers to operate with. Geometry and physics continue inorganic nature, while natural history continues the study already commenced in geography. Then come Greek and Latin, and here is opened up a great field of study into the embryology of our civilization. In the dead languages we have the three great threads running through the history of human progress. The Greek, with its literature and aesthetic art and its philosophy, showing the higher forms of human freedom in contrast with the Egyptian, which showed only the struggle for freedom and never the man separated from the animal and the inorganic world. The Roman, with the continual gaze upon the will of man, seeks the true forms of contracts and treaties and corporations, whereby one man may combine with another; and it essays the conquering of men and reducing them to obedience to civil law, not only external conquest but internal conquest as well. The Hebrew thread is the religious one, which we recognize in the celebration of worship one day each week and in the various holy days. We acknowledge this the most essential thread of our civilization. So, with the secondary education we begin to get the embryology of our forms of life. The higher or collegiate education is the comparative step of education. Each branch is studied in the light of all the others. Natural science and sociology are investigated; logic and mental philosophy; ethics and rhetoric; as well as the philosophy of history and of literature, and the comparative sciences, which furnish the light for the whole method of higher education. The first, or elementary education, then, is but superficial, a mere inventory; the secondary insists on some reflection on what has been learned; and the third, or higher education, is the unity and comparison of all that has been learned, so that each is explained by the Whole. Give the child possession of the embryology of civilization, and his insight into the evolution of civilization is insured. Educators have adopted the course of study as it exists, led by an unconscious or blind impulse. Herbert Spencer should have investigated and discovered its purpose, which is a far deeper one than he has thought out when he advocates its overthrow for the sake of knowledge that leads to direct self-preservation.

19

Report of the Committee of Ten on Secondary School Studies

National Education Association, 1894

In the 1890s, the Committee of Ten's landmark report significantly impacted the high school curriculum. Concerned with the problem of inconsistent college entrance requirements, the National Education Association (NEA), at a meeting in 1892, authorized the Committee of Ten to recommend standards for the various core subjects in the secondary school curriculum. The Committee of Ten was comprised of nine separate sub-conferences based upon the academic disciplines of (1) Latin, (2) Greek, (3) English, (4) Modern Languages, (5) Mathematics, (6) Physics, Astronomy, and Chemistry, (7) Natural History, (8) History, Civil Government, and Political Economy, and (9) Geography.

Nicholas Murray Butler, who became the NEA President in 1894, and who later served as Columbia University President, was instrumental in appointing the ten members of the Committee. Charles W. Eliot, the Harvard University President responsible for ushering in the elective course system, served as the chairman of the Committee of Ten. Other prominent members of the Committee included William Torrey Harris, Commissioner of Education and James Burrill Angell, President of the University of Michigan. Butler believed

American Educational Thought: Essays from 1640–1940, pages 269–320
Copyright © 2010 by Information Age Publishing

that the group comprised a remarkable committee, but the all white male members predominantly hailed from elite eastern institutions. Published in 1893 by the U.S. Government Printing office and one year later by the American Book Company, the report recommended four different courses of study in high school and advised against curricular distinction for students preparing for college and students preparing for life. —CHB

The Committee of Ten appointed at the meeting of the National Educational Association at Saratoga on the 9th of July, 1892, have the honor to present the following report: At the meeting of the National Council of Education in 1891, a Committee appointed at a previous meeting made a valuable report through their Chairman, Mr. James H. Baker, then Principal of the Denver High School, on the general subject of uniformity in school programmes and in requirements for admission to college. The Committee was continued, and was authorized to procure a Conference on the subject of uniformity during the meeting of the National Council in 1892, the Conference to consist of representatives of leading colleges and secondary schools in different parts of the country. This Conference was duly summoned, and held meetings at Saratoga on July 7th, 8th, and 9th, 1892. There were present between twenty and thirty delegates. Their discussions took a wide range, but resulted in the following specific recommendations, which the Conference sent to the National Council of Education then in session.

1. That it is expedient to hold a conference of school and college teachers of each principal subject which enters into the programmes of secondary schools in the United States and into the requirements for admission to college—as, for example, of Latin, of geometry, or of American history—each conference to consider the proper limits of its subject, the best methods of instruction, the most desirable allotment of time for the subject, and the best methods of testing the pupils' attainments therein, and each conference to represent fairly the different parts of the country.
2. That a Committee be appointed with authority to select the members of these conferences and to arrange their meetings, the results of all the conferences to be reported to this Committee for such action as it may deem appropriate, and to form the basis of a report to be presented to the Council by this Committee.
3. That this Committee consist of the following gentlemen:

CHARLES W. ELIOT

President of Harvard University, Cambridge, Mass., *Chairman.*

WILLIAM T. HARRIS
Commissioner of Education, Washington, D. C.
JAMES B. ANGELL
President of the University of Michigan, Ann Arbor, Mich.
JOHN TETLOW
Head Master of the Girls' High School and the Girls' Latin
School, Boston, Mass.
JAMES M. TAYLOR
President of Vassar College, Poughkeepsie, N. Y.
OSCAR D. ROBINSON
Principal of the High School, Albany, N. Y.
JAMES H. BAKER
President of the University of Colorado, Boulder, Colo.
RICHARD H. JESSE
President of the University of Missouri, Columbia, Mo.
JAMES C. MACKENZIE
Head Master of the Lawrenceville School, Lawrenceville, N. J.
HENRY C. KING
Professor in Oberlin College, Oberlin, Ohio.

These recommendations of the Conference were adopted by the National Council of Education on the 9th of July, and the Council communicated the recommendations to the Directors of the National Educational Association, with the further recommendation that an appropriation not exceeding $2500 be made by the Association towards the expenses of these conferences. On the 12th of July the Directors adopted a series of resolutions under which a sum not exceeding $2500 was made available for this undertaking during the academic year 1892–93.

Every gentleman named on the above Committee of Ten accepted his appointment; and the Committee met, with every member present, at Columbia College, New York City, from the 9th to the 11th of November, 1892, inclusive.

In preparation for this meeting, a table had been prepared by means of a prolonged correspondence with the principals of selected secondary schools in various parts of the country, which showed the subjects taught in forty leading secondary schools in the United States, and the total number of recitations, or exercises, allotted to each subject. Nearly two hundred schools were applied to for this information; but it did not prove practicable to obtain within three months verified statements from more than forty schools. This table proved conclusively, first, that the total number of subjects taught in these secondary schools was nearly forty, thirteen of which, however, were found in only a few schools; secondly, that many of these subjects were taught for such short periods that little training could be derived from them; and thirdly, that the time allotted to the same subject in the different schools varied widely. Even for the older subjects, like Latin and algebra, there appeared to be a wide diversity of practice with regard to the time allotted to them. Since this table was comparative in its nature,— that is, permitted comparisons to be made between different schools,— and could be easily misunderstood and misapplied by persons who had small acquaintance with school programmes, it was treated as a confidential document; and was issued at first only to the members of the Committee of Ten and the principals of the schools mentioned in the table. Later, it was sent—still as a confidential paper—to the members of the several conferences organized by the Committee of Ten.

The Committee of Ten, after a preliminary discussion on November 9th, decided on November 10th to organize conferences on the following subjects:— 1. Latin; 2. Greek; 3. English; 4. Other Modern Languages; 5. Mathematics; 6. Physics, Astronomy, and Chemistry; 7. Natural History (Biology, including Botany, Zoölogy, and Physiology); 8. History, Civil Government, and Political Economy; 9. Geography (Physical Geography, Geology, and Meteorology). They also decided that each Conference should consist of ten members. They then proceeded to select the members of each of these Conferences, having regard in the selection to the scholarship and experience of the gentlemen named, to the fair division of the members between colleges on the one hand and schools on the other, and to the proper geographical distribution of the total membership. After selecting ninety members for the nine Conferences, the Committee decided on an additional number of names to be used as substitutes for persons originally chosen who should decline to serve, from two to four substitutes being selected for each Conference. In the selection of substitutes the Committee found it difficult to regard the geographical distribution of the persons selected with as much strictness as in the original selection; and, accordingly, when it became necessary to call on a considerable number of substitutes, the accurate geographical distribution of membership was somewhat impaired. The lists of the members of the several Conferences were finally adopted at a meeting of the Committee on November 11th; and the Chairman and Secretary of the Committee were then empowered to fill any vacancies which might occur.

The Committee next adopted the following list of questions as a guide for the discussions of all the Conferences, and directed that the Conferences be called together on the 28th of December:—

1. In the school course of study extending approximately from the age of six years to eighteen years—a course including the periods of both elementary and secondary instruction—at what age should the study which is the subject of the Conference be first introduced?

2. After it is introduced, how many hours a week for how many years should be devoted to it?

3. How many hours a week for how many years should be devoted to it during the last four years of the complete course; that is, during the ordinary high school period?

4. What topics, or parts, of the subject may reasonably be covered during the whole course?

5. What topics, or parts, of the subject may best be reserved for the last four years?

6. In what form and to what extent should the subject enter into college requirements for admission? Such questions as the sufficiency of translation at sight as a test of knowledge of a language, or the superiority of a laboratory examination in a scientific subject to a written examination on a text-book, are intended to be suggested under this head by the phrase "in what form."

7. Should the subject be treated differently for pupils who are going to college, for those who are going to a scientific school, and for those who, presumably, are going to neither?

8. At what stage should this differentiation begin, if any be recommended ?

9. Can any description be given of the best method of teaching this subject throughout the school course?

10. Can any description be given of the best mode of testing attainments in this subject at college admission examinations?

11. For those cases in which colleges and universities permit a division of the admission examination into a preliminary and a final examination separated by at least a year, can the best limit between the preliminary and final examinations be approximately defined?

The Committee further voted that it was expedient that the Conferences on Latin and Greek meet at the same place. Finally, all further questions of detail with regard to the calling and the instruction of the Conferences were referred to the Chairman with full power.

During the ensuing six weeks, the composition of the nine Conferences was determined in accordance with the measures adopted by the Committee of Ten. Seventy persons originally selected by the Committee accepted the invitation of the Committee, and sixty-nine of these persons were present at the meetings of their respective Conferences on the 28th of December. Twenty substitutes accepted service, of whom twelve were persons selected by the Committee of Ten, and eight were selected under the authority granted to the Chairman and Secretary of the Committee in emergencies. One of these eight gentlemen was selected by a Conference at its first meeting. Two gentlemen who accepted service—one of the original members and one substitute—absented themselves from the meetings of their respective Conferences without giving any notice to the Chairman of the Committee of Ten, who was therefore unable to fill their places. With these two exceptions, all the Conferences met on December 28th with full membership.

The places of meeting were as follows:—for the Latin and Greek Conferences, the University of Michigan, Ann Arbor, Mich.; for the English Conference, Vassar College, Poughkeepsie, N. Y.; for the Conference on Other Modern Languages, the Bureau of Education, Washington, D. C.; for the Conference on Mathematics, Harvard University, Cambridge, Mass.; for the Conferences on Physics, Astronomy, and Chemistry, and on Natural History, the University of Chicago, Chicago, Ill.; for the Conference on History, Civil Government, and Political Economy, the University of Wisconsin, Madison, Wis., for the Conference on Geography, the Cook County Normal School, Englewood, Ill. The Committee of Ten and all the Conferences enjoyed the hospitality of the several institutions at which they met, and the members were made welcome at private houses during the sessions. Through the exertions of Mr. N. A. Calkins, Chairman of the Trustees of the National Educational Association, important reductions of railroad fares were procured for some members of the Committee and of the Conferences; but the reductions obtainable were less numerous and considerable than the National Council of Education had hoped. In filling a few vacancies of which notice was received shortly before December 28th, it was necessary to regard as one qualification nearness of residence to the appointed places of meeting; but on the whole the weight and effectiveness of the several Conferences were not impaired by the necessary replacement of twenty of the members originally selected by the Committee of Ten. The list of the members of the Conferences on the 28th of December was as follows:—

   1. LATIN.
       Professor CHARLES E. BENNETT
           Cornell University, Ithaca, N. Y.
       FREDERICK L. BLISS
           Principal of the Detroit High School, Detroit, Mich.

JNO.T. BUCHANAN

> Principal of the Kansas City High School, Kansas City, Mo.

WILLIAM C. COLLAR

> Head Master of the Roxbury Latin School, Roxbury, Mass.

JOHN S. CROMBIE

> Principal of the Adelphi Academy, Brooklyn, N. Y.

Professor JAMES H. DILLARD

> Tulane University, New Orleans, La.

Rev. WILLIAM GALLAGHER

> Principal of Williston Seminary, Easthampton, Mass.

Professor WILLIAM G. HALE

> University of Chicago, Chicago, Ill.

Professor JOHN C. ROLFE

> University of Michigan, Ann Arbor, Mich.

JULIUS SACHS

> Principal of the Collegiate Institute for Boys, 38 West 59th
> Street, New York City.

2. GREEK.

E. W. COY

> Principal of the Hughes High School, Cincinnati, O.

Professor MARTIN L. D'OOGE

> University of Michigan, Ann Arbor, Mich.

A. F. FLEET

> Superintendent of the Missouri Military Academy, Mexico,
> Mo.

ASHLEY D. HURT

> Head Master of the High School, Tulane University, New
> Orleans, La.

ROBERT D. KEEP

> Principal of the Free Academy, Norwich, Conn.

Professor ABBY LEACH

> Vassar College, Poughkeepsie, N. Y.

CLIFFORD H. MOORE

> Phillips Academy, Andover, Mass.

WILLIAM H. SMILEY

> Principal of the High School, Denver, Colo.

Professor CHARLES F. SMITH

> Vanderbilt University, Nashville, Tenn.

Professor BENJAMIN I. WHEELER

> Cornell University, Ithaca, N. Y.

3. ENGLISH.
    Professor EDWARD A. ALLEN
        University of Missouri, Columbia, Mo.
    F. A. BARBOUR
        Michigan State Normal School, Ypsilanti, Mich.
    Professor FRANK A., BLACKBURN
        University of Chicago, Chicago, Ill.
    Professor CORNELIUS B. BRADLEY
        University of California, Berkeley, Calif.
    Professor FRANCIS B. GUMMERE
        Haverford College, Pa.
    Professor EDWARD E. HALE, Jr.
        University of Iowa, Iowa City, Iowa.
    Professor GEORGE L. KITTREDGE
        Harvard University, Cambridge, Mass.
    CHARLES L. LOOS, Jr.
        High School, Dayton, Ohio.
    W. H. MAXWELL
        Superintendent of Schools, Brooklyn, N. Y.
    SAMUEL THURBER
        Master in the Girls' High School, Boston, Mass.
4. OTHER MODERN LANGUAGES.
    Professor JOSEPH L. ARMSTRONG
        Trinity College, Durham, N. C.
    THOMAS B. BRONSON
        Lawrenceville School, Lawrenceville, N. J.
    Professor ALPHONSE N. VAN DAELL
        Massachusetts Institute of Technology, Boston, Mass.
    CHARLES H. GRANDGENT
        Director of Modern Language Instruction in the Public
        Schools, Boston, Mass.
    Professor CHARLES HARRIS
        Oberlin College, Oberlin, Ohio.
    WILLIAM T. PECK
        High School, Providence, R. I.
    Professor SYLVESTER PRIMER
        University of Texas, Austin, Texas.
    JOHN J. SCHOBINGER
        Principal of a Private School for Boys, Chicago, Ill.
    ISIDORE H. B. SPIERS
        William Penn Charter School, Philadelphia, Pa.

Professor WALTER D. TOY
  University of North Carolina, Chapel Hill, N. C.
5. MATHEMATICS.
  Professor WILLIAM E. BYERLY
    Harvard University, Cambridge, Mass.
  Professor FLORIAN CAJORI
    Colorado College, Colorado Springs, Colo.
  ARTHUR H. CUTLER
    Principal of a Private School for Boys, New York City.
  Professor HENRY B. FINE
    College of New Jersey, Princeton, N. J.
  VV. A. GREESON
    Principal of the High School, Grand Rapids, Mich.
  ANDREW INGRAHAM
    Swain Free School, New Bedford, Mass.
  Professor SIMON NEWCOMB
    Johns Hopkins University, and Washington, D. C.
  Professor GEORGE D. OLDS
    Amherst College, Amberst, Mass.
  JAMES L. PATTERSON
    Lawrenceville School, Lawrenceville, N. J.
  Professor T. H. SAFFORD
    Williams College, Williamstown, Mass.
6. PHYSICS, ASTRONOMY, AND CHEMISTRY.
  Professor BROWN AYERS
    Tulane University, New Orleans, La.
  IRVING W. FAY
    The Belmont School, Belmont, Calif.
  ALFRED P. GAGE
    English High School, Boston, Mass.
  GEORGE WARREN KRALL
    Manual Training School, Washington University, St. Louis,
    Mo.
  Professor WILLIAM W. PAYNE
    Carleton College, Northfield, Minn.
  WILLIAM MCPHERSON, Jr.
    2901 Collinwood Avenue, Toledo, Ohio.
  Professor IRA REMSEN
    Johns Hopkins University, Baltimore, Md.
  Professor JAMES H. SHEPARD
    South Dakota Agricultural College, Brookings, So. Dak.

Professor WILLIAM J. WAGGENER
   University of Colorado, Boulder, Colo.
GEORGE R. WHITE
   Phillips Exeter Academy, Exeter, N. H.[\SUNL]
7. NATURAL HISTORY (BIOLOGY, INCLUDING BOTANY, ZOOL-
   OGY, AND PHYSIOLOGY).
Professor CHARLES E. BESSEY
   University of Nebraska, Lincoln, Neb.
ARTHUR C. BOYDEN
   Normal School, Bridgewater, Mass.
Professor SAMUEL F. CLARKE
   Williams College, Williamstown, Mass.
Professor DOUGLAS H. CAMPBELL
   Leland Stanford Jr. University, Palo . Alto, Calif.
President JOHN M. COULTER
   Indiana University, Bloomington, Ind.
Principal S. A. MERRITT
   Helena, Montana.
W. B. POWELL
   Superintendent of Schools, Washington, D. C.
CHARLES B. SCOTT
   High School, St. Paul, Minn.
Professor ALBERT H. TUTTLE
   University of Virginia, Charlottesville, Va.
O. S. WESTCOTT
   Principal of the North Division High School, Chicago, Ill.
8. HISTORY, CIVIL GOVERNMENT, AND POLITICAL ECONOMY.
President CHARLES K. ADAMS
   University of Wisconsin, Madison, Wis.
Professor EDWARD G. BOURNE
   Adelbert College, Cleveland, Ohio.
ABRAM BROWN
   Principal of the Central High School, Columbus, Ohio.
Professor A. B. HART
   Harvard University, Cambridge, Mass.
RAY GREENE HULING
   Principal of the High School, New Bedford, Mass.
Professor JESSE MACY
   Iowa College, Grinnell, Iowa.
Professor JAMES HARVEY ROBINSON
   University of Pennsylvania, Philadelphia, Pa.

Professor WILLIAM A. SCOTT
University of Wisconsin, Madison, Wis.
HENRY P. WARREN
Head Master of the Albany Academy, Albany, N. Y.
Professor WOODROW WILSON
College of New Jersey, Princeton, N. J.

9. GEOGRAPHY (PHYSICAL GEOGRAPHY, GEOLOGY, AND ME-
   TEOROLOGY).
   Professor THOMAS C. CHAMBERLIN
   University of Chicago, Chicago, Ill.
   Professor GEORGE L. COLLIE
   Beloit College, Beloit, Wis.
   Professor W. M. DAVIS
   Harvard University, Cambridge, Mass.
   DELWIN A. HAMLIN
   Master of the Rice Training School, Boston, Mass.
   Professor EDWIN J. HOUSTON
   Central High School, Philadelphia, Pa.
   Professor MARK W. HARRINGTON
   The Weather Bureau, Washington, D. C.
   CHARLES F. KING
   Dearborn School, Boston, Mass.
   FRANCIS W. PARKER
   Principal of the Cook County Normal School, Englewood,
   Ill.
   G. M. PHILIPS
   Principal of the State Normal School, West Chester, Pa.
   Professor ISRAEL C. RUSSELL
   University of Michigan, Ann Arbor, Mich.

The ninety members of the Conferences were divided as follows,—for-
ty-seven were in the service of colleges or universities, forty-two in the service of schools, and one was a government official formerly in the service of
a university. A considerable number of the college men, however, had also
had experience in schools. Each Conference, in accordance with a recommendation of the Committee of Ten, chose its own Chairman and Secretary; and these two officers prepared the report of each Conference. Six of
the Chairmen were college men, and three were school men; while of the
Secretaries, two were college men and seven school men. The Committee
of Ten requested that the reports of the Conferences should be sent to their
Chairman by the 1st of April, 1893—three months being thus allowed for

the preparation of the reports. Seven Conferences substantially conformed to this request of the Committee; but the reports from the Conferences on Natural History and Geography were delayed until the second week in July. The Committee of Ten, being of course unable to prepare their own report until all the reports of the December Conferences had been received, were prevented from presenting their report, as they had intended, at the Education Congress which met at Chicago July 27th–29th.

All the Conferences sat for three days; their discussions were frank, earnest, and thorough; but in every Conference an extraordinary unity of opinion was arrived at. The nine reports are characterized by an amount of agreement which quite surpasses the most sanguine anticipations. Only two Conferences present minority reports, namely, the Conference on Physics, Astronomy, and Chemistry, and the Conference on Geography; and in the first case, the dissenting opinions touch only two points in the report of the majority, one of which is unimportant. In the great majority of matters brought before each Conference, the decision of the Conference was unanimous. When one considers the different localities, institutions, professional experiences, and personalities represented in each of the Conferences, the unanimity developed is very striking, and should carry great weight.

Before the 1st of October, 1893, the reports of the Conferences had all been printed, after revision in proof by the chairmen of the Conferences respectively, and had been distributed to the members of the Committee of Ten, together with a preliminary draft of a report for the Committee. With the aid of comments and suggestions received from members of the Committee a second draft of this report was made ready in print to serve as the ground-work of the deliberations of the Committee at their final meeting. This meeting was held at Columbia College from the 8th to the 11th of November, 1893, inclusive, every member being present except Professor King, who is spending the current academic year in Europe. The points of view and the fields of work of the different members of the Committee being fortunately various, the discussions at this prolonged meeting were vigorous and comprehensive, and resulted in a thorough revision of the preliminary report. This third revise having been submitted to the members of the Committee, a cordial agreement on both the form and the substance of the present report, with the exceptions stated in the minority report of President Baker, was arrived at after a correspondence which extended over three weeks. The report itself embodies the numerous votes and resolutions adopted by the Committee. Professor King, having received in Europe the Conference reports, the two preliminary drafts of the Committee's report, and the third revise, desired to have his name signed to the final report.

The Council and the public will doubtless be impressed, at first sight, with the great number and variety of important changes urged by the Conferences; but on a careful reading of the appended reports it will appear that the spirit of the Conferences was distinctly conservative and moderate, although many of their recommendations are of a radical nature. The Conferences which found their tasks the most difficult were the Conferences on Physics, Astronomy, and Chemistry; Natural History; History, Civil Government, and Political Economy; and Geography; and these four Conferences make the longest and most elaborate reports, for the reason that these subjects are to-day more imperfectly dealt with in primary and secondary schools than are the subjects of the first five Conferences. The experts who met to confer together concerning the teaching of the last four subjects in the list of Conferences all felt the need of setting forth in an ample way what ought to be taught, in what order, and by what method. They ardently desired to have their respective subjects made equal to Latin, Greek, and Mathematics in weight and influence in the schools; but they knew that educational tradition was adverse to this desire, and that many teachers and directors of education felt no confidence in these subjects as disciplinary material. Hence the length and elaboration of these reports. In less degree, the Conferences on English and Other Modern Languages felt the same difficulties, these subjects being relatively new as substantial elements in school programmes. The Committee of Ten requested the Conferences to make their reports and recommendations as specific as possible. This request was generally complied with; but, very naturally, the reports and recommendations are more specific concerning the selection of topics in each subject, the best methods of instruction, and the desirable appliances or apparatus, than concerning the allotment of time to each subject. The allotment of time is a very important matter of administrative detail; but it presents great difficulties, requires a comprehensive survey of the comparative claims of many subjects, and in different parts of the country is necessarily affected by the various local conditions and historical developments. Nevertheless, there will be found in the Conference reports recommendations of a fundamental and far-reaching character concerning the allotment of programme time to each subject.

It might have been expected that every Conference would have demanded for its subject a larger proportion of time than is now commonly assigned to it in primary and secondary schools; but, as a matter of fact, the reports are noteworthy for their moderation in this respect,—especially the reports on the old and well-established subjects. The Latin Conference declares that,—"In view of the just demand for more and better work in several other subjects of the preparatory course, it seemed clear to the Conference that no increase in the quantity of the preparation in Latin should be asked for." Among the votes passed by the Greek Conference will be noticed the following:— "That in making the following recommendations, this Conference desires that the average age at which pupils now enter college should be lowered rather than raised; and the Conference urges that no addition be made in the advanced requirements in Greek for admission to college." The Mathematical Conference recommends that the course in arithmetic in elementary schools should be abridged, and recommends only a moderate assignment of time to algebra and geometry. The Conference on Geography says of the present assignment of time to geography in primary and secondary schools that "it is the judgment of the Conference that too much time is given to the subject in proportion to the results secured. It is not their judgment that more time is given to the subject than it merits, but that either more should be accomplished, or less time taken to attain it."

Anyone who reads these nine reports consecutively will be struck with the fact that all these bodies of experts desire to have the elements of their several subjects taught earlier than they now are; and that the Conferences on all the subjects except the languages desire to have given in the elementary schools what may be called perspective views, or broad surveys, of their respective subjects—expecting that in later years of the school course parts of these same subjects will be taken up with more amplitude and detail. The Conferences on Latin, Greek, and the Modern Languages agree in desiring to have the study of foreign languages begin at a much earlier age than now,—the Latin Conference suggesting by a reference to European usage that Latin be begun from three to five years earlier than it commonly is now. The Conference on Mathematics wish to have given in elementary schools not only a general survey of arithmetic, but also the elements of algebra, and concrete geometry in connection with drawing. The Conference on Physics, Chemistry, and Astronomy urge that nature studies should constitute an important part of the elementary school course from the very beginning. The Conference on Natural History wish the elements of botany and zoology to be taught in the primary schools. The Conference on History wish the systematic study of history to begin as early as the tenth year of age, and the first two years of study to be devoted to mythology and to biography for the illustration of general history as well as of American history. Finally, the Conference on Geography recommend that the earlier course treat broadly of the earth, its environment and inhabitants, extending freely into fields which in later years of study are recognized as belonging to separate sciences.

In thus claiming entrance for their subjects into the earlier years of school attendance, the Conferences on the newer subjects are only seeking an advantage which the oldest subjects have long possessed. The elements of language, number, and geography have long been imparted to young children. As things now are, the high school teacher finds in the pupils fresh from the grammar schools no foundation of elementary mathematical conceptions outside of arithmetic; no acquaintance with algebraic language; and no accurate knowledge of geometrical forms. As to botany, zoology, chemistry, and physics, the minds of pupils entering the high school are ordinarily blank on these subjects. When college professors endeavor to teach chemistry, physics, botany, zoology, meteorology, or geology to persons of eighteen or twenty years of age, they discover that in most instances new habits of observing, reflecting, and recording have to be painfully acquired by the students,—habits which they should have acquired in early childhood. The college teacher of history finds in like manner that his subject has never taken any serious hold on the minds of pupils fresh from the secondary schools. He finds that they have devoted astonishingly little time to the subject; and that they have acquired no habit of historical investigation, or of the comparative examination of different historical narratives concerning the same periods or events. It is inevitable, therefore, that specialists in any one of the subjects which are pursued in the high schools or colleges should earnestly desire that the minds of young children be stored with some of the elementary facts and principles of their subject; and that all the mental habits, which the adult student will surely need, begin to be formed in the child's mind before the age of fourteen. It follows, as a matter of course, that all the Conferences except the Conference on Greek, make strong suggestions concerning the programmes of primary and grammar schools,—generally with some reference to the subsequent programmes of secondary schools. They desire important changes in the elementary grades; and the changes recommended are all in the direction of increasing simultaneously the interest and the substantial training quality of primary and grammar school studies.

If anyone feels dismayed at the number and variety of the subjects to be opened to children of tender age, let him observe that while these nine Conferences desire each their own subject to be brought into the courses of elementary schools, they all agree that these different subjects should be correlated and associated one with another by the programme and by the actual teaching. If the nine Conferences had sat all together as a single body, instead of sitting as detached and even isolated bodies, they could not have more forcibly expressed their conviction that every subject recommended for introduction into elementary and secondary schools should help every other; and that the teacher of each single subject should feel responsible for the advancement of the pupils in all subjects, and should distinctly contribute to this advancement.

On one very important question of general policy which affects profoundly the preparation of all school programmes. the Committee of Ten and all the Conferences are absolutely, unanimous. Among the questions suggested for discussion in each Conference were the following:—

7. Should the subject be treated differently for pupils who are going to college, for those who are going to a scientific school, and for those who, presumably, are going to neither?

8. At what age should this differentiation begin, if any be recommended?

The 7th question is answered unanimously in the negative by the Conferences, and the 8th therefore needs no answer. The Committee of Ten unanimously agree with the Conferences. Ninety-eight teachers, intimately concerned either with the actual work of American secondary schools, or with the results of that work as they appear in students who come to college, unanimously declare that every subject which is taught at all in a secondary school should be taught in the same way and to the same extent to every pupil so long as he pursues it, no matter what the probable destination of the pupil may be, or at what point his education is to cease. Thus, for all pupils who study Latin, or history, or algebra, for example, the allotment of time and the method of instruction in a given school should be the same year by year. Not that all the pupils should pursue every subject for the same number of years; but so long as they do pursue it, they should all be treated alike. It has been a very general custom in American high schools and academies to make up separate courses of study for pupils of supposed different destinations, the proportions of the several studies in the different courses being various. The principle laid down by the Conferences will, if logically carried out, make a great simplification in secondary school programmes. It will lead to each subject's being treated by the school in the same way by the year for all pupils, and this, whether the individual pupil be required to choose between courses which run through several years, or be allowed some choice among subjects year by year.

Persons who read all the appended reports will observe the frequent occurrence of the statement that, in order to introduce the changes recommended, teachers more highly trained will be needed in both the elementary and the secondary schools. There are frequent expressions to the effect that a higher grade of scholarship is needed in teachers of the lower classes, or that the general adoption of some method urged by a Conference must depend upon the better preparation of teachers in the high schools, model schools, normal schools, or colleges in which they are trained. The experienced principal or superintendent in reading the reports will be apt to say to himself,— "This recommendation is sound, but cannot be carried out without teachers who have received a training superior to that of the teachers now at my command." It must be remembered, in connection with these admissions, or expressions of anxiety, that the Conferences were urged by the Committee of Ten to advise the Committee concerning the best possible—almost the ideal—treatment of each subject taught in a secondary school course, without, however, losing sight of the actual condition of American schools, or pushing their recommendations beyond what might reasonably be considered attainable in a moderate number of years. The Committee believe that the Conferences have carried out wisely the desire of the Committee, in that they have recommended improvements, which, though great and seldom to be made at once and simultaneously, are by no means unattainable. The existing agencies for giving instruction to teachers already in service are numerous; and the normal schools and the colleges are capable of making prompt and successful efforts to supply the better trained and equipped teachers for whom the reports of the Conferences call.

Many recommendations will be found to be made by more than one Conference. Thus, all the Conferences on foreign languages seem to agree that the introduction of two foreign languages in the same year is inexpedient; and all of them insist on practice in reading the foreign language aloud, on the use of good English in translating, and on practice in translating the foreign language at sight, and in writing it. Again, all the Conferences on scientific subjects dwell on laboratory work by the pupils as the best means of instruction, and on the great utility of the genuine laboratory note-book; and they all protest that teachers of science need at least as thorough a special training as teachers of languages or mathematics receive. In reading the reports, many instances will be noticed in which different Conferences have reached similar conclusions without any consultation, or have followed a common line of thought.

Your Committee now proceed to give summaries of the most important recommendations made by the Conferences as regards topics and methods, reserving the subject of time-allotment. But in so doing, they desire to say that the reading of these summaries should not absolve anyone interested in the general subject from reading with care the entire report of every Conference. The several reports are so full of suggestions and recommendations concisely and cogently stated that it is impossible to present adequate abstracts of them.

1. Latin

An important recommendation of the Latin Conference is the recommendation that the study of Latin be introduced into American schools earlier than it now is. They recommend that translation at sight form a constant and increasing part of the examinations for admission to college and of the work of preparation. They next urge that practice in writing Latin should not be dissociated from practice in reading and translating; but, on the contrary, that the two should be carried on with equal steps. The Conference desire the schools to adopt a greater variety of Latin authors for beginners, and they give good reasons against the exclusive use of Caesar's Gallic War. They object to the common practice of putting the teaching of beginners into the hands of the youngest teachers, who have the slenderest equipment of knowledge and experience. They dwell on the importance of attending to pronunciation and reading aloud, to forms, vocabulary, syntax, and order, and to the means of learning to understand the Latin before translating it; and they describe and urge the importance of a higher ideal in translation than now prevails in secondary schools. The formal recommendations of the Conference, fourteen in number, will be found concisely stated in numbered paragraphs at the close of their report.

2. Greek

The Conference on Greek agree with the Conference on Latin in recommending the cultivation of reading at sight in schools, and in recommending that practice in translation into the foreign language should be continued throughout the school course. They urge that three years be the minimum time for the study of Greek in schools; provided that Latin be studied four years. They would not have a pupil begin the study of Greek without a knowledge of the elements of Latin. They recommend the substitution of portions of the Hellenica for two books of the Anabasis in the requirements for admission to college, and the use of some narrative portions of Thucydides in schools. They urge that Homer should continue to be studied in all schools which provide instruction in Greek through three years, and they suggest that the Odyssey is to be preferred to the Iliad. They regret "that so few colleges through their admission examinations encourage reading at sight in schools." Like the Latin Conference, the Greek Conference urge that the reading of the text be constantly practiced by both teacher and pupil, "and that teachers require from their pupils no less intelligent reading of the text than accurate translation of the same."

The Greek Conference also adopted a vote "to concur with the Latin Conference as to the age at which the study of Latin should be begun." The specific recommendations of the Conference will be found in brief form in the paragraphs at the head of the eleven numbered sections into which their report is divided.

3. English

The Conference on English found it necessary to deal with the study of English in schools below the high school grade as well as in the high school. Their opening recommendations deal with the very first years of school, and one of the most interesting and admirable parts of their report relates to English in the primary and the grammar schools. The Conference are of the opinion that English should be pursued in the high school during the entire course of four years; but in making this recommendation the Conference have in mind both study of literature and training in the expression of thought. To the study of rhetoric they assign one hour a week in the third year of the high school course. To the subject of historical and systematic grammar they assign one hour a week in the fourth year of the high school course. The intelligent reader of the report of this Conference will find described in it the means by which the study of English in secondary schools is to be made the equal of any other study in disciplinary or developing power. The Conference claim for English as much time as the Latin Conference claim for Latin in secondary schools; and it is clear that they intend that the study shall be in all respects as serious and informing as the study of Latin. One of the most interesting opinions expressed by the Conference is "that the best results in the teaching of English in high schools cannot be secured without the aid given by the study of some other language; and that Latin and German, by reason of their fuller inflectional system, are especially suited to this end." In the case of high schools, as well as in schools of lower grade, the Conference declare that every teacher, whatever his department, should feel responsible for the use of good English on the part of his pupils. In several passages of this report the idea recurs that training in English must go hand in hand with the study of other subjects. Thus the Conference hope for the study of the history and geography of the English-speaking people, so far as these illustrate the development of the English language. They mention that "the extent to which the study of the sources of English words can be carried in any school or class will depend on the acquaintance the pupils possess with Latin, French, and German." They say that the study of words should be so pursued as to illustrate the political, social, intellectual, and religious development of the English race; and they urge that the admission of a student to college should be made to depend largely on his ability to write English, as shown in his examination books on other subjects. It is a fundamental idea in this report that the study of every other subject should contribute to the pupil's training in English; and that the pupil's capacity to write English should be made available, and be developed, in every other department. The very specific recommendations of the Conference as to English requirements for admission to colleges and scientific schools are especially wise and valuable.

4. Other Modern Languages

The most novel and striking recommendation made by the Conference on Modern Languages is that an elective course in German or French be provided in the grammar school, the instruction to be open to children at about ten years of age. The Conference made this recommendation "in the firm belief that the educational effects of modern language study will be of immense benefit to all who are able to pursue it under proper guidance." They admit that the study of Latin presents the same advantages; but living languages seem to them better adapted to grammar school work. The recommendations of this Conference with regard to the number of lessons a week are specific. They even construct a table showing the time which should be devoted to modern languages in each of the last four years of the elementary schools and in each year of the high school. They plead that "all pupils of the same intelligence and the same degree of maturity be instructed alike, no matter whether they are subsequently to enter a college or scientific school, or intend to pursue their studies no farther." The Conference also state with great precision what in their judgment may be expected of pupils in German and French at the various stages of their progress. An important passage of the report treats of the best way to facilitate the progress of beginners;—pupils should be lifted over hard places; frequent reviews are not to be recommended; new texts stimulate interest and enlarge the vocabulary. Their recommendations concerning translation into English, reading aloud, habituating the ear to the sounds of the foreign language, and translating into the foreign language, closely resemble the recommendations of the Conferences on Latin, Greek, and English regarding the best methods of instruction in those languages. In regard to college requirements, the Conference agree with several other Conferences in stating "that college requirements for admission should coincide with the high school requirements for graduation." Finally, they declare that "the worst obstacle to modern language study is the lack of properly equipped instructors; and that it is the duty of universities, states, and cities to provide opportunities for the special preparation of modern language teachers."

5. Mathematics

The form of the report of the Conference on Mathematics differs somewhat from that of the other reports. This report is subdivided under five headings:—1st, General Conclusions. 2nd, The Teaching of Arithmetic. 3rd, The Teaching of Concrete Geometry. 4th, The Teaching of Algebra. 5th, The Teaching of Formal or Demonstrative Geometry.

The first general conclusion of the Conference was arrived at unanimously. The Conference consisted of one government official and university professor, five professors of mathematics in as many colleges, one principal of a high school, two teachers of mathematics in endowed schools, and one proprietor of a private school for boys. The professional experience of these gentlemen and their several fields of work were various, and they came from widely separated parts of the country; yet they were unanimously of opinion "that a radical change in the teaching of arithmetic was necessary." They recommend "that the course in arithmetic be at once abridged and enriched; abridged by omitting entirely those subjects which perplex and exhaust the pupil without affording any really valuable mental discipline, and enriched by a greater number of exercises in simple calculation, and in the solution of concrete problems." They specify in detail the subjects which they think should be curtailed, or entirely omitted; and they give in their special report on the teaching of arithmetic a full statement of the reasons on which their conclusion is based. They map out a course in arithmetic which, in their judgment, should begin about the age of six years, and be completed at about the thirteenth year of age.

The Conference next recommend that a course of instruction in concrete geometry with numerous exercises be introduced into the grammar schools; and that this instruction should, during the earlier years, be given in connection with drawing. They recommend that the study of systematic algebra should be begun at the age of fourteen; but that, in connection with the study of arithmetic, the pupils should earlier be made familiar with algebraic expressions and symbols, including the method of solving simple equations. "The Conference believe that the study of demonstrative geometry should begin at the end of the first year's study of algebra, and be carried on by the side of algebra for the next two years, occupying about two hours and a half a week." They are also of opinion "that if the introductory course in concrete geometry has been well taught, both plane and solid geometry can be mastered at this time." Most of the improvements in teaching arithmetic which the Conference suggest "can be summed up under the two heads of giving the teaching a more concrete form, and paying more attention to facility and correctness in work. The concrete system should not be confined to principles, but be extended to practical applications in measuring and in physics."

In regard to the teaching of concrete geometry, the Conference urge that while the student's geometrical education should begin in the kindergarten, or at the latest in the primary school, systematic instruction in concrete or experimental geometry should begin at about the age of ten for the average student, and should occupy about one school hour a week for at least three years. From the outset of this course, the pupil should be required to express himself verbally as well as by drawing and modelling. He should learn to estimate by the eye, and to measure with some degree of accuracy, lengths, angular magnitudes, and areas; to make accurate plans from his own measurements and estimates; and to make models of simple geometrical solids. The whole work in concrete geometry will connect itself on the one side with the work in arithmetic, and on the other with elementary instruction in physics. With the study of arithmetic is therefore to be intimately associated the study of algebraic signs and forms, of concrete geometry, and of elementary physics. Here is a striking instance of the interlacing of subjects which seems so desirable to every one of the nine Conferences.

Under the head of teaching algebra, the Conference set forth in detail the method of familiarizing the pupil with the use of algebraic language during the study of arithmetic. This part of the report also deals clearly with the question of the time required for the thorough mastery of algebra through quadratic equations. The report on the teaching of demonstrative geometry is a clear and concise statement of the best method of teaching this subject. It insists on the importance of elegance and finish in geometrical demonstration, for the reason that the discipline for which geometrical demonstration is to be chiefly prized is a discipline in complete, exact, and logical statement. If slovenliness of expression, or awkwardness of form, is tolerated, this admirable discipline is lost. The Conference therefore recommend an abundance of oral exercises in geometry—for which there is no proper substitute—and the rejection of all demonstrations which are not exact and formally perfect. Indeed throughout all the teaching of mathematics the Conference deem it important that great stress be laid by the teacher on accuracy of statement and elegance of form as well as on clear and rigorous reasoning. Another very important recommendation in this part of the report is to be found the following passage,—"As soon as the student has acquired the art of rigorous demonstration, his work should cease to be merely receptive. He should begin to devise constructions and demonstrations for himself. Geometry cannot be mastered, by reading the demonstrations of a text-book, and while there is no branch of elementary mathematics in which purely receptive work, if continued too long, may lose its interest more completely, there is also none in which independent work can be made more attractive and stimulating." These observations are entirely in accordance with the recent practice of some colleges in setting admission examination papers in geometry which demand of the candidates some capacity to solve new problems, or rather to make new application of familiar principles.

6. Physics, Chemistry, and Astronomy

The Conference on this subject were urgent that the study of simple natural phenomena be introduced into elementary schools; and it was the sense of the Conference that at least one period a day from the first year of the primary school should be given to such study. Apparently the Conference entertained the opinion that the present teachers in elementary schools are ill prepared to teach children how to observe simple natural phenomena; for their second recommendation was that special science teachers or superintendents be appointed to instruct the teachers of elementary schools in the methods of teaching natural phenomena. The Conference was clearly of opinion that from the beginning this study should be pursued by the pupil chiefly, though not exclusively, by means of experiments and by practice in the use of simple instruments for making physical measurements. The report dwells repeatedly on the importance of the study of things and phenomena by direct contact. It emphasizes the necessity of a large proportion of laboratory work in the study of physics and chemistry, and advocates the keeping of laboratory note-books by the pupils, and the use of such note-books as part of the test for admission to college. At the same time the report points out that laboratory work must be conjoined with the study of a text-book and with attendance at lectures or demonstrations; and that intelligent direction by a good teacher is as necessary in a laboratory as it is in the ordinary recitation or lecture room. The great utility of the laboratory note-book is emphatically stated. To the objection that the kind of instruction described requires much time and effort on the part of the teacher, the Conference reply that to give good instruction in the sciences requires of the teacher more work than to give good instruction in mathematics or the languages; and that the sooner this fact is recognized by those who have the management of schools the better for all concerned. The science teacher must regularly spend much time in collecting materials, preparing experiments, and keeping collections in order; and this indispensable labor should be allowed for in programmes and salaries. As regards the means of testing the progress of the pupils in physics and chemistry, the Conference were unanimously of opinion that a laboratory examination should always be combined with an oral or written examination, neither test taken singly being sufficient. There was a difference of opinion in the Conference on the question whether physics should precede chemistry, or chemistry physics. The logical order would place physics first; but all the members of the Conference but one advised that chemistry be put first for practical reasons which are stated in the majority report. A sub-committee of the Conference has prepared lists of experiments in physics and chemistry for the use of secondary schools,—not, of course, as a prescription, but only as a suggestion, and a somewhat precise indication of the topics which the Conference had in mind, and of the limits of the instruction.

7. Natural History

The Conference on Natural History unanimously agreed that the study of botany and zoölogy ought to be introduced into the primary schools at the very beginning of the school course, and be pursued steadily, with not less than two periods a week, throughout the whole course below the high school. In the next place they agreed that in these early lessons in natural science no text-book should be used; but that the study should constantly be associated with the study of literature, language, and drawing. It was their opinion that the study of physiology should be postponed to the later years of the high school course; but that in the high school, some branch of natural history proper should be pursued every day throughout at least one year. Like the report on Physics, Chemistry, and Astronomy, the report on Natural History emphasizes the absolute necessity of laboratory work by the pupils on plants and animals; and would have careful drawing insisted on from the beginning of the instruction. As the laboratory note-book is recommended by the Conference on Physics, so the Conference on Natural History recommends that the pupils should be made to express themselves clearly and exactly in words, or by drawings, in describing the objects which they observe; and they believe that this practice will be found a valuable aid in training the pupils in the art of expression. They agree with the Conference on Physics, Chemistry, and Astronomy that science examinations should include both a written and a laboratory test, and that the laboratory note-books of the pupils should be produced at the examination. The recommendations of this Conference are therefore very similar to those of the sixth Conference, so far as methods go; but there are appended to the general report of the Conference on Natural History sub-reports which describe the proper topics, the best order of topics, and the right methods of instruction in botany for schools below the high school, and for the high school itself, and in zoölogy for the secondary schools. Inasmuch as both the subject matter and the methods of instruction in natural history are much less familiar to ordinary school teachers than the matter and the methods in the languages and mathematics, the Conference believed that descriptive details were necessary in order to give a clear view of the intentions of the Conference. In another sub-report the Conference give their reasons for recommending the postponement to the latest possible time of the study of physiology and hygiene. Like the sixth Conference, the Conference on Natural History protest that no person should be regarded as qualified to teach natural science who has not had special training for this work,—a preparation at least as thorough as that of their fellow teachers of mathematics and the languages.

8. History, Civil Government, and Political Economy

The Conference on History, Civil Government, and Political Economy had a task different in some respects from those of other Conferences. It is now-a-days admitted that language, natural science, and mathematics should each make a substantial part of education; but the function of history in education is still very imperfectly apprehended. Accordingly, the eighth Conference were at pains to declare their conception of the object of studying history and civil government in schools, and their belief in the efficiency of these studies in training the judgment, and in preparing children for intellectual enjoyments in after years, and for the exercise at maturity of a salutary influence upon national affairs. They believed that the time devoted in schools to history and the allied subjects should be materially increased; and they have therefore presented arguments in favor of that increase. At the same time, they state strongly their conviction that they have recommended "nothing that was not already being done in some good schools, and that might not reasonably be attained wherever there is an efficient system of graded schools." This Conference state quite as strongly as any other their desire to associate the study of their particular subject with that of other subjects which enter into every school programme. They declare that the teaching of history should be intimately connected with the teaching of English; that pupils should be encouraged to avail themselves of their knowledge of ancient and modern languages; and that their study of history should be associated with the study of topography and political geography, and should be supplemented by the study of historical and commercial geography, and the drawing of historical maps. They desire that historical works should be used for reading in schools, and that subjects of English composition should be drawn from the lessons in history. They would have historical poems committed to memory, and the reading of biographies and historical novels encouraged. While they are of opinion that political economy should not be taught in secondary schools, they urge that, in connection with United States history, civil government, and commercial geography, instruction should be given in the most important economic topics. The Conference would therefore have the instruction in history made contributary to the work in three other school departments, namely, English, geography, and drawing. The subject of civil government they would associate with both history and geography. They would introduce it into the grammar school by means of oral lessons, and into the high school by means of a text-book with collateral reading and oral lessons. In the high school they believe that the study of civil government may be made comparative,—that is, that the American method may be compared with foreign systems.

Although the Conference was made up of very diverse elements, every member of the Conference was heartily in favor of every vote adopted. This remarkable unanimity was not obtained by the silence of dissentients, or the withdrawal of opposition on disputed points. It was the natural result of the strong conviction of all the members, that history, when taught by the methods advocated in their report, deserves a position in school programmes which would give it equal dignity and importance with any of the most favored subjects, and that the advantages for all children of the rational study of history ought to be diffused as widely as possible. On one point they made a clearer declaration than any other Conference; although several other Conferences indicate similar opinions. They declared that their interest was chiefly "in the school children who have no expectation of going to college, the larger number of whom will not even enter a high school," and that their "recommendations are in no way directed to building up the colleges, or increasing the number of college students." Like every other Conference, they felt anxious about the qualifications of the teachers who are to be entrusted with the teaching of history, and they urged that only teachers who have had adequate special training should be employed to teach history and civil government. In their specific recommendations they strongly urge that the historical course be made continuous from year to year, and extend through eight years, and in this respect be placed upon the same footing with other substantial subjects.

The answers of this Conference to the questions contained in the memorandum sent to the Conferences by the Committee of Ten were specific and clear. In regard to the time to be devoted to history in school programmes, this Conference ask for not less than three periods a week throughout a course of eight years; and they suggest that some of this time can be found by contracting the course in arithmetic, and using for history a part of the time now given to political geography and to language study. Of these eight years they suggest that four should be in the high school and four in the grammar school. They "especially recommend such a choice of subjects as will give pupils in the grammar schools an opportunity of studying the history of other countries, and to the high schools one year's study on the intensive method."

A large portion of the report is necessarily taken up with the description of what the Conference consider the most suitable historical topics and the best methods of teaching history. This portion of the report does not admit of any useful presentation in outline; it must be read in full.

With regard to examinations in history for admission to college, the Conference protest "against the present lax and inefficient system," and seem to sum up their own desires on this subject in the statement that "the requirements for college ought to be so framed that the methods of teaching best adapted to meet them will also be best for all pupils."

Like the Conferences on scientific subjects the Conference on History insist on note-books, abstracts, special reports, and other written work, as desirable means of teaching. If the recommendations of the nine Conferences should be carried out in grammar and high schools, there would certainly be at least one written exercise a day for every pupil,—a result which persons interested in training children to write English deem it important to accomplish.

The observations of the Conference on geographical training in connection with history are interesting and suggestive, as are also the recurring remarks on the need of proper apparatus for teaching history, such as maps, reference-libraries, historical pictures, and photographs. It is not the natural sciences alone which need school apparatus.

9. Geography

Considering that geography has been a subject of recognized value in elementary schools for many generations, and that a considerable portion of the whole school time of children has long been devoted to a study called by this name, it is somewhat startling to find that the report of the Conference on Geography deals with more novelties than any other report; exhibits more dissatisfaction with prevailing methods; and makes, on the whole, the most revolutionary suggestions. This Conference had but nine members present at its sessions; and before the final revision of its report had been accomplished, one of the most valued of its members died. Seven members sign the majority report, and the minority report is presented by one member. The dissenting member, however, while protesting against the views of the majority on many points, concurs with the majority in some of the most important conclusions arrived at by the Conference.

It is obvious on even a cursory reading of the majority and minority reports that geography means for all the members of this Conference something entirely different from the term geography as generally used in school programmes. Their definition of the word makes it embrace not only a description of the surface of the earth, but also the elements of botany, zoölogy, astronomy, and meteorology, as well as many considerations pertaining to commerce, government, and ethnology. "The physical environment of man" expresses as well as any single phrase can the Conference's conception of the principal subject which they wish to have taught. No one can read the reports without perceiving that the advanced instruction in geography which the Conference conceive to be desirable and feasible in high schools cannot be given until the pupils have mastered many of the elementary facts of botany, zoölogy, geometry, and physics. It is noteworthy also that this ninth Conference, like the seventh, dealt avowedly and unreservedly with the whole range of instruction in primary and secondary schools. They did not pretend to treat chiefly instruction in secondary schools, and incidentally instruction in the lower schools; but, on the contrary, grasped at once the whole problem, and described the topics, methods, and apparatus appropriate to the entire course of twelve years. They recognized that complete descriptions would be necessary in all three branches of the subject,—topics, methods, and equipment; and they have given these descriptions with an amplitude and force which leave little to be desired. More distinctly than any other Conference, they recognized that they were presenting an ideal course which could not be carried into effect everywhere or immediately. Indeed at several points they frankly state that the means of carrying out their recommendations are not at present readily accessible; and they exhibit the same anxiety which is felt by several other Conferences about training teachers for the kind of work which the Conference believe to be desirable. After the full and interesting descriptions of the relations and divisions of geographical science, as the Conference define it, the most important sections of their report relate to the methods and means of presenting the subject in schools, and to the right order in developing it. The methods which they advocate require not only better equipped teachers, but better means of illustrating geographical facts in the schoolroom, such as charts, maps, globes, photographs, models, lantern slides, and lanterns. Like all the other Conferences on scientific subjects, the ninth Conference dwell on the importance of forming from the start good habits of observing correctly and stating accurately the facts observed. They also wish that the instruction in geography may be connected with the instruction in drawing, history, and English. They believe that meteorology may he taught as an observational study in the earliest years of the grammar school, the scholars being even then made familiar with the use of the thermometer, the wind-vane, and the rain-gauge; and that it may be carried much farther in the high school years, after physics has been studied, so that the pupils may then attain a general understanding of topographical maps, of pressure and wind charts, of isothermal charts, and of such complicated subjects as weather prediction, rainfall and the distribution of rain, storms, and the seasonal variations of the atmosphere. Their conception of physiography is a very comprehensive one. In short, they recommend a study of physical geography which would embrace in its scope the elements of half-a-dozen natural sciences, and would bind together in one sheaf the various glean-ings which the pupils would have gathered from widely separated fields. There can be no doubt that the study would be interesting, informing, and developing, or that it would be difficult and in every sense substantial.

Allotment of School Time

It already appears that the nine Conferences have attended carefully to three out of the five subjects which it was the intention of the National Council of Education that they should examine. They have discussed fully the proper limits of the several subjects of instruction in secondary schools, the best methods of instruction, and the best methods of testing pupils' attainments. The Conferences were equally faithful in discussing the other two subjects committed to them by the Council, namely, the most desirable allotment of time for each subject, and the requirements for admission to college.

The next subject which the Committee of Ten, following the guidance of the Conferences, desire to present to the Council is, therefore, the al-lotment of school time among the various subjects of study. It is the obvi-ous duty of the Committee, in the first place, to group together in tabular form the numerous suggestions on this subject made by the Conferences. Having exhibited the programme-time suggestions of the Conferences, it will remain for the Committee to construct a flexible and comprehensive schedule of studies, based on the recommendations of the Conferences.

[Table 1] exhibits the demands for programme time made by all the Conferences. It will be seen at once that this table does not yield, with-out modification, a practical programme. The nine Conferences acted separately, and were studying each its own needs, and not the comparative needs of all the subjects. It was not for them to balance the different inter-ests, but for each to present strongly one interest. It will further be noticed that some of their demands are not specific,— that is, they do not call for any specified number of recitation periods for a definite number of weeks during a stated number of years. The Conferences on Languages and His-tory are the most definite in their recommendations, the Conferences on

TABLE 1 Recommendations of the Nine Conferences of the Committee of 10

Subject	Elementary Grades—Primary and Grammar School								Secondary School—High School or Academy			
	1st year	2nd year	3rd year	4th year	5th year	6th year	7th year	8th year	9th year	10th year	11th year	12th year
	Age 6–7	7–8	8–9	9–10	10–11	11–12	12–13	13–14	14–15	15–16	16–17	17–18
1. Latin	Reasons given for beginning Latin earlier than is now the custom								5p. a wk.	5p. a wk.	5p. a wk.	5p. a wk.
2. Greek	Latin to be begun a year before Greek									5p. a wk.	4p. a wk.	4p. a wk.
3. English	Pupils to reproduce orally stories told them, to invent stories and describe objects.		Supplementary reading begun—and continued through all the grades. Composition begun—writing narratives and descriptions—oral and written exercises on forms and the sentence.				From this grade no reader to be used	Grammar 3p. a wk.	Literature 3p. a wk. Composition 2p. a wk.	Literature 3p. a wk. Composition 2p. a wk.	Literature 3p. a wk. Composition 1p. a wk. Rhetoric 1p. a wk.	Literature 3p. a wk. Composition 1p. a wk. Grammar 1p. a wk.
4. Modern Languages					Elective German or French 5p. a wk.	Elective German or French 4p. a wk.	Elective German or French 3p. a wk. at least	Elective German or French 3p. a wk. at least	The language begun below 4p. a wk.	The same language 4p. a wk., Second language 4p. a wk.	The same language 4p. a wk., Second language 4p. a wk.	The same language 4p. a wk., Second language 4p. a wk.

Subject								
5. Mathematics	Arithmetic during first eight years, with algebraic expressions and symbols and simple equations—no specific number of hours being recommended.	Concrete Geometry, 1p. a wk.	Concrete Geometry, 1p. a wk.	Concrete Geometry, 1p. a wk.	Concrete Geometry, 1p. a wk.	Algebra, 5p. a wk.	Algebra *or* Bookkeeping and Commercial Arithmetic, 2.5p a wk. Geometry 2.5p. a wk.	Algebra *or* Bookkeeping and Commercial Arithmetic, 2.5p a wk. Geometry 2.5p. a wk.	Trigonometry and higher Algebra for candidates for scientific schools.
6. Physics, Chemistry, & Astronomy	Study of natural phenomena 5p. a wk. through first eight years by experiments, including physical measurements and the recommendation of Conferences 7 & 9						Elective Astronomy, 5p. a wk. 12 wks.	Chemistry, 5p. a wk.	Physics, 5p. a wk.
7. Natural History	Through first eight years 2p. a wk., of not less than 30 minutes each, devoted to plants and animals; the instruction to be correlated with language, drawing, literature, and geography.					One yr. (which yr. not specified) 5p. a wk. for botany or zoology. Half-yr. (late in course) anatomy, physiology, and hygiene, 5p. a wk.			
8. History		Biography & Mythology, 3p. a wk.		American History and elements of civil government, 3 p. a wk.	Greek and Roman History, 3 p. a wk.	French History, 3 p. a wk.	English History, 3p. a wk.	American History, 3p. a wk.	A special period intensively, and civil government, 3 p. a wk.
9. Geography	Time allotted in first eight years to equal that given to number work. The subject—the earth, its environment and inhabitants, including the elements of astronomy, meteorology, zoology; botany; history; commerce, races, religions, and governments.				Physical Geography	(Physiography, geology, or meteorology at some part of the high school course. Possibly more than one of these where election is allowed.)	Elective Meteorology, 1/2 this year or next.	Elective Geology or Physiography, 1/2 yr.

Mathematics and the Sciences being much less definite. Table 1 is therefore not a programme, but the materials from which serviceable programmes may be constructed.

The Committee of Ten deliberately placed in this one table the recommendations of the Conferences for the elementary grades and the recommendations for secondary schools, in order that the sequence of the recommendations for each subject might be clearly brought out. The recommendations made for the secondary schools presuppose in many cases that the recommendations made for the elementary schools have been fulfilled; or, at least, in many cases the Conferences would have made different recommendations for the secondary schools, if they had been compelled to act on the assumption that things must remain just as they are in the elementary schools.

At this point it is well to call attention to the list of subjects which the Conferences deal with as proper for secondary schools. They are: 1. languages—Latin, Greek, English, German, and French, (and locally Spanish); 2. mathematics—algebra, geometry, and trigonometry; 3. general history, and the intensive study of special epochs; 4. natural history—including descriptive astronomy, meteorology, botany, zoölogy, physiology, geology, and ethnology, most of which subjects may be conveniently grouped under the title of physical geography; and 5. physics and chemistry. The Committee of Ten assent to this list, both for what it includes and for what it excludes, with some practical qualifications to be mentioned below.

Table 2 exhibits the total amount of instruction (estimated by the number of weekly periods assigned to each subject) to be given in a secondary school during each year of a four years' course, on the supposition that the recommendations of the Conferences are all carried out.

TABLE 2   Total Amount of Instruction Recommended by Nine Conferences

		Total
1st Secondary School Year		
Latin		5.0 p.
English Literature	3.0 p.	5.0 p.
English Composition	2.0 p.	
German or French	⇀	4.0 p.
Algebra		5.0 p.
History		3.0 p.
	Total	22.0 p.

2nd Secondary School Year

Latin		5.0 p.
Greek		5.0 p.
English Literature	3.0 p.	5.0 p.
English Composition	2.0 p.	
German		4.0 p.
French		4.0 p.
Algebra (or bookkeeping and commercial arithmetic)	2.5 p.	5.0 p.
Geometry	2.5 p.	
Astronomy (12 weeks)		5.0 p.
Botany or Zoology		5.0 p.
History		3.0 p.
Total		37.5 p.

3rd Secondary School Year

Latin		5.0 p.
Greek		4.0 p.
English Literature	3.0 p.	5.0 p.
English Composition	1.0 p.	
Rhetoric	1.0 p.	
German		4.0 p.
French		4.0 p.
Algebra (or bookkeeping and commercial arithmetic)	2.5 p.	5.0 p.
Geometry	2.5 p.	
Chemistry		5.0 p.
History		3.0 p.
Total		35.0 p.

4th Secondary School Year

Latin		5.0 p.
Greek		4.0 p.
English Literature	3.0 p.	5.0 p.
English Composition	1.0 p.	
English Grammar	1.0 p.	
German		4.0 p.
French		4.0 p.
Trigonometry (½ yr.)	2.0 p.	2.0 p.
Higher Algebra (½ yr.)	2.0 p.	
Physics		5.0 p.
Anatomy, Physiology, and Hygiene (½ yr.)		5.0 p.
History		3.0 p.
Geol. or Physiography (½ yr.)	3.0 p.	3.0 p.
Meteorology (½ yr.)	3.0 p.	
Total		37.5 p.

The method of estimating the amount of instruction offered in any subject by the number of recitation periods assigned to it each week for a given number of years or half years is in some respects an inadequate one, for it takes no account of the scope and intensity of the instruction given during the periods; but so far as it goes, it is trustworthy and instructive. It represents with tolerable accuracy the proportional expenditure which a school is making on a given subject, and therefore the proportional importance which the school attaches to that subject. It also represents roughly the proportion of the pupil's entire school time which he can devote to a given subject, provided he is free to take all the instruction offered in that subject. All experience shows that subjects deemed important get a large number of weekly periods, while those deemed unimportant get a small number. Moreover, if the programme time assigned to a given subject be insufficient, the value of that subject as training cannot be got, no matter how good the quality of the instruction.

Every one of these years, except the first, contains much more instruction than any one pupil can follow; but, looking at the bearing of the table on the important question of educational expenditure, it is encouraging to observe that there are already many secondary schools in this country in which quite as many subjects are taught as are mentioned in this table, and in which there are more weekly periods of instruction provided for separate classes than are found in any year of the table. In some urban high schools which provide from five to nine different courses of three to five years each, and in some endowed secondary schools which maintain two or three separate courses called Classical, Latin-scientific, and English, or designated by similar titles, the total number of weekly periods of unrepeated instruction given to distinct classes is even now larger than the largest total of weekly periods found in Table 2. The annual expenditure in such schools is sufficient to provide all the instruction called for by Table 2. The suggestions of the Conferences presuppose that all the pupils of like intelligence and maturity in any subject study it in the same way and to the same extent, so long as they study it at all,—this being a point on which all the Conferences insist strongly. No provision is made, therefore, for teaching Latin, or algebra, or history to one portion of a class four times a week, and to another portion of the same class only thrice or twice a week. Such provisions are very common in American schools; but the recommendations of the Conferences, if put into effect, would do away with all expenditures of this sort.

It clearly appears from Table 2 that the recommendations of the Conferences on scientific subjects have been moderate so far as the proposed allotment of time to them is concerned. The Conferences on Physics, Chemistry and Astronomy, Natural History, and Geography held one combined session in Chicago, and passed a resolution that one-fourth of the whole high school course ought to be devoted to natural science, their intention doubtless being that each pupil should devote one quarter of his time to science; yet if all the time asked for in secondary schools by the scientific Conferences be added together, it will appear, first, that the rare pupil who should take all the scientific instruction provided would need for it only one quarter of his time, and secondly, that less than one-sixth of the whole instruction to be given in accordance with the combined recommendations of all the Conferences is devoted to subjects of natural science. The first year of the secondary school course according to Table 2 will contain no science at all; and it is only in the last year of the secondary school that the proportion of natural science teaching rises to one-fourth of the whole instruction.

In studying these two tables which result from the recommendations of the Conferences, the Committee of Ten perceived at once, that if the recommendations are to be carried out, so far as offering the instruction proposed is concerned, a selection of studies for the individual pupil must be made in the second, third, and fourth years of the secondary school course. This selection will obviously be made in different ways in different schools. Any school principal may say,— "With the staff at my command I can teach only five subjects out of those proposed by the Conferences in the manner proposed. My school shall therefore be limited to these five." Another school may be able to teach in the thorough manner proposed five subjects, but some or all of these five may be different from those selected by the first school. A larger or richer school may be able to teach all the subjects mentioned, and by the methods and with the apparatus described. In the last case, each pupil, under the supervision of the teachers, and with the advice of parents or friends, may make choice between several different four-years' courses arranged by the school; or, if the school authorities prefer, the pupil may be allowed to make year by year a carefully guided choice among a limited number of subjects; or these two methods may be combined. Selection for the individual is necessary to thoroughness, and to the imparting of power as distinguished from information; for any large subject whatever, to yield its training value, must be pursued through several years and be studied from three to five times a week, and if each subject studied is thus to claim a considerable fraction of the pupil's school time, then clearly the individual pupil can give attention to only a moderate number of subjects.

In Table 2 the number of weekly periods assigned to a single subject varies from two to five, about half of the assignments being made for five periods a week. There is an obvious convenience in the number five because it ordinarily gives one period a day for five days in the week; but there is also an obvious disadvantage in making too free use of the number five. It practically limits to three or, at most, four, the number of subjects which the individual pupil may pursue simultaneously; and this limit is inexpedient in a four years' programme.

The Committee have therefore prepared the following modification of Table 2, using four as the standard number of weekly periods, excepting the first year of a new language, and in the few cases in which the Conferences advise a number smaller than four. By this means the total number of periods is somewhat reduced, except in the first year, and the numbers of periods allotted to different subjects are made more consonant, each with the others. The result is only a correlation and adjustment of the recommendations of the Conferences, no judgment or recommendation of the Committee being expressed in it.

The adoption of the number four as the standard number of weekly periods will not make it impossible to carry into effect the fundamental conception of all the Conferences, namely,— that all the subjects which make part of the secondary school course should be taught consecutively enough and extensively enough to make every subject yield that training which it is best fitted to yield,—provided that the proposed correlation and association of subjects are carried out in practice. With regard to the arrangement or sequence of subjects, the Committee follow in this table the recommendations of the Conferences with only slight modifications. They insert in the first year applied geography, using the term in the sense in which it is used by the Conference on Geography; and they make this insertion in order that natural science may be represented in the programme of that year, and that a complete break of continuity, as regards science subjects, between the eighth grade and the second year of the secondary school may be avoided. They have felt obliged to put physics into the third year, and chemistry into the fourth, in order that the subject of physics may precede meteorology and physiography; and they have slightly increased the number of lessons in astronomy. With regard to the proportions of school time to be devoted to the different subjects, Table 3 reduces somewhat the proportional time devoted to Latin, English, and mathematics, and increases the proportional time to be devoted to natural science. In a secondary school which teaches all the subjects recommended by the Conferences, and to the extent contemplated in Table 3, nearly one-fifth of the whole instruction given will be devoted to natural science.

The Committee regard Table 3 not, of course, as a feasible programme, but as the possible source of a great variety of good secondary school pro-

TABLE 3   Committee of 10 Modifications of the Total Amount of Instruction Recommended by Nine Conferences

		Total
1st Secondary School Year		
Latin		5.0 p.
English Literature	2.0 p.	4.0 p.
English Composition	2.0 p.	
German or French		5.0 p.
Algebra		4.0 p.
History of Italy, Spain, and France		3.0 p.
Applied Geography (European political—continental and oceanic flora and fauna)		4.0 p.
Total		25.0 p.
2nd Secondary School Year		
Latin		4.0 p.
Greek		5.0 p.
English Literature	2.0 p.	4.0 p.
English Composition	2.0 p.	
German, continued		4.0 p.
French, begun		5.0 p.
Algebra (or bookkeeping and commercial arithmetic)	2.0 p.	4.0 p.
Geometry	2.0 p.	
Botany or Zoology		4.0 p.
English History to 1688		3.0 p.
Total		33.0 p.
3rd Secondary School Year		
Latin		4.0 p.
Greek		4.0 p.
English Literature	2.0 p.	4.0 p.
English Composition	1.0 p.	
Rhetoric	1.0 p.	
German		4.0 p.
French		4.0 p.
Algebra (or bookkeeping and commercial arithmetic)	2.0 p.	4.0 p.
Geometry	2.0 p.	
Physics		4.0 p.
History, English and American		3.0 p.
Astronomy 1st ½ yr.	3.0 p.	4.0 p.
Meteorology 2nd ½ yr.	3.0 p.	
Total		33.0 p.

(continued)

TABLE 3 Committee of 10 Modifications of the Total Amount of Instruction Recommended by Nine Conferences (continued)

		Total
4th Secondary School Year		
Latin		4.0 p.
Greek		4.0 p.
English Literature	2.0 p.	4.0 p.
English Composition	1.0 p.	
English Grammar	1.0 p.	
German		4.0 p.
French		4.0 p.
Trigonometry		2.0 p.
Higher Algebra		
Chemistry		4.0 p.
History (intensive) and Civil Government		3.0 p.
Geol. or Physiography (½ yr.)	4.0 p.	4.0 p.
Anatomy, Physiology, Hygiene (½ yr.)	4.0 p.	
	Total	33.0 p.

grammes. It would be difficult to make a bad programme out of the materials contained in this table, unless indeed the fundamental principles advocated by the Conferences should be neglected. With some reference to Table 1, excellent six years' and five years' programmes for secondary schools can readily be constructed by spreading the subjects contained in Table 3 over six or five years instead of four,—of course with some changes in the time-allotment.

The details of the time-allotment for the several studies which enter into the secondary school programme may seem to some persons mechanical, or even trivial—a technical matter to be dealt with by each superintendent of schools, or by each principal of a secondary school, acting on his own individual experience and judgment; but such is not the opinion of the Committee of Ten. The Committee believe that to establish just proportions between the several subjects, or groups of allied subjects, on which the Conferences were held, it is essential that each principal subject shall be taught thoroughly and extensively, and therefore for an adequate number of periods a week on the school programme. If twice as much time is given in a school to Latin as given to mathematics, the attainments of the pupils in Latin ought to be twice as great as they are in mathematics, provided that equally good work is done in the two subjects; and Latin will have twice the educational value of mathematics. Again, if in a secondary school Latin is steadily pursued for four years with four or five hours a week devoted to it, that subject will be worth more to the pupil than the sum of half a dozen other subjects, each of which has one sixth of the time allotted to Latin. The good effects of continuous study in one subject will be won for the pupil through the Latin, and they will not be won through the six other subjects among which only so much time as is devoted to the single language has been divided. If every subject studied at all is to be studied thoroughly and consecutively, every subject must receive an adequate time-allotment. If every subject is to provide a substantial mental training, it must have a time-allotment sufficient to produce that fruit. Finally, since selection must be exercised by or on behalf of the individual pupil, all the subjects between which choice is allowed should be approximately equivalent to each other in seriousness, dignity, and efficacy. Therefore they should have approximately equal time-allotments. The Conferences have abundantly shown how every subject which they recommend can be made a serious subject of instruction, well fitted to train the pupil's powers of observation, expression, and reasoning. It remains for makers of school programmes to give every subject the chance of developing a good training capacity by giving it an adequate time-allotment.

The schedule of studies contained in Table 3 permits flexibility and variety in three respects. First, it is not necessary that any school should teach all the subjects which it contains, or any particular set of subjects. Secondly, it is not necessary that the individual pupil should everywhere and always have the same number of periods of instruction per week. In one school the pupils might have but sixteen periods a week, in another twenty; or in some years of the course the pupils might have more periods a week than in other years. Within the schedule many particular arrangements for the convenience of a school, or for the welfare of an individual pupil would be possible. Thirdly, it is not necessary that every secondary school should begin its work at the level which is assumed as the starting point of secondary instruction in Tables 1, 2, and 3. If in any community the high school has no such grammar school foundation beneath it as is imagined in Table 1 it will simply have to begin its work lower down in the table. The sequence of studies recommended by the Conferences would still serve as a guide; but the demarcation between the elementary schools and the high school would occur in that community at a lower point. From this point of view, Tables 1, 2, and 3 may be considered to set a standard towards which secondary schools should tend; and not a standard to which they can at once conform.

The adoption of a programme based on Table 3 would not necessarily change at all the relation of a school to the colleges or universities to which it habitually sends pupils. Any such programme would lend itself either to the examination method of admission to college, or to the certificate method; and it could be slightly modified in such a way as to meet the present admission requirements of any college in the country. Future changes in admission requirements might fairly be made with a view to the capabilities of programmes based on Table 3.

As samples of school programmes constructed within the schedules of Table 3, the Committee present the following working programmes, which they recommend for trial wherever the secondary school period is limited to four years. All four combined might, of course, be tabulated as one programme with options by subject.

These four programmes taken together use all the subjects mentioned in Table 3, and usually, but not always, to about the amounts there indicated. History and English suffer serious contraction in the Classical programme. All four programmes conform to the general recommendations of the Conferences, that is,—they treat each subject in the same way for all pupils with trifling exceptions; they give time enough to each subject to win from it the kind of mental training it is fitted to supply; they put the different principal subjects on an approximate equality so far as time-allotment is concerned; they omit all short information courses; and they make sufficiently continuous the instruction in each of the main lines, namely, language, science, history and mathematics. With slight modifications, they would prepare the pupils for admission to appropriate courses in any American college or university on the existing requirements; and they would also meet the new college requirements which are suggested below.

In preparing these programmes, the Committee were perfectly aware that it is impossible to make a satisfactory secondary school programme, limited to a period of four years, and founded on the present elementary school subjects and methods. In the opinion of the Committee, several subjects now reserved for high schools,—such as algebra, geometry, natural science, and foreign languages,—should be begun earlier than now, and therefore within the schools classified as elementary; or, as an alternative, the secondary school period should be made to begin two years earlier than at present, leaving six years instead of eight for the elementary school period. Under the present organization, elementary subjects and elementary methods are, in the judgment of the Committee, kept in use too long.

The most striking differences in the four programmes will be found, as is intimated in the headings, in the relative amounts of time given to foreign languages. In the Classical programme the foreign languages get a large share of time; in the English programme a small share. In compensation, English and history are more developed in the English programme than in the Classical.

Many teachers will say, at first sight, that physics comes too early in these programmes and Greek too late. One member of the Committee is firmly of the opinion that Greek comes too late. The explanation of the positions assigned to these subjects is that the Committee of Ten attached great importance to two general principles in programme making:—In the first place they endeavored to postpone till the third year the grave choice between the Classical course and the Latin-Scientific. They believed that this bifurcation should occur as late as possible, since the choice between these two roads often determines for life the youth's career. Moreover, they believed that it is possible to make this important decision for a boy on good grounds, only when he has had opportunity to exhibit his quality and discover his tastes by making excursions into all the principal fields of knowledge. The youth who has never studied any but his native language cannot know his own capacity for linguistic acquisition; and the youth who has never made a chemical or physical experiment cannot know whether or not he has a taste for exact science. The wisest teacher, or the most observant parent, can hardly predict with confidence a boy's gift for a subject which he has never touched. In these considerations the Committee found strong reasons for postponing bifurcation, and making the subjects of the first two years as truly representative as possible. Secondly, inasmuch as many boys and girls who begin the secondary school course do not stay in school more than two years, the Committee thought it important to select the studies of the first two years in such a way that linguistic, historical, mathematical, and scientific subjects should all be properly represented. Natural history being represented by physical geography, the Committee wished physics to represent the inorganic sciences of precision. The first two years of any one of the four programmes presented above will, in the judgment of the Committee, be highly profitable by themselves to children who can go no farther.

Although the Committee thought it expedient to include among the four programmes, one which included neither Latin nor Greek, and one which included only one foreign language (which might be either ancient or modern), they desired to affirm explicitly their unanimous opinion that, under existing conditions in the United States as to the training of teachers and the provision of necessary means of instruction, the two programmes called respectively Modern Languages and English must in practice be distinctly inferior to the other two.

TABLE 4   Four Working Programmes for Secondary Schools

Year	Classical Three foreign languages (one modern)	Latin-Scientific Two foreign languages (one modern)	Modern Languages Two foreign languages (both modern)	English One foreign language (ancient or modern)
I.	Latin — 5 p.	Latin — 5 p.	French [or German] begun — 5 p.	Latin, or German, or French begun — 5 p.
	English — 4 p.	English — 4 p.	English — 4 p.	English — 4 p.
	Algebra — 4 p.	Algebra — 4 p.	Algebra — 4 p.	Algebra — 4 p.
	History — 4 p.	History — 4 p.	History — 4 p.	History — 4 p.
	Physical Geography — 3 p.	Physical Geography — 3 p.	Physical Geography — 3 p.	Physical Geography — 3 p.
	20 p.	20 p.	20 p.	20 p.
II.	Latin — 5 p.	Latin — 5 p.	French [or German] — 5 p.	Latin, or German, or French — 5 or 4 p.
	English — 2 p.	English — 2 p.	English — 2 p.	English — 3 or 4 p.
	German [or French] begun[a] — 4 p.	German [or French] begun — 4 p.	German [or French] begun — 4 p.	Geometry — 3 p.
	Geometry — 3 p.	Geometry — 3 p.	Geometry — 3 p.	Physics — 3 p.
	Physics — 3 p.	Physics — 3 p.	Physics — 3 p.	History — 3 p.
	History — 3 p.	Botany or Zoology — 3 p.	Botany or Zoology — 3 p.	Botany or Zoology — 3 p.
	20 p.	20 p.	20 p.	20 p.

III.

Programme 1:

Subject	Periods
Latin	4 p.
Greek	5 p.
English	3 p.
German [or French]	4 p.
Mathematics — Algebra (2 p.), Geometry (2 p.)	4 p.
Astronomy (½ yr), Meteorology (½ yr)	3 p.
History	
	20 p.

Programme 2:

Subject	Periods
Latin	4 p.
Greek	5 p.
English	2 p.
German [or French]	4 p.
Mathematics — Algebra (2 p.), Geometry (2 p.)	4 p.
Astronomy (½ yr) & Meteorology (½ yr)	3 p.
History	2 p.
	20 p.

Programme 3:

Subject	Periods
French [or German]	4 p.
English	3 p.
German [or French]	4 p.
Mathematics — Algebra (2 p.), Geometry (2 p.)	4 p.
Astronomy (½ yr) & Meteorology (½ yr)	3 p.
History	2 p.
	20 p.

Programme 4:

Subject	Periods
Latin, or German, or French	4 p.
English — As in others (3 p.), Additional (2 p.)	5 p.
Mathematics — Algebra (2 p.), Geometry (2 p.)	4 p.
Astronomy (½ yr) & Meteorology (½ yr)	3 p.
History — As in Latin-Scientific (2 p.), Additional (2 p.)	4 p.
	20 p.

IV.

Programme 1:

Subject	Periods
Latin	4 p.
Greek	5 p.
English	2 p.
German [or French]	3 p.
Chemistry	3 p.
Trigonometry & Higher Algebra *or* History	3 p.
	20 p.

Programme 2:

Subject	Periods
Latin	4 p.
Greek	4 p.
English	
German [or French]	3 p.
Chemistry	3 p.
Trigonometry & Higher Algebra *or* History	3 p.
Geology or Physiography (½ yr) & Anatomy, Physiology, & Hygiene (½ yr)	3 p.
	20 p.

Programme 3:

Subject	Periods
Latin	4 p.
Greek	4 p.
English	
German [or French]	3 p.
Chemistry	3 p.
Trigonometry & Higher Algebra *or* History	3 p.
Geology or Physiography (½ yr) & Anatomy, Physiology, & Hygiene (½ yr)	3 p.
	20 p.

Programme 4:

Subject	Periods
Latin	4 p.
English — As in Classical (2 p.), Additional (2 p.)	5 p.
German [or French]	3 p.
Chemistry	3 p.
Trigonometry & Higher Algebra *or* History	3 p.
Geology or Physiography (½ yr) & Anatomy, Physiology, & Hygiene (½ yr)	3 p.
	20 p.

---

a In any school in which Greek can be better taught than a modern language, or in which local public opinion or the history of the school makes it desirable to teach Greek in an ample way, Greek may be substituted for German or French in the second year of the Classical programme.

In the construction of the sample programmes the Committee adopted twenty as the maximum number of weekly periods, but with two qualifications, namely, that at least five of the twenty periods should be given to unprepared work, and that laboratory subjects should have double periods whenever that prolongation should be possible.

The omission of music, drawing, and elocution from the programmes offered by the Committee was not intended to imply that these subjects ought to receive no systematic attention. It was merely thought best to leave it to local school authorities to determine, without suggestions from the Committee, how these subjects should be introduced into the programmes in addition to the subjects reported on by the Conferences.

The Committee were governed in the construction of the first three programmes by the rule laid down by the language Conferences, namely, that two foreign languages should not be begun at the same time. To obey this rule is to accept strict limitations in the construction of a four years' Classical programme. A five years' or six years' programme can be made much more easily under this restriction. The Committee were anxious to give five weekly periods to every foreign language in the year when it was first attacked; but did not find it possible to do so in every case.

The four programmes can be carried out economically in a single school; because, with a few inevitable exceptions, the several subjects occur simultaneously in at least three programmes and with the same number of weekly periods.

Numerous possible transpositions of subjects will occur to every experienced teacher who examines these specimen programmes. Thus, in some localities it would be better to transpose French and German; the selection and order of science subjects might be varied considerably to suit the needs or circumstances of different schools; and the selection and order of historical subjects admit of large variety.

Many subjects now familiar in secondary school courses of study do not appear in Table 3 or in the specimen programmes given above; but it must not be supposed that the omitted subjects are necessarily to be neglected. If the recommendations of the Conference were carried out, some of the omitted subjects would be better dealt with under any one of the above programmes than they are now under familiar high school and academy programmes in which they figure as separate subjects. Thus, drawing does not appear as a separate subject in the specimen programmes; but the careful reader of the Conference reports will notice that drawing, both mechanical and free-hand, is to be used in the study of history, botany, zoölogy, astronomy, meteorology, physics, geography, and physiography, and that the kind of drawing recommended by the Conferences is the most useful kind,—namely, that which is applied to recording, describing, and discussing observations. This abundant use of drawing might not prevent the need of some special instruction in drawing, but it ought to diminish the number of periods devoted exclusively to drawing. Again, neither ethics nor economics, neither metaphysics nor aesthetics appear in the programmes; but in the large number of periods devoted to English and history there would be some time for incidental instruction in the elements of these subjects. It is through the reading and writing required of pupils, or recommended to them, that the fundamental ideas on these important topics are to be inculcated. Again, the industrial and commercial subjects do not appear in these programmes; but book-keeping and commercial arithmetic are provided for by the option for algebra designated in Table 3; and if it were desired to provide more amply for subjects thought to have practical importance in trade or the useful arts, it would be easy to provide options in such subjects for some of the science contained in the third and fourth years of the "English" programme.

The Committee of Ten think much would be gained if, in addition to the usual programme hours, a portion of Saturday morning should be regularly used for laboratory work in the scientific subjects. Laboratory work requires more consecutive time than the ordinary period of recitation affords; so that an hour and a half is about the shortest advantageous period for a laboratory exercise. The Committee venture to suggest further that, in addition to the regular school sessions in the morning, one afternoon in every week should be used for out-of-door instruction in geography, botany, zoölogy, and geology, these afternoon and Saturday morning exercises being counted as regular work for the teachers who conduct them. In all laboratory and field work, the Committee believe that it will be found profitable to employ as assistants to the regular teachers,—particularly at the beginning of laboratory and field work in each subject,—recent graduates of the secondary schools who have themselves followed the laboratory and field courses; for at the beginning the pupil will need a large amount of individual instruction in the manipulation of specimens, the use of instruments, and the prompt recording of observations. One teacher without assistants cannot supervise effectively the work of thirty or forty pupils, either in the laboratory or in the field. The laboratory work on Saturday mornings could be maintained throughout the school year; the afternoon excursions would of course be difficult, or impossible, for perhaps a third of the school year.

In general, the Committee of Ten have endeavored to emphasize the principles which should govern all secondary school programmes, and to show how the main recommendations of the several Conferences may be carried out in a variety of feasible programmes.

College Admissions

One of the subjects which the Committee of Ten were directed to consider was requirements for admission to college; and particularly they were expected to report on uniform requirements for admission to colleges, as well as on a uniform secondary school programme. Almost all the Conferences have something to say about the best mode of testing the attainments of candidates at college admission examinations; and some of them, notably the Conferences on History and Geography, make very explicit declarations concerning the nature of college examinations. The improvements desired in the mode of testing the attainments of pupils who have pursued in the secondary schools the various subjects which enter into the course will be found clearly described under each subject in the several Conference reports; but there is a general principle concerning the relation of the secondary schools to colleges which the Committee of Ten, inspired and guided by the Conferences, feel it their duty to set forth with all possible distinctness.

The secondary schools of the United States, taken as a whole, do not exist for the purpose of preparing boys and girls for colleges. Only an insignificant percentage of the graduates of these schools go to colleges or scientific schools. Their main function is to prepare for the duties of life that small proportion of all the children in the country—a proportion small in number, but very important to the welfare of the nation—who show themselves able to profit by an education prolonged to the eighteenth year, and whose parents are able to support them while they remain so long at school. There are, to be sure, a few private or endowed secondary schools in the country, which make it their principal object to prepare students for the colleges and universities; but the number of these schools is relatively small. A secondary school programme intended for national use must therefore be made for those children whose education is not to be pursued beyond the secondary school. The preparation of a few pupils for college or scientific school should in the ordinary secondary school be the incidental, and not the principal object. At the same time, it is obviously desirable that the colleges and scientific schools should be accessible to all boys or girls who have completed creditably the secondary school course. Their parents often do not decide for them, four years before the college age, that they shall go to college, and they themselves may not, perhaps, feel the desire to continue their education until near the end of their school course. In order that any successful graduate of a good secondary school should be free to present himself at the gates of the college or scientific school of his choice, it is necessary that the colleges and scientific schools of the country should accept for admission to appropriate courses of their instruction the attainments of any youth who has passed creditably through a good secondary school course, no matter to what group of subjects he may have mainly devoted himself in the secondary school. As secondary school courses are now too often arranged, this is not a reasonable request to prefer to the colleges and scientific schools; because the pupil may now go through a secondary school course of a very feeble and scrappy nature—studying a little of many subjects and not much of any one, getting, perhaps, a little information in a variety of fields, but nothing which can be called a thorough training. Now the recommendations of the nine Conferences, if well carried out, might fairly be held to make all the main subjects taught in the secondary schools of equal rank for the purposes of admission to college or scientific school. They would all be taught consecutively and thoroughly, and would all be carried on in the same spirit; they would all be used for training the powers of observation, memory, expression, and reasoning; and they would all be good to that end, although differing among themselves in quality and substance. In preparing the programmes of Table 4, the Committee had in mind that the requirements for admission to colleges might, for schools which adopted a programme derived from that table, be simplified to a considerable extent, though not reduced. A college might say,—We will accept for admission any groups of studies taken from the secondary school programme, provided that the sum of the studies in each of the four years amounts to sixteen, or eighteen, or twenty periods a week,—as may be thought best,—and provided, further, that in each year at least four of the subjects presented shall have been pursued at least three periods a week, and that at least three of the subjects shall have been pursued three years or more. For the purposes of this reckoning, natural history, geography, meteorology, and astronomy might be grouped together as one subject. Every youth who entered college would have spent four years in studying a few subjects thoroughly; and, on the theory that all the subjects are to be considered equivalent in educational rank for the purposes of admission to college, it would make no difference which subjects he had chosen from the programme—he would have had four years of strong and effective mental training. The Conferences on Geography and Modern Languages make the most explicit statement to the effect that college requirements for admission should coincide with high-school requirements for graduation. The Conference on English is of opinion "that no student should be admitted to college who shows in his English examination and his other examinations that he is very deficient in ability to write good English." This recommendation suggests that an ample English course in the secondary school should be required of all persons who intend to enter college. It would of course be possible for any college to require for admission any one subject, or any group of subjects, in the table, and the requirements of different colleges, while all kept within the table, might differ in many respects; but the Committee are of opinion that the satisfactory completion of any one of the four years' courses of study embodied in the foregoing programmes should admit to corresponding courses in colleges and scientific schools. They believe that this close articulation between the secondary schools and the higher institutions would be advantageous alike for the schools, the colleges, and the country.

Training of Teachers

Every reader of this report and of the reports of the nine Conferences will be satisfied that to carry out the improvements proposed more highly trained teachers will be needed than are now ordinarily to be found for the service of the elementary and secondary schools. The Committee of Ten desire to point out some of the means of procuring these better trained teachers. For the further instruction of teachers in actual service, three agencies already in existence may be much better utilized than they now are. The Summer Schools which many universities now maintain might be resorted to by much larger numbers of teachers, particularly if some aid, such as the payment of tuition fees and travelling expenses, should be given to teachers who are willing to devote half of their vacations to study, by the cities and towns which these teachers serve. Secondly, in all the towns and cities in which colleges and universities are planted, these colleges or universities may usefully give stated courses of instruction in the main subjects used in the elementary and secondary schools to teachers employed in those towns and cities. This is a reasonable service which the colleges and universities may render to their own communities. Thirdly, a superintendent who has himself become familiar with the best mode of teaching any one of the subjects which enter into the school course can always be a very useful instructor for the whole body of teachers under his charge. A real master of any one subject will always have many suggestions to make to teachers of other subjects. The same is true of the principal of a high school, or other leading teacher in a town or city. In every considerable city school system the best teacher in each department of instruction should be enabled to give part of his time to helping the other teachers by inspecting and criticising their work, and showing them, both by precept and example, how to do it better.

In regard to preparing young men and women for the business of teaching, the country has a right to expect much more than it has yet obtained from the colleges and normal schools. The common expectation of attainment for pupils of the normal schools has been altogether too low the country over. The normal schools, as a class, themselves need better apparatus, libraries, programmes, and teachers. As to the colleges, it is quite as much an enlargement of sympathies as an improvement of apparatus or of teaching that they need. They ought to take more interest than they have heretofore done, not only in the secondary, but in the elementary schools; and they ought to take pains to fit men well for the duties of a school superintendent. They already train a considerable number of the best principals of high schools and academies; but this is not sufficient. They should take an active interest, through their presidents, professors, and other teachers, in improving the schools in their respective localities, and in contributing to the thorough discussion of all questions affecting the welfare of both the elementary and the secondary schools.

Finally, the Committee venture to suggest, in the interest of secondary schools, that uniform dates—such as the last Thursday, Friday, and Saturday, or the third Monday, Tuesday, and Wednesday of June and September—be established for the admission examinations of colleges and scientific schools throughout the United States. It is a serious inconvenience for secondary schools which habitually prepare candidates for several different colleges or scientific schools that the admission examinations of different institutions are apt to occur on different dates, sometimes rather widely separated.

The Committee also wish to call attention to the service which Schools of Law, Medicine, Engineering, and Technology, whether connected with universities or not, can render to secondary education by arranging their requirements for admission, as regards selection and range of subjects, in conformity with the courses of study recommended by the Committee. By bringing their entrance requirements into close relation with any or all of the programmes recommended for secondary schools, these professional schools can give valuable support to high schools, academies, and preparatory schools.

CHARLES W. ELIOT
WILLIAM T. HARRIS
JAMES B. ANGELL
JOHN TETLOW
JAMES M. TAYLOR,
OSCAR D. ROBINSON
JAMES H. BAKER
RICHARD H. JESSE
JAMES C. MACKENZIE
HENRY C. KING
4 December, 1893.

Minority Report

President Baker signs the above report, but adds the following statement:—

TO THE NATIONAL COUNCIL OF EDUCATION: I beg leave to note some exceptions taken to parts of the report of the Committee of Ten. Had the Committee not been limited in time, doubtless fuller discussion would have resulted in modifying some statements embodied in the report. The great value of the reports of the Conferences upon the subjects referred to them, as to matter, place, time, methods, adequate and continuous work for each subject, and identity of work in different courses, and the masterly summary and tabulation of their recommendations, made by the Chairman of the Committee of Ten, can but invite cordial commendation. Objections are raised to parts of the special work of the Committee.

1. I cannot endorse expressions that appear to sanction the idea that the choice of subjects in secondary schools may be a matter of comparative indifference. I note especially the following sentences, referring the reader to their context for accurate interpretation.

> "Any school principal may say:—'With the staff at my command I can teach only five subjects out of those proposed by the Conferences in the manner proposed. My school shall, therefore, be limited to these five.' Another school may be able to teach in the thorough manner proposed five subjects, but some or all of these five may be different from those selected by the first school."

> "If twice as much time is given in a school to Latin as is given to mathematics, the attainments of the pupils in Latin ought to be twice as great as they are in mathematics, provided that equally good work is done in the two subjects; and Latin will have twice the educational value of mathematics."

> "The schedule of studies contained in Table 3 permits flexibility and variety in three respects. First, it is not necessary that any school should teach all the subjects which it contains, or any particular set of subjects."

> "Every youth who entered college would have spent four years in studying a few subjects thoroughly; and on the theory that all the subjects are to be considered equivalent in educational rank for the purpose of admission to college, it would make no difference which subjects he had chosen from the programme—he would have had four years of strong and effective mental training."

All such statements are based upon the theory that, for the purposes of general education, one study is as good as another,—a theory which appears to me to ignore Philosophy, Psychology and Science of Education. It is a theory which makes education formal and does not consider the nature and value of the content. Power comes through knowledge; we can not conceive of observation and memory in the abstract. The world which offers to the human mind several distinct views is the world in which our power that comes through knowledge is to be used, the world which we are to understand and enjoy. The relation between the subjective power and the objective—or subjective—knowledge is inseparable and vital. On any other theory, for general education, we might well consider the study of Egyptian hieroglyphics as valuable as that of physics, and Choctaw as important as Latin. Secondary school programmes can not well omit mathematics, or science, or history, or literature, or the culture of the ancient classics. An education which gives a view in all directions is the work of elementary and secondary schools. Such an education is the necessary preparation for the special work of the university student. If I rightly understood, the majority of the Committee rejected the theory of equivalence of studies for general education. Studies vary in value for the training of the different powers, and for this additional reason the choice can not be regarded as a matter of indifference.

The training of "observation, memory, expression and reasoning" (inductive) is a very important part of education, but is not all of education. The imagination, deductive reasoning, the rich possibilities of emotional life, the education of the will through ethical ideas and correct habit, all are to be considered in a scheme of learning. Ideals are to be added to the scientific method.

The dilemma which appears on an examination of the time demands of the various conferences offers to the programme maker the alternatives of omitting essential subjects and of a rational adjustment of the time element, while retaining all essential subjects. Reason and experience point toward the latter alternative. By wise selection of matter within the lines of study adequate and consecutive time can be given to each.

2. The language of the second paragraph following Table 2 might be misconstrued to mean that the Committee favor the multiplication of courses with a loss of the thoroughness attainable when the teaching force is devoted to one or two courses. Intension rather than extension of effort, both in respect to the number of courses and in respect to the number of studies or topics under each principal subject, is to be strongly recommended.

3. It may seem trivial to offer criticism of the specimen programmes made by the Committee, and yet I believe that each member felt that with ample deliberation results somewhat different would have been reached. Note for instance that in some of the programmes history is entirely omit-

ted in the second year, and physics is given only three hours per week, —no more time than is allowed for botany or zoölogy. There are many symmetrical secondary school programmes in actual operation today which furnish continuous instruction in all important subjects throughout the four years, allowing to each an amount of time adequate to good results. For most high schools the first, the Classical programme, and the last programme, the one offering one foreign language, will commend themselves because they are economical, and they combine a good finishing course with adequate college preparation.

4. On the basis of the tabulated results of the Conferences I believe that by earnest scientific examination a scheme of work can be formulated that will meet the views of the members of the Committee and of most educators. As an afterthought it may be an occasion for regret that the strength of the discussion was not devoted to Table 3. Instead of considering the work of the Committee as ended, I would recommend that the National Council hold itself responsible for further examination of the data furnished by the Conferences. I have not presumed to offer a substitute report, because I believe that the importance of the work demands further effort of an entire Committee.

Respectfully submitted,

JAMES H. BAKER.

20

The Child (From Talks on Pedagogics*)*

Francis W. Parker, 1894

Francis W. Parker (1837–1902) was one of the pioneers of the Progressive education movement in the United States. Parker began his teaching career at the age of 16. After serving in the Union Army during the Civil War, Parker resumed his teaching career and studied the ideas of European thinkers such as Rousseau, Froebel, Herbart, and Pestalozzi, as well as Americans such as Horace Mann. In 1875, Parker became a superintendent in Quincy, Massachusetts and launched an experimental program that emphasized the progressive concepts of a child-centered curriculum, the school as a community of learners, and the development of the whole child in preparation for democratic citizenship. The success of the Quincy Plan drew international attention to Parker and his progressive ideas. The following is a chapter from Parker's 1894 book Talks on Pedagogics. In this chapter, Parker asks us to consider what we as teachers can learn from the "spontaneous activities" of children. Parker asks us to look to the nature of the child as we form our educational goals. —AJM

I propose in this and the following talks to present a general exposition of the theory of *concentration.* The least that can be said for this theory is that

American Educational Thought: Essays from 1640–1940, pages 321–334

it presents to some extent an outline of a rounded educational doctrine for the study and criticism of teachers. In the beginning of these discussions, the question of all questions, and indeed the everlasting question, is: What is the being to be educated? What is the child? What is this little lump of flesh, breathing life and singing the song of immorality? The wisdom and philosophy of ages upon ages have asked this question, and still it remains unanswered. It is the central problem of the universe. The child is the climax and culmination of all God's creations, and to answer the question, "What is the child?" is to approach nearer the still greater question: What is the Creator and Giver of Life?

I can answer the question tentatively. It is a question for you and for me, and for the teachers of the present and the future, to answer; and still it will ever remain the unanswered question. We should study the child, as we study all phenomena, by its actions, and by its tendencies to act. The child is born, we are told by scientists, deaf, dumb, and blind, yet, in design, possessing marvelous possibilities for development. It is well for us to stand by the cradle of a little child who has drawn his first breath, and is ready to be acted upon by the external energies which surround him.

One hypothesis we can accept as true: the inherited organism of bone, muscle and brain determines exactly the limits or boundaries of the baby's development. Each nerve-fiber or convolution of the brain says: "Thus far shall thou go and no farther;" and it is well to say in the same breath that no human being ever had the external conditions for growth by which the full possibilities, predetermined and fixed by the organism, have been realized. The organism itself determines the external conditions for development. Every muscle, every nerve, every fiber, every convolution of the brain, their nature and power, are in themselves possibilities for the reception of those external energies which act upon the body of the child, and make their way to the brain through the sensorium. The child itself is a central energy, or complex of energies, upon which and through which certain external energies act. No simple energy can enter a child's brain except by first touching the child's body (the end-organs), and countless energies touch the child's body which do not enter the brain at all; others enter, but lie below the plane of consciousness.

Forms or waves of light touch the eye and create elementary ideas of color in the brain, but just what colors there shall be in the brain is determined by the passive power and delicacy of the organism itself. Vibrations of air touch and enter the brain through the ear. Strongest and most effective of all is the contact and resistance of the body to objects more dense than waves of air or waves of ether. The great giant sense of touch begins its creative power in the brain at the birth of the child, and even before birth. It is well for us to understand thoroughly that the child, an organic complex of energies, is acted upon and through by external energies, and, whatever matter may be in itself, the mind is conscious of nothing but pure energy, and is primarily developed by external energies which, we infer, act through forms and qualities of matter. Stimuli come from all the surroundings of the child. The products of the stimuli create in the child's mind concepts corresponding to external objects. These concepts are activities in themselves, or phases of differentiated energy. Units of elementary ideas, individual concepts, enable the mind to react upon externality. The child begins to move under the stimulus created by external activities, to smile, to laugh, to stretch out its hands, to see, to hear, to touch, to taste, and to smell.

It is not possible for me to state the exact order of the succession of the arousing to action of the different senses. Our questions here are: What are the spontaneous activities of the child? In other words, what must the child do from the nature of its being, the nature of the stimulus acting through its body and in its mind, and the potentialities of the ego? What are the tendencies of these spontaneous activities? The child's consciousness begins in obscurity, weakness, and vagueness, and still in this very obscurity and vagueness there is great activity. The very few weak and obscure ideas of color and sound and form set the whole being into motion. Before there is any consciousness, before the child has the most obscure feeling of itself, music affects it in a wonderful way. Lullaby songs will soothe it to sleep, changing vague pain into vague pleasure. The whole being is sensitive to the rhythm of music. Not only can it be soothed and lulled to sleep with music, but its first dawning consciousness of life is marked by a smile aroused by a song. The first spiritual breath of external life comes with musical cadences. One the first sounds that it makes is an imitation of rhythm. What is this marvelous gift that makes the child so sensitive to musical cadence? The whole universe moves in rhythm: the avalanche thunders from the mountainside in, deep cadences; the ocean surf roars in musical cadence. The rippling of the brook and the soughing of the breeze in the foliage are the simple music of nature. The little child is the centre of all this rhythm, and the feeling of this rhythm is the truth of the universe whispering its sweet songs to the child's soul.

Perhaps the most marked mental action of the little child is the fanciful creation of new ideas and images. A little vague color and sound, and a few percepts of touch, are sufficient to set the little being into most vigorous action. External objects act upon the child and produce their correspondences, individual concepts, in its mind. As I have already said, these concepts are very vague, obscure, and indistinct.

Notwithstanding all this, creation is the moving, central power and delight of the child. The baby creates out of its meager store of ideas a new world, its own world, in which it lives and moves and has its being. Let us pause a moment, and look at the marvelous meaning of this wonderful power of the child in the creations of fancy. If the little human being were limited to actuality, that is, to the vague reflex of external objects, if it were bound by its own meager store of so-called facts, it would indeed live in a dark and dismal prison; but it bursts the bands of reality and goes out into a higher world to the invisible life. It lives over again the childhood of the race in the myth. It revels in fanciful forms of its own weak but vivid creations; it spontaneously seeks the invisible.

Next to the cradle song is the cradle story. You know very well how eager a child is for stories that arouse its love for rhythm and excite its fancy. The child most delights in fairy tales, the mythical treasures of the ages. The cruel bonds of stern reality are broken; and it enters a beautiful and invisible world, peopled by creations of its own fancy. If a child were limited in its early stages to the world of reality, if it could not go out into the unknown world, the invisible world, it would lead the life of a brute. The human animal differs from the brute in its faith in an invisible world. The self-created, invisible world, to the child, is the fire-mist heaven; it is the chaos that precedes the spiritual life. Banish myth from the child, and you take away that beauty which is the essence of truth. Parents who forbid the myth because they conceive, forsooth, it is not the truth, limit the child to the baldest materialism, or prepare the way for fancy to run riot to ruin.

What is the myth? The record of the human race is full of myths. Myth comes from the imperfect answer which nature gives to the childish soul of man. The answers are not false, but they are imperfect and partial, and are, to childish souls, the solution of their great problems. Every answer given to a spontaneous and innocent question contains a golden kernel of intrinsic truth. It is that truth which a child can bear in its early years. It cannot grasp precepts and logic, but it can understand the truth, like those who crowded around the Saviour,— in parables. The myth is common to all tribes and nations on the face of the earth. All myths have a wonderful similarity, proving that the human spirit in every stage of growth, and in every clime, and under all environments, has the same strong everlasting tendency upward. Every myth contains a lesson to man. Out of the ignorance of the nature of the child, and from the spirit of dogmatism and bigotry, there has come the falsehood that says the myth does not contain the whole truth, and therefore must be rejected. Who knows the whole truth? Shall the child be robbed of that which delights its soul and lays the foundation of true religious life? No greater mistake can be made in regard to the spontaneous activities of the child, for the myth is the true fire-mist of character, it contains golden symbols that point upward to God and to heaven. The myth is the foundation of faith in the future life, the foundation of all spiritual growth. The fairies and trolls change, as the soul changes, to real folks and real life.

The myth is the beginning of history. The creatures of fancy foreshadow the real people with whom the child must live. It is, indeed, the child seeing through a glass darkly, but that obscurity of truth and tendency towards it are absolutely essential to its growth. Myth, I say, is the beginning of history. The myths presented to the child should contain in themselves the guiding stare of life and immortality.

The myth is the beginning of science. The human race began, we are told, with a firm belief that every object in the universe was animated, life-like, human-like. This was the childish study of science, but it sustained a great truth. The stone and the mountain are not organisms for life, it is true, but there breathes through them an irresistible energy, which comes from the Giver of all Life. The myth of the early ages points towards the marvelous revelations of the scientific truth of the present. The myth is an imperfect and partial apprehension of truth. The myth clears away under the steady light of the ever-moving mind; it is essential to the weak state of the child. "The night veileth the morning."

Just as the human race arose in its development from the myths of antiquity, so the child must rise from the myths of childhood. The lack of ideality, the failure in spiritual growth, in true religious life, are caused more by the failure of the parents to recognize the true nature of the child and his inborn love for myth than any other cause whatever. The rankest materialism in its worst form has never struck harder blows at true spiritual life than the ignorance of misguided parents, who keep their child from fairy life and fairy land. Fairy land is over the border of the present, into the future, and the truest tendency of the human life is to live in the ideal of the future, to reach forward towards the invisible and the unknown. Slowly the human beings have arisen—guided by a glimmering light—and have climbed spiritually from the earth and the clod, from the shrub and tree up the broad walls of the arched sky, to stars, and moon, and sun, and then beyond the sun, for the divinity seeking and striving imagination stretches away to the invisible, all powerful, all-controlling, all-loving, One who permeates the universe, lives in it, and breathes His life through it, the eternal life to be taken into the human soul. The myth is the obscure image, in the child's soul, of God Himself. There are many parents who shudder at the myth of Santa Claus, an invisible being that brings the child gifts; but that invisible being, to the child's weak apprehension, is the foreshadowing of the All-Giver, the forerunner of the One who came to man on the blessed Christmas night. No rough voice and no ignorant soul should ever tell the little child that Santa Claus does not exist, for Santa Claus is the foreshadowing of the All-Giver, All-Lover, the One who gives because He loves.

It is impossible to take a child into history, science, ethics, and religion without the continued exercise of these spontaneous fanciful tendencies. You may reply that a child may live in myth and fancy all its life. I admit that this is possible. Many people do live in myth all their lives just because myth is not put into the crucible of highest reason; just because the conditions are not presented for myth to change to history, to science, to ethics, and to religion. This is no proof that the strongest spontaneous tendency of the child is wrong; it is only a proof of neglect to build upon it. I think we can take it for granted that, as God, the loving Creator of the child, made the child His highest creation, He put into that child Himself, His divinity, and that this divinity manifests itself in the seeking for truth through the visible and tangible.

The child is brought into direct contact with its mother, its father, and the whole family, and who will dare to say that the child is not, above all, a student of human nature? Who will say that its eyes, when they touch one's face, cannot read the soul better than older people? The child looks at you with the innocence and purity of childhood, and no hypocrisy, no dissimulation, though it may veil the truth from older eyes, can keep it from little ones. It studies the relation of being to being, father to mother, parents to children. It may be that I use too strong a word when I say it "studies", but still it is something very like study. The study of family life is the child's beginning of the study of anthropology and of history. The child is not only a student of individual life, but of community life, the life of the family, the life of neighbors, of the children he meets at play, in the house, in the yard, in the street; and the measure of the child's judgment of community life is the measure in its after study of history. It may study history in school or the university, but in all life the judgments formed at home, in the nursery, in the parlor, in the kitchen, in the street, are the strongest, ever-enduring measures in all his after-judgments of the record of the human life taught by experience and in history. Every human being with whom he comes in contact is a new study to him. The looks, the manners, the dress, the attitude, and the facial expression lead him to make his childish inferences. Then comes the kindergarten and the school, the first step in a broader community life than that which home furnishes. Here, the study, not only of history, but of civics, begins. The true foundation of civics is community life. The child's home measure of life, the government of his home, give him democratic, monarchical, or socialistic principles. Whatever the rule of the home or school may be, that rule is ever afterwards either loved or hated by the child. Thus the child spontaneously begins the study of anthropology, ethnology, and history, and in these studies he has a profound, abiding interest, in these studies he forms habits of judgment which to a great extent are fixed and permanent.

It needs no argument to prove that the child studies or, at least, is exceedingly interested in zoology. Few beings, except, perhaps, the father and mother, can interest a child more deeply than the brute life which surrounds him. The cat is "a thing of beauty and a joy forever"; the dog is its particular friend. It stretches out its little hands before it can speak, and its first utterances follow the attempts of its original ancestors in imitating the voice of the dog. The child delights in birds, butterflies, and bees. Place any moving, living thing before the child, and it moves towards it with an excited interest. It wants to touch it, to stroke it, to know more about it. Endowed with the original idea of animism, it no doubt believes every brute that it sees to have a mind like its own. It will imitate the dog, the cat, and the birds, and will talk to them as to its own companions. He studies zoology in that he becomes acquainted with the animals he meets: every insect, every animal, wild or tame, the grasshopper, the locust, bugs that scurry away when he lifts a stone, the fish-worms which he digs for bait, are objects of intense interest. He knows the difference between the white grub and the common earth-worm. The animals in the woods are his friends. The birds, their habits, their nests, their little ones, and their songs fill him with joy. He can take a lesson from the timid partridge, who is ever ready to give her life for her children. He knows the sly habit of the crows, studies the psychology of their reasoning. The horses, and oxen, and sheep are all his friends. What farm-boy has not cried over the loss of a favorite sheep, taken away by the cruel butcher?

The child has a great love for vegetable life. There never was a child that lived who did not worship flowers, reach out for them, desire to hold them in its hands, gaze at them, and smell them. Of course, the spontaneous activities of the child are governed to a great degree by its environment. Take a little boy with the environment of a farm—such an instance comes to me—a boy upon a rocky farm in New England. He studies spontaneously his entire environment. It is safe to say that he knows every plant upon the farm, every kind of grass, every weed. He comes in direct contact with worm-wood, sorrel, rag-weed. He can tell all the kinds of grass from the graceful silver grass to the stately timothy. He knows the mosses and lichens that cling to the rocks and carpet the marshy land. He knows the shrubs and bushes; the huckleberry-bush is his delight. The strawberry in the rich meadow he watches from blossom to fruit with a keen sense of the joy which is to follow. Every tree he knows—the magnificent pine, the stately maple, the spreading chestnut in the pasture. He can tell you the shape of the tree; its trunk, its foliage: its fruit he spontaneously classifies. Thus, every child is an earnest, indefatigable lover of botany. In his future life, the farm-boy carries his botany of the farm with him wherever he goes. He compares all other plants and classifies them according to the spontaneous classifications made on the farm. He says: "This was on the old farm; this was not." "This is something new." "This is like something I've seen before." "This bush is like the lilac; this rose is like the rose in the old garden."

Not only is the boy on the farm a student of life, but he extends his study to the forces of earth, and air, and water. The earth touches him, heaven bends down to him and asks him questions. The clouds he knows, from the rounded thunderhead to the mackerel sky. He knows also the winds; he can foretell the weather. He looks with intense joy to the next rainy day; that will bring him rest, or, something better, fishing. He watches the sun with a deep interest. It will be a very stupid boy who cannot tell exactly the noon hour by the sun, aided by that internal monitor, his stomach. Winds, clouds, air, and heat, everything that influences vegetation, come within the mental range of the farm-boy.

Mineralogy, especially upon a rocky farm, comes very close to the boy in clearing the ground, in picking stones, in building stone walls, in quarrying ledges. Watch a crowd of children upon the beach gathering pebbles and curious stones. They are interested in the color and form of the pebbles, and may be made exceedingly interested in the origin of the different forms, if some kind, observant friend is there to continue the questions which the stones themselves ask. Children naturally take to playing in the dirt as ducks to water. The different kinds of soils attract their attention—sand, gravel, and clay. They never tire of playing in the sand, or expressing crude fancies by modeling in the clay. The changes which natural forces bring about on the earth's surface are of deep interest to children, especially the changes brought about by running water, after a rain, or the wind swirling the sand into piles. They never tire of damming up a temporary stream or changing its current, and of watching its effects when it spreads out silt, or the guts it makes in the soft earth. The brooks and rivers are never-ceasing sources of delight to children; they watch them at flood-time, when the water spreads out over the meadows; they notice the caving in of banks, the carrying of earth by water and its deposition on the shelving shores.

Real geography, or the appearance of the earth's surface, is a subject of intense, though unconscious, interest on the part of the child. Let a boy hunt stray cows or sheep over a large farm; he soon learns to know every crook, every turn and corner in the whole farm, every hiding-place. He knows the hills, valleys, springs, and meadows. Of all the mental pictures that remain vivid through life and are recalled with ever-renewed pleasure, are the pictures of the country surrounding the birthplace, or the house in which we lived when children. The house itself, the fireplace, paper on the wall, furniture, everything is distinct in our minds when other pictures fade or are blurred by time. The country round about, every hillock, every depression, brook, and rivulet are never-fading in the brain.

To sum up, the subjects of the child's spontaneous study and persistent interest include all the central subjects of study—geography, geology, mineralogy, botany, zoology, anthropology, etc. In fact, the child begins every subject spontaneously and unconsciously. He must begin these subjects because he lives and because his environment acts upon him and educates him. Of course, the difference in environment makes a great difference in the child's mental action, the child's individual concepts; still, in all children there are the same spontaneous tendencies. The boy, for instance, on a farm may have a large range of vegetation to study, and the poor little child in the dark city may worship with his whole soul some potted plant and from it draw lessons of inspiration and love. The child studies the clouds, the sky, the stars, the earth, vegetation, animal life, history, every hour of the day. To be sure, he may have more interest in one subject than another, but to him all these subjects are related one to the other, as the cloud is related to rain, and the rain is related to vegetation and soil. It is the tendency of pedantry to search in the far distance for facts and mysteries, but the truth is that the marvelous is close to us, that miracles are of the most common occurrence.

I wish to call your attention to the wonderful powers acquired by the child in the first three years of its life, and the wonderful persistence there is in such acquirement. Take, for instance, the art of locomotion, the creeping and walking. Watch the face of the child standing for the first time upon its little legs, attracted by the outstretched arms of its mother, who stands across the room; look at the mingled courage and fear in the baby's face. He has a great ambition to move, as he has seen others move, upon his two feet. He stretches out his arms, he fears, he takes courage, he moves one foot and is successful, and then the other; he looks at his mother's encouraging smile, takes another step, and then another, until the great feat of walking across the room is accomplished. From the time he first stands upon his feet to the time he runs around with perfect unconsciousness of his power of movement, there takes place a succession of experiments, of trials, and of failures and successes, all guided and controlled by his desire to walk.

More wonderful than learning to walk is learning to hear language and to talk. In the beginning the child creates his own language of gesture by means of his own body. He hears language, words that are in themselves complex. Oral words act upon his consciousness and are associated by a fixed and everlasting law of the mind. Idioms are acquired by hearing and association, and with it all comes an intense desire to express thought. With his voice he creates at first his own language, which consists of crudely articulate sounds, and then follows the acquisition of the vernacular which he hears. It is well for us to consider carefully the processes of learning to talk. The child must learn to hear first; that is, the words must act upon consciousness and their correspondences must be associated with the appropriate activities in consciousness. The idioms must act in the same way and be associated with their appropriate activities or relations of ideas. Then follows the making of oral words. He learns enunciation, or the utterance of single sounds. He learns articulation, or the unity of sounds in words. He learns accent, pronunciation, and syntax, all by hearing language and under the one controlling motive of expressing his own thought. He begins, it is true, with crude utterances, but these utterances are to him the best possible expression of his thought. He learns any language and every language that he hears. If we could understand the psychological mechanical processes by which a child learns his own vernacular from the first step of hearing to the last step by which the sentence is in his power, we should understand the whole theory of learning any language. Those who have tried to speak a foreign language will readily understand something of the struggle the child goes through in order to master one single phonic element. You see that he does all this unconsciously, that all these efforts are natural and to a great degree automatic. He never for a moment thinks of a single sound by itself unless that sound is a whole word. He knows nothing at all of the complex elements of a language, nothing of slow pronunciation, nothing of syntax, still he masters the language by a natural process. This word natural is variously interpreted. It is exceedingly ambiguous, almost as ambiguous as the word "abstract." Still I believe that we can find a scientific definition of the word natural. If the word natural means anything, it means strict, conformity to God's laws. That is, a child learns every oral word by the same law under which every oral or written word in any and every language must be learned. The child does not know the law, but he obeys the law by instinct. If the child makes these marvelous acquisitions naturally, in conformity to law, why not have him continue that conformity to law in all his after-acquisitions?

Learning to write is far easier in itself, if we follow the law, than learning to hear language or learning to speak. The great lesson to teachers is, find the law, follow the law; give the child conditions in learning to write like those he has had in learning to speak. Indeed, the conditions can be made far better, for learning to speak is left very much to accident and to desultory instruction, while learning to write may be under the most careful guidance.

It goes without saying that the child is a student of form and color. Everything that enters his brain, as I have already said, must touch the end-organs, and these attributes or objects which touch the end-organs are forms of matter. Froebel, who had such divine insight, understood the great value of the tactual sense. Color is representative in its power. It brings into consciousness the correspondences to forms of external objects.

Not only does the child study form, but he makes intuitively a systematic preparation for the study of number. The child begins with no idea of distance. He grasps for the moon with the same confidence as he does for an object near at hand. The ideas of distance, size, weight, are preparations for number. The child first learns to measure by constantly reaching out its hands, creeping and walking, and after that it measures distance by sight. Not only does it begin to measure and estimate distances, but it judges area and bulk, and compares different sizes, areas, weights, and bulks. The study of weight to him also has its charms, the difference of pressure upon his hand, his own weight in the effort of other children to lift him. He measures force and time in the same unconscious way, the time of sleeping, the time between a promised pleasure and its anticipated realization, and soon he learns to look at the clock to help him put in his judgment. He estimates very carefully the value of a cent and a stick of candy. All these spontaneous activities are in the direction of number study, are mingled with all his activities and are absolutely necessary to his mental and physical action. It is true these measures are very inadequate and imperfect, but they are the beginnings of the power of accurate measuring, that mode of judgment which will end, if he continues to have the right conditions, in exact measuring and weighing, and in accurate knowledge of values.

There is at first a perfect unity of thought and action. Hear the voice and watch the movements of a little child! No dancing teacher, no teacher of elocution, no actor, can ever successfully imitate the voice of the child, or the perfectly unconscious beauty and grace of its movements. Indeed it is the highest aim of artists in acting and elocution to acquire the unconscious grace and power of a child. Listen to the voice of the child, melodious, harmonious, perfect in emphasis, it is the immediate pulsations of his soul, the instantaneous reflex of his consciousness, with unconsciousness of his body, his organs of expression, his forms of speech. The child, until education intervenes, is a unit of action and expression, and that unity is acquired and maintained by action under a motive with no overpowering consciousness of the means or forms of expression. Must that beautiful unity be broken? Can it be perpetuated, and strengthened?

There never was such a thing as a lazy child born on earth. Childhood is full of activities of every kind, stimulated by external energies and shaped by internal power. The child experiments continually until it gains its ends. It will reach hundreds of times for an object, and at last succeed. What modes of expression, excepting speech, does a child acquire in the first years of its life? I should say that all children love music, though there is a vast difference in individual organisms in this as in all other modes of expression. Most children strive to imitate that which they hear in rhythm. Making, or manual work, is really the natural element of the child. I think I can say, without fear of dispute, that a child tries to make everything that he sees made. The little girl wishes to use the scissors, needle and thread. In the kitchen, unless repressed by the mother, she makes cakes and bread. In fact, the whole round of housekeeping in the beginning furnishes countless objects for activity and a desire to imitate. Boys in the shop, or on the farm, strive to do what they see done. They harness each other in teams, they drive the dog and the goat, they make mill-wheels and dams. The tendency to imitate, the desire to make the objects they see made, is intensely strong in every child.

Every child has the artist element born in him; he loves to model objects out of sand and clay. Paint is a perfect delight to children, bright colors charm them. Give the child a paint-brush, and though his expression of thought will be exceedingly crude, it will be very satisfactory to him; he will paint any object with the greatest confidence. It is very interesting to watch the crowd of little children near Lake Chautauqua, as busy as bees and as happy as angels. Let us look at the forms the children make out of the pliable sand. Here are caves where the fairies dwell, mountains, volcanoes, houses where the giants live. All these fantastic forms spring from the brain of the child and are expressed by means of this plastic material. See that little three-year-old girl with the model of a house in her brain: she is now wheeling a wheel-barrow, assisted by a little companion; in the barrow is the wood, and in her brain is the house. Energetic, persistent, happy, in what direction? In the direction of true growth! The little girl in the kitchen is not happy until she can mould and change the flour into dough, and dough into forms for baking; and here begin her first lessons in chemistry, the wonderful changes which heat brings about. She will dress her doll, working patiently for hours. Inexpert beholders may not know what the crude forms mean, but the child knows and is satisfied,—nay, delighted.

Give a child a piece of chalk, and its fancy runs riot: people, horses, houses, sheep, trees, birds, spring up in the brave confidence of childhood. In fact, all the modes of expression are spontaneously and persistently exercised by the child from the beginning except writing. It sings, it makes, it moulds, it paints, it draws, it expresses thought in all the forms of thought-expression, with the one exception.

I have very imperfectly presented, in this brief outline, some of the spontaneous activities of the little child. The more I strive to present them, the more imperfect seems the result, so much lies beyond in the interpretation of the child's instinctive activities, so much seems to exceed all present discovery. The question, my fellow-teachers, is, what should these lessons teach us? The child instinctively begins all subjects known in the curriculum of the university. He begins them because he cannot help it; his very nature impels him. These tendencies, these spontaneous activities of the child spring from the depths of its being, spring from all the past, for the child is the fruit of all the past, and the seed of all the future. These quiet, persistent, powerful tendencies we must examine and continue with the greatest care. The child overcomes great obstacles by persistent energy, always acting with great confidence of himself and his powers. He overcomes these obstacles because his whole being is a unit of action, controlled by one motive. The spontaneous tendencies of the child are the records of inborn divinity; we are here, my fellow-teachers, for one purpose, and that purpose is to understand these tendencies and continue them in all these directions, following nature. First of all, we should recognize the great dignity of the child, the child's divine power and divine possibilities, and then we are to present the conditions for their complete outworking. We are here that the child may take one step higher; we are here to find and present the conditions adapted to the divine nature of the child.

I have tried to show that the whole round of knowledge is begun by the child, and begun because it breathes, because it lives. If the child loves science and history, and studies or attends to them instinctively, then he should go on, and we must know the conditions or subjects and means which should be presented to him for each new demand or need.

I grant that in the past of education attention has been directed too much to dead forms of thought, and for one good reason at least: the sciences are a modern creation of man and have not yet reached the child. Now we have these marvelous subjects presented to us, worked out by great thinkers of the present, and we are to choose whether we will continue the dead formalism that too often leads to pedantry and bigotry, or whether we are to lead the child's soul in that direction which God designed in His creation of the human being.

In conclusion I commend to you, in the words of our greatest American philosopher:

> *"A babe by its mother lies, bathed in joy;*
> *Glide the hours uncounted, the sun is its toy;*
> *Shines the peace of all being without cloud in its eyes,*
> *And the sum of the world in soft miniature lies."*

I commend to you the "sum of the world" for your study, for in this direction lies all the future progress of humanity.

21

The Function of Education in Democratic Society

Charles W. Eliot, 1898

Charles W. Eliot (1834–1926) served as the President of Harvard for 40 years (1869–1909). During his administration, Eliot enacted a variety of reforms such as an extended elective system, the addition of new courses, flexible student discipline, higher standards for professional degrees, required written examinations, and a larger faculty. In 1892, Eliot served as chairman of the National Education Association's (NEA) Committee of Ten. The committee organized conferences that each included eminent professors and educators from selected academic subjects: 1) Latin, 2) Greek, 3) English, 4) Other Modern Languages, 5) Mathematics, 6) Physics, Astronomy, and Chemistry, 7) Natural History, 8) History, Civil Government, and Political Economy, and 9) Geography. Each conference was charged with developing recommendations on issues such as when the subject should be introduced to children, how much time should be devoted to the subject, which topics should be taught in high school, which are the best methods for teaching the subject, and how should proficiency in the subject be measured and factored into college entrance requirements. The report of the Committee of Ten recommended a greater degree of standardization in American secondary schools.

American Educational Thought: Essays from 1640–1940, pages 335–345

Although Eliot is known primarily for his reform of Harvard and his service on the Committee of Ten, he was very interested in the improvement of secondary schools and the broader purposes of education in a democracy. In the following essay from 1898, Eliot outlines what he believes to be the function of education in a democratic society. —AJM

What the function of education shall be in a democracy will depend on what is meant by democratic education. Too many of us think of education for the people as if it meant only learning to read, write, and cipher. Now, reading, writing, and simple ciphering are merely the tools by the diligent use of which a rational education is to be obtained through years of well-directed labor. They are not ends in themselves, but means to the great end of enjoying a rational existence. Under any civilized form of government, these arts ought to be acquired by every child by the time it is nine years of age. Competent teachers, or properly conducted schools, now teach reading, writing, and spelling simultaneously, so that the child writes every word it reads, and, of course, in writing spells the word. Ear, eye, and hand thus work together from the beginning in the acquisition of the arts of reading and writing. As to ciphering, most educational experts have become convinced that the amount of arithmetic which an educated person who is not some sort of computer needs to make use of is but small, and that real education should not be delayed or impaired for the sake of acquiring a skill in ciphering which will be of little use either to the child or to the adult. Reading, writing, and arithmetic, then, are not the goal of popular education.

The goal in all education, democratic or other, is always receding before the advancing contestant, as the top of a mountain seems to retreat before the climber, remoter and higher summits appearing successively as each apparent summit is reached. Nevertheless, the goal of the moment in education is always the acquisition of knowledge, the training of some permanent capacity for productiveness or enjoyment, and the development of character. Democratic education being a very new thing in the world, its attainable objects are not yet fully perceived. Plato taught that the laborious classes in a model commonwealth needed no education whatever. That seems an extraordinary opinion for a great philosopher to hold; but, while we wonder at it, let us recall that only one generation ago in some of our Southern States it was a crime to teach a member of the laborious class to read. In feudal society education was the privilege of some of the nobility and clergy, and was one source of the power of these two small classes. Universal education in Germany dates only from the Napoleonic wars and its object has been to make intelligent soldiers and subjects, rather than happy freemen. In England the system of public instruction is but twenty-seven years old. Moreover, the fundamental object of democratic education—to lift the whole population to a higher plane of intelligence, conduct, and happiness —has not yet been perfectly apprehended even in the United States. Too many of our own people think of popular education as if it were only a protection against dangerous superstitions, or a measure of police, or a means of increasing the national productiveness in the arts and trades. Our generation may, therefore, be excused if it has but an incomplete vision of the goal of education in a democracy.

I proceed to describe briefly the main elements of instruction and discipline in a democratic school. As soon as the easy use of what I have called the tools of education is acquired, and even while this familiarity is being gained, the capacities for productiveness and enjoyment should begin to be trained through the progressive acquisition of an elementary knowledge of the external world. The democratic school should begin early—in the very first grades—the study of nature; and all its teachers should, therefore, be capable of teaching the elements of physical geography, meteorology, botany, and zoology, the whole forming in the child's mind one harmonious sketch of its complex environment. This is a function of the primary-school teacher which our fathers never thought of, but which every passing year brings out more and more clearly as a prime function of every instructor of little children. Somewhat later in the child's progress toward maturity the great sciences of chemistry and physics will find place in its course of systematic training. From the seventh or eighth year, according to the quality and capacity of the child, plane and solid geometry, the science of form, should find a place among the school studies, and some share of the child's attention that great subject should claim for six or seven successive years. The process of making acquaintance with external nature through the elements of these various sciences should be interesting and enjoyable for every child. It should not be painful, but delightful; and throughout the process the child's skill in the arts of reading, writing, and ciphering should be steadily developed.

[handwritten margin note: Curriculum /method]

There is another part of every child's environment with which he should early begin to make acquaintance, namely, the human part. The story of the human race should be gradually conveyed to the child's mind from the time he begins to read with pleasure. This story should be conveyed quite as much through biography as through history; and with the descriptions of facts and real events should be entwined charming and uplifting products of the imagination. I cannot but think, however, that the wholly desirable imaginative literature for children remains, in large measure, to be written. The mythologies, Old Testament stories, fairy tales, and historical romances on which we are accustomed to feed the childish mind contain a great deal that is perverse, barbarous, or trivial; and to this infiltration into children's minds, generation after generation, of immoral, cruel, or foolish ideas, is probably to be attributed, in part, the slow ethical progress of the race. The common justification of our practice is that children do not apprehend the evil in the mental pictures with which we so rashly supply them. But what should we think of a mother who gave her child dirty milk or porridge, on the theory that the child would not assimilate the dirt? Should we be less careful of mental and moral food-materials? It is, however, as undesirable as it is impossible to try to feed the minds of children only upon facts of observation or record. The immense product of the imagination in art and literature is a concrete fact with which every educated human being should be made somewhat familiar, such products being a very real part of every individual's actual environment.

Into the education of the great majority of children there enters as an important part their contribution to the daily labor of the household and the farm, or, at least, of the household. It is one of the serious consequences of the rapid concentration of population into cities and large towns, and of the minute division of labor which characterizes modern industries, that this wholesome part of education is less easily secured than it used to be when the greater part of the population was engaged in agriculture. Organized education must, therefore, supply in urban communities a good part of the manual and moral training which the cooperation of children in the work of father and mother affords in agricultural communities. Hence the great importance in any urban population of facilities for training children to accurate hand-work, and for teaching them patience, forethought, and good judgment in productive labor.

Lastly, the school should teach every child, by precept, by example, and by every illustration its reading can supply, that the supreme attainment for any individual is vigor and loveliness of character. Industry, persistence, veracity in word and act, gentleness, and disinterestedness should be made to thrive and blossom during school life in the hearts of the children who bring these virtues from their homes well started, and should be planted and tended in the less fortunate children. Furthermore, the pupils should be taught that what is virtue in one human being is virtue in any group of human beings, large or small—a village, a city, or a nation; that the ethical principles which should govern an empire are precisely the same as those which should govern an individual; and that selfishness, greed, falseness, brutality, and ferocity are as hateful and degrading in a multitude as they are in a single savage.

The education thus outlined is what I think should be meant by democratic education. It exists today only among the most intelligent people, or in places singularly fortunate in regard to the organization of their schools; but though it be the somewhat distant ideal of democratic education, it is by no means an unattainable ideal. It is the reasonable aim of the public school in a thoughtful and ambitious democracy. It, of course, demands a kind of teacher much above the elementary-school teacher of the present day, and it also requires a larger expenditure upon the public school than is at all customary as yet in this country. But that better kind of teacher and that larger expenditure are imperatively called for, if democratic institutions are to prosper, and to promote continuously the real welfare of the mass of the people. The standard of education should not be set at the now attained or the now attainable. It is the privilege of public education to press toward a mark remote.

From the total training during childhood there should result in the child a taste for interesting and improving reading, which should direct and inspire its subsequent intellectual life. That schooling which results in this taste for good reading, however unsystematic or eccentric the schooling may have been, has achieved a main end of elementary education; and that schooling which does not result in implanting this permanent taste has failed. Guided and animated by this impulse to acquire knowledge and exercise his imagination through reading, the individual will continue to educate himself all through life. Without that deep-rooted impulsion he will soon cease to draw on the accumulated wisdom of the past and the new resources of the present, and, as he grows older, he will live in a mental atmosphere which is always growing thinner and emptier. Do we not all know many people who seem to live in a mental vacuum—to whom, indeed, we have great difficulty in attributing immortality, because they apparently have so little life except that of the body? Fifteen minutes a day of good reading would have given any one of this multitude a really human life. The uplifting of the democratic masses depends on this implanting at school of the taste for good reading.

Another important function of the public school in a democracy is the discovery and development of the gift or capacity of each individual child. This discovery should be made at the earliest practicable age, and, once made, should always influence, and sometimes determine, the education of the individual. It is for the interest of society to make the most of every useful gift or faculty which any member may fortunately possess; and it is one of the main advantages of fluent and mobile democratic society that it is more likely than any other society to secure the fruition of individual capacities. To make the most of any individual's peculiar power, it is important to discover it early, and then train it continuously and assiduously. It is wonderful what apparently small personal gifts may become the means of conspicuous service or achievement, if only they get discovered, trained, and applied. A quick eye for shades of color enables a blacksmith to earn double wages in sharpening drills for quarrymen. A delicate sense of touch makes the fortune of a wool-buyer. An extraordinarily perceptive forefinger gives a surgeon the advantage over all his competitors. A fine voice, with good elocution and a strong memory for faces and parliamentary rules, may give striking political success to a man otherwise not remarkable. In the ideal democratic school no two children would follow the same course of study or have the same tasks, except that they would all need to learn the use of the elementary tools of education—reading, writing, and ciphering. The different children would hardly have any identical needs. There might be a minimum standard of attainment in every branch of study, but no maximum. The perception or discovery of the individual gift or capacity would often be effected in the elementary school, but more generally in the secondary; and the making of these discoveries should be held one of the most important parts of the teacher's work. The vague desire for equality in a democracy has worked great mischief in democratic schools. There is no such thing as equality of gifts, or powers, or faculties, among either children or adults. On the contrary, there is the utmost diversity; and education and all the experience of life increase these diversities, because school, and the earning of a livelihood, and the reaction of the individual upon his surroundings, all tend strongly to magnify innate diversities. The pretended democratic school with an inflexible programme is fighting not only against nature, but against the interests of democratic society. Flexibility of programme should begin in the elementary school, years before the period of secondary education is reached. There should be some choice of subjects of study by ten years of age, and much variety by fifteen years of age. On the other hand, the programmes of elementary as well as of secondary schools should represent fairly the chief divisions of knowledge, namely, language and literature, mathematics, natural science, and history, besides drawing, manual work, and music. If school programmes fail to represent the main varieties of intellectual activity, they will not afford the means of discovering the individual gifts and tendencies of the pupils.

As an outcome of successful democratic education, certain habits of thought should be well established in the minds of all the children before any of them are obliged to leave school in order to help in the support of the family. In some small field each child should acquire a capacity for exact observation, and as a natural result of this acquirement it should come to admire and respect exact observation in all fields. Again, in some small field it should acquire the capacity for exact description, and a respect for exact description in all fields. And, lastly, it should attain, within the limited range of its experience and observation, the power to draw a justly limited inference from observed facts. I need not say that this power of just inference is an admirable one, which many adults never attain as the combined result of their education in childhood and their experience in after life. Yet democratic institutions will not be safe until a great majority of the population can be trusted not only to observe accurately and state precisely the results of observation, but also to draw just inferences from those results. The masses of the people will always be liable to dangerous delusions so long as their schools fail to teach the difference between a true cause and an event preceding or accompanying a supposed effect. Thus, a year ago our nation came to the very brink of a terrible disaster because millions of our people thought the fall in the price of silver during the past twenty years was the cause of the fall in price of many other American products; whereas the prime cause of the general fall of prices, including the price of silver, was the immense improvement which has taken place since the Civil War in the manufacture and distribution of mechanical power—an operating cause which, in the near future, is going to produce much more striking effects than it has yet produced.

Any one who has attained to the capacity for exact observation and exact description, and knows what it is to draw a correct inference from well-determined premises, will naturally acquire a respect for these powers when exhibited by others in fields unknown to him. Moreover, any one who has learned how hard it is to determine a fact, to state it accurately, and to draw from it the justly limited inference, will be sure that he himself cannot do these things, except in a very limited field. He will know that his own personal activity must be limited to a few subjects, if his capacity is to be really excellent in any. He will be sure that the too common belief that a Yankee can turn his hand to anything is a mischievous delusion. Having, as the result of his education, some vision of the great range of knowledge and capacity needed in the business of the world, he will respect the trained capacities which he sees developed in great diversity in other people. In short, he will come to respect and confide in the expert in every field of human activity. Confidence in experts, and willingness to employ them and abide by their decisions, are among the best signs of intelligence in an educated individual or an educated community; and in any democracy which is to thrive, this respect and confidence must be felt strongly by the majority of the population. In the conduct of private and corporation business in the United States the employment of experts is well recognized as the only rational and successful method. No one would think of building a bridge or a dam, or setting up a power station or a cotton-mill, without relying absolutely upon the advice of intelligent experts. The democracy must learn, in governmental affairs, whether municipal, state, or national, to employ experts and abide by their decisions. Such complicated subjects as taxation, finance, and public works cannot be wisely managed by popular assemblies or their committees, or by executive officers who have no special acquaintance with these most difficult subjects. American experience during the last twenty years demonstrates that popular assemblies have become absolutely incapable of dealing wisely with any of these great subjects. A legislature or a Congress can indicate by legislation the object it wishes to attain; but to devise the means of attaining that object in taxation, currency, finance, or public works, and to expend the money appropriated by the constituted authorities for the object, must be functions of experts. Legislators and executives are changed so frequently, under the American system of local representation, that few gain anything that deserves to be called experience in legislation or administration; while the few who serve long terms are apt to be so absorbed in the routine work of carrying on the government and managing the party interests, that they have no time either for thorough research or for invention. Under present conditions, neither expert knowledge nor intellectual leadership can reasonably be expected of them. Democracies will not be safe until the population has learned that governmental affairs must be conducted on the same principles on which successful private and corporate business is conducted; and therefore it should be one of the principal objects of democratic education so to train the minds of the children, that when they become adult they shall have within their own experience the grounds of respect for the attainments of experts in every branch of governmental, industrial, and social activity, and of confidence in their advice.

The next function of education in a democracy should be the firm planting in every child's mind of certain great truths which lie at the foundation of the democratic social theory. The first of these truths is the intimate dependence of each human individual on a multitude of other individuals, not in infancy alone, but at every moment of life—a dependence which increases with civilization and with the development of urban life. This sense of mutual dependence among multitudes of human beings can be brought home to children during school life so clearly and strongly that they will never lose it. By merely teaching children whence come their food, drink, clothing, and means of getting light and heat, and how these materials are supplied through the labors of many individuals of many races scattered all over the world, the school may illustrate and enforce this doctrine of intricate interdependence, which really underlies modern democracy—a doctrine never more clearly expressed than in these two Christian sentences: "No man liveth to himself," and "We are every one members one of another." The dependence of every family, and indeed every person, on the habitual fidelity of mechanics, purveyors, railroad servants, cooks, and nurses can easily be brought home to children. Another mode of implanting this sentiment is to trace in history the obligations of the present generation to many former generations. These obligations can be easily pointed out in things material, such as highways, waterworks, fences, houses, and barns, and, in New England at least, the stone walls and piles of stone gathered from the arable fields by the patient labor of predecessors on the family farm. But it may also be exhibited to the pupils of secondary schools, and, in some measure, to the pupils of elementary schools, in the burdens and sufferings which former generations have borne for the establishment of freedom of conscience and of speech, and of toleration in religion, and for the development of the institutions of public justice. Of course history is full of examples of the violation of this fundamental democratic doctrine of mutual help. Indeed, history, as commonly written, consists chiefly in the story of hideous violations of this principle, such as wars and oppressions, and the selfish struggles of class against class, church against church, and nation against nation. But these violations, with the awful sufferings that follow from them, may be made to point and emphasize the truth of the fundamental doctrine; and unless the teaching of history in our public schools does this, it were better that the subject should not be taught at all.

Democratic education should also inculcate on every child the essential unity of a democratic community, in spite of the endless diversities of function, capacity, and achievement among the individuals who compose the community. This is a doctrine kindred with that just mentioned, but not identical. It is a doctrine essential to diffused democratic contentment and self-respect, but materially different from the ordinary conception of equality of condition as a result of democracy; for unity is attainable, while equality of condition is unnatural and unattainable. The freedom and social mobility which characterize the democratic state permit, and indeed bring about, striking inequalities of condition; and if the surface of democratic society should be leveled off any day, inequalities would reappear on the morrow, unless individual freedom and social mobility should be destroyed. The children of a democratic society should, therefore, be taught at school, with the utmost explicitness, and with vivid illustrations, that inequalities of condition are a necessary result of freedom; but that through all inequalities should flow the constant sense of essential unity in aim and spirit. This unity in freedom is the social goal of democracy, the supreme good of all ranks of society, of the highest no less than of the lowest.

Another ethical principle which a democracy should teach to all its children is the familiar Christian doctrine that service rendered to others is the surest source of one's own satisfaction and happiness. This doctrine is a tap-root of private happiness among all classes and conditions of men; but in a democracy it is important to public happiness and well-being. In a democracy the public functionary is not a master, but a trusted servant. By excellence of service he earns not only a pecuniary consideration, but also respect and gratitude. This statement applies just as well to a letter-carrier, a fireman, or a village selectman, as it does to a high-school teacher, a judge, or a governor. Democracy applies literally the precept, "If any man would be great among you, let him be your servant." The quality of this faithful service and its rewards should be carefully taught in school to all children of a democracy. The children should learn that the desire to be of great public service is the highest of all ambitions; and they should be shown in biography and in history how the men and women who, as martyrs, teachers, inventors, legislators, and judges, have rendered great service, have thereby won enduring gratitude and honor.

Since it is a fundamental object of a democracy to promote the happiness and well-being of the masses of the population, the democratic school should explicitly teach children to see and utilize the means of happiness which lie about them in the beauties and splendors of nature. The school should be a vehicle of daily enjoyment, and the teacher should be to the child a minister of joy. Democratic society has already learned how to provide itself—at least, in the more intelligent communities—with open grounds in cities, and parks in suburbs, and has in these ways begun to provide directly for the wholesome pleasures of the population. It should be a recognized function of the democratic school to teach the children and their parents how to utilize all accessible means of innocent enjoyment.

Finally, the democratic school must teach its children what the democratic nobility is. The well-trained child will read in history and poetry about patricians, nobles, aristocrats, princes, kings, and emperors, some of them truly noble, but many vile; and he will also read with admiring sympathy of the loyalty and devotion which through all the centuries have been felt by generous men and women of humbler condition toward those of higher. He will see what immense virtues these personal loyalties have developed, even when the objects of loyalty have been unworthy; and he will ask himself, "What are to be the corresponding virtues in a democracy?" The answer is, Fidelity to all forms of duty which demand courage, self-denial, and zeal, and loyal devotion to the democratic ideals of freedom, serviceableness, unity, toleration, public justice, and public joyfulness. The children should learn that the democratic nobility exists, and must exist if democracy is to produce the highest types of character; but that it will consist only of men and women of noble character, produced under democratic conditions by the combined influences of fine inherited qualities, careful education, and rich experience. They should learn to admire and respect persons of this quality, and to support them, on occasion, in preference to the ignoble. They should learn that mere wealth has no passport to the democratic nobility, and that membership in it can be transmitted to children only through the transmission of the sound mental and moral qualities which are its sole warrant. This membership should be the rightful ambition of parents for their children, and of children for their future selves. Every person of the true quality, no matter what his station or vocation, is admitted of right to this simple democratic nobility, which home, church, and school unite in recruiting; and there are, consequently, more real nobles under the democratic form of government than under any other.

22

Excerpts from Talks to Teachers on Psychology and to Students on Some of Life's Ideals

William James, 1899

William James (1842–1910) is commonly referred to as the Father of American Psychology and the Father of Pragmatism. These two titles reflect James' work in the fields of psychology and philosophy. James believed that psychological study must be informed by philosophical principles. Psychologists who wanted to focus solely on the observable elements of human psychology and behavior criticized him for his attention to "the consciousness of the self" and the soul. Pragmatism was conceived by James and others as a method for determining the truth of an idea in terms of its agreement with reality and its personal utility. Thus, the mind of the truth seeker has a role to play in the process of determining the truth of an idea.

James taught at Harvard from 1875 until 1907 and published numerous books, such as *The Principles of Psychology* (1890), *Varieties of Religious Experiences* (1902), and *Pragmatism* (1907). In 1892, James began a series of lectures on psychology for teachers in Cambridge. The lectures, based on his *Principles of*

American Educational Thought: Essays from 1640–1940, pages 347–359
Copyright © 2010 by Information Age Publishing
All rights of reproduction in any form reserved.

Psychology, were very popular, and he subsequently spoke to teachers throughout the country. James remarked that the purpose of his lectures was to "dispel the mystification" of psychology for teachers. The lectures were published
in installments in the *Atlantic Monthly,* and in 1899 they were collected and
published as a book entitled, *Talks to Teachers on Psychology and to Students on
Some of Life's Ideals.* The book became required reading in many teacher education programs in the early decades of the 20th century. The following are
the first four chapters of *Talks to Teachers.* —AJM

Psychology and the Teaching Art

In the general activity and uprising of ideal interests which every one with
an eye for fact can discern all about us in American life, there is perhaps no
more promising feature than the fermentation which for a dozen years or
more has been going on among the teachers. In whatever sphere of education their functions may lie, there is to be seen among them a really inspiring amount of searching of the heart about the highest concerns of their
profession. The renovation of nations begins always at the top, among the
reflective members of the State, and spreads slowly outward and downward.
The teachers of this country, one may say, have its future in their hands.
The earnestness which they at present show in striving to enlighten and
strengthen themselves is an index of the nation's probabilities of advance in
all ideal directions. The outward organization of education which we have
in our United States is perhaps, on the whole, the best organization that exists in any country. The State school systems give a diversity and flexibility,
an opportunity for experiment and keenness of competition, nowhere else
to be found on such an important scale. The independence of so many of
the colleges and universities; the give and take of students and instructors
between them all; their emulation, and their happy organic relations to
the lower schools; the traditions of instruction in them, evolved from the
older American recitation-method (and so avoiding on the one hand the
pure lecture-system prevalent in Germany and Scotland, which considers
too little the individual student, and yet not involving the sacrifice of the instructor to the individual student, which the English tutorial system would
seem too often to entail),—all these things (to say nothing of that coeduca-
tion of the sexes in whose benefits so many of us heartily believe), all these
things, I say, are most happy features of our scholastic life, and from them
the most sanguine auguries may be drawn.

Having so favorable an organization, all we need is to impregnate it
with geniuses, to get superior men and women working more and more
abundantly in it and for it and at it, and in a generation or two America may

well lead the education of the world. I must say that I look forward with no little confidence to the day when that shall be an accomplished fact.

No one has profited more by the fermentation of which I speak, in pedagogical circles, than we psychologists. The desire of the school-teachers for a completer professional training, and their aspiration toward the 'professional' spirit in their work, have led them more and more to turn to us for light on fundamental principles. And in these few hours which we are to spend together you look to me, I am sure, for information concerning the mind's operations, which may enable you to labor more easily and effectively in the several schoolrooms over which you preside.

Far be it from me to disclaim for psychology all title to such hopes. Psychology ought certainly to give the teacher radical help. And yet I confess that, acquainted as I am with the height of some of your expectations, I feel a little anxious lest, at the end of these simple talks of mine, not a few of you may experience some disappointment at the net results. In other words, I am not sure that you may not be indulging fancies that are just a shade exaggerated. That would not be altogether astonishing, for we have been having something like a 'boom' in psychology in this country. Laboratories and professorships have been founded, and reviews established. The air has been full of rumors. The editors of educational journals and the arrangers of conventions have had to show themselves enterprising and on a level with the novelties of the day. Some of the professors have not been unwilling to co-operate, and I am not sure even that the publishers have been entirely inert. 'The new psychology' has thus become a term to conjure up portentous ideas withal; and you teachers, docile and receptive and aspiring as many of you are, have been plunged in an atmosphere of vague talk about our science, which to a great extent has been more mystifying than enlightening. Altogether it does seem as if there were a certain fatality of mystification laid upon the teachers of our day. The matter of their profession, compact enough in itself, has to be frothed up for them in journals and institutes, till its outlines often threaten to be lost in a kind of vast uncertainty. Where the disciples are not independent and critical-minded enough (and I think that, if you teachers in the earlier grades have any defect—the slightest touch of a defect in the world—it is that you are a mite too docile), we are pretty sure to miss accuracy and balance and measure in those who get a license to lay down the law to them from above.

As regards this subject of psychology, now, I wish at the very threshold to do what I can to dispel the mystification. So I say at once that in my humble opinion there is no 'new psychology' worthy of the name. There is nothing but the old psychology which began in Locke's time, plus a little physiology of the brain and senses and theory of evolution, and a few refinements of introspective detail, for the most part without adaptation to the teacher's use. It is only the fundamental conceptions of psychology which are of real value to the teacher; and they, apart from the aforesaid theory of evolution, are very far from being new—I trust that you will see better what I mean by this at the end of all these talks.

I say moreover that you make a great, a very great mistake, if you think that psychology, being the science of the mind's laws, is something from which you can deduce definite programmes and schemes and methods of instruction for immediate schoolroom use. Psychology is a science, and teaching is an art; and sciences never generate arts directly out of themselves. An intermediary inventive mind must make the application, by using its originality.

The science of logic never made a man reason rightly, and the science of ethics (if there be such a thing) never made a man behave rightly. The most such sciences can do is to help us to catch ourselves up and check ourselves, if we start to reason or to behave wrongly; and to criticize ourselves more articulately after we have made mistakes. A science only lays down lines within which the rules of the art must fall, laws which the follower of the art must not transgress; but what particular thing he shall positively do within those lines is left exclusively to his own genius. One genius will do his work well and succeed in one way, while another succeeds as well quite differently; yet neither will transgress the lines.

The art of teaching grew up in the schoolroom, out of inventiveness and sympathetic concrete observation. Even where (as in the case of Herbart) the advancer of the art was also a psychologist, the pedagogics and the psychology ran side by side, and the former was not derived in any sense from the latter. The two were congruent, but neither was subordinate. And so everywhere the teaching must *agree* with the psychology, but need not necessarily be the only kind of teaching that would so agree; for many diverse methods of teaching may equally well agree with psychological laws.

To know psychology, therefore, is absolutely no guarantee that we shall be good teachers. To advance to that result, we must have an additional endowment altogether, a happy tact and ingenuity to tell us what definite things to say and do when the pupil is before us. That ingenuity in meeting and pursuing the pupil, that tact for the concrete situation, though they are the alpha and omega of the teacher's art, are things to which psychology cannot help us in the least.

The science of psychology, and whatever science of general pedagogics may be based on it, are in fact much like the science of war. Nothing is simpler or more definite than the principles of either. In war, all you have to do is to work your enemy into a position from which the natural obstacles prevent him from escaping if he tries to; then to fall on him in numbers superior to his own, at a moment when you have led him to think you far away; and so, with a minimum of exposure of your own troops, to hack his force to pieces, and take the remainder prisoners. Just so, in teaching, you must simply work your pupil into such a state of interest in what you are going to teach him that every other object of attention is banished from his mind; then reveal it to him so impressively that he will remember the occasion to his dying day; and finally fill him with devouring curiosity to know what the next steps in connection with the subject are. The principles being so plain, there would be nothing but victories for the masters of the science, either on the battlefield or in the schoolroom, if they did not both have to make their application to an incalculable quantity in the shape of the mind of their opponent. The mind of your own enemy, the pupil, is working away from you as keenly and eagerly as is the mind of the commander on the other side from the scientific general. Just what the respective enemies want and think, and what they know and do not know, are as hard things for the teacher as the general to find out. Divination and perception, not psychological pedagogics or theoretic strategy, are the only helpers here.

But, if the use of psychological principles thus be negative rather than positive, it does not follow that it may not be a great use, all the same. It certainly narrows the path for experiments and trials. We know in advance, if we are psychologists, that certain methods will be wrong, so our psychology saves us from mistakes. It makes us, moreover, more clear as to what we are about. We gain confidence in respect to any method which we are using as soon as we believe that it has theory as well as practice at its back. Most of all, it fructifies our independence, and it reanimates our interest, to see our subject at two different angles,—to get a stereoscopic view, so to speak, of the youthful organism who is our enemy, and, while handling him with all our concrete tact and divination, to be able, at the same time, to represent to ourselves the curious inner elements of his mental machine. Such a complete knowledge as this of the pupil, at once intuitive and analytic, is surely the knowledge at which every teacher ought to aim.

Fortunately for you teachers, the elements of the mental machine can be clearly apprehended, and their workings easily grasped. And, as the most general elements and workings are just those parts of psychology which the teacher finds most directly useful, it follows that the amount of this science which is necessary to all teachers need not be very great. Those who find themselves loving the subject may go as far as they please, and become possibly none the worse teachers for the fact, even though in some of them one might apprehend a little loss of balance from the tendency observable in all of us to overemphasize certain special parts of a subject when we are studying it intensely and abstractly. But for the great majority of you a general view is enough, provided it be a true one; and such a general view, one may say, might almost be written on the palm of one's hand.

Least of all need you, merely *as teachers,* deem it part of your duty to become contributors to psychological science or to make psychological observations in a methodical or responsible manner. I fear that some of the enthusiasts for child-study have thrown a certain burden on you in this way. By all means let child-study go on, —it is refreshing all our sense of the child's life. There are teachers who take a spontaneous delight in filling syllabuses, inscribing observations, compiling statistics, and computing the percent. Child-study will certainly enrich their lives. And, if its results, as treated statistically, would seem on the whole to have but trifling value, yet the anecdotes and observations of which it in part consists do certainly acquaint us more intimately with our pupils. Our eyes and ears grow quickened to discern in the child before us processes similar to those we have read of as noted in the children, —processes of which we might otherwise have remained inobservant. But, for Heaven's sake, let the rank and file of teachers be passive readers if they so prefer, and feel free not to contribute to the accumulation. Let not the prosecution of it be preached as an imperative duty or imposed by regulation on those to whom it proves an exterminating bore, or who in any way whatever miss in themselves the appropriate vocation for it. I cannot too strongly agree with my colleague, Professor Munsterberg, when he says that the teacher's attitude toward the child, being concrete and ethical, is positively opposed to the psychological observer's, which is abstract and analytic. Although some of us may conjoin the attitudes successfully, in most of us they must conflict.

The worst thing that can happen to a good teacher is to get a bad conscience about her profession because she feels herself hopeless as a psychologist. Our teachers are overworked already. Every one who adds a jot or tittle of unnecessary weight to their burden is a foe of education. A bad conscience increases the weight of every other burden; yet I know that child-study, and other pieces of psychology as well, have been productive of bad conscience in many a really innocent pedagogic breast. I should indeed be glad if this passing word from me might tend to dispel such a bad conscience, if any of you have it; for it is certainly one of those fruits of more or less systematic mystification of which I have already complained. The best teacher may be the poorest contributor of child-study material, and the best contributor may be the poorest teacher. No fact is more palpable than this.

So much for what seems the most reasonable general attitude of the teacher toward the subject which is to occupy our attention.

The Stream of Consciousness

I said a few minutes ago that the most general elements and workings of the mind are all that the teacher absolutely needs to be acquainted with for his purposes.

Now the *immediate* fact which psychology, the science of mind, has to study is also the most general fact. It is the fact that in each of us, when awake (and often when asleep), *some kind of consciousness is always going on.* There is a stream, a succession of states, or waves, or fields (or of whatever you please to call them), of knowledge, of feeling, of desire, of deliberation, etc., that constantly pass and repass, and that constitute our inner life. The existence of this stream is the primal fact, the nature and origin of it form the essential problem, of our science. So far as we class the states or fields of consciousness, write down their several natures, analyze their contents into elements, or trace their habits of succession, we are on the descriptive or analytic level. So far as we ask where they come from or why they are just what they are, we are on the explanatory level.

In these talks with you, I shall entirely neglect the questions that come up on the explanatory level. It must be frankly confessed that in no fundamental sense do we know where our successive fields of consciousness come from, or why they have the precise inner constitution which they do have. They certainly follow or accompany our brain states, and of course their special forms are determined by our past experiences and education. But, if we ask just *how* the brain conditions them, we have not the remotest inkling of an answer to give; and, if we ask just how the education moulds the brain, we can speak but in the most abstract, general, and conjectural terms. On the other hand, if we should say that they are due to a spiritual being called our Soul, which reacts on our brain states by these peculiar forms of spiritual energy, our words would be familiar enough, it is true; but I think you will agree that they would offer little genuine explanatory meaning. The truth is that we really *do not know* the answers to the problems on the explanatory level, even though in some directions of inquiry there may be promising speculations to be found. For our present purposes I shall therefore dismiss them entirely, and turn to mere description. This state of things was what I had in mind when, a moment ago, I said there was no 'new psychology' worthy of the name.

We have thus fields of consciousness, —that is the first general fact; and the second general fact is that the concrete fields are always complex. They contain sensations of our bodies and of the objects around us, memories of past experiences and thoughts of distant things, feelings of satisfaction and dissatisfaction, desires and aversions, and other emotional conditions, together with determinations of the will, in every variety of permutation and combination.

In most of our concrete states of consciousness all these different class-es of ingredients are found simultaneously present to some degree, though the relative proportion they bear to one another is very shifting. One state will seem to be composed of hardly anything but sensations, another of hardly anything but memories, etc. But around the sensation, if one consid-er carefully, there will always be some fringe of thought or will, and around the memory some margin or penumbra of emotion or sensation.

In most of our fields of consciousness there is a core of sensation that is very pronounced. You, for example, now, although you are also thinking and feeling, are getting through your eyes sensations of my face and figure, and through your ears sensations of my voice. The sensations are the *centre* or *focus,* the thoughts and feelings the *margin,* of your actually present con-scious field.

On the other hand, some object of thought, some distant image, may have become the focus of your mental attention even while I am speaking, —your mind, in short, may have wandered from the lecture; and, in that case, the sensations of my face and voice, although not absolutely vanished from your conscious field, may have taken up there a very faint and margin-al place. Again, to take another sort of variation, some feeling connected with your own body may have passed from a marginal to a focal place, even while I speak.

The expressions 'focal object' and 'marginal object,' which we owe to Mr. Lloyd Morgan, require, I think, no further explanation. The distinction they embody is a very important one, and they are the first technical terms which I shall ask you to remember.

In the successive mutations of our fields of consciousness, the process by which one dissolves into another is often very gradual, and all sorts of inner rearrangements of contents occur. Sometimes the focus remains but little changed, while the margin alters rapidly. Sometimes the focus alters, and the margin stays. Sometimes focus and margin change places. Some-times, again, abrupt alterations of the whole field occur. There can seldom be a sharp description. All we know is that, for the most part, each field has a sort of practical unity for its possessor, and that from this practical point of view we can class a field with other fields similar to it, by calling it a state of emotion, of perplexity, of sensation, of abstract thought, of volition, and the like.

Vague and hazy as such an account of our stream of consciousness may be, it is at least secure from positive error and free from admixture of conjecture or hypothesis. An influential school of psychology, seeking to avoid haziness of outline, has tried to make things appear more exact and scientific by making the analysis more sharp. The various fields of consciousness, according to this school, result from a definite number of perfectly definite elementary mental states, mechanically associated into a mosaic or chemically combined. According to some thinkers,—Spencer, for example, or Taine,—these resolve themselves at last into little elementary psychic particles or atoms of 'mind-stuff,' out of which all the more immediately known mental states are said to be built up. Locke introduced this theory in a somewhat vague form. Simple 'ideas' of sensation and reflection, as he called them, were for him the bricks of which our mental architecture is built up. If I ever have to refer to this theory again, I shall refer to it as the theory of 'ideas.' But I shall try to steer clear of it altogether. Whether it be true or false, it is at any rate only conjectural; and, for your practical purposes as teachers, the more unpretending conception of the stream of consciousness, with its total waves or fields incessantly changing, will amply suffice.

The Child as a Behaving Organism

I wish now to continue the description of the peculiarities of the stream of consciousness by asking whether we can in any intelligible way assign its *functions*. It has two functions that are obvious: it leads to knowledge, and it leads to action. Can we say which of these functions is the more essential? An old historic divergence of opinion comes in here. Popular belief has always tended to estimate the worth of a man's mental processes by their effects upon his practical life. But philosophers have usually cherished a different view. "Man's supreme glory," they have said, "is to be a *rational* being, to know absolute and eternal and universal truth. The uses of his intellect for practical affairs are therefore subordinate matters. 'The theoretic life' is his soul's genuine concern." Nothing can be more different in its results for our personal attitude than to take sides with one or the other of these views, and emphasize the practical or the theoretical ideal. In the latter case, abstraction from the emotions and passions and withdrawal from the strife of human affairs would be not only pardonable, but praiseworthy; and all that makes for quiet and contemplation should be regarded as conducive to the highest human perfection. In the former, the man of contemplation would be treated as only half a human being, passion and practical resource would become once more glories of our race, a concrete victory over this earth's outward powers of darkness would appear an equivalent for any amount of passive spiritual culture, and conduct would remain as the test of every education worthy of the name.

It is impossible to disguise the fact that in the psychology of our own day the emphasis is transferred from the mind's purely rational function, where Plato and Aristotle, and what one may call the whole classic tradition in philosophy had placed it, to the so long neglected practical side. The theory of evolution is mainly responsible for this. Man, we now have reason to believe, has been evolved from infra-human ancestors, in whom pure reason hardly existed, if at all, and whose mind, so far as it can have had any function, would appear to have been an organ for adapting their movements to the impressions received from the environment, so as to escape the better from destruction. Consciousness would thus seem in the first instance to be nothing but a sort of superadded biological perfection, —useless unless it prompted to useful conduct, and inexplicable apart from that consideration.

Deep in our own nature the biological foundations of our consciousness persist, undisguised and undiminished. Our sensations are here to attract us or to deter us, our memories to warn or encourage us, our feelings to impel, and our thoughts to restrain our behavior, so that on the whole we may prosper and our days be long in the land. Whatever of transmundane metaphysical insight or of practically inapplicable aesthetic perception or ethical sentiment we may carry in our interiors might at this rate be regarded as only part of the incidental excess of function that necessarily accompanies the working of every complex machine.

I shall ask you now—not meaning at all thereby to close the theoretic question, but merely because it seems to me the point of view likely to be of greatest practical use to you as teachers—to adopt with me, in this course of lectures, the biological conception, as thus expressed, and to lay your own emphasis on the fact that man, whatever else he may be, is primarily a practical being, whose mind is given him to aid in adapting him to this world's life.

In the learning of all matters, we have to start with some one deep aspect of the question, abstracting it as if it were the only aspects; and then we gradually correct ourselves by adding those neglected other features which complete the case. No one believes more strongly than I do that what our senses know as 'this world' is only one portion of our mind's total environment and object. Yet, because it is the primal portion, it is the *sine qua non* of all the rest. If you grasp the facts about it firmly, you may proceed to higher regions undisturbed. As our time must be so short together, I prefer being elementary and fundamental to being complete, so I propose to you to hold fast to the ultra-simple point of view.

The reasons why I call it so fundamental can be easily told. First, human and animal psychology thereby becomes less discontinuous. I know that to some of you this will hardly seem an attractive reason, but there are others whom it will affect. Second, mental action is conditioned by brain action, and runs parallel therewith. But the brain, so far as we understand it, is given us for practical behavior. Every current that runs into it from skin or eye or ear runs out again into muscles, glands, or viscera, and helps to adapt the animal to the environment from which the current came. It therefore generalizes and simplifies our view to treat the brain life and the mental life as having one fundamental kind of purpose. Third, those very functions of the mind that do not refer directly to this world's environment, the ethical utopias, aesthetic visions, insights into eternal truth, and fanciful logical combinations, could never be carried on at all by a human individual, unless the mind that produced them in him were also able to produce more practically useful products. The latter are thus the more essential, or at least the more primordial results. Fourth, the inessential 'unpractical' activities are themselves far more connected with our behavior and our adaptation to the environment than at first sight might appear. No truth, however abstract, is ever perceived, that will not probably at some time influence our earthly action. You must remember that, when I talk of action here, I mean action in the widest sense. I mean speech, I mean writing, I mean yeses and noes, and tendencies 'from' things and tendencies 'toward' things, and emotional determinations; and I mean them in the future as well as in the immediate present. As I talk here, and you listen, it might seem as if no action followed. You might call it a purely theoretic process, with no practical result. But it *must* have a practical result. It cannot take place at all and leave your conduct unaffected. If not today, then on some far future day, you will answer some question differently by reason of what you are thinking now. Some of you will be led by my words into new veins of inquiry, into reading special books. These will develop your opinion, whether for or against. That opinion will in turn be expressed, will receive criticism from others in your environment, and will affect your standing in their eyes. We cannot escape our destiny, which is practical; and even our most theoretic faculties contribute to its working out.

These few reasons will perhaps smooth the way for you to acquiescence in my proposal. As teachers, I sincerely think it will be a sufficient conception for you to adopt of the youthful psychological phenomena handed over to your inspection if you consider them from the point of view of their relation to the future conduct of their possessor. Sufficient at any rate as a first conception and as a main conception. You should regard your professional task as if it consisted chiefly and essentially in *training the pupil to behavior;* taking behavior, not in the narrow sense of his manners, but in the very widest possible sense, as including every possible sort of fit reaction on the circumstances into which he may find himself brought by the vicissitudes of life.

The reaction may, indeed, often be a negative reaction. *Not* to speak, *not* to move, is one of the most important of our duties, in certain practical emergencies. "Thou shalt refrain, renounce, abstain!" This often requires a great effort of will power, and, physiologically considered, is just as positive a nerve function as is motor discharge.

Education and Behavior

In our foregoing talk we were led to frame a very simple conception of what an education means. In the last analysis it consists in the organizing of *resources* in the human being, of powers of conduct which shall fit him to his social and physical world. An 'uneducated' person is one who is nonplussed by all but the most habitual situations. On the contrary, one who is educated is able practically to extricate himself, by means of the examples with which his memory is stored and of the abstract conceptions which he has acquired, from circumstances in which he never was placed before. Education, in short, cannot be better described than by calling it *the organization of acquired habits of conduct and tendencies to behavior.*

To illustrate—You and I are each and all of us educated, in our several ways; and we show our education at this present moment by different conduct. It would be quite impossible for me, with my mind technically and professionally organized as it is, and with the optical stimulus which your presence affords, to remain sitting here entirely silent and inactive. Something tells me that I am expected to speak, and must speak; something forces me to keep on speaking. My organs of articulation are continuously innervated by outgoing currents, which the currents passing inward at my eyes and through my educated brain have set in motion; and the particular movements which they make have their form and order determined altogether by the training of all my past years of lecturing and reading. Your conduct, on the other hand, might seem at first sight purely receptive and inactive,—leaving out those among you who happen to be taking notes. But the very listening which you are carrying on is itself a determinate kind of conduct. All the muscular tensions of your body are distributed in a peculiar way as you listen. Your head, your eyes, are fixed characteristically. And, when the lecture is over, it will inevitably eventuate in some stroke of behavior, as I said on the previous occasion: you may be guided differently in some special emergency in the schoolroom by words which I now let fall—So it is with the impressions you will make there on your pupil. You should get into the habit of regarding them all as leading to the acquisition by him of capacities for behavior,—emotional, social, bodily, vocal, technical, or what not. And, this being the case, you ought to feel willing, in a general way, and without hair-splitting or farther ado, to take up for the purpose of these lectures with the biological conception of the mind, as of something given us for practical use. That conception will certainly cover the greater part of your own educational work.

If we reflect upon the various ideals of education that are prevalent in the different countries, we see that what they all aim at is to organize capacities for conduct. This is most immediately obvious in Germany, where the explicitly avowed aim of the higher education is to turn the student into an instrument for advancing scientific discovery. The German universities are proud of the number of young specialists whom they turn out every year, —not necessarily men of any original force of intellect, but men so trained to research that when their professor gives them an historical or philological thesis to prepare, or a bit of laboratory work to do, with a general indication as to the best method, they can go off by themselves and use apparatus and consult sources in such a way as to grind out in the requisite number of months some little pepper-corn of new truth worthy of being added to the store of extant human information on that subject. Little else is recognized in Germany as a man's title to academic advancement than his ability thus to show himself an efficient instrument of research.

In England, it might seem at first sight as if the higher education of the universities aimed at the production of certain static types of character rather than at the development of what one may call this dynamic scientific efficiency. Professor Jowett, when asked what Oxford could do for its students, is said to have replied, "Oxford can teach an English gentleman how to *be* an English gentleman." But, if you ask what it means to '*be*' an English gentleman, the only reply is in terms of conduct and behavior. An English gentleman is a bundle of specifically qualified reactions, a creature who for all the emergencies of life has his line of behavior distinctly marked out for him in advance. Here, as elsewhere, England expects every man to do his duty.

23

Selected Writings of John Dewey

Most educational historians consider John Dewey (1859–1952) to be America's most influential philosopher. Dewey was a prolific writer who produced popular works in the areas of education, metaphysics, epistemology, ethics, aesthetics, and social/political philosophy. Dewey was born in Burlington, Vermont, on October 20, 1859. After graduating from the University of Vermont in 1879, he taught high school for two years in Oil City, Pennsylvania. While teaching high school, he became interested in philosophy and chose to pursue graduate study at Johns Hopkins University. After graduating from Johns Hopkins in 1883 with a PhD in philosophy, Dewey accepted an appointment to teach philosophy at the University of Michigan. He remained at Michigan for ten years. In 1894, he began to teach in the Department of Pedagogy, Psychology, and Philosophy at the University of Chicago. During his ten-year stay in Chicago, Dewey became famous for his revolutionary ideas on pedagogy. In 1904, Dewey left the University of Chicago to teach in the department of philosophy at Columbia University. During his forty-eight years in New York, Dewey also taught regularly at Teachers College. He remained active as a writer and so-

American Educational Thought: Essays from 1640–1940, pages 361–399
Copyright © 2010 by Information Age Publishing

cial thinker throughout retirement, until his death on June 2, 1952. During his 75-year writing career, Dewey produced dozens of books and hundreds of articles, many of which remain influential today. Dewey's books *The Child and the Curriculum* and *School and Society*, excerpted below, inspired the Progressive education movement, which emphasized child development and the adaptation of curriculum to the interests and needs of students. The somewhat extreme child-centered view that Dewey espouses in *The Child and the Curriculum* and *School and Society* is counterbalanced by *Experience and Education,* a book Dewey published in 1938. "My Pedagogic Creed" is a noteworthy piece of scholarship from Dewey not only because it displays the rhetorical side of his work, but also because it shows how his early life was strongly influenced by his faith. —JWN

My Pedagogic Creed, 1897

ARTICLE I: What Education Is

I believe that all education proceeds by the participation of the individual in the social consciousness of the race. This process begins unconsciously almost at birth, and is continually shaping the individual's powers, saturating his consciousness, forming his habits, training his ideas, and arousing his feelings and emotions. Through this unconscious education the individual gradually comes to share in the intellectual and moral resources which humanity has succeeded in getting together. He becomes an inheritor of the funded capital of civilization. The most formal and technical education in the world cannot safely depart from this general process. It can only organize it or differentiate it in some particular direction.

I believe that the only true education comes through the stimulation of the child's powers by the demands of the social situations in which he finds himself. Through these demands he is stimulated to act as a member of a unity, to emerge from his original narrowness of action and feeling, and to conceive of himself from the standpoint of the welfare of the group to which he belongs. Through the responses which others make to his own activities he comes to know what these mean in social terms. The value which they have is reflected back into them. For instance, through the response which is made to the child's instinctive babblings the child comes to know what those babblings mean; they are transformed into articulate language and thus the child is introduced into the consolidated wealth of ideas and emotions which are now summed up in language.

I believe that this educational process has two sides—one psychological and one sociological; and that neither can be subordinated to the other or neglected without evil results following. Of these two sides, the psychological is the basis. The child's own instincts and powers furnish the material and give the starting point for all education. Save as the efforts of the educator connect with some activity which the child is carrying on of his own initiative independent of the educator, education becomes reduced to a pressure from without. It may, indeed, give certain external results, but cannot truly be called educative. Without insight into the psychological structure and activities of the individual, the educative process will, therefore, be haphazard and arbitrary. If it chances to coincide with the child's activity it will get a leverage; if it does not, it will result in friction, or disintegration, or arrest of the child's nature.

I believe that knowledge of social conditions, of the present state of civilization, is necessary in order properly to interpret the child's powers. The child has his own instincts and tendencies, but we do not know what these mean until we can translate them into their social equivalents. We must be able to carry them back into a social past and see them as the inheritance of previous race activities. We must also be able to project them into the future to see what their outcome and end will be. In the illustration just used, it is the ability to see in the child's babblings the promise and potency of a future social intercourse and conversation which enables one to deal in the proper way with that instinct.

I believe that the psychological and social sides are organically related and that education cannot be regarded as a compromise between the two, or a superimposition of one upon the other. We are told that the psychological definition of education is barren and formal—that it gives us only the idea of a development of all the mental powers without giving us any idea of the use to which these powers are put. On the other hand, it is urged that the social definition of education, as getting adjusted to civilization, makes of it a forced and external process, and results in subordinating the freedom of the individual to a preconceived social and political status.

I believe that each of these objections is true when urged against one side isolated from the other. In order to know what a power really is we must know what its end, use, or function is; and this we cannot know save as we conceive of the individual as active in social relationships. But, on the other hand, the only possible adjustment which we can give to the child under existing conditions, is that which arises through putting him in complete possession of all his powers. With the advent of democracy and modern industrial conditions, it is impossible to foretell definitely just what civilization will be twenty years from now. Hence it is impossible to prepare the child for any precise set of conditions. To prepare him for the future life means to give him command of himself; it means so to train him that he will have the full and ready use of all his capacities; that his eye and ear and hand may be tools ready to command, that his judgment may be capable of grasping the conditions under which it has to work, and the executive forces be trained to act economically and efficiently. It is impossible to reach this sort of adjustment save as constant regard is had to the individual's own powers, tastes, and interests—say, that is, as education is continually converted into psychological terms.

In sum, I believe that the individual who is to be educated is a social individual and that society is an organic union of individuals. If we eliminate the social factor from the child we are left only with an abstraction; if we eliminate the individual factor from society, we are left only with an inert and lifeless mass. Education, therefore, must begin with a psychological insight into the child's capacities, interests, and habits. It must be controlled at every point by reference to these same considerations. These powers, interests, and habits must be continually interpreted—we must know what they mean. They must be translated into terms of their social equivalents—into terms of what they are capable of in the way of social service.

ARTICLE II: What the School Is

I believe that the school is primarily a social institution. Education being a social process, the school is simply that form of community life in which all those agencies are concentrated that will be most effective in bringing the child to share in the inherited resources of the race, and to use his own powers for social ends.

I believe that education, therefore, is a process of living and not a preparation for future living.

I believe that the school must represent present life—life as real and vital to the child as that which he carries on in the home, in the neighborhood, or on the playground.

I believe that education which does not occur through forms of life, or that are worth living for their own sake, is always a poor substitute for the genuine reality and tends to cramp and to deaden.

I believe that the school, as an institution, should simplify existing social life; should reduce it, as it were, to an embryonic form. Existing life is so complex that the child cannot be brought into contact with it without either confusion or distraction; he is either overwhelmed by the multiplicity of activities which are going on, so that he loses his own power of orderly reaction, or he is so stimulated by these various activities that his powers are prematurely called into play and he becomes either unduly specialized or else disintegrated.

I believe that as such simplified social life, the school life should grow gradually out of the home life; that it should take up and continue the activities with which the child is already familiar in the home.

I believe that it should exhibit these activities to the child, and reproduce them in such ways that the child will gradually learn the meaning of them, and be capable of playing his own part in relation to them.

I believe that this is a psychological necessity, because it is the only way of securing continuity in the child's growth, the only way of giving a background of past experience to the new ideas given in school.

I believe that it is also a social necessity because the home is the form of social life in which the child has been nurtured and in connection with which he has had his moral training. It is the business of the school to deepen and extend his sense of the values bound up in his home life.

I believe that much of present education fails because it neglects this fundamental principle of the school as a form of community life. It conceives the school as a place where certain information is to be given, where certain lessons are to be learned, or where certain habits are to be formed. The value of these is conceived as lying largely in the remote future; the child must do these things for the sake of something else he is to do; they are mere preparation. As a result they do not become a part of the life experience of the child and so are not truly educative.

I believe that the moral education centers upon this conception of the school as a mode of social life, that the best and deepest moral training is precisely that which one gets through having to enter into proper relations with others in a unity of work and thought. The present educational systems, so far as they destroy or neglect this unity, render it difficult or impossible to get any genuine, regular moral training.

I believe that the child should be stimulated and controlled in his work through the life of the community.

I believe that under existing conditions far too much of the stimulus and control proceeds from the teacher, because of neglect of the idea of the school as a form of social life.

I believe that the teacher's place and work in the school is to be interpreted from this same basis. The teacher is not in the school to impose certain ideas or to form certain habits in the child, but is there as a member of the community to select the influences which shall affect the child and to assist him in properly responding to these influences.

I believe that the discipline of the school should proceed from the life of the school as a whole and not directly from the teacher.

I believe that the teacher's business is simply to determine on the basis of larger experience and riper wisdom, how the discipline of life shall come to the child.

I believe that all questions of the grading of the child and his promotion should be determined by reference to the same standard. Examinations are of use only so far as they test the child's fitness for social life and reveal the place in which he can be of the most service and where he can receive the most help.

ARTICLE III: The Subject-Matter of Education

I believe that the social life of the child is the basis of concentration, or correlation, in all his training or growth. The social life gives the unconscious unity and the background of all his efforts and of all his attainments.

I believe that the subject-matter of the school curriculum should mark a gradual differentiation out of the primitive unconscious unity of social life.

I believe that we violate the child's nature and render difficult the best ethical results, by introducing the child too abruptly to a number of special studies, of reading, writing, geography, etc., out of relation to this social life.

I believe, therefore, that the true center of correlation on the school subjects is not science, nor literature, nor history, nor geography, but the child's own social activities.

I believe that education cannot be unified in the study of science, or so called nature study, because apart from human activity, nature itself is not a unity; nature in itself is a number of diverse objects in space and time, and to attempt to make it the center of work by itself, is to introduce a principle of radiation rather than one of concentration.

I believe that literature is the reflex expression and interpretation of social experience; that hence it must follow upon and not precede such experience. It, therefore, cannot be made the basis, although it may be made the summary of unification.

I believe once more that history is of educative value in so far as it presents phases of social life and growth. It must be controlled by reference to social life. When taken simply as history it is thrown into the distant past and becomes dead and inert. Taken as the record of man's social life and progress it becomes full of meaning. I believe, however, that it cannot be so taken excepting as the child is also introduced directly into social life.

I believe accordingly that the primary basis of education is in the child's powers at work along the same general constructive lines as those which have brought civilization into being.

I believe that the only way to make the child conscious of his social heritage is to enable him to perform those fundamental types of activity which make civilization what it is.

I believe, therefore, in the so-called expressive or constructive activities as the center of correlation.

I believe that this gives the standard for the place of cooking, sewing, manual training, etc., in the school.

I believe that they are not special studies which are to be introduced over and above a lot of others in the way of relaxation or relief, or as additional accomplishments. I believe rather that they represent, as types, fundamental forms of social activity; and that it is possible and desirable that the child's introduction into the more formal subjects of the curriculum be through the medium of these activities.

I believe that the study of science is educational in so far as it brings out the materials and processes which make social life what it is.

I believe that one of the greatest difficulties in the present teaching of science is that the material is presented in purely objective form, or is treated as a new peculiar kind of experience which the child can add to that which he has already had. In reality, science is of value because it gives the ability to interpret and control the experience already had. It should be introduced, not as so much new subject-matter, but as showing the factors already involved in previous experience and as furnishing tools by which that experience can be more easily and effectively regulated.

I believe that at present we lose much of the value of literature and language studies because of our elimination of the social element. Language is almost always treated in the books of pedagogy simply as the expression of thought. It is true that language is a logical instrument, but it is fundamentally and primarily a social instrument. Language is the device for communication; it is the tool through which one individual comes to share the ideas and feelings of others. When treated simply as a way of getting individual information, or as a means of showing off what one has learned, it loses its social motive and end.

I believe that there is, therefore, no succession of studies in the ideal school curriculum. If education is life, all life has, from the outset, a scientific aspect, an aspect of art and culture, and an aspect of communication. It cannot, therefore, be true that the proper studies for one grade are mere reading and writing, and that at a later grade, reading, or literature, or science, may be introduced. The progress is not in the succession of studies but in the development of new attitudes towards, and new interests in, experience.

I believe finally, that education must be conceived as a continuing re-construction of experience; that the process and the goal of education are one and the same thing.

I believe that to set up any end outside of education, as furnishing its goal and standard, is to deprive the educational process of much of its meaning and tends to make us rely upon false and external stimuli in dealing with the child.

ARTICLE IV: The Nature of Method

I believe that the question of method is ultimately reducible to the question of the order of development of the child's powers and interests. The law for presenting and treating material is the law implicit within the child's own nature. Because this is so I believe the following statements are of supreme importance as determining the spirit in which education is carried on:

I believe that the active side precedes the passive in the development of the child nature; that expression comes before conscious impression; that the muscular development precedes the sensory; that movements come before conscious sensations; I believe that consciousness is essentially motor or impulsive; that conscious states tend to project themselves in action.

I believe that the neglect of this principle is the cause of a large part of the waste of time and strength in school work. The child is thrown into a passive, receptive, or absorbing attitude. The conditions are such that he is not permitted to follow the law of his nature; the result is friction and waste.

I believe that ideas (intellectual and rational processes) also result from action and devolve for the sake of the better control of action. What we term reason is primarily the law of orderly or effective action. To attempt to develop the reasoning powers, the powers of judgment, without reference to the selection and arrangement of means in action, is the fundamental fallacy in our present methods of dealing with this matter. As a result we present the child with arbitrary symbols. Symbols are a necessity in mental development, but they have their place as tools for economizing effort; presented by themselves they are a mass of meaningless and arbitrary ideas imposed from without.

I believe that the image is the great instrument of instruction. What a child gets out of any subject presented to him is simply the images which he himself forms with regard to it.

I believe that if nine tenths of the energy at present directed towards making the child learn certain things, were spent in seeing to it that the child was forming proper images, the work of instruction would be indefinitely facilitated.

I believe that much of the time and attention now given to the preparation and presentation of lessons might be more wisely and profitably expended in training the child's power of imagery and in seeing to it that he was continually forming definite, vivid, and growing images of the various subjects with which he comes in contact in his experience.

I believe that interests are the signs and symptoms of growing power. I believe that they represent dawning capacities. Accordingly the constant and careful observation of interests is of the utmost importance for the educator.

I believe that these interests are to be observed as showing the state of development which the child has reached.

I believe that they prophesy the stage upon which he is about to enter.

I believe that only through the continual and sympathetic observation of childhood's interests can the adult enter into the child's life and see what it is ready for, and upon what material it could work most readily and fruitfully.

I believe that these interests are neither to be humored nor repressed. To repress interest is to substitute the adult for the child, and so to weaken intellectual curiosity and alertness, to suppress initiative, and to deaden interest. To humor the interests is to substitute the transient for the permanent. The interest is always the sign of some power below; the important thing is to discover this power. To humor the interest is to fail to penetrate below the surface and its sure result is to substitute caprice and whim for genuine interest.

I believe that the emotions are the reflex of actions.

I believe that to endeavor to stimulate or arouse the emotions apart from their corresponding activities, is to introduce an unhealthy and morbid state of mind.

I believe that if we can only secure right habits of action and thought, with reference to the good, the true, and the beautiful, the emotions will for the most part take care of themselves.

I believe that next to deadness and dullness, formalism and routine, our education is threatened with no greater evil than sentimentalism.

I believe that this sentimentalism is the necessary result of the attempt to divorce feeling from action.

ARTICLE V: The School and Social Progress

I believe that education is the fundamental method of social progress and reform.

I believe that all reforms which rest simply upon the enactment of law, or the threatening of certain penalties, or upon changes in mechanical or outward arrangements, are transitory and futile.

I believe that education is a regulation of the process of coming to share in the social consciousness; and that the adjustment of individual activity on the basis of this social consciousness is the only sure method of social reconstruction.

I believe that this conception has due regard for both the individualistic and socialistic ideals. It is duly individual because it recognizes the formation of a certain character as the only genuine basis of right living. It is socialistic because it recognizes that this right character is not to be formed by merely individual precept, example, or exhortation, but rather by the influence of a certain form of institutional or community life upon the individual, and that the social organism through the school, as its organ, may determine ethical results.

I believe that in the ideal school we have the reconciliation of the individualistic and the institutional ideals.

I believe that the community's duty to education is, therefore, its paramount moral duty. By law and punishment, by social agitation and discussion, society can regulate and form itself in a more or less haphazard and chance way. But through education society can formulate its own purposes, can organize its own means and resources, and thus shape itself with definiteness and economy in the direction in which it wishes to move.

I believe that when society once recognizes the possibilities in this direction, and the obligations which these possibilities impose, it is impossible to conceive of the resources of time, attention, and money which will be put at the disposal of the educator.

I believe that it is the business of every one interested in education to insist upon the school as the primary and most effective interest of social progress and reform in order that society may be awakened to realize what the school stands for, and aroused to the necessity of endowing the educator with sufficient equipment properly to perform his task.

I believe that education thus conceived marks the most perfect and intimate union of science and art conceivable in human experience.

I believe that the art of thus giving shape to human powers and adapting them to social service, is the supreme art; one calling into its service the best of artists; that no insight, sympathy, tact, executive power, is too great for such service.

I believe that with the growth of psychological service, giving added insight into individual structure and laws of growth; and with growth of social science, adding to our knowledge of the right organization of individuals, all scientific resources can be utilized for the purposes of education.

I believe that when science and art thus join hands the most commanding motive for human action will be reached; the most genuine springs of human conduct aroused and the best service that human nature is capable of guaranteed.

I believe, finally, that the teacher is engaged, not simply in the training of individuals, but in the formation of the proper social life.

I believe that every teacher should realize the dignity of his calling; that he is a social servant set apart for the maintenance of proper social order and the securing of the right social growth.

I believe that in this way the teacher always is the prophet of the true God and the usherer in of the true kingdom of God.

Excerpt from *School and Society,* 1900

The School and Social Progress

We are apt to look at the school from an individualistic standpoint, as something between teacher and pupil, or between teacher and parent. That which interests us most is naturally the progress made by the individual child of our acquaintance, his normal physical development, his advance in ability to read, write, and figure, his growth in the knowledge of geography and improvement in manners, habits of promptness, order, and industry—it is from such standards as these that we judge the work of the school. And rightly so. Yet the range of the out-look needs to be enlarged. What the best and wisest parents wants for his own child, that must the community want for all of its children. Any other ideal for our schools is narrow and unlovely; acted upon, it destroys our democracy. All that society has accomplished for itself is put, through the agency of the school, at the disposal of its future members. All its better thoughts of itself it hopes to realize through the new possibilities thus opened to its future self. Here individualism and socialism are at one. Only by being true to the full growth of all the individuals who make it up, can society by any chance be true to itself. And in the self-direction thus given, nothing counts as much as the school, for, as Horace Mann said, "Where anything is growing, one former is worth a thousand re-formers."

Whenever we have in mind the discussion of a new movement in education, it is especially necessary to take the broader, or social, view. Otherwise, changes in the school institution and tradition will be looked at as the arbitrary inventions of particular teachers, at the worst transitory fads, and at the best merely improvements in certain details—and this is the plane upon which it is too customary to consider school changes. It is as rational to conceive of the locomotive or the telegraph as personal devices. The modification going on in the method and curriculum of education is as much a product of the changed social situation, and as much an effort to meet the needs of the new society that is forming, as are changes in modes of industry and commerce.

It is to this, then, that I especially ask your attention: the effort to conceive what roughly may be termed the "New Education" in the light of larger changes in society. Can we connect this "New Education" with the general march of events? If we can, it will lose its isolated character; it will cease to be an affair which proceeds only from the over-ingenious minds of pedagogues dealing with particular pupils. It will appear as part and parcel of the whole social evolution, and, in its more general features at least, as inevitable. Let us then ask after the main aspects of the social movement; and afterward turn to the school to find what witness it gives of effort to put itself in line. And since it is quite impossible to cover the whole ground, I shall for the most part confine myself in this chapter to one typical thing in the modern school movement—that which passes under the name of manual training—hoping, if the relation of that to changed social conditions appears, we shall be ready to concede the point as well regarding other educational innovations.

I make no apology for not dwelling at length upon the social changes in question. Those I shall mention are writ so large that he who runs may read. The change that comes first to mind, the one that overshadows and even controls all others, is the industrial one—the application of science resulting in the great inventions that have utilized the forces of nature on a vast and inexpensive scale: the growth of a world-wide market as the object of production, of vast manufacturing centers to supply this market, of cheap and rapid means of communication and distribution between all its parts. Even as to its feebler beginnings, this change is not much more than a century old; in many of its most important aspects it falls within the short span of those now living. One can hardly believe there has been a revolution in all history so rapid, so extensive, so complete. Through it the face of the earth is making over, even as to its physical forms; political boundaries are wiped out and moved about, as if they were indeed only lines on a paper map; population is hurriedly gathered into cities from the ends of the earth; habits of living are altered with startling abruptness and thoroughness; the search for the truths of nature is infinitely stimulated and facilitated, and their application to life made not only practicable, but commercially necessary. Even our moral and religious ideas and interests, the most conservative because the deepest-lying things in our nature, are profoundly affected. That this revolution should not affect education in some other than a formal and superficial fashion is inconceivable.

Back of the factory system lies the household and neighborhood system. Those of us who are here today need go back only one, two, or at most three generations, to find a time when the household was practically the center in which were carried on, or about which were clustered, all the typical forms of industrial occupation. The clothing worn was for the most part made in the house; the members of the household were usually familiar also with the shearing of the sheep, the carding and spinning of the wool, and the plying of the loom. Instead of pressing a button and flooding the house with electric light, the whole process of getting illumination was followed in its toilsome length from the killing of the animal and the trying of fat to the making of wicks and dipping of candles. The supply of flour, of lumber, of foods, of building materials, of household furniture, even of metal ware, of nails, hinges, hammers, etc., was produced in the immediate neighborhood, in shops which were constantly open to inspection and often centers of neighborhood congregation. The entire industrial process stood revealed, from the production on the farm of the raw materials till the finished article was actually put to use. Not only this, but practically every member of the household had his own share in the work. The children, as they gained in strength and capacity, were gradually initiated into the mysteries of the several processes. It was a matter of immediate and personal concern, even to the point of actual participation.

We cannot overlook the factors of discipline and of character-building involved in this kind of life: training in habits of order and of industry, and in the idea of responsibility, of obligation to do something, to produce something, in the world. There was always something which really needed to be done, and a real necessity that each member of the household should do his own part faithfully and in co-operation with others. Personalities which became effective in action were bred and tested in the medium of action. Again, we cannot overlook the importance for educational purposes of the close and intimate acquaintance got with nature at first hand, with real things and materials, with the actual processes of their manipulation, and the knowledge of their social necessities and uses. In all this there was continual training of observation, of ingenuity, constructive imagination, of logical thought, and of the sense of reality acquired through first-hand contact with actualities. The educative forces of the domestic spinning and weaving, of the sawmill, the gristmill, the cooper shop, and the blacksmith forge, were continuously operative.

No number of object-lessons, got up as object-lessons for the sake of giving information, can afford even the shadow of a substitute for acquaintance with the plants and animals of the farm and garden acquired through actual living among them and caring for them. No training of sense-organs in school, introduced for the sake of training, can begin to compete with the alertness and fullness of sense-life that comes through daily intimacy and interest in familiar occupations. Verbal memory can be trained in committing tasks, a certain discipline of the reasoning powers can be acquired through lessons in science and mathematics; but, after all, this is somewhat remote and shadowy compared with the training of attention and of judgment that is acquired in having to do things with a real motive behind and a real outcome ahead. At present, concentration of industry and division of labor have practically eliminated household and neighborhood occupations—at least for educational purposes. But it is useless to bemoan the departure of the good old days of children's modesty, reverence, and implicit obedience, if we expect merely by bemoaning and by exhortation to bring them back. It is radical conditions which have changed, and only an equally radical change in education suffices. We must recognize our compensations—the increase in toleration, in breadth of social judgment, the larger acquaintance with human nature, the sharpened alertness in reading signs of character and interpreting social situations, greater accuracy of adaptation to differing personalities, contact with greater commercial activities. These considerations mean much to the city-bred child of today. Yet there is a real problem: how shall we retain these advantages, and yet introduce into the school something representing the other side of life-occupations which exact personal responsibilities and which train the child in relation to the physical realities of life?

When we turn to the school, we find that one of the most striking tendencies at present is toward the introduction of so-called manual training, shopwork, and the household arts—sewing and cooking.

This has not been done "on purpose," with a full consciousness that the school must now supply that factor of training formerly taken care of in the home, but rather by instinct, by experimenting and finding that such work takes a vital hold of pupils and gives them something which was not to be got in any other way. Consciousness of its real import is still so weak that the work is often done in a half-hearted, confused, and unrelated way. The reasons assigned to justify it are painfully inadequate or sometimes even positively wrong.

If we were to cross-examine even those who are most favorably disposed to the introduction of this work into our school system, we should, I imagine, generally find the main reasons to be that such work engages the full spontaneous interest and attention of the children. It keeps them alert and active, instead of passive and receptive; it makes them more useful, more capable, and hence more inclined to be helpful at home; it prepares them to some extent for the practical duties of later life—the girls to be more efficient house managers, if not actually cooks and seamstresses; the boys (were our educational system only adequately rounded out into trade schools) for their future vocations. I do not underestimate the worth of these reasons. Of those indicated by the changed attitude of the children I shall indeed have something to say in the next chapter, when speaking directly of the relationship of the school to the child. But the point of view is, upon the whole, unnecessarily narrow. We must conceive of work in wood and metal, of weaving, sewing, and cooking, as methods of living and learning, not as distinct studies.

We must conceive of them in their social significance, as types of the processes by which society keeps itself going, as agencies for bringing home to the child some of the primal necessities of community life, and as ways in which these needs have been met by the growing insight and ingenuity of man; in short, as instrumentalities through which the school itself shall be made a genuine form of active community life, instead of a place set apart in which to learn lessons.

A society is a number of people held together because they are working along common lines, in a common spirit, and with reference to common aims. The common needs and aims demand a growing interchange of thought and growing unity of sympathetic feeling. The radical reason that the present school cannot organize itself as a natural social unit is because just this element of common and productive activity is absent. Upon the playground, in game and sport, social organization takes place spontaneously and inevitably. There is something to do, some activity to be carried on, requiring natural divisions of labor, selection of leaders and followers, mutual co-operation and emulation. In the schoolroom the motive and the cement of social organization are alike wanting. Upon the ethical side, the tragic weakness of the present school is that it endeavors to prepare future members of the social order in a medium in which the conditions of the social spirit are eminently wanting.

The difference that appears when occupations are made the articulating centers of school life is not easy to describe in words; it is a difference in motive, of spirit and atmosphere. As one enters a busy kitchen in which a group of children are actively engaged in the preparation of food, the psychological difference, the change from more or less passive and inert recipiency and restraint to one of buoyant outgoing energy, is so obvious as fairly to strike one in the face. Indeed, to those whose image of the school is rigidly set the change is sure to give a shock. But the change in the social attitude is equally marked. The mere absorbing of facts and truths is so exclusively individual an affair that it tends very naturally to pass into selfishness. There is no obvious social motive for the acquirement of mere learning, there is no clear social gain in success thereat. Indeed, almost the only measure for success is a competitive one, in the bad sense of that term—a comparison of results in the recitation or in the examination to see which child has succeeded in getting ahead of others in storing up, in accumulating, the maximum of information. So thoroughly is this the prevailing atmosphere that for one child to help another in his task has become a school crime. Where the school work consists in simply learning lessons, mutual assistance, instead of being the most natural form of co-operation and association, becomes a clandestine effort to relieve one's neighbor of his proper duties. Where active work is going on, all this is changed. Helping others, instead of being a form of charity which impoverishes the recipient, is simply an aid in setting free the powers and furthering the impulse of the one helped. A spirit of free communication, of interchange of ideas, suggestions, results, both successes and failures of previous experiences, becomes the dominating note of the recitation. So far as emulation enters in, it is in the comparison of individuals, not with regard to the quantity of information personally absorbed, but with reference to the quality of work done—the genuine community standard of value. In an informal but all the more pervasive way, the school life organizes itself on a social basis.

Within this organization is found the principle of school discipline or order. Of course, order is simply a thing which is relative to an end. If you have the end in view of forty or fifty children learning certain set lessons, to be recited to a teacher, your discipline must be devoted to securing that result. But if the end in view is the development of a spirit of social co-operation and community life, discipline must grow out of and be rela-

School + school discipline merely mimics real life.

tive to such an aim. There is little of one sort of order where things are in process of construction; there is a certain disorder in any busy workshop; there is not silence; persons are not engaged in maintaining certain fixed physical postures; their arms are not folded; they are not holding their books thus and so. They are doing a variety of things, and there is the confusion, the bustle, that results from activity. But out of the occupation, out of doing things that are to produce results, and out of doing these in a social and co-operative way, there is born a discipline of its own kind and type. Our whole conception of school discipline changes when we get this point of view. In critical moments we all realize that the only discipline that stands by us, the only training that becomes intuition, is that got through life itself. That we learn from experience, and from books or the sayings of others only as they are related to experience, are not mere phrases. But the school has been so set apart, so isolated from the ordinary conditions and motives of life, that the place where children are sent for discipline is the one place in the world where it is most difficult to get experience—the mother of all discipline worth the name. It is only when a narrow and fixed image of traditional school discipline dominates that one is in any danger of overlooking that deeper and infinitely wider discipline that comes from having a part to do in constructive work, in contributing to a result which, social in spirit, is none the less obvious and tangible in form—and hence in a form with reference to which responsibility may be exacted and accurate judgment passed.

The great thing to keep in mind, then, regarding the introduction into the school of various forms of active occupation, is that through them the entire spirit of the school is renewed. It has a chance to affiliate itself with life, to become the child's habitat, where he learns through directed living, instead of being only a place to learn lessons having an abstract and remote reference to some possible living to be done in the future. It gets a chance to be a miniature community, an embryonic society. This is the fundamental fact, and from this arise continuous and orderly streams of instruction. Under the industrial regime described, the child, after all, shared in the work, not for the sake of the sharing, but for the sake of the product. The educational results secured were real, yet incidental and dependent. But in the school the typical occupations followed are freed from all economic stress. The aim is not the economic value of the products, but the development of social power and insight. It is this liberation from narrow utilities, this openness to the possibilities of the human spirit, that makes these practical activities in the school allies of art and centers of science and history.

The unity of all the sciences is found in geography. The significance of geography is that it presents the earth as the enduring home of the occupations of man. The world without its relationship to human activity is less than a world. Human industry and achievement, apart from their roots in the earth, are not even a sentiment, hardly a name. The earth is the final source of all man's food. It is his continual shelter and protection, the raw material of all his activities, and the home to whose humanizing and idealizing all his achievement returns. It is the great field, the great mine, the great source of the energies of heat, light, and electricity; the great scene of ocean, stream, mountain, and plain, of which all our agriculture and mining and lumbering, all our manufacturing and distributing agencies, are but the partial elements and factors. It is through occupations determined by this environment that mankind has made its historical and political progress. It is through these occupations that the intellectual and emotional interpretation of nature has been developed. It is through what we do in and with the world that we read its meaning and measure its value.

In educational terms, this means that these occupations in the school shall not be mere practical devices or modes of routine employment, the gaining of better technical skill as cooks, seam-stresses, or carpenters, but active centers of scientific insight into natural materials and processes, points of departure whence children shall be led out into a realization of the historic development of man. The actual significance of this can be told better through one illustration taken from actual school work than by general discourse.

There is nothing which strikes more oddly upon the average intelligent visitor than to see boys as well as girls of ten, twelve, and thirteen years of age engaged in sewing and weaving. If we look at this from the standpoint of preparation of the boys for sewing on buttons and making patches, we get a narrow and utilitarian conception—a basis that hardly justifies giving prominence to this sort of work in the school. But if we look at it from another side, we find that this work gives the point of departure from which the child can trace and follow the progress of mankind in history, getting an insight also into the materials used and the mechanical principles involved. In connection with these occupations the historic development of man is recapitulated. For example, the children are first given the raw material— the flax, the cotton plant, the wool as it comes from the back of the sheep (if we could take them to the place where the sheep are sheared, so much the better). Then a study is made of these materials from the standpoint of their adaptation to the uses to which they may be put. For instance, a comparison of the cotton fiber with wool fiber is made. I did not know, until the children told me, that the reason for the late development of the cotton industry as compared with the woolen is that the cotton fiber is so very difficult to free by hand from the seeds. The children in one group worked thirty minutes freeing cotton fibers from the boll and seeds, and succeeded in getting out less than one ounce. They could easily believe that one person could gin only one pound a day by hand, and could understand why their ancestors wore woolen instead of cotton clothing. Among other things discovered as affecting their relative utilities was the shortness of the cotton fiber as compared with that of wool, the former averaging, say, one-third of an inch in length, while the latter run to three inches in length; also that the fibers of cotton are smooth and do not cling together, while the wool has a certain roughness which makes the fibers stick, thus assisting the spinning. The children worked this out for themselves with the actual material, aided by questions and suggestions from the teacher.

They then followed the processes necessary for working the fibers up into cloth. They reinvented the first frame for carding the wool—a couple of boards with sharp pins in them for scratching it out. They re-devised the simplest process for spinning the wool—a pierced stone or some other weight through which the wool is passed, and which as it is twirled draws out the fiber; next the top, which was spun on the floor, while the children kept the wool in their hands until it was gradually drawn out and wound upon it. Then the children are introduced to the invention next in historic order, working it out experimentally, thus seeing its necessity, and tracing its effects, not only upon that particular industry, but upon modes of social life—in this way passing in review the entire process up to the present complete loom, and all that goes with the application of science in the use of our present available powers. I need not speak of the science involved in this—the study of the fibers, of geographical features, the conditions under which raw materials are grown, the great centers of manufacture and distribution, the physics involved in the machinery of production; nor, again, of the historical side—the influence which these inventions have had upon humanity. You can concentrate the history of all mankind into the evolution of the flax, cotton, and wool fibers into clothing. I do not mean that this is the only, or the best, center. But it is true that certain very real and important avenues to the consideration of the history of the race are thus opened—that the mind is introduced to much more fundamental and controlling influences than appear in the political and chronological records that usually pass for history.

Now what is true of this one instance of fibers used in fabrics (and, of course, I have only spoken of one or two elementary phases of that) is true in its measure of every material used in every occupation, and of the processes employed. The occupation supplies the child with a genuine motive; it gives him experience at first hand; it brings him into contact with realities. It does all this, but in addition it is liberalized throughout by

Deeper knowledge/ understanding

translation into its historic and social values and scientific equivalencies. With the growth of the child's mind in power and knowledge it ceases to be a pleasant occupation merely and becomes more and more a medium, an instrument, an organ of understanding—and is thereby transformed.

This, in turn, has its bearing upon the teaching of science. Under present conditions, all activity, to be successful, has to be directed somewhere and somehow by the scientific expert—it is a case of applied science. This connection should determine its place in education. It is not only that the occupations, the so-called manual or industrial work in the school, give the opportunity for the introduction of science which illuminates them, which makes them material, freighted with meaning, instead of being mere devices of hand and eye; but that the scientific insight thus gained becomes an indispensable instrument of free and active participation in modern social life. Plato somewhere speaks of the slave as one who in his actions does not express his own ideas, but those of some other man. It is our social problem now, even more urgent than in the time of Plato, that method, purpose, understanding, shall exist in the consciousness of the one who does the work, that his activity shall have meaning to himself.

When occupations in the school are conceived in this broad and generous way, I can only stand lost in wonder at the objections so often heard, that such occupations are out of place in the school because they arc materialistic, utilitarian, or even menial in their tendency. It sometimes seems to me that those who make these objections must live in quite another world. The world in which most of us live is a world in which everyone has a calling and occupation, something to do. Some are managers and others are subordinates. But the great thing for one as for the other is that each shall have had the education which enables him to see within his daily work all there is in it of large and human significance. How many of the employed are today mere appendages to the machines which they operate! This may be due in part to the machine itself or the regime which lays so much stress upon the products of the machine; but it is certainly due in large part to the fact that the worker has had no opportunity to develop his imagination and his sympathetic insight as to the social and scientific values found in his work. At present, the impulses which lie at the basis of the industrial system are either practically neglected or positively distorted during the school period. Until the instincts of construction and production are systematically laid hold of in the years of childhood and youth, until they are trained in social directions, enriched by historical interpretation, controlled and illuminated by scientific methods, we certainly are in no position even to locate the source of our economic evils, much less to deal with them effectively.

If we go back a few centuries, we find a practical monopoly of learning. The term possession of learning is, indeed, a happy one. Learning was a class matter. This was a necessary result of social conditions. There were not in existence any means by which the multitude could possibly have access to intellectual resources. These were stored up and hidden away in manuscripts. Of these there were at best only a few, and it required long and toilsome preparation to be able to do anything with them. A high-priesthood of learning, which guarded the treasury of truth and which doled it out to the masses under severe restrictions, was the inevitable expression of these conditions. But, as a direct result of the industrial revolution of which we have been speaking, this has been changed. Printing was invented; it was made commercial. Books, magazines, papers were multiplied and cheapened. As a result of the locomotive and telegraph, frequent, rapid, and cheap intercommunication by mails and electricity was called into being. Travel has been rendered easy; freedom of movement, with its accompanying exchange of ideas, indefinitely facilitated. The result has been an intellectual revolution. Learning has been put into circulation. While there still is, and probably always will be, a particular class having the special business of inquiry in hand, a distinctively learned class is henceforth out of the question. It is an anachronism. Knowledge is no longer an immobile solid; it has been liquefied. It is actively moving in all the currents of society itself.

It is easy to see that this revolution, as regards the materials of knowledge, carries with it a marked change in the attitude of the individual. Stimuli of an intellectual sort pour in upon us in all kinds of ways. The merely intellectual life, the life of scholarship and of learning, thus gets a very altered value. Academic and scholastic, instead of being titles of honor, are becoming terms of reproach.

But all this means a necessary change in the attitude of the school, one of which we are as yet far from realizing the full force. Our school methods, and to a very considerable extent our curriculum, are inherited from the period when learning and command of certain symbols, affording as they did the only access to learning, were all-important. The ideals of this period are still largely in control, even where the outward methods and studies have been changed. We sometimes hear the introduction of manual training, art, and science into the elementary, and even the secondary, schools deprecated on the ground that they tend toward the production of specialists—that they detract from our present scheme of generous, liberal culture. The point of this objection would be ludicrous if it were not often so effective as to make it tragic. It is our present education which is highly specialized, one-sided, and narrow. It is an education dominated almost entirely by the mediaeval conception of learning. It is something which appeals for the most part simply to the intellectual aspect of our natures, our desire to learn, to accumulate information, and to get control of the symbols of learning; not to our impulses and tendencies to make, to do, to create, to produce, whether in the form of utility or of art. The very fact that manual training, art, and science are objected to as technical, as tending toward mere specialism, is of itself as good testimony as could be offered to the specialized aim which controls current education. Unless education had been virtually identified with the exclusively intellectual pursuits, with learning as such, all these materials and methods would be welcome, would be greeted with the utmost hospitality.

While training for the profession of learning is regarded as the type of culture, or a liberal education, the training of a mechanic, a musician, a lawyer, a doctor, a farmer, a merchant, or a rail-road manager is regarded as purely technical and professional. The result is that which we see about us everywhere—the division into "cultured" people and "workers," the separation of theory and practice. Hardly 1 per cent of the entire school population ever attains to what we call higher education; only 5 per cent to the grade of our high school; while much more than half leave on or before the completion of the fifth year of the elementary grade. The simple facts of the case are that in the great majority of human beings the distinctively intellectual interest is not dominant. They have the so-called practical impulse and disposition. In many of those in whom by nature intellectual interest is strong, social conditions prevent its adequate realization. Consequently by far the larger number of pupils leave school as soon as they have acquired the rudiments of learning, as soon as they have enough of the symbols of reading, writing, and calculating to be of practical use to them in getting a living. While our educational leaders are talking of culture, the development of personality, etc., as the end and aim of education, the great majority of those who pass under the tuition of the school regard it only as a narrowly practical tool with which to get bread and butter enough to eke out a restricted life. If we were to conceive our educational end and aim in a less exclusive way, if we were to introduce into educational processes the activities which appeal to those whose dominant interest is to do and to make, we should find the hold of the school upon its members to be more vital, more prolonged, containing more of culture.

But why should I make this labored presentation? The obvious fact is that our social life has undergone a thorough and radical change. If our education is to have any meaning for life, it must pass through an equally complete transformation. This transformation is not something to appear suddenly, to be executed in a day by conscious purpose. It is already in progress. Those modifications of our school system which often appear (even to

Experiential learning

those most actively concerned with them, to say nothing of their spectators) to be mere changes of detail, mere improvement within the school mechanism, are in reality signs and evidences of evolution. The introduction of active occupations, of nature-study, of elementary science, of art, of history; the relegation of the merely symbolic and formal to a secondary position; the change in the moral school atmosphere, in the relation of pupils and teachers—of discipline; the introduction of more active, expressive, and self-directing factors—all these are not mere accidents, they are necessities of the larger social evolution. It remains but to organize all these factors, to appreciate them in their fullness of meaning, and to put the ideas and ideals involved into complete, uncompromising possession of our school system. To do this means to make each one of our schools an embryonic community life, active with types of occupations that reflect the life of the larger society and permeated throughout with the spirit of art, history, and science. When the school introduces and trains each child of society into membership within such a little community, saturating him with the spirit of service, and providing him with the instruments of effective self-direction, we shall have the deepest and best guaranty of a larger society which is worthy, lovely, and harmonious.

The School and the Life of the Child

In the last chapter I tried to set forth the relationship between the school and the larger life of the community, and the necessity for certain changes in the methods and materials of school work, that it might be better adapted to present social needs.

Here I wish to look at the matter from the other side and consider the relationship of the school to the life and development of the children in the school. As it is difficult to connect general principles with such thoroughly concrete things as little children, I have taken the liberty of introducing a great deal of illustrative matter from the work of the University Elementary School, that in some measure you may appreciate the way in which the ideas presented work themselves out in actual practice.

Some few years ago I was looking about the school supply stores in the city, trying to find desks and chairs which seemed thoroughly suitable from all points of view—artistic, hygienic, and educational—to the needs of the children. We had a great deal of difficulty in finding what we needed, and finally one dealer, more intelligent than the rest, made this remark: "I am afraid we have not what you want. You want something at which the children may work; these are all for listening." That tells the story of the traditional education. Just as the biologist can take a bone or two and reconstruct the whole animal, so, if we put before the mind's eye the ordinary schoolroom, with its rows of ugly desks placed in geometrical order, crowded together so that there shall be as little moving room as possible, desks almost all of the same size, with just space enough to hold books, pencils, and paper, and add a table, some chairs, the bare walls, and possibly a few pictures, we can reconstruct the only educational activity that can possibly go on in such a place. It is all made "for listening"—because simply studying lessons out of a book is only another kind of listening; it marks the dependency of one mind upon another. The attitude of listening means, comparatively speaking, passivity, absorption; that there are certain ready-made materials which are there, which have been prepared by the school superintendent, the board, the teacher, and of which the child is to take in as much as possible in the least possible time.

There is very little place in the traditional schoolroom for the child to work. The workshop, the laboratory, the materials, the tools with which the child may construct, create, and actively inquire, and even the requisite space, have been for the most part lacking. The things that have to do with these processes have not even a definitely recognized place in education. They are what the educational authorities who write editorials in the daily papers generally term "fads" and "frills." A lady told me yesterday that she had been visiting different schools trying to find one where activity on the part of the children preceded the giving of information on the part of the teacher, or where the children had some motive for demanding the information. She visited, she said, twenty-four different schools before she found her first instance. I may add that that was not in this city.

Another thing that is suggested by these schoolrooms, with their set desks, is that everything is arranged for handling as large numbers of children as possible; for dealing with children en masse, as an aggregate of units; involving, again, that they be

treated passively. The moment children act they individualize themselves; they cease to be a mass and become the intensely distinctive beings that we are acquainted with out of school, in the home, the family, on the playground, and in the neighborhood.

On the same basis is explicable the uniformity of method and curriculum. If everything is on a "listening" basis, you can have uniformity of material and method. The ear, and the book which reflects the ear, constitute the medium which is alike for all. There is next to no opportunity for adjustment to varying capacities and demands. There is a certain amount—a fixed quantity—of ready-made results and accomplishments to be acquired by all children alike in a given time. It is in response to this demand that the curriculum has been developed from the elementary school up through the college. There is just so much desirable knowledge, and there are just so many needed technical accomplishments in the world. Then comes the mathematical problem of dividing this by the six, twelve, or sixteen years of school life. Now give the children every year just the proportionate fraction of the total, and by the time they have finished they will have mastered the whole. By covering so much ground during this hour or day or week or year, everything comes out with perfect evenness at the end—provided the children have not forgotten what they have previously learned. The outcome of all this is Matthew Arnold's report of the statement, proudly made to him by an educational authority in France, that so many thousands of children were studying at a given hour, say eleven o'clock, just such a lesson in geography; and in one of our own western cities this proud boast used to be repeated to successive visitors by its superintendent.

I may have exaggerated somewhat in order to make plain the typical points of the old education: its passivity of attitude, its mechanical massing of children, its uniformity of curriculum and method. It may be summed up by stating that the center of gravity is outside the child. It is in the teacher, the textbook, anywhere and everywhere you please except in the immediate instincts and activities of the child himself. On that basis there is not much to be said about the life of the child. A good deal might be said about the studying of the child, but the school is not the place where the child lives. Now the change which is coming into our education is the shifting of the center of gravity. It is a change, a revolution, not unlike that introduced by Copernicus when the astronomical center shifted from the earth to the sun. In this case the child becomes the sun about which the appliances of education revolve; he is the center about which they are organized.

If we take an example from an ideal home, where the parent is intelligent enough to recognize what is best for the child, and is able to supply what is needed, we find the child learning through the social converse and constitution of the family. There are certain points of interest and value to him in the conversation carried on: statements are made, inquiries arise, topics are discussed, and the child continually learns. He states his experiences, his misconceptions are corrected. Again the child participates in the household occupations, and thereby gets habits of industry, order, and regard for the rights and ideas of others, and the fundamental habit of subordinating his activities to the general interest of the household. Participation in these household tasks becomes an opportunity for gaining knowledge. The ideal home would naturally have a workshop where the child could work out his constructive instincts. It would have a miniature laboratory in which his inquiries could be directed. The life of the child would extend out of doors to the garden, surrounding fields, and forests. He would have his excursions, his walks and talks, in which the larger world out of doors would open to him.

Now, if we organize and generalize all of this, we have the ideal school. There is no mystery about it, no wonderful discovery of pedagogy or educational theory. It is simply a question of doing systematically and in a large, intelligent, and competent way what for various reasons can be done in most households only in a comparatively meager and haphazard manner. In the first place, the ideal home has to be enlarged. The child must be brought into contact with more grown people and with more children in order that there may be the freest and richest social life. Moreover, the occupations and relationships of the home environment are not specially selected for the growth of the child; the main object is something else, and what the child can get out of them is incidental. Hence the need of a school. In this school the life of the child becomes the all-controlling aim. All the media necessary to further the growth of the child center there. Learning certainly, but living primarily, and learning through and in relation to this living. When we take the life of the child centered and organized in this way, we do not find that he is first of all a listening being; quite the contrary.

The statement so frequently made that education means "drawing out" is excellent, if we mean simply to contrast it with the process of pouring in. But, after all, it is difficult to connect the idea of drawing out with the ordinary doings of the child of three, four, seven, or eight years of age. He is already running over, spilling over, with activities of all kinds. He is not a purely latent being whom the adult has to approach with great caution and skill in order gradually to draw out some hidden germ of activity. The child is already intensely active, and the question of education is the question of taking hold of his activities, of giving them direction. Through direction, through organized use, they tend toward valuable results, instead of scattering or being left to merely impulsive expression.

If we keep this before us, the difficulty I find uppermost in the minds of many people regarding what is termed the new education is not so much solved as dissolved; it disappears. A question often asked is: If you begin with the child's ideas, impulses, and interests, all so crude, so random and scattering, so little refined or spiritualized, how is he going to get the necessary discipline, culture, and information? If there were no way open to us except to excite and indulge these impulses of the child, the question might well be asked. We should either have to ignore and repress the activities or else to humor them. But if we have organization of equipment and of materials, there is another path open to us. We can direct the child's activities, giving them exercise along certain lines, and can thus lead up to the goal which logically stands at the end of the paths followed.

"If wishes were horses, beggars would ride." Since they are not, since really to satisfy an impulse or interest means to work it out, and working it out involves running up against obstacles, becoming acquainted with materials, exercising ingenuity, patience, persistence, alertness, it of necessity involves discipline—ordering of power—and supplies knowledge. Take the example of the little child who wants to make a box. If he stops short with the imagination or wish, he certainly will not get discipline. But when he attempts to realize his impulse, it is a question of making his idea definite, making it into a plan, of taking the right kind of wood, measuring the parts needed, giving them the necessary proportions, etc. There is involved the preparation of materials, the sawing, planing, the sandpapering, making all the edges and corners to fit. Knowledge of tools and processes is inevitable. If the child realizes his instinct and makes the box, there is plenty of opportunity to gain discipline and perseverance, to exercise effort in overcoming obstacles, and to attain as well a great deal of information.

So undoubtedly the little child who thinks he would like to cook has little idea of what it means or costs, or what it requires. It is simply a desire to "mess around," perhaps to imitate the activities of older people. And it is doubtless possible to let ourselves down to that level and simply humor that interest. But here, too, if the impulse is exercised, utilized, it rims up against the actual world of hard conditions, to which it must accommodate itself; and there again come in the factors of discipline and knowledge. One of the children became impatient, recently, at having to work things out by a long method of experimentation, and said, "Why do we bother with this? Let's follow a recipe in a cookbook." The teacher asked the children where the recipe came from, and the conversation showed that if they simply followed this they would not understand the reasons for what they were doing. They were then quite willing to go on with the experimental work. To follow that work will, indeed, give an illustration of just the point in question. Their occupation happened that day to be the cooking of eggs, as making a transition from the cooking of vegetables to that of meats. In order to get a basis of comparison they first summarized the constituent food elements in the vegetables and made a preliminary comparison with those found in meat. Thus they found that the woody fiber or cellulose in vegetables corresponded to the connective tissue in meat, giving the element of form and structure. They found that starch and starchy products were characteristic of the vegetables, that mineral salts were found in both alike, and that there was fat in both—a small quantity in vegetable food and a large amount in animal. They were prepared then to take up the study of albumen as the characteristic feature of animal food, corresponding to starch in the vegetables, and were ready to consider the conditions requisite for the proper treatment of albumen—the eggs serving as the material of experiment.

They experimented first by taking water at various temperatures, finding out when it was scalding, simmering, and boiling hot, and ascertained the effect of the various degrees of temperature on the white of the egg. That worked out, they were prepared, not simply to cook eggs, but to understand the principle involved in the cooking of eggs. I do not wish to lose sight of the universal in the particular incident. For the child simply to desire to cook an egg, and accordingly drop it in water for three minutes, and take it out when he is told, is not educative. But for the child to realize his own impulse by recognizing the facts, materials, and conditions involved, and then to regulate his impulse through that recognition, is educative. This is the difference, upon which I wish to insist, between exciting or indulging an interest and realizing it through its direction.

Another instinct of the child is the use of pencil and paper. All children like to express themselves through the medium of form and color. If you simply indulge this interest by letting the child go on indefinitely, there is no growth that is more than accidental. But let the child first express his impulse, and then through criticism, question, and suggestion bring him to consciousness of what he has done, and what he needs to do, and the result is quite different. Here, for example, is the work of a seven-year-old child. It is not average work, it is the best work done among the little children, but it illustrates the particular principle of which I have been speaking. They had been talking about the primitive conditions of social life when people lived in caves. The child's idea of that found expression in this way: the cave is neatly set up on the hillside in an impossible way. You see the conventional tree of childhood—a vertical line with horizontal branches on each side. If the child had been allowed to go on repeating this sort of thing day by day, he would be indulging his instinct rather than exercising it. But the child was now asked to look closely at trees, to compare those seen with the one drawn, to examine more closely and consciously into the conditions of his work. Then he drew trees from observation.

Finally he drew again from combined observation, memory, and imagination. He made again a free illustration, expressing his own imaginative thought, but controlled by detailed study of actual trees. The result was a scene representing a bit of forest; so far as it goes, it seems to me to have as much poetic feeling as the work of an adult, while at the same time its trees are, in their proportions, possible ones, not mere symbols.

If we roughly classify the impulses which are available in the school, we may group them under four heads. There is the social instinct of the children as shown in conversation, personal intercourse, and communication. We all know how self-centered the little child is at the age of four or five. If any new subject is brought up, if he says anything at all, it is: "I have seen that"; or, "My papa or mamma told me about that." His horizon is not large; an experience must come immediately home to him, if he is to be sufficiently interested to relate it to others and seek theirs in return. And yet the egoistic and limited interest of little children is in this manner capable of infinite expansion. The language instinct is the simplest form of the social expression of the child. Hence it is a great, perhaps the greatest of all, educational resources.

Then there is the instinct of making—the constructive impulse. The child's impulse to do finds expression first in play, in movement, gesture, and make-believe, becomes more definite, and seeks outlet in shaping materials into tangible forms and permanent embodiment. The child has not much instinct for abstract inquiry. The instinct of investigation seems to grow out of the combination of the constructive impulse with the conversational. There is no distinction between experimental science for little children and the work done in the carpenter shop. Such work as they can do in physics or chemistry is not for the purpose of making technical generalizations or even arriving at abstract truths. Children simply like to do things and watch to see what will happen. But this can be taken advantage of, can be directed into ways where it gives results of value, as well as be allowed to go on at random.

And so the expressive impulse of the children, the art instinct grows also out of the communicating and constructive instincts. It is their refinement and full manifestation. Make the construction adequate, make it full, free, and flexible, give it a social motive, something to tell, and you have a work of art. Take one illustration of this in connection with the textile work—sewing and weaving. The children made a primitive loom in the shop; here the constructive instinct was appealed to. Then they wished to do something with this loom, to make something. It was the type of the Indian loom, and they were shown blankets woven by the Indians. Each child made a design kindred in idea to those of the Navajo blankets, and the one which seemed best adapted to the work in hand was selected. The technical resources were limited, but the coloring and form were worked out by the children. Examination of the work of the twelve-year-olds shows that it took patience, thoroughness, and perseverance. It involved not merely discipline and information of both a historical sort and the elements of technical design, but also something of the spirit of art in adequately conveying an idea.

One more instance of the connection of the art side with the constructive side: The children had been studying primitive spinning and carding, when one of them, twelve years of age, made a picture of one of the children spinning. Here is still another piece of work which is not quite average; it is better than the average. It is an illustration of two hands and the drawing out of the wool to get it ready for spinning. This was done by a child eleven years of age. But, upon the whole, with the younger children especially, the art impulse is connected mainly with the social instinct—the desire to tell, to represent.

Now, keeping in mind these fourfold interests—the interest in conversation or communication; in inquiry, or finding out things; in making things, or construction; and in artistic expression—we may say they are the natural resources, the uninvested capital, upon the exercise of which depends the active growth of the child. I wish to give one or two illustrations, the first from the work of children seven years of age. It illustrates in a way the dominant desire of the children to talk, particularly about folks and of things in relation to folks. If you observe little children, you will find they are interested in the world of things mainly in its connection with people, as a background and medium of human concerns. Many anthropologists have told us there are certain identities in the child interests with those of primitive life. There is a sort of natural recurrence of the child mind to the typical activities of primitive peoples; witness the hut which the boy likes to build in the yard, playing hunt, with bows, arrows, spears, and so on. Again the question comes: What are we to do with this interest—are we to ignore it, or just excite and draw it out? Or shall we get hold of it and direct it to something ahead, something better? Some of the work that has been planned for our seven-year-old children has the latter end in view—to utilize this interest so that it shall become a means of seeing the progress of the human race. The children begin by imagining present conditions taken away until they are in contact with nature at first hand. That takes them back to a hunting people, to a people living in caves or trees and getting a precarious subsistence by hunting and fishing. They imagine as far as possible the various natural physical conditions adapted to that sort of life; say, a hilly, woody slope, near mountains, and a river where fish would be abundant. Then they go on in imagination through the hunting to the semi-agricultural stage, and through the nomadic to the settled agricultural stage. The point I wish to make is that there is abundant opportunity thus given for actual study for inquiry which results in gaining information. So, while the instinct primarily appeals to the social side, the interest of the child in people and their doings is carried on into the larger world of reality. For example, the children had some idea of primitive weapons, of the stone arrowhead, etc. That provided occasion for the testing of materials as regards their friability, their shape, texture, etc., resulting in a lesson in mineralogy, as they examined the different stones to find which was best suited to the purpose. The discussion of the iron age supplied a demand for the construction of a smelting oven made out of clay and of considerable size. As the children did not get their drafts right at first, the mouth of the furnace not being in proper relation to the vent as to size and position, instruction in the principles of combustion, the nature of drafts and of fuel, was required. Yet the instruction was not given ready-made; it was first needed, and then arrived at experimentally. Then the children took some material, such as copper, and went through a series of experiments, fusing it, working it into objects; and the same experiments were made with lead and other metals. This work has been also a continuous course in geography, since the children have had to imagine and work out the various physical conditions necessary to the different forms of social life implied. What would be the physical conditions appropriate to pastoral life? to the beginning of agriculture? to fishing? What would be the natural method of exchange between these peoples? Having worked out such points in conversation, they have afterward represented them in maps and sand-molding. Thus they have gained ideas of the various forms of the configuration of the earth, and at the same time have seen them in their relation to human activity, so that they are not simply external facts, but are fused and welded with social conceptions regarding the life and progress of humanity. The result, to my mind, justifies completely the conviction that children, in a year of such work (of five hours a week altogether), get infinitely more acquaintance with facts of science, geography, and anthropology than they get where information is the professed end and object, where they are simply set to learning facts in fixed lessons. As to discipline, they get more training of attention, more power of interpretation, of drawing inferences, of acute observation and continuous reflection, than if they were put to working out arbitrary problems simply for the sake of discipline.

I should like at this point to refer to the recitation. We all know what it has been—a place where the child shows off to the teacher and the other children the amount of information he has succeeded in assimilating from the textbook. From this other standpoint the recitation becomes pre-eminently a social meeting-place; it is to the school what the spontaneous conversation is at home, excepting that it is more organized, following definite lines. The recitation becomes the social clearing-house, where experiences and ideas are exchanged and subjected to criticism, where misconceptions are corrected, and new lines of thought and inquiry are set up.

This change of the recitation, from an examination of knowledge already acquired to the free play of the children's communicative instinct, affects and modifies all the language work of the school. Under the old regime it was unquestionably a most serious problem to give the children a full and free use of language. The reason was obvious. The natural motive for language was seldom offered. In the pedagogical textbooks language is defined as the medium of expressing thought. It becomes that, more or less, to adults with trained minds, but it hardly needs to be said that language is primarily a social thing, a means by which we give our experiences to others and get theirs again in return. When it is taken away from its natural purpose, it is no wonder that it becomes a complex and difficult problem to teach language. Think of the absurdity of having to teach language as a thing by itself. If there is anything the child will do before he goes to school, it is to talk of the things that interest him. But when there are no vital interests appealed to in the school, when language is used simply for the repetition of lessons, it is not surprising that one of the chief difficulties of school work has come to be instruction in the mother-tongue. Since the language taught is unnatural, not growing out of the real desire to communicate vital impressions and convictions, the freedom of children in its use gradually disappears, until finally the high-school teacher has to invent all kinds of devices to assist in getting any spontaneous and full use of speech. Moreover, when the language instinct is appealed to in a social way, there is a continual contact with reality. The result is that the child always has something in his mind to talk about, he has something to say; he has a thought to express, and a thought is not a thought unless it is one's own. On the traditional method, the child must say something that he has merely learned. There is all the difference in the world between having something to say and having to say something. The child who has a variety of materials and facts wants to talk about them, and his language becomes more refined and full, because it is controlled and informed by realities. Reading and writing, as well as the oral use of language, may be taught on this basis. It can be done in a related way, as the outgrowth of the child's social desire to recount his experiences and get in return the experiences of others, directed always through contact with the facts and forces which determine the truth communicated.

I do not have space to speak of the work of the older children, where the original crude instincts of construction and communication have been developed into something like scientifically directed inquiry, but I will give an illustration of the use of language following upon this experimental work. The work was on the basis of a simple experiment of the commonest sort, gradually leading the children out into geological and geographical study. The sentences that I am going to cite seem to me poetic as well as "scientific." "A long time ago when the earth was new, when it was lava, there was no water on the earth, and there was steam all round the earth up in the air, as there were many gases in the air. One of them was carbon dioxide. The steam became clouds, because the earth began to cool off, and after a while it began to rain, and the water came down and dissolved the carbon dioxide from the air." There is a good deal more science in that than probably would be apparent at the outset. It represents some three months of work on the part of the child. The children kept daily and weekly records, but this is part of the summing up of the quarter's work. I call this language poetic, because the child has a clear image and has a personal feeling for the realities imaged. I extract sentences from two other records to illustrate further the vivid use of language when there is a vivid experience back of it. "When the earth was cold enough to condense, the Water, with the help of carbon dioxide, pulled the calcium out of the rocks into a large body of water where the little animals could get it." The other reads as follows: "When the earth cooled, calcium was in the rocks. Then the carbon dioxide and water united and formed a solution, and, as it ran, it tore out the calcium and carried it on to the sea, where there were little animals who took it out of solution." The use of such words as "pulled" and "tore" in connection with the process of chemical combination evidences a personal realization which compels its own appropriate expression.

If I had not taken so much space in my other illustrations, I should like to show how, beginning with very simple material things, the children are led on to larger fields of investigation and to the intellectual discipline that is the accompaniment of such research. I will simply refer to the experiment in which the work began. It consisted in making precipitated chalk, used for polishing metals. The children, with simple apparatus—a tumbler, lime water, and a glass tube—precipitated the calcium carbonate out of the water; and from this beginning went on to a study of the processes by which rocks of various sorts, igneous, sedimentary, etc., had been formed on the surface of the earth and the places they occupy; then to points in the geography of the United States, Hawaii, and Puerto Rico; to the effects of these various bodies of rock, in their various configurations, upon the human occupations; so that this geological record finally rounded itself out into the life of man at the present time. The children saw and felt the connection between these geologic processes, taking place ages and ages ago, and the physical conditions determining the industrial occupations of today.

Of all the possibilities involved in the subject, "The School and the Life of the Child," I have selected but one, because I have found that it gives people more difficulty, is more of a stumbling-block, than any other. One may be ready to admit that it would be most desirable for the school to be a place in which the child should really live, and get a life-experience in which he should delight and find meaning for its own sake. But then we hear this inquiry: How, upon this basis, shall the child get the needed information; how shall he undergo the required discipline? Yes, it has come to this, that with many, if not most, people the normal processes of life appear to be incompatible with getting information and discipline. So I have tried to indicate, in a highly general and inadequate way (for only the school itself, in its daily operation, could give a detailed and worthy representation), how the problem works itself out—how it is possible to lay hold upon the rudimentary instincts of human nature, and, by supplying a proper medium, so to control their expression as not only to facilitate and enrich the growth of the individual child, but also to supply the same results, and far more, of technical information and discipline that have been the ideals of education in the past.

But although I have selected this especial way of approach (as a concession to the question almost universally raised), I am not willing to leave the matter in this more or less negative and explanatory condition. Life is the great thing after all; the life of the child at its time and in its measure no less than the life of the adult. Strange would it be, indeed, if intelligent and serious attention to what the child now needs and is capable of in the way of a rich, valuable, and expanded life should somehow conflict with the needs and possibilities of later, adult life. "Let us live with our children" certainly means, first of all, that our children shall live—not that they shall be hampered and stunted by being forced into all kinds of conditions, the most remote consideration of which is relevancy to the present life of the child. If we seek the kingdom of heaven, educationally, all other things shall be added unto us—which, being interpreted, is that if we identify ourselves with the real instincts and needs of childhood, and ask only after its fullest assertion and growth, the discipline and information and culture of adult life shall all come in their due season.

Speaking of culture reminds me that in a way I have been speaking only of the outside of the child's activity—only of the outward expression of his impulses toward saying, making, finding out, and creating. The real child, it hardly need be said, lives in the world of imaginative values and ideas which find only imperfect outward embodiment. We hear much nowadays about the cultivation of the child's "imagination." Then we undo much of our own talk and work by a belief that the imagination is some special part of the child that finds its satisfaction in some one particular direction—generally speaking, that of the unreal and make-believe, of the myth and made-up story. Why are we so hard of heart and so slow to believe? The imagination is the medium in which the child lives. To him there is everywhere and in everything which occupies his mind and activity at all a surplusage of value and significance. The question of the relation of the school to the child's life is at bottom simply this: Shall we ignore this native setting and tendency, dealing, not with the living child at all, but with the dead image we have erected, or shall we give it play and satisfaction? If we once believe in life and in the life of the child, then will all the occupations and uses spoken of, then will all history and science, become instruments of appeal and materials of culture to his imagination, and through that to the richness and the orderliness of his life. Where we now see only the outward doing and the outward product, there, behind all visible results, is the readjustment of mental attitude, the enlarged and sympathetic vision, the sense of growing power, and the willing ability to identify both insight and capacity with the interests of the world and man. Unless culture be a superficial polish, a veneering of mahogany over common wood, it surely is this—the growth of the imagination in flexibility, in scope, and in sympathy, till the life which the individual lives is informed with the life of nature and of society. When nature and society can live in the schoolroom, when the forms and tools of learning are subordinated to the substance of experience, then shall there be an opportunity for this identification, and culture shall be the democratic password.

Excerpt from *Experience and Education*, 1938

Reprinted with permission of Kappa Delta Pi, International Honor Society in Education

Traditional vs. Progressive Education

Mankind likes to think in terms of extreme opposites. It is given to formulating its beliefs in terms of *Either–Ors*, between which it recognizes no intermediate possibilities. When forced to recognize that the extremes cannot be acted upon, it is still inclined to hold that they are all right in theory but that when it comes to practical matters circumstances compel us to compromise. Educational philosophy is no exception. The history of educational theory is marked by opposition between the idea that education is development from within and that it is formation from without; that it is based upon natural endowments and that education is a process of overcoming natural inclination and substituting in its place habits acquired under external pressure.

At present, the opposition, so far as practical affairs of the school are concerned, tends to take the form of contrast between traditional and progressive education. If the underlying ideas of the former are formulated broadly, without the qualifications required for accurate statement, they are found to be about as follows: The subject-matter of education consists of bodies of information and of skills that have been worked out in the past; therefore, the chief business of the school is to transmit them to the new generation. In the past, there have also been developed standards and rules of conduct; moral training consists in forming habits of action in conformity with these and rules and standards. Finally, the general pattern of school organization (by which I mean the relations of pupils to one another and to the teachers) constitutes the school a kind of institution sharply marked off from other social institutions. Call up in imagination the ordinary school-room, its time-schedules, schemes of classification, of examination and promotion, of rules of order, and I think you will grasp what is meant by "pattern of organization" If then you contrast this scene with what goes on in the family, for example, you will appreciate what is meant by the school being a kind of institution sharply marked off from any other form of social organization.

The three characteristics just mentioned fix the aims and methods of instruction and discipline. The main purpose or objective is to prepare the young for future responsibilities and for success in life, by means of acquisition of the organized bodies of information and prepared forms of skill which comprehend the material of instruction. Since the subject-matter as well as standards of proper conduct are handed down from the past, the attitude of pupils must, upon the whole, be one of docility, receptivity, and obedience. Books, especially textbooks, are the chief representatives of the lore and wisdom of the past, while teachers are the organs through which pupils are brought into effective connection with the material. Teachers are the agents through which knowledge and skills are communicated and rules of conduct enforced.

I have not made this brief summary for the purpose of criticizing the underlying philosophy. The rise of what is called new education and progressive schools is of itself a product of discontent with traditional education. In effect it is a criticism of the latter. When the implied criticism is made explicit it reads somewhat as follows: The traditional scheme is, in essence, one of imposition from above and from outside. It imposes adult standards, subject-matter, and methods upon those who are only growing slowly toward maturity. The gap is so great that the required subject-matter, the methods of learning and of behaving are foreign to the existing capacities of the young. They are beyond the reach of the experience the young learners already possess. Consequently, they must be imposed; even though good teachers will use devices of art to cover up the imposition so as to relieve it of obviously brutal features.

But the gulf between the mature or adult products and the experience and abilities of the young is so wide that the very situation forbids much active participation by pupils in the development of what is taught. Theirs is to do—and learn, as it was the part of the six hundred to do and die. Learning here means acquisition of what already is incorporated in books and in the heads of the elders. Moreover, that which is taught is thought of as essentially static. It is taught as a finished product, with little regard either to the ways in which it was originally built up or to changes that will surely occur in the future. It is to a large extent the cultural product of societies that assumed the future would be much like the past, and yet it is used as educational food in a society where change is the rule, not the exception.

If one attempts to formulate the philosophy of education implicit in the practices of the new education, we may, I think, discover certain common principles amid the variety of progressive schools now existing. To imposition from above is opposed expression and cultivation of individuality; to external discipline is opposed free activity; learning from texts and teachers, learning through experience; to acquisition of isolated skills and techniques by drill, is opposed acquisition of them as means of attaining ends which make direct vital appeal; to preparation for a more or less remote future is opposed making the most of the opportunities of present life; to static aims and materials is opposed acquaintance with a changing world.

Now, all principles by themselves are abstract. They become concrete only in the consequences which result from their application. Just because the principles set forth are so fundamental and far-reaching, everything depends upon the interpretation given them as they are put into practice in the school and the home. It is at this point that the reference made earlier to *Either–Or* philosophies becomes peculiarly pertinent. The general philosophy of the new education may be sound, and yet the difference in abstract principles will not decide the way in which the moral and intellectual preference involved shall be worked out in practice. There is always the danger in a new movement that in rejecting the aims and methods of that which it would supplant, it may develop its principles negatively rather than positively and constructively. Then it takes its clew in practice from that which is rejected instead of from the constructive development of its own philosophy.

I take it that the fundamental unity of the newer philosophy is found in the idea that there is an intimate and necessary relation between the processes of actual experience and education. If this be true, then a positive and constructive development of its own basic idea depends upon having a correct idea of experience. Take, for example, the question of organized subject-matter—which will be discussed in some detail later. The problem for progressive education is: What is the place and meaning of subject-matter and of organization *within* experience? How does subject-matter function? Is there anything inherent in experience which tends towards progressive organization of its contents? What results follow when the materials of experience are not progressively organized? A philosophy which proceeds on the basis of rejection, of sheer opposition, will neglect these questions. It will tend to suppose that because the old education was based on ready-made organization, therefore it suffices to reject the principle of organization *in toto,* instead of striving to discover what it means and how it is to be attained on the basis of experience. We might go through all the points of difference between the new and the old education and reach similar conclusions. When external control is rejected, the problem becomes that of finding the factors of control that are inherent within experience. When external authority is rejected, it does not follow that all authority should be rejected, but rather that there is need to search for a more effective source of authority. Because the older education imposed the knowledge, methods, and the rules of conduct of the mature person upon the young, it does not follow, except upon the basis of the extreme *Either–Or* philosophy, that the knowledge and skill of the mature person has no directive value for the experience of the immature. On the contrary, basing education upon personal experience may mean more multiplied and more intimate contacts between the mature and the immature than ever existed in the traditional school, and consequently more, rather than less, guidance by others. The problem, then, is: how these contacts can be established without violating the principle of learning through personal experience. The solution of this problem requires a well thought-out philosophy of the social factors that operate in the constitution of individual experience.

What is indicated in the foregoing remarks is that the general principles of the new education do not of themselves solve any of the problems of the actual or practical conduct and management of progressive schools. Rather, they set new problems which have to be worked out on the basis of a new philosophy of experience. The problems are not even recognized, to say nothing of being solved, when it is assumed that it suffices to reject the ideas and practices of the old education and then go to the opposite extreme. Yet I am sure that you will appreciate what is meant when I say that many of the newer schools tend to make little or nothing of organized subject-matter of study; to proceed as if any form of direction and guidance by adults were an invasion of individual freedom, and as if the idea that education should be concerned with the present and future meant that acquaintance with the past has little or no role to play in education. Without pressing these defects to the point of exaggeration, they at least illustrate what is meant by a theory and practice of education which proceeds negatively or by reaction against what has been current in education rather than by a positive and constructive development of purposes, methods, and subject-matter on the foundation of a theory of experience and its educational potentialities.

It is not too much to say that an educational philosophy which professes to be based on the idea of freedom may become as dogmatic as ever was the traditional education which is reacted against. For any theory and set of practices is dogmatic which is not based upon critical examination of its own underlying principles. Let us say that the new education emphasizes the freedom of the learner. Very well. A problem is now set. What does freedom mean and what are the conditions under which it is capable of realization? Let us say that the land of external imposition which was so common in the traditional school limited rather than promoted the intellectual and moral development of the young. Again, very well. Recognition of this serious defect sets a problem. Just what is the role of the teacher and of books in promoting the educational development of the immature? Admit that traditional education employed as the subject-matter for study facts and ideas so bound up with the past as to give little help in dealing with the issues of the present and future. Very well. Now we have the problem of discovering the connection which actually exists *within* experience between the achievements of the past and the issues of the present. We have the problem of ascertaining how acquaintance with the past may be translated into a potent instrumentality for dealing effectively with the future. We may reject knowledge of the past as the *end* of education and thereby only emphasize its importance as a *means*. When we do that we have a problem that is new in the story of education: How shall the young become acquainted with the past in such a way that the acquaintance is a potent agent in appreciation of the living present?

24

The Ideal School as Based on Child Study

G. Stanley Hall, 1901

G. Stanley Hall (1844–1924) was born on a farm in Ashfield, Massachusetts in 1844. He graduated from Williams College in 1867. After some early interest in theology as his chosen profession, Hall decided to study psychology and philosophy at Harvard. At Harvard, he studied with William James and Henry P. Bowditch. In 1878, Hall received the first doctoral degree in psychology in the United States, from Harvard. He began his first professorship in 1882 at Johns Hopkins University, where he taught psychology and pedagogics. Hall's views on education draw upon the ideas of individuals such as Jean-Jacques Rousseau, Friedrich Froebel, and Charles Darwin. In works such as "The Contents of Children's Minds" and "The Ideal School Based as on Child Study," Hall sets forth his "recapitulation of the race" theory. He argues that, as children develop, they follow the same pattern as the development of the human race. Hall was an influential promoter of the "new psychology," which was developing in the U.S. during the late 19th

American Educational Thought: Essays from 1640–1940, pages 401–410
Copyright © 2010 by Information Age Publishing
All rights of reproduction in any form reserved.

century. He helped to establish journals such as *American Journal of Psychology* and *The Pedagogical Seminary*, both of which were deeply influential in the fields of American psychology and education. Through works such as "The Ideal School as Based on Child Study," Hall brought the power of empirical science to the study of teaching and children. His efforts laid the foundation for movements such as child-centered learning, developmentalism, and Progressive education. Through his work at Johns Hopkins University and Clark University, Hall influenced individuals such as John Dewey, James McKeen Cattell, and Lewis Terman. —JWN

I shall try in this paper to break away from all current practices, traditions, methods, and philosophies, for a brief moment, and ask what education would be if based solely upon a fresh and comprehensive view of the nature and needs of childhood. Hitherto the data for such a construction of the ideal school have been inefficient, and soon they will be too manifold for any one mind to make the attempt; so the moment is opportune. What follows is based almost solely, point by point, upon the study of the stages of child development, and might, perhaps, without presumption be called a first attempt to formulate a practical program of this great movement. In my limited space I can do little more than barely state the conclusions that affect the practical work of teachers.

The school I shall describe exists nowhere, but its methods, unless I err, are valid everywhere. Altho' many of its features exist already, and could be pieced together in a mosaic from many lands and ages, it is essentially the school invisible, not made with hands. But, as there is nothing so practical as the truly ideal, altho' my school today exists nowhere, it might be organized anywhere tomorrow; and I hope that the most and the least conservative will agree that it is the true goal of all endeavor, and will not differ except as to whether it may be realized at once or only at the end of a long period of labor. I confess that something like this has from the first animated all my own feeble educational endeavors, and that without it I should be without hope and without goal in the world of pedagogy.

Beginning within the deep philosophy often imbedded in words, "school," or "schole," means leisure, exemption from work, the perpetuation of the primeval paradise created before the struggle for existence began. It stands for the prolongation of human infancy, and the no whit less important prolongation of adolescence. It is sacred to health, growth, and heredity, a pound of which is worth a ton of instruction. The guardians of the young should strive first of all to keep out of nature's way, and to prevent harm, and should merit the proud title of defenders of the happiness and rights of children. They should feel profoundly that childhood, as it comes fresh from the hand of God, is not corrupt, but illustrates the survival of the most consummate thing in the world, they should be convinced that there is nothing else so worthy of love, reverence, and service as the body and soul of the growing child.

Practically, this means that every invasion of this leisure, the provision of a right measure of which is our first duty to youth, has a certain presumption against it, and must justify itself by conclusive reasons. Before we let the pedagog loose upon childhood, not only must each topic in his curriculum give an account of itself, but his inroads must be justified in the case of each child. We must overcome the fetishism of the alphabet, of the multiplication table, of grammars, of scales, and of bibliolatry, and must reflect that but a few generations ago the ancestors of all of us were illiterate; that the invention of Cadmus seemed the sowing of veritable dragon's teeth in the brain; that Charlemagne and many other great men of the world could not read or write; that scholars have argued that Cornelia, Ophelia, Beatrice, and even the blessed mother of our Lord knew nothing of letters. The knights, the elite leaders of the Middle Ages, deemed writing a mere clerk's trick beneath the attention of all those who scorned to muddle their wits with others' ideas, feeling that their own were good enough for them.

Nay more: there are many who ought not to be educated, and who would be better in mind, body, and morals if they knew no school. What shall it profit a child to gain the world of knowledge and lose his own health? Cramming and over-schooling have impaired many a feeble mind, for which, as the proverb says, nothing is so dangerous as ideas too large for it. We are coming to understand the vanity of mere scholarship and erudition, and to know that even ignorance may be a wholesome poultice for weakly souls; while scribes, sophists, scholastics, and pedants suggest how much of the learning of the past is now seen to be vanity, and how incompetent pedagogs have been as guardians of the sacred things of culture. Thus, while I would abate no whit from the praise of learning and education for all who are fit for them, I would bring discrimination down to the very basis of our educational pyramid.

The kindergarten age is from two or three to six or seven. Here, before the ideal school can be inaugurated, we need some work of rescue from the symbolists. Now the body needs most attention, and the soul least. The child needs more mother, and less teacher; more of the educated nurse, and less of the metaphysician. We must largely eliminate, and partly reconstruct, the mother-plays, while transforming and vastly enlarging the repertory of the gifts and occupations. We must develop the ideal nursery, playgrounds, and rooms, where light, air, and water are at their best. The influences of the new hygiene have been felt least here, where they are needed most. The neglect of these basal principles suggests that we have still among us those whose practice implies a belief that any old place is good enough to hatch out beautiful souls, provided only Froebelian orthodoxy of doctrine and method is steadfastly maintained...

The kindergarten should fill more of the day, and should strive to kill time. In the Berlin Institute children sleep at noon in a darkened room, with music, crackers, or even bottles, and thus resist man's enemy, fatigue, and restore paradise for themselves. Part of the cult here should be idleness and the intermediate state of reverie. We should have a good excuse to break into these, and at this age children should be carefully shielded from all suspicion of any symbolic sense. Thus in play, and play only, life is made to seem real. Imitation should have a far larger scope. Children should hear far more English and better, and in the later years the ear should be trained for French or German. Color should never be taught as such. The children of the rich, generally prematurely individualized or over-individualized, especially when they are children, must be disciplined and subordinated; while the children of the poor, usually under-individualized, should be indulged. We should lose no syllable of the precious positive philosophy of Froebel, the deepest of all modern educational thinkers; but we must profoundly reconstruct every practical expression that he attempted of his ideas, and must strive to induce at least a few college-trained men and women to turn their attention to the kindergarten, thus making the training schools feel, what they have hitherto known so little of, the real spirit and influence of modern science. Teachers should study every child, not necessarily by any of the current technical methods. They should learn far more than they can teach, and in place of the shallow manikin child of books they should see, know, and love only the real thing. After this metempsychosis, the kindergarten should be, and should become, an integral part of every school system.

The age of about seven or eight is a transition period of the greatest interest for science. Then most children have less chewing surface by three or four teeth; there is a year or more of increased danger to the heart; the breath is shorter and fatigue easier; lassitude, nervousness, visual disorders, and cough are somewhat more imminent; and the blood is more often impoverished. The brain has practically finished for life its growth in weight and size; and all work and strain must be reduced. Some important corner in its time of development, not yet fully understood, is turned.

At eight or nine there begins a new period, which, for nearly four years, to the dawn of puberty, constitutes a unique stage of life, marked off by many important differences from the period which precedes and that which follows it. During these years there is a decreased rate of growth, so that the body relatively rests, but there is a striking increase of vitality, activity, and power to resist disease. Fatigue, too, is now best resisted, and it is amazing to see how much can be endured. The average child now plays more games, and has more daily activity, in proportion to size and weight, than at any other stage. It would seem, as I have proposed elsewhere with ground for the theory, as tho these four years represented, on the recapitulation theory, a long period in some remote age, well above the simian, but mainly before the historic, period, when our early forebears were well adjusted to their environment. Before a higher and much more modern story was added to human nature, the young in warmer climates, where most human traits were evolved, became independent of their parents, and broke away to subsist for themselves at an early age. In this age, which we will call the juvenile, the individual boy today is a precious key for the reconstruction of a stage in the history of the race otherwise very obscure.

However this may be, child nature suggests very plainly that this period should be mainly devoted to drill, habituation, and mechanism. The age of reason is only dawning, and is not yet much in order; but discipline should be the watchword here. Writing, and even reading, for instance, should be neglected in our system before eight, and previous school work should focus on stories, the study of nature, and education by play and other activities. Now writing and reading should be first taught with stress. Their nascent period is now beginning. If we teach them before, we are apt to make the average child a bad writer for life by precocious overemphasis on the finer muscles. Modern studies show that the zigzag of the eye back and forth along the printed line is as dangerous as is the too early wigwag of the pen. At best the strain laid upon these tiny muscles is dangerous. Too early drill in read-writing is also enormously wasteful, because intensive effort gives facility now in an amazingly short time. Now first the smaller muscles in the average child, so important for mind- and will-training, can bear hard work and much strain. Accuracy, which, when out of its season, is fraught with so many dangers for mind and body, is now in order.

Verbal memory is now at its very best, and should be trained far more than it is. We are now educating the automatic bases of both mind and morals, and habits are never so easily formed or made stable. Manual training and games should be extremely diverse, manifold, and thoro. It is the time to break in the human colt, which is by nature, in some sense, the wildest of all wild animals. If the piano or any other musical instrument is to be learned, this is the time for drill, especially on scales and exercises. An instrumentalist's technique is rarely good if its foundations are not laid in this age. Names, even technical ones, come now. Drawing, too, should now come into prominence, beginning in its large and perfectly free form before writing, and only near the end of the period becoming severely methodic and accurate. Art training should not result in intimidation, but first everything should be drawn—battles, fires, shipwrecks, and railroad accidents, with plenty of human figures and action, and no angles, straight lines, or regular curves, which have come very late in the history of the race. This would make drawing, as it should be, a real expression of the child's soul, and the child should copy what he, and not what the adult, sees.

The mother-tongue will be the vehicle of nearly all the work of this period; but it will be on the short circuit from ear to mouth, which existed for unknown eons before reading and writing, and not chiefly on the long circuit and, biologically, very recent brain-path from eye to hand. Teachers praise written work in home and at school—compositions, essays, class work; but all these appeal to new and undeveloped powers of nerve and muscle. It is because we try to establish good English upon these foundations, so precarious at this stage, that we have so much and so just complaint of bad English. We ruin both handwriting and idiomatic speech by precocity. The child should live in a world of sonorous speech. He should hear and talk for hours each day; and then he would lay foundations for terse and correct English, and would keep read-writing, as it should forever be, subordinate to hearing and speaking. He would write as he speaks, and we should escape the abominations of bookish talk. At this stage written work should be required far less than at present.

Further, to secure these ends, we must first lay stress upon correct spelling—which is, after all, of far less importance than we think—and also upon correct, adult Addisonian syntax. Good grammar is too much to expect yet. We must strive first for utterance and expression, which may be homely, if only vigorous and adequate. Hence, much that we call slang has its place, and is really a revival of English in its most formative stage. The prim proprieties we idolize are not yet, but it is the hour of delight in cogency of expression. We do not yet know what slang to teach, or how to teach it, but we ought to give the best of it an important place. The boy is not totally depraved because he loves the speech of Chimmie Fadden, of Mr. Ade, or of "The Charwoman," because such language is fresh from the mint where all words were made. Our end is the cultivation of expression, which must bring out clearly and strongly what is in the boy's soul. This expression must be of a kind at least no less effective for other boys than for us. A training that gives the power of writing, or even talking, upon any subject or upon none in particular, is bad and vicious. Children have no right to write unless it is upon some subject that they know, and upon which they feel strongly. Theme and composition should be strictly confined to the fields of interest, and then expression will find or make a vent for itself. Moreover, we should not teach language, as such, or apart from objects, acts, amid concrete reality-truth. We must burn most of our language books.

At this stage, arithmetic, so greatly overdone in American schools, should be mechanized, with plenty of mental exercises, and later with rules and processes for written work, with only little attempt at explanation. The elements of geometry, especially on the constructive side, and the metric system should come early, and the rudiments of algebra later. This is the stage, too, for beginning one or two foreign languages. These should always first be taught by ear and mouth. The child has a natural desire to express himself in many other vocal forms than the vernacular, for it is the age when all kinds of gibberish, dog Latin, and inventive words culminate. It represents the stage when human speech evolved fastest. If these languages are taught earlier, they jeopardize idiomatic English; if later, they are never pronounced or used with precision, and are not immediate vehicles of thought. Psychology has shown that speech is greatly reinforced by appeals to the eye, not in the form of the written or printed word, but thru pictures, and that even color intensifies the linguistic effect. Many a French or German word that could not otherwise be recalled is reproduced, or first taught more permanently, if the object or picture is shown, or the appropriate action is performed at the same instant. Books should be by no means discarded, but the chief stress should be laid on the oral work and thought. The object should be brought into immediate action without the intervention of the English word.

As to the dead languages, if they are to be taught, Latin should be begun not later than ten or eleven, and Greek never later than twelve or thirteen. Here both object and method are very different. These languages are taught thru English, and the eye-hand circuit should have much more prominence. Word-matching and translation are the goal. The chief reason why the German boy of fifteen or sixteen in Unter Secunda does so easily here what seems to us prodigious is because he is taught to study; and the teacher's chief business in class is not to hear recitations, but to study with the boys. One of the best of these teachers told me that the boy should never see a dictionary or even a vocabulary, but the teacher must be a "pony." The pupil should never be brought face to face with an unknown sentence, but everything must be carefully translated for him; he must note all the unknown words from the teacher's lips and all the special grammatical points, so that home study and the first part of the next lesson will be merely repetitions of what the teacher had told and done.

The modern school geography should be reduced to about one-fourth or even one-eighth of its present volume. It is too often a mosaic of geology, topography, physical geography, botany, zoology, anthropology, meteorology, and astronomy. The facts of each of these sciences, however, are not taught in their natural or logical order; but the associations are mainly those of place and contiguity, not of similarity and cause. Even in these days of correlation of studies the facts of these sciences are separated from their logical connection with each other; and by the use of a more fortuitous local association the reason is injured. Our geographies do not respect the unity of the child's mind. Their facts are connected neither with each other nor with the nascent stages of growth. The interest in primitive man and animals culminates from nine to ten; that in trade and governmental parts of geography comes from sixteen to twenty. The geographies of the last two or three years have mitigated, but by no means healed, these evils; and, as we speak of Turkey as "the sick man of Europe," we may still speak of geography as the sick subject of our curriculum.

Instead of reverencing this relic of mediaevalism, as its history shows it to be, we should greatly reduce the time given to it, and should first teach Heimatskunde; make maps more abundant, but more incidental to every topic, especially history; develop and teach elementary and illustrated anthropology and zoology, broadening to elementary astronomy, geology, meteorology, and botany, taught by and for themselves to bring out their disciplinary value, and so on in ways I have here no space to dwell upon. When we have reduced the enormous time now given in geography, the elements of each of these sciences will be taught in primers—some of which are now begun before the end of this period—which will continue the nature work of the period before seven or eight.

The hand is in a sense never so near the brain as now; knowledge never so strongly tends to become practical; muscular development never so conditions mental. Muscle-training of every kind, from play up to manual work, must now begin. Instead of the Swedish or other curricularized and exactly finished objects made, we should have a curriculum of toys at first and of rude scientific apparatus later, where everything will focus more upon the ulterior use of the object than upon the process of making it. All these things will be chosen from the field of the child's interests.

Singing will be prominent in the ideal school at this age; but far more time will be given to rote singing than to singing from notes, especially at first. The chief aim will be, not to develop the power to read music, important as the place of this is, but to educate the sentiments, and especially to attune them to love of home, nature, fatherland, and religion—the four chief themes of song in all ages, past and present. Music is the language of the feelings, just as speech is of the intellect. It is as absurd to teach notes to children before they can sing well as it would be to teach them reading before they can speak. The object of musical education in the public school is to express and train the emotions, and, thru these, the will and character; to perform joys and conduct, and not to make musicians.

Reason is still very undeveloped. The child's mind is at a stage when there is little in it that has not been brought in by way of sense. We must open wide the eye-gate and the ear-gate. "Show," "demonstrate," and "envisage" should be our watchwords, not "explain." We can easily make casuists and prigs, but we jeopardize thereby the ultimate vigor of reason. Hence we should explain very little. Even with respect to morals and conduct the chief duty of the child at this age is to obey. In most cases to try to explain brings self-consciousness and conceit. This method is the resource of teachers and parents whose personality is deficient in authoritativeness. Obedience should still be a law, if not a passion. If it is lacking, this is due to imperfect character or perverted methods in adults.

In fine, this is the age for training, with plenty of space and time, however, for spontaneity and voluntary action. The good teacher is a true *Pedotrieb*, or boy driver. He needs some method, but much more matter. He or she finds relatively little sentiment, but much selfishness, bound up in the hearts of children at this age. One of the chronic errors of too fond mothers and of modern teachers is to overestimate the capacities of children, especially boys, at this age for sympathy with adult feelings or interests. The world we live in is not theirs. We are "Olympians," and can enforce our will because we are stronger. We must be tolerated and respected, and must be treated within all the forms of respect and obedience that we require; but the interest of children at this age is almost exclusively in each other, and in each other's ways, not in adults. This breaks out suddenly, but just later.

Just before this period ends, boys and girls in the ideal school will be chiefly, tho not exclusively, placed under the care of teachers of their own sex. At the close of this period the ideal child, ideally trained, will be first of all helpful and active in body and mind; will read and write well; will know a great deal about the different aspects of nature in his home environment; will not be bookish, but will already know a few dozen well-chosen books; will understand and read simple French and German; and will perhaps have a good start in Latin and Greek. Some buds of specialization will have begun to bourgeon. This child will be able to play several dozen games; will know something of a number of industries....

I have spoken frankly, and have dealt only with general principles over a vast field, far too large to be adequately discussed here. I have carefully avoided all details, altho, I have fully worked them out on paper at great length, for each topic to the close of the high-school period or the age of nineteen, when physical growth is essentially completed. This material will soon appear in a volume. The chief petition in my daily prayer now is for a millionaire. With the means at hand, I have no shadow of doubt or fear but that in five years from the date of any adequate gift we shall be able to invite all interested to a system of education, covering this ground, which will be a practical realization of much present prophecy, and which will commend itself even to the most conservative defenders of things as they are and have been, because the best things established will be in it. But it will be essentially pedocentric rather than scholiocentric; it may be a little like the Reformation, which insisted that the sabbath, the Bible, and the church were made for man and not he for them; it will fit both the practices and the results of modern science and psychological study; it will make religion and morals more effective; and, perhaps above all, it will give individuality in the school its full rights as befits a republican form of government, and will contribute something to bring the race to the higher maturity of the superman that is to be, effectiveness in developing which is the highest and final test of art, science, religion, home, state, literature, and every human institution.

25

Excerpt from **Up From Slavery**

Booker T. Washington (1901)

Booker T. Washington (1856–1915) was born a slave in Hale's Ford, Virginia. At the end of the Civil War, Washington and his family lived in poverty and worked in salt furnaces and coal mines. At the age of 16, Washington began attending the Hampton Institute and paid for his school by working as a janitor. In 1881, Washington became the leader of a new school for African Americans that opened in Tuskegee, Alabama. Washington designed the Tuskegee Normal and Industrial Institute to teach self-discipline and self-reliance through training in agriculture or an industrial trade. He believed that industrial education such as this would lead to economic and social progress for African Americans. In 1901, Washington's autobiography, *Up From Slavery*, was published. In the excerpt that follows, Washington describes the living condition of African Americans in Alabama when he arrived at Tuskegee. He explains how these early experiences at Tuskegee confirmed his beliefs about the importance of industrial education that avoided "mere book learning" in the struggle for African American equality. —AJM

American Educational Thought: Essays from 1640–1940, pages 411–424
Copyright © 2010 by Information Age Publishing
All rights of reproduction in any form reserved.

411

Early Days at Tuskegee

During the time that I had charge of the Indians and the night-school at Hampton, I pursued some studies myself, under the direction of the instructors there. One of these instructors was the Rev. Dr. H. B. Frissell, the present Principal of the Hampton Institute, General Armstrong's successor.

In May, 1881, near the close of my first year in teaching the night-school, in a way that I had not dared expect, the opportunity opened for me to begin my life-work. One night in the chapel, after the usual chapel exercises were over, General Armstrong referred to the fact that he had received a letter from some gentlemen in Alabama asking him to recommend some one to take charge of what was to be a normal school for the coloured people in the little town of Tuskegee in that state. These gentlemen seemed to take it for granted that no coloured man suitable for the position could be secured, and they were expecting the General to recommend a white man for the place. The next day General Armstrong sent for me to come to his office, and, much to my surprise, asked me if I thought I could fill the position in Alabama. I told him that I would be willing to try. Accordingly, he wrote to the people who had applied to him for the information, that he did not know of any white man to suggest, but if they would be willing to take a coloured man, he had one whom he could recommend. In this letter he gave them my name.

Several days passed before anything more was heard about the matter. Some time afterward, one Sunday evening during the chapel exercises, a messenger came in and handed the General a telegram. At the end of the exercises he read the telegram to the school. In substance, these were its words: "Booker T. Washington will suit us. Send him at once."

There was a great deal of joy expressed among the students and teachers, and I received very hearty congratulations. I began to get ready at once to go to Tuskegee. I went by way of my old home in West Virginia, where I remained for several days, after which I proceeded to Tuskegee. I found Tuskegee to be a town of about two thousand inhabitants, nearly one-half of whom were coloured. It was in what was known as the Black Belt of the South. In the county in which Tuskegee is situated the coloured people outnumbered the whites by about three to one. In some of the adjoining and near-by counties the proportion was not far from six coloured persons to one white.

I have often been asked to define the term "Black Belt." So far as I can learn, the term was first used to designate a part of the country which was distinguished by the colour of the soil. The part of the country possessing this thick, dark, and naturally rich soil was, of course, the part of the South where the slaves were most profitable, and consequently they were taken there in the largest numbers. Later, and especially since the war, the term seems to be used wholly in a political sense—that is, to designate the counties where the black people outnumber the white.

Before going to Tuskegee I had expected to find there a building and all the necessary apparatus ready for me to begin teaching. To my disappointment, I found nothing of the kind. I did find, though, that which no costly building and apparatus can supply,—hundreds of hungry, earnest souls who wanted to secure knowledge.

Tuskegee seemed an ideal place for the school. It was in the midst of the great bulk of the Negro population, and was rather secluded, being five miles from the main line of railroad, with which it was connected by a short line. During the days of slavery, and since, the town had been a centre for the education of the white people. This was an added advantage, for the reason that I found the white people possessing a degree of culture and education that is not surpassed by many localities. While the coloured people were ignorant, they had not, as a rule, degraded and weakened their bodies by vices such as are common to the lower class of people in the large cities. In general, I found the relations between the two races pleasant. For example, the largest, and I think at that time the only hardware store in the town was owned and operated jointly by a coloured man and a white man. This copartnership continued until the death of the white partner.

I found that about a year previous to my going to Tuskegee some of the coloured people who had heard something of the work of education being done at Hampton had applied to the state Legislature, through their representatives, for a small appropriation to be used in starting a normal school in Tuskegee. This request the Legislature had complied with to the extent of granting an annual appropriation of two thousand dollars. I soon learned, however, that this money could be used only for the payment of the salaries of the instructors, and that there was no provision for securing land, buildings, or apparatus. The task before me did not seem a very encouraging one. It seemed much like making bricks without straw. The coloured people were overjoyed, and were constantly offering their services in any way in which they could be of assistance in getting the school started.

My first task was to find a place in which to open the school. After looking the town over with some care, the most suitable place that could be secured seemed to be a rather dilapidated shanty near the coloured Methodist church, together with the church itself as a sort of assembly-room. Both the church and the shanty were in about as bad condition as was possible. I recall that during the first months of school that I taught in this building it was in such poor repair that, whenever it rained, one of the older students would very kindly leave his lessons and hold an umbrella over me while I heard the recitations of the others. I remember, also, that on more than one occasion my landlady held an umbrella over me while I ate breakfast.

At the time I went to Alabama the coloured people were taking considerable interest in politics, and they were very anxious that I should become one of them politically, in every respect. They seemed to have a little distrust of strangers in this regard. I recall that one man, who seemed to have been designated by the others to look after my political destiny, came to me on several occasions and said, with a good deal of earnestness: "We wants you to be sure to vote jes' like we votes. We can't read de newspapers very much, but we knows how to vote, an' we wants you to vote jes' like we votes." He added: "We watches de white man, and we keeps watching de white man till we finds out which way de white man's gwine to vote; an' when we finds out which way de white man's gwine to vote, den we votes 'xactly de other way. Den we knows we's right."

I am glad to add, however, that at the present time the disposition to vote against the white man merely because he is white is largely disappearing, and the race is learning to vote from principle, for what the voter considers to be for the best interests of both races.

I reached Tuskegee, as I have said, early in June 1881. The first month I spent in finding accommodations for the school, and in traveling through Alabama, examining into the actual life of the people, especially in the country districts, and in getting the school advertised among the class of people that I wanted to have attend it. The most of my traveling was done over the country roads, with a mule and a cart or a mule and a buggy wagon for conveyance. I ate and slept with the people, in their little cabins. I saw their farms, their schools, their churches. Since, in the case of the most of these visits, there had been no notice given in advance that a stranger was expected, I had the advantage of seeing the real, everyday life of the people.

In the plantation districts I found that, as a rule, the whole family slept in one room, and that in addition to the immediate family there sometimes were relatives, or others not related to the family, who slept in the same room. On more than one occasion I went outside the house to get ready for bed, or to wait until the family had gone to bed. They usually contrived some kind of a place for me to sleep, either on the floor or in a special part of another's bed. Rarely was there any place provided in the cabin where one could bathe even the face and hands, but usually some provision was made for this outside the house, in the yard.

The common diet of the people was fat pork and corn bread. At times I have eaten in cabins where they had only corn bread and "black-eye peas" cooked in plain water. The people seemed to have no other idea than to live on this fat meat and corn bread,—the meat, and the meal of which the bread was made, having been bought at a high price at a store in town, notwithstanding the fact that the land all about the cabin homes could easily have been made to produce nearly every kind of garden vegetable that is raised anywhere in the country. Their one object seemed to be to plant nothing but cotton; and in many cases cotton was planted up to the very door of the cabin.

In these cabin homes I often found sewing-machines which had been bought, or were being-bought, on installments, frequently at a cost of as much as sixty dollars, or showy clocks for which the occupants of the cabins had paid twelve or fourteen dollars. I remember that on one occasion when I went into one of these cabins for dinner, when I sat down to the table for a meal with the four members of the family, I noticed that, while there were five of us at the table, there was but one fork for the five of us to use. Naturally there was an awkward pause on my part. In the opposite corner of that same cabin was an organ for which the people told me they were paying sixty dollars in monthly installments. One fork, and a sixty-dollar organ!

In most cases the sewing-machine was not used, the clocks were so worthless that they did not keep correct time—and if they had, in nine cases out of ten there would have been no one in the family who could have told the time of day—while the organ, of course, was rarely used for want of a person who could play upon it.

In the case to which I have referred, where the family sat down to the table for the meal at which I was their guest, I could see plainly that this was an awkward and unusual proceeding, and was done in my honour. In most cases, when the family got up in the morning, for example, the wife would put a piece of meat in a frying-pan and put a lump of dough in a "skillet," as they called it. These utensils would be placed on the fire, and in ten or fifteen minutes breakfast would be ready. Frequently the husband would take his bread and meat in his hand and start for the field, eating as he walked. The mother would sit down in a corner and eat her breakfast, perhaps from a plate and perhaps directly from the "skillet" or frying-pan, while the children would eat their portion of the bread and meat while running about the yard. At certain seasons of the year, when meat was scarce, it was rarely that the children who were not old enough or strong enough to work in the fields would have the luxury of meat.

The breakfast over, and with practically no attention given to the house, the whole family would, as a general thing, proceed to the cotton-field. Every child that was large enough to carry a hoe was put to work, and the baby—for usually there was at least one baby—would be laid down at the end of the cotton row, so that its mother could give it a certain amount of attention when she had finished chopping her row. The noon meal and the supper were taken in much the same way as the breakfast.

All the days of the family would be spent after much this same routine, except Saturday and Sunday. On Saturday the whole family would spend at least half a day, and often a whole day, in town. The idea in going to town was, I suppose, to do shopping, but all the shopping that the whole family had money for could have been attended to in ten minutes by one person. Still, the whole family remained in town for most of the day, spending the greater part of the time in standing on the streets, the women, too often, sitting about somewhere smoking or dipping snuff. Sunday was usually spent in going to some big meeting. With few exceptions, I found that the crops were mortgaged in the counties where I went, and that the most of the coloured farmers were in debt. The state had not been able to build schoolhouses in the country districts, and, as a rule, the schools were taught in churches or in log cabins. More than once, while on my journeys, I found that there was no provision made in the house used for school purposes for heating the building during the winter, and consequently a fire had to be built in the yard, and teacher and pupils passed in and out of the house as they got cold or warm. With few exceptions, I found the teachers in these country schools to be miserably poor in preparation for their work, and poor in moral character. The schools were in session from three to five months. There was practically no apparatus in the schoolhouses, except that occasionally there was a rough blackboard. I recall that one day I went into a schoolhouse—or rather into an abandoned log cabin that was being used as a schoolhouse—and found five pupils who were studying a lesson from one book. Two of these, on the front seat, were using the book between them; behind these were two others peeping over the shoulders of the first two, and behind the four was a fifth little fellow who was peeping over the shoulders of all four.

What I have said concerning the character of the schoolhouses and teachers will also apply quite accurately as a description of the church buildings and the ministers.

I met some very interesting characters during my travels. As illustrating the peculiar mental processes of the country people, I remember that I asked one coloured man, who was about sixty years old, to tell me something of his history. He said that he had been born in Virginia, and sold into Alabama in 1845. I asked him how many were sold at the same time. He said, "There were five of us; myself and brother and three mules."

In giving all these descriptions of what I saw during my month of travel in the country around Tuskegee, I wish my readers to keep in mind the fact that there were many encouraging exceptions to the conditions which I have described. I have stated in such plain words what I saw, mainly for the reason that later I want to emphasize the encouraging changes that have taken place in the community, not wholly by the work of the Tuskegee school, but by that of other institutions as well.

Teaching School in a Stable and a Hen-House

I confess that what I saw during my month of travel and investigation left me with a very heavy heart. The work to be done in order to lift these people up seemed almost beyond accomplishing. I was only one person, and it seemed to me that the little effort which I could put forth could go such a short distance toward bringing about results. I wondered if I could accomplish anything, and if it were worthwhile for me to try.

Of one thing I felt more strongly convinced than ever, after spending this month in seeing the actual life of the coloured people, and that was that, in order to lift them up, something must be done more than merely to imitate New England education as it then existed. I saw more clearly than ever the wisdom of the system which General Armstrong had inaugurated at Hampton. To take the children of such people as I had been among for a month, and each day give them a few hours of mere book education, I felt would be almost a waste of time.

After consultation with the citizens of Tuskegee, I set July 4, 1881, as the day for the opening of the school in the little shanty and church which had been secured for its accommodation. The white people, as well as the coloured, were greatly interested in the starting of the new school, and the opening day was looked forward to with much earnest discussion. There were not a few white people in the vicinity of Tuskegee who looked with some disfavour upon the project. They questioned its value to the coloured people, and had a fear that it might result in bringing about trouble between the races. Some had the feeling that in proportion as the Negro received education, in the same proportion would his value decrease as an economic factor in the state. These people feared the result of education would be that the Negroes would leave the farms, and that it would be difficult to secure them for domestic service.

The white people who questioned the wisdom of starting this new school had in their minds pictures of what was called an educated Negro, with a high hat, imitation gold eye-glasses, a showy walking-stick, kid gloves, fancy boots, and what not—in a word, a man who was determined to live by his wits. It was difficult for these people to see how education would produce any other kind of a coloured man.

In the midst of all the difficulties which I encountered in getting the little school started, and since then through a period of nineteen years, there are two men among all the many friends of the school in Tuskegee upon whom I have depended constantly for advice and guidance; and the success of the undertaking is largely due to these men, from whom I have never sought anything in vain. I mention them simply as types. One is a white man and an ex-slaveholder, Mr. George W. Campbell; the other is a black man and an ex-slave, Mr. Lewis Adams. These were the men who wrote to General Armstrong for a teacher.

Mr. Campbell is a merchant and banker, and had had little experience in dealing with matters pertaining to education. Mr. Adams was a mechanic, and had learned the trades of shoemaking, harness-making, and tinsmithing during the days of slavery. He had never been to school a day in his life, but in some way he had learned to read and write while a slave. From the first, these two men saw clearly what my plan of education was, sympathized with me, and supported me in every effort. In the days which were darkest financially for the school, Mr. Campbell was never appealed to when he was not willing to extend all the aid in his power. I do not know two men, one an ex-slaveholder, one an ex-slave, whose advice and judgment I would feel more like following in everything which concerns the life and development of the school at Tuskegee than those of these two men.

I have always felt that Mr. Adams, in a large degree, derived his unusual power of mind from the training given his hands in the process of mastering well three trades during the days of slavery. If one goes today into any Southern town, and asks for the leading and most reliable coloured man in the community, I believe that in five cases out of ten he will be directed to a Negro who learned a trade during the days of slavery.

On the morning that the school opened, thirty students reported for admission. I was the only teacher. The students were about equally divided between the sexes. Most of them lived in Macon County, the county in which Tuskegee is situated, and of which it is the county seat. A great many more students wanted to enter the school, but it had been decided to receive only those who were above fifteen years of age, and who had previously received some education. The greater part of the thirty were public-school teachers, and some of them were nearly forty years of age. With the teachers came some of their former pupils, and when they were examined it was amusing to note that in several cases the pupil entered a higher class than did his former teacher. It was also interesting to note how many big books some of them had studied, and how many high-sounding subjects some of them claimed to have mastered. The bigger the book and the longer the name of the subject, the prouder they felt of their accomplishment. Some had studied Latin, and one or two Greek. This they thought entitled them to special distinction.

In fact, one of the saddest things I saw during the month of travel which I have described was a young man, who had attended some high school, sitting down in a one-room cabin, with grease on his clothing, filth all around him, and weeds in the yard and garden, engaged in studying a French grammar.

The students who came first seemed to be fond of memorizing long and complicated "rules" in grammar and mathematics, but had little thought or knowledge of applying these rules to the everyday affairs of their life. One subject which they liked to talk about, and tell me that they had mastered, in arithmetic, was "banking and discount," but I soon found out that neither they nor almost any one in the neighbourhood in which they lived had ever had a bank account. In registering the names of the students, I found that almost every one of them had one or more middle initials. When I asked what the "J" stood for, in the name of John J. Jones, it was explained to me that this was a part of his "entitles." Most of the students wanted to get an education because they thought it would enable them to earn more money as schoolteachers.

Notwithstanding what I have said about them in these respects, I have never seen a more earnest and willing company of young men and women than these students were. They were all willing to learn the right thing as soon as it was shown them what was right. I was determined to start them off on a solid and thorough foundation, so far as their books were concerned. I soon learned that most of them had the merest smattering of the high-sounding things that they had studied. While they could locate the Desert of Sahara or the capital of China on an artificial globe, I found out that the girls could not locate the proper places for the knives and forks on an actual dinner table, or the places on which the bread and meat should be set.

I had to summon a good deal of courage to take a student who had been studying cube root and "banking and discount," and explain to him that the wisest thing for him to do first was thoroughly to master the multiplication table.

The number of pupils increased each week, until by the end of the first month there were nearly fifty. Many of them, however, said that, as they could remain only for two or three months, they wanted to enter a high class and get a diploma the first year if possible.

At the end of the first six weeks a new and rare face entered the school as a co-teacher. This was Miss Olivia A. Davidson, who later became my wife. Miss Davidson was born in Ohio, and received her preparatory education in the public schools of that state. When little more than a girl, she heard of the need of teachers in the South. She went to the state of Mississippi and began teaching there. Later she taught in the city of Memphis. While teaching in Mississippi, one of her pupils became ill with smallpox. Every one in the community was so frightened that no one would nurse the boy. Miss Davidson closed her school and remained by the bedside of the boy night and day until he recovered. While she was at her Ohio home on her vacation, the worst epidemic of yellow fever broke out in Memphis, Tenn., that perhaps has ever occurred in the South. When she heard of this, she at once telegraphed the Mayor of Memphis, offering her services as a yellow-fever nurse, although she had never had the disease.

Miss Davidson's experience in the South showed her that the people needed something more than mere book learning. She heard of the Hampton system of education, and decided that this was what she wanted in order to prepare herself for better work in the South. The attention of Mrs. Mary Hemenway, of Boston, was attracted to her rare ability. Through Mrs. Hemenway's kindness and generosity, Miss Davidson, after graduating at Hampton, received an opportunity to complete a two years' course of training at the Massachusetts State Normal School at Framingham.

Before she went to Framingham, someone suggested to Miss Davidson that, since she was so very light in colour, she might find it more comfortable not to be known as a coloured woman in this school in Massachusetts. She at once replied that under no circumstances and for no considerations would she consent to deceive any one in regard to her racial identity.

Soon after her graduation from the Framingham institution, Miss Davidson came to Tuskegee, bringing into the school many valuable and fresh ideas as to the best methods of teaching, as well as a rare moral character and a life of unselfishness that I think has seldom been equaled. No single individual did more toward laying the foundations of the Tuskegee Institute so as to insure the successful work that has been done there than Olivia A. Davidson.

Miss Davidson and I began consulting as to the future of the school from the first. The students were making progress in learning books and in developing their minds; but it became apparent at once that, if we were to make any permanent impression upon those who had come to us for training, we must do something besides teach them mere books. The students had come from homes where they had had no opportunities for lessons which would teach them how to care for their bodies. With few exceptions, the homes in Tuskegee in which the students boarded were but little improvement upon those from which they had come. We wanted to teach the students how to bathe; how to care for their teeth and clothing. We wanted to teach them what to eat, and how to eat it properly, and how to care for their rooms. Aside from this, we wanted to give them such a practical knowledge of some one industry, together with the spirit of industry, thrift, and economy, that they would be sure of knowing how to make a living after they had left us. We wanted to teach them to study actual things instead of mere books alone.

We found that the most of our students came from the country districts, where agriculture in some form or other was the main dependence of the people. We learned that about eighty-five per cent of the coloured people in the Gulf states depended upon agriculture for their living. Since this was true, we wanted to be careful not to educate our students out of sympathy with agricultural life, so that they would be attracted from the country to the cities, and yield to the temptation of trying to live by their wits. We wanted to give them such an education as would fit a large proportion of them to be teachers, and at the same time cause them to return to the plantation districts and show the people there how to put new energy and new ideas into farming, as well as into the intellectual and moral and religious life of the people.

All these ideas and needs crowded themselves upon us with a seriousness that seemed well-nigh overwhelming. What were we to do? We had only the little old shanty and the abandoned church which the good coloured people of the town of Tuskegee had kindly loaned us for the accommodation of the classes. The number of students was increasing daily. The more we saw of them, and the more we traveled through the country districts, the more we saw that our efforts were reaching, to only a partial degree, the actual needs of the people whom we wanted to lift up through the medium of the students whom we should educate and send out as leaders.

The more we talked with the students, who were then coming to us from several parts of the state, the more we found that the chief ambition among a large proportion of them was to get an education so that they would not have to work any longer with their hands.

This is illustrated by a story told of a coloured man in Alabama, who, one hot day in July, while he was at work in a cotton-field, suddenly stopped, and, looking toward the skies, said:"O Lawd, de cotton am so grassy, de work am so hard, and the sun am so hot dat I b'lieve dis darky am called to preach!"

About three months after the opening of the school, and at the time when we were in the greatest anxiety about our work, there came into the market for sale an old and abandoned plantation which was situated about a mile from the town of Tuskegee. The mansion house—or "big house," as it would have been called—which had been occupied by the owners during slavery, had been burned. After making a careful examination of this place, it seemed to be just the location that we wanted in order to make our work effective and permanent.

But how were we to get it? The price asked for it was very little—only five hundred dollars—but we had no money, and we were strangers in the town and had no credit. The owner of the land agreed to let us occupy the place if we could make a payment of two hundred and fifty dollars down, with the understanding that the remaining two hundred and fifty dollars must be paid within a year. Although five hundred dollars was cheap for the land it was a large sum when one did not have any part of it.

In the midst of the difficulty I summoned a great deal of courage and wrote to my friend General J. F. B. Marshall, the Treasurer of the Hampton Institute, putting the situation before him and beseeching him to lend me the two hundred and fifty dollars on my own personal responsibility. Within a few days a reply came to the effect that he had no authority to lend me money belonging to the Hampton Institute, but that he would gladly lend me the amount needed from his own personal funds.

I confess that the securing of this money in this way was a great surprise to me, as well as a source of gratification. Up to that time I never had had in my possession so much money as one hundred dollars at a time, and the loan which I had asked General Marshall for seemed a tremendously large sum to me. The fact of my being responsible for the repaying of such a large amount of money weighed very heavily upon me.

I lost no time in getting ready to move the school on to the new farm. At the time we occupied the place there were standing upon it a cabin, formerly used as the dining room, an old kitchen, a stable, and an old hen-house. Within a few weeks we had all of these structures in use. The stable was repaired and used as a recitation-room, and very presently the hen-house was utilized for the same purpose.

I recall that one morning, when I told an old coloured man who lived near, and who sometimes helped me, that our school had grown so large that it would be necessary for us to use the hen-house for school purposes, and that I wanted him to help me give it a thorough cleaning out the next day, he replied, in the most earnest manner: "What you mean, boss? You sholy ain't gwine clean out de hen-house in de day-time?"

Nearly all the work of getting the new location ready for school purposes was done by the students after school was over in the afternoon. As soon as we got the cabins in condition to be used, I determined to clear up some land so that we could plant a crop. When I explained my plan to the young men, I noticed that they did not seem to take to it very kindly. It was hard for them to see the connection between clearing land and an education. Besides, many of them had been schoolteachers, and they questioned whether or not clearing land would be in keeping with their dignity. In order to relieve them from any embarrassment, each afternoon after school I took my axe and led the way to the woods. When they saw that I was not afraid or ashamed to work, they began to assist with more enthusiasm. We kept at the work each afternoon, until we had cleared about twenty acres and had planted a crop.

In the meantime Miss Davidson was devising plans to repay the loan. Her first effort was made by holding festivals, or "suppers." She made a personal canvass among the white and coloured families in the town of Tuskegee, and got them to agree to give something, like a cake, a chicken, bread, or pies, that could be sold at the festival. Of course the coloured people were glad to give anything that they could spare, but I want to add that Miss Davidson did not apply to a single white family, so far as I now remember, that failed to donate something; and in many ways the white families showed their interest in the school.

Several of these festivals were held, and quite a little sum of money was raised. A canvass was also made among the people of both races for direct gifts of money, and most of those applied to gave small sums. It was often pathetic to note the gifts of the older coloured people, most of whom had spent their best days in slavery. Sometimes they would give five cents, sometimes twenty-five cents. Sometimes the contribution was a quilt, or a quantity of sugarcane. I recall one old coloured woman, who was about seventy years of age, who came to see me when we were raising money to pay for the farm. She hobbled into the room where I was, leaning on a cane. She was clad in rags; but they were clean. She said: "Mr. Washin'ton, God knows I spent de bes' days of my life in slavery. God knows I's ignorant an' poor; but," she added, "I knows what you an' Miss Davidson is tryin' to do.

I knows you is tryin' to make better men an' better women for de coloured race. I ain't got no money, but I wants you to take dese six eggs, what I's been savin' up, an' I wants you to put dese six eggs into de eddication of dese boys an' gals."

Since the work at Tuskegee started, it has been my privilege to receive many gifts for the benefit of the institution, but never any, I think, that touched me so deeply as this one.

26

Selected Writings of W.E.B. DuBois

William Edward Burghardt DuBois (1868–1963) began thinking and writing about the social status of African Americans at an early age. He wrote articles for the New York Globe at age 15 and completed a doctorate at Harvard when he was 26. He was convinced that Blacks must push and agitate for social advancement to occur. He was opposed to the methods of "submission" and "adjustment" pursued by Booker T. Washington. DuBois wrote prolifically and served as the editor-in-chief of *Crisis* magazine, published by the NAACP, for 25 years. His scathing editorials often provoked conflict with the NAACP leadership. DuBois grew increasingly frustrated by the persistence of racial injustice in the United States and the failure of Black leaders to be aggressive in their demands for change. He embraced radical social causes and ideologies, such as Pan-Africanism and communism, which alienated him from the mainstream. He lived in Ghana during the last years of his life and became a Ghanaian citizen shortly before his death in 1963. In the following selections, DuBois explains his views on the role of education in the social advancement of African Americans and his disagreements with the philosophy and methods of Booker T. Washington. —AJM

American Educational Thought: Essays from 1640–1940, pages 425–447
Copyright © 2010 by Information Age Publishing

Of the Training of Black Men, 1902

From the shimmering swirl of waters where many, many thoughts ago the slave-ship first saw the square tower of Jamestown have flowed down to our day three streams of thinking: one from the larger world here and overseas, saying, the multiplying of human wants in culture lands calls for the world-wide co-operation of men in satisfying them. Hence arises a new human unity, pulling the ends of earth nearer, and all men, black, yellow, and white. The larger humanity strives to feel in this contact of living nations and sleeping hordes a thrill of new life in the world, crying, If the contact of Life and Sleep be Death, shame on such Life. To be sure, behind this thought lurks the afterthought of force and dominion,—the making of brown men to delve when the temptation of beads and red calico cloys.

The second thought streaming from the death-ship and the curving river is the thought of the older South: the sincere and passionate belief that somewhere between men and cattle God created a tertium quid, and called it a Negro,—a clownish, simple creature, at times even lovable within its limitations, but straitly foreordained to walk within the Veil. To be sure, behind the thought lurks the afterthought, —some of them with favoring chance might become men, but in sheer self-defense we dare not let them, and build about them walls so high, and hang between them and the light a veil so thick, that they shall not even think of breaking through.

And last of all there trickles down that third and darker thought, the thought of the things themselves, the confused half-conscious mutter of men who are black and whitened, crying Liberty, Freedom, Opportunity— vouchsafe to us, O boastful World, the chance of living men! To be sure, behind the thought lurks the afterthought: suppose, after all, the World is right and we are less than men? Suppose this mad impulse within is all wrong, some mock mirage from the untrue?

So here we stand among thoughts of human unity, even through conquest and slavery; the inferiority of black men, even if forced by fraud; a shriek in the night for the freedom of men who themselves are not yet sure of their right to demand it. This is the tangle of thought and afterthought wherein we are called to solve the problem of training men for life.

Behind all its curiousness, so attractive alike to sage and dilettante, lie its dim dangers, throwing across us shadows at once grotesque and awful. Plain it is to us that what the world seeks through desert and wild we have within our threshold; —a stalwart laboring force, suited to the semi-tropics; if, deaf to the voice of the Zeitgeist, we refuse to use and develop these men, we risk poverty and loss. If, on the other hand, seized by the brutal afterthought, we debauch the race thus caught in our talons, selfishly sucking their blood and brains in the future as in the past, what shall save us from national decadence? Only that saner selfishness which, Education teaches men, can find the rights of all in the whirl of work.

Again, we may decry the color prejudice of the South, yet it remains a heavy fact. Such curious kinks of the human mind exist and must be reckoned with soberly. They cannot be laughed away, nor always successfully stormed at, nor easily abolished by act of legislature. And yet they cannot be encouraged by being let alone. They must be recognized as facts, but unpleasant facts; things that stand in the way of civilization and religion and common decency. They can be met in but one way: by the breadth and broadening of human reason, by catholicity of taste and culture. And so, too, the native ambition and aspiration of men, even though they be black, backward, and ungraceful, must not lightly be dealt with. To stimulate wildly weak and untrained minds is to play with mighty fires; to flout their striving idly is to welcome a harvest of brutish crime and shameless lethargy in our very laps. The guiding of thought and the deft coordination of deed is at once the path of honor and humanity.

And so, in this great question of reconciling three vast and partially contradictory streams of thought, the one panacea of Education leaps to the lips of all; such human training as will best use the labor of all men without enslaving or brutalizing; such training as will give us poise to encourage the prejudices that bulwark society, and stamp out those that in sheer barbarity deafen us to the wail of prisoned souls within the Veil, and the mounting fury of shackled men.

But when we have vaguely said Education will set this tangle straight, what have we uttered but a truism? Training for life teaches living; but what training for the profitable living together of black men and white? Two hundred years ago our task would have seemed easier. Then Dr. Johnson blandly assured us that education was needed solely for the embellishments of life, and was useless for ordinary vermin. Today we have climbed to heights where we would open at least the outer courts of knowledge to all, display its treasures to many, and select the few to whom its mystery of Truth is revealed, not wholly by truth or the accidents of the stock market, but at least in part according to deftness and aim, talent and character. This programme, however, we are sorely puzzled in carrying out through that part of the land where the blight of slavery fell hardest, and where we are dealing with two backward peoples. To make here in human education that ever necessary combination of the permanent and the contingent—of the ideal and the practical in workable equilibrium—has been there, as it ever must be in every age and place, a matter of infinite experiment and frequent mistakes.

In rough approximation we may point out four varying decades of work in Southern education since the Civil War. From the close of the war until 1876 was the period of uncertain groping and temporary relief. There were army schools, mission schools, and schools of the Freedmen's Bureau in chaotic disarrangement, seeking system and cooperation. Then followed ten years of constructive definite effort toward the building of complete school systems in the South. Normal schools and colleges were founded for the freedmen, and teachers trained there to man the public schools. There was the inevitable tendency of war to underestimate the prejudice of the master and the ignorance of the slave, and all seemed clear sailing out of the wreckage of the storm. Meantime, starting in this decade yet especially developing from 1885 to 1895, began the industrial revolution of the South. The land saw glimpses of a new destiny and the stirring of new ideals. The educational system striving to complete itself saw new obstacles and a field of work ever broader and deeper. The Negro colleges, hurriedly founded, were inadequately equipped, illogically distributed, and of varying efficiency and grade; the normal and high schools were doing little more than common school work, and the common schools were training but a third of the children who ought to be in them, and training these too often poorly. At the same time the white South, by reason of its sudden conversion from the slavery ideal, by so much the more became set and strengthened in its racial prejudice, and crystallized it into harsh law and harsher custom; while the marvelous pushing forward of the poor white daily threatened to take even bread and butter from the mouths of the heavily handicapped sons of the freedmen. In the midst, then, of the larger problem of Negro education sprang up the more practical question of work, the inevitable economic quandary that faces a people in the transition from slavery to freedom, and especially those who make that change amid hate and prejudice, lawlessness and ruthless competition.

The industrial school springing to notice in this decade, but coming to full recognition in the decade beginning with 1895, was the proffered answer to this combined educational and economic crisis, and an answer of singular wisdom and timeliness. From the very first in nearly all the schools some attention had been given to training in handiwork, but now was this training first raised to a dignity that brought it in direct touch with the South's magnificent industrial development, and given an emphasis which reminded black folk that before the Temple of Knowledge swing the Gates of Toil.

Yet after all they are but gates, and when turning our eyes from the temporary and the contingent in the Negro problem to the broader question of the permanent uplifting and civilization of black men in America, we have a right to inquire, as this enthusiasm for material advancement mounts to its height, if after all the industrial school is the final and sufficient answer in the training of the Negro race; and to ask gently, but in all sincerity, the ever recurring query of the ages, Is not life more than meat, and the body more than raiment? And men ask this today all the more eagerly because of sinister signs in recent educational movements. The tendency is here born of slavery and quickened to renewed life by the crazy imperialism of the day, to regard human beings as among the material resources of a land to be trained with an eye single to future dividends. Race prejudices, which keep brown and black men in their "places," we are coming to regard as useful allies with such a theory, no matter how much they may dull the ambition and sicken the hearts of struggling human beings. And above all, we daily hear that an education that encourages aspiration, that sets the loftiest of ideals and seeks as an end culture and character than bread-winning, is the privilege of white men and the danger and delusion of black.

Especially has criticism been directed against the former educational efforts to aid the Negro. In the four periods I have mentioned, we find first boundless, planless enthusiasm and sacrifice; then the preparation of teachers for a vast public school system; then the launching and expansion of that school system amid increasing difficulties; and finally the training of workmen for the new and growing industries. This development has been sharply ridiculed as a logical anomaly and flat reversal of nature. Soothly we have been told that first industrial and manual training should have taught the Negro to work, then simple schools should have taught him to read and write, and finally, after years, high and normal schools could have completed the system, as intelligence and wealth demanded.

That a system logically so complete was historically impossible, it needs but a little thought to prove. Progress in human affairs is more often a pull than a push, surging forward of the exceptional man, and the lifting of his duller brethren slowly and painfully to his vantage ground. Thus it was no accident that gave birth to universities centuries before the common schools, that made fair Harvard the first flower of our wilderness. So in the South: the mass of the freedmen at the end of the war lacked the intelligence so necessary to modern workingmen. They must first have the common school to teach them to read, write, and cipher. The white teachers who flocked South went to establish such a common school system. They had no idea of founding colleges; they themselves at first would have laughed at the idea. But they faced, as all men since them have faced, that central paradox of the South, the social separation of the races. Then it was the sudden volcanic rupture of nearly all relations between black and white, in work and government and family life. Since then a new adjustment of relations in economic and political affairs has grown up,—an adjustment subtle and difficult to grasp, yet singularly ingenious, which leaves still that frightful chasm at the color line across which men pass at their peril.

Thus, then and now, there stand in the South two separate worlds; and separate not simply in the higher realms of social intercourse, but also in church and school, on railway and street car, in hotels and theatres, in streets and city sections, in books and newspapers, in asylums and jails, in hospitals and graveyards. There is still enough of contact for large economic and group cooperation, but the separation is so thorough and deep, that it absolutely precludes for the present between the races anything like that sympathetic and effective group training and leadership of the one by the other, such as the American Negro and all backward peoples must have for effectual progress.

This the missionaries of 1868 soon saw; and if effective industrial and trade schools were impractical before the establishment of a common school system, just as certainly no adequate common schools could be founded until there were teachers to teach them. Southern whites would not teach them; Northern whites in sufficient numbers could not be had. If the Negro was to learn, he must teach himself, and the most effective help that could be given him was the establishment of schools to train Negro teachers. This conclusion was slowly but surely reached by every student of the situation until simultaneously, in widely separated regions, without consultation or systematic plan, there arose a series of institutions designed to furnish teachers for the untaught. Above the sneers of critics at the obvious defects of this procedure must ever stand its one crushing rejoinder: in a single generation they put thirty thousand black teachers in the South; they wiped out the illiteracy of the majority of the black people of the land, and they made Tuskegee possible.

Such higher training schools tended naturally to deepen broader development: at first they were common and grammar schools, then some became high schools. And finally, by 1900, some thirty-four had one year or more of studies of college grade. This development was reached with different degrees of speed in different institutions: Hampton is still a high school, while Fisk University started her college in 1871, and Spelman Seminary about 1896. In all cases the aim was identical: to maintain the standards of the lower training by giving teachers and leaders the best practicable training; and above all to furnish the black world with adequate standards of human culture and lofty ideals of life. It was not enough that the teachers of teachers should be trained in technical normal methods; they must also, so far as possible, be broad-minded, cultured men and women, to scatter civilization among a people whose ignorance was not simply of letters, but of life itself.

It can thus be seen that the work of education in the South began with higher institutions of training, which threw off as their foliage common schools, and later industrial schools, and at the same time strove to shoot their roots ever deeper toward college and university training. That this was an inevitable and necessary development, sooner or later, goes without saying; but there has been, and still is, a question in many minds if the natural growth was not forced, and if the higher training was not either overdone or done with cheap and unsound methods. Among white Southerners this feeling is widespread and positive. A prominent Southern journal voiced this in a recent editorial: "The experiment that has been made to give the colored students classical training has not been satisfactory. Even though many were able to pursue the course, most of them did so in a parrot-like way, learning what was taught, but not seeming to appropriate the truth and import of their instruction, and graduating without sensible aim or valuable occupation for their future. The whole scheme has proved a waste of time, efforts, and the money of the state."

While most far-minded men would recognize this as extreme and over-drawn, still without doubt many are asking, Are there a sufficient number of Negroes ready for college training to warrant the undertaking? Are not too many students prematurely forced into this work? Does it not have the effect of dissatisfying the young Negro with his environment? And do these graduates succeed in real life? Such natural questions cannot be evaded, nor on the other hand must a nation naturally skeptical as to Negro ability assume an unfavorable answer without careful inquiry and patient openness to conviction. We must not forget that most Americans answer all queries regarding the Negro a priori, and that the least that human courtesy can do is to listen to evidence.

The advocates of the higher education of the Negro would be the last to deny the incompleteness and glaring defects of the present system: too many institutions have attempted to do college work, the work in some cases has not been thoroughly done, and quantity rather than quality has sometimes been sought. But all this can be said of higher education throughout the land: it is the almost inevitable incident of educational growth, and leaves the deeper question of the legitimate demand for the higher training of Negroes untouched. And this latter question can be settled in but one way—by a first-hand study of the facts. If we leave out of view all institutions which have not actually graduated students from a course higher than that of a New England high school, even though they be called colleges; if then we take the thirty-four remaining institutions, we may clear up many misapprehensions by asking searchingly, What kind of institutions are they, what do they teach, and what sort of men do they graduate?

And first we may say that this type of college, including Atlanta, Fisk and Howard, Wilberforce and Lincoln, Biddle, Shaw, and the rest, is peculiar, almost unique. Through the shining trees that whisper before me as I write, I catch glimpses of a boulder of New England granite, covering a grave, which graduates of Atlanta University have placed there:

> "IN GRATEFUL MEMORY OF THEIR FORMER TEACHER AND FRIEND AND OF THE UNSELFISH LIFE HE LIVED, AND THE NOBLE WORK HE WROUGHT; THAT THEY, THEIR CHILDREN, AND THEIR CHILDREN'S CHILDREN MIGHT BE BLESSED."

This was the gift of New England to the freed Negro: not alms, but a friend; not cash, but character. It was not and is not money these seething millions want, but love and sympathy, the pulse of hearts beating with red blood; a gift which to-day only their own kindred and race can bring to the masses, but which once saintly souls brought to their favored children in the crusade of the sixties, that finest thing in American history, and one of the few things untainted by sordid greed and cheap vainglory. The teachers in these institutions came not to keep the Negroes in their place, but to raise them out of their places where the filth of slavery had wallowed them. The colleges they founded were social settlements; homes where the best of the sons of the freedmen came in close and sympathetic touch with the best traditions of New England. They lived and ate together, studied and worked, hoped and harkened in the dawning light. In actual formal content their curriculum was doubtless old-fashioned, but in educational power it was supreme, for it was the contact of living souls.

From such schools about two thousand Negroes have gone forth with the bachelor's degree. The number in itself is enough to put at rest the argument that too large a proportion of Negroes are receiving higher training. If the ratio to population of all Negro students throughout the land, in both college and secondary training, be counted, Commissioner Harris assures us "it must be increased to five times its present average" to equal the average of the land.

Fifty years ago the ability of Negro students in any appreciable numbers to master a modern college course would have been difficult to prove.

Today it is proved by the fact that four hundred Negroes, many of whom have been reported as brilliant students, have received the bachelor's degree from Harvard, Yale, Oberlin, and seventy other leading colleges. Here we have, then, nearly twenty-five hundred Negro graduates, of whom the crucial query must be made. How far did their training fit them for life? It is of course extremely difficult to collect satisfactory data on such a point,— difficult to reach the men, to get trustworthy testimony, and to gauge that testimony by any generally acceptable criterion of success. In 1900, the Conference at Atlanta University undertook to study these graduates, and published the results. First they sought to know what these graduates were doing, and succeeded in getting answers from nearly two thirds of the living. The direct testimony was in almost all cases corroborated by the reports of the colleges where they graduated, so that in the main the reports were worthy of credence. Fifty-three per cent of these graduates were teachers,— presidents of institutions, heads of normal schools, principals of city school systems, and the like. Seventeen per cent were clergymen; another seventeen per cent were in the professions, chiefly as physicians. Over six per cent were merchants, farmers, and artisans, and four per cent were in the government civil service. Granting even that a considerable proportion of the third unheard from are unsuccessful, this is a record of usefulness. Personally I know many hundreds of these graduates and have corresponded with more than a thousand; through others I have followed carefully the life-work of scores; I have taught some of them and some of the pupils whom they have taught, lived in homes which they have builded, and looked at life through their eyes. Comparing them as a class with my fellow students in New England and in Europe, I cannot hesitate in saying that nowhere have I met men and women with a broader spirit of helpfulness, with deeper devotion to their life-work, or with more consecrated determination to succeed in the face of bitter difficulties than among Negro college-bred men. They have, to be sure, their proportion of ne'er-do-wells, their pedants and lettered fools, but they have a surprisingly small proportion of them; they have not that culture of manner which we instinctively associate with university men, forgetting that in reality it is the heritage from cultured homes, and that no people a generation removed from slavery can escape a certain unpleasant rawness and gaucherie, despite the best of training.

With all their larger vision and deeper sensibility, these men have usually been conservative, careful leaders. They have seldom been agitators, have withstood the temptation to head the mob, and have worked steadily and faithfully in a thousand communities in the South. As teachers they have given the South a commendable system of city schools and large numbers of private normal schools and academies. Colored college-bred men have worked side by side with white college graduates at Hampton; almost from the beginning the backbone of Tuskegee's teaching force has been formed of graduates from Fisk and Atlanta. And today the institute is filled with college graduates, from the energetic wife of the principal down to the teacher of agriculture, including nearly half of the executive council and a majority of the heads of departments. In the professions, college men are slowly but surely leavening the Negro church, are healing and preventing the devastations of disease, and beginning to furnish legal protection for the liberty and property of the toiling masses. All this is needful work. Who would do it if Negroes did not? How could Negroes do it if they were not trained carefully for it? If white people need colleges to furnish teachers, ministers, lawyers, and doctors, do black people need nothing of the sort?

If it be true that there are an appreciable number of Negro youth in the land capable by character and talent to receive that higher training, the end of which is culture, and if the two and a half thousand who have had something of this training in the past have in the main proved themselves useful to their race and generation, the question then comes, What place in the future development of the South might the Negro college and college-bred man to occupy? That the present social separation and acute race sensitiveness must eventually yield to the influences of culture as the South grows civilized is clear. But such transformation calls for singular wisdom and patience. If, while the healing of this vast sore is progressing, the races are to live for many years side by side, united in economic effort, obeying a common government, sensitive to mutual thought and feeling, yet subtly and silently separate in many matters of deeper human intimacy—if this unusual and dangerous development is to progress amid peace and order, mutual respect and growing intelligence, it will call for social surgery at once the delicatest and nicest in modern history. It will demand broad-minded, upright men both white and black, and in its final accomplishment American civilization will triumph. So far as white men are concerned, this fact is today being recognized in the South, and a happy renaissance of university education seems imminent. But the very voices that cry Hail! to this good work are, strange to relate, largely silent or antagonistic to the higher education of the Negro.

Strange to relate! for this is certain, no secure civilization can be built in the South with the Negro as an ignorant, turbulent proletariat. Suppose we seek to remedy this by making them laborers and nothing more: they are not fools, they have tasted of the Tree of Life, and they will not cease to think, will not cease attempting to read the riddle of the world. By taking away their best equipped teachers and leaders, by slamming the door of opportunity in the faces of their bolder and brighter minds, will you make them satisfied with their lot? or will you not rather transfer their leading from the hands of men taught to think to the hands of untrained demagogues? We ought not to forget that despite the pressure of poverty, and despite the active discouragement and even ridicule of friends, the demand for higher training steadily increases among Negro youth: there were, in the years from 1875 to 1880, twenty-two Negro graduates from Northern colleges; from 1885 to 1895 there were forty-three, and from 1895 to 1900, nearly 100 graduates. From Southern Negro colleges there were, in the same three periods, 143, 413, and over 500 graduates.

Here, then, is the plain thirst for training; by refusing to give this Talented Tenth the key to knowledge can any sane man imagine that they will lightly lay aside their yearning and contentedly become hewers of wood and drawers of water?

No. The dangerously clear logic of the Negro's position will more and more loudly assert itself in that day when increasing wealth and more intricate social organization preclude the South from being, as it so largely is, simply an armed camp for intimidating black folk. Such waste of energy cannot be spared if the South is to catch up with civilization. And as the black third of the land grows in thrift and skill, unless skillfully guided in its larger philosophy, it must more and more brood over the red past and the creeping, crooked present, until it grasps a gospel of revolt and revenge and throws its new-found energies athwart the current of advance. Even today the masses of the Negroes see all too clearly the anomalies of their position and the moral crookedness of yours. You may marshal strong indictments against them, but their counter-cries, lacking though they be in formal logic, have burning truths within them which you may not wholly ignore, O Southern Gentlemen! If you deplore their presence here, they ask, Who brought us? When you shriek, Deliver us from the vision of intermarriage, they answer, that legal marriage is infinitely better than systematic concubinage and prostitution. And if in just fury you accuse their vagabonds of violating women, they also in fury quite as just may wail: the rape which your gentlemen have done against helpless black women in defiance of your own laws is written on the foreheads of two millions of mulattoes, and written in ineffaceable blood. And finally, when you fasten crime upon this race as its peculiar trait, they answer that slavery was the arch-crime, and lynching and lawlessness its twin abortion; that color and race are not crimes, and yet they it is which in this land receive most unceasing condemnation, North, East, South, and West.

I will not say such arguments are wholly justified—I will not insist that there is no other side to the shield; but I do say that of the nine millions of

Negroes in this nation, there is scarcely one out of the cradle to whom these arguments do not daily present themselves in the guise of terrible truth. I insist that the question of the future is how best to keep these millions from brooding over the wrongs of the past and the difficulties of the present, so that all their energies may be bent toward a cheerful striving and cooperation with their white neighbors toward a larger, juster, and fuller future. That one wise method of doing this lies in the closer knitting of the Negro to the great industrial possibilities of the South is a great truth. And this the common schools and the manual training and trade schools are working to accomplish. But these alone are not enough. The foundations of knowledge in this race, as in others, must be sunk deep in the college and university if we would build a solid, permanent structure. Internal problems of social advance must inevitably come,—problems of work and wages, of families and homes, of morals and the true valuing of the things of life; and all these and other inevitable problems of civilization the Negro must meet and solve largely for himself, by reason of his isolation; and can there be any possible solution other than by study and thought and an appeal to the rich experience of the past? Is there not, with such a group and in such a crisis, infinitely more danger to be apprehended from half-trained minds and shallow thinking than from over-education and over-refinement? Surely we have wit enough to found a Negro college so manned and equipped as to steer successfully between the dilettante and the fool. We shall hardly induce black men to believe that if their bellies be full it matters little about their brains. They already dimly perceive that the paths of peace winding between honest toil and dignified manhood call for the guidance of skilled thinkers, the loving, reverent comradeship between the black lowly and black men emancipated by training and culture.

The function of the Negro college then is clear: it must maintain the standards of popular education, it must seek the social regeneration of the Negro, and it must help in the solution of problems of race contact and cooperation. And finally, beyond all this, it must develop men. Above our modern socialism, and out of the worship of the mass, must persist and evolve that higher individualism which the centres of culture protect; there must come a loftier respect for the sovereign human soul that seeks to know itself and the world about it; that seeks a freedom for expansion and self-development; that will love and hate and labor in its own way, untrammeled alike by old and new. Such souls aforetime have inspired and guided worlds, and if we be not wholly bewitched by our Rhine-gold, they shall again. Herein the longing of black men must have respect: the rich and bitter depth of their experience, the unknown treasures of their inner life, the strange rendings of nature they have seen, may give the world new points of view and make their loving, living, and doing precious to all human hearts. And to themselves in these the days that try their souls the chance to soar in the dim blue air above the smoke is to their finer spirits boon and guerdon for what they lose on earth by being black.

I sit with Shakespeare and he winces not. Across the color line I move arm in arm with Balzac and Dumas, where smiling men and welcoming women glide in gilded halls. From out the caves of Evening that swing between the strong-limbed earth and the tracery of the stars, I summon Aristotle and Aurelius and what soul I will, and they come all graciously with no scorn nor condescension. So, wed with Truth, I dwell above the Veil. Is this the life you grudge us, O knightly America? Is this the life you long to change into the dull red hideousness of Georgia? Are you so afraid lest peering from this high Pisgah, between Philistine and Amalekite, we sight the Promised Land?

Of Mr. Booker T. Washington and Others, 1903

From birth till death enslaved; in word, in deed, unmanned!
Hereditary bondsmen! Know ye not
Who would be free themselves must strike the blow?
BYRON

Easily the most striking thing in the history of the American Negro since 1876 is the ascendancy of Mr. Booker T. Washington. It began at the time when war memories and ideals were rapidly passing; a day of astonishing commercial development was dawning; a sense of doubt and hesitation over-took the freedmen's sons,—then it was that his leading began. Mr. Washington came, with a simple definite programme, at the psychological moment when the nation was a little ashamed of having bestowed so much sentiment on Negroes, and was concentrating its energies on Dollars. His programme of industrial education, conciliation of the South, and submission and silence as to civil and political rights, was not wholly original; the Free Negroes from 1830 up to war-time had striven to build industrial schools, and the American Missionary Association had from the first taught various trades; and Price and others had sought a way of honorable alliance with the best of the Southerners. But Mr. Washington first indissolubly linked these things; he put enthusiasm, unlimited energy, and perfect faith into his programme, and changed it from a by-path into a veritable Way of Life. And the tale of the methods by which he did this is a fascinating study of human life.

It startled the nation to hear a Negro advocating such a programme after many decades of bitter complaint; it startled and won the applause of the South, it interested and won the admiration of the North; and after a confused murmur of protest, it silenced if it did not convert the Negroes themselves.

To gain the sympathy and cooperation of the various elements comprising the white South was Mr. Washington's first task; and this, at the time Tuskegee was founded, seemed, for a black man, well-nigh impossible. And yet ten years later it was done in the word spoken at Atlanta; "In all things purely social we can be as separate as the five fingers, and yet one as the hand in all things essential to mutual progress." This "Atlanta Compromise" is by all odds the most notable thing in Mr. Washington's career. The South interpreted it in different ways: the radicals received it as a complete surrender of the demand for civil and political equality; the conservatives, as a generously conceived working basis for mutual understanding. So both approved it, and today its author is certainly the most distinguished Southerner since Jefferson Davis, and the one with the largest personal following,

Next to this achievement comes Mr. Washington's work in gaining place and consideration in the North. Others less shrewd and tactful had formerly essayed to sit on these two stools and had fallen between them; but as Mr. Washington knew the heart of the South from birth and training, so by singular insight he intuitively grasped the spirit of the age which was dominating the North. And so thoroughly did he learn the speech and thought of triumphant commercialism, and the ideals of material prosperity, that the picture of a lone black boy poring over a French grammar amid the weeds and dirt of a neglected home soon seemed to him the acme of absurdities. One wonders what Socrates and St. Francis of Assisi would say to this.

And yet this very singleness of vision and thorough oneness with his age is a mark of the successful man. It is as though Nature must needs make men narrow in order to give them force. So Mr. Washington's cult has gained unquestioning followers, his work has wonderfully prospered, his friends are legion, and his enemies are confounded. Today he stands as the one recognized spokesman of his ten million fellows, and one of the most notable figures in a nation of seventy millions. One hesitates, therefore, to criticise a life which, beginning with so little, has done so much. And yet the time is come when one may speak in all sincerity and utter courtesy of the mistakes and shortcomings of Mr. Washington's career, as well as of his triumphs, without being thought captious or envious, and without forgetting that it is easier to do ill than well in the world.

The criticism that has hitherto met Mr. Washington has not always been of this broad character. In the South especially has he had to walk warily to avoid the harshest judgments, —and naturally so, for he is dealing with the one subject of deepest sensitiveness to that section. Twice—once when at the Chicago celebration of the Spanish-American War he alluded to the color-prejudice that is "eating away the vitals of the South," and once when he dined with President Roosevelt—has the resulting Southern criticism been violent enough to threaten seriously his popularity. In the North the reeling has several times forced itself into words, that Mr. Washington's counsels of submission overlooked certain elements of true manhood, and that his educational programme was unnecessarily narrow. Usually, however, such criticism has not found open expression, although, too, the spiritual sons of the Abolitionists have not been prepared to acknowledge that the schools founded before Tuskegee, by men of broad ideals and self-sacrificing spirit, were wholly failures or worthy of ridicule. While, then, criticism has not railed to follow Mr. Washington, yet the prevailing public opinion of the land has been but too willing to deliver the solution of a wearisome problem into his hands, and say, "If that is all you and your race ask, take it."

Among his own people, however, Mr. Washington has encountered the strongest and most lasting opposition, amounting at times to bitterness, and even today continuing strong and insistent even though largely silenced in outward expression by the public opinion of the nation. Some of this opposition is, of course, mere envy; the disappointment of displaced demagogues and the spite of narrow minds. But aside from this, there is among educated and thoughtful colored men in all parts of the land a feeling of deep regret, sorrow, and apprehension at the wide currency and ascendancy which some of Mr. Washington's theories have gained. These same men admire his sincerity of purpose, and are willing to forgive much to honest endeavor which is doing something worth the doing. They cooperate with Mr. Washington as far as they conscientiously can; and, indeed, it is no ordinary tribute to this man's tact and power that, steering as he must between so many diverse interests and opinions, he so largely retains the respect of all.

But the hushing of the criticism of honest opponents is a dangerous thing. It leads some of the best of the critics to unfortunate silence and paralysis of effort, and others to burst into speech so passionately and intemperately as to lose listeners. Honest and earnest criticism from those whose interests are most nearly touched, —criticism of writers by readers, —this is the soul of democracy and the safeguard of modern society. If the best of the American Negroes receive by outer pressure a leader whom they had not recognized before, manifestly there is here a certain palpable gain. Yet there is also irreparable loss, —a loss of that peculiarly valuable education which a group receives when by search and criticism it finds and commissions its own leaders. The way in which this is done is at once the most elementary and the nicest problem of social growth. History is but the record of such group-leadership; and yet how infinitely changeful is its type and character! And of all types and kinds, what can be more instructive than the leadership of a group within a group? —that curious double movement where real progress may be negative and actual advance be relative retrogression. All this is the social student's inspiration and despair.

Now in the past the American Negro has had instructive experience in the choosing of group leaders, founding thus a peculiar dynasty which in the light of present conditions is worthwhile studying. When sticks and stones and beasts form the sole environment of a people, their attitude is largely one of determined opposition to and conquest of natural forces. But when to earth and brute is added an environment of men and ideas, then the attitude of the imprisoned group may take three main forms, —a feeling of revolt and revenge; an attempt to adjust all thought and action to the will of the greater group; or, finally, a determined effort at self-realization and self-development despite environing opinion. The influence of all of these attitudes at various times can be traced in the history of the American Negro, and in the evolution of his successive leaders.

Before 1750, while the fire of African freedom still burned in the veins of the slaves, there was in all leadership or attempted leadership but the one motive of revolt and revenge, —typified in the terrible Maroons, the Danish blacks, and Cato of Stono, and veiling all the Americas in fear of insurrection. The liberalizing tendencies of the latter half of the eighteenth century brought, along with kindlier relations between black and white, thoughts of ultimate adjustment and assimilation. Such aspiration was especially voiced in the earnest songs of Phyllis, in the martyrdom of Attucks, the fighting of Salem and Poor, the intellectual accomplishments of Banneker and Derham, and the political demands of the Cuffes.

Stern financial and social stress after the war cooled much of the previous humanitarian ardor. The disappointment and impatience of the Negroes at the persistence of slavery and serfdom voiced itself in two movements. The slaves in the South, aroused undoubtedly by vague rumors of the Haytian revolt, made three fierce attempts at insurrection, —in 1800 under Gabriel in Virginia, in 1822 under Vesey in Carolina, and in 1831 again in Virginia under the terrible Nat Turner. In the Free States, on the other hand, a new and curious attempt at self-development was made. In Philadelphia and New York color-prescription led to a withdrawal of Negro

communicants from white churches and the formation of a peculiar so-
cio-religious institution among the Negroes known as the African Church,
—an organization still living and controlling in its various branches over a
million of men.

Walker's wild appeal against the trend of the times showed how the
world was changing after the coming of the cotton gin. By 1830 slavery
seemed hopelessly fastened on the South, and the slaves thoroughly cowed
into submission. The free Negroes of the North, inspired by the mulatto immigrants from the West Indies, began to change the basis of their demands;
they recognized the slavery of slaves, but insisted that they themselves were
freemen, and sought assimilation and amalgamation with the nation on
the same terms with other men. Thus, Forten and Purvis of Philadelphia,
Shad of Wilmington, Du Bois of New Haven, Barbadoes of Boston, and others, strove singly and together as men, they said, not as slaves; as "people
of color," not as "Negroes." The trend of the times, however, refused them
recognition save in individual and exceptional cases, considered them as
one with all the despised blacks, and they soon found themselves striving to
keep even the rights they formerly had of voting and working and moving
as: freemen. Schemes of migration and colonization arose among them;
but these they refused to entertain, and they eventually turned to the Abolition movement as a final refuge.

Here, led by Remond, Nell, Wells-Brown, and Douglass, a new period of
self-assertion and self-development dawned. To be sure, ultimate freedom
and assimilation was the ideal before the leaders, but the assertion of the
manhood rights of the Negro by himself was the main reliance, and John
Brown's raid was the extreme of its logic. After the war and emancipation,
the great form of Frederick Douglass, the greatest of American Negro leaders, still led the host. Self-assertion, especially in political lines, was the main
programme, and behind Douglass came Elliot, Bruce, and Langston, and
the Reconstruction politicians, and, less conspicuous but of greater social
significance, Alexander Crummell and Bishop Daniel Payne.

Then came the Revolution of 1876, the suppression of the Negro votes,
the changing and shifting of ideals, and the seeking of new lights in the
great night. Douglass, in his old age, still bravely stood for the ideals of his
early manhood, — ultimate assimilation through self-assertion, and on no
other terms. For a time Price arose as a new leader, destined, it seemed, not
to give up, but to re-state the old ideals in a form less repugnant to the white
South. But he passed away in his prime. Then came the new leader. Nearly
all the former ones had become leaders by the silent suffrage of their fellows, had sought to lead their own people alone, and were usually, save

Douglass, little known outside their race. But Booker T. Washington arose as essentially the leader not of one race but of two, —a compromiser between the South, the North, and the Negro. Naturally the Negroes resented, at first bitterly, signs of compromise which surrendered their civil and political rights, even though this was to be exchanged for larger chances of economic development. The rich and dominating North, however, was not only weary of the race problem, but was investing largely in Southern enterprises, and welcomed any method of peaceful cooperation. Thus, by national opinion, the Negroes began to recognize Mr. Washington's leadership; and the voice of criticism was hushed.

Mr. Washington represents in Negro thought the old attitude of adjustment and submission; but adjustment at such a peculiar time as to make his programme unique. This is an age of unusual economic development, and Mr. Washington's programme naturally takes an economic cast, becoming a gospel of Work and Money to such an extent as apparently almost completely to overshadow the higher aims of life. Moreover, this is an age when the more advanced races are coming in closer contact with the less developed races, and the race-feeling is therefore intensified; and Mr. Washington's programme practically accepts the alleged inferiority of the Negro races. Again, in our own land, the reaction from the sentiment of war time has given impetus to race-prejudice against Negroes, and Mr. Washington withdraws many of the high demands of Negroes as men and American citizens. In other periods of intensified prejudice all the Negro's tendency to self-assertion has been called forth; at this period a policy of submission is advocated. In the history of nearly all other races and peoples the doctrine preached at such crises has been that manly self-respect is worth more than lands and houses, and that a people who voluntarily surrender such respect, or cease striving for it, are not worth civilizing.

In answer to this, it has been claimed that the Negro can survive only through submission. Mr. Washington distinctly asks that black people give up, at least for the present, three things, —First, political power, Second, insistence on civil rights, Third, higher education of Negro youth, —and concentrate all their energies or industrial education, and accumulation of wealth, and the conciliation of the South. This policy has been courageously and insistently advocated for over fifteen years, and has been triumphant for perhaps ten years. As a result of this tender of the palm-branch, what has been the return? In these years there have occurred:

1. The disfranchisement of the Negro.
2. The legal creation of a distinct status of civil inferiority for the Negro.

3. The steady withdrawal of aid from institutions for the higher training of the Negro.

These movements are not, to be sure, direct results of Mr. Washington's teachings; but his propaganda has, without a shadow of doubt, helped their speedier accomplishment. The question then comes: Is it possible, and probable, that nine millions of men can make effective progress in economic lines if they are deprived of political rights, made a servile caste, and allowed only the most meagre chance for developing their exceptional men? If history and reason give any distinct answer to these questions, it is an emphatic NO. And Mr. Washington thus faces the triple paradox of his career:

1. He is striving nobly to make Negro artisans, businessmen and property-owners; but it is utterly impossible, under modern competitive methods, for workingmen and property-owners to defend their rights and exist without the right of suffrage.
2. He insists on thrift and self-respect, but at the same time counsels a silent submission to civic inferiority such as is bound to sap the manhood of any race in the long run.
3. He advocates common-school and industrial training, and depreciates institutions of higher learning; but neither the Negro common-schools, nor Tuskegee itself, could remain open a day were it not for teachers trained in Negro colleges, or trained by their graduates.

This triple paradox in Mr. Washington's position is the object of criticism by two classes of colored Americans. One class is spiritually descended from Toussaint the Savior, through Gabriel, Vesey, and Turner, and they represent the attitude of revolt and revenge; they hate the white South blindly and distrust the white race generally, and so far as they agree on definite action, think that the Negro's only hope lies in emigration beyond the borders of the United States. And yet, by the irony of fate, nothing has more effectually made this programme seem hopeless than the recent course of the United States toward weaker and darker peoples in the West Indies, Hawaii, and the Philippines, —for where in the world may we go and be safe from lying and brute force?

The other class of Negroes who cannot agree with Mr. Washington has hitherto said little aloud. They deprecate the sight of scattered counsels, of internal disagreement; and especially they dislike making their just criticism of a useful and earnest man an excuse for a general discharge of venom from small-minded opponents. Nevertheless, the questions involved are so fundamental and serious that it is difficult to see how men like the Grimkes, Kelly Miller, J. W. E. Bowen, and other representatives of this group, can much longer be silent. Such men feel in conscience bound to ask of this nation three things:

1. The right to vote.
2. Civic equality.
3. The education of youth according to ability.

They acknowledge Mr. Washington's invaluable service in counseling patience and courtesy in such demands; they do not ask that ignorant black men vote when ignorant whites are debarred, or that any reasonable restrictions in the suffrage should not be applied; they know that the low social level of the mass of the race is responsible for much discrimination against it, but they also know, and the nation knows, that relentless color-prejudice is more often a cause than a result of the Negro's degradation; they seek the abatement of this relic of barbarism, and not its systematic encouragement and pampering by all agencies of social power from the Associated Press to the Church of Christ. They advocate, with Mr. Washington, a broad system of Negro common schools supplemented by thorough industrial training; but they are surprised that a man of Mr. Washington's insight cannot see that no such educational system ever has rested or can rest on any other basis than that of the well-equipped college and university, and they insist that there is a demand for a few such institutions throughout the South to train the best of the Negro youth as teachers, professional men, and leaders.

This group of men honor Mr. Washington for his attitude of conciliation toward the white South; they accept the "Atlanta Compromise" in its broadest interpretation; they recognize, with him, many signs of promise, many men of high purpose and fair judgment, in this section; they know that no easy task has been laid upon a region already tottering under heavy burdens. But, nevertheless, they insist that the way to truth and right lies in straightforward honesty, not in indiscriminate flattery; in praising those of the South who do well and criticising uncompromisingly those who do ill; in taking advantage of the opportunities at hand and urging their fellows to do the same, but at the same time in remembering that only a firm adherence to their higher ideals and aspirations will ever keep those ideals within the realm of possibility. They do not expect that the free right to vote, to enjoy civic rights, and to be educated, will come in a moment; they do not expect to see the bias and prejudices of years disappear at the blast of a trumpet; but they are absolutely certain that the way for a people to gain their reasonable rights is not by voluntarily throwing them away and insisting that they do not want them; that the way for a people to gain respect is not by continually belittling and ridiculing themselves; that, on the contrary, Negroes must insist continually, in season and out of season, that voting is necessary to modern man-hood, that color discrimination is barbarism, and that black boys need education as well as white boys.

In failing thus to state plainly and unequivocally the legitimate demands of their people, even at the cost of opposing an honored leader, the thinking classes of American Negroes would shirk a heavy responsibility, —a responsibility to themselves, a responsibility to the struggling masses, a responsibility to the darker races of men whose future depends so largely on this American experiment, but especially a responsibility to this nation, —this common Fatherland. It is wrong to encourage a man or a people in evil-doing; it is wrong to aid and abet a national crime simply because it is unpopular not to do so. The growing spirit of kindliness and reconciliation between the North and South after the frightful difference of a generation ago ought to be a source of deep congratulation to all, and especially to those whose mistreatment caused the war; but if that reconciliation is to be marked by the industrial slavery and civic death of those same black men, with permanent legislation into a position of inferiority, then those black men, if they are really men, are called upon by every consideration of patriotism and loyalty to oppose such a course by all civilized methods, even though such opposition involves disagreement with Mr. Booker T. Washington. We have no right to sit silently by while the inevitable seeds are sown for a harvest of disaster to our children, black and white.

First, it is the duty of black men to judge the South discriminatingly. The present generation of Southerners are not responsible for the past, and they should not be blindly hated or blamed for it. Furthermore, to no class is the indiscriminate endorsement of the recent course of the South toward Negroes more nauseating than to the best thought of the South. The South is not "solid"; it is a land in the ferment of social change, wherein forces of all kinds are fighting for supremacy; and to praise the ill the South is today perpetrating is just as wrong as to condemn the good. Discriminating and broad-minded criticism is what the South needs, —needs it for the sake of her own white sons and daughters. . . .

Today even the attitude of the Southern whites toward the blacks is not, as so many assume, in all cases the same; the ignorant Southerner hates the Negro, the workingmen fear his competition, the money-makers wish to use him as a laborer, some of the educated see a menace in his upward development, while others—usually the sons of the masters—wish to help him to rise. National opinion has enabled this last class to maintain the Negro common schools, and to protect the Negro partially in property, life, and limb. Through the pressure of the money-makers, the Negro is in danger of being reduced to semi-slavery, especially in the country districts; the workingmen, and those of the educated who fear the Negro, have united to disfranchise him, and some have urged his deportation; while the passions of the ignorant are easily aroused to lynch and abuse any black man. To praise this intricate whirl of thought and prejudice is nonsense; to inveigh indiscriminately against "the South" is unjust; but to use the same breath in praising Governor Aycock, exposing Senator Morgan, arguing with Mr. Thomas Nelson Page, and denouncing Senator Ben Tillman, is not only sane, but the imperative duty of thinking black men.

It would be unjust to Mr. Washington not to acknowledge that in several instances he has opposed movements in the South which were unjust to the Negro; he sent memorials to the Louisiana and Alabama constitutional conventions, he has spoken against lynching, and in other ways has openly or silently set his influence against sinister schemes and unfortunate happenings. Notwithstanding this, it is equally true to assert that on the whole the distinct impression left by Mr. Washington's propaganda is, first, that the South is justified in its present attitude toward the Negro because of the Negro's degradation; secondly, that the prime cause of the Negro's failure to rise more quickly is his wrong education in the past; and, thirdly, that his future rise depends primarily on his own efforts. Each of these propositions is a dangerous half-truth. The supplementary truths must never be lost sight of: first, slavery and race-prejudice are potent if not sufficient causes of the Negro's position; second, industrial and common-school training were necessarily slow in planting because they had to await the black teachers trained by higher institutions, —it being extremely doubtful if any essentially different development was possible, and certainly a Tuskegee was unthinkable before 1880; and, third, while it is a great truth to say that the Negro must strive and strive mightily to help himself, it is equally true that unless his striving be not simply seconded, but rather aroused and encouraged, by the initiative of the richer and wiser environing group, he cannot hope for great success.

In his failure to realize and impress this last point, Mr. Washington ... shift[s] the burden of the Negro problem to the Negro's shoulders and stand[s] aside as critical and rather pessimistic spectators; when in fact the burden belongs to the nation, and the hands of none of us are clean if we bend not our energies to righting these great wrongs.

The South ought to be led, by candid and honest criticism, to assert her better self and do her full duty to the race she has cruelly wronged and is still wronging. The North—her co-partner in guilt—cannot salve her conscience by plastering it with gold. We cannot settle this problem by diplomacy and suaveness, by "policy" alone. If worse come to worst, can the moral fibre of this country survive the slow throttling and murder of nine millions of men?

The black men of America have a duty to perform, a duty stern and delicate, —a forward movement to oppose a part of the work of their greatest leader. So far as Mr. Washington preaches Thrift, Patience, and Industrial Training for the masses, we must hold up his hands and strive with him, rejoicing in his honors and glorying in the strength of this Joshua called of God and of man to lead the headless host. But so far as Mr. Washington apologizes for injustice, North or South, does not rightly value the privilege and duty of voting, belittles the emasculating effects of caste distinctions, and opposes the higher training and ambition of our brighter minds, —so far as he, the South, or the Nation, does this, —we must unceasingly and firmly oppose them. By every civilized and peaceful method we must strive for the rights which the world accords to men, clinging unwaveringly to those great words which the sons of the Fathers would fain forget: "We hold these truths to be self-evident: That all men are created equal; that they are endowed by their Creator with certain unalienable rights; that among these are life, liberty, and the pursuit of happiness."

27

Why Teachers Should Organize

Margaret Haley, 1904

Margaret Haley (1861–1939) was born in Joliet, Illinois, shortly after the Civil War began. She began her career as a teacher in Chicago in 1876 at the age of sixteen. She left teaching in 1901 to become of full time employee of the Chicago Teachers Federation, the local teachers union. Haley spent most of her career lobbying on behalf of teachers, in order to improve wages and working conditions. She became the President of the National Federation of Teachers and used this position to develop the stronger National Education Association (NEA). She was the first woman to speak from the floor of the NEA, and she was a close associate of Ella Flagg Young, a progressive educator, who was the first female President of the NEA. Haley was a strong voice in national education politics. She and her colleagues acquired the nickname, "Lady Labor Sluggers."

In this essay, Haley's appeal to teachers to organize in unions derives from her belief in the responsibilities of citizenship demanded in a democratic form of government. In this sense, Haley's arguments are similar to the pleas made by the founding fathers in the early republic. She quotes Horace Mann and John Dewey, who both influenced her thinking, in an attempt to demonstrate support for public schools and the teaching profession. She observed first-

American Educational Thought: Essays from 1640–1940, pages 449–454
Copyright © 2010 by Information Age Publishing

hand the poor working conditions for teachers, and the increasing similarity of teaching to factory work, which she called "factoryization," and treating teachers like "automatons." She articulated her desire for teachers to be recognized as educators with the power to think and make decisions. Her remarks are relevant today as increasing standardization haunts the world of education; the ability of teachers to make educational decisions about content, methods, and processes has decreased. —CHB

The responsibility for changing existing conditions so as to make it possible for the public school to do its work rests with the people, the whole people. Any attempt on the part of the public to evade or shift this responsibility must result in weakening the public sense of civic responsibility and the capacity for civic duty, besides further isolating the public school from the people, to the detriment of both.

The sense of responsibility for the duties of citizenship in a democracy is necessarily weak in a people so lately freed from monarchical rule as are the American people, and who still retain in their educational, economic, and political systems so much of their monarchical inheritance, with growing tendencies for retaining and developing the essential weaknesses of that inheritance instead of overcoming them.

Practical experience in meeting the responsibilities of citizenship directly, not in evading or shifting them, is the prime need of the American people. However clever or cleverly disguised the schemes for relieving the public of these responsibilities by vicarious performance of them, or however appropriate those schemes in a monarchy, they have no place in a government of the people, by the people, and for the people, and such schemes must result in defeating their object; for to the extent that they obtain they destroy in a people the capacity for self-government.

If the American people cannot be made to realize and meet their responsibility to the public school, no self-appointed custodians of the public intelligence and conscience can do it for them. Horace Mann, speaking of the dependence of the prosperity of the schools on the public intelligence, said:

> The people will sustain no better schools and have no better education than they personally see the need of; and therefore the people are to be informed and elevated as a preliminary step toward elevating the schools.

Sometimes, in our impatience at the slowness with which the public moves in these matters, we are tempted to disregard this wise counsel.

The methods as well as the objects of teachers' organizations must be in harmony with the fundamental object of the public school in a democracy, to preserve and develop the democratic ideal. It is not enough that this ideal be realized in the administration of the schools and the methods of teaching; in all its relations to the public, the public school must conform to this ideal.

Nowhere in the United States today does the public school, as a branch of the public service, receive from the public either the moral or financial support needed to enable it properly to perform its important function in the social organism. The conditions which are militating most strongly against efficient teaching, and which existing organizations of the kind under discussion here are directing their energies toward changing briefly stated are the following:

1. Greatly increased cost of living, together with constant demands for higher standards of scholarship and professional attainments and culture, to be met with practically stationary and wholly inadequate teachers' salaries.
2. Insecurity of tenure of office and lack of provision for old age.
3. Overwork in overcrowded schoolrooms, exhausting both mind and body.
4. And, lastly, lack of recognition of the teacher as an educator in the school system, due to the increased tendency toward "factoryizing education," making the teacher an automaton, a mere factory hand, whose duty it is to carry out mechanically and unquestioningly the ideas and orders of those clothed with the authority of position, and who may or may not know the needs of the children or how to minister to them.

The individuality of the teacher and her power of initiative are thus destroyed, and the result is courses of study, regulations, and equipment which the teachers have had no voice in selecting, which often have no relation to the children's needs, and which prove a hindrance instead of a help in teaching.

Dr. John Dewey, of the University of Chicago, in the *Elementary School Teacher* for December, 1903, says:

As to the teacher: If there is a single public-school system in the United States where there is official and constitutional provision made for submitting questions of methods of discipline and teaching, and the questions of the curriculum, text-books, etc., to the discussion of those actually engaged in the work of teaching, that fact has escaped my notice. Indeed, the opposite situation is so common that it seems, as a rule, to be absolutely taken for granted as the normal and final condition of affairs. The number of persons to whom any other course has occurred as desirable, or even possible—to say nothing of necessary—is apparently very limited. But until the public-school system is organized in such a way that every teacher has some regular and representative way in which he or she can register judgment upon matters of educational importance, with the assurance that this judgment will somehow affect the school system, the assertion that the present system is not, from the internal standpoint, democratic seems to be justified. Either we come here upon some fixed and inherent limitation of the democratic principle, or else we find in this fact an obvious discrepancy between the conduct of the school and the conduct of social life—a discrepancy so great as to demand immediate and persistent effort at reform.

A few days ago Professor George F. James, dean of pedagogy of the State University of Minnesota, said to an audience of St. Paul teachers:

One hundred thousand teachers will this year quit an occupation which does not yield them a living wage. Scores and hundreds of schools are this day closed in the most prosperous sections of this country because the bare pittance offered will not attract teachers of any kind.

Professor James further maintained that school-teachers are not only underpaid, but that they are paid much less proportionately than they received eight years ago. It is necessary that the public understand the effect which teaching under conditions is having upon the education of the children.

A word, before closing, on the relations of the public-school teachers and the public schools to the labor unions. As the professional organization furnishes the motive and ideal which shall determine the character and methods of the organized effort of teachers to secure better conditions for teaching, so is it the province of the educational agencies in a democracy to furnish the motive and ideal which shall determine the character and methods of the organization of its members for self-protection.

There is no possible conflict between the good of society and the good of its members, of which the industrial workers are the vast majority. The organization of these workers for mutual aid has shortened the hours of labor, raised and equalized the wages of men and women, and taken the children from the factories and workshops. These humanitarian achievements of the labor unions—and many others which space forbids enumerating— in raising the standard of living of the poorest and weakest members of society, are a service to society which for its own welfare it must recognize. More than this, by intelligent comprehension of the limitations of the labor unions and the causes of these limitations, by just, judicious, and helpful criticism and cooperation, society must aid them to feel the inspiration of higher ideals, and to find the better means to realize these ideals.

If there is one institution on which the responsibility to perform this service rests most heavily, it is the public school. If there is one body of public servants of whom the public has a right to expect the mental and moral equipment to face the labor question, and other issues vitally affecting the welfare of society and urgently pressing for a rational and scientific solution, it is the public school teachers, whose special contribution to society is their own power to think, the moral courage to follow their convictions, and the training of citizens to think and to express thought in free and intelligent action.

The narrow conception of education which makes the mechanics of reading, and arithmetic, and other subjects, the end and aim of the schools, instead of a means to an end—which mistakes the accidental and incidental for the essential—produces the unthinking, mechanical mind in teacher and pupil, and prevents the public school as an institution, and the public school teachers as a body, from becoming conscious of their relation to society and its problems, and from meeting their responsibilities. On the other hand, that teaching which is most scientific and rational gives the highest degree of power to think and to select the most intelligent means of expressing thought in every field of activity. The ideals and methods of the labor unions are in a measure a test of the efficiency of the schools and other educational agencies.

How shall the public school and the industrial workers, in their struggle to secure the rights of humanity thru a more just and equitable distribution of the products of their labor, meet their mutual responsibility to each other and to society?

Whether the work of coordinating these two great educational agencies, manual and mental labor, with each other and with the social organism, shall be accomplished thru the affiliation of the organizations of brain and manual workers is a mere matter of detail and method to be decided by the exigencies in each case. The essential thing is that the public-school teachers recognize the fact that their struggle to maintain the efficiency of the schools thru better conditions for themselves is a part of the same great struggle which the manual workers—often misunderstood and unaided— have been making for humanity thru their efforts to secure living conditions for themselves and their children; and that back of the unfavorable conditions of both is a common cause.

Two ideals are struggling for supremacy in American life today: one the industrial ideal, dominating thru the supremacy of commercialism, which subordinates the worker to the product and the machine; the other, the ideal of democracy, the ideal of the educators, which places humanity above all machines, and demands that all activity shall be the expression of life. If this ideal of the educators cannot be carried over into the industrial field, then the ideal of industrialism will be carried over into the school. Those two ideals can no more continue to exist in American life than our nation could have continued half slave and half free. If the school cannot bring joy to the work of the world, the joy must go out of its own life, and work in the school as in the factory will become drudgery.

Viewed in this light, the duty and responsibility of the educators in the solution of the industrial question is one which must thrill and fascinate while it awes, for the very depth of the significance of life is shut up in this question. But the first requisite is to put aside all prejudice, all preconceived notions, all misinformation and half-information, and to take to this question what the educators have long recognized must be taken to scientific investigation in other fields. There may have been justification for failure to do this in the past, but we cannot face the responsibility of continued failure and maintain our title as thinkers and educators. When men organize and go out to kill, they go surrounded by pomp, display, and pageantry, under the inspiration of music and with the admiration of the throng. Not so the army of industrial toilers who have been fighting humanity's battles, unhonored and unsung.

It will be well indeed if the teachers have the courage of their convictions and face all that the labor unions have faced with the same courage and perseverance.

Today, teachers of America, we stand at the parting of the ways: Democracy is not on trial, but America is.

28

The Certification of Teachers

A Consideration of Present Conditions with Suggestions as to Future Improvement

Ellwood P. Cubberley, 1906

Ellwood Patterson Cubberley (1868–1941) was born and educated in Antioch, Indiana. Although not initially enamored with school, he met a high school teacher named Arthur Kautz who inspired his interest in a life of education. Cubberley's father wanted him to continue this interest by studying pharmacy at Purdue University so he could take up the family drug-store business, but Cubberley heard a lecture during the summer from the president of Indiana University on "The Value of Higher Education" that inspired him to take a different direction. He attended Indiana University and studied math and science with the goal of becoming a geologist. His expertise in science earned him a teaching position at Ridgeville College (Indiana) and later at Vincennes University (Indiana), of which he eventually became president. From that point on, Cubberley moved down the career path of educational administration. He later became Superintendent of the San Diego Board of Education, on which he served. In 1899, he accepted a position as professor of education at Stanford University's young school of education, where he

American Educational Thought: Essays from 1640–1940, pages 455–471
Copyright © 2010 by Information Age Publishing
455

taught until his retirement in 1933. At Stanford, Cubberley became a major progressive reformer in the emerging field of educational administration. He envisioned the public schools as the most efficient way for the state to educate the millions of southern and eastern European immigrants who were then flocking to America's shores. The strong political and racial views that motivated Cubberley's work are evident when, speaking of these immigrants, he wrote they "served to dilute tremendously our national stock and to weaken and corrupt our political life." Since immigrant culture was sustained in the family, the state education system Cubberley envisioned would need to provide an alternative influence under the guiding hand of scientifically trained administrators. As one of Cubberley's works celebrated, "each year the child is coming to belong more and more to the state, and less and less to the parent." To ensure that the state guided students toward productive vocational ends in the nation's social order, public schools needed trained teachers. Thus, in his books such as *Public School Administration* (1916), Cubberley outlined his case for making schools more efficient by using modern scientific techniques such as standardized tests and scientific training. In the essay below, Cubberley focuses on the need to use tests and teacher certification to improve the effectiveness of teacher training. —PLG

From small beginnings we have gradually evolved, during the past fifty to seventy-five years, a series of American school systems of which we may feel justly proud. Though each state and territory has a different school system, the systems in different states often differing greatly in important features, there is nevertheless such a similarity of aim and purpose between the different state school systems that we not uncommonly group them all together and speak of them collectively as our American public-school system. In this so-called American public-school system we teach sixteen and a half millions of children each year, nearly half a million teachers are required for the work, and for this system we yearly expend over a quarter of a billion of dollars...

For the training of future teachers for the work of instruction we maintain about 180 state normal schools, upon which we expend about four millions of dollars each year. In addition, more than fifty cities maintain city training-schools for the preparation of future teachers for the schools of these cities, and about 100 private normal schools assist in giving some kind of training to those who expect to teach. Two hundred and thirty colleges and universities also offer special courses and contribute their quota of teachers for the higher work of instruction. In 1903–4, 449 private high schools and 272 public high schools also offered some courses of instruction intended for the preparation of future teachers.

All of these institutions tend to increase the number of trained teachers in the schools, and in most states the number of such is slowly increasing;

but so large is the number who teach but a short time, and so easy is it to enter upon the work of teaching, in most states without the necessity of any training of a professional nature, that the number of trained teachers actually teaching in the different states is not very large. Perhaps, averaging all the different states of the Union, 15 to 20 per cent, of all the teachers in our schools have received some special training before entering upon the work of a teacher. The remaining 80 to 85 per cent, have been prepared by private study, and tested wholly by examination and experience, and have had no special professional preparation whatever for the work of teaching.

Not only is the largest item of expense in all schools that for the salary of the teacher, but the teacher is also the most important single factor in determining the efficiency of our educational system. Hence it is very important not only that the teacher possess an adequate academic and professional education, but that he or she also be imbued with the right attitude toward the institutions of democracy which we cherish, and toward those ethical principles which we as a people hold to be of abiding worth.

Obviously so costly and important a work as that of educating the future citizens of our nation cannot be thrown open without qualification to anyone who wishes to enter it. Just as the state must from time to time, determine what requirements it deems advisable to enforce as to subjects of instruction, length of school term, minimum tax-rate to be levied for education, attendance at school, additional advantages which must be provided, and other items looking toward the enforcing of the educational rights of children, so also must the state, from time to time, set the educational and professional requirements which it must exact from those who expect to teach in the schools which the state has deemed it wise to provide.

To determine whether or not any individual possesses these educational prerequisites for admission to the profession of teaching, two methods are available. One is to examine the candidate by giving him or her a written or oral examination, or both, the examination to be given either by the laymen of the school committee or by a professional examining body; and the other is to accept satisfactory evidence of proper education and professional training, such as college or normal-school diplomas, or certificates of qualification issued elsewhere, as being the equivalent of the oral or written test. It is not possible, in most states, under present conditions, to use the second method alone, though it is obviously much the better of the two; so for some time to come the two methods must exist side by side.

The idea of requiring those who wish to teach to pass an examination to prove their fitness is an old one. In its rudimentary beginnings it is as old as schools themselves. The examination of the candidate for master was one of the functions of the mediaeval university, and in some form or other it has been in use ever since. With the rapid development of state and national systems of public education during the nineteenth century, an examination of candidates for entry to the teaching profession has come to be one of the established rights and duties of the state. In our own country it has been customary, from the earliest colonial time, for communities to appoint a committee to examine the prospective schoolmaster, and to satisfy themselves that he possessed the requisite moral and scholastic qualifications to be worthy of being entrusted with the task of instructing the young. Unless he could pass this test, he could not be employed as a teacher; and the survival of this old custom, once so common among our people, is still found in parts of New England, where it is made the duty of the school committee to "require full and satisfactory evidence of the moral character" of new teachers, and to "ascertain by personal examination their qualifications for teaching and their capacity for the government of schools." Likewise the very common legal requirement that "no teacher shall be employed in any school supported by the public funds, or any part thereof, until he has received a certificate of qualification therefor,"— issued and signed by the proper authority upon a public examination, or upon the presentation of acceptable credential, is only an elaboration of the early idea. To provide for this examination we consider to be not only the right, but also the duty, of the state.

To this end each of our states and territories has established some form of examination and certification system, by which the selection from among those who wish to teach may be made and the best of a number of applicants may be selected. The different systems vary much in nature, scope, and standards, and some are certainly much more effective than are others in obtaining a well-educated and a professional body of teachers for the schools, and in keeping them alive professionally after they have once been obtained. In certain New England states, as we have just said, we find a survival of the old colonial system, where a body of laymen, representing the local community, passes upon the qualifications of those whom they wish to employ. In a few other states, as for example Oklahoma, the county has been made the unit and the county examination is supreme. Under this system all teachers must take the county examination in the county in which they expect to teach, and the county certificates are not valid in other counties, and are good but for a limited period. In other states, as for example Alabama, the state examination system rules. All teachers must pass the regular state examination set by the state examining board, even including the graduates of the normal schools of the state. Between these extremes there are many variations and combinations, the usual plan being a combination by which the county grants two or three grades of county certificates, while the state certificating authorities grant professional state certificates and life diplomas to experienced teachers. In most states the two systems exist side by side and frequently overlap in their functions.

Among the plans in use in the different states there is so great a diversity in standards and procedure that the ability of a teacher to transfer from one county to another or from one state to another is in many cases most unnecessarily restricted. Many of these restrictions are unwarranted by any educational standard and serve no useful educational purpose, and some are so absolutely unnecessary and so narrowly restrictive that they almost seem to have been established for the purpose of providing per diem work for the board of examiners, or for the purpose of preventing teachers from elsewhere coming into the county or state to interfere with the law of supply and demand in the home field. From an educational point of view many of the restrictions are indefensible.

In the number and nature of the subjects required for the examinations, the kinds of certificates issued, and the recognition of diplomas of graduation and proficiency in lieu of an examination, there is also great diversity, though there is here a possibility of reducing these to common units so as to provide for a much wider interchange. . . .

In the study of present conditions, perhaps the two most significant weaknesses revealed in our systems of certification were the low standards and the great lack of uniformity. To raise and to standardize our certification requirements ought to be the keynotes of future progress.

The amount of common knowledge which we as a people have is increasing so rapidly, our elementary-school curriculum is being enriched so fast, and the general intelligence of our people is becoming of such a standard that the teacher with a meager intellectual equipment should no longer have a place in our educational system. Yet . . . for the twenty-eight states tabulated, it is possible to secure a third-grade teacher's certificate in 90 per cent, of the number with no educational test beyond the common-school branches; and for the thirty-seven states tabulated it is possible to secure a first-grade certificate, in two-thirds of these states, without giving evidence of knowing anything about a single high-school subject except algebra, and in two-fifths of the states without knowing even this. These low-standard certificates are wholly out of place today and ought to be eliminated at the earliest possible moment.

The great diversity of our requirements and our unwillingness to recognize equivalents are two of our marked educational characteristics. So great is the diversity that a good teacher today is unnecessarily hampered in his ability to move about, not only from state to state, but also from county to county, and often from county to city or from one city to another. Many of these restrictions are not warranted by any educational standards, but are more of the nature of a protective tariff levied on foreign capacity and in favor of home production. This makes the local examination system, with its accompanying barriers, in the nature of a protected industry, and this is not in the interests of good education. The strict county system too often perpetuates the rule of the weak by shielding them from the competition of the strong. All barriers to competency are wrong.

That these barriers exist has been pointed out frequently. . . . In fourteen states there is no admission to the teaching profession except on examination. In eleven of these states forty or more subjects are required to secure the highest certificate granted, and all must be secured by examination. In fourteen states no recognition is given to diplomas from normal schools or other institutions of learning within the state. The graduates of such institutions are placed on a par with the "graduates" of the country school. In nineteen states absolutely no recognition is given to any form of credential from another state. Only eleven states recognize normal-school diplomas from other states; seventeen recognize college or university diplomas from outside the state; and eighteen recognize a life-diploma or state professional certificate from elsewhere. In a number of our states there is no recognition of certificates from one county to another within the state. Many of these barriers are indefensible, while the defense of others can be eliminated with ease by raising and standardizing requirements.

. . . We ought to work toward greater uniformity by the establishment of educational prerequisites, common requirements or norms within subjects, options and equivalents as between subjects, and the entire abolition of certain other subjects from the list of tests. We need to do in the examinations for teachers' certificates what the colleges have done in the matter of entrance requirements—viz., unify as much as possible and then accept evidences of education, equivalent subjects, and equivalent certificates, so far as they go, leaving the candidate to supply the balance by an examination instead of requiring him to pass on the entire list. If this cannot be done by arrangements within states and between states, then we would better work for national uniformity by establishing a national examining and certificating board, after the plan of the College Entrance Examination Board, which will examine teachers, pass on credentials, and issue certificates of such a high standard that our states would be forced to accept them, just as the colleges have been forced to accept the certificates of the above board.

The low standards are also apparent in the requirements for life-certificates. While a state life-diploma ought to be of such a standard that it would be accepted willingly anywhere in the United States, many of the low-standard life-diplomas now granted certainly ought not to be recognized from state to state. A life-certificate ... ought to be led up to by a series of graded certificates, each demanding higher and higher standards; and the state life-certificate, the culmination of a teacher's certificating career, should be given only to those whose education and professional standing single them out as the state's most capable teachers. In a number of our states, on the contrary, a life-diploma is obtainable on the single basis of a definite number of months of teaching, and hence involves no educational standards of any consequence and really stands for nothing.

Each state must, of course, be allowed to set its own standards, and it cannot be expected to accept certificates or diplomas from states having a distinctly lower standard. This should be recognized and accepted, and reciprocity should not be expected. Instead of being "uppish" about it and striking back by way of retaliation, as certain states do because their credentials are not accredited by some more progressive state, they should on the contrary welcome a teacher from such a state because of his better training and what he may bring.

It is possible, though, for most of our states to determine the value of credentials from elsewhere, and to recognize them as far as they apply. The work of California in this respect is most commendable. This state has a published list of accredited universities and normal schools throughout the United States and Canada, and a list of accredited state diplomas. Anyone possessing any of these credentials may be certificated in any county in the state, without examination, and on the same terms as the holders of similar local documents. A fundamental principle in California is that the certification door should always be open for competency, from whatever quarter it may come.

In almost every state, too, these low-standard certificates are good for teaching in any part of the school system in which the holders can secure employment. This should not be allowed to continue, but a separate high-school certificate should be erected for high-school work.... Teachers in all branches of the service should be required to know more than they are expected to teach, and the importance of this for high-school teachers cannot be overemphasized.

In the matter of examinations, there is great need of our decreasing the emphasis which we now place on the written test. We could greatly improve our certificating systems by erecting certain educational prerequisites and accepting evidence of education in lieu of at least part of the examinations. As fast as can be done, the periodical written examination ought to be diminished in importance as a means of recruiting our teaching force. We ought to insist more and more on securing the educated and trained teacher instead of the raw recruit. Not only should the number of examinations be decreased, but teachers of training or of long and satisfactory experience ought to be relieved of the necessity of frequent tests.

There is no valid excuse, for example, for compelling a graduate of a state normal school to pass a county examination before she can teach. If her normal-school diploma does not stand for better education and better professional preparation than the county examination represents, and if she is not superior to the untrained product of the county examination method, then it is time either to renovate the normal schools of the state and put in a corps of teachers who can produce a better output, or to abolish them entirely and save an unnecessary expense.

The securing of the educated and trained teacher instead of the raw recruit is, however, an economic problem as well as an educational one, though this economic problem has an educational aspect as well. There never can be high educational standards for teachers in such states as Indiana, Illinois, Wisconsin, Missouri, or Kansas — states using the very objectionable census basis for the apportionment of their school funds, and raising but a small general tax—until there is a radical reform in the methods of raising school funds and of apportioning the funds after they have been raised.... There are, in their ultimate analysis, but three primary problems in education. The first is that of how properly to finance a school system. The second is how to secure a trained teaching force for it. The third is how to supervise it to produce leaders for its management and improvement. The financial one always underlies the other two.

By way of giving concreteness to these suggestions, we will indicate a possible general plan for certification, based on the best of our current practice and theory. While not claiming that the proposed plan is perfect, we nevertheless feel that it, or its substantial equivalent, could be somewhat generally adopted with the greatest advantage to our educational work. The aim of the plan is the ultimate establishment and maintenance of high standards for our teaching work, and the method by which it is proposed to attain such standards is that of gradually raising requirements, and thus gradually cutting off the great mass of poorly educated and poorly trained teachers who today work on low standards, work for small wages, and too often serve to discredit the name and work of a teacher.

Proposed Plan for the Certification of Teachers

Types of Certificates

Five types of certificates shall be provided for, as follows:

I. Elementary-School Certificate,
II. High-School Certificates,
III. Special Certificates,
IV. Supervisory Certificates,
V. State Life-Certificates.

I. Elementary-School Certificate. —Good only for teaching in the first nine grades of the public schools, but not good for the ninth grade if the same is part of an organized high school. This certificate to be (at first) of three grades, as follows:

1. Third-grade elementary certificate. —To be granted only upon examination. Subjects to be all the common-school branches, English composition, civics, physiology and hygiene, and the principles of teaching and school management. Certificate good for one year, and only in the county where issued. Intended as a trial certificate, not renewable, and not more than two such certificates to be granted to any applicant. Success while teaching under this to be considered in granting future certificates. (Such a certificate ought not to be granted at all, but is included as a concession to present practice in so many of our states. As soon as the question of taxation and appropriation of funds can be attended to, this certificate ought to be abolished entirely. The first step would be to provide that not more than one such certificate should be granted to any applicant, the second step to provide that it should not be valid to teach in any city or town graded school or any rural school enrolling over twenty-five pupils, and the third step would be to abolish it entirely.)

2. Second-grade elementary certificate. —To be granted upon an examination on all the subjects required for a third-grade certificate, and, in addition, algebra or geometry, elements of bookkeeping, physical geography and the elements of one other science, and those parts of the school law which have to do with the relations of teachers to pupils, parents, and school officers. Good in the county where issued, and optional recognition in other counties of the same state. No interstate recognition of this certificate. Good for two years, and renewable for three-year periods, without examination, if the teaching continues to be satisfactory to the supervisor. This certificate to be granted also, without examination, to the graduates

of the state normal schools within the state, and to the graduates of accredited normal schools from without the state, where the normal-school training is based on a common-school education, and hence has not been preceded by a high-school training. (In time to come this certificate should be abolished also. The first step would be to refuse to renew it without a new examination, and to limit it strictly to the county where issued. California reached the point, in 1901, where a certificate somewhat equivalent to this could be entirely abolished, and it was done.)

3. First-grade elementary certificate. —To be granted upon an examination on all the subjects required for the second grade certificate, and, in addition, vocal music, drawing, general history, English and American literature, one additional science, and one other subject of high-school rank to be determined by the candidate. This certificate not to be granted to any applicant who has not had either at least two years of successful experience as a teacher, or normal-school training as required for the certificate. This certificate to be good in any county of the state, to be issued for five- or six-year periods, and to be renewable, without examination, so long as the holder continues to teach or to be engaged in educational work. Full interstate recognition of this certificate. Successful teachers, holding live second-grade certificates, may, on recommendation of the supervisor, be credited with all the subjects required for a second-grade certificate, and be granted a first-grade certificate on passing a satisfactory examination on the additional subjects. This certificate to be granted also, without examination, to the graduate of any state normal school within the State, and to the graduates of accredited normal schools without the state, where the normal-school training has been of not less than two years' duration and based upon a full four-year high-school course, or its equivalent in a private institution; and also to the graduates of accredited colleges and universities who have also completed a normal-school course intended for college graduates, and who intend to teach in the elementary school. In the case of normal-school and college graduates who have not had two years of experience as a teacher, this certificate to be issued at first for two years only. If recommended as successful, then the certificate to be renewed for five- or six-year periods, as indicated above. (In time, this should come to be the only elementary-school certificate granted, and it should be recognized between states as freely as between counties within the state.)

4. Examinations for these certificates. —Examinations for these certificates should be given in each county, on questions uniform throughout the state, and not oftener than four times a year. Whether these examinations should be under the control of the state board of education or the county superintendent is not of fundamental importance. As soon as the number

entering teaching on credentials will warrant, the examinations ought to be reduced to twice a year, say December and July, and later they can be reduced to once a year, which should be in the summer. When the number taking these examinations has been so reduced that many counties have no applicants, and most of the others only a few, as is the case now in California, then the state board of education should take charge of the examinations and arrange for them to be held at a stated time each year, and at only five or six places in the state.

II. High-School Certificates. —Good for teaching in any regular high school, six-year high school, or the seventh and eighth grades in graded city schools. May also be accepted by a county superintendent for elementary-school work in his county. This certificate to be, at first, of two grades, as follows:

1. Second-grade high-school certificate. —To be granted on the presentation of evidence that the applicant has taught successfully at least one year, and has completed at least two years of study beyond a full high-school course in some reputable college or university, and on a written examination covering (1) oral and written English; (2) two lines of high-school work which the candidate is prepared to teach; and (3) the general theory of secondary education, the theory and methods of instruction in the two lines of work offered, and class management. This certificate to be issued at first for two years. If the candidate is reported as a satisfactory high-school teacher, it may be renewed for three-year periods, without examination, so long as the holder continues to teach. Optional recognition between counties, but good only in "non-commissioned" high schools or "unaccredited" ones, or for grade work, as indicated or accepted. (This certificate in the nature of a transition certificate, while the state is growing used to the idea of a separate high-school certificate. At first, it might be necessary to accept normal-school training as a substitute for the required college work, but this is inadvisable. As soon as the supply of college-trained teachers equals the demand, this certificate ought to be abandoned entirely.)

2. First-grade high-school certificates. —To be granted on the presentation of evidence of having completed a full college course in some reputable college or university, and of having made preparation to teach one or more lines of high-school work. The diploma of graduation to be accepted as evidence of general academic preparation, but the candidate must also either —a) Pass a written examination on the general theory of secondary education; the purpose and methods of instruction in the subject or subjects he has prepared to teach; and class management, or b) Submit a satisfactory recommendation from the faculty of the institution in which he secured his training to the effect that he has satisfactorily completed such

pedagogical courses. This exemption from the pedagogical examination to expire after two years, unless the candidate engages in teaching or some form of educational work. This certificate to be issued at first for two years. If the candidate is reported as a satisfactory teacher, then the certificate to be renewed for five- or six-year periods, and to be valid so long as the holder continues to teach or to be engaged in educational work. This certificate to be good in any county in the state, and to be recognized freely between states. Good in any kind of a high school. (California has gone even farther. The number of properly certificated high-school teachers was so in excess of the demand that in 1905 the requirements were raised to include one year of graduate study.)

3. Examinations for high-school certificates. —No examinations to be given by which a teacher can secure a high-school certificate wholly on the basis of an examination. The educational prerequisite must be insisted upon. The examinations as provided for above to be given not oftener than twice a year. (Later this ought to be reduced to one examination, held in the summer.) These examinations should be under the control of the state board of education or examiners, or the state superintendent, as county boards will frequently find difficulty in examining candidates for this certificate. The questions and grading should be uniform throughout the state, the county superintendent acting for the state authorities in giving the examinations and transmitting the papers.

III. Special Certificates. —In recognition of certain special lines of school work, a few special certificates will need to be granted.

1. Kindergarten certificates. —To be granted to those who hold or secure a first-grade elementary certificate, or who present evidence showing that they are graduates of an accredited normal school, or of a four-year high school (or an equivalent private school), and who present satisfactory evidence that they have completed a kindergarten training course in a state normal school or in a reputable private kindergarten training-school. Certificates granted at first for two years, and on satisfactory evidence of successful teaching to be renewable for five- to six-year periods so long as the holder continues to teach. Valid in any county of the state, and optional interstate recognition.

2. Special certificates. —To be granted to those who hold or secure a first-grade certificate, or who present satisfactory evidence that they are graduates of an accredited normal school, or of a four-year high school, and who, in addition, present satisfactory evidence of having made special preparation to teach the special subject or subjects for which a certificate is asked. Such special certificates to be granted at first for two years. If the can-

didate is reported as a satisfactory teacher, then the certificate to be renewable for five- or six-year periods, so long as the holder continues to teach. Special certificates shall not be issued except for music, drawing, physical training, manual training, domestic science, instruction in special schools for the deaf and blind, and commercial, industrial, and technical work. (It is very desirable to limit special certificates rather closely, and to insist on, as nearly as possible, the standards required of regular teachers in the same kind of school work. The great danger of the specially certificated teacher is that he may represent a decidedly lower general educational level than the regular teachers of the school. Special certificates should not be granted to teach the regular studies of a high-school course, but a general high-school certificate should be insisted upon.)

IV. Supervisory Certificates. —These to be primarily for the encouragement and singling out of the educational leader, and to be of two grades, as follows:

1. Second-grade supervisory certificate. —To be granted to the graduate of any accredited normal school who has taught at least two years in the state where the certificate is issued, or to the holder of a first-grade certificate who has had at least thirty months of teaching experience, one-half of which must have been in the state where the certificate is issued, and who, in addition, passes a satisfactory examination on educational psychology, the theory and administration of education, school hygiene, the history of the state's educational system, and the school law of the state, and who prepares a satisfactory thesis on one of a number of assigned topics. Said thesis is not expected to be "original" in its treatment, but should show grasp of the subject and power to think clearly. Only one examination each year. This to be uniform throughout the state and under the direction of the state board of education, the state board of examiners, or the state superintendent. This certificate to be issued for a five- or six-year period, and to be renewable, without examination, on the presentation of satisfactory evidence that the holder has been a successful principal or supervisor, so long as the holder continues to teach. Certificates to be valid anywhere in the state, with optional interstate recognition. This certificate to be good for supervisory work or for any form of teaching for which a first-grade elementary certificate would be valid. (This certificate is intended to recognize the successful practitioner who can give evidence that, by private study, he has kept himself abreast of the times.)

2. First-grade supervisory certificate. —To be granted to any teacher who has had at least two years of teaching experience, who holds a baccalaureate degree from a college requiring a four-year course, and who, in ad-

dition, either —a) Submits a recommendation from the faculty of the college stating that he has completed a thorough pedagogical course of study which has included all the examination subjects required for a second-grade supervisory certificate, and, in the estimation of said faculty, is fitted to do supervisory work in the schools of the state; or b) Passes the written pedagogical examination as required for a second-grade supervisory certificate. This certificate to have the same validity as the second-grade supervisory certificate, and in addition to be recognized freely between states.

V. State Life-Certificates or Diplomas. —With the standards just given for first-grade certificates, state life-certificates become of much less importance and significance. Each of the higher grades of certificates so far given, with their general state validity and repeated renewals, is practically a life-certificate. Still, as these diplomas have a certain recognition and standing, it will be wise to continue them, though gradually raising the standards for granting them and making them stand for distinguished excellence. These life-certificates should be of three forms, but be recognized as of somewhat equivalent rank and dignity. Each form of certificate to be for life, and to be good anywhere in the state, and for the same grade of instruction as local certificates of the same name. Such life-diplomas should be given full and complete interstate recognition. But one examination to be given each year for these certificates. This to be given under the direction of the state superintendent or the state board of education, and at only a few places (eight to ten) in the state.

1. State life elementary certificate. —To be granted only to those who have taught at least fifty months, one-half of which has been in the state where the certificate is issued, and who have taught for at least two years on a first-grade elementary certificate. Adequate evidence of successful experience and professional growth must be submitted. In addition, candidates must pass a written examination on educational psychology, the history of education, current theory, and problems of the elementary school, and prepare a short paper on some topic relating to method as applied to the elementary curriculum or to the theory of education as applied to the elementary school. A number of topics for this paper to be announced at the examination from which candidates may select.

2. State life high-school certificates. —To be granted only to those who have taught at least fifty months, one-half of which has been in high-school work in the state where the certificate is issued, and who have been teaching for at least two years on a first-grade high-school certificate. Adequate evidence of successful experience and professional growth must be submitted. In addition, candidates must pass a written examination on the history and

theory of secondary education, present problems of secondary education (comparative as well as local), and prepare a paper of some length on one of a number of topics to be assigned at the time of the examination, covering some point in the method and purpose of instruction of some subject taught in the secondary school, or the general theory of secondary education.

3. State life supervisory certificate. —To be granted only to those who have taught at least fifty months, at least one-half of which has been as a principal or supervisor and on first- or second-grade supervisory certificate in the state where the certificate is issued. Adequate evidence of successful experience as a supervisor and of professional growth must be submitted. In addition, candidates must pass a written examination on the history of education, the theory (or philosophy) of education, principles of city and state school administration, education in the leading European states as compared with America (general principles, based on assigned reading), and must prepare a paper of some length on one of a number of topics, submitted at the time of the examination, and covering some point in the administration or the theory of education.

Certain Features of the Plan

1. No city certificates to be issued, except perhaps in a few of our very largest cities. Cities must accept the state certificates, so far as they go, but are at liberty to refuse to employ those not holding first-grade certificates; and those not having had a certain degree of education, professional training, and teaching experience; and to subject those who meet these standards to a further professional and competitive test.
2. No temporary or special certificates to be issued except to those whose credentials would insure them a regular certificate, without examination, at the next meeting of the board of examiners or the county board of education.
3. No state professional certificates as distinguished from life diplomas, as the standards set for the first-grade certificate and their general state validity make a state professional certificate unnecessary.
4. Gradual separation and erection of a high-school certificate, based on education and training, and with no method of securing it wholly on examination.
5. Definite provision for the development of the educated leader as opposed to the successful practitioner.
6. Gradual curtailment of special and temporary certificates, and the insistence, as fast as possible, that the educational standard for

these shall be somewhat equivalent to that demanded for regular certificates of equivalent grade.

7. Gradual curtailment of the number of examinations given for all grades of certificates, with a view to emphasizing training and education.

8. Abolition of all fees for examinations, certificates, or renewals. Evidence as to good moral character to be required for all forms of certificate.

9. Freeing the successful teacher from the necessity of continual re-examinations, so long as he (or she) continues to teach in a satisfactory manner, but limiting him in the matter of movement and availability for the best positions unless he obtains a high grade of certificate.

10. Close association of the supervisory and certificating functions, thus making reports as to a teacher's efficiency of some real value.

11. Providing for the renewal of certificates, after the probationary period has been passed, rather than granting full life-certification on any standard lower than that required for a state life-certificate. Under an adequate system of supervision the renewal could be made of educational significance. There would be no serious objection, however, to making a first-grade certificate a permanent county certificate, after the second renewal, valid so long as the holder continues to teach in the county.

12. The full recognition of normal-school and college diplomas, though at first for only temporary two-year certificates. After evidence of successful experience, these to guarantee the holder a long-time renewable certificate of general validity, which is practically a life-certificate.

13. The recognition of normal-school and college diplomas of equal rank from other states, and on the same basis as similar local documents.

14. As fast as can be done, our state normal schools should pass from an elementary-school to a high-school basis of admission, and then concentrate their efforts on giving two years of high-grade academic and professional training. This has already been accomplished in a few states and should be extended as rapidly as possible to all. The graduates of such schools would then receive first-grade certificates without examination.

15. Full inter-county and interstate recognition, for teachers of experience, of all regular first-grade certificates.

16. Recognition of equivalents and options in examinations, and in measuring the value of certificates from other states.

If some such plan for the certification of teachers were adopted generally by our leading states, it would be a most potent factor in the elevation and improvement of the schools of the entire country. The effect of such standards in California has been most beneficial from every point of view. Each increase of standards has been accompanied by certain "growing pains," but the result has soon demonstrated the wisdom of the action. Such doubtless will be the case elsewhere. A movement looking toward the general adoption of some such standards ought to be urged in our various state teachers' associations, and might well enlist the active efforts of our National Educational Association as well. It would be a cause worthy of their steel.

29

Selected Writings of Jane Addams

Jane Addams (1860–1935) is best known as the founder of Hull House in Chicago. Addams and her friend Ellen Starr opened Hull House in 1899 in a section of Chicago populated by immigrants who were primarily industrial workers. The settlement house served as a community meeting place and provided a variety of social services to the community such as daycare, music and art classes, employment assistance, social clubs, a labor museum, and a library. Hull House became a center for social activism, and Addams became well known for her work in the labor, women's, and peace movements of the late 19th and early 20th centuries. She wrote and spoke prolifically about the work at Hull House and her views on the social issues of the day. In 1931, she was awarded the Nobel Peace prize for her work. In the following selections, Addams remarks on the connections that should be fostered between the school and the society in which it exists. The first selection is an address to the National Education Association in which Addams discusses the special role of the school in immigrant communities. In the second selection, Addams promotes the teaching of current events as a strategy for connecting the school curriculum with immediate social concerns. —AJM

American Educational Thought: Essays from 1640–1940, pages 473–484
Copyright © 2010 by Information Age Publishing
473

The Public School and the Immigrant Child, 1908

I am always diffident when I come before a professional body of teachers, realizing as I do that it is very easy for those of us who look on to bring indictments against results; and realizing also that one of the most difficult situations you have to meet is the care and instruction of the immigrant child, especially as he is found where I see him, in the midst of crowded city conditions.

And yet in spite of the fact that the public school is the great savior of the immigrant district, and the one agency which inducts the children into the changed conditions of American life, there is a certain indictment which may justly be brought, in that the public school too often separates the child from his parents and widens that old gulf between fathers and sons which is never so cruel and so wide as it is between the immigrants who come to this country and their children who have gone to the public school and feel that they have there learned it all. The parents are thereafter subjected to certain judgment, the judgment of the young which is always harsh and in this instance founded upon the most superficial standard of Americanism. And yet there is a notion of culture which we would define as a knowledge of those things which have been long cherished by men, the things which men have loved because thru generations they have softened and interpreted life, and have endowed it with value and meaning. Could this standard have been given rather than the things which they see about them as the test of so-called success, then we might feel that the public school has given at least the beginnings of culture which the child ought to have. At present the Italian child goes back to its Italian home more or less disturbed and distracted by the contrast between the school and the home. If he throws off the control of the home because it does not represent the things which he has been taught to value he takes the first step toward the Juvenile Court and all the other operations of the law, because he has prematurely asserted himself long before he is ready to take care of his own affairs.

We find in the carefully prepared figures which Mr. Commons and other sociologists have published that while the number of arrests of immigrants is smaller than the arrests of native born Americans, the number of arrests among children of immigrants is twice as large as the number of arrests among the children of native born Americans. It would seem that in spite of the enormous advantages which the public school gives to these children it in some way loosens them from the authority and control of their parents, and tends to send them, without a sufficient rudder and power of self-direction, into the perilous business of living. Can we not say, perhaps, that the schools ought to do more to connect these children with the best things of the past, to make them realize something of the beauty and charm of the language, the history, and the traditions which their parents represent. It is easy to cut them loose from their parents, it requires cultivation to tie them up in sympathy and understanding. The ignorant teacher cuts them off because he himself cannot understand the situation, the cultivated teacher fastens them because his own mind is open to the charm and beauty of that old-country life. In short, it is the business of the school to give to each child the beginnings of a culture so wide and deep and universal that he can interpret his own parents and countrymen by a standard which is world-wide and not provincial.

The second indictment which may be brought is the failure to place the children into proper relation to-ward the industry which they will later enter. Miss Arnold has told us that children go into industry for a very short time. I believe that the figures of the United States census show the term to be something like six years for the women in industry as over against twenty-four years for men, in regard to continuity of service. Yet you cannot disregard the six years of the girls nor the twenty-four years of the boys, because they are the immediate occupation into which they enter after they leave the school—even the girls are bound to go thru that period—that is, the average immigrant girls are—before they enter the second serious business of life and maintain homes of their own. Therefore, if they enter industry unintelligently, without some notion of what it means, they find themselves totally unprepared for their first experience with American life, they are thrown out without the proper guide or clue which the public school might and ought to have given to them. Our industry has become so international, that it ought to be easy to use the materials it offers for immigrant children. The very processes and general principles which industry represents give a chance to prepare these immigrant children in a way which the most elaborated curriculum could not present. Ordinary material does not give the same international suggestion as industrial material does.

Third, I do not believe that the children who have been cut off from their own parents are going to be those who, when they become parents themselves, will know how to hold the family together and to connect it with the state. I should begin to teach the girls to be good mothers by teaching them to be good daughters. Take a girl whose mother has come from South Italy. The mother cannot adjust herself to the changed condition of housekeeping, does not know how to wash and bake here, and do the other things which she has always done well in Italy, because she has suddenly been transported from a village to a tenement house. If that girl studies these household conditions in relation to the past and to the present needs of the family, she is undertaking the very best possible preparation for her future obligations to a household of her own. And to my mind she can undertake it in no better way. Her own children are mythical and far away, but the little brothers and sisters pull upon her affections and her loyalty, and she longs to have their needs recognized in the school so that the school may give her some help. Her mother complains that the baby is sick in America because she cannot milk her own goat; she insists if she had her own goat's milk the baby would be quite well and flourishing, as the children were in Italy. If that girl can be taught that the milk makes the baby ill because it is not clean and be provided with a simple test that she may know when milk is clean, it may take her into the study not only of the milk within the four walls of the tenement house, but into the inspection of the milk of her district. The milk, however, remains good educational material, it makes even more concrete the connection which you would be glad to use between the household and the affairs of the American city. Let her not follow the mother's example of complaining about changed conditions; let her rather make the adjustment for her mother's entire household. We cannot tell what adjustments the girl herself will be called upon to make ten years from now; but we can give her the clue and the aptitude to adjust the family with which she is identified to the constantly changing conditions of city life. Many of us feel that, splendid as the public schools are in their relation to the immigrant child, they do not understand all of the difficulties which surround that child—all of the moral and emotional perplexities which constantly harass him. The children long that the school teacher should know something about the lives they lead and should be able to reprove the hooting children who make fun of the Italian mother because she wears a kerchief on her head, not only because they are rude but also because they are stupid. We send young people to Europe to see Italy, but we do not utilize Italy when it lies about the schoolhouse. If the body of teachers in our great cities could take hold of the immigrant colonies, could bring out of them their handicrafts and occupations, their traditions, their folk songs and folk lore, the beautiful stories which every immigrant colony is ready to tell and translate; could get the children to bring these things into school as the material from which culture is made and the material upon which culture is based, they would discover that by comparison that which they give them now is a poor meretricious and vulgar thing. Give these children a chance to utilize the historic and industrial material which they see about them and they will begin to have a sense of ease in America, a first consciousness of being at home. I believe if these people are welcomed upon the basis of the resources which they represent and the contributions which they bring, it may come to pass that these schools which deal with immigrants will find that they have a wealth of cultural and industrial material which will make the schools in other neighborhoods positively envious. A girl living in a tenement household, helping along this tremendous adjustment, healing over this great moral upheaval which the parents have suffered and which leaves them bleeding and sensitive—such a girl has a richer experience and a finer material than any girl from a more fortunate household can have at the present moment.

I wish I had the power to place before you what it seems to me is the opportunity that the immigrant colonies present to the public school: the most endearing occupation of leading the little child, who will in turn lead his family, and bring them with him into the brotherhood for which they are longing. The immigrant child cannot make this demand upon the school because he does not know how to formulate it; it is for the teacher both to perceive it and to fulfill it.

Education by the Current Event, 1930

The settlements early founded their educational theories upon a conviction that in every social grade and class in the whole circle of genuine occupations there are mature men and women of moral purpose and specialized knowledge, who because they have become efficient unto life, may contribute an enrichment to the pattern of human culture. We knew that much of this possible enrichment was lost because he who would incorporate these experiences into the common heritage must constantly depend upon fresh knowledge and must further be equipped with a wide and familiar acquaintance with the human spirit and its productions. The difficulties involved would be almost insurmountable but that life has a curious trick of suddenly regarding as a living moral issue, vital and unappeasable, some old outworn theme which has been kicked about for years as mere controversial material. The newly moralized issue, almost as if by accident, suddenly takes fire and sets whole communities in a blaze, lighting up human relationships and public duty with new meaning. The event suddenly transforms abstract social idealism into violent political demands, entangling itself with the widest human aspiration.

When that blaze actually starts, when the theme is heated, molten as it were with human passion and desire, the settlement can best use it in its unending effort to make culture and the issue of things go together. From time to time during the last twenty years, when such a blaze did start it seemed for the moment that the peculiar aspect of the world which marks each age for what it is—the summary of its experiences, knowledge and affections, in which are found the very roots of its social existence was fused into a glowing whole. At such a moment, it seemed possible to educate the entire community by a wonderful unification of effort and if the community had been able to command open discussion and a full expression of honest opinion the educational opportunity would have been incomparable. As an example of sudden interest, resulting in widespread education upon a given theme, the trial at Dayton, Tennessee, upon the general subject of the theory of evolution, forms a striking example....

During the trial the situation was so sharply defined that it brought before the entire country a public discussion of fundamentalism versus evolution. That such a situation arose was in one sense a demonstration of our democratic purpose, which is, after all, an attempt at self-expression for each man. Democracy believes that the man at the bottom may realize his aim only through an unfolding of his own being, and that he must have an efficacious share in the regulation of his own life. While there was no doubt that the overwhelming public opinion concerning the Tennessee trial was on the side of liberality both in politics and religion, the group of so-called narrow-minded men had made their own contribution to our national education. In the first place, they had asserted the actuality of religion. It is always difficult to convince youth that reality reaches upward as well as outward, and that the higher planes of life contain anything but chilly sentiments. The educator dealing with religious topics often finds that young people receive his statements with polite attention, but when it comes to action, they who are fretting with impatience to throw themselves into the stream of life and to become a part of its fast-flowing current, carefully imitate the really desirable world inhabited by successful men of affairs. But suddenly there came from a group of remote mountaineers a demonstration of a vivid and sustained interest in matters of religion, resulting in a sharp clash of doctrine between themselves and thousands of our fellow citizens, who all hung upon the issues of the trial with avid interest. It was at times almost comic to hear the "hard-boiled" city youth in his bewilderment talk about the situation.

In the first place, modern economics had taught him—or he thought that it had—that a man was abjectly dependent upon the material world about him and must succumb to the iron clamp which industry imposes upon life; moreover, the youth himself gravely asserted that man's *very* freedom, morality and progress is determined by the material conditions which surround him and he had bodily taken over this theory into ethics and philosophy. He quoted those students of the social order who in what they considered the scientific spirit had collected and arranged data, to demonstrate the sole reaction of economic forces upon human life. These young people had for the most part lightly disregarded all teleological considerations, as they had long before renounced the theological explanations of a final cause. And yet many of them were secretly glad of this opportunity for discussion with old Jewish fathers who had never ceased to attest to the life of the spirit and who on their side caught their first glimpse in those sons hotly defending the theory of evolution, of the same zeal which they and their fathers had expended upon religion. These same young men so devoted to economic determinism as a theory of life had been already somewhat disconcerted by a recent movement in psychiatry with the emphasis upon the emotional and subconscious life versus the exclusive response to environmental stimuli. But if they were startled they were also much interested in this ardent inner life which was apparently to be found among so many different types of people who were everywhere responding to the blaze of interest started in Tennessee.

The repercussions of the trial were the more interesting because the incident brought into the circle of their discussion a large number of people who had hitherto been quite outside their zone of interest. These remote farmers were isolated, save on the occasional Sundays when a circuit rider came to preach, by their discouraging occupation of extracting a living from a rock-bound soil. Nothing could have been further from the experiences and mental processes of the intelligentsia of a cosmopolitan city than these mountaineers, nothing more diverse than the two methods of approach to the time-old question of the origin of man. Only a molten current event could have accomplished a simultaneous discussion upon the same theme by these two bodies of people.

Although these young Chicago intelligentsia I have been describing lived among colonies of immigrants, each one with its own history and conscious religious background, and had moreover naturally been interested in the normative sciences, they had known little about such descendants of early Americans so Anglo-Saxon and "Nordic" in background that they still had remnants of Elizabethan English in their daily speech. It was interesting to hear these young men talk of the effects of isolation whether the group were encompassed by mountains or by the invisible boundaries of a ghetto.

Another instance of discussion spreading to thousands of people in the United States was demonstrated when the Labor Party of England first came into power. While the discussion of such international events varies from community to community with local experiences; traditions and problems of human relationship, it has an enormous influence upon the situation as a whole. Many people for the first time get an impression of our own national situation in comparison with the economic situation in other nations and certain words lose their national connotation and more nearly approach international usage. The fact that in many European nations the socialists were among the major political parties, that a "Labor" Party had come to office in England was in itself an education in the use of words as they are current throughout civilization. Perhaps more important still the man of affairs began to contrast such attempts at political control of industrial situations with the associative business control which has been worked out in the United States. . . .

It would seem obvious that the most important condition for the peaceful and fruitful development of the world would be at the lowest, a theory of live and let live between countries organized on different economic systems. If the Soviet Republics are to foment revolution and unrest in countries where the basis of communism does not exist, and if countries organized by private business are determined to keep Russia outside the comity of nations, it is clear that the two economic systems will never learn much from one another. A mixed type of state with competitive and cooperative elements may have the greatest survival value and prove to be the most serviceable. But the line of demarkation between private business and public business will differ both between countries and in different stages in the same country. Obviously each country should have a basis of comparison and learn to work out its own opportunities both by the successes and failures of its world neighbors. Of course it ought to be possible to do this in the spirit of scientific detachment, for Russia is now conducting perhaps the largest piece of conscious social laboratory experiment that history records. It looks for the moment, however, as if Russia would evoke such a strong emotional reaction for so long a time that it will still remain impossible for Americans. . . .

Another instance of education through the discussion of current social developments, took place in regard to the problem of race relations when the industrial needs of war-time and the immigration restriction following the war, resulted in a great increase of Negroes in the urban populations throughout the country. This was brought to a head in Chicago as in many other places by the question of housing, when real estate values became confused as always with the subject of segregation. Whatever may be the practical solution it is still true that a complete segregation of the Negro in definite parts of the city, tends in itself to put him outside the immediate action of that imperceptible but powerful social control which influences the rest of the population. Those inherited resources of civilization which are embodied in custom and kindly intercourse, make more for social restraint than does legal enactment itself. . . .

Another result of race antagonism is the readiness to irritation which inevitably results when one race is forced to demand as a right from the other those things which should be accorded as a courtesy. Every chance meeting between representatives of the two races is easily characterized either by insolence or arrogance. To the friction of city life and the complications of modern intercourse is added this primitive race animosity.

Happily in the midst of this current event discussion, there came to Chicago a distinguished Negro singer, various plays concerning colored people which portrayed something of that inner life upon which the kinship of races is founded and the Race Relations Committee of the Chicago Woman's Club arranged for a week of exhibits at the Art Institute and for recitals and lectures by well-known artists, poets and scholars. We have no exact knowledge of what has been and is being lost by the denial of free expression on the part of the Negro, it is difficult even to estimate it. One can easily suggest the sense of humor, unique and spontaneous, so different from the wit of the Yankee or the inimitable story telling prized in the South; the natural use of rhythm and onomatopoeia which is now so often travestied in the grotesqueness of long words: the use of varied colors which makes it natural perhaps that the only scientific study made in America of the use of common clay as coloring material in the building of simple houses should have been done by a Negro so that we may hope some day to rival the pinks, yellows and blues of those European houses which afford the traveler such perpetual joy.

There is one exception to this lack of recognition, in the admiration of those melodies which we have learned to call the only American folksongs and which have become the basis of the Negroes' contribution to American music. Perhaps because an oppressed people have always been sustained by their dreams the spirituals became the support of their failing spirits. It may be that the wish-fulfillment was too slowly transferred to actual life but certainly an ever-increasing respect is coming from the Negroes' own achievements in the arts. Through their plays they have found the stimulus for conduct in the very field where it was possible to make the initial step toward social efficiency. It may be significant that the curtain falls on an advanced play like "Porgy" while the Negroes of Catfish Row are singing, "I'm on my way."

But even though fine demonstrations have been made by smaller groups of cultivated Negroes, we cannot truthfully say, however much we should like to do so, that recognition lies with the colored man himself and that the worthy will be worthily received. To make even the existing degree of recognition more general requires first of all a modicum of leisure and freedom from grinding poverty. An investigation made in 1929 by the Woman's Bureau of the Department of Labor gives an analysis of *Colored Women in Industry* from studies made in fifteen states. Their earnings were found to be far below the earnings of most white women, *although* they too must somehow meet the expenses of food, shelter and clothing. A great American industrialist had said, almost at the moment of the publication of the report, "American industry must for the future be based not on a living wage alone, nor on a saving wage, but on a cultural wage." No one needs the benefit of this dictum more than the ambitious Negro.

Because we are no longer stirred as the Abolitionists were, to remove fetters, to prevent cruelty, to lead the humblest to the banquet of civilization, we have allowed ourselves to become indifferent to the gravest situation in our American life. The abolitionists grappled with an evil intrenched since the beginning of recorded history and it seems at moments that we are not even preserving what was so hardly won. To continually suspect, suppress or fear any large group in a community must finally result in a loss of enthusiasm for that type of government which gives free play to the self-development of a majority of its citizens. It means an enormous loss of capacity to the nation when great ranges of human life are hedged about with antagonism. We forget that whatever is spontaneous in a people, in an individual, a class or a nation, is always a source of life.

In the world-wide effort to relieve the colored races from the odium and discrimination which white races have placed upon them, no man living on the planet today has done more than has Mahatma Gandhi, first in South Africa in the struggle for civil rights against the Transvaal Government, which absorbed his energy for almost twenty years, and later in the undertaking, the most difficult of all, directed against customs intrenched in the religious traditions of India, to free the fifty million untouchables or pariahs, who are subject to many *harsh* rules of segregation. While the differences of race between the Brahmans and Pariahs is not the sole basis of the insupportable division between them, the situation is essentially the same as that which faces any effort to break down barriers of race or caste. Gandhi's most striking success in his protest against untouchability was the opening of the roads, which because they passed near the temples were forbidden to the Pariahs. His followers faced a cordon of police for twelve hours every day during a year and four months before the orthodox Brahmans yielded. Such devotion opened to the untouchables not only that one forbidden road but all the roads that had been forbidden to them in southern India and gave the doctrine of untouchability its severest blow. Such a long and courageous effort may indicate that only sustained moral energy will be able to break through long established restrictions.

Problems of race relations may arise in situations where a group of people regard themselves, or are regarded by others, as racially homogeneous, even where such an assumption does not correspond to scientific reality. Merely to inform people that such and such a group conflict is based upon an ethnological misunderstanding, will not do away either with the conflict or its emotional associations in the minds of those implicated. The entire race situation demonstrates once more that mere information is not enough and that the various research bodies need to be constantly supplemented.

During its first two decades, Hull-House with other American settlements, issued various studies and fact-finding analyses of the city areas with which they were most familiar. The settlements had antedated by three years the first sociological departments in the universities and by ten years the establishment of the first Foundations so that in a sense we were the actual pioneers in field research. We based the value of our efforts not upon any special training, but upon the old belief that he who lives near the life of the poor, he who knows the devastating effects of disease and vice, has at least an unrivaled opportunity to make a genuine contribution to their understanding. . . .

In the third decade of our existence [we developed] as a sort of settlement creed [the conviction] that the processes of social amelioration are of necessity the results of gradual modification. We learned to act upon a belief that the hoary abominations of society can only be done away with through the "steady effort to accumulate facts and exalt the human will." But because such an undertaking requires the cooperation of many people and because with the best will in the world it is impossible to get the interest of the entire community centered upon any given theme, we gradually discovered that the use of the current event is valuable beyond all other methods of education. In time we came to define a settlement as an institution attempting to learn from life itself in which undertaking we did not hesitate to admit that we encountered many difficulties and failures. . . .

The settlements have often been accused of scattering their forces; as institutions they are both philanthropic and educational; in their approach to social problems they call now upon the sociologist, now upon the psychiatrist; they seek the services of artists, economists, gymnasts, case-workers, dramatists, trained nurses; one day they beg the anthropologist for a clue to a new immigration, and the next they boast that one of their pupils is playing in the symphony orchestra. In response to the irrefutable charge of weakness in multiform activity, we are accustomed to reply that even so we are not as varied and complex as life itself. I recall my sense of relief the first time I heard a sociologist use the phrase, "vortex causation"; the universities were at last defining the situation and it was possible that they would later enter this inner-related field of personal difficulties, bewildering legal requirements, ill health and conflicting cultures which the settlements find so baffling.... Each current event in this interrelated world may be the result of a repercussion from any part of the globe, or due to the same impulse manifesting itself in widely separated areas.... It seems at moments as if we were about to extend indefinitely what we call our public, and that unless it were stretched to world dimensions, the most significant messages of our times might easily escape us.

30

The Contribution of Psychology to Education

E.L. Thorndike, 1910

E.L. Thorndike (1874–1949) made his mark on American education through his work as a psychologist. He was born on August 31, 1874, in Williamsburg, Massachusetts. He received a B.A. degree from Wesleyan University in 1895. In 1896, he earned a second B.A. degree from Harvard. The following year, 1897, he took his Master's degree, also from Harvard. At Harvard, he studied the pragmatic philosophy of William James. Thorndike continued his study of psychology by completing his Ph.D. degree in 1897 at Columbia University. At Columbia, he studied with prominent scientist James McKeen Cattell. For his dissertation, Thorndike conducted research on animal learning and intelligence. He was particularly interested in the behavior of chickens. In his dissertation, "Animal Intelligence: An Experimental Study of the Associative Processes in Animals," Thorndike sought to discover how understanding the way animals learn can be applied to learning in humans. Following graduation from Columbia, Thorndike taught and conducted psychological research, also at Columbia, from 1909 to 1940. His work on learning theory influenced thousands of educational psychologists during his long career. Thorndike is probably best known for his work with animals. The goal with his efforts was

American Educational Thought: Essays from 1640–1940, pages 485–492
Copyright © 2010 by Information Age Publishing

to discover how animals, including humans, learned. Through his study of the responses of cats and dogs to various stimuli, Thorndike believed that he could discover how all animals, including humans, learn. Thorndike became a leading proponent of behavioral psychology, which contends that all learning takes place through reflex actions, stimulus-response associations, and reinforcement. In the essay below, "The Contribution of Psychology to Education," Thorndike makes the case for what the new empirical science has to offer education after a time when philosophy and other humanities fields had served as the foundation for curriculum, teaching, and learning. —JWN

Psychology is the science of the intellects, characters and behavior of animals including man. Human education is concerned with certain changes in the intellects, characters and behavior of men, its problems being roughly included under these four topics: Aims, materials, means and methods.

Psychology contributes to a better understanding of the aims of education by defining them, making them clearer; by limiting them, showing us what can be done and what can not; and by suggesting new features that should be made parts of them.

Psychology makes ideas of educational aims clearer. When one says that the aim of education is culture, or discipline, or efficiency, or happiness, or utility, or knowledge, or skill, or the perfection of all one's powers, or development, one's statements and probably one's thoughts, need definition. Different people, even amongst the clearest-headed of them, do not agree concerning just what culture is, or just what is useful. Psychology helps here by requiring us to put our notions of the aims of education into terms of the exact changes that education is to make, and by describing for us the changes which do actually occur in human beings.

Psychology helps to measure the probability that an aim is attainable. For example, certain writers about education state or imply that the knowledge and skill and habits of behavior which are taught to the children of today are of service not only to this generation and to later generations through the work this generation does, but also to later generations forever through the inheritance of increased capacity for knowledge and skill and morals. But if the mental and moral changes made in one generation are not transmitted by heredity to the next generation, the improvement of the race by direct transfer of acquisitions is a foolish, because futile aim.

Psychology enlarges and refines the aim of education. Certain features of human nature may be and have been thought to be unimportant or even quite valueless because of ignorance of psychology. Thus for hundreds of years in the history of certain races even the most gifted thinkers of the race have considered it beneath the dignity of education to make physical health an important aim. Bodily welfare was even thought of as a barrier to spiritual growth, an undesirable interferer with its proper master. Education aimed to teach it its proper place, to treat it as a stupid and brutish slave. It is partly because psychology has shown the world that the mind is the servant and co-worker as well as the master of the body, that the welfare of our minds and morals is intimately bound up with the welfare of our bodies, particularly of our central nervous systems, that today we can all see the eminence of bodily health as an aim of education. To an understanding of the material of education, psychology is the chief contributor.

Psychology shares with anatomy, physiology, sociology, anthropology, history and the other sciences that concern changes in man's bodily or mental nature the work of providing thinkers and workers in the field of education with knowledge of the material with which they work. Just as the science and art of agriculture depend upon chemistry and botany, so the art of education depends upon physiology and psychology.

A complete science of psychology would tell every fact about every one's intellect and character and behavior, would tell the cause of every change in human nature, would tell the result which every educational force—every act of every person that changed any other or the agent himself—would have. It would aid us to use human beings for the world's welfare with the same surety of the result that we now have when we use falling bodies or chemical elements. In proportion as we get such a science we shall become masters of our own souls as we now are masters of heat and light. Progress toward such a science is being made.

Psychology contributes to understanding of the means of education, first, because the intellects and characters of any one's parents, teachers and friends are very important means of educating him, and, second, because the influence of any other means, such as books, maps or apparatus, cannot be usefully studied apart from the human nature which they are to act upon.

Psychology contributes to knowledge of methods of teaching in three ways. First, methods may be deduced outright from the laws of human nature. For instance, we may infer from psychology that the difficulty pupils have in learning to divide by a fraction is due in large measure to the habit established by all the thousands of previous divisions which they have done or seen, the habit, that is, of "division—decrease" or "number divided—result smaller than the number." We may then devise or select such a method as will reduce this interference from the old habits to a minimum without weakening the old habits in their proper functioning.

Second, methods may be chosen from actual working experience, re-gardless of psychology, as a starting point. Thus it is believed that in the el-ementary school a class of fifteen pupils for one teacher gives better results than either a class of three or a class of thirty. Thus, also, it is believed that family life is better than institutional life in its effects upon character and enterprise. Thus, also, it is believed that in learning a foreign language the reading of simple discussions of simple topics is better than the translation of difficult literary masterpieces that treat subtle and complex topics. Even in such cases psychology may help by explaining *why* one method does suc-ceed better and so leading the way to new insights regarding other ques-tions not yet settled by experience.

Third, in all cases psychology, by its methods of measuring knowledge and skill, may suggest means to test and verify or refute the claims of any method. For instance, there has been a failure on the part of teachers to decide from their classroom experience whether it is better to teach the spelling of a pair of homonyms together or apart in time. But all that is required to decide the question for any given pair is for enough teachers to use both methods with enough different classes, keeping everything else ex-cept the method constant, and to measure the errors in spelling the words thereafter in the two cases. Psychology, which teaches us how to measure changes in human nature, teaches us how to decide just what the results of any method of teaching are.

So far I have outlined the contribution of psychology to education from the point of view of the latter's problems. I shall now outline very briefly the work being done by psychologists which is of special significance to the theory and practice of education and which may be expected to result in the largest and most frequent contributions.

It will, of course, be understood that directly or indirectly, soon or late, every advance in the sciences of human nature will contribute to our suc-cess in controlling human nature and changing it to the advantage of the common weal. If certain lines of work by psychologists are selected for men-tion here, it is only because they are the more obvious, more direct and, so far as can now be seen, greater aids to correct thinking about education.

The first line of work concerns the discovery and improvement of means of measurement of intellectual functions. (The study of means of measur-ing moral functions such as prudence, readiness to sacrifice an immediate for a later good, sympathy, and the like, has only barely begun.) Beginning with easy cases such as the discrimination of sensory differences, psychology has progressed to measuring memory and accuracy of movement, fatigue, improvement with practice, power of observing small details, the quantity, rapidity and usefulness of associations, and even to measuring so complex a function as general intelligence and so subtle a one as suggestibility.

The task of students of physical science in discovering the thermometer, galvanometer and spectroscope, and in defining the volt, calorie erg, and ampère, is being attempted by psychologists in the sphere of human nature and behavior. How important such work is to education should be obvious. At least three-fourths of the problems of educational practice are problems whose solution depends upon the *amount* of some change in boys and girls. Of two methods, which gives the *greater* skill? Is the gain in general ability from a "disciplinary" study so great as to outweigh the loss in specially useful habits? Just how much more does a boy learn when thirty dollars a year is spent for his teaching than when only twenty dollars is spent? Units in which to measure the changes wrought by education are essential to an adequate science of education. And, though the students of education may establish these units by their own investigations, they can use and will need all the experience of psychologists in the search for similar units.

The second line of work concerns race, sex, age and individual differences in all the many elements of intellect and character and behavior. How do the Igorottes, Ainus, Japanese and Esquimaux differ in their efficiency in learning to operate certain mechanical contrivances? Is the male sex more variable than the female in mental functions? What happens to keenness of sensory discrimination with age? How do individuals of the same race, sex and age differ in efficiency in perceiving small visual details or in accuracy in equaling a given length, or in the rapidity of movement? These are samples of many questions which psychologists have tried to answer by appropriate measurements. Such knowledge of the differences which exist amongst men for whatever reason is of service to the thinker about the particular differences which education aims to produce between a man and his former self.

These studies of individual differences or variability are being supplemented by studies of correlations. How far does superior vividness and fidelity in imagery from one sense go with inferiority in other sorts of imagery? To what extent is motor ability a symptom of intellectual ability? Does the quick learner soon forget? What are the mental types that result from the individual variations in mental functions and their inter-correlations? Psychology has already determined with more or less surety the answers to a number of such questions instructive in their bearing upon both scientific insight into human nature and practical arrangements for controlling it.

The extent to which the intellectual and moral differences found in human beings are consequences of their original nature and determined by the ancestry from which they spring, is a matter of fundamental importance for education. So also is the manner in which ancestral influence operates. Whether such qualities as leadership, the artistic temperament, originality, persistence, mathematical ability, or motor skill are represented in the germs each by one or a few unit characters so that they "Mendelize" in inheritance, or whether they are represented each by the cooperation of so many unit characters that the laws of their inheritance are those of "blending" is a question whose answer will decide in great measure the means to be employed for racial improvement. Obviously both the amount and the mode of operation of ancestral influence upon intellect and character are questions which psychology should and does investigate.

The results and methods of action of the many forces which operate in childhood and throughout life to change a man's original nature are subjects for study equally appropriate to the work of a psychologist, a sociologist or a student of education, but the last two will naturally avail themselves of all that the first achieves. Although as yet the studies of such problems are crude, speculative and often misguided, we may hope that the influence of climate, food, city life, the specialization of industry, the various forms of the family and of the state, the different "studies" of the schools, and the like will come to be studied by as careful psychologists and with as much care as is now the case with color-vision or the perception of distance.

The foundation upon which education builds is the equipment of instincts and capacity given by nature apart from training. Just as knowledge of the peculiar inheritance characteristic of any individual is necessary to efficient treatment of him, so knowledge of the unlearned tendencies of man as a species is necessary to efficient planning for education in general. Partly in conscious response to this demand and partly as a result of growing interest in comparative and genetic psychology, there have been in the last two decades many studies by psychologists of both the general laws of instinct and their particular natures, dates of appearance and disappearance, and conditions of modifiability. The instincts of attitude—of interest and aversion—are of course to be included here, as well as the tendencies to more obviously effective responses.

It is unfortunately true that the unlearned tendencies to respond of ants and chickens have been studied with more care than those of men, and also that the extreme complexity and intimate mixture with habits in the case of human instincts prevent studies of them, even when made with great care, from giving entirely unambiguous and elegant results. But the educational theorist or practitioner who should conclude that his casual observations of children in homes and schools needs no reinforcement from the researches of psychologists would be making the same sort of, thought [sic] not so great, an error as the pathologist or physician who should neglect the scientific studies of bacteria and protozoa. Also the psychologist who condemns these studies *in toto* because they lack the precision and surety of his own studies of sensations and perceptual judgments is equally narrow, though from a better motive.

The modifications of instincts and capacities into habits and powers and the development of the latter are the subjects of researches in dynamic psychology which are replacing the vague verbal and trite maxims of what used to be called "applied psychology" by definite insights into reality far in advance of those which common-sense sagacity alone can make. We are finding out when and why "practice makes perfect" and when and why it does not; wherein the reinforcement of a connection between situation and response by resulting satisfaction is better than the inhibition of alternative connections by discomfort and wherein it is not; what the law of diminishing returns from equal amounts of practice is, what it implies, and how it is itself limited; how far the feelings of achievement, of failure and of fatigue are symptomatic of progress, retardation and unfitness for work. Such a list of topics could be much extended even now and is being increased rapidly as more psychologists and more gifted psychologists come to share in the study of the learning process.

Only twenty years ago a student could do little more than add to his own common-sense deductions from the common facts of life the ordered series of similar deductions by the sagacious Bain. Bain utilized all the psychology of his day as well as the common fund of school-room experience, but today his book is hopelessly outgrown. Although it was the source of the minor books on the topic during the eighties and nineties, no one would now think of presenting the facts of the science of education by a revised edition of Bain.

Other lines of psychological work deserve more than mention. Incidental contributions from studies of sensory and perceptual processes, imagery and memory, attention and distraction, facilitation, inhibition and fatigue, imitation and suggestion, the rate and accuracy of movement and other topics—even from studies made with little or no concern about the practical control of human nature—sum up to a body of facts which do extend and economize that control. The special psychology of babies, children and adolescents is obviously important to education. False infant psychology or false child psychology is harmful, not because it is infant psychology, but because it is false.

I give only mention to these so as to save space in which to call attention to another relation between psychology and education which is not sufficiently known. The science of education can and will itself contribute abundantly to psychology. Not only do the laws derived by psychology from simple, specially arranged experiments help us to interpret and control mental action under the conditions of school-room life. School-room life itself is a vast laboratory in which are made thousands of experiments of the utmost interest to "pure" psychology. Not only does psychology help us to understand the mistakes made by children in arithmetic. These mistakes afford most desirable material for studies of the action of the laws of association, analysis and selective thinking. Experts in education studying the responses to school situations for the sake of practical control will advance knowledge not only of the mind as a learner under school conditions but also of the mind for every point of view.

Indeed I venture to predict that this journal will before many years contain a notable proportion of articles reporting answers to psychological questions got from the facts of educational experience, in addition to its list of papers reporting answers to educational questions got from the experiments of the laboratory.

All that is here written may seem very obvious and needless, and meet the tragic fate of being agreed with by every one who reads it. I hope that it is obvious and needless, and that the relation between psychology and education is not, in the mind of any competent thinker, in any way an exception to the general case that action in the world should be guided by the truth about the world; and that any truth about it will directly or indirectly, soon or late, benefit action.

31

Equal Pay for Equal Work

Grace Strachan, 1910

Grace Strachan (n.d–1922) was an educator who was born in Buffalo, New York. When she married Timothy Forsythe, she took her husband's surname. She began teaching at the age of sixteen, and gained fame as the District Superintendent of Schools in New York City in the early 1900s. She also headed the Interborough Association of Women Teachers (IAWT), a New York City teachers union, founded in 1906. During this time period, the campaign "Equal Pay for Equal Work" began in which local female teachers fought to earn the same salaries as their male counterparts. In the essay that Strachan had published in the *New York Times*, she explains why she rejects the proposed salary increase for female teachers. Focusing on the single issue of salary, she notes that a raise for women teachers from $600 to $750 was still less than the $900 male teachers earned. She makes several additional arguments in support of equal pay, and was ultimately successful in her campaign. In 1912, a new law was implemented in New York City which stated that "in the salaries of teachers hereafter appointed, there shall be no discrimination on account of the sex of the teacher." —CHB

American Educational Thought: Essays from 1640–1940, pages 493–497
Copyright © 2010 by Information Age Publishing
All rights of reproduction in any form reserved.

Preface

Salary—A periodical allowance made as compensation to a person
for his official or professional services or for his regular work.
—Funk and Wagnalls.

Notice the words, "a person." Here is no differentiation between male persons and female persons. Yet the City of New York pays a "male" person for certain "professional services" $900, while paying a "female" person only $600 for the same "professional services." Stranger still, it pays for certain experience of a "male" person $105, while paying a "female" person only $40 for the identical experience. These are but samples of the "glaring inequalities" in the teachers' salary schedules.

Why is the male in the teaching profession differentiated from the male in every other calling, when his salary is concerned?

Why does the city differentiate the woman it hires to teach its children from the woman it hires to take stenographic notes, use a typewriter, follow up truants, inspect a tenement, or issue a license?

Why are not the appointees from the eligible lists established by the Department of Education, entitled to the same privileges and rights as appointees from Civil Service lists from other City and State Departments?

Some ask, "Shall the single woman, in teaching, be given the married woman's wage?" I do not know what they mean, But I say, "Why not the single woman in teaching just as much as the single woman in washing, in farming, in dressmaking, in nursing, in telephoning?"

Again, some ask, is there such a thing as "equal work" by two people?

Technically, no. No two people do exactly the same work in the same way. This is true of all professional and official work. Compare Mayor Gaynor's work with Mayor McClellan's. Will any one say their work as Mayor is "Equal Work"? And yet the pay is the same. Do all policemen do "Equal Work"? Yet they receive equal pay. So with firemen, school physicians, tenement house inspectors. The taxpayers, no doubt, believe that, judged by his work, Mayor Gaynor is worth a far higher salary than many of his predecessors. But a great corporation like the City of New York cannot attempt to pay each of its employees according to the work of that particular street cleaner or fireman or stenographer, and so must be content with classifying its positions, and fixing a salary for each. So should it do for its teachers. That is all we ask.

The Family-to-Support Argument

It is rather a sad commentary on our profession that its men members are the only men who object to women members of the same profession getting the same pay for the same work. Who ever heard of a man lawyer fighting a woman lawyer in this way? A man doctor arguing that another doctor should give her services for less pay simply because she happened to be a woman? And leaving the professions, what attitude do we find the men who form our "Labor Unions" taking on this question? They form a solid phalanx on the side of "Equal Pay." The most powerful of all unions in many respects—"Big Six"—has a By-Law making it a misdemeanor to pay a woman less than a man working at the same form. All Labor Unions fight "two prices on a job."

Is it not sad to see men, American men, shoving aside, trampling down, and snatching the life preservers from their sisters? I say life preservers seriously and mean it literally. For to the woman obliged to support herself, is not her wage earning ability truly a life preserver. How can any man except one whom she is legally privileged to assist, take from a woman any part of the wages she has earned and remain worthy even in his own eyes? The excuses he makes to himself and to others in the attempt to justify his act, tend to belittle him more and more.

And yet some men whose blood sisters have by teaching provided the money to enable them, their brothers, to become teachers, oppose those very sisters in their efforts to obtain "Equal Pay for Equal Work." Can one ask for stronger proof of the insidious danger to our manhood which lurks in unjust standards of salary for service rendered? The true man, the good man, ought to put the woman who earns a respectable living, on a pedestal, as a beacon of encouragement to other women to show them one who wanted clothes to wear, and food to eat, and a place to live, and who obtained them by honorable labor. . . .

I am firmly convinced that while teaching is a natural vocation for most women, it is rarely the true vocation of a man. And that those who enter the profession without the love for it which overshadows even the pocket returns, invariably deteriorate. Their lives are spent largely among those whom they consider their subordinates—in position or in salary, if not in intellect—the children and the women teachers. They grow to have an inordinate opinion of themselves. No matter how ridiculous or absurd or unfair may be the attitudes they take and the things they say, there is no one to say, "Nonsense!" as would one of his peers in the outer world. The novelist David Graham Phillips in the following description of one of his characters expresses my opinion better than I can myself: "Peter was not to blame for his weakness. He had not had the chance to become otherwise. He had been deprived of that hand-to-hand strife with life which alone makes a man strong. Usually, however, the dangerous truth as to his weakness was well hidden by the fictitious seeming of strength which obstinacy, selfishness and the adulation of a swarm of sycophants and dependents combine to give a man of means and position."

Recently in one of our schools, a male assistant to the principal resigned. The vacancy thus caused was filled by a woman. This woman is doing the same work as the man did, but with greater satisfactions to the principal. But she is being paid $800 a year less than the man was.

In another school I know there was a woman assistant to principal. As a grade teacher she had married and resigned, expecting—as most girls do when they marry—that she wouldn't have to work outside the home any more. But her husband became a victim of tuberculosis, and they went to Colorado in search of health for him. Time passed, their funds were exhausted, the invalid was unable to work, and so they came back, and the wife—after certifying, as our by-laws require, that her husband was unable to support her and had been so for two years—was reappointed. Later she secured promotion to assistant to principal. During the day she labored in a large, progressive school, composed almost wholly of children born in Russia, or of Russian parentage. At night she taught a class of foreign men. Now, although she actually had a family to support, she was receiving $800 a year less than a man in her position would receive. A married man? Oh, no, not necessarily. He might be a millionaire bachelor, or the pet of a wealthy wife—it is only necessary for him to be a "male" assistant to principal. Possibly on account of her family responsibilities, probably because she was ambitious, she strove for a principalship. During the school year, she traveled to Columbia University and took post graduate courses after school and on Saturdays; during the summer, when she should have been resting, she was studying with Professor This and Professor That. Last September she took the examination for a principal's license: in October, she died— typhoid, the doctors said. The husband she had cheerfully and lovingly supported for years survived her but a few weeks.

Why have I dwelt on this? To show the absurdity of the "family wage" argument of the male teacher. . . . Under a system of equal pay, where services should be paid for irrespective of sex, some women who now marry would remain single. But there are some men to-day who remain single because of relative economic independence, which they desire to maintain. These men are, however, relatively few. Women are as instinctive and as normal as men are, and independence, which they feared to lose, would prevent very few from marrying when they could make marriages which were attractive to them. Independence of women would improve marriage, since fewer women would marry because of necessity. By the same means divorce would be decreased, and human happiness would have a boom.

Our Association early in 1908 gathered some statistics. They showed 377 women—eleven of them married and six widows—supporting 707 others besides themselves. These teachers are, all women, but the people depending wholly upon them or partly upon them are their mothers or their fathers or both or a brother or a sister or a niece or a nephew. These are actual figures collated from written answers to our questionnaire.

You see, then, that here is an average of two people for every woman to support besides herself. Now, what salary is offered to these young women of twenty-one years of age, after they have spent all these years in preparing for the position of teacher? What salary is she being paid by the City of New York, the greatest city in the world, with the greatest public school system in the world? $11.53 a week. A woman in charge of one of the stations in the city gets more than that. Does the latter have to spend as much money on clothes? No. She can wear the same clothes from one end of the year to the other if she wants to, and not be criticized. But I know when I go into a classroom, among the things that I notice is the teacher's dress—whether it is neat, whether it is appropriate. She must be a model for her class. Besides, the teacher must live in a respectable neighborhood and make a good appearance at home and abroad, and she must continue her studies in order to give satisfactory service.

32

Report of the Commission of the Reorganization of Secondary Education

National Education Association, 1918

The Report of the Commission on the Reorganization of Secondary Education, also known as the Cardinal Principles Report, was published during a time of great change in American education. Since the late 1880s, immigrants had been flocking to America's shores, causing the public school system to educate students from increasingly diverse backgrounds. In addition to an influx of immigrants, more students who already lived in America had begun to attend school through high school age due to the passage of compulsory education laws. Students who had never had a chance to attend school before began to spend increasingly more time in school. The curriculum as well as the teaching methods used in high schools, however, had changed little since before the Civil War. To deal with the problem of how to adapt curriculum to this new diverse body of students, the National Education Association established a commission, known as the Commission on the Reorganization of Secondary Education (CRSE), to review curricula across the country and issue a report that would direct the future of secondary education curriculum. The document below is the result of the Commission's work. The report became known as the "Cardinal Principles Report" because

American Educational Thought: Essays from 1640–1940, pages 499–509
Copyright © 2010 by Information Age Publishing
All rights of reproduction in any form reserved.

the Commission gave it this title. They outline seven "Cardinal Principles" they believe should serve as the foundation for high school curriculum. The authors of the report adopted the Progressive notion that the purpose of education and the content of the curriculum should be responsive to social trends, societal needs, and the interests of individual students. They noted that these seven principles were relevant for their time, but suggested that future generations revisit the question of purpose and determine which principles should guide secondary education.

Defenders of a traditional academic curriculum criticized the report (and continue to do so) as an attempt to remove academic rigor from high school curriculum, thereby lowering standards and failing to challenge students. On the other hand, supporters contend that the CRSE presented a vision for high school curriculum that retains an emphasis on intellectual excellence while at the same time broadening the scope of what high schools should seek to accomplish. Readers in the twenty-first century can read the report themselves and decide if the Commission presents a bold enough vision for high school curriculum. —JWN

I. The Need for Reorganization

Secondary education should be determined by the needs of the society to be served, the character of the individuals to be educated, and the knowledge of educational theory and practice available. These factors are by no means static. Society is always in process of development; the character of the secondary-school population undergoes modification; and the sciences on which educational theory and practice depend constantly furnish new information. Secondary education, however, like any other established agency of society, is conservative and tends to resist modification. Failure to make adjustments when the need arises leads to the necessity for extensive reorganization at irregular intervals. The evidence is strong that such a comprehensive reorganization of secondary education is imperative at the present time.

1. *Changes in society.*—Within the past few decades changes have taken place in American life profoundly affecting the activities of the individual. As a citizen, he must to a greater extent and in a more direct way cope with problems of community life, State and National Governments, and international relationships. As a worker, he must adjust himself to a more complex economic order. As a relatively independent personality, he has more leisure. The problems arising from these three dominant phases of life are closely interrelated and call for a degree of intelligence and efficiency on the part of every citizen that can not be secured through elementary education alone, or even through secondary education unless the scope of that education is broadened.

The responsibility of the secondary school is still further increased because many social agencies other than the school afford less stimulus for education than heretofore. In many vocations there have come such significant changes as the substitution of the factory system for the domestic system of industry; the use of machinery in place of manual labor; the high specialization of processes with a corresponding subdivision of labor; and the breakdown of the apprentice system. In connection with home and family life have frequently come lessened responsibility on the part of the children; the withdrawal of the father and sometimes the mother from home occupations to the factory or store; and increased urbanization, resulting in less unified family life. Similarly, many important changes have taken place in community life, in the church, in the State, and in other institutions. These changes in American life call for extensive modifications in secondary education.

2. *Changes in the secondary-school population.*—In the past 25 years there have been marked changes in the secondary-school population of the United States. The number of pupils has increased, according to Federal returns, from one for every 210 of the total population in 1889–90, to one for every 121 in 1899–1900, to one for every 89 in 1909–10, and to one for every 73 of the estimated total population in 1914–15. The character of the secondary-school population has been modified by the entrance of large numbers of pupils of widely varying capacities, aptitudes, social heredity, and destinies in life. Further, the broadening of the scope of secondary education has brought to the school many pupils who do not complete the full course but leave at various stages of advancement. The needs of these pupils can not be neglected, nor can we expect in the near future that all pupils will be able to complete the secondary school as fulltime students.

At present only about one-third of the pupils who enter the first year of the elementary school reach the four-year high school, and only about one in nine is graduated. Of those who enter the seventh school year, only one-half to two-thirds reach the first year of the four-year high school. Of those who enter the four-year high school about one-third leave before the beginning of the second year, about one-half are gone before the beginning of the third year, and fewer than one-third are graduated. These facts can no longer be safely ignored.

3. *Changes in educational theory.*—The sciences on which educational theory depends have within recent years made significant contributions. In particular, educational psychology emphasizes the following factors:

(*a*) *Individual differences in capacities and aptitudes among secondary-school pupils.*—Already recognized to some extent, this factor merits fuller attention.

(*b*) *The reexamination and reinterpretation of subject values and the teaching methods with reference to "general discipline."*—While the final verdict of modern psychology has not as yet been rendered, it is clear that former conceptions of "general values" must be thoroughly revised.

(*c*) *Importance of applying knowledge.*—Subject values and teaching methods must be tested in terms of the laws of learning and the application of knowledge to the activities of life, rather than primarily in terms of the demands of any subject as a logically organized science.

(*d*) *Continuity in the development of children.*—It has long been held that psychological changes at certain stages are so pronounced as to overshadow the continuity of development. On this basis secondary education has been sharply separated from elementary education. Modern psychology, however, goes to show that the development of the individual is in most respects a continuous process and that, therefore, any sudden or abrupt break between the elementary and the secondary school or between any two successive stages of education is undesirable.

The foregoing changes in society, in the character of the secondary school population, and in educational theory, together with many other considerations, call for extensive modifications of secondary education. Such modifications have already begun in part. The present need is for the formulation of a comprehensive program of reorganization, and its adoption, with suitable adjustments, in all the secondary schools of the Nation. Hence it is appropriate for a representative body like the National Education Association to outline such a program. This is the task entrusted by that association to the Commission on the Reorganization of Secondary Education.

II. The Goal of Education in a Democracy

Education in the United States should be guided by a clear conception of the meaning of democracy. It is the ideal of democracy that the individual and society may find fulfillment each in the other. Democracy sanctions neither the exploitation of the individual by society, nor the disregard of the interests of society by the individual. More explicitly—

> The purpose of democracy is so to organize society that each member may develop his personality primarily through activities designed for the well-being of his fellow members and of society as a whole.

This ideal demands that human activities be placed upon a high level of efficiency; that to this efficiency be added an appreciation of the significance of these activities and loyalty to the best ideals involved; and that the individual choose that vocation and those forms of social service in which his personality may develop and become most effective. For the achievement of these ends democracy must place chief reliance upon education. Consequently, education in a democracy, both within and without the school, should develop in each individual the knowledge, interests, ideals, habits, and powers whereby he will find his place and use that place to shape both himself and society toward ever nobler ends.

III. The Main Objectives of Education

In order to determine the main objectives that should guide education in a democracy, it is necessary to analyze the activities of the individual. Normally he is a member of a family, of a vocational group, and of various civic groups, and by virtue of these relationships he is called upon to engage in activities that enrich the family life, to render important vocational services to his fellows, and to promote the common welfare. It follows, therefore, that worthy home membership, vocation, and citizenship demand attention as three of the leading objectives.

Aside from the immediate discharge of these specific duties, every individual should have a margin of time for the cultivation of personal and social interests. This leisure, if worthily used, will recreate his powers and enlarge and enrich life, thereby making him better able to meet his responsibilities. The unworthy use of leisure impairs health, disrupts home life, lessens vocational efficiency, and destroys civic-mindedness. The tendency in industrial life, aided by legislation, is to decrease the working hours of large groups of people. While shortened hours tend to lessen the harmful reactions that arise from prolonged strain, they increase, if possible, the importance of preparation for leisure. In view of these considerations, education for the worthy use of leisure is of increasing importance as an objective.

To discharge the duties of life and to benefit from leisure, one must have good health. The health of the individual is essential also to the vitality of the race and to the defense of the Nation. Health education is, therefore, fundamental.

There are various processes, such as reading, writing, arithmetical computations, and oral and written expression, that are needed as tools in the affairs of life. Consequently, command of these fundamental processes, while not an end in itself, is nevertheless an indispensable objective.

And, finally, the realization of the objectives already named is dependent upon ethical character, that is, upon conduct founded upon right principles, clearly perceived and loyally adhered to. Good citizenship, vocational excellence, and the worthy use of leisure go hand in hand with ethical character; they are at once the fruits of sterling character and the channels through which such character is developed and made manifest. On the one hand, character is meaningless apart from the will to discharge the duties of life, and, on the other hand, there is no guaranty that these duties will be rightly discharged unless principles are substituted for impulses, however well-intentioned such impulses may be. Consequently, ethical character is at once involved in all the other objectives and at the same time requires specific consideration in any program of national education.

This commission, therefore, regards the following as the main objectives of education: 1. Health. 2. Command of fundamental processes. 3. Worthy home membership. 4. Vocation. 5. Citizenship. 6. Worthy use of leisure. 7. Ethical character.

The naming of the above objectives is not intended to imply that the process of education can be divided into separated fields. This can not be, since the pupil is indivisible. Nor is the analysis all-inclusive. Nevertheless, we believe that distinguishing and naming these objectives will aid in directing efforts; and we hold that they should constitute the principal aims in education.

IV. The Role of Secondary Education in Achieving these Objectives

The objectives outlined above apply to education as a whole—elementary, secondary, and higher. It is the purpose of this section to consider specifically the role of secondary education in achieving each of these objectives. This commission favors such reorganization that secondary education may be defined as applying to all pupils of approximately 12 to 18 years of age.

1. *Health.*—Health needs can not be neglected during the period of secondary education without serious danger to the individual and the race. The secondary school should therefore provide health instruction, inculcate health habits, organize an effective program of physical activities, regard health needs in planning work and play, and cooperate with home and community in safeguarding and promoting health interests.

To carry out such a program it is necessary to arouse the public to recognize that the health needs of young people are of vital importance to society, to secure teachers competent to ascertain and meet the needs of individual pupils and able to inculcate in the entire student body a love for clean sport: to furnish adequate equipment, for physical activities, and to make the school building, its rooms and surroundings, conform to the best standards of hygiene and sanitation.

2. *Command of fundamental processes.*—Much of the energy of the elementary school is properly devoted to teaching certain fundamental processes, such as reading, writing, arithmetical computations, and the elements of oral and written expression. The facility that a child of 12 or 14 may acquire in the use of these tools is not sufficient for the needs of modern life. This is particularly true of the mother tongue. Proficiency in many of these processes may be increased more effectively by their application to new material than by the formal reviews commonly employed in grades seven and eight. Throughout the secondary school, instruction and practice must go hand in hand, but as indicated in the report of the committee on English, only so much theory should be taught at any one time as will show results in practice.

3. *Worthy home membership.*—Worthy home membership as an objective calls for the development of those qualities that make the individual a worthy member of a family, both contributing to and deriving benefit from that membership. This objective applies to both boys and girls. The social studies should deal with the home as a fundamental social institution and clarify its relation to the wider interests outside. Literature should interpret and idealize the human elements that go to make the home.

Music and art should result in more beautiful homes and in greater joy therein. The coeducational school with a faculty of men and women should, in its organization and its activities, exemplify wholesome relations between boys and girls and men and women.

Home membership as an objective should not be thought of solely with reference to future duties. These are the better guaranteed if the school helps the pupils to take the right attitude toward present home responsibilities and interprets to them the contribution of the home to their development.

In the education of every high-school girl, the household arts should have a prominent place because of their importance to the girl herself and to others whose welfare will be directly in her keeping. The attention now devoted to this phase of education is inadequate, and especially so for girls preparing for occupations not related to the household arts and for girls planning for higher institutions. The majority of girls who enter wage-earning occupations directly from the high school remain in them for only a few years, after which home making becomes their lifelong occupation. For them the high-school period offers the only assured opportunity to prepare for that lifelong occupation, and it is during this period that they are most likely to form their ideals of life's duties and responsibilities. For girls planning to enter higher institutions—our traditional ideals of preparation for higher institutions are particularly incongruous with the actual needs and future responsibilities of girls. It would seem that such high-school work as is carefully designed to develop capacity for, and interest in, the proper management and conduct of a home should be regarded as of importance at least equal to that of any other work. We do not understand how society can properly continue to sanction for girls high-school curriculums that disregard this fundamental need, even though such curriculums are planned in response to the demands made by some of the colleges for women.

In the education of boys, some opportunity should be found to give them a basis for the intelligent appreciation of the value of the well-appointed home and of the labor and skill required to maintain such a home, to the end that they may cooperate more effectively. For instance, they should understand the essentials of food values, of sanitation, and of household budgets.

4. *Vocation.*—Vocational education should equip the individual to secure a livelihood for himself and those dependent on him, to serve society well through his vocation, to maintain the right relationships toward his fellow workers and society, and, as far as possible, to find in that vocation his own best development.

This ideal demands that the pupil explore his own capacities and aptitudes, and make a survey of the world's work, to the end that he may select his vocation wisely. Hence, an effective program of vocational guidance in the secondary school is essential.

Vocational education should aim to develop an appreciation of the significance of the vocation to the community and a clear conception of right relations between the members of the chosen vocation, between different vocational groups, between employer and employee, and between producer and consumer. These aspects of vocational education, heretofore neglected, demand emphatic attention.

The extent to which the secondary school should offer training for a specific vocation depends upon the vocation, the facilities that the school can acquire, and the opportunity that the pupil may have to obtain such training later. To obtain satisfactory results those proficient in that vocation should be employed as instructors and the actual conditions of the vocation should be utilized either within the high school or in cooperation with the home, farm, shop, or office. Much of the pupil's time will be required to produce such efficiency.

5. *Civic education.*—should develop in the individual those qualities whereby he will act well his part as a member of neighborhood, town or city, State, and Nation, and give him a basis for understanding international problems.

For such citizenship the following are essential: A many-sided interest in the welfare of the communities to which one belongs; loyalty to ideals of civic righteousness; practical knowledge of social agencies and institutions; good judgment as to means and methods that will promote one social end without defeating others; and as putting all these into effect, habits of cordial cooperation in social undertakings.

The school should develop the concept that the civic duties of men and women, while in part identical, are also in part supplementary. Differentiation in civic activities is to be encouraged, but not to the extent of loss of interest in the common problems with which all should cope.

Among the means for developing attitudes and habits important in a democracy are the assignment of projects and problems to groups of pupils for cooperative solution and the socialized recitation whereby the class as a whole develops a sense of collective responsibility. Both of these devices give training in collective thinking. Moreover, the democratic organization and administration of the school itself as well as the cooperative relations of pupil and teacher, pupil and pupil, and teacher and teacher, are indispensable. While all subjects should contribute to good citizenship, the social studies—geography, history, civics, and economics—should have this as their dominant aim. Too frequently, however, does mere information, conventional in value and remote in its bearing, make up the content of the social studies. History should so treat the growth of institutions that their present value may be appreciated. Geography should show the interdependence of men while it shows their common dependence on nature. Civics should concern itself less with constitutional questions and remote governmental functions, and should direct attention to social agencies close at hand and to the informal activities of daily life that regard and seek the common good. Such agencies as child-welfare organizations and consumers' leagues afford specific opportunities for the expression of civic qualities by the older pupils.

The work in English should kindle social ideals and give insight into social conditions and into personal character as related to these conditions. Hence the emphasis by the committee on English on the importance of a knowledge of social activities, social movements, and social needs on the part of the teacher of English.

The comprehension of the ideals of American democracy and loyalty to them should be a prominent aim of civic education. The pupil should feel that he will be responsible, in cooperation with others, for keeping the Nation true to the best inherited conceptions of democracy, and he should also realize that democracy itself is an ideal to be wrought out by his own and succeeding generations.

Civic education should consider other nations also. As a people we should try to understand their aspirations and ideals that we may deal more sympathetically and intelligently with the immigrant coming to our shores, and have a basis for a wiser and more sympathetic approach to international problems. Our pupils should learn that each nation, at least potentially, has something of worth to contribute to civilization and that humanity would be incomplete without that contribution. This means a study of specific nations, their achievements and possibilities, not ignoring their limitations. Such a study of dissimilar contributions in the light of the ideal of human brotherhood should help to establish a genuine internationalism, free from sentimentality, founded on fact, and actually operative in the affairs of nations.

6. *Worthy use of leisure.* —Education should equip the individual to secure from his leisure the recreation of body, mind, and spirit, and the enrichment and enlargement of his personality.

This objective calls for the ability to utilize the common means of enjoyment, such as music, art, literature, drama, and social intercourse, together with the fostering in each individual of one or more special vocational interests.

Heretofore the high school has given little conscious attention to this objective. It has so exclusively sought intellectual discipline that it has seldom treated literature, art, and music so as to evoke right emotional response and produce positive enjoyment. Its presentation of science should aim, in part, to arouse a genuine appreciation of nature.

The school has failed also to organize and direct the social activities of young people as it should. One of the surest ways in which to prepare pupils worthily to utilize leisure in adult life is by guiding and directing their use of leisure in youth. The school should, therefore, see that adequate recreation is provided both within the school and by other proper agencies in the community. The school, however, has a unique opportunity in this field because it includes in its membership representatives from all classes of society and consequently is able through social relationships to establish bonds of friendship and common understanding that can not be furnished by other agencies. Moreover, the school can so organize recreational activities that they will contribute simultaneously to other ends of education, as in the case of the school pageant or festival.

7. *Ethical character.*—In a democratic society ethical character becomes paramount among the objectives of the secondary school. Among the means for developing ethical character may be mentioned the wise selection of content and methods of instruction in all subjects of study, the social contacts of pupils with one another and with their teachers, the opportunities afforded by the organization and administration of the school for the development on the part of pupils of the sense of personal responsibility and initiative and, above all, the spirit of service and the principles of true democracy which should permeate the entire school—principal, teachers, and pupils.

33

The Project Method

William H. Kilpatrick, 1918

William Heard Kilpatrick (1871–1965), the son of a Baptist minister, was born in White Plains, Georgia. He attended Mercer University for his undergraduate degree and attended The Johns Hopkins University for graduate study. He went on to teach at an elementary-secondary school in Georgia for four years, after which he accepted a teaching job at Mercer. Following six years of teaching at Mercer, he became acting president of the University, but he abruptly left after being accused of atheism by the trustees. Kilpatrick went back to teaching for a year, but then accepted a scholarship to begin as a Ph.D. student in educational philosophy at Teachers College, Columbia University. Kilpatrick remained at Teachers College as a student and then a professor for the rest of his life. At Columbia, Kilpatrick became the favorite disciple of John Dewey, who once called him "the best student I ever had." Kilpatrick returned the praise by helping to popularize Dewey's ideas. As Kilpatrick put it, "I feel in some measure that I am best qualified of those about here to interpret Dewey. His own lectures are frequently impenetrable to even intelligent students." As a fierce advocate of Progressive education, Kilpatrick became the most popular professor at Teachers College, the leading graduate school of education in the country. A charismatic figure, Kilpatrick lectured to large audiences of graduate students about progressive themes such as the

American Educational Thought: Essays from 1640–1940, pages 511–524
Copyright © 2010 by Information Age Publishing

importance of learning by doing. Due primarily to the extremely large classes that he taught, often numbering close to 1000 students, Kilpatrick became known as "the million dollar professor." By the end of his career, Kilpatrick had taught more than 35,000 students. Kilpatrick himself claimed Teachers College had trained "3 out of every four educational supervisors" in the United States by 1921. In the essay below, Kilpatrick describes an educational approach that some would consider one of the model statements of the Progressive movement. —PLG

The word 'project' is perhaps the latest arrival to knock for admittance at the door of educational terminology. Shall we admit the stranger? Not widely until two preliminary questions have first been answered in the affirmative: First, is there behind the proposed term and waiting even now to be christened a valid notion or concept which promises to render appreciable service in educational thinking? Second, if we grant the foregoing, does the term 'project' fitly designate the waiting concept? Because the question as to the concept and its worth is so much more significant than any matter of mere names, this discussion will deal almost exclusively with the first of the two inquiries. It is indeed entirely possible that some other term, as 'purposeful act', for example, would call attention to a more important element in the concept, and, if so, might prove superior as a term to the word 'project'. At the outset it is probably wise to caution the reader against expecting any great amount of novelty in the idea here presented. The metaphor of christening is not to be taken too seriously; the concept to be considered is not in fact newly born. Not a few readers will be disappointed that after all so little new is presented.

A little of the personal may perhaps serve to introduce the more formal discussion. In attacking with successive classes in educational theory the problem of method, I had felt increasingly the need of unifying more completely a number of important related aspects of the educative process. I began to hope for some one concept which might serve this end. Such a concept, if found, must, so I thought, emphasize the factor of action, preferably wholehearted vigorous activity. It must at the same time provide a place for the adequate utilization of the laws of learning, and no less for the essential elements of the ethical quality of conduct. The last named looks of course to the social situation as well as to the individual attitude. Along with these should go, as it seemed, the important generalization that education is life—so easy to say and so hard to delimit. Could now all of these be contemplated under one workable notion? If yes, a great gain. In proportion as such a unifying concept could be found in like proportion would the work of presenting educational theory be facilitated: in like proportion should be the rapid spread of a better practice.

But could this unifying idea be found? Here was in fact the age-old problem of effective logical organization. My whole philosophic outlook had made me suspicious of so-called 'fundamental principles'. Was there yet another way of attaining unity? I do not mean to say that I asked these questions, either in these works or in this order. Rather is this a retrospective ordering of the more important outcomes. As the desired unification lay specifically in the field of method, might not some typical unit of concrete procedure supply the need—some unit of conduct that should be, as it were, a sample of life, a fair sample of the worthy life and consequently of education? As these questionings rose more definitely to mind, there came increasingly a belief—corroborated on many sides—that the unifying ideas I sought was to be found in the conception of a wholehearted purposeful activity proceeding in a social environment, or more briefly, in the unit element of such activity, the hearty purposeful act.

It is to this purposeful act with the emphasis on the word purpose that I myself apply the term 'project'. I did not invent the term nor did I start it on its educational career. Indeed, I do not know how long it has already been in use. I did, however, consciously appropriate the word to designate the typical unit of the worthy life described above. Others who were using the term seemed to me either to use it in a mechanical and partial sense or to be intending in a general way what I tried to define more exactly. The purpose of this article is to attempt to clarify the concept underlying the term as much as it is to defend the claim of the concept to a place in our educational thinking. The actual terminology with which to designate the concept is, as was said before, to my mind a matter of relatively small moment. If, however, we think of a project as a pro-ject, something pro-jected, the reason for its adoption may better appear.

Postponing yet a little further the more systematic presentation of the matter, let us from some typical instances see more concretely what is contemplated under the term project or hearty purposeful act? Suppose a girl makes a dress. If she did in hearty fashion purpose to make the dress, if she planned it, if she made it herself, then I should say the instance is that of a typical project. We have a wholehearted purposeful act carried on amid social surroundings. That the dressmaking was purposeful is clear; the purpose once formed dominated each succeeding step in the process and gave unity to the whole. That the girl was wholeheartedly in the work was assured in the illustration. That the activity proceeded in a social environment is clear; other girls at least are to see the dress. As another instance, suppose a boy undertakes to get out a school newspaper. If he is in earnest about it, we again have the effective purpose being the essence of the project. So we may instance a pupil writing a letter (if the hearty purpose is present), a child listening absorbedly to a story, Newton explaining the motion of the moon on the principles of terrestrial dynamics, Demosthenes trying to arouse the Greeks against Philip, Da Vinci painting the *Last Supper,* my writing this article, a boy solving with felt purpose an 'original' in geometry. All of the foregoing have been acts of individual in purposing, but this is not to rule out group projects: a class presents a play, a group of boys organize a baseball nine, three pupils prepare to read a story to their comrades. It is clear then that projects may present every variety that purposes present life. It is also clear that a mere description of outwardly observable facts might not disclose the essential factor, namely the presence of a dominating purpose. It is equally true that there can be every degree of approximation to full projects according as the animating purpose varies in clearness and strength. If we conceive activities as ranging on a scale from those performed under dire compulsion up to those into which one puts his 'whole heart', the argument herein made restricts the term 'project' or purposeful act to the upper portions of the scale. An exact dividing line is hard to draw, and yields indeed in importance to the notion that psychological value increases with degree of approximation to 'wholeheartedness'. As to the social environment element, some may feel that, however important this is to the fullest educative experience, it is still not essential to the conception of the purposeful act as here presented. These might therefore wish to leave this element out of the defining discussion. To this I should not object if it were clearly understood that the resulting concept—now essentially psychological in character—generally speaking, demands the social situation both for its practical working and for the comparative valuation of proffered projects.

With this general introduction, we may, in the first place, say that the purposeful act is the typical unit of the worthy life. Not that all purposes are good, but that the worthy life consists of purposive activity and not mere drifting. We scorn the man who passively accepts what fate or some other chance brings to him. We admire the man who is master of his fate, who with deliberate regard for a total situation forms clear and far-reaching purposes, who plans and executes with nice care the purposes formed. A man who habitually so regulates his life with reference to worthy social aims meets at once the demands for practical efficiency and of moral responsibility. Such a one presents the ideal of democratic citizenship. It is equally true that the purposeful act is not the unit of life for the serf or the slave. These poor unfortunates must in the interest of the overmastering system be habituated to act with a minimum their own purposing and with a maximum of servile acceptance of others' purposes. In important matters they merely follow plans handed down to them from above, and execute these according to prescribed directions. For them another carries responsibility and upon the results of their labor another passes judgment. No such plan as that here advocated would produce the kind of docility required for their hopeless fate. But it is a democracy which we contemplate and with which we are here concerned.

As the purposeful act is thus the typical unit of the worthy life in a democratic society, so also should it be made the typical unit of school procedure. We of America have for years increasingly desired that education be considered as life itself and not as a mere preparation for later living. The conception before us promises a definite step toward the attainment of this end. If the purposeful act be in reality the typical unit of the worthy life, then it follows that to base education on purposeful acts is exactly to identify the process of education with worthy living itself. The two become then the same. All the arguments for placing education on a life basis seem, to me at any rate, to concur in support of this thesis. On this basis education has become life. And if the purposeful act thus makes of education life itself, could we reasoning in advance expect to find a better preparation for later life than practice in living now? We have heard of old that "we learn to do by doing" and much wisdom resides in this saying. If the worthy life of the coming day is to consist of well-chosen purposeful acts, what preparation for that time could promise more than practice now, under discriminating guidance, in forming and executing worthy purposes? To this end must the child have within rather large limits the opportunity to purpose. For the issues of his act he must—in like limits—be held accountable. That the child may properly progress, the total situation—all the factors of life, including comrades—speaking, if need be through the teacher, must make clear its selective judgment upon what he does, approving the better, rejecting the worse. In a true sense the whole remaining discussion is but to support the contention here argued in advance that education based on the purposeful act prepares best for life while at the same time it constitutes the present worthy life itself.

A more explicit reason for making the purposeful act the typical unit of instruction is found in the utilization of the laws of learning which this plan affords. I am assuming that it is not necessary in this magazine to justify or even explain at length these laws. (The discussion which here follows is adapted from Thorndike's *Educational Psychology*, Vol. II, pp. 1–16). Any act of conduct consists of a response to the existing situation. That response and not some other followed the given situation because there existed in the nervous system a bond or connection joining the stimulus of that situation with that response. Some such bonds come with us into the world as, for example, the infant cries (responds) when he is very hungry (situation acting as stimulus). Other bonds are acquired, as when the child later asks in words for food when he is hungry. The process of acquiring or otherwise changing bonds we call learning. The careful statements of the conditions under which bonds are built or changed are the laws of learning. Bonds are not always equally *ready* to act: when I am angry, the bonds that have to do with smiling are distinctly unready; other bonds controlling uglier behavior are quite ready. When a bond is ready to act, to act gives *satisfaction* and not to act gives *annoyance*. When a bond is not ready to act, to act gives annoyance and not to act gives satisfaction. These two statements constitute the Law of Readiness. The law that most concerns us in this discussion is that of Effect: when a modifiable bond acts, it is strengthened or weakened according as satisfaction or annoyance results. The ordinary psychology of common observation has not been so conscious of these two laws as it has of the third law, that of Exercise; but for our present purposes, repetition simply means the continued application of the law of Effect. (The law of Exercise does of course include more than this, as the successful educator must know if he would meet all situations.) There are yet other laws necessary for a full explanation of the facts of learning. Our available space allows for only one more, that of 'set' or attitude, the others we have to assume without explicit reference. When a person is very angry, he is sometimes colloquially said to be "mad all over." Such a phrase implies that many bonds are ready to act conjointly to an end, in this case, the end of overcoming or doing damage to the object of anger. Under such conditions there is (a) available and at work a stock of energy for attaining the end, (b) a state of readiness in the bonds pertaining to the activity at hand, and (c) a correlative unreadiness on the part of the bonds that might thwart the attainment of the end contemplated by the 'set'. The reader is asked to note (a) how a 'set' towards an end means readiness and action of pertinent bonds with reference to that end, (b) how this end defines success, (c) how readiness means satisfaction when success is attained, and (d) how satisfaction strengthens the bonds whose action brought success. These facts fit well with the generalization that man's mental powers and capacities came into being in connection with the continual attaining of ends demanded by the life of the organism. The capacity for 'set' means in the case of man the capacity for determined and directed action. Such action means for our discussion not only that (objective) success is more likely to result, but that learning better takes place. The bonds whose action brought success are by the resulting satisfaction more firmly fixed, both as distinct bonds separately considered and as a system of bonds working together under the 'set'. Set, readiness, determined action, success, satisfaction, and learning are inherently connected.

How then does the purposeful act utilize the laws of learning? A boy is intent upon making a kite that will fly. So far he has not succeeded. The purpose is clear. This purpose is but the 'set' consciously and volitionally bent on its end. As set the purpose is the inner urge that carries the boy on in the face of hindrance and difficulty. It brings 'readiness' to pertinent inner resources of knowledge and thought. Eye and hand are made alert. The purpose of acting as aim guides the boy's thinking, directs his examination of plan and material, elicits from within appropriate suggestions, and tests these several suggestions by their pertinency to the end in view. The purpose in that it contemplates a specific end defines success: the kite must fly or he has failed. The progressive attaining of success with reference to subordinate aims brings satisfaction at the successive stages of completion. Satisfaction in detail and in respect of the whole by the automatic working of the second law of learning (Effect) fixes the several bonds which by their successive successes brought the finally successful kite. The purpose thus supplies the motive power, makes available inner resources, guides the process to its pre-conceived end, and by this satisfactory success fixes in the boy's mind and character the successful steps as part and parcel of one whole. The purposeful act does utilize the laws of learning.

But this account does not yet exhaust the influence of the purpose on the resulting learning. Suppose as extreme cases two boys making kites, the one with wholeheartedness of purpose, as we have just described, the other under direct compulsion as a most unwelcome task. For simplicity's sake suppose the latter under enforced directions makes a kite identical with the other. Call the identical movements in the two cases the 'primary' responses of kite-making. These furnish the kind of responses that we can and customarily do assign as tasks the external and irreducible minimum for the matter at hand. Upon such we can feasibly insist, even to the point of punishment if we so decide. Follow now the thinking of the two boys as they make their kites. Besides the thinking necessarily involved in the 'primary' responses, other thoughts, few or many, will come; some perhaps of materials or processes involved, penumbrae as it were of the primary responses; others more personal or by way of comment upon the process. The penumbrae of the primary we may call the 'accessory' or the complementary responses; the others, the 'concomitants' or by-products of the activity. The terminology is not entirely happy, and the exact lines of division are not easy to draw; but the distinctions may perhaps help us to see a further function of purpose.

As for the primary responses we need do little more than recall the discussion of the immediately preceding paragraphs. The factor of 'set' conditions the learning process. A strong set acting through the satisfaction which attends success fixes quickly and strongly the bonds which brought success. In the case of coercion, however, a different state of affairs holds. There are in effect two sets operating: one set kept in existence solely through coercion is concerned to make a kite that will pass muster; the other set has a different end and would pursue a different course were the coercion removed. Each set in so far as it actually exists means a possible satisfaction and in that degree a possible learning. But the two sets being opposed mean at times a confusion as to the object of success, and in every case each set destroys a part of the other's satisfaction and so hampers the primary learning. So far then as concerns even the barest mechanics of kite-making, the boy of wholehearted purpose will emerge with a higher degree of skill and knowledge and his learning will longer abide with him.

In the case of the accessory or complementary responses, the difference is equally noticeable. The unified set of wholeheartedness will render available all the pertinent connected inner resources. A wealth of marginal responses will be ready to come forward at every opportunity. Thoughts will be turned over and over, and each step will be connected in many ways with other experiences. Alluring leads in various allied directions will open before the boy, which only the dominant present purpose could suffice to postpone. The element of satisfaction will attend connections seen, so that the complex of allied thinking will the longer remain as a mental possession. All of this is exactly not so with the other boy. The forbidden 'set' so long as it persists will pretty effectually quench the glow of thought. Unreadiness will rather characterize his attitude. Responses accessory to the work at hand will be few in number, and the few that come will lack the element of satisfaction to fix them. Where the one boy has a wealth of accessory ideas, the other has poverty. What abides with the one, is fleeting with the other. Even more pronounced is the difference in the by-products of *concomitants* from these contrasted activities. The one boy looks upon his school activity with joy and confidence and plans yet other projects; the other counts his school a bore and begins to look elsewhere for the expression there denied. To the one the teacher is a friend and a comrade; to the other, a taskmaster and enemy. The one easily feels himself on the side of the school and other social agencies, the other with equal ease considers them all instruments of suppression.

The contrasts here made are consciously of extremes. Most children live between the two. The question is whether we shall not consciously put before us as an ideal the one type of activity and approximate it as closely as we can rather than supinely rest content to live as close to the other type as do the general run of our American schools. Does not the ordinary school among us put its almost exclusive attention on the *primary* responses and the learning of these in the second fashion here described? Do we not too often reduce the subject matter of instruction to the level of this type alone? Does not our examination system—even our scientific tests at times—tend to carry us in the same direction? How many children at the close of a course decisively shut the book and say, "Thank gracious, I am through with that!" How many people 'get an education' and yet hate books and hate to think?

The thought suggested at the close of the preceding paragraph may be generalized into a criterion more widely applicable. The richness of life is seen upon reflection to depend, in large measure at least, upon the tendency of what one does to suggest and prepare for succeeding activities. Any activity—beyond the barest physical wants—which does not thus 'lead on' becomes in time stale and flat. Such 'leading on' means that the individual has been modified so that he sees what before he did not see or does what before he could not do. But this is exactly to say that the activity has had an educative effect. Not to elaborate the argument, we may assert that the richness of life depends exactly on its tendency to lead one on to other like fruitful activity; that the degree of this tendency consists exactly in the educative effect of the activity involved; and that we may therefore take as the criterion of the value of any activity—whether intentionally educative or not—its tendency directly or indirectly to lead the individual and others whom he touches on to other like fruitful activity. If we apply this criterion to the common run of American schools we get exactly the discouraging results indicated above. It is the thesis of this paper that these evil results must inevitably follow the effort to found our educational procedure on an unending round of set tasks in conscious disregard of the element of dominant purpose in those who perform the tasks. This again is not to say that every purpose is good nor that the child is a suitable judge as between purposes nor that he is never to be forced to act against a purpose which he entertains. We contemplate no scheme of subordination of teacher or school to childish whim; but we do mean that any plan of educational procedure which does not aim consciously and insistently at securing and utilizing vigorous purposing on the part of the pupils is founded essentially on an ineffective and unfruitful basis. Nor is the quest for desirable purposes hopeless. There is no necessary conflict in kind between the social demands and the child's interests. Our whole fabric of institutional life grew out of human interests. The path of the race is here a possible path for the individual. There is no normal boy but has already many socially desirable interests and is capable of many more. It is the special duty and opportunity of the teacher to guide the pupil through his present interests and achievement into the wider interests and achievement demanded by the wider social life of the older world.

The question of moral education was implicitly raised in the preceding paragraph. What is the effect on morals of the plan herein advocated? A full discussion is unfortunately impossible. Speaking for myself, however, I consider the possibilities for building moral character in a regime of purposeful activity one of the strongest points in its favor; and contrariwise the tendency toward a selfish individualism one of the strongest counts against our customary set-task sit-alone-at-your-own-desk procedure. Moral character is primarily an affair of shared social relationships, the disposition to determine one's conduct and attitudes with reference to the welfare of the group. This means, psychologically, building stimulus-response bonds such that when certain ideas are present as stimuli certain approved responses will follow. We are then concerned that children get a goodly stock of ideas to serve as stimuli for conduct, that they develop good judgment for selecting the idea appropriate in a given case, and that they have firmly built such response bonds as will bring—as inevitably as possible—the appropriate conduct once the proper idea has been chosen. In terms of this (necessarily simplified) analysis we wish such school procedure as will most probably result in the requisite body of ideas, in the needed skill in judging a moral situation, and in unfailing appropriate response bonds. To get these three can we conceive of a better way than by living in a social *milieu* which provides, under competent supervision, for shared coping with a variety of social situations? In the school procedure here advocated children are living together in the pursuit of a rich variety of purposes, some individually sought, many conjointly. As must happen in social commingling, occasions of moral stress will arise, but here—fortunately—under conditions that exclude extreme and especially harmful cases. Under the eye of the skillful teacher the children as an embryonic society will make increasingly finer discriminations as to what is right and proper. Ideas and judgment come thus. Motive and occasion arise together; the teacher has but to steer the process of evaluating the situation. The teacher's success—if we believe in democracy—will consist in gradually eliminating himself or herself from the success of the procedure.

Not only do defined ideas and skill in judging come from such a situation, but response bonds as well. The continual sharing of purposes in such a school offers ideal conditions for forming the necessary habits of give and take. The laws of learning hold here as elsewhere, especially the Law of Effect. If the child is to set up habits of acting, satisfaction must attend the doing or annoyance the failure. Now there are few satisfactions so gratifying and few annoyances so distressing as the approval and the disapproval of our comrades. Anticipated approval will care for most cases; but the positive social disapproval of one's fellows has peculiar potency. When the teacher merely coerces and the other pupils side with their comrade, a contrary 'set'—such as we earlier discussed—is almost inevitable, often so definite as to prevent the fixing in the child's character of the desired response. Conformity may be but outward. But when all concerned take part in deciding what is just—if the teacher act wisely—there is far less likelihood of an opposing 'set'. Somehow disapproval by those who understand from one's own point of view tends to dissolve an opposing 'set', and one acts then more fully from his own decision. In such cases the desired bond is better built in one's moral character. Conformity is not merely outward. It is necessary to emphasize the part the teacher plays in this group building of bonds. Left alone, as 'the gentlemen's grade' in college indicates, pupils may develop habits of dawdling. Against this purposelessness the present thesis is especially directed; but proper ideals must be built up in the school group. As an ideal is but an idea joined with tendencies to act, the procedure for building has been discussed; but the teacher is responsible for the results. The pupils working under his guidance must through the social experiences encountered build the ideals necessary for approved social life. The regime of purposeful activity offers then a wider variety of educative moral experiences more nearly typical of life itself than does our usual school procedure, lends itself better to the educative evaluation of these, and provides better for the fixing of all as permanent acquisitions in the intelligent moral character.

The question of the growth or building of interests is important in the theory of the plan here discussed. Many points still prove difficult, but some things can be said. Most obvious is the fact of 'maturing' (itself a difficult topic). At first an infant responds automatically to his environment. Only later, after many experiences have been organized, can he, properly speaking, entertain purposes; and in this there are many gradations. Similarly, the earliest steps involved in working out a set are those that have been instinctively joined with the process. Later on, steps may be taken by 'suggestion' (the relatively automatic working of acquired associations). Only comparatively late do we find true adaptation of means to end, the conscious choice of steps to the attainment of deliberately formed purposes. These considerations must qualify any statements made regarding child purposes. In this connection a quotation from Woodworth's new book is pertinent; "almost any object, almost any act, and particularly almost any process or change in objects that can be directed by one's own activity toward some definite end, is interesting on its own account, and furnishes its own drive, once it is fairly initiated." (*Dynamic Psychology*, p. 202). One result of the growth here discussed is the 'leading on' it affords. A skill acquired as end can be applied as means to new purposes. Skill or idea arising first in connection with means may be singled out for special consideration and so forms new ends. This last is one of the most fruitful sources of new interests, particularly of the intellectual kind.

In connection with this 'maturing' goes a general increase in the 'interest span', the length of time during which a set will remain active, the time within which a child will—if allowed—work at any given project. What part of this increase is due to nature and physical maturing, what part to nurture, why the span is long for some activities and short for others, how we can increase the span in any given cases, are questions of the greatest moment for the educator. It is a matter of common knowledge that within limits 'interests' may be built up, the correlative interest spans appreciably increased. Whatever else may be said, this must mean that stimulus-response bonds have been formed and this in accordance with the laws of learning. We have already seen the general part played by the factor of purpose in utilizing the laws of learning. There seems no reason to doubt that like considerations hold here. In particular the discussion of coercion with its two opposed sets holds almost unchanged. Since the 'set' of external origin has its correlative goal and its consequent possible success, there is a theoretical possibility of learning. In this way we may conceive a new interest built by coercion. Two factors, however, greatly affect the practical utilization of this possibility, the one inherently to hinder, the other possibly to help. The inherent hindrance is the opposed (internal) set, which in proportion to its intensity and persistence will confuse the definition of success and lessen the satisfaction of attainment. Acquiring a new interest is in this respect accordingly doubly and inherently hindered by coercion. The second factor, which may chance favorably, is the possibility that what (reduced) learning takes place may connect with some already potentially existent interest giving such expression to it that the inner opposition to the enforced activity is won over, and the opposing set dissolved. This second factor is of especial significance for the light it throws upon the relation of teacher and pupils in this matter of coercion. It seems from these considerations that if compulsion will result in such learning as sets free some self-continuing activity and these before harmful concomitants have been set up, we may approve such compulsion as a useful temporary device. Otherwise, so far as concerns the building of interests, the use of coercion seems a choice of evils with the general probabilities opposing. (Coercion may be permissible as a particular expedient in some other instances, as when damage is about to be done either to others or to property or to the child himself. Clearly this is a temporary device and, even in these cases, generally a choice of evils. There are some who needlessly confuse coercion with purposeful action in the face of difficulty. A certain stress of difficulty is healthy, probably necessary to wholeheartedness. Without it there is likely mere routine action of functions already learned. On the other hand, too great a difficulty means failure often with discouragement. In between these extremes lies the most educative activity).

It may be well to come closer to the customary subject matter of the school. Let us consider the classification to the different types of projects: Type 1, where the purpose is to embody some idea or plan in external form, as building a boat, writing a letter, presenting a play; Type 2, where the purpose is to enjoy some (esthetic) experience, as listening to a story, hearing a symphony, appreciating a picture; Type 3, where the purpose is to straighten out some intellectual difficulty, to solve some problem, as to find out whether or not dew falls, to ascertain how New York outgrew Philadelphia; Type 4, where the purpose is to obtain some item or degree of skill or knowledge, as learning to write grade 14 on the Thorndike Scale, learning the irregular verbs in French. It is at once evident that these groupings more or less overlap and that one type may be used as means to another as end. It may be of interest to note that with these definitions the project method logically includes the problem method as a special case. The value of such a classification as that here given seems to me to lie in the light it should throw on the kind of projects teachers may expect and on the procedure that normally prevails in the several types.

For type 1 the following steps have been suggested: purposing, planning, executing and judging. It is in accord with the general theory here advocated that the child as far as possible take each step himself. Total failure, however, may hurt more than assistance. The opposed dangers seem to be on the one hand that the child may not come out master of the process, on the other that he may waste time. The teacher must steer the child through these narrows, taking care meanwhile to avoid the other dangers previously discussed. The function of the purpose and the place of thinking in the process need but be mentioned. Attention may be called to the fourth step, that the child as he grows older may increasingly judge the result in terms of the aim and with increasing care and success draw from the process its lessons for the future.

Type 2, enjoying an esthetic experience, may seem to some hardly to belong in the list of projects. But the factor of purpose undoubtedly guides the process and—I must think—influences the growth of appreciation. I have, however, as yet no definite procedure steps to point out.

Type 3, the solving of some problem, is of all the best known, owing to the work of Professors Dewey and McMurray. The steps that have been used are those of the Dewey analysis of thought (Dewey, *How We Think*,

Chap. VI). This type lends itself, next to type 4, best of all to our ordinary school-room work. For this reason I have myself feared its overemphasis. Our schools—at least in my judgment—do emphatically need a great increase in the social activity possible in type 1.

Type 4, where the purpose has to do with specific items of knowledge or skill, would seem to call for the same steps as type 1, purposing, planning, executing, and judging. Only here, the planning had perhaps best come from the psychologist. In this type also there is danger of over-emphasis. Some teachers indeed may not closely discriminate between the drill as a project and a drill as a set task, although the results will be markedly different.

The limits of the article forbid a discussion of other important aspects of the topic: the changes necessitated by this plan in room furniture and equipment, perhaps in school architecture, the new type of text-book, the new kind of curriculum and program, possibly new plans of grading and promotion, most of all a changed attitude as to what to wish for in the way of achievement. Nor can we consider what this type of procedure means for democracy in furnishing us better citizens, alert, able to think and act, too intelligently critical to be easily hoodwinked either by politicians or by patent-medicines, self-reliant, ready of adaptation to the new social conditions that impend. The question of difficulties would itself require a separate article: opposition of tradition, of taxpayers; unprepared and incompetent teachers; the absence of a worked-out procedure; problems of administration and supervision. All these and more would suffice to destroy the movement were it not deeply grounded.

In conclusion, then, we may say that the child is naturally active, especially along social lines. Heretofore a regime of coercion has only too often reduced our schools to aimless dawdling and our pupils to selfish individualists. Some in reaction have resorted to foolish humoring of childish whims. The contention of this paper is that wholehearted purposeful activity in a social situation as the typical unit of school procedure is the best guarantee of the utilization of the child's native capacities now too frequently wasted. Under proper guidance purpose means efficiency, not only in reaching the projected end of the activity immediately at hand, but even more in securing from the activity the learning which it potentially contains. Learning of all kinds and in its all desirable ramifications best proceeds in proportion as wholeheartedness of purpose is present. With the child naturally social and with the skillful teacher to stimulate and guide his purposing, we can especially expect that kind of learning we call character building. The necessary reconstruction consequent upon these considerations offers a most alluring 'project' to the teacher who but dares to purpose.

34

Selected Writings of Mary McLeod Bethune

Mary Jane McLeod Bethune was born in South Carolina in 1875, the fifteenth of seventeen children to parents who had been slaves. She became a prominent Civil Rights leader, as well as an important African American educator. Early in life, she took an interest in her own education. She attended a local missionary school and then received a scholarship to attend Scotia Seminary and Moody Bible Institute. In 1904, she established the Daytona Educational and Industrial Institute for Negro Girls, which merged in 1923 to become the co-educational Bethune-Cookman College.

Bethune-Cookman was the first fully accredited four year college for blacks in the state of Florida. Bethune remained the President of the college until 1942. In addition to her educational work, Bethune was deeply involved in politics and the advancement of blacks. She served as the director of the Office of Minority Affairs in the National Youth Administration (the first federal office for a black woman), and was a member of Franklin D. Roosevelt's Black Cabinet, and became friends with Eleanor Roosevelt through her role as the

American Educational Thought: Essays from 1640–1940, pages 525–532
Copyright © 2010 by Information Age Publishing
All rights of reproduction in any form reserved.

President of the National Association of Colored Women's Clubs. She died in 1955, having been named one of the fifty women who had done the most for the welfare of the United States. —CHB

A Philosophy of Education for Negro Girls, 1926

For the past seventy years the Negro has experienced various degrees of freedom. That which was given him in the early years of emancipation was more genuine and perhaps more benign than that which, today, he must take. Today he must free himself by reason of his ability and by merit, and by whatever trust and confidence may be found in himself.

A great deal of this new freedom rests upon the type of education which the Negro woman will receive. Early emancipation did not concern itself with giving advantages to Negro girls. The domestic realm was her field and no one sought to remove her. Even here, she was not given special training for her tasks. Only those with extraordinary talents were able to break the shackles of bondage. Phyllis Wheatley is to be remembered as an outstanding example of this ability—for through her talents she was able to free herself from house hold cares that devolved upon Negro women and make a contribution in literary art which is never to be forgotten. The years still re-echo her words.

> *"Remember, Christians, Negroes, black as Cain May be refined, and join the Angelic train."*

Very early in my life, I saw the vision of what our women might contribute to the growth and development of the race—if they were given a certain type of intellectual training. I longed to see women, Negro women, hold in their hands diplomas which bespoke achievement; I longed to see them trained to be inspirational wives and mothers; I longed to see their accomplishments recognized side by side with any woman, anywhere. With this vision before me, my life has been spent.

Has the Negro girl proved herself worthy of the intellectual advantages which have been given her? What is your answer when I tell you that Negro women stand at the helm of outstanding enterprises; such are Nannie Burroughs, Charlotte Hawkins Brown; they are proprietors of business. We recall Madame Walker and Annie Malone; they are doing excellent work in the field of Medicine, Literary Art, Painting and Music. Of that large group let us mention Mary Church Terrell and Jessie Fauset; Hazel Harrison, Caterina Jarboro and Marian Anderson as beacon lights. One very outstanding woman is a banker. Others are leaders in Politics.

In the rank of average training we witness strivings of Negro women in the school rooms of counties and cities pouring out their own ambitions to see them achieved in the lives of the next generation. The educated Negro girl has lifted the standard of the Negro home so that the present generation is better born and therefore has the promise of a better future.

If there is to be any distinctive difference between the education of the Negro girl and the Negro boy, it should be that of consideration for the unique responsibility of this girl in the world today. The challenge to the Negro home is one which dares the Negro to develop initiative to solve his own problems, to work out his own problems, to work out his difficulties in a superior fashion, and to finally come into his right as an American Citizen, because he is tolerated. This is the moral responsibility of the education of the Negro girl; it must become a part of her thinking; her activities must lead her into such endeavors early in her educational life; this training must be inculcated into the school curricula so that the result may be a natural expression born into her children. Such is the natural endowment which her education must make it possible for her to bequeath to the future of the Negro race.

The education of the Negro girl must embrace a larger appreciation for good citizenship in the home. Our girls must be taught cleanliness, beauty and thoughtfulness and their application in making home life possible. For proper home life provides the proper atmosphere for life everywhere else. The ideals of home must not forever be talked about; they must be living factors built into the everyday educational experiences of our girls.

Negro girls must receive also a peculiar appreciation for the expression of the creative self. They must be taught to realize their responsibility and find ways whereby the home and the schoolroom may encourage our youth to be creative; to develop to the fullest extent the inner urges that make them distinctive and that will lead them to be worthy contributors to the life of the little worlds in which they will live. This in itself will do more to remove the walls of inter-racial prejudice and build up intra-racial confidence and pride than many of our educational tools and devices. This is the Gibraltar that we need. Lest it be sunken in the sea of carelessness and improper emphasis, let us, quickly, set it upon the table and let us stress this standard of conduct and individual creative nurture in the education of our girls. The spiritual reactions are sure to harmonize when we safeguard this phase of our education:

Negro women have always known struggle. This heritage is just as much to be desired as any other. Our girls should be taught to appreciate it and welcome it.

Let mine be a hearty soul that wins
By mettle and fairness and pluck
A heart with the freedom of soaring winds
That never depends on luck!

This characteristic should be sought in that ardent way. Every Negro girl should pray for that pioneering spirit. Let her Arithmetic, History, Economics and what not, be taught with the zeal of struggle; the determination to win by mettle and fairness and pluck. For such she needs after she leaves the school life and enters the Life's school.

God give us girls—the time demands
Strong girls, good girls, true girls with willing hands;
Girls whom the world's gold cannot buy,
Girls who possess opinions and a will;
Girls who honor and will not lie
Girls who can stand before the motley crowd
And down its treacherous flatteries without winking
Tall girls, sun-crowned Girls whose voices cry aloud
And give us a challenge to the whole world's thinking.

The Educational Values of the College Bred, 1934

Mr. Chairman:

May I express my gratitude to your committee for your gracious invitation to be present with you on this historic day and to participate in the parting greetings to this remarkable class that must soon find its way out into the world of service.

One's heart is moved with emotions as we look backward and think of the seed-sowers of this grand old Institution, and of thousands who have arisen from the lowly fields of ignorance and poverty to the great fields of knowledge ripened with opportunities to serve. We think today in terms of deep appreciation and affection of those who have been faithfully carrying on during all of the long, long years, enduring hardness, very often, like good soldiers. We congratulate you upon the standard of this Institution, for what it means to a race and to a Nation. Its influences are seeping through to all races and classes with its fine, new-day program of Education.

Education is the great American Adventure, the world's most colossal democratic experiment. Education is the largest public enterprise in the United States; in my opinion, the country's most important business. This is emphasized when I remind you that, according to Edgar Knight of the

University of North Carolina, the public school property of this country amounts to seven billion dollars; that three billion dollars are spent annually for school support; that one million two hundred thousand teachers are employed; and that there are thirty million students enrolled in our various types of institutions; that two persons out of every seven in the United States are giving full time to this education.

Why this large investment in education? Why do we educate people, anyhow? Why do we spend these huge sums? Obviously, it is just this: Nature has stored up in individuals native powers, possibilities, potentialities, and it is the problem, the work of education to release these powers—to make actual and real these possibilities and potentialities in order that the individual himself may live life to the fullest and make a contribution to the sum total of human happiness.

In my mind there are three factors that have contributed to make Education the great enterprise it is today: The first is Science with its powers of production, distribution, transportation and communication. The second is the Ideal of Democracy. In former years education was a luxury to be enjoyed by the members of higher castes; now it is within the reach of the masses. The third is Religion. All science points toward God—God the maker, the Preserver, the Director of all of our lives. As you grow in the knowledge of Science, young people, strive to grow more like God. Amid the collapse and crumbling of economic and social structures, religion is the vitalizing element in all education.

I believe, as does Glenn Frank, President of the University of Wisconsin, that our colleges are charged with tremendous responsibilities, chief among them being, in my opinion, the underprivileged masses who are impatiently awaiting the sane, sympathetic, patient, Christian leadership that must come year after year from the colleges of our country. Further, colleges have three other responsibilities: 1) to produce the Investigator, 2) to produce the Interpreter, 3) to produce the Inspirer.

Schools have two giant responsibilities: THE RESPONSIBILITY OF INVESTIGATION and THE RESPONSIBILITY OF INTERPRETATION. The man in the laboratory may investigate; the man in the lecture room may interpret. But the teacher must deal with the minds of his students—minds that are plastic and can be shaped into whatever the teacher's own character may design. Schools have many functions, but their chief function is to furnish society with three sorts of servants: investigators, interpreters, inspirers. Speaking loosely for a moment, the teacher is of the third sort. The teacher's primary business is that of a stirrer-up. He is not, save secondarily, a salesman of knowledge. He is primarily a stimulator of knowledge and curiosity. But the good teacher is an investigator. He is not content to squat behind the breast-works of accumulated knowledge; he flirts with the unknown out on the frontiers of knowledge; only so can he bring the spirit of intellectual adventure and conquest into his classroom; an incurious teacher cannot stimulate curiosity.

The good teacher is also an INTERPRETER. He not only knows more about his own subject than any other subjects but he knows enough about other subjects to keep his own subject in perspective. The good teacher is an INSPIRER. He knows that the art of teaching lies in starting something in the student's mind. He is not content with merely putting something into the student's mind as a butcher stuffs a sausage-skin. In short, therefore, the good teacher is an INVESTIGATOR, an INTERPRETER, an INSPIRER.

The future of America, young men, young women, is in the hands of two men—the investigator and the interpreter. We shall never lack for the administrator, the third man needed to complete this trinity of social servants. And we have an ample supply of investigators, but there is a shortage of readable and responsible interpreters, men who can effectively play mediator between specialist and layman. The practical value of every social invention or material discovery depends upon its being adequately interpreted to the masses. Are we willing to blaze the way to that shut-in mass that we may interpret to them the way up, out, and over to the real realm of American Citizenship? They are calling for the interpreter, who will answer—"Here I am, send me."

Our fathers and mothers prayed for the leadership and the interpretation, young men and women, that you are able to give today. Will you give it? Science owes its effective ministry as much to the interpretative mind as to the creative mind. The knowledge of mankind is advanced by the investigator, but the investigator is not always the best interpreter of his discoveries. Rarely, in fact, do the genius for exploration and the genius for exposition meet in the same mind. The interpreter stands between the layman and the investigator, whose knowledge of one thing is authoritative. The investigator advances knowledge. The interpreter advances progress. History affords abundant evidence that civilization has advanced in direct ratio to the efficiency with which the thought of the thinkers has been translated into the language of the workers. A dozen fields of thought are today congested with knowledge that the physical and social sciences have unearthed, and the whole tone and temper of American life can be lifted by putting this knowledge into general circulation.

But where are the interpreters with the training and the willingness to think their way through this knowledge and translate it into the language of the street? Young men, young women, I raise the recruiting trumpet for the Interpreters.

Now, in order to do properly the work of the college-bred, there are certain very essential qualities. In the days of King Arthur, it was customary for the knights, if they would go on their pilgrimages, to take certain vows in the prosecution of their work. I am going to do a similar thing here today and ask you—as Crusaders of Knowledge—to take with me certain pledges or vows for the performance of your task. I would have you take with me, first, the vow of definite and specific preparation—for, to recognize the major needs of our fellowmen is often a difficult task. To face the sacrifice necessary for training, even though hearts are consecrated, is more difficult. Only the spiritually determined with triumph.

Second—the vow of a sympathetic attitude. To fortify you with supreme tolerance of the groping, ofttimes slow and pain-filled efforts of those we are dedicated to serve—for how often are these efforts interspersed with frequent disillusionment for both teacher and student.

Third—the vow of industry. The bud of determination cannot reach fruition until it has blossomed forth into labor—consistent, steady, untiring labor, the force of which, whether manual or mental, may carve alike beauty from rugged native stone or keen thinking from untried minds.

Fourth—the vow of idealism. Seek your ideals from Nature's plan of perfection, for in it is reflected Deity. Strive for the heights of the mountains, the turbulent strength of the sea, the fine and delicate loveliness of the primrose, the shining glory of the stars.

Fifth—the vow of courage. When the inevitable obstacles, pitfalls, frustrations, misunderstandings, even failures confront you, this vow will stand in good stead, for your spirit will be permeated with a veritable armor of Courage, which is the heritage only of those who are sure of their way—and being sure, scorn the undergrowth or the bypath.

Sixth—the vow of Faith. Has it ever occurred to you that Faith—simple Faith—so often made complex by our own clumsy efforts to force it into our consciousness—is merely the serene confidence, the inward smiling assurance of rightness begetting rightness? Faith is the substance of things hoped for, the evidence of things not seen.

In the rural section of the South, farmers on an occasion viewed with alarm the parching of their crops from drought. Days of piercing sun cracked the earth, and the plants, upon which the very subsistence of the group depended, withered in agony. One devout woman suggested a concentrated prayer for rain at the little meeting house. At the time indicated every soul blended in supplication for material salvation. And the rain came in torrents even as they prayed. Following the glorious thanksgiving, the farmer folk made ready to go home but alas, the blessed rain prevented their venturing out—all but one little girl. "I brought my umbrella," she said, "for I KNEW if we prayed for rain, it would come." Hers was the Vow of Faith!

May I earnestly exhort YOU to have faith—in God, in yourselves, your possibilities—faith in Mankind.

35

Excerpt from Dare the School Build a New Social Order?

George S. Counts, 1932

George S. Counts (1889–1974) was one of the most influential educational thinkers of the early 20th century. His address "Dare the School Build a New Social Order," which he delivered in 1932, served to refocus democratic education in a more socially oriented direction. Counts was a social and political activist who challenged members of the Progressive Education Association and others to focus their efforts on teaching children to contribute to the common good, rather than only meeting their individual wants, needs, and desires. Counts was born and reared in rural Kansas. He began graduate school at the University of Chicago in 1913. John Dewey had left Chicago in 1904, but the School of Education remained deeply influenced by Dewey's efforts. When Counts arrived, Charles H. Judd was Dean of the School of Education. Counts studied under Judd, as well as with Albion W. Small from the department of sociology. Counts completed his doctoral degree at Chicago in 1916, with a dissertation on the psychology of arithmetic. Upon graduation, he accepted his first academic appointment as professor of education at Delaware College. Between the years 1918 and 1927, he held academic appointments at Harris Teachers College, the University of Washington, Yale University, and

American Educational Thought: Essays from 1640–1940, pages 533–549
Copyright © 2010 by Information Age Publishing
533

the University of Chicago, his alma mater. In 1927, he accepted a position at Teachers College, Columbia University, where he remained until his retirement in 1955. While at Teachers College, Counts served as a president of the American Federation of Teachers. He also was a leader of New York's Liberal Party. During his long and prolific career, Counts produced numerous books, articles, and lectures. He first became well known in the early 1930s during the Depression. His work, which was influenced deeply by Russian educational thought, challenged teachers to view themselves as leaders in the building of a new social order, rather than as technicians who merely followed other people's dictates. Counts often was at odds with political conservatives who thought his views were too radical, unrealistic, and vague. Despite the criticism that he sometimes encountered, Counts remains a critical figure in the field of American educational thought. —JWN

Like all simple and unsophisticated peoples we Americans have a sublime faith in education. Faced with any difficult problem of life we set our minds at rest sooner or later by the appeal to the school. We are convinced that education is the one unfailing remedy for every ill to which man is subject, whether it be vice, crime, war, poverty, riches, injustice, racketeering, political corruption, race hatred, class conflict, or just plain original sin. We even speak glibly and often about the general reconstruction of society through the school. We cling to this faith in spite of the fact that the very period in which our troubles have multiplied so rapidly has witnessed an unprecedented expansion of organized education. This would seem to suggest that our schools, instead of directing the course of change, are themselves driven by the very forces that are transforming the rest of the social order.

The bare fact, however, that simple and unsophisticated peoples have unbounded faith in education does not mean that the faith is untenable. History shows that the intuitions of such folk may be nearer the truth than the weighty and carefully reasoned judgments of the learned and the wise. Under certain conditions education may be as beneficent and as powerful as we are wont to think. But if it is to be so, teachers must abandon much of their easy optimism, subject the concept of education to the most rigorous scrutiny, and be prepared to deal much more fundamentally, realistically, and positively with the American social situation than has been their habit in the past. Any individual or group that would aspire to lead society must be ready to pay the costs of leadership: to accept responsibility, to suffer calumny, to surrender security, to risk both reputation and fortune. If this price, or some important part of it, is not being paid, then the chances are that the claim to leadership is fraudulent. Society is never redeemed without effort, struggle, and sacrifice. Authentic leaders are never found breathing that rarefied atmosphere lying above the dust and smoke of battle. With regard to the past we always recognize the truth of this principle, but when we think of our own times we profess the belief that the ancient roles have been reversed and that now prophets of a new age receive their rewards among the living.

That the existing school is leading the way to a better social order is a thesis which few informed persons would care to defend. Except as it is forced to fight for its own life during times of depression, its course is too serene and untroubled. Only in the rarest of instances does it wage war on behalf of principle or ideal. Almost everywhere it is in the grip of conservative forces and is serving the cause of perpetuating ideas and institutions suited to an age that is gone. But there is one movement above the educational horizon which would seem to show promise of genuine and creative leadership. I refer to the Progressive Education movement. Surely in this union of two of the great faiths of the American people, the faith in progress and the faith in education, we have reason to hope for light and guidance. Here is a movement which would seem to be completely devoted to the promotion of social welfare through education.

Even a casual examination of the program and philosophy of the Progressive schools, however, raises many doubts in the mind. To be sure, these schools have a number of large achievements to their credit. They have focused attention squarely upon the child; they have recognized the fundamental importance of the interest of the learner; they have defended the thesis that activity lies at the root of all true education; they have conceived learning in terms of life situations and growth of character; they have championed the rights of the child as a free personality. Most of this is excellent, but in my judgment it is not enough. It constitutes too narrow a conception of the meaning of education; it brings into the picture but one-half of the landscape.

If an educational movement, or any other movement, calls itself progressive, it must have orientation; it must possess direction. The word itself implies moving forward, and moving forward can have little meaning in the absence of clearly defined purposes. We cannot, like Stephen Leacock's horseman, dash off in all directions at once. Nor should we, like our presidential candidates, evade every disturbing issue and be all things to all men. Also we must beware lest we become so devoted to motion that we neglect the question of direction and be entirely satisfied with movement in circles. Here, I think, we find the fundamental weakness, not only of Progressive Education, but also of American education generally. Like a baby shaking a rattle, we seem to be utterly content with action, provided it is sufficiently vigorous and noisy. In the last analysis a very large part of American educational thought, inquiry, and experimentation is much ado about nothing.

And, if we are permitted to push the analogy of the rattle a bit further, our consecration to motion is encouraged and supported in order to keep us out of mischief. At least we know that so long as we thus busy ourselves we shall not incur the serious displeasure of our social elders.

The weakness of Progressive Education thus lies in the fact that it has elaborated no theory of social welfare, unless it be that of anarchy or extreme individualism. In this, of course, it is but reflecting the viewpoint of the members of the liberal-minded upper middle class who send their children to the Progressive schools—persons who are fairly well-off, who have abandoned the faiths of their fathers, who assume an agnostic attitude towards all important questions, who pride themselves on their open-mindedness and tolerance, who favor in a mild sort of way fairly liberal programs of social reconstruction, who are full of good will and humane sentiment, who have vague aspirations for world peace and human brotherhood, who can be counted upon to respond moderately to any appeal made in the name of charity, who are genuinely distressed at the sight of *unwonted* forms of cruelty, misery, and suffering, and who perhaps serve to soften somewhat the bitter clashes of those real forces that govern the world; but who, in spite of all their good qualities, have no deep and abiding loyalties, possess no convictions for which they would sacrifice over-much, would find it hard to live without their customary material comforts, are rather insensitive to the accepted forms of social injustice, are content to play the role of interested spectator in the drama of human history, refuse to see reality in its harsher and more disagreeable forms, rarely move outside the pleasant circles of the class to which they belong, and in the day of severe trial will follow the lead of the most powerful and respectable forces in society and at the same time find good reasons for so doing. These people have shown themselves entirely incapable of dealing with any of the great crises of our time—war, prosperity, or depression. At bottom they are romantic sentimentalists, but with a sharp eye on the main chance. That they can be trusted to write our educational theories and shape our educational programs is highly improbable.

Among the members of this class the number of children is small, the income relatively high, and the economic functions of the home greatly reduced. For these reasons an inordinate emphasis on the child and child interests is entirely welcome to them. They wish to guard their offspring from too strenuous endeavor and from coming into too intimate contact with the grimmer aspects of industrial society. They wish their sons and daughters to succeed according to the standards of their class and to be a credit to their parents. At heart feeling themselves members of a superior human strain, they do not want their children to mix too freely with the children of the poor or of the less fortunate races. Nor do they want them to accept radical social doctrines, espouse unpopular causes, or lose themselves in quest of any Holy Grail. According to their views education should deal with life, but with life at a distance or in a highly diluted form. They would generally maintain that life should be kept at arm's length, if it should not be handled with a poker.

If Progressive Education is to be genuinely progressive, it must emancipate itself from the influence of this class, face squarely and courageously every social issue, come to grips with life in all of its stark reality, establish an organic relation with the community, develop a realistic and comprehensive theory of welfare, fashion a compelling and challenging vision of human destiny, and become less frightened than it is today at the bogies of *imposition* and *indoctrination*. In a word, Progressive Education cannot place its trust in a child-centered school.

This brings us to the most crucial issue in education—the question of the nature and extent of the influence which the school should exercise over the development of the child. The advocates of extreme freedom have been so successful in championing what they call the rights of the child that even the most skillful practitioners of the art of converting others to their opinions disclaim all intention of molding the learner. And when the word indoctrination is coupled with education there is scarcely one among us possessing the hardihood to refuse to be horrified. This feeling is so widespread that even Mr. Lunacharsky, Commissar of Education in the Russian Republic until 1929, assured me on one occasion that the Soviet educational leaders do not believe in the indoctrination of children in the ideas and principles of communism. When I asked him whether their children become good communists while attending the schools, he replied that the great majority do. On seeking from him an explanation of this remarkable phenomenon he said that Soviet teachers merely tell their children the truth about human history. As a consequence, so he asserted, practically all of the more intelligent boys and girls adopt the philosophy of communism. I recall also that the Methodist sect in which I was reared always confined its teachings to the truth!

The issue is no doubt badly confused by historical causes. The champions of freedom are obviously the product of an age that has broken very fundamentally with the past and is equally uncertain about the future. In many cases they feel themselves victims of narrow orthodoxies which were imposed upon them during childhood and which have severely cramped their lives. At any suggestion that the child should be influenced by his elders they therefore envisage the establishment of a state church, the formulation of a body of sacred doctrine, and the teaching of this doctrine as fixed and final. If we are forced to choose between such an unenlightened form of pedagogical influence and a condition of complete freedom for the child, most of us would in all probability choose the latter as the lesser of two evils. But this is to create a wholly artificial situation: the choice should not be limited to these two extremes. Indeed today neither extreme is possible.

I believe firmly that a critical factor must play an important role in any adequate educational program, at least in any such program fashioned for the modern world. An education that does not strive to promote the fullest and most thorough understanding of the world is not worthy of the name. Also there must be no deliberate distortion or suppression of facts to support any theory or point of view. On the other hand, I am prepared to defend the thesis that all education contains a large element of imposition, that in the very nature of the case this is inevitable, that the existence and evolution of society depend upon it, that it is consequently eminently desirable, and that the frank acceptance of this fact by the educator is a major professional obligation. I even contend that failure to do this involves the clothing of one's own deepest prejudices in the garb of universal truth and the introduction into the theory and practice of education of an element of obscurantism. In the development of this thesis I shall examine a number of widespread fallacies which seem to me to underlie the theoretical opposition to all forms of imposition. Although certain of these fallacies are very closely related and to some extent even cover the same territory, their separate treatment will help to illuminate the problem.

Chapter 2

1. There is the fallacy that man is born free. As a matter of fact, he is born helpless. He achieves freedom, as a race and as an individual, through the medium of culture. The most crucial of all circumstances conditioning human life is birth into a particular culture. By birth one becomes a Chinese, an Englishman, a Hottentot, a Sioux Indian, a Turk, or a one-hundred-percent American. Such a range of possibilities may appear too shocking to contemplate, but it is the price that one must pay in order to be born. Nevertheless, even if a given soul should happen by chance to choose a Hottentot for a mother, it should thank its lucky star that it was born into the Hottentot culture rather than entirely free. By being nurtured on a body of culture, however backward and limited it may be comparatively, the individual is at once imposed upon and liberated. The child is terribly imposed upon by being compelled through the accidents of birth to learn one language rather than another, but without some language man would never become man. Any language, even the most poverty-stricken, is infi-

nitely better than none at all. In the lifecycle of the individual many choices must of necessity be made, and the most fundamental and decisive of these choices will always be made by the group. This is so obvious that it should require no elaboration. Yet this very obvious fact, with its implications, is commonly disregarded by those who are fearful of molding the child.

One of the most important elements of any culture is a tradition of achievement along a particular line—a tradition which the group imposes upon the young and through which the powers of the young are focused, disciplined, and developed. One people will have a fine hunting tradition, another a maritime tradition, another a musical tradition, another a military tradition, another a scientific tradition, another a baseball tradition, another a business tradition, and another even a tradition of moral and religious prophecy. A particular society of the modern type commonly has a vast number of different traditions all of which may be bound together and integrated more or less by some broad and inclusive tradition. One might argue that the imposing of these traditions upon children involves a severe restriction upon their freedom. My thesis is that such imposition, provided the tradition is vital and suited to the times, releases the energies of the young, sets up standards of excellence, and makes possible really great achievement. The individual who fails to come under the influence of such a tradition may enjoy a certain kind of freedom, but it is scarcely a kind of freedom that anyone would covet for either himself or his children. It is the freedom of mediocrity, incompetence, and aimlessness.

2. There is the fallacy that the child is good by nature. The evidence from anthropology, as well as from common observation, shows that on entering the world the individual is neither good nor bad; he is merely a bundle of potentialities which may be developed in manifold directions. Guidance is, therefore, not to be found in child nature, but rather in the culture of the group and the purposes of living. There can be no good individual apart from some conception of the character of the *good* society; and the good society is not something that is given by nature: it must be fashioned by the hand and brain of man. This process of building a good society is to a very large degree an educational process. The nature of the child must of course be taken into account in the organization of any educational program, but it cannot furnish the materials and the guiding principles of that program. Squirm and wriggle as we may, we must admit that the bringing of materials and guiding principles from the outside involves the molding of the child.

3. There is the fallacy that the child lives in a separate world of his own. The advocates of freedom often speak of the adult as an alien influence

in the life of the child. For an adult to intrude himself or his values into the domain of boys and girls is made to take on the appearance of an invasion by a foreign power. Such a dualism is almost wholly artificial. Whatever may be the view of the adult, the child knows but one society; and that is a society including persons of all ages. This does not mean that conflicts of interest may not occur or that on occasion adults may not abuse and exploit children. It does mean that in a proper kind of society the relationship is one of mutual benefit and regard in which the young repay in trust and emulation the protection and guidance provided by their elders. The child's conception of his position in society is well expressed in the words of Plenty-coups, the famous Crow chieftain, who spoke thus of his boyhood: "We followed the buffalo herds over our beautiful plains, fighting a battle one day and sending out a war-party against the enemy the next. My heart was afire. I wished so to help my people, to distinguish myself, so that I might wear an eagle's feather in my hair. How I worked to make my arms strong as a grizzly's, and how I practiced with my bow! A boy never wished to be a man more than I." Here is an emphatic and unequivocal answer to those who would raise a barrier between youth and age. Place the child in a world of his own and you take from him the most powerful incentives to growth and achievement. Perhaps one of the greatest tragedies of contemporary society lies in the fact that the child is becoming increasingly isolated from the serious activities of adults. Some would say that such isolation is an inevitable corollary of the growing complexity of the social order. In my opinion it is rather the product of a society that is moved by no great commanding ideals and is consequently victimized by the most terrible form of human madness—the struggle for private gain. As primitive peoples wisely protect their children from the dangers of actual warfare, so we guard ours from the acerbities of economic strife. Until school and society are bound together by common purposes the program of education will lack both meaning and vitality.

4. There is the fallacy that education is some pure and mystical essence that remains unchanged from everlasting to everlasting. According to this view, genuine education must be completely divorced from politics, live apart from the play of social forces, and pursue ends peculiar to itself. It thus becomes a method existing independently of the cultural milieu and equally beneficent at all times and in all places. This is one of the most dangerous of fallacies and is responsible for many sins committed in different countries by American educators traveling abroad. They have carried the same brand of education to backward and advanced races, to peoples living under relatively static conditions and to peoples passing through periods of rapid and fundamental transition. They have called it Education with a cap-

ital *E*, whereas in fact it has been American education with a capital *A* and a small *e*. Any defensible educational program must be adjusted to a particular time and place, and the degree and nature of the imposition must vary with the social situation. Under ordinary conditions the process of living suffices in itself to hold society together, but when the forces of disintegration become sufficiently powerful it may well be that a fairly large measure of deliberate control is desirable and even essential to social survival.

5. There is the fallacy that the school should be impartial in its emphases, that no bias should be given instruction. We have already observed how the individual is inevitably molded by the culture into which he is born. In the case of the school a similar process operates and presumably is subject to a degree of conscious direction. My thesis is that complete impartiality is utterly impossible, that the school must shape attitudes, develop tastes, and even impose ideas. It is obvious that the whole of creation cannot be brought into the school. This means that some selection must be made of teachers, curricula, architecture, methods of teaching. And in the making of the selection the dice must always be weighted in favor of this or that. Here is a fundamental truth that cannot be brushed aside as irrelevant or unimportant; it constitutes the very essence of the matter under discussion. Nor can the reality be concealed beneath agreeable phrases. Professor Dewey states in his *Democracy and Education* that the school should provide a *purified* environment for the child. With this view I would certainly agree; probably no person reared in our society would favor the study of pornography in the schools. I am sure, however, that this means stacking the cards in favor of the particular systems of value which we may happen to possess. It is one of the truisms of the anthropologist that there are no maxims of purity on which all peoples would agree. Other vigorous opponents of imposition unblushingly advocate the "cultivation of democratic sentiments" in children or the promotion of child growth in the direction of "a better and richer life." The first represents definite acquiescence in imposition; the second, if it does not mean the same thing, means nothing. I believe firmly that democratic sentiments should be cultivated and that a better and richer life should be the outcome of education, but in neither case would I place responsibility on either God or the order of nature. I would merely contend that as educators we must make many choices involving the development of attitudes in boys and girls and that we should not be afraid to acknowledge the faith that is in us or mayhap the forces that compel us.

6. There is the fallacy that the great object of education is to produce the college professor, that is, the individual who adopts an agnostic attitude towards every important social issue, who can balance the pros against the cons with the skill of a juggler, who sees all sides of every question and

never commits himself to any, who delays action until all the facts are in, who knows that all the facts will never come in, who consequently holds his judgment in a state of indefinite suspension, and who before the approach of middle age sees his powers of action atrophy and his social sympathies decay. With Peer Gynt he can exclaim:

> *Ay, think of it—wish it done—will it to boot,—*
> *But do it—! No, that's past my understanding!*

This type of mind also talks about waiting until the solutions of social problems are found, when as a matter of fact there are no solutions in any definite and final sense. For any complex social problem worthy of the name there are probably tens and even scores, if not hundreds, of "solutions," depending upon the premises from which one works. The meeting of a social situation involves the making of decisions and the working out of adjustments. Also it involves the selection and rejection of values. If we wait for a solution to appear like the bursting of the sun through the clouds or the resolving of the elements in an algebraic equation, we shall wait in vain. Although college professors, if not too numerous, perform a valuable social function, society requires great numbers of persons who, while capable of gathering and digesting facts, are at the same time able to think in terms of life, make decisions, and act. From such persons will come our real social leaders.

7. There is the closely related fallacy that education is primarily intellectualistic in its processes and goals. Quite as important is that ideal factor in culture which gives meaning, direction, and significance to life. I refer to the element of faith or purpose which lifts man out of himself and above the level of his more narrow personal interests. Here, in my judgment, is one of the great lacks in our schools and in our intellectual class today. We are able to contemplate the universe and find that all is vanity. Nothing really stirs us, unless it be that the bath water is cold, the toast burnt, or the elevator not running; or that perchance we miss the first section of a revolving door. Possibly this is the fundamental reason why we are so fearful of molding the child. We are moved by no great faiths; we are touched by no great passions. We can view a World order rushing rapidly towards collapse with no more concern than the outcome of a horserace; we can see injustice, crime and misery in their most terrible forms all about us and, if we are not directly affected, register the emotions of a scientist studying white rats in a laboratory. And in the name of freedom, objectivity, and the open mind, we would transmit this general attitude of futility to our children. In my opinion this is a confession of complete moral and spiritual bankruptcy.

We cannot, by talk about the interests of children and the sacredness of personality, evade the responsibility of bringing to the younger generation a vision which will call forth their active loyalties and challenge them to creative and arduous labors. A generation without such a vision is destined, like ours, to a life of absorption in self, inferiority complexes, and frustration. The genuinely free man is not the person who spends the day contemplating his own navel, but rather the one who loses himself in a great cause or glorious adventure.

8. There is the fallacy that the school is an all-powerful educational agency. Every professional group tends to exaggerate its own importance in the scheme of things. To this general rule the teachers offer no exception. The leaders of Progressive Education in particular seem to have an overweening faith in the power of the school. On the one hand, they speak continually about reconstructing society through education; and on the other, they apparently live in a state of perpetual fear lest the school impose some one point of view upon all children and mold them all to a single pattern. A moment's reflection is sufficient to show that life in the modern world is far too complex to permit this: the school is but one formative agency among many, and certainly not the strongest at that. Our major concern consequently should be, not to keep the school from influencing the child in a positive direction, but rather to make certain that every Progressive school will use whatever power it may possess in opposing and checking the forces of social conservatism and reaction. We know full well that, if the school should endeavor vigorously and consistently to win its pupils to the support of a given social program, unless it were supported by other agencies, it could act only as a mild counterpoise to restrain and challenge the might of less enlightened and more selfish purposes.

9. There is the fallacy that ignorance rather than knowledge is the way of wisdom. Many who would agree that imposition of some kind is inevitable seem to feel that there is something essentially profane in any effort to understand, plan, and control the process. They will admit that the child is molded by his environment, and then presumably contend that in the fashioning of this environment we should close our eyes to the consequences of our acts, or at least should not endeavor to control our acts in the light of definite knowledge of their consequences. To do the latter would involve an effort to influence deliberately the growth of the child in a particular direction—to cause him to form this habit rather than that, to develop one taste rather than another, to be sensitive to a given ideal rather than its rival. But this would be a violation of the "rights of the child," and therefore evil. Apparently his rights can be protected only if our influence upon him is thoroughly concealed under a heavy veil of ignorance. If the school can

do no better than this, it has no reason for existence. If it is to be merely an arena for the blind play of psychological forces, it might better close its doors. Here is the doctrine of *laissez faire,* driven from the field of social and political theory, seeking refuge in the domain of pedagogy. Progressive Education wishes to build a new world but refuses to be held accountable for the kind of world it builds. In my judgment, the school should know what it is doing, in so far as this is humanly possible, and accept full responsibility for its acts.

10. Finally, there is the fallacy that in a dynamic society like ours the major responsibility of education is to prepare the individual to adjust himself to social change. The argument in support of this view is fairly cogent. The world is changing with great rapidity; the rate of change is being accelerated constantly; the future is full of uncertainty. Consequently the individual who is to live and thrive in this world must possess an agile mind, be bound by no deep loyalties, hold all conclusions and values tentatively, and be ready on a moment's notice to make even fundamental shifts in outlook and philosophy. Like a lumberjack riding a raft of logs through the rapids, he must be able with lightning speed to jump from one insecure foundation to another, if he is not to be overwhelmed by the onward surge of the cultural stream. In a word, he must be as willing to adopt new ideas and values as to install the most up-to-the-minute labor saving devices in his dwelling or to introduce the latest inventions into his factory. Under such a conception of life and society, education can only bow down before the gods of chance and reflect the drift of the social order. This conception is essentially anarchic in character, exalts the irrational above the rational forces of society, makes of security an individual rather than a social goal, drives every one of us into an insane competition with his neighbors, and assumes that man is incapable of controlling in the common interest the creatures of his brain. Here we have imposition with a vengeance, but not the imposition of the teacher or the school. Nor is it an enlightened form of imposition. Rather is it the imposition of the chaos and cruelty and ugliness produced by the brutish struggle for existence and advantage. Far more terrifying than any indoctrination in which the school might indulge is the prospect of our becoming completely victimized and molded by the mechanics of industrialism. The control of the machine requires a society which is dominated less by the ideal of individual advancement and more by certain far-reaching purposes and plans for social construction. In such a society, instead of the nimble mind responsive to every eddy in the social current, a firmer and more steadfast mentality would be preferable.

Chapter 3

If we may now assume that the child will be imposed upon in some fashion by the various elements in his environment, the real question is not whether imposition will take place, but rather from what source it will come. If we were to answer this question in terms of the past, there could, I think, be but one answer: on all genuinely crucial matters the school follows the wishes of the groups or classes that actually rule society; on minor matters the school is sometimes allowed a certain measure of freedom. But the future may be unlike the past. Or perhaps I should say that teachers, if they could increase sufficiently their stock of courage, intelligence, and vision, might become a social force of some magnitude. About this eventuality I am not over sanguine, but a society lacking leadership as ours does, might even accept the guidance of teachers. Through powerful organizations they might at least reach the public conscience and come to exercise a larger measure of control over the schools than hitherto. They would then have to assume some responsibility for the more fundamental forms of imposition which, according to my argument, cannot be avoided.

That the teachers should deliberately reach for power and then make the most of their conquest is my firm conviction. To the extent that they are permitted to fashion the curriculum and the procedures of the school they will definitely and positively influence the social attitudes, ideals, and behavior of the coming generation. In doing this they should resort to no subterfuge or false modesty. They should say neither that they are merely teaching the truth nor that they are unwilling to wield power in their own right. The first position is false and the second is a confession of incompetence. It is my observation that the men and women who have affected the course of human events are those who have not hesitated to use the power that has come to them. Representing as they do, not the interests of the moment or of any special class, but rather the common and abiding interests of the people, teachers are under heavy social obligation to protect and further those interests. In this they occupy a relatively unique position in society. Also since the profession should embrace scientists and scholars of the highest rank, as well as teachers working at all levels of the educational system, it has at its disposal, as no other group, the knowledge and wisdom of the ages. It is scarcely thinkable that these men and women would ever act as selfishly or bungle as badly as have the so-called "practical" men of our generation—the politicians, the financiers, the industrialists. If all of these facts are taken into account, instead of shunning power, the profession should rather seek power and then strive to use that power fully and wisely and in the interests of the great masses of the people.

The point should be emphasized that teachers possess no magic secret to power. While their work should give them a certain moral advantage, they must expect to encounter the usual obstacles blocking the road to leadership. They should not be deceived by the pious humbug with which public men commonly flatter the members of the profession. To expect ruling groups or classes to give precedence to teachers on important matters, because of age or sex or sentiment, is to refuse to face realities. It was one of the proverbs of the agrarian order that a spring never rises higher than its source. So the power that teachers exercise in the schools can be no greater than the power they wield in society. Moreover, while organization is necessary, teachers should not think of their problem primarily in terms of organizing and presenting a united front to the world, the flesh, and the devil. In order to be effective they must throw off completely the slave psychology that has dominated the mind of the pedagogue more or less since the days of ancient Greece. They must be prepared to stand on their own feet and win for their ideas the support of the masses of the people. Education as a force for social regeneration must march hand in hand with the living and creative forces of the social order. In their own lives teachers must bridge the gap between school and society and play some part in the fashioning of those great common purposes which should bind the two together.

This brings us to the question of the kind of imposition in which teachers should engage, if they had the power. Our obligations, I think, grow out of the social situation. We live in troublous times; we live in an age of profound change; we live in an age of revolution. Indeed it is highly doubtful whether man ever lived in a more eventful period than the present. In order to match our epoch we would probably have to go back to the fall of the ancient empires or even to that unrecorded age when men first abandoned the natural arts of hunting and fishing and trapping and began to experiment with agriculture and the settled life. Today we are witnessing the rise of a civilization quite without precedent in human history—a civilization founded on science, technology, and machinery, possessing the most extraordinary power, and rapidly making of the entire world a single great society. Because of forces already released, whether in the field of economics, politics, morals, religion, or art, the old molds are being broken. And the peoples of the earth are everywhere seething with strange ideas and passions. If life were peaceful and quiet and undisturbed by great issues, we might with some show of wisdom center our attention on the nature of the child. But with the world as it is, we cannot afford for a single instant to remove our eyes from the social scene or shift our attention from the peculiar needs of the age.

In this new world that is forming, there is one set of issues which is peculiarly fundamental and which is certain to be the center of bitter and prolonged struggle. I refer to those issues which may be styled economic. President Butler has well stated the case: "For a generation and more past," he says, "the center of human interest has been moving from the point which it occupied for some four hundred years to a new point which it bids fair to occupy for a time equally long. The shift in the position of the center of gravity in human interest has been from politics to economics; from considerations that had to do with forms of government, with the establishment and protection of individual liberty, to considerations that have to do with the production, distribution, and consumption of wealth."

Consider the present condition of the nation. Who among us, if he had not been reared amid our institutions, could believe his eyes as he surveys the economic situation, or his ears as he listens to solemn disquisitions by our financial and political leaders on the cause and cure of the depression! Here is a society that manifests the most extraordinary contradictions: a mastery over the forces of nature, surpassing the wildest dreams of antiquity, is accompanied by extreme material insecurity; dire poverty walks hand in hand with the most extravagant living the world has ever known; an abundance of goods of all kinds is coupled with privation, misery, and even starvation; an excess of production is seriously offered as the underlying cause of severe physical suffering; breakfastless children march to school past bankrupt shops laden with rich foods gathered from the ends of the earth; strong men by the million walk the streets in a futile search for employment and with the exhaustion of hope enter the ranks of the damned; great captains of industry close factories without warning and dismiss the workmen by whose labors they have amassed huge fortunes through the years; automatic machinery increasingly displaces men and threatens society with a growing contingent of the permanently unemployed; racketeers and gangsters with the connivance of public officials fasten themselves on the channels of trade and exact toll at the end of the machine gun; economic parasitism, either within or without the law, is so prevalent that the tradition of honest labor is showing signs of decay; the wages paid to the workers are too meager to enable them to buy back the goods they produce; consumption is subordinated to production and a philosophy of deliberate waste is widely proclaimed as the highest economic wisdom; the science of psychology is employed to fan the flames of desire so that men may be enslaved by their wants and bound to the wheel of production; a government board advises the cotton-growers to plow under every third row of cotton in order to bolster up the market; both ethical and aesthetic considerations are commonly over-ridden by "hard-headed business men" bent on material gain; federal aid to the unemployed is opposed on the ground that it would pauperize the masses when the favored members of society have always lived on a dole; even responsible leaders resort to the practices of the witch doctor and vie with one another in predicting the return of prosperity; an ideal of rugged individualism, evolved in a simple pioneering and agrarian order at a time when free land existed in abundance, is used to justify a system which exploits pitilessly and without thought of the morrow the natural and human resources of the nation and of the world. One can only imagine what Jeremiah would say if he could step out of the pages of the Old Testament and cast his eyes over this vast spectacle so full of tragedy and of menace.

The point should be emphasized, however, that the present situation is also freighted with hope and promise. The age is pregnant with possibilities. There lies within our grasp the most humane, the most beautiful, the most majestic civilization ever fashioned by any people. This much at least we know today. We shall probably know more tomorrow. At last men have achieved such a mastery over the forces of nature that wage slavery can follow chattel slavery and take its place among the relics of the past. No longer are there grounds for the contention that the finer fruits of human culture must be nurtured upon the toil and watered by the tears of the masses. The limits to achievement set by nature have been so extended that we are today bound merely by our ideals, by our power of self-discipline, by our ability to devise social arrangements suited to an industrial age. If we are to place any credence whatsoever in the word of our engineers, the full utilization of modern technology at its present level of development should enable us to produce several times as much goods as were ever produced at the very peak of prosperity, and with the working day, the working year, and the working life reduced by half. We hold within our hands the power to usher in an age of plenty, to make secure the lives of all, and to banish poverty forever from the land. The only cause for doubt or pessimism lies in the question of our ability to rise to the stature of the times in which we live.

Our generation has the good or the ill fortune to live in an age when great decisions must be made. The American people, like most of the other peoples of the earth, have come to the parting of the ways; they can no longer trust entirely the inspiration which came to them when the Republic was young; they must decide afresh what they are to do with their talents. Favored above all other nations with the resources of nature and the material instrumentalities of civilization, they stand confused and irresolute before the future. They seem to lack the moral quality necessary to quicken, discipline, and give direction to their matchless energies. In a recent paper Professor Dewey has, in my judgment, correctly diagnosed our troubles;

"the schools, like the nation," he says, "are in need of a central purpose which will create new enthusiasm and devotion, and which will unify and guide all intellectual plans."

This suggests, as we have already observed, that the educational problem is not wholly intellectual in nature. Our Progressive schools therefore cannot rest content with giving children an opportunity to study contemporary society in all of its aspects. This of course must be done, but I am convinced that they should go much farther. If the schools are to be really effective, they must become centers for the building, and not merely for the contemplation, of our civilization. This does not mean that we should endeavor to promote particular reforms through the educational system. We should, however, give to our children a vision of the possibilities which lie ahead and endeavor to enlist their loyalties and enthusiasms in the realization of the vision. Also our social institutions and practices, all of them, should be critically examined in the light of such a vision.

36

Selected Writings of William C. Bagley

During his lifetime, William C. Bagley (1874–1946) was America's most influential philosopher of teacher education. Although he has become known as the father of "Essentialism," his central focus throughout this career was the education of teachers and, more specifically, curriculum for the education of teachers. During his nearly fifty-year career, Bagley wrote numerous books and articles on topics such as teacher education, curriculum, educational philosophy and psychology, higher education, and secondary education.

Bagley was born in Detroit, Michigan on March 15, 1874. After graduating from Michigan Agricultural College in 1895, he taught in a rural, one-room school in upstate Michigan. He attended graduate school at the University of Wisconsin (Madison) and Cornell University. After completing his Ph.D. in psychology at Cornell in 1900, Bagley chose to dedicate his life to the education of teachers for public school service. He taught for four years at Montana State Normal School in Dillon, Montana, and then for two more years at Oswego State Normal School in Oswego, New York. In 1908, he accepted a position as Professor of Education at the University of Illinois. At Illinois, Bagley

American Educational Thought: Essays from 1640–1940, pages 551–580
Copyright © 2010 by Information Age Publishing

established the University of Illinois' School of Education. After serving as the School's Inaugural Dean, he departed Illinois for Teachers College, Columbia University. At Teachers College, he served as chair of Teachers College's department of teacher education. He taught at Teachers College from 1917 to 1939, when he retired at the age of 65.

During his Teachers College tenure, Bagley wrote numerous books and hundreds of articles and editorials, all of which related directly to the discipline of teacher education. Late in his career, Bagley became critical of extremism within educational thought, specifically the ideas of William Heard Kilpatrick. Bagley believed that Kilpatrick and others had misinterpreted the complex work of John Dewey. During the 1930s, Bagley joined with numerous others to found Essentialism, an educational philosophy that sought to retain the valuable aspects of Progressive education while at the same time emphasizing a unique philosophy of professional education. Bagley's philosophy of professional education always sought to integrate the subject-matter disciplines, the technique of teaching, and the critically important question of purpose. —JWN

An Essentialist's Platform for the Advancement of American Education, 1938

Prefatory Note

The first three sections of this paper were prepared by the writer for discussion by a small group which met at Atlantic City on February 26, 1938, and which adopted the name, The Essentialist Committee for the Advancement of American Education. An unauthorized release to the press including a few statements from this paper gave rise to rather wide publicity and led to somewhat fiery denunciations by prominent leaders in American educational theory. For this reason the first three sections are here published essentially as they were first presented. The article is published on the sole responsibility of the writer, and not as an official pronouncement of the Committee, although the members of the Committee are in substantial agreement with the position here taken and have suggested only minor changes, almost all of which have been made in revising the original draft. The Managing Editor of Educational Administration and Supervision has kindly agreed to publish further articles dealing with the same problem. It is hoped that other members of the Committee will make contributions. The Committee includes in addition to the writer: Dr. M. Demiashkevich; Dr. Walter H. Ryle; Dr. M. L. Shane; Mr. F. Alden Shaw, *Chairman and Organizer*; Dr. Louis Shores; Dr. Guy M. Whipple.

I. *The Situation*

In spite of its vast extent and its heavy cost to society, public education in the United States is in many ways appallingly weak and ineffective. For the sake of brevity only a few outstanding evidences of this weakness will be set forth here:

1. Age for age, the average pupil of our elementary schools does not meet the standards of achievement in the fundamentals of education that are attained in the elementary schools of many other countries. In so far as English-speaking countries are concerned, this statement can be and has been substantiated by the scores made in the elementary schools of these countries on American achievement tests, the norms of which represent the average scores of large, unselected groups of American pupils. In the most extended investigation of this type, the differences revealed are so wide as to justify no other inference than that American elementary-school achievement is far below what it could be and what it should be.

2. Similar comparisons relative to secondary education cannot be made because the secondary schools of practically all other countries are not intended for "all the children of all the people" as are our high schools. It is generally agreed among competent students of the problem that our average 18-year-old high-school graduate is scholastically far behind the average 18-year-old graduates of the secondary schools of many other countries. This difference has been recognized in the practice of admitting the latter to junior-year standing in many American colleges. But even granting that secondary education elsewhere is in general selective, there is abundant evidence that in our laudable efforts to send everyone to and through high school standards have been unnecessarily lowered. Both the bright and slow pupils are handicapped by weaknesses in the fundamentals that all except those hopelessly subnormal are able to master. Within the past decade the effectiveness of high-school instruction has been weakened by increasing disabilities in so basic an accomplishment as reading. It is scarcely too much to say, indeed, that increasing proportions of pupils in the junior and senior high schools are essentially illiterate. Failures in such high-school studies as mathematics and natural science are in many cases traceable to the fact that pupils cannot read effectively. Classes in "remedial" reading are now necessary on the secondary level to bring pupils to a standard of literacy that primary and intermediate grade instruction could and should have insured. Equally lamentable weaknesses in basic arithmetic are reported. And it is now taken for granted by high-school teachers of Latin and modern languages that one of their chief duties is to teach their pupils the rudiments of English grammar.

3. In other and not at all exclusively scholastic accomplishments, American education is relatively ineffective. A recent study suggests that juvenile delinquency may be correlated in many cases with these reading disabilities which we contend are almost always unnecessary and easily avoidable by appropriate elementary education. And while no causal relationship is claimed, it is well to know that during the one hundred years in which universal elementary education has been increasingly the policy of all civilized countries, ours is apparently the only country in which the expansion of the universal school has not been paralleled by a significant and in some cases a remarkable decrease in the ratios of serious crime.

II. The Causes: A. General Economic and Social Factors

4. American education has been confronted with uniquely difficult and complicated problems which have arisen from a rapid growth in population; from a constantly advancing frontier; from the increase in national wealth; from the arrival year after year and decade after decade of millions of immigrants of widely diverse national origins; from the complex social and political situations involved in racial differences; from the profound changes brought about by the transition from a predominantly agricultural to a predominantly industrial civilization; from the growth of cities; from an ever-increasing mobility of the population; and from a multitude of other factors which have operated here with a force unprecedented in history and unparalleled in any other part of the world.

The American public school has met some of these problems with a notable measure of success. Of outstanding significance is the fact that among the states which by any test would be rated as the most advanced in civilization are those which have had the heaviest burden of immigration from backward countries to assimilate. And it should be said that, in general, the states that have had the most substantial (but not necessarily the most "Progressive") school systems have by far the lowest ratios of serious crime. In a notable degree, too, these same states, many of which do not rank high in per capita wealth, are those that have been least dependent upon the federal government for "relief" during the depression years. Beyond all this, the schools can claim a very high degree of definitely measurable success for their programs of physical development and health education.

5. The upward expansion of mass-education first to the secondary and now to the college level, which is probably the chief cause of our educational ineffectiveness, has been an outcome, not alone of a pervasive faith in education, to the realization of which the material wealth of the country was fairly adequate, but also and perhaps more fundamentally of economic factors. Power-driven machinery, while in many cases reducing occupational

opportunities on the purely routine levels, quite as markedly opened new occupational opportunities in types of work that could not be done by machinery; work that involved deliberation and judgment; work for which a broad foundation in general education as well as specialized technical and vocational training was advantageous and often essential. That increasing numbers of young persons should seek the advantages of an extended education has been inevitable. Fortunately the wealth of the country has enabled the people of many sections to meet this demand. In opening the high schools and colleges to ever-increasing numbers, however, it was just as inevitable that scholastic standards should be relaxed, and when such a need arises it is only natural that those responsible for the administration of education should welcome any theory or philosophy which justifies or rationalizes such a policy—any theory of education which can make a virtue of necessity. Under such a condition, it is easy to understand why the relaxation of standards has been carried far beyond the actual needs of the case.

III. The Causes: B. Educational Theories that are Essentially Enfeebling

6. Throughout the long history of education—and organized education is practically as old as civilization—two opposing theories have been in evidence. Although over-simplification is always dangerous, one with this caution may contrast these two theories of education by certain conflicting concepts summed up in pairing such opposites as "individual vs. society," "freedom vs. discipline," "interest vs. effort," "play vs. work,"—or to use more recently current expressions, "immediate needs vs. remote goals," "personal experience vs. race experience," "psychological organization vs. logical organization," "pupil-initiative vs. teacher-initiative." The fundamental dualism suggested by these terms has persisted over the centuries. It came out sharply in Greek education during the Age of the Sophists. It was reflected in the educational changes brought about by the Italian Renaissance. It appeared in the 17th Century in a definite school of educational theory the adherents of which even at that time styled themselves the "Progressives." It was explicit in the successive educational reforms proposed by Rousseau, Pestalozzi, Froebel, and Herbart. In American education it was reflected in the theories advocated and practiced by Bronson Alcott, in the work of Horace Mann, and later in the work of E.A. Sheldon and Francis W. Parker; while the present outstanding leader, John Dewey, first came into prominence during the last decade of the 19th Century in an effort to resolve the dualism through an integration expressed in the title of his classic essay, now called "Interest and Effort in Education."

7. Under the necessity which confronted American education of rationalizing the loosening of standards and the relaxation of rigor if mass-

education were to be expanded upward, the theories which emphasized interest, freedom, immediate needs, personal experience, psychological organization, and pupil-initiative, and which in so doing tended to discredit and even condemn their opposites—effort, discipline, remote goals, race-experience, logical sequence, and teacher-initiative—naturally made a powerful appeal. Over more than a generation these theories have increasingly influenced the lower schools. They find specific expression today in a variety of definite movements so numerous that even the more outstanding can here be listed.

(a) The complete abandonment in many school systems of rigorous standards of scholastic achievement as a condition of promotion from grade to grade, and the passing of all pupils "on schedule." This policy which found a strong initial support thirty years ago in the studies of "retardation and elimination" has of late been given even a wider appeal by the teachings of mental hygiene regarding the possible effects of failure in disintegrating personality. The problem is extremely complicated as a later reference to it will show, but the movement has already resulted in at least one very important change. Instead of having "overage" pupils piling up in the intermediate grades, we now have "overgraded" pupils handicapped in the work of the junior and senior high schools by their lack of thorough training in the fundamentals already referred to.

(b) The disparagement of system and sequence in learning and a dogmatic denial of any value in, even of any possibility of learning through, the logical, chronological, and causal relationships of learning materials. This has led to an enthronement of the doctrine of incidental learning. Only as one becomes acquainted with facts and principles through applying them to vital problems that appeal to one as worth solving at the moment (so the theory holds) can one truly learn such facts and principles. And on the side of skills—such as the fundamental arts of language, measurement, and computation—mastery as far as possible should await an occasion when one of them is needed. As someone has said in effect, "These things are only tools, and when a workman needs a tool he goes to the shop and gets it." And yet this theory that "mind will not learn what is alien to its fundamental vital purposes," Thorndike has pronounced on the basis of extended experimentation, "to be attractive and plausible but definitely false." The disparagement of systematic and sequential learning has also been criticized in no uncertain terms by John Dewey.

(c) The wide vogue of the so-called "activity movement." This is an outgrowth of the so-called "project-method" which in its turn was an effort to find, or to encourage the learner to find, problems or vital purposes in the solution of

which desirable learnings could be effected. The activity movement and the resulting "activity programs" and "activity curricula," like the project-method, have an important place—a central function in the primary school, and a very useful supplementary function on all educational levels. The tendency to make them a substitute for systematic and sequential learning and to go even further and regard activity, as a sufficient end in itself irrespective of whether or not, anything is learned through the activity is another matter. It is, however, an intriguing proposal. As one enthusiastic activist said, "Let us not use activities as pegs on which to hang subject-matter." If the schools only provide an abundance of "rich experiences" for the learner, it seems, other things will miraculously take care of themselves. This is not at all absurd if one accepts the premises; it is a thoroughly consistent result of the theory of incidental learning carried to its logical conclusion.

(d) The discrediting of the exact and exacting studies. The most significant barrier to opening the high schools to the masses was at the outset the practically universal requirement of Latin, algebra, and geometry in the secondary program. Perhaps inherently and certainly as commonly taught, the difficulties in mastering these subjects were quite beyond a large proportion of pupils. At the same time the practical value of the subjects was difficult to defend. Their central place in the curriculum, however, was believed to be justified in a high degree by the mental discipline that their mastery involved: Anything that would tend to discredit this justification was seized upon by those responsible for the upward expansion of mass-education. Most fortunately for their purposes there appeared just at the turn of the century the report of the first careful psychological experiments testing the validity of the theory of mental discipline. These really classic experiments of Thorndike and Woodworth were followed by a long series of similar investigations that aimed to determine in how far learnings acquired in one subject were, or could be, applied in other situations. The results in general indicated that such a "transfer" was far from inevitable and in some cases either quite negative or so slight as to bring the whole theory into question.

The proponents of the universal high school and of other educational movements that were impeded by the requirement of subjects inherently difficult to the average mind were not slow to capitalize these experimental findings. As is natural under conditions of this sort, the evidence was generalized to a far greater extent than the experiments warranted, and with far-reaching results in school practice. Although the absolute number enrolled in Latin classes has increased, only a small proportion of pupils graduating from the high schools during the past ten years have even been exposed to Latin. Increasing proportions, too, are quite innocent of any training in elementary mathematics beyond the increasingly ineffective modicum of arithmetic acquired in the elementary schools. But the important part is that there has been a growing practice of discouraging even competent learners from undertaking the studies that are exact though exacting; hence the upward expansion of mass-education, while sincerely a democratic movement, is not guarding itself against the potentially most fatal pitfall of democracy. It has deliberately adopted the easy policy of leveling-down rather than facing resolutely the difficult task of leveling-up—and upon the possibility of leveling-up the future of democracy indisputably depends. As John Dewey has contended, the older curriculum of classics and mathematics does have a unique value to those competent to its mastery—a value for which the so-called reform movements have not as yet, in his judgment, provided a substitute.

(e) An increasingly heavy emphasis upon the "social studies." While the exact and exacting studies were in effect being discredited, the primrose path of least resistance was opened ever wider in the field known as the social studies. The argument here is plausible and appealing. "Education for citizenship" is a ringing slogan with limitless potentialities, especially in an age when high-sounding shibboleths, easily formulated, can masquerade as fundamental premises and postulates wrought through the agony of hard thinking.

Obviously no fundamental premise in educational thinking could fail to recognize the importance of a firm foundation in the history of human institutions, or of an acquaintance with present and pressing social problems especially in the light of their genesis, or of an acquaintance with such principles of economics, sociology, and political science as have been well established.

But just as obviously the social sciences, so called, are not in the same class with the natural sciences. Their generalizations permit trustworthy predictions only in a few cases and then only in a slight degree. When the human element enters, uncertainty enters—else the world could have anticipated and adjusted itself to Hitler and Mussolini and Stalin and the military oligarchy of Japan and would not be standing dazed and impotent as it stands today. And while to expect an educational pabulum of social studies in the lower schools essentially to overcome this inherent limitation of the social sciences is an alluring prospect, it is to expect nothing less than a miracle. It is, indeed, just as sensible as would be a brave and desperate effort to incite immature minds to square the circle.

(f) Using the lower schools to establish a new social order. The proposal definitely and deliberately to indoctrinate immature learners in the interest of a specific social order and one that involves wide departures from that

which prevails in our country is to be questioned, if for no other reasons, upon the grounds set forth in the preceding paragraphs. With the growing ineffectiveness of the lower schools in failing to lay adequate foundations in fundamental and established learnings of unquestioned permanence and value, such efforts would necessarily be superficial in the last degree. It would be an extreme case of building what may be characterized for the sake of argument as a perfectly splendid edifice on shifting sands—in this case, quicksands would be the more appropriate metaphor. And here we might well study certain peoples that have actually achieved a social order which is pointed to by our idealists as exemplifying in many ways the realization of their dreams. Reference is made, of course, to such countries as Sweden, Denmark, Norway, and New Zealand. An outstanding fact of fundamental significance is that these countries have not achieved these laudable results by emasculating their educational systems. Their peoples indeed would stand aghast at the very suggestion.

(g) *The "curriculum-revision" movement and its vagaries.* The various reform proposals just discussed have culminated in the general movement known as curriculum-revision which has dominated the lower schools for nearly twenty years. A primary emphasis has been the alleged need of building the programs of instruction around the local community. As long ago as 1933 more than 30,000 different curricula were on file in the curriculum-laboratory of Teachers College, Columbia University. Most of these had been prepared during the preceding decade by committees of teachers in local school systems throughout the country. Sometimes the committees were personally directed by a "curriculum-expert"; in practically all cases a rapidly developing theory evolved by these specialists guided the work. In so far as we can learn, this theory has never explicitly recognized that the state or the nation has a stake in the content of school instruction. The need of common elements in the basic culture of all people, especially in a democracy, has in effect been denied. Furthermore, with the American people the most mobile in the world, with stability of residence over the period of school attendance the exception and not the rule in many sections of the country, and with a significantly higher average of school failure among pupils whose parents move from place to place than among those who remain in the same community, the curriculum theorists have been totally insensitive to the need of a certain measure of uniformity in school requirements and in the grade-placement of crucial topics. In addition to all this, the clear tendency of the curriculum-revision movement has been to minimize basic learnings, to magnify the superficial, to belittle sequence and system, and otherwise to aggravate the weakness and ineffectiveness of the lower schools.

IV. The Problem and the Platform

8. It is particularly unfortunate that American education should be un-necessarily weak at a time, when the situation both at home and abroad is critical in the last degree.

The American people are facing an economic problem which both in nature and in magnitude is without an even remotely similar precedent in all history. In the richest country in the world, two thirds of the world's un-employment is now concentrated. In the midst of potential abundance, the cogs in the wheels of production, distribution, exchange, and consumption have lamentably failed to mesh.

It is the indicated and imminent task of the present dominant genera-tion to solve this problem under whatever expert guidance at the hands of the economist and the social engineer it may find and accept. The student of education must cooperate with all other citizens in this task. It is his own specific duty, however, to consider the problems in his field that are bound to arise in the changes that seem now to be inevitable, regardless of the form which the solution of the present desperate economic situation may take—this with one exception, for if in desperation the American people discard democracy and yield to a dictator the sincere student of education will have no function and consequently no duty. The yes-man and the rub-ber-stamp will take his place. He will be a luxury without a purpose; and the dictators have standardized a simple but effective technique for liquidating luxuries of this sort.

9. We shall assume, however, that "it can't happen here" and that, whatever may be the new economic and social order, the political order based upon representative government and the Bill of Rights will persist. Hence a primary function of American education will be to safeguard and strengthen these ideals of American democracy, with especial emphasis upon freedom of speech, freedom of the press, freedom of assembly, and freedom of religion. It is clear enough now that whenever any one of these is permitted to collapse, the whole democratic structure will topple like a house of cards. These, then, are among the first essentials in the platform of the Essentialist.

10. Democracy is now distinctly on trial. It is under criticism and sus-picion. Every weakness will be watched for and welcomed by its enemies. Inevitably the future will bring competition if not clashes and conflicts with the now militantly anti-democratic peoples. Democratic societies can-not survive either competition or conflict with totalitarian states unless there is a democratic discipline that will give strength and solidarity to the democratic purpose and ideal. If the theory of democracy finds no place

for discipline, then, the theory will have before long only historical signifi- cance. French education, much closer to the danger, has recognized this imperative need. Still unswerving in fidelity to the ideals of democracy, and still giving its first emphasis to clarity of thought and independence in individual thinking as the time-honored objectives of French education, it recognizes no less the fundamental importance of social solidarity in the defense of democracy.

American educational theory long since dropped the term "discipline" from its vocabulary. Today its most vocal and influential spokesmen en- throne the right even of the immature learner to choose what he shall learn. They condemn as "authoritarian" all learning tasks that are imposed by the teacher. They deny any value in the systematic and sequential mastery of the lessons that the race has learned at so great a cost. They condone and rationalize the refusal of the learner to attack a task that does not interest him. In effect they open wide the lines of least resistance and least effort. Obedience they stigmatize as a sign of weakness. All this they advocate in the magic names of "democracy" and "freedom."

Now, obviously, the freedom of the immature to choose what they shall learn is of negligible consequence compared with their later freedom from the want, fear, fraud, superstition, and error which may fetter the ignorant as cruelly as the chains of the slave-driver—and the price of this freedom is systematic and sustained effort often devoted to the mastery of materials the significance of which must at the time be taken on faith.

11. This problem is far more than merely personal or individual in its reference. A democratic society has a vital, collective stake in the informed intelligence of every individual citizen. That a literate electorate is abso- lutely indispensable not only to its welfare but to its very survival is clearly demonstrated by the sorry fate that so speedily overtook every unschooled and illiterate democracy founded as a result of the War that was to "Make the world safe for democracy."

And literacy in this sense means, of course, far more than the mere ability to translate printed letters into spoken words; it means the develop- ment and expansion of ideas; it means the basis for intelligent understand- ing and for the collective thought and judgment which are the essence of democratic institutions. These needs are so fundamental in an effective democracy that it would be folly to leave them to the whim or caprice of either learner or teacher.

Among the essentials of the Essentialist, then, is a recognition of the right of the immature learner to guidance and direction when these are needed either for his individual welfare or for the welfare and progress of the democratic group. The responsibility of the mature for the instruction and control of the immature is the biological meaning of the extended period of human immaturity and necessary dependence. It took the human race untold ages to recognize this responsibility. It is literally true that until this recognition dawned man remained a savage. Primitive societies, as numerous students have observed (and their testimony seems to be unanimous), pamper and indulge their young. Freedom of children from control, guidance, and discipline is with them a rule so nearly universal that its only brief but significant exception during the nearly universal savage ceremonies marking the adolescent onset of maturity is regarded as the first faint beginning of consciously directed human education.

It would be futile to deny that control and discipline may be stupid and brutal and used for unworthy ends. It would be futile to deny the need for the development of self-discipline and for the relaxation of external discipline with the growth of volitional maturity. But all this does not alter the fundamental truth that freedom must go hand in hand with responsibility and that responsible freedom is always a conquest, never a gift.

12. An effective democracy demands a community of culture. Educationally this means that each generation be placed in possession of a common core of ideas, meanings, understandings, and ideals representing the most precious elements of the human heritage.

There can be little question as to the essentials. It is by no means a mere accident that the arts of recording, computing, and measuring have been among the first concerns of organized education. They are basic social arts. Every civilized society has been founded upon these arts, and when these arts have been lost, civilization has invariably and inevitably collapsed. Egypt, Asia Minor, and Mesopotamia are strewn with the ruins of civilizations that forgot how to read and write. Contemporary civilization, for the first time in history has attempted to insure its continuance by making these arts in so far as possible the prerogative of all.

Nor is it at all accidental that a knowledge of the world that lies beyond one's immediate experience has been among the recognized essentials of universal education, and that at least a speaking acquaintance with man's past and especially with the story of one's own country was early provided for in the program of the universal school. Widening the space horizon and extending the time perspective are essential if the citizen is to be protected from the fallacies of the local and the immediate.

Investigation, invention, and creative art have added to the heritage and the list of recognized essentials has been extended and will be further extended. Health instruction and the inculcation of health practices are now basic phases of the work of the lower schools. The elements of natural science have their place. Neither the fine arts nor the industrial arts are neglected.

We repeat that there can be little question as to the essentials of universal education. As Charles A. Beard has so well said; "While education constantly touches the practical affairs of the hour and day, and responds to political and economic exigencies, it has its own treasure heavy with the thought and sacrifice of the centuries. It possesses a heritage of knowledge and heroic examples—accepted values stamped with the seal of permanence."

13. A specific program of studies including these essentials should be the heart of a democratic system of education. In a country like ours with its highly mobile population there should be an agreement as to the order and grade-placement of subjects and especially of crucial topics. There is no valid reason for the extreme localism that has come to characterize American education. There is no valid reason for the failure of the American elementary school to lay as firm a foundation in the fundamentals of education as do the elementary schools of other democracies. It. is especially regrettable that contemporary educational theory should in effect condone and rationalize scamped work by ridiculing such traits as thoroughness, accuracy, persistence, and the ideal of good workmanship for its own sake. One may be very sure that democracy schooled to the easy way will have short shrift in competition or conflict with any social order dominated by objectives which, however reprehensible, are clear-cut and appealing, and are consequently embraced even by disfranchised masses.

14. Generally speaking, the recognized essentials should be taught, as such through a systematic program of studies and activities for the carrying out, of which the teachers should be responsible. Informal learning through experiences initialed by the learners is important, and abundant opportunities should be provided for such experiences throughout the range of organized education. Beyond the primary grades, however, where as we have said it may well predominate, informal learning should be regarded as supplementary rather than central.

15. Failure in school is unpleasant and the repetition of a grade is costly and often not very effective. On the other hand, the lack of a stimulus that will keep the learner to his task is a serious injustice both to him and to the democratic group which, we repeat, has a fundamental stake in his effective education. Too severe a stigma has undoubtedly been placed upon school failure by implying that it is symptomatic of permanent weakness. By no means is this always the case. No less a genius than Pasteur did so poorly in his first year at the Higher Normal School of Paris that he had

to go home for further preparation. One of the outstanding scientists of the present century had a hard time in meeting the requirements of the secondary school, failing, it is said, in the most elementary work of the field in which he later became world-famous. The list could be extended almost indefinitely.

Obviously not all learners can progress at the same rate. Some will go very, very slowly. Others will have trouble in getting started but will progress rapidly when they overcome the initial handicaps. Let us not stigmatize failure as we have done in the past. On the other hand, if education abandons rigorous standards and consequently provides no effective stimulus to the effort that learning requires, many persons will pass through twelve years of schooling only to find themselves in a world in which ignorance and lack of fundamental training are increasingly heavy handicaps. This in an all too literal sense is to throw the baby out with the bath.

16. The transition from a predominantly rural to a predominantly urban life has laid increasing burdens upon American education. For four decades or more we have been told that the school must provide opportunities for types of education that the normal bringing-up of children once provided on the farm and in the home. Manual training and the household arts were among the first responses to this demand. The parallel development of physical training with its later ramifications into various forms of health education are traceable in part to the same causes. Playgrounds, gymnasiums, and swimming pools are material expressions of the effort to meet these recognized needs. School and college athletics are lusty by-products representing in a very real sense the importance of finding a substitute for the vigorous physical work that once devolved of necessity upon the great majority of young people.

With the profound changes in the conditions of life already in progress, and with their clearly predictable extension and intensification in the immediate future, analogous substitutes must be sought for other educative experiences which the simpler conditions of life naturally and normally provided. Bread-winning employment is now postponed for vast numbers of young people. Willy-nilly they must remain dependent upon society, whether in attendance at school or college, or in such highly important educational enterprises as the Civilian Conservation Corps, or in "made work" of one variety or another.

The analogy of our civilization with the older civilizations based upon slavery is in no sense far-fetched. It has, indeed, a profound significance. Our slaves, it is true, are mechanical and not human. They are power-driven and increasingly they are being automatically controlled. They can do much more economically than human slaves the heavy work and the routine work. In some tasks they can perceive distinctions far too fine to be detected by the human senses, and they can respond far more quickly and far more accurately and dependably than can human nerves and muscles. Fortunately they can neither feel nor suffer, and so the grossest evils of the old slave civilizations are avoided. The fact remains, however, that the perils to those who are the supposed beneficiaries of a slave civilization are in no significant degree changed, whether the slaves be men or robots. Every slave civilization has within it the seeds of degeneration, decay, and ultimate extinction. Struggle and competition, selection and rejection, have often been cruel, but in both biological and social evolution they have been primary factors of progress. In societies that have lifted themselves above the plane of the brute and the savage, a most powerful steadying and civilizing force has been the ideal of personal economic responsibility for one's own survival and for one's old age and the care of one's dependents.

Generally speaking, then, "social security," like responsible freedom, has been a conquest, not a gift. Making it a gift involves some definite dangers. In our own country, few families have long survived the social security that comes through inherited wealth. "Three generations from shirt-sleeves to shirt-sleeves" has usually told the story. But this rule has had its exceptions. Here, as in some other countries, social security has, with occasional families, remained secure over a much longer time—but under the condition that each generation has been rigorously disciplined to its responsibilities and made clearly aware of the pitfalls that await the spendthrift and the idler. These exceptions, and especially those among them that have exemplified the development in each generation of a vigorous and highly sensitized social conscience, warrant the hope that an economy of abundance with social security for all may be so organized that our machine-slave civilization can escape that fate of the slave civilizations that have gone before. Herein lies an educational problem of the first magnitude which our educational theorists seem not even dimly to have sensed—so busy have they been in condemning out of hand the economic system which has made possible an economy of abundance based upon a machine-slave civilization.

A clear and primary duty of organized education at the present time is to recognize the fundamental character of the changes that are already taking place, and to search diligently for means of counteracting their dangers. Let us repeat that an educational theory meet to these needs must be strong, virile, and positive, not feeble, effeminate, and vague. The theories that have increasingly dominated American education during the past generation are at basis distinctly of the latter type. The Essentialists have recognized and still recognize the contributions of real value that these theories have made to educational practice. They believe, however, that these positive elements can be preserved in an educational theory which finds its basis in the necessary dependence of the immature upon the mature for guidance, instruction, and discipline. This dependence is inherent in human nature, "What has been ordained among the prehistoric protozoa," said Huxley, "cannot be altered by act of Parliament" — nor, we may add, by the wishful thinking of educational theorists, however sincere their motives. "Authoritarianism" is an ugly word. But when those who detest it carry their laudable rebellion against certain of its implications so far as to reject the authority of plain facts, their arguments, while well adapted perhaps to the generation of heat, become lamentably lacking in light.

The Significance of the Essentialist Movement in Educational Theory, 1939

I.

In 1935, the late Michael Demiashkevich suggested the term "Essentialists" as an appropriate designation for the advocates of an educational theory which places relatively heavy emphasis upon the induction of each generation into its social heritage as the primary function of education as a social institution. This was by way of contrast with the teachings of the school of educational theory which has become increasingly dominant in the United States during the past generation and which, in its well-intended efforts to improve American education, has, in effect, discredited and belittled the significance of a mastery of what we commonly call subject-matter, or in a large generic sense, knowledge.

From another angle, the contrast may be drawn by saying that the Essentialist emphasizes the basic significance of the accumulated experience of the race, and affirms the chief concern of education to be the transmission to each generation of the most important lessons that have come out of this experience, while the prevailing American theory lays its emphasis upon personal or individual experience, and affirms the chief concern of education to be the direction of individual growth with the mastery of race experience a relatively unimportant matter except as the individual himself recognizes a need for certain of its lessons as instruments or tools in the solution of problems that appeal to him at the time as worth solving,

Numerous terms that loom large in current discussions illustrate this unmistakable tendency of the theory that now dominates American education. Some of these have become stereotypes and like all stereotypes and shibboleths have become heavily charged with emotion, which, whether justified or unjustified, certainly does not promote clarity of thought. Such words as "freedom," "liberty," and "democracy" make a strong popular appeal, and are readily and often unfairly coupled with such alleged opposites as "discipline," "control," and "authority." Of a somewhat more technical nature, but similarly charged with emotion to the initiated, are such ringing adjectives as "functional," "dynamic," "experimental," "instrumental," and "progressive," and such noble nouns as "activity" and "integration." Not very much skill in dialectic is needed to make these words carry conviction when brought into contrast with such unsavory adjectives as "structural," "static," "traditional," "formal," and "reactionary," or with such unpalatable nouns as "passivity," and "atomism."

Some ten years ago an Australian educator, in reporting a first-hand study of American education, remarked upon the way in which words were used in connection with the curriculum-revision movement, then in full swing. He said in effect that, in our educational discussions, we always contrasted a static curriculum with a fluid, adjustable, dynamic curriculum. We never used an analogous pair of contrasting adjectives: we never spoke of a "stable" curriculum as opposed to an "unstable" curriculum. Thus in the mere choice of words the dice are deliberately "loaded."

The Essentialist, then, labors from the outset under a serious handicap. This was revealed clearly enough in February of 1938, when a very small group adopted the name, "The Essentialist Committee for the Advancement of American Education." This name attracted attention even before the Committee met. It was assumed at once that the group would stand in opposition to the Progressive school of educational theory. When fragments from a set of theses that had been prepared for informal discussion were, without authorization, released to the press and given wide publicity, the Progressive leaders rushed to the defense, although the word "Progressive" appeared in the theses only once and then only in a brief reference to a group of European educators who, in the seventeenth century, adopted that name. The Essentialists' criticisms of the prevailing American theory of education, however, were taken by the present-day Progressives as directed toward them, and in spite of the fact that some of their best-known leaders, particularly Mr. John Dewey and Mr. Boyd H. Bode, were already on record as voicing many of the same criticisms, the Essentialists were assailed as reactionaries and were aligned by Mr. Dewey himself with the religious "Fundamentalists" and the social and economic stand-patters.

Because these denunciations were widely disseminated by the press, the term "Essentialist" achieved, literally overnight, something akin to a vogue on a nation-wide basis—a result quite unexpected and not altogether welcomed by the members of the Essentialist Committee. "Essentialist" proved itself to be a "winged word." Whether the analogy should be with the wings of the eagle or the wings of the vulture depends upon one's point of view, but be that as it may, the quick and widespread response clearly indicated a certain measure of unrest and dissatisfaction upon the part of at least a certain segment of the lay public regarding some of the policies and practices that have increasingly come to characterize American education, particularly on the elementary and secondary levels. Never, in my professional experience covering now more than forty years, has there been anything approaching so general an interest in educational theory as this incident aroused. Mr. Gallup even prepared to submit the controversy to one of his famous polls of public opinion, but, according to reports, gave it up as a hopeless task when two questions acceptable to both sides apparently promised to be equally unintelligible to the ubiquitous man in the street. But the interest still continues. Within the month I have been interviewed by feature writers representing four general magazines of wide circulation. Each of these writers was at the time preparing an article dealing with certain phases of the controversy.

These evidences of public interest in some of the basic problems of educational theory are symptomatic, not of a public concern in educational theory as such, but rather of a public distrust of the practical consequences which seem, to the public, to result when the theories are put into practice. The letters that I have received since last February have come in largest numbers not from teachers and school administrators but from parents who are sincerely concerned regarding what their children are learning or, rather, failing to learn in school. They complain of the lack of thoroughness in what the parents regard as the "fundamentals," of the preoccupation of pupils in school with activities which they (the parents) regard as of trivial importance, of the indisposition to undertake tasks that are not initially appealing, of the general attitude of irresponsibility which seems, in some cases at least, to carry over from the school to the home.

II.

I turn now to the real significance of the position taken by the Essentialists. This position was based primarily upon certain incontestable weaknesses in American education. These weaknesses were traced to the vast upward expansion of the universal school. Until the beginning of the present century, educational opportunities beyond the sixth school year had been in effect selective in the sense that a large proportion of the pupils never even attempted to avail themselves of them. Half the drafted soldiers at the time when we entered the World War had not progressed further than the sixth grade. Most of these men were in school in the first decade of the century. Many of them, of course, had attended school more than six years, but had been retarded one or more years and had left school at the end of the compulsory-schooling period. The work of the upper elementary grades and of the high school could be and was very distinctly limited to, and adapted to, the groups more favored from the point of view of mental ability. It was not adapted to the average mind.

In that same decade beginning in 1900, however, the upward expansion of mass-education gained some momentum. Increasing efforts were made to reduce school failures in the lower grades. The proportion passing from the elementary schools to the high schools was far higher in 1910 than in 1900. This movement was greatly accelerated during the second decade of the century. By 1920, the high school had become essentially non-selective, and another ten years found secondary education almost as nearly universal in many communities as elementary education had been at the turn of the century. By that time, too, the institutions of higher education—particularly the tax supported colleges and universities which admitted high-school graduates without examination-found themselves facing, in their turn, the difficult problem of dealing with an increasingly heterogeneous student-body.

It was this vast upward expansion of mass-education on a scale unprecedented in history and unparalleled elsewhere in the contemporary world that the Essentialists emphasized as the primary causal factor in the relative weakness of American education. It was not that the Essentialists opposed this movement. Even if they had been so disposed, their efforts would have been as foolishly futile as were the legendary efforts of Mrs. Partington to sweep back the sea. The Essentialists recognized that the expansion of the universal school had come about through the operation of fundamental social and economic forces, chief among which, very obviously, had been the marvelous technological developments which had reduced occupational opportunities on the routine levels and which, almost as spectacularly, had created new demands on the stepped-up levels—the levels represented by types of work that cannot be done by the machine, and for which, in many instances, an extensive equipment in both general educational and technical training is a prerequisite.

It is the Essentialist's contention that, because the opening of the upper grades and the high schools to unselected and increasingly heterogeneous groups was inevitable, so a modification of the older standards was inevitable. Rigorous requirements simply had to be relaxed, and they have been progressively relaxed over a period now of more than thirty years. The result is a matter of statistical record. Not only do we have in proportion to our population more persons above the age of fourteen in full-time attendance at school and college than any other country—this would be expected of the world's wealthiest country—but we have gone much further than this. Our high-school and college enrollment probably equals or exceeds in absolute numbers the enrollment in institutions of the same grade in all other countries combined.

The Essentialists are as proud of this record as is any other American educational group, but apparently alone in our profession the Essentialists are not blind to the fact that American education has paid a high price for the achievement, and, in their belief, an unnecessarily high price. They point especially to the fact that, in lowering standards and relaxing rigor, American education has yielded to quite natural temptation. It has, in effect, made low standards and relaxed rigor virtues and has carried these practices much farther than the situation demanded.

In proof of this the Essentialists have adduced some compelling evidence. It is now possible to compare the efficiency of our elementary schools with the elementary schools of other English-speaking countries on the basis of scores made by large unselected groups on achievement tests. The *elementary* schools of all civilized countries are, like ours, non-selective, universal schools, hence such comparisons are justified. Similar comparisons of high schools with the *secondary* schools of other countries are, of course, impossible, since in all other comparable countries secondary education is still highly selective and not universal as with us.

Elementary-school comparisons of this type have been made, in some cases on an extensive scale and with meticulous care. In every instance of which I am informed, the contention that American education has been unnecessarily weakened by the relaxation of standards is emphatically confirmed. Age for age, our elementary-school pupils fall far behind the pupils of other English-speaking countries in their mastery of those elements of knowledge and skill that are generally accepted as the fundamentals of organized education.

It would be very difficult if not impossible to compare American elementary schools with those of non-English-speaking countries on the basis of relative scores on standardized achievement tests. One may venture a guess, however, that if such comparisons could be made with the elementary schools of France, Holland, Switzerland, and the Scandinavian countries, equal or greater differences would be found.

There are other methods of comparing various countries as to the possible relative efficiency of their systems of universal schooling. One must, of course, emphasize the adjective, *possible,* for either definitely to credit favorable social conditions to school efficiency or definitely to charge unfavorable social conditions against school inefficiency would obviously be a foolhardy procedure. One fairly trustworthy available measure is the *per-capita* consumption of "solid" literature as reflected in the statistics of book publication exclusive of fiction. When we make these comparisons on the hypothesis that an educational system plays a significant part in determining such consumption, we find that we are far below practically all other literate countries, and while it is possible that the opportunities provided by our public libraries may account for some part of these differences, it is doubtful whether they will completely straighten out the discrepancies.

Still another possible index of the efficiency of American education is the proportion in which our countrymen have found such world recognition as is represented by Nobel-Prize awards—and particularly the awards in physics, chemistry, and physiology and medicine. In these fields we can boast of a Michelson, a Compton, a Richards, a Urey, and a Carrel—five in all, of whom one, Alexis Carrel, was born and educated in France. This is a distinguished list, but in proportion either to our total population or to the numbers enrolled in our graduate schools our status in relation to other countries is far below what it should be. If we add the three American prize-winners in literature—Sinclair Lewis, Eugene O'Neil, and Pearl Buck—the list is extended in distinction, but our relative status is not perceptibly improved. Only in connection with the peace awards—to Theodore Roosevelt, Woodrow Wilson, Charles G. Dawes, Nicholas Murray Butler, Jane Addams, and Frank B. Kellogg—do we have a representation at all commensurate with our population.

There is another comparison which may or may not be significant. For more than twenty-five years I have repeatedly pointed out that, among all the countries that have embraced the idea of universal elementary education, ours is apparently the only one in which the expansion of the universal school has not been paralleled by decreasing ratios of serious crime. I have not maintained that the schools are responsible for our very high crime-rates, but in a country where this problem and the somewhat analogous problems involved in the world's second-highest divorce rate and in the wide prevalence of political corruption remain unsolved, I have maintained, the proponents and defenders of relaxed standards and the lines of least resistance in education should recognize their serious responsibility and assume the burden of evidence in defense of their policies. I have raised the question whether the educational theories which have increasingly influenced and now dominate American schools are not likely to compound rather than correct these unquestioned weaknesses of our national life. Certain it is that the sections of the country that have been and still are the most law-abiding are also the sections which have so far been least influenced by these now dominant educational theories. I refer particularly to New England and the Middle Atlantic states.

III.

Taking all available evidence into consideration, the contention of the Essentialists that American education is on the whole "appallingly weak and ineffective" seems clearly to be justified. This was the primary contention in the theses discussed by the Essentialist Committee in February of 1938, and this charge was among the fragmentary statements sent out in the unauthorized news reports which brought instant rebuke from the leaders of the Progressive school of educational theory.

An interesting side-light on the present situation in American education is revealed by the character of these rebukes. In so far as they came to my attention they were, with one exception, limited to the type of denunciation represented by Mr. Dewey's charge, already referred to, that the Essentialists were cut from the same cloth as the religious "Fundamentalists" and the economic royalists. They were pictured as reactionaries, incurably wedded to "comfortable old habits" and stupidly defending long outmoded practices. The one instance in which a critic referred to the charge that American education was weak and ineffective used the following defense:

> As for the statement that American children do not show up so well as foreign ones on standardized tests, in so far as it is true, it is a criticism of the traditional methods which are still largely used in this country despite the advance of progressivism.

This statement attributed to one of the best-known Progressive leaders is so widely at variance with the facts that it could have been made only on the spur of the moment and perhaps at the importunity of a newspaper reporter who called late at night over the telephone and aroused the critic only partially from a deep sleep. Anyone at all familiar with the situation knows that the so-called "traditional methods" of teaching have been far more generally abandoned in American schools than anywhere else in the world. A study based upon a nation-wide sampling of actual classroom procedures, made in 1931, reported such informal procedures as the "socialized recitation" and the project method as much more frequently found in the town and city elementary schools than the formal recitation based on a textbook assignment. The former are among the approved Progressive practices, and they are, in a very real sense, indigenous to American schools.

I refer to this criticism because it is a favorite contention of the Progressives that their teachings have affected the actual teaching in American schools only in a slight degree. One would be rash to assert that teachers use Progressive practices exclusively or consistently or efficiently, but it is equally rash to maintain that the Progressive educational theories have not significantly influenced what we may without disrespect call the rank and file of American teachers. Trustworthy studies have shown that a very substantial majority of the leaders in public education throughout the country are very sympathetic toward the Progressive doctrines. For more than twenty-five years, too, these theories have been taught both to prospective teachers-in-training and, in summer sessions and extension classes, to teachers in service. When one remembers that, during a large part of this period, from one-fifth to one-fourth of the total public-school teaching personnel have been enrolled annually in summer-session classes alone, to maintain that public-school practice has not been affected by our dominant educational theory is to imply that the instructors under whom these teachers studied must have been inconceivably incompetent.

Another evidence of the favor with which the Progressive doctrines have been received is found in the fact that practically all of the schools that have been pointed to as models of what good schools should be, the schools that have been most prominently in the professional eye, the schools that have been noted most frequently in the public press, have been dominated by the Progressive theories. Teachers College of Columbia University, for example, operates two schools—Lincoln School and Horace Mann School. The latter has two divisions under separate administrations. Lincoln School was established and endowed for the avowed purpose of demonstrating the Progressive theories and has done so consistently for twenty years. One of the Horace Mann schools is also of the Progressive stripe although not so far toward the left as Lincoln School. The other Horace Mann School—the Horace Mann School for Boys—is frankly and consistently dominated by the Essentialist doctrines. I have no intention of comparing these schools as to their work or its results. They are all, in my judgment, excellent schools of their respective types. What I do wish to emphasize, however, is that the Progressive schools are far more widely known and very much more frequently visited than is the Essentialist school. Indeed it will doubtless come as a surprise to many of my readers that Teachers College actually operates a school that is not dominated by the Progressive theories, just as many persons to whom I am introduced as a member of the Teachers College staff assume as a matter of course that I must see eye to eye with Mr. Dewey and Mr. Kilpatrick.

What I have just said does not concern the validity of the Progressive doctrines nor their desirability as guides to American education. It is simply a refutation of the contention that these doctrines have not influenced the work of the schools, and especially the elementary schools. It is not difficult to understand, indeed, why some of the doctrines have been very eagerly embraced by those responsible for the schools. I have already referred to the relaxation of rigor and the loosening of standards necessitated by the upward expansion of mass-education, which, in its turn, was necessitated by the operation of deep-lying economic forces. It was inevitable that any theory which justified or rationalized the loosening of standards should be received with favor. Generally speaking, the doctrines espoused by the Progressives are admirably adapted to meet this need. In a very real sense, these doctrines served passing well to make a virtue of necessity.

A most interesting illustration of the operation of this factor is furnished by the discrediting of the so-called doctrine of mental discipline. The first serious criticisms of this doctrine came late in the nineteenth century from a group of educational theorists who claimed Herbart as their patron saint. The Herbartians were the Progressives of their day. Indeed, the present Progressive school of educational theory stems in part from the disciples of Herbart.

The Herbartian protest against formal discipline, however, had little effect at the time. The upward expansion of mass-education was still in the future. The high school was still essentially a selective institution. By the turn of the century, however, this movement was well started, and just at the turn of the century the first substantial experiments on the transfer of training were reported. While neither the early "transfer experiments" nor those that followed were in any sense a product of the Progressive school of educational theory, the interpretation given to the findings as overthrowing the doctrine of mental discipline has been quite in line with the Progressive teachings. The fact which I wish to emphasize, however, is that the doctrine of formal discipline stood squarely in the way of the movement that was opening the high schools to the masses. Consequently anything that would tend to discredit this doctrine was seized upon with avidity.

In the same way and for the same reason, the principal Progressive theories have found a sympathetic hearing, especially during the past twenty-five years. The doctrine of formal discipline was not the only obstacle that handicapped the upward expansion of the universal school. Any formal requirement in any school will turn away some pupils or students if they are free to enter or leave. A typical Progressive tenet had an early expression in Charles W. Eliot's advocacy of the elective system in the colleges.

The elective system soon found a place in the larger high schools, and with the development of the high schools as non-selective institutions of mass-education, prescriptions and requirements have been reduced almost to the vanishing point.

Other tenets of the Progressive school of educational theory have fitted in passing well with the need of relaxing rigor and reducing standards if the universal school was to be expanded upward. The limitations of space preclude me from doing more than merely list a few of the more significant.

There is, for example, a general denial—sometimes implicit, often explicit—of any virtue in the systematic and sequential mastery of subject-matter as such. In other words, the organization of learning materials on the basis of what may be called their internal relationships—logical, chronological, spatial, causal—has been questioned, in some cases to the point of discredit. All learnings should come as instruments in the solution of immediate problems or the realization of immediate purposes. In effect, this excludes the recognition of any educational values except those now called "functional" or "instrumental" but which were long referred to in educational discussions as "utilitarian."

A very clear tendency in recent years has been still further to extend this limitation, and to view with suspicion any learnings that are not initiated by the learner himself. Imposed assignments, even if presented in the form of problems, are frowned upon. Some Progressive leaders believe that learnings planned in advance by the teacher are in the nature of an injustice to the learner. One of my students who was employed as a teacher in an extreme left-wing school was so thoughtless as to ask the principal for a copy of the course of study. She was promptly rebuked by the principal's question, "How can you tell in advance where the mind of the child will lead you?"

However infrequent such extreme practice may be, the undeniable effect of the Progressive teachings is to belittle the significance of organized knowledge, to subordinate the tested lessons of race-experience to the unpredictable learning-outcomes of personal and incidental experience, and, despite the lip-service given by the Progressives to social values, to exalt and even enthrone individual interests and desires above social needs.

It is well known, of course, that some of the Progressive leaders have spoken in no uncertain terms against the extremes to which some of the Progressive tenets have been carried. More than ten years ago, Mr. Dewey sent out the following warning to his followers:

> There is a tendency in so-called advanced schools of educational thought . . .
> to say, in effect, let us surround pupils with certain materials, tools, appli-

ances, etc., and then let pupils respond to these things according to their own desires. Above all let us not suggest any end or plan to the students; let us not suggest to them what they shall do, for that is an unwarranted trespass upon their sacred intellectual individuality since the essence of such individuality is to set up ends and aims. Now such a method is really stupid. For it attempts the impossible, which is always stupid; and it misconceives the conditions of independent thinking...

In his recent book, *Experience and Education,* Mr. Dewey carries his criticisms still further. Mr. Bode in his *Progressive Education at the Crossroads* speaks forcefully against the Progressives' rejection of systematic and sequential learning. And numerous sympathizers with many of the Progressive tenets have expressed regret that the Progressive group has what some of them frankly call a "lunatic fringe."

While these evidences of dissatisfaction are reassuring, I am not convinced that they solve the problem. Twenty-five years ago, in a review of Mr. Dewey's *Schools of Tomorrow,* I called attention to the discrediting of race-experience and the enthronement of individualism as inherent in the theory. By this I meant that a carrying-out of the theory to its logical conclusions would result precisely in just what has eventuated.

IV.

If this paper has been critical rather than constructive, it should not be inferred that the Essentialists are entirely negative in their attitude toward present tendencies in American education. In a paper published last spring I set forth "An Essentialist's Platform for the Advancement of American Education." My colleague, Mr. I. L. Kandel, will shortly publish from the Essentialist point of view a book entitled *Conflicting Theories of Education.* Mr. Frederick S. Breed also published early in January a thoroughgoing analysis of educational theory from the same point of view.

What I wish to say here is that no reasonable program for American education could omit many of the policies and practices that the Progressives have emphasized. The Essentialist certainly would indorse the functional approach to the problems of teaching and learning; the effort always to build the lessons of race-experience upon the individual, first-hand experience of the learner; the condemnation always of stupid, parrot-like learning; the importance in the earlier school years especially of the procedures that are reflected in such concepts as the project method and the activity program; and the efforts to make school life a happy as well as a profitable series of learning experiences.

On the other hand, the Essentialists would hold that out of the experience of the race have come certain lessons so important to social welfare and social progress that it would be the height of folly to leave their mastery to the whim or caprice of either teacher or learner. They would hold that "the freedom of the immature to choose what they shall learn is of small consequence compared with their later freedom from the want, fear, fraud, superstition, and error which may fetter the ignorant as cruelly as the chains of the slave-driver—and the price of this freedom is systematic and sustained effort often devoted to the mastery of materials the significance of which must at the time be taken on faith."

The Essentialists, while recognizing the relaxation of rigor as necessary to the upward expansion of mass-education, would protest against the implication that such relaxation itself spells progress. They would protest especially against the present tendency to discredit the studies that are inherently exact and exacting, that demand concentrated and sustained effort. It is one thing to say that large numbers of persons lack the mental ability essential to the mastery of such subjects. It is quite another to discourage really competent learners from attempting such mastery. This is being done, if not always intentionally, certainly in effect. May I quote a brief statement from the "Platform" just referred to:

> While the exact and exacting studies were in effect being discredited, the primrose path of least resistance was opened ever wider in the field known as the social studies. The argument here is plausible and appealing. "Education for citizenship" is a ringing slogan with limitless potentialities, especially in an age when high-sounding shibboleths, easily formulated, can masquerade as fundamental premises and postulates wrought through the agony of hard thinking.

> Obviously no fundamental premise in educational thinking could fail to recognize the importance of a firm foundation in the history of human institutions, or of an acquaintance with present and pressing social problems especially in the light of their genesis, or of an acquaintance with such principles of economics, sociology, and political science as have been well established.

> But just as obviously the social sciences, so called, are not in the same class with the natural sciences. Their generalizations permit trustworthy predictions only in a few cases and then only in a slight degree. When the human element enters, uncertainty enters—else the world could have anticipated and adjusted itself to Hitler and Mussolini and Stalin and the military oligarchy of Japan and would not be standing dazed and impotent as it stands today. And while to expect an educational pabulum of social studies in the lower schools essentially to overcome this inherent limitation of the social

sciences is an alluring prospect, it is to expect nothing less than a miracle. It is, indeed, just as sensible as would be a brave and desperate effort to incite immature minds to square the circle.

V.

It is in this connection, and in conclusion, that I would make a brief reference to the Essentialists' attitude toward the field of teaching represented by the classicists.

Foreign languages, and particularly the ancient languages, have long been under fire. They represent the kind of learning that requires concentrated and sustained effort. Skilful teaching can do much to enliven this process, but even the best teaching cannot be a substitute for the learner's determined and dogged effort.

There is a widely accepted tenet, strongly emphasized by the Progressives, that there are few learnings which cannot safely await the motivating force of a "vital" need on the part of the learner. Foreign languages have been disposed of by certain educational theorists in this nonchalant way. As one writer expressed it, "These are only tools, and when one needs a tool one goes to the shop and gets it."

I should like to record an emphatic condemnation of this type of educational advice. I have been, in a very real sense, a victim of it. Although my undergraduate college work was begun nearly fifty years ago, it included only a negligible amount of work in only one of the foreign languages. A few years afterward, when I began my graduate work, it was necessary for me to read French and German. As I tell my own graduate students, we did not in those ancient times have examinations in these languages in order to matriculate for the doctorate. We did not have examinations because such elementary literacy was taken for granted; and we were given assignments in French and German scientific literature as a matter of course. I indeed had a really vital need for these important tools at that time, and willy-nilly I "went to the shop to get them." If anyone tells me that this is a way to come into possession of these tools that is easier and better than organized, systematic instruction by a good teacher in advance of a vital need I should like to tell him from my own bitter experience that he is talking nonsense.

Now, of course and quite fortunately, only a minute fraction of high-school pupils will go on for the doctor's degree, yet I should wish to encourage any person who can possibly do so to undertake a mastery of at least one foreign language. I believe that this advice can be defended from many points of view—of not the least significance in the present stage of educational development is the fact that about the only way for an American pupil to get some instruction in the rudiments of English grammar is at the hands of a teacher of a foreign language. The National Council of Teachers of English has officially relegated English grammar to the senior high school and there to be an elective subject open only to those who "take to it kindly."

As for Latin I should be even more emphatic in my advice that no competent student be discouraged from undertaking its study. Especially unfortunate, I believe, is the disposition of many educational theorists not only to belittle the significance of Latin, but even to suggest that its value is less than zero—a negative quantity —and that, except for a very few who are to become highly specialized scholars, time spent in the study of Latin is time wasted.

Pertinent here are the results of an interesting investigation reported in 1931. In connection with the problem of selecting students for admission to teachers colleges, Mr. H. L. Kriner attempted to find whether there was anything in the high-school record of an applicant for admission to a professional school for teachers that would indicate whether such an applicant would be likely to become a good teacher. He arranged with the superintendents of certain school systems in Pennsylvania to list for him the best teachers and the poorest teachers serving in their schools. He took only about ten per cent of the teachers who represented the two extremes of high efficiency and low efficiency. Then he went back to the records that these teachers had made as high-school pupils. Without going further into the details of the study, he found some very interesting facts which may be summarized as follows:

1. The best single index of a prospective teacher's chances of success in teaching, either in the elementary school or in the high school, is whether he or she has successfully completed in high school more than two years of Latin.
2. The second best index is whether he or she has completed in high school more than two years of mathematics.
3. The third best index is whether he or she has completed in high school more than two years in the natural sciences.
4. If the prospective teacher has taken in high school more than two years of the social studies, he or she is a poor risk.

Whether the exact and exacting studies select the pupils who are the more competent and hence the more likely to succeed in anything that they undertake, or whether the exact and exacting studies have after all somewhat of a disciplinary influence for those who succeed in them is not disclosed by Mr. Kriner's study, but it seems fairly clear that the pursuit of such subjects is not altogether disastrous. And I may say in passing that the question of mental discipline is by no means a closed question, as most students are led to believe in their classes in educational theory. The preponderance of evidence from more than one hundred published experiments on the transfer of training, far from justifying the sweeping negation of the possibilities of mental discipline, actually justifies the hypothesis that, under certain conditions, disciplinary values can be realized. It would be most unfortunate to assume that this end is easy to achieve or that it can be achieved in any appreciable degree with learners of limited mentality. It would be equally unfortunate to adopt the policy clearly sanctioned by contemporary educational theory which, in condemning out of hand the studies that are exact and exacting, opens wide the lines of least resistance and actually works an injustice to a certain proportion of competent but immature pupils and students.

My own objection to Progressivism is that, in spite of many salutary virtues, it is at basis a weak theory. It lacks virility not in the sense that it is feminine but rather in the sense that it is effeminate. It is my contention that its virtues and its worthy contributions to educational progress can be preserved without committing American education to its weaknesses and its shortcomings, especially at a stage of social evolution when education among the few remaining democratic nations needs most emphatically to be fused through and through with a virile and dynamic idealism.

37

Selection from Progressive Education at the Crossroads

Boyd H. Bode, 1938

Boyd H. Bode (1873–1953) spent most of his academic career at Ohio State University, where he served as a philosophy of education professor and head of the university's department of education for more than twenty years. Prior to arriving at Ohio State in 1921, Bode completed his PhD degree in philosophy at Cornell University in 1900. Between 1900 and 1921, he served as professor of philosophy at the University of Wisconsin and the University of Illinois. At Illinois, Bode was attracted to the field of education by his former Ph.D. classmate at Cornell, William Bagley. Bode gradually dedicated more and more time to writing in the field of educational philosophy and less time to the field of philosophy itself. He had a tendency to reject fads and fashions in the Progressive education movement and instead take a middle position on controversial issues. For example, he appreciated the point that teachers should attend to the needs and interests of students, but he also recognized that this view was often overemphasized, leaving subject-matter and the organized disciplines behind as part of a school's curriculum. Bode also argued consistently that educational philosophy must take into account social ideals, not just the developmental stages of children. Bode argued this position during the heyday of child-centered Progressivism, when making the case for any kind of social ideal was unpopular. When the 1930s rolled around and a social vision for schooling became popular, Bode once again criticized an extreme position. This time, however, he argued against the kind of social planning that he worried would overwhelm individual rights. This kind of balanced, pragmatic approach is evident in this selection from *Progressive Education at the Crossroads*. As Bode's most well-known book, *Crossroads* was his attempt to help Progressive education find its way back to influence during a time of intense criticism. He argues that Progressives should avoid extremes while at the same time placing their faith in the everyday abilities of the common man to solve society's problems. —JWN

Progressive Education and Democracy

The strongest and most evangelistic movement in American education at the present time is the movement known as progressive education. A visitor to our schools ordinarily has no difficulty in recognizing a so-called progressive school. He can usually tell the difference the moment he opens the door. The progressive school cultivates an atmosphere of activity and freedom which is all its own. In academic language, the progressive school is a place where children go, not primarily to learn, but to carry on a way of life.

The Progressives' Paradox

In spite of this distinctiveness, however, our visitor, if he is a reflective person, is likely to have peculiar difficulty in defining a progressive school. Any trait or aspect which he may select as a distinguishing characteristic presently turns out to have significant limitations. In other words, we seem to encounter a variety of contradictions when we try to state the qualities of such a school.

It emphasizes freedom, yet it also attaches major importance to guidance and direction. It plays up method, but it is also critical of the content of the more conventional curriculum. It places the individual at the center of the stage; yet it perpetually criticizes the competitive character of the present social order, which indicates that it rejects the philosophy of individualism. It insists that intelligence must be permitted to operate freely; yet it seldom alarms its constituents, who, in the case of private schools, are generally the more prosperous element in society. It commonly regards the college as the citadel of its enemy; yet its chief business is often preparation for college. It holds that learning takes place through doing; yet physical activity tapers off sharply as we go up the educational scale. To the earnest observer all this is very confusing.

These real or apparent contradictions naturally invite the conclusion that the progressive movement draws its chief inspiration from a certain sentimentality about children. This sentimentality, so it appears, leads to a lot of unedifying fussiness, which is camouflaged as "respect for personality," but is not intended to be really subversive. There is no intention of changing the established values of society beyond the point of spreading more sweetness and light. With respect to these values the teachers in our progressive schools are frequently as conventional as the buttons on the sleeve of a man's coat.

A New Organizing Principle

Such a conclusion, however, would be a bit too simple. The continuing vitality of the progressive movement is evidence that it is based on something of larger significance. The emphasis of progressive education on the individual, on the sinfulness of "imposition," and on the necessity of securing free play for intelligence, whether rightly or wrongly applied, is a reflection of the growing demand, outside of the school, for recognition of the common man. Similarly, the confusion in progressive education is a reflection of the confusion in the outside world resulting from this demand.

We are gradually discovering that the admission of the common man to the status of full recognition means more than an extension of privilege. It is not on a par, for example, with opening the door of an art gallery to all comers, instead of merely to the chosen few. In its application to industry this recognition obviously means an extensive revision of our conception of property rights and of the function of government. As applied to organized religion it means a shift of emphasis from eternal salvation to progress through social control. In relation to the values of scholarship and esthetic appreciation it means a transformation of these values so that they will not remain a detached occupation for a leisure class and for specialists, but will become incorporated in the affairs of everyday experience. In brief, the recognition of the common man—which is what we call democracy—introduces a point of view which is so far-reaching in its implications as to make democracy a distinctive and competing way of life.

Unless progressive education is content to be simply a method which is available to any teacher and for any purpose, it had better play out its string and become an exponent of that specific way of life for which the name "democracy" is perhaps as good as any. The refusal to take this step would leave progressive education with no guiding principle except random interests and hypothetical needs, and so would justify most of the hard things that have been said about it by its critics. On the other hand, taking this step means that the question of reorganizing or reinterpreting the established values and institutions of our civilization must receive major attention. These values took their character and form in large part at a time when the common man had not yet secured a prominent place in the picture. As was intimated a moment ago, there is considerable ground for the suspicion that our concern for the common man will evaporate into idle words and sentiments, unless we gain some perception of what is required to give the common man his proper share in our social and cultural heritage. To leave our conception of this heritage unchanged means that in our attempts to "socialize" the school population we are really practicing "imposition" on the sly.

In a word, the rise of the common man is the disturbing factor, both on the social and on the educational level. As long as he remained submerged, the situation was comparatively simple. It was commonly taken for granted that the higher cultural values were not for him. It was even supposed that he was too earth-earthy to appreciate them. This supposition was refuted as he gained wider opportunities, but it also appears that his scale of values is somewhat different from that of the aristocratic class by which he was ruled so long in the past. The difference is making itself felt in certain areas, such as industrial relations and organized religion, although it is not any too clear as yet just what kind of reorganization in ideals and practice is required in these areas by the application of the principle of democracy. What reorganization the principle of democracy calls for in the field of education is perhaps even more obscure. This problem must be faced, however, if we are to arrive at a significant and defensible conception of the meaning of the progressive movement in education...

The Choice Required

Progressive education is confronted with the choice of becoming the avowed exponent of democracy or else of becoming a set of ingenious devices for tempering the wind to the shorn lamb. If democracy is to have a deep and inclusive human meaning, it must have also a distinctive educational system.

Since the whole weight of tradition is on the side of absolutes, which are abstractions that serve to maintain an aristocratic form of society, such a system must have direct and constant reference to the conflict between the aristocratic and the democratic ways of life. It must have a psychology based on the conception of knowledge and truth as functions in the control of experience—the kind of psychology which is pointed toward in what is sometimes called "organismic" psychology. It must have a theory of values which has as its center the continuous improvement of human living through voluntary reciprocity or the constant widening of common interests and common concerns. Lastly, it must undertake to point out how the acceptance of such a standard for growth and progress requires continuous and frequently extensive reconstruction or revision of traditional beliefs and attitudes, in accordance with growing insight and changing circumstances. In a word, progressive education must become clearly conscious of the implications contained in its basic attitude and to use these implications as a vantage point from which to reorganize its thinking and procedures.

38

Prejudice the Garden Toward Roses?

Isaac Kandel, 1939

Isaac L. Kandel (1881–1965), often referred to as the father of comparative education in America, spent most of his career as a professor of education at Teachers College, Columbia University. Kandel's title as the father of comparative education is indeed appropriate, but it also obscures the many other contributions that he made to American education. Kandel was born in Romania, but he grew up in Manchester, England, after his parents emigrated there when Kandel was a young child. After completing his early education at Manchester Grammar School, Kandel entered the University of Manchester in 1899 where he studied Classics. After completing his undergraduate degree in 1903, Kandel then earned an M.A. degree in Education, also at Manchester, in 1906. Following three years of teaching in England and Ireland, Kandel made a major decision to leave Europe and travel to the U.S. to complete a Ph.D. in Education at Teachers College. Kandel

American Educational Thought: Essays from 1640–1940, pages 587–596
Copyright © 2010 by Information Age Publishing

enjoyed New York City so much that he decided to live the reminder of his life in the city.

After the completion of his Ph.D. degree in 1908, Kandel worked as a writer of encyclopedia entries and as an assistant to Paul Monroe, a Teachers College professor. Monroe served as Kandel's dissertation advisor and was a major supporter of Kandel's work. Monroe played a significant role in helping Kandel to earn a position as a professor of education at Teachers College beginning in 1921. In accepting this position, Kandel became the first Jew to hold a professorship at Teachers College. During the next twenty-five years, Kandel produced an incredible amount of scholarship, totaling more than fifty books and several hundred articles.

The book that established Kandel as the founder of comparative education is his book entitled, appropriately enough, *Comparative Education,* which appeared in 1933. *Comparative Education* is a massive 920-page behemoth that provides an exhaustive survey of education in England, France, Germany, Italy, Russia, and the United States. In addition to his work in comparative education, Kandel became well known for his publications on the history and philosophy of education. The 1920s and 1930s saw Kandel become an increasingly vocal and insightful critic of Progressive education. In numerous books and articles, he argued that Progressives had abandoned subject-matter, rejected the importance of social goals, dealt an irreversible blow to moral education, worshipped at the altar of individual whims and desires, and, in a shocking reversal during the 1930s, had begun to advocate collectivism. In his unforgettably titled "Prejudice the Garden Toward Roses?," Kandel makes the case for a structured curriculum that shapes students toward desired character traits, as opposed to an unmanaged approach that leaves the "garden" to do whatever it wishes. —JWN

The conflict between the traditionalists or, as they have recently begun to be described, the essentialists, and the progressives in education is more than the batrachomyomachia which it appears to be to laymen and to a large part of the profession of teachers. It is a conflict between idealism in one form or another and pragmatism, between classicism and romanticism, between those who believe that the experience of the race has something to contribute to the enlightenment of the individual in the modern world and those who stress the primacy of immediate experiencing by the individual in and through the environment in which he lives. It is, therefore, a conflict which is more fundamental than the question whether instruction shall center round "subjects" or grow out of the "needs" of the pupil. Both the essentialists and the progressives believe in the principle of education as "growth," but the former hold that growth must have a definite direction whereas the latter advocate growth with nothing fixed in advance, or as an "on-going process" without direction; the latter concentrate their attention on change and constant reconstruction of values, while the former believe in the existence of certain eternal and permanent values which have grown out of the experience of the race. Frederick J. E. Woodbridge well summarized the nature of the conflict when he wrote "For that complex of human performances which we call civilization turns out, as we examine it closely, to be a changing and shifting scene which has nonetheless a definable background. To discover that background, and to exhibit the varied lights and shadows as thrown up from it, is a proper task for philosophy." It may be added that this is a task for education also. The progressives stress the changing and shifting scene, the pre-cariousness of life and the unpredictable future; "the votaries of progress," as Dean Inge has pointed out, "mistake the flowing tide for the river of eternity." The essentialists start with a definable background, not because they wish to be conservative or, as the progressives charge, static, but because they believe, as Mr. Woodbridge puts it, that "the background is thus the important factor, at once conservative and propelling."

It is on the whole because of the failure to trace back to their origins the philosophical bases of the conflict between essentialists and progressives that education in the United States has reached its present state of chaos and uncertainty. The essentialists, relying on the persistence of their point of view through the ages and remembering that much that is claimed by the progressives is not new, have failed until recently to put forward a philosophical defense of their position, whereas the progressives, with the fervor of evangelists, have rallied round the new movement which, as John Dewey has recently warned, "takes its clew in practice from that which is rejected instead of from the constructive development of its own philosophy." And this has been easier in a cultural atmosphere whose chief tradition is to have no traditions and whose predominant interest is in change. It has been rejection of the past and desire for novelty rather than a clear-cut philosophy that have attracted adherents; *omne ignotum pro magnifico*. A certain sentimentality about the child, emphasis on respect for personality, and stress on activity are other factors that have appealed to the American mind. There has in addition been an active campaign which has presented a distorted picture of the traditional school to the public.

What is the picture of the traditional school which the progressive educators portray in such a way as to play upon the slenderest feeling of parents—their desire to give their children the best possible start in life? The child, they say, goes to the traditional school unwillingly and is kept there under control discipline until the close of the day, when he has a chance to explode into freedom. School equipment, with its long orderly rows of desks, is designed for maintenance of discipline and for the enforcement of obedience to authority. The classroom is arranged essentially for listening, for passivity rather than for movement and activity. Education is regarded as a preparation for adult life with deferred values to be appreciated and understood later and, therefore, with little or no meaning for the child in his immediate present. The child is to be shaped and molded to conform to a fixed pattern. Therefore the emphasis in the curriculum is not upon the child's immediate needs and interests but upon the social heritage, built up under an authoritarian concept of society, shaped by adult needs and logically arranged into a patchwork of compartmentalized subjects. The methods of instruction stress drill and study which mean memorization of formal material from books to be repeated or recited to the teacher. Such learning is not an active process but merely the uncritical accumulation of facts and information. In the social and moral fields the emphasis is upon accepted doctrines and upon authority as sacred and beyond question. Most of the work of the school is intellectual and displays an almost total disregard of the emotions. Individual differences are disregarded and promotion is determined by a standardized lockstep. Finally, the traditional school concentrates attention upon the past and ignores the contemporary life of and around the child.

If anyone is disposed to question this statement of the way in which progressive education has built itself up he is reminded of the "March of Time" film shown a little over a year ago. In this film the traditional school was represented exactly as described above; the teacher with cane in hand was calculated to strike terror into the hearts of his pupils who, as they entered the classroom to face a blackboard covered with arithmetic tables and spelling lists, abandoned all their happiness and joy outside. In the modern progressive school which was shown in contrast the pupils were happy, active, moving about and "doing things." Observers who watched closely noticed that the traditional school was of the vintage of about 50 years ago; whereas the progressive school was one of the most modern experimental schools.

This in essence has been the strategy of the protagonists of progressive education. They take a school which has all but disappeared, call it traditional and compare it with the best of the progressive type. Rarely is any mention made of the fact that the traditional school has itself been undergoing a process of transformation, that the number of children who go unwillingly to school has almost completely disappeared, that curricula and courses have been revised in order that the formal, useless and meaningless may be eliminated and that what is significant for understanding the world of the present should receive its due emphasis. Rarely, if ever, is the essentialist given any credit for building his educational theory and practice on a philosophy which is perfectly valid and acceptable or for having values which he believes to be as important for the welfare of society as for the education of the child for that society. To the impression which progressive educators have sought to convey—that the essentialist is simply seeking to carry on the school as he has inherited it from the past, without any adjustment to changing needs—they have more recently begun to add the argument that the traditionalist in education is by the same token reactionary in political and social affairs. By implication, therefore, progressives are radicals who advocate their educational theories and practices to reconstruct society and to change the social order.

The criticisms of the traditional school are thus manufactured out of whole cloth to make the flesh of parents creep. And as if these criticisms are not enough, some progressives have woven into their arguments a little of the jargon drawn from psychoanalysis. What parent will want, if he has a choice, to send his child to a school in which he will be unhappy and thwarted at every turn—with the added dangers of acquiring inhibitions, complexes and repressions and developing a dual personality? The parents will accept at its face value the implication that nothing happens to a child in the way of learning and education unless he is active, moving about, criticizing, discussing, solving problems and expressing himself.

Progressive education, however, has not always been concerned with social change. It started out 30 years ago with the theory that school and society must be brought more closely together, that the curriculum should be made more meaningful and significant to the learner and that the child or the learner with his needs and interests should be made the starting-point of a process through which his experience would be constantly reconstructed. Education must no longer be a preparation for life; education is life, arising out of the experiences and needs of the child and promoting his growth. Rejecting what was criticized as excessive emphasis on formal subject matter the progressives began to worship at the altar of the child. Children should be allowed to grow in accordance with their needs and interests; nothing must be interposed between them and their own direct and immediate experiences; knowledge is valuable only as it is acquired in a real situation; the teacher must be present to provide the proper environment for experiencing but must not intervene except to guide and advise. There must, in fact, be "nothing-fixed-in-advance" and subjects must not be "set-out-to-be-learned," for such a practice is imposition of external experience and authority and, therefore, opposed to free and natural development. Thus the purpose of the new movement was for very many years defined by the Progressive Education Association in the following terms: "(1) The pupils shall be allowed freedom to develop naturally; (2) interest of the child shall be the motive of all work; and (3) the teacher shall be considered a guide and not a taskmaster." No reference was ever made to the curriculum or its content. Nor is there, in the latest resolutions of the Association, any suggestion of what the curriculum should be except that it must be directed to the reconstruction of culture and the promotion of a new social order: "In order to establish integration again in our culture and to utilize our recent gains over the physical world, our next great period of progress must be in the direction of creating new institutional controls designed by the people for their common welfare." This task is to be begun in the school by "providing for pupils a selected and stimulating environment out of which may emerge purposes which will lead children and youth through relevant experiences to the understanding of the possibilities for human betterment in modern techniques providing we can design democratic institutions suited to the new conditions." There has thus been a shift in emphasis from the child with his needs and interests and education for growth with nothing-fixed-in-advance, to a speculative study of a vague form of social order which has not yet emerged.

The essentialist rejects the progressive theory of growth with nothing-fixed-in-advance, a planless education based upon the unselected experiences and needs of the child or even selected by cooperative, shared discussions of pupils and teachers. Growth cannot be self-directed; it needs direction through a carefully chosen environment to an end or ends in the minds of those who have been entrusted by society with the child's education. The problem is not new; it was first posed in modern times by Rousseau and has been the subject of controversy ever since. It was answered for all time by Coleridge nearly 100 years ago in the following story:

> Thelwall thought it very unfair to influence a child's mind by inculcating any opinions before it should have come to years of discretion, and be able to choose for itself. I showed him my garden, and told him it was my botanical garden. "How so?" said he, "it is covered with weeds."—"Oh," I replied, *"that* is only because it has not yet come to its age of discretion and choice. The weeds, you see, have taken the liberty to grow, and I thought it unfair in me to prejudice the soil towards roses and strawberries."

What has been said of growth applies equally to the theory of building an education on the needs and experiences of the child. Such needs and experiences must be guided by and selected in the light of ends and purposes. And yet attempts have been made and are still being made to follow the needs and experiences of the child without a plan and with as little interference as possible from the teacher. Nothing must be done, according to this view, to determine the future thought and conduct of the child. The child is to grow in response to his own needs and through solving his own problems as they emerge out of his own experience. Despite this theory progressive schools do become conventionalized and adopt certain patterns—all students are exposed to one pattern of social studies, all build ships one year and the next turn out ashtrays and book-ends, all alike, and so on. The product, it is claimed, is unimportant; it *is* important that free rein be given the creative urge and self-expression—before there is anything to express or create. And this is carried over into the moral field; for since there are, for the progressive, no eternal verities or permanent values, and it is immoral for adults to impose their standards of morality on the child, the child must discover standards of conduct for himself, and what works is true.

The full weight of the progressive attack is against subject matter and the planned organization of a curriculum in terms of subjects. There are three reasons for this attack: First, the theory that the work of the school must grow out of the interests and experiences of the child; second, the objection that a subject-matter organization is in terms of facts, information and knowledge to be acquired and not in terms of problems, situations and activities in and out of which the need for knowledge arises; and third, the criticism that such subject matter is acquired through books and that education therefore becomes formal, verbal, and bookish. The child must be left to find out things for himself in order to solve a problem or meet a situation, but nothing is said as to how problems are recognizable without knowledge. What the traditionalist calls the essentials can, it is maintained by the progressive, be acquired incidentally without the waste of effort and formal drill. The teacher is not entirely discarded; he is part of the environment to guide and to give help when called upon, but he must have no long-range plan based on his greater and richer background of experience, because he cannot anticipate the situations and problems that will confront the child. Creative activity leading to more activity is the goal to be attained, but this goal is at best vague and places the emphasis on method at the expense of content. One is reminded of the conversation between the cat and Alice. "'Then it doesn't matter which way you *go*,' said the cat.—'So long as I get somewhere,' Alice added as an explanation."

It is that "somewhere" that is the crux of the present problem, for if the course is to be planless and improvised according to the immediate needs and urges of the child the result will be a patchwork as meaningless as a Surrealist or Dadaistic painting, which is also the product of nothing-fixed-in-advance except an inner urge to express oneself. But the progres-

594 ■ *American Educational Thought: Essays from 1640–1940*

sives are not really as black as they would like to paint themselves. They hold up the child-centered school as the ideal, but on close investigation it is found that the child-centered school is a teacher-centered school, that when the teacher who has been successful in turning out poets leaves the school the Pierian springs dry up. In actual practice the teacher who is acclaimed for creating situations in which pupils produce poetry, music and art is the teacher who is inspired by a rich command of her subjects and who makes the pupils over into a pattern already "fixed-in-advance" in her mind. There is no spontaneous germination of poetry, music, art, or of anything else in the child-centered school, and the successful teacher does more than stand by and suggest.

The ranks of progressive educators are today splitting into a number of groups. There are those who, still stressing the child, would bring the community into the school in order to provide for growth through real experiences, to develop critical attitudes and to lay the basis for social reconstruction. This group, in general—usually concerned with young children whose experiences are still wholes and not yet organized—would extend its theory upwards through the grades and into the high school. A second group is opposed to a curriculum fixed-in-advance and seeks to build up an education on the immediate experiences of the pupils and the problems arising therefrom. Both groups are opposed to subjects as such.

The danger of chaos which threatens education from both points of view has recently been pointed out by leaders of what may become a third group. B. H. Bode in his *Progressive Education at the Crossroads* has attacked the theory of education based on the unselected needs and interests of the child and of growth without a sense of direction, and the theory that the school must "teach the child, not the subject." "To raise a hue and cry against subjects," writes Mr. Bode, "is to pour out the baby with the bath. The traditional subjects stood for an educational value, which we neglect at our peril." And again, "if we may assume that the purpose of teaching is to liberate the intelligence of the pupil, it appears that we must go into 'logical organization' and beyond it. The pupil must acquire some capacity for thinking as the specialist thinks; and, in addition, he must see the bearing of the subject on the question of absolute standards." At almost the same time Mr. Dewey sounded the same note of warning in his latest book, *Experience and Education*, and as the following quotations indicate urges a return to subject matter:

> But finding the material of learning within experience is only the first step. The next step is the progressive development of what is already experienced into a fuller and richer and also more organized form, a form

that gradually approximates that in which subject matter is presented to the skilled, mature person ... That up to the present the weakest point in progressive schools is the matter of selection and organization of intellectual subject matter is, I think, inevitable under the circumstances. ... The educator cannot start with knowledge already organized and proceed to ladle it out in doses. But as an ideal the active process of organizing facts and ideas is an ever-present educational process.

Thus the serious misgivings of the essentialists are being allayed and a bridge is being prepared for a reconciliation between the essentialist and progressive points of view. Certain doctrinal differences will continue to exist. The progressive will, no doubt, continue to stress the early experiences of the child; the essentialist will from the start select those experiences in consonance with a planned organization of education as a whole. The progressive is likely to emphasize the immediate and draw on the past only for illustrative purposes; the essentialist will seek to avoid a disorderly and discontinuous fumbling with needs, activities and experiences, and by inducting the pupil into what Charles A. Beard has described as "the treasures heavy with the thought and sacrifices of the centuries" and "a heritage of knowledge and heroic examples—accepted values stamped with the seal of permanence" he will endeavor to produce men and women possessing the understanding that comes through knowledge, men and women critical because they possess a mastery of facts and an ability to think objectively and free because they have disciplined themselves for a life of duty and responsibility.

The essentialist starts with the premise that the school is an institution created to achieve some definite purpose. He agrees with the general progressive formula that education is life, but believes that formal education must confront the pupil with a certain body of experiences selected from what is called life. He is no less interested than the progressive in the principle that learning cannot be successful unless it is based on the capacities, interests and purpose of the learner, but he believes those interests and purposes must be made over by the skill of a teacher who is master of that "logical organization" called subjects and who understands the processes of educational development. The essentialist no longer believes that that development is wholly intellectual: he recognizes that education must not be directed to the mind alone but to the whole human being, if this is to grow into a well-rounded personality. He welcomes the call of the progressive leaders for subjects and subject matter, for he has felt that when the lid was taken off the universe the bottom began to fall out of education. He is willing to learn and has learned much from progressive theory on methods of instruction; he believes, indeed, that the chief contribution of what is called the pragmatic philosophy has been to methodology. Finally, he is still concerned about the future of American education because adequate attention has not been given to the proper selection and professional preparation of teachers. Until this is done and until there is a shift of emphasis from both subject matter and the child to the teacher he has no reason to expect success from any theory of education. For ultimately it is the teacher with a broad liberal education, mastery of a special field, understanding of the process of learning and a strong conviction on the contribution that education can make to social welfare and progress who is the key to the situation.

Sources

Addams, J. (1908). The public school and the immigrant child. *National Education Association Journal of Proceedings and Addresses*, 47th annual meeting, 99–102.

Addams, J. (1930). *The second twenty years at Hull-House.* New York: Macmillan, chapter 12.

Bagley, W. C. (1938). An essentialist's platform for the advancement of American education. *Educational Administration and Supervision, 24,* 241–256.

Bagley, W. C. (1938). The significance of the essentialist movement in educational theory. *Classical Journal, 34,* 326–344.

Bangs, N., Bond, T. E., & Peck, G. (1840-41). Memorial of a committee of the Methodist Episcopal Church. *Documents of the board of Aldermen, of the City of New York, VII* (40), 480–485.

Beecher, C. (1835). *An essay on the education of female teachers.* New York: Van Nostrand & Dwight.

Beecher, C. (1846). *The evils suffered by American women and American children, the cause and the remedy.* New York: Harper.

Bethune, M. M. (1926). *Mary McLeod Bethune Papers: A philosophy of education for negro girls.* New Orleans: Amistad Research Center, Tulane University, Box 2, Folder 13.

Bethune, M. M. (1934). *Mary McLeod Bethune Papers: The educational values of the college bred.* Daytona Beach: Mary McLeod Foundation, Bethune-Cookman College, Amistad Box 2, Folder 15.

Bode, B. H. (1938). *Progressive education at the crossroads.* New York: Newson and Co., pp. 9–14, 26–27.

American Educational Thought: Essays from 1640–1940, pages 597–600

Bushnell, H. (1853). *Common schools: a discourse on the modifications demanded by the Roman Catholics delivered in the North Church, Hartford, on the day of the late fast, March 25, 1853.* Hartford: Press of Case, Tiffany and Co, pp. 1–24.

Cotton, J. (1656). *Spiritual milk for Boston babes in either England: Drawn out of the breasts of both testaments for their souls nourishment, but may be of like use to any children.* Cambridge: Samuel Green.

Counts, G. (1932). *Dare the school build a new social order.* New York: John Day Company, pp. 1–34.

Cubberley, E. P. (1906). The certification of teachers. *The fifth yearbook of the national society for the scientific study of education.* Chicago: University of Chicago Press, pp. 73–77.

Dabney, R. (1879). Secularized education. *The Princeton Review, 55,* 377–400.

Dewey, J. (1929). *My pedagogic creed.* Washington: Progressive Education Association.

Dewey, J. (2001). *School and society; &, the child and the curriculum.* Mineola, NY: Dover Publications, pp. 6–62.

Dewey, J. (1938). *Experience and education.* New York: Macmillan, pp. 1–11.

Dodge, A. W. (1840). Report to the committee on education of the House of Representatives. *Documents printed by order of the House of Representations of Massachusetts, 1840,* Number 49.

Du Bois, W. E. B. (1907). *The souls of black folk.* Chicago: A.C. McClurg and Co., pp. 41–59, 88–109.

Eliot, C. W. (1898). *Educational reform: Essays and addresses.* New York: Century Co, pp. 401–418.

Emerson, R. W. (1883) *Education, an essay and other selections.* Boston: Houghton Mifflin, pp. 18–34.

Franklin, B. (1749). *Proposals relating to the education of youth in Pensilvania.* Philadelphia: B. Franklin and D. Hall.

Haley, M. (1904). Why teachers should organize, *National Education Association Journal of Proceedings and Addresses,* 43rd annual meeting, pp. 145–151.

Hall, G. S. (1901). The ideal school as based on child study, *National Education Association Journal of Proceedings and Addresses,* 40th annual meeting, pp. 475–482, 488.

Harris, W. T. (1885). *Compulsory education in relation to crime and social morals.* Washington, DC: s.n., pp. 1–13.

Harris, W. T. (1893). *The philosophy of education.* Baltimore, pp. 269–277.

Hughes, J. (1866). Petition of the Catholic of New York for a portion of the common school funds. In L. Kehoe (Ed.), *Complete works of the most Reverend John Hughes* (pp. 102–107). New York: Lawrence Kehoe.

James, W. (1899). *Talks to teachers on psychology, and to students on some of life's ideals.* New York: Holt, pp. 3–32.

Jefferson, T. (1904-05). A bill for the more general diffusion of knowledge. In P.L. Ford (Ed.), *The works of Thomas Jefferson, Vol. 2* (pp. 414–426). New York and London: G.P. Putnam's Sons.

Jefferson, T. (1829). Letter to John Banister. In T.J. Randolph. *Memoirs, Correspondence, and Private Papers of Thomas Jefferson* (pp. 345–347). London: Henry Colburn and Richard Benley.

Jefferson, T. (1904–05). Letter to Nathaniel Burwell. In P.L. Ford (Ed.), *The works of Thomas Jefferson, Vol. 12* (pp. 90–92). New York and London: G.P. Putnam's Sons.

Kandel, I. L. (1939). Prejudice the garden toward roses. *The American Scholar 18*, 72–82.

Kilpatrick, W.H. (1918). The project method. *Teachers College Record 19*(4) 319–335.

Lyon, M. (1997). *The Mary Lyon collection: Series B writings and documents: Mount Holyoke Female Seminary: the character of the young ladies.* Five Colleges, Inc.

Mann, H. (1892). *Life and works of Horace Mann, vol. II.* Boston: Lee and Shephard Publishers, 39–86.

Mann, H. (1891). *Life and works of Horace Mann, vol. IV.* Boston: Lee and Shephard Publishers, 232–34, 235–36, 243–44, 245, 246–47, 250–52, 259–60, 268–69, 277–78, 283–84, 297–98, 299, 312–13, 334–37.

Mather, C. (1708). *An essay about the good education of children.* Boston: John Allen.

National Education Association. (1893). Report of the Committee of ten on secondary school studies appointed at the meeting of the National educational association July, 9, 1892, with the reports of the conferences arranged by this committee and held December 28–30, 1892. Washington, D.C.: Government Printing Office.

National Education Association of the United States. Commission on the Reorganization of Secondary Education. (1918). *Cardinal principles of secondary education. A report of the commission on the reorganization of secondary education.* Washington, D.C.: Government Printing Office.

Parker, F. W. (1894). *Talks on pedagogics. An outline of the theory of concentration.* New York and Chicago, E. L. Kellogg & Co., pp. 3–24.

Penn, W. (1775/1904). *Fruits of solitude in reflections and maxims.* London: Headley Brothers, pp. 21–28, 54–57.

Report of the special committee of the board of aldermen. (1840–41). *Documents of the board of Aldermen, of the City of New York, VII* (40), 458–563.

Rush, B. (1786). *A plan for the establishment of public schools and the diffusion of knowledge in Pennsylvania; to which are added thoughts upon the mode of education, proper in a republic. Addressed to the Legislature and citizens of the State.* Philadelphia: Thomas Dobson.

Rush, B. (1787). *Thoughts upon female education, accommodated to the present state of society, manners, and government, in the United States of America.* Philadelphia: Prichard & Hall.

Stanton, E. C. (1881). The declaration of sentiments. In E.C. Stanton, S.B. Anthony, M.J. Gage (Eds.). *A history of woman suffrage, Vol. 1* (pp. 70–71). Rochester, NY: Fowler and Wells.

Strachan, G. C. (1910). *Equal pay for equal work: The story of the struggle for justice being made by the women teachers of the city of New York.* New York: B. F. Buck & Company, 7–8, 120–121.

Thorndike, E. L. (1910). The contribution of psychology to education. *Journal of Educational Psychology 1,* 5–12.

Washington, B. (1901/1919). *Up from slavery.* New York: Doubleday, Page and Company, pp. 106–32.

Webster, N. (1790). *A collection of essays and fugitive [sic] writings on moral, historical, political and literary subjects.* Boston: Thomas and E.T. Andrews, pp. 1–36.

Willard, E. H. (1819). *An address to the public, particularly to the members of the legislature of New-York, proposing a plan for improving female education* (2nd ed.). Middlebury: J.W. Copeland, pp. 26–35.

About the Editors

Andrew J. Milson is an Associate Professor in the Department of Teacher Education & Administration at the University of North Texas in Denton, Texas. He earned his Ph.D. in 1999 from the University of Georgia, where he studied social science education and geography. His research interests include geographic education and the use of geospatial technologies in educational environments. He has published articles in journals such as, *Journal of Geography, Theory and Research in Social Education, Social Education, Educational Policy,* and *Journal of Educational Research.* He co-edited, with Marsha Alibrandi, the book, *Digital Geography: Geospatial Technologies in the Social Studies Classroom* (Information Age, 2008). He also contributed a chapter on GIS and critical map literacy to the recent book *The Electronic Republic?: The Impact of Technology on Education for Citizenship* (Purdue, 2008). He lives in McKinney, Texas with his wife, Lori, and their son, Colin.

Chara Haeussler Bohan, Ph.D., is Associate Professor in the Department of Middle-Secondary Education at Georgia State University in Atlanta, Georgia. She earned her doctoral degree at The University of Texas at Austin, her master's degree at Teachers College, Columbia University, and her bachelor's degree at Cornell University. Her research interests include education history, social studies education, and women's studies. She authored, *Go to the Sources: Lucy Maynard Salmon and the Teaching of History* (Peter Lang, 2004). She has also written several journal articles in publications such as *Theory and Research in Social Education, Social Studies Research and Practice,* the *Journal of Curriculum and Supervision,* and *Social Studies and the Young Learner.*

American Educational Thought: Essays from 1640–1940, pages 601–602
601

She has contributed numerous chapters, in recent books such as, *Addressing Social Issues in the Classroom and Beyond* (Information Age, 2007), *John Dewey in My Classroom* (Kappa Delta Pi, 2004) and *Social Education in the Twentieth Century: Curriculum and Context for Citizenship* (Peter Lang, 2004). She lives in Marietta, Georgia with her husband, Tom, and her two wonderful children, Caleb and Chloë.

Perry L. Glanzer, Ph.D. is an Associate Professor in the School of Education and an Affiliate Faculty Member with the Institute for Church-State Studies at Baylor University in Waco, Texas. His research and teaching interests include moral and character education, the relationship between religion, education and politics, and the philosophy of education. He is the author of *The Quest for Russia's Soul: Evangelicals and Moral Education in Post-Communist Russia* (Baylor University Press, 2002) and coauthor with Todd Ream of *Christian Faith and Scholarship: An Exploration of Contemporary Developments* (Wiley and Jossey-Bass, 2007). His recent journal articles can be found in *Phi Delta Kappan*, *British Journal of Education Studies*, *Journal of Values and Belief*, *Religious Education*, *Educational Theory* and the *Journal of Church and State*. He lives in Hewitt, Texas with his wife, Rhonda, and his sons, Bennett and Cody.

J. Wesley Null is Associate Professor of Curriculum & Foundations of Education in the School of Education and the Honors College at Baylor University in Waco, Texas. He completed his Ph.D. degree at The University of Texas at Austin, where he studied curriculum theory and the history of education. At Baylor, Null teaches foundations of education in the School of Education and interdisciplinary courses on social science and great texts in the Honors College. Null is the author of *Peerless Educator: The Life and Work of Isaac Leon Kandel* (Peter Lang, 2007) and *A Disciplined Progressive Educator: The Life and Career of William Chandler Bagley* (Peter Lang, 2004). He also is co-editor, with Diane Ravitch, of *Forgotten Heroes of American Education: The Great Tradition of Teaching Teachers* (Information Age, 2006). He has co-edited several other books as well, including *Readings in American Educational Thought: From Puritanism to Progressivism* (Information Age, 2004) and *The Pursuit of Curriculum: Schooling and the Public Interest* (2006). Null serves as Editor of the *American Educational History Journal*. He lives in Hewitt, Texas with his wife, Dana, and their two children, Corbin and Raegan.